Memoirs
of
Duc de Saint-Simon

1710 - 1715

A shortened version

Edited and translated by
LUCY NORTON

Warwick, NY

Text copyright © 2007 by Lucy Norton
Design © copyright © Carlton Books Limited 2007
This edition copyright © 1500 Books 2007

Photo credit: Hubert Josse/Musée de l'Armée/Dist. Réunion des musées nationaux/Art Resource, NY
Used with permission.

ISBN 10: 1-933698-15-2
ISBN 13: 978-1-933698-15-1

SYNOPSIS OF CONTENTS

PART THREE
POLITICS

Chapter 6
1715

MAP
(drawn by Drawn by H.J. Blackman)

ACKNOWLEDGMENTS

Once again I should like to thank Sir Denis Brogan, Mrs Joy Law, Mme Chantal Coural, Miss Irene Clephane, and Mr Christopher Sinclair-Stevenson for their continued help and support.

NOTE ON COINAGE

1 silver livre	=	1 franc (which before 1914 = 10d.)
1 écu	=	3 livres
1 gold Louis	=	24 livres

BOOKS CONSULTED

Mémoires de Saint-Simon. Ed. A. de Boislisle. Paris, Hachette, 1879-1928, 43 vols.

Saint-Simon par lui-même. François-Régis Bastide. Paris, Editions du Seuil, 1953.

Saint-Simon Mémoires. Ed. Gonzague Truc. Paris, Bibliothèque de la Pléiade, Gallimard, 1953, 7 vols.

Saint-Simon et sa Comédie Humaine. La Varende. Paris, Hachette, 1955.

Sur Saint-Simon. Emmanuel d'Astier. Paris, Gallimard, 1962.

Louis XIV et Vingt Millions de Français. Pierre Goubert. Paris, Fayard, 1966.

Introduction to Eighteenth-Century France. John Lough. London, 1954.

The Letters of Madame. Ed. Gertrude Scott Stevenson. London, 1924.

Marlborough, his Life and Times. Sir Winston Churchill. London, 1947.

The Ancien Régime. C. B. A. Behrens. London, 1967.

THE ROYAL FAMILY IN 1710

Louis XIV
aged 72

His Son
Monseigneur le Grand Dauphin aged 49

His Grandsons
Louis, Duc de Bourgogne
aged 28

Philippe d'Anjou, Philip V, King of Spain
aged 27

Charles, Duc de Berry
aged 25

His Great-grandsons
Louis
aged 3

Louis (later Louis XV)
infant

His Sister-in-law
Elisabeth Charlotte d'Orléans,
Princess of the Palatinate
aged 58

His Nephew
Philippe II, Duc d'Orléans aged 36

His Great-nephew and -nieces
Louis (later Duc d'Orléans)
aged 7

Marie Louise Elisabeth m. Duc de Berry
aged 15

Louise Adélaïde
aged 12

Charlotte Aglaë
aged 10

Louise Elisabeth
aged 1

His Bastards

By Mme de Montespan:
Louis, Duc du Maine,
aged 10
Louis, Comte de Toulouse,
aged 32
Louise Françoise (Madame la Duchesse) m. Monsieur le Duc
aged 37
Françoise Marie (Duchesse d'Orléans)
aged 33
By Mme de La Vallière:
Marie Anne (Dowager Princesse de Conti)
aged 44

Princes of the Blood
of the
Condé and Conti Families

Condé
Louis III de Condé, Duc de Bourbon (Monsieur le Duc)
aged 42 (d. 1710)

His Children
Louis Henri (Monsieur le Duc)
aged 18
Charles, Comte de Charolais
aged 10
Louis, Comte de Clermont
aged 3
Louise Elisabeth (m. Louis Armand de Conti)
aged 17
Five other daughters

Conti
Louis Armand, Prince de Conti
aged 15
Marie Anne (Mlle de Conti)
aged 21
Louise Adélaïde (Mlle de La Roche-sur-Yon)
aged 14

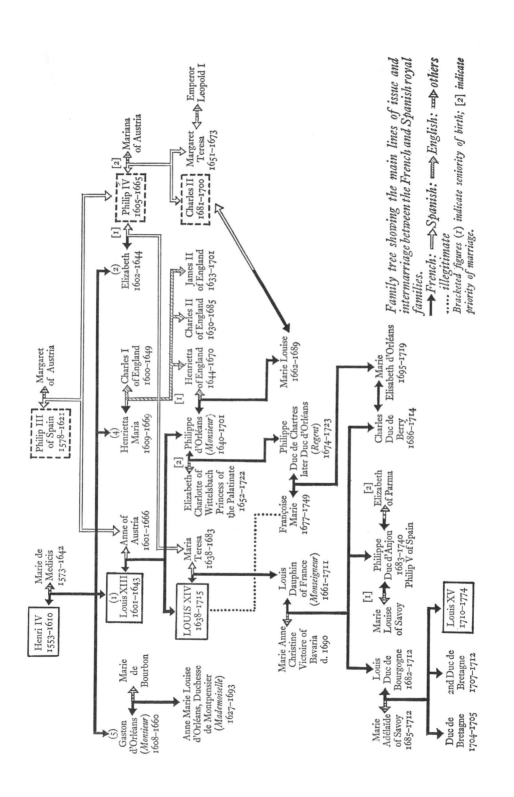

Family tree showing the main lines of issue and intermarriage between the French and Spanish royal families.

→ *French:* ⇒ *Spanish:* ⟹ *English:* ⟹ *others*

.... *illegitimate*

Bracketed figures (1) indicate seniority of birth; [2] indicate priority of marriage.

Henri IV
1553–1610

Marie de Medicis
1573–1642

Philip III of Spain
1578–1621

Margaret of Austria

Gaston d'Orléans (*Monsieur*)
1608–1660

Marie de Bourbon

Anne Marie Louise d'Orléans, Duchesse de Montpensier (*Mademoiselle*)
1627–1693

Louis XIII
1601–1643

Anne of Austria
1601–1666

Henrietta Maria
1609–1669

Charles I of England
1600–1649

Elizabeth
1602–1644

Philip IV
1605–1665

Mariana of Austria

Margaret Teresa
1651–1673

Emperor Leopold I

Charles II
1661–1700

Maria Teresa
1638–1683

LOUIS XIV
1638–1715

Elizabeth Charlotte of Wittelsbach Princess of the Palatinate
1652–1722

Philippe d'Orléans (*Monsieur*)
1640–1701

Henrietta of England
1644–1670

Charles II of England
1630–1685

James II of England
1633–1701

Marie Anne Christine Victoire of Bavaria
d. 1690

Louis Dauphin of France (*Monseigneur*)
1661–1711

Françoise Marie
1677–1749

Philippe Duc de Chartres later Duc d'Orléans (*Regent*)
1674–1723

Marie Louise
1662–1689

Louis Duc de Bourgogne
1682–1712

Marie Louise of Savoy

Philippe Duc d'Anjou
1683–1740
Philip V of Spain

Elizabeth of Parma

Charles Duc de Berry
1686–1714

Marie Elisabeth d'Orléans
1695–1719

Marie Adélaïde of Savoy
1685–1712

Duc de Bretagne
1704–1705

2nd Duc de Bretagne
1707–1712

Louis XV
1710–1774

PART III
POLITICS

CHAPTER I

1710

[At the end of 1709 the future for France and M. le Duc de Saint-Simon looked very black indeed. After the cruel winter and the famine that followed, the people of France, the money, and the army were completely exhausted. The fifth year of the War of the Spanish Succession had ended with the appalling slaughter of the Battle of Malplaquet. The enemy were at the very gates of France. Saint-Simon was in disgrace; many of his friends (notably, the Duc d'Orléans and Chamillart) were also out of favour, and the rest were powerless to help him; his enemies at the court of Monseigneur, le Grand Dauphin, were successfully doing their utmost to ruin him with the King. Seeing no hope of recovery, and having lost his lodging at Versailles after the death of his father-in-law the Maréchal de Lorges, Saint-Simon made up his mind to retire for ever from the Court to his estate of La Ferté, in Brittany. At the very end of the year, however, Mme de Saint-Simon and his friends the Chancellor and Mme de Pontchartrain persuaded him to make one last effort to right himself with the King. Very unwillingly he agreed to let Maréchal, the King's surgeon, ask for an audience on his behalf, and to accept, as a makeshift, a room and a privy in the Pontchartrains' Versailles apartment. But although his mind was thus occupied by the crisis in his personal affairs, he turned all his energies to retrieving the lost character of his friend M. le Duc d'Orléans by persuading him to part with his mistress, Mme d'Argenton.]

Conversations with M. le Duc d'Orléans to effect his separation from Mme d'Argenton - The rupture is effected - The King appoints a time for my audience - My audience is successful - My intimacy with Mme la Duchesse d'Orléans - The King gives no New Year presents - Mme la Duchesse de Bourgogne gives birth to a son (one day to be Louis XV) - Death of the Duchesse de Foix - Death of the Maréchale de La Meilleraye - Death of Monsieur le Duc - Mme la Duchesse d'Orléans claims a novel rank for her children - The King gives a ruling - First step towards the marriage of Mademoiselle to the Duc de Berry - Mourning for Monsieur le Duc - Extraordinary scene in the King's study - The King of Spain asks for Vendôme - Vendôme's shabby marriage to Mlle d'Enghien - The Duc de Beauvilliers suggests my writing an essay on Mgr le Duc de Bourgogne - Character of that prince - I form a cabal on behalf of Mademoiselle - Terrors of M. le Duc d'Orléans - Horrible insinuations concerning M. le Duc d'Orléans - Mme de Saint-Simon required to be lady-in-waiting - We object - We finally accept - We have a most agreeable apartment - Marriage of Mademoiselle to M. le Duc de Berry - Villars is disgraced and recovers immediately - Situation in Flanders - Berwick granted a peerage - Quarrels in Flanders - Vendôme again asked for by

Spain - Battle of Villaviciosa - Death of the Abbé de Pompadour - The King's
tithe - Inconceivable gullibility of Monseigneur - I am vilely slandered - The future
terrible to contemplate - M. and Mme la Duchesse de Berry obtain an establishment
- Death of the Duchess of Mantua - A bogus alchemist - Character of Boudin -
The King orders plays and other diversions at Versailles

THE FIRST four days of 1710 were so full of interest that they almost warrant the
treatment of a journal, not only for the part I played in them, but because they
set off a whole train of important happenings. On the first day of the year M. le
Duc d'Orléans returned to Versailles for the traditional rites and visits of courtesy. I saw him after the King's vespers, when he led me into his dark inner study,
overlooking the great gallery. At first, as so often occurs after long separations, the
talk was fragmentary and purposeless; but after a while I inquired about his relations with the King and Monseigneur. He replied with some hesitation, 'Not bad;
not good'; and when I remarked that that was not saying much, he admitted to
having given a banquet at Saint-Cloud for the Elector of Bavaria and to having
invited some ladies, including the Elector's former mistress Mme d'Arco. In such
circumstances he had seen no harm in asking Mme d'Argenton also; but the King
had taken offence, and after sulking for a few days had mentioned it. All that was
now forgotten, he continued, and they were back on their normal footing. I asked
what that was, for as I had been absent four months, this conveyed nothing to me;
whereupon he began to beat about the bush until it suddenly dawned on him that
I knew something, and he asked what people were saying.

I told him frankly that I had it on good authority that the King was much
displeased with him, indeed could scarcely be more so; that Monseigneur was
infinitely worse and making even less attempt at concealment; that following their
example most people were avoiding him, and that I had been hearing so many
distressing details that I had begun to despair for him altogether. He listened
attentively, and after a long pause agreed with all I had said. He thought it the
result of the Spanish affair which, despite his innocence, had been inflated out
of all proportion by the mischief-makers; that unfortunately he could do nothing
about it, and that it must be left for time to cure. I looked at him severely, saying
that time obliterated certain bad impressions but implanted others more deeply,
and that the Spanish trouble was unhappily of the latter kind. He had only to
reflect and he would see that the King and Monseigneur were far colder to him
now than in the first days after that episode. He considered deeply and admitted
that I spoke truly. I seized on that as an opportunity to extract a similar admission regarding his avoidance by Society. He complained bitterly; but when I saw
he grew resentful, I explained that under such an absolute ruler the entire Court

and everyone else suited their behaviour to that of the monarch, watching for him to give them the lead. People sometimes acted thus from servility, more often from a wish to flatter; but in this case it was simply from terror, for everyone fully understood why the King had changed. Thus, however unkind, however unjust, however monstrous he might feel the desertion of his friends to be, he could not rightly blame anyone, nor hope to end it save by altering the King's opinion of him, whereafter the rest of the world would follow suit.

That unexpected attack so much discomposed the prince that I was encouraged to continue. At first I had intended only to sound him, not broach the whole matter; but I now lost all my qualms and resolved to chance my luck should the occasion offer, as it very soon did; for M. le Duc d'Orléans was visibly impressed and no longer refused to face the facts. After a long silence he rose and began to pace the room. I also rose, and leaning my back against the wall was observing him closely, when he suddenly looked up, gave a deep sigh, and exclaimed, 'Well! What must I do?', as though he expected some reply. 'What should you do?' said I, 'what should you do?', my voice becoming full of meaning. 'I know very well what you should do, but I cannot possibly tell you. What a pity! for it is your only chance.' 'Ah! I see what you mean,' he replied as though struck by a thunderbolt; and still muttering, 'I see what you mean,' he flung himself on a seat at the farther end of the room. Sure now that he had grasped my meaning, and almost as stunned as he appeared to be, I turned my face to the wall to give myself time to recover and to spare him the embarrassment of being watched in those first moments. A long silence followed, during which I could hear him jerking convulsively in his chair, and I anxiously wondered where next the conversation would lead me. I then heard sighs amidst his restless movements, and guessed that suffering played a greater part than anger in his turmoil.

I turned round, still not looking at him, and broke the silence that was becoming too long-drawn-out by telling him that my words were the result of a conversation between myself and Bezons, who were, as I truly believed, his most loyal and trusty servants. I then continued that, horror-stricken by all that was told me on my return from La Ferté, and by what I had since discovered from those with knowledge, I had vainly sought for some other means of extricating him from his tragic isolation. There seemed no other way; but appalled at the cruelty of it, I had consulted the Maréchal de Bezons, who had pronounced it the only certain remedy. After this brief explanation I said no more. His bodily agitation grew no worse, but he said nothing and continued to heave deep sighs. I turned away once more to allow him more privacy, from time to time giving vent to monosyllabic utterances as though confirming my opinion. 'It is the one cure! The one chance!' and other such phrases. At long last M. le Duc d'Orléans rose and walked towards me, saying with a wretchedness that defies description, 'What would you have me do?' 'Regain your royal dignity,' I answered, 'and return to your rightful sphere, better even than you were before.' A few moments later, I added, 'How I wish Bezons were here!' For some time he made no reply, and then almost absent-mindedly said, 'But he is here.' 'What!' I cried, 'here at Versailles?' 'Yes, indeed,' said he, 'I saw him this morning in the King's ante-room.' 'Well, Sir, will you not send for him?' He thought for a while, I pressed him, he consented, and I instantly left the room to tell the servants that he was asking for the Maréchal de Bezons.

At that moment they announced Mgr le Duc de Bourgogne; it was customary on New Year's Day for the Sons of France to return the visits of the Grandsons (but never those of the princes of the blood). We left the study to receive him. The visit took place in the State-bedroom, standing, and lasted barely a quarter of an hour. M. le Duc d'Orléans was so perfectly composed that had I not known better I should have suspected nothing. They went afterwards by way of M. le Duc d'Orléans's study to Mme la Duchesse d'Orléans's room, where, catching sight of the Duchesse de Villeroy, I signed to her to come and keep me company in the inner study, where I had been left alone. She came very unwillingly, saying that she cared too much for Mme la Duchesse d'Orléans to feel at home in that place. I made some laughing reply. Then, hearing the sounds of departure, she invited me to supper and conversation with herself, her husband, and his brother-in-law the Duc de La Rocheguyon. I tried to make excuses on the plea that I was already engaged to sup with the Pontchartrains, but she was disappointed, and refused to let me go until I had promised.

Meanwhile they had told me that Bezons was nowhere to be found, and I therefore decided to wait until M. le Duc d'Orléans returned, so as to pursue the matter further and not leave him too much alone. He was not long gone. I asked him whether he had news of Bezons, to which he replied that Bezons had gone back to Paris; but although I showed my disappointment he seemed somewhat relieved, saying that they were bound to meet soon. I had originally intended to suggest asking him to return, but in view of that reply I thought it best to say nothing and to write myself. I therefore gently brought M. le Duc d'Orléans back to the point where we were interrupted, less to egg him on than to accustom him gradually to the idea. I put it to him that love-affairs of that kind were not for life; that he had reached an age when this one appeared so unbecoming that he would in any event soon end it; that his present situation was the perfect moment; that he knew how very seldom I protested and then only with the greatest reluctance; that I should never have advised a complete rupture had not the emergency quite overcome all my qualms, and that he should regard this surmounting of my very real unwillingness as the best possible proof of my devotion.

He listened in a silence broken only by heavy sighs and, when I had finished speaking, said he could well believe that I disliked making such a proposal, but that he understood my motives and was obliged to me. At that point, glad to have succeeded so far at a first encounter and reluctant to spoil it by taking all the heart out of him, I let the conversation drop and took my leave. Having nowhere else to go, since my refuge at the Chancellor's was not yet ready, I went to Pontchartrain's study, and finding him alone asked leave to write at his table. There and then I sent an urgent note to Bezons, informing him that the subject was broached and asking him to meet me next day during the King's mass, when I would tell him all. Later I went as I had promised to sup with the Duchesse de Villeroy. As we were leaving the dining-room she said again that she could not endure the room to which I had beckoned her that morning. Whereat I laughed, saying that such distaste might not last long; that what had upset her was equally displeasing to me, and that I was perhaps not unprofitably employed when she last saw me. 'Excellent!' she exclaimed, 'that at least will be something to look forward to. Will you promise?' At that moment the two dukes joined us and we talked of other matters.

On the following day, Thursday, 2 January, Bezons's reply arrived while I was dressing; and at first I was vexed because I imagined that it was an excuse. When I opened it, however, I was reassured, for he said I was the best friend in the world and that he would meet me at the King's mass. He was there waiting for me in the tribune and was vastly surprised to hear all that had happened on the previous day. He even remarked on my audacity; but although matters had progressed far beyond our hopes he still was not sure of success. None the less he agreed that we should press on with all speed, not relaxing our efforts for a moment, and not letting M. le Duc d'Orléans out of our sight until we had compelled him to win this great triumph over himself, or were forced to admit defeat. Directly the King had returned to his own apartments Bezons and I went to M. le Duc d'Orléans's study. We were just about to enter when someone drew Bezons aside and the prince said to me with a smile, 'Now confess that you sent for him!' I smiled also, adding that I had almost suggested doing so on the previous evening but had been afraid of being told to do nothing. Whereat the prince replied that I was right, for he would certainly have forbidden me to write. Bezons then joined us and we all sat down.

I spoke first, addressing my remarks to Bezons and repeating all over again the gist of the earlier conversation, not so much for his benefit as to remind M. le Duc d'Orléans. Bezons then turned to the prince, asking how he rated a friend like myself and inviting him to admire my courage in daring to act. He went on to reason briefly but very sensibly and with great urgency so as to force the prince to a decision. After that he was silent. M. le Duc d'Orléans's reply was incoherent, the sudden uncontrolled outburst of a man in extreme anguish, attempting to relieve his feelings in words of anger. I left him for a while to rave and sigh and complain, and then said that it hurt me more than him, to have to attack him on this tender spot and for that reason alone he should try to master himself. The time was come, I said, to finish with this scandal that had plunged him into a bottomless abyss from which, if only he were firm, he might emerge to make a triumphal progress to honour, favour and glory, leading shortly to greater heights than he had ever yet attained. Bezons echoed these closing words of mine, re-emphasizing and acclaiming them. We then continued for some considerable time to throw the ball from one to another so as to avoid annoying him by urging too much, and to give him time to digest our remarks. After a long pause M. le Duc d'Orléans asked us both, but looking at me in particular, how we expected that he should be raised so high for an action which, though the King would undoubtedly approve of it, had nothing whatever to do with the main cause of his anger. Since I had begun the conversation, and the prince had seemed to address me rather than Bezons, I thought that I had best be the one to speak and bring the whole issue into daylight.

I began by saying that by giving up a life that was so shocking to many who, though heedless of their own consciences, were very sensitive to the morals of Society, he would clear himself of all blame for that unseemly attachment and for all the offences ascribed to him during its course. A great passion, I continued, may make a man incapable of reflection and lead him into all manner of scrapes, but his unhealthy interest in the future, though he believed it had attracted little notice and was now forgotten, had lately been revived and exaggerated until it appeared as a crime of the first magnitude as well as appalling blasphemy. Even to friendly eyes it had seemed a weakness that sadly belied his nobler nature; he was now regarded as a man devoured by a longing to reign, a longing born no doubt of human weakness, but nourished and increased by what he had seen at séances.[1] Such manifestations, feared by some and ridiculed by others, were regarded by all as the source of ideas of grandeur out of character for a wise man and still more so for a loyal subject. That, I contended, was at the root of the Spanish suspicions and their sinister misinterpretation, and of other suspicions too, which I could not bring myself to name. He pressed me to speak, which was just what I wanted. After hesitating long enough to arouse his interest and prepare him for most dreadful revelations, I said that since he ordered me to tell him and no one else would dare, he must know of the rumour that he had made a pact with the Viennese court to marry the Dowager-Queen of Spain, whose

[1] In 1706, before leaving to take up his command in Italy, the Duc d'Orléans had attended a séance at Mme d'Argenton's house, and had seen an apparition, resembling himself, and wearing a crown.

vast fortune would pave the way for him to ascend the Spanish throne without too much opposition from the Allies. He was said already to be intriguing to have his marriage annulled by Rome and his children declared bastards, with the intention of waiting until her great age had carried the old queen off, and of then marrying Mme d'Argenton, for whom the spirits had already prophesied a crown. All told, it was indeed fortunate that Mme la Duchesse d'Orléans had survived her recent confinement for, apart from her preservation, it had stilled the wicked tongues of the monsters who spread the rumour that she was poisoned. Not for nothing, they had said, was he the son of Monsieur.[1]

At this terrible recital M. le Duc d'Orléans was horrified beyond measure, and at the same time indescribably affected by having been attacked with such malicious cruelty. He cried out several times, but I, not wishing to have to drain the bitter cup a second time, pressed on until I had told all. When I had finished I was silent; so also was the prince, who by this time was beyond words. Bezons, quite overcome by what he had heard, stared fixedly at the floor; as he said later, he felt like sinking beneath it and positively dared not raise his eyes. Not that what I said was in any way new to him; it was hearing me state it so boldly to the prince's face that had made him feel faint. After a few moments M. le Duc d'Orléans broke the silence with a bitter tirade against the wicked people who invented such abominations, such wild and barbarous plots, and dared to father them on him. I thought it more prudent to let him vent his outraged feelings, and to give Bezons time to recover. I then resumed, for as yet I had told only half, observing that M. le Duc d'Orléans would now understand the cause of his isolation and the King's aversion, and would doubtless also have perceived the connection between the ending of his shocking love-affair and his reinstatement. There I paused once more so as to enable him to accept gradually and without too much indignation a line of thought doubly distressing because it was both honest and immediate. Moreover I had no wish to stun him with too many hard blows.

The Maréchal de Bezons, who had hitherto said very little, now began to speak. He had only to continue the road which I had opened by force of arms, and he fought on steadily and well. The prince, furious and exhausted by more than one very real distress, said nothing; it was already much that he listened. Bezons and I kept the ball rolling, as it were, acclaiming everything the other said in order to drive home our arguments less brutally than when addressing the prince directly. At times we allowed the conversation to lapse, because we did not wish to fatigue him unbearably. Suddenly, he made a loud exclamation as though waking from a trance. 'But how can I do it? What can I say to her?' These ejaculations, wrung from him by our endeavours, gave me fresh hope, and I swiftly seized

---

[1] Monsieur the King's brother had been suspected of poisoning his first wife Henrietta of England. She was widely believed to have been poisoned, but more probably she died of a burst appendix.

the moment to say that he was wise to know that such decisions must be taken at once and acted upon with all speed. If how were the only question, I begged him to be patient and let me speak again. I continued that it was my firm conviction and that of Bezons also, or so I believed, that it would be folly to break with Mme d'Argenton if she still lived in Paris. He would never resist the temptation to see her, and seeing her would mean reunion. Here he interrupted me, asking impatiently what I expected him to do, and how could he avoid seeing her at least once more, since their parting was not from anger or repugnance. I replied calmly and coldly that if he saw her for any reason whatsoever our endeavours would all have been in vain, and Bezons, echoing my words, fought manfully on, became heated, and finally exclaimed, 'For God's sake, do not make that mistake. You will repent it to your dying day!' I supported him with all my might, and when the prince produced fresh reasons, I countered them, saying that ours was surely the kindest way since it bore witness to an overmastering passion that dared not risk meeting the beloved object once the decision had been taken.

Everything depended, I said, on Mme d'Argenton's removal from Paris; but great though M. le Duc d'Orléans was he had neither the authority nor indeed the heart to banish her. That alone should tell him what to do, and at the same time offer him the means to restore his fortunes. He must immediately go to the King, and implore him for protection against himself, saying that his overpowering passion was now more than he could morally endure, and that he could no longer face its disastrous consequences. Remembering the King's past kindnesses, he should appeal to him to forget his anger and rescue him from an affair which he had not the strength to end. He must then beg King Louis to seize this moment when a fleeting glimpse of reason and his duty had been vouchsafed to him, and order Mme d'Argenton to leave Paris. I concluded that by speaking thus to an uncle who had once loved him dearly,[1] a father-in-law outraged by his daughter's misery,[2] a king easily moved by a subject's trust, a man who knew the fatal power of a grand passion, he would change the King in an instant to the father of a prodigal, as in the Bible story. I knew for a fact, I added, that what had most antagonized the King in the Spanish affair was the sensation that his love was not returned; indeed, he had been heard to say as much to Mme de Maintenon one day, his lips trembling with anger as he vowed it was a personal affront. An appeal to the King in this loving, trustful way, complaining of nothing but admitting all, and concealing beneath the veil of his embarrassment everything that was

---

[1] This would appear to contradict Saint-Simon's usual description of their relationship, but he did not overmuch mind such contradictions, and, in any case, the feelings of the King and his nephew fluctuated considerably.
[2] The Duchesse d'Orléans was a daughter of Louis XIV by Mme de Montespan.

better not spoken, might persuade the King to forget his hurt in the satisfaction of knowing that his nephew had sought help from him alone. That, in turn, would readily dispose him to believe that all his nephew's offences, all the grave imputations, the suspect and reprehensible séances, and even the affair in Spain were the evil effects of passionate love.

M. le Duc d'Orléans had no patience to hear more. 'What?' he exclaimed, 'are you telling me to accuse her of all the crimes laid at my door, and to save myself at her expense? Is it not enough to break with her, without entangling her in the Spanish trouble, in which she had no part whatsoever? I am surprised that you of all people should offer me this way out.' 'Love makes you blind, Sir,' I replied. 'You imagine that I wish to make Mme d'Argenton a scapegoat, and you bristle up as though I were proposing something dishonourable. That indeed is what I have in mind, I do not deny it.' I then asked him if it were not a fact that his mistress had encouraged him to experiment further in the supernatural arts which he had previously banished from his house. He had already admitted as much, and I thus had every reason to think that his love-affair had in literal truth led him into great errors. That was not only the truth, I said, but common knowledge; thus nothing he told the King about Mme d'Argenton would be either new or a betrayal, and he need not restrain himself on that account. As for harm coming to that lady, any such notion seemed absurd to me. Parted from him and away from Paris, which was one and the same, she would be in no danger. He would no doubt provide for her comfort, even beyond what he had already given her, for cessation of intercourse need not mean the end of protection. Moreover, the King had been in love too often not to understand the niceties and obligations of such partings. Mme d'Argenton had nothing to fear from him, but on the contrary much to gain; and as for the prince himself, I could wish him no kinder judge. With Mme d'Argenton protected, deception done with, truth preserved, every advantage would be gained without the smallest shred of a scruple rightly attaching to the honourable means employed to that end. M. le Duc d'Orléans, however, still persisted in maintaining that it was a courtier's trick; and even Bezons appeared to be having some difficulty in accommodating himself to my line of thought. I then had the idea of asking what had so shocked them. Bezons tried to answer but, finding no solid ground beneath his feet and feeling that the prime issue of the parting with Mme d'Argenton was being overshadowed by the question of the prince's faults, he merely looked discomfited. M. le Duc d'Orléans no longer argued, though he would not yet admit defeat; and declaring that the whole matter was irrelevant until he had decided on the main point, he relapsed into a gloomy silence which neither the maréchal nor I cared to interrupt.

I soon perceived that something further was distressing him, but that he was in two minds whether or not to speak. He began a sentence; then with an effort cut it short. When this had occurred several times, I plucked up courage to say that I begged him to recollect that we were his most devoted servants, and that in his present situation he would do well to tell us all. There was a long and bitter struggle, after which he announced that one other matter did greatly oppress him, although he was most reluctant to broach it, for what most of all afflicted him was the thought of his family and the life to which he would be expected to return. I answered that I had half-suspected this trouble and was truly glad that he had decided to be frank; and I opened my attack by saying that I was not surprised that he feared to begin a life so wholly new to him whose tender pleasures he had not yet experienced. At these words, which he repeated in a kind of fury, he confessed to having so strong an aversion for his wife that he thought he should never conquer it.[1] I thereupon turned to Bezons, saying that I had thought as much, but that it was the least of my anxieties. What was more natural than that M. le Duc d'Orléans, forced into an unworthy marriage, should have fallen victim to bad companions and an overmastering passion and have become estranged from his wife in this unhappy way. Now was the time for good feeling and wiser counsels to prevail, and to begin a new life, in which he might find peace and true nobility in the enduring dignity of his home.

Bezons supported me strongly, praising Mme la Duchesse d'Orléans and giving me the opportunity to do likewise; but strangely enough this seemed only to infuriate the prince, who promptly lapsed into his former despondent state. At last he unburdened himself, and this time gave us all his confidence, concealing neither names nor details, making accusations, and telling us much that we should by far have preferred never to know; but it was better out. Bezons took refuge in platitudes, all very true in themselves; I, however, had the good fortune, through channels very privately mine but none the less accurate, to be able to produce proofs so clear and positive that, despite himself, M. le Duc d'Orléans had to be convinced, although he remarked that even had I known something against his wife, I should not have told it. 'Indeed, Sir!' said I, 'I should most certainly not have told; but neither should I have spoken with such authority had I not been, as well as sure, totally without the smallest suspicion concerning her. To speak ill of her, even truthfully, would be abominable; to persuade you wrongly would be against my conscience and a betrayal of your trust.' That statement, so certain, so sincere, left him no further room for doubt, and he did not conceal his joy. He enlarged on the abominable accusation, and now that it was destroyed gave us ample opportunity to do the same regarding its inventors,

---

[1] According to Madame things had become so strained between them that he would consent to visit her once a day only on condition that she promised not to lose her temper.

whom he named as being Madame la Duchesse, Mme d'Argenton, and other shameless women, most of them members of that clique.[1] We were successful in making him ashamed of ever having believed them, considering their reputations. In conclusion, I said that he would live to bless the day on which he had chanced to find such convincing proof, and reason had compelled him to admit and repent of his credulity.

We then proceeded to praise Mme la Duchesse d'Orléans, I waxing very eloquent on the subject of her uncomplaining patience and her lively interest in his honour. Bezons once again supported me strongly, and the prince listened quietly enough as we described to him the joys of a happy marriage, in which also we carried conviction, for we both spoke from felicitous experience. At that point we left him despite his protests, for it was late and we were quite worn out by our hard and dangerous work. He implored us not to desert him in the awful struggle to which we had committed him. As we left, Bezons again said that I was the best friend imaginable, but that my violence had more than once left him trembling and breathless. He also admitted that it had been very necessary, for without violence we should never have prevailed. We promptly separated for fear of giving M. le Duc d'Orléans's servants cause to gossip, on account of this long session following so close upon my visit of the previous day, and we agreed to return after dinner and devote the rest of that day to being with the prince.

When I returned shortly before three o'clock, I found M. le Duc d'Orléans already in his *entresol*-study, in the company of Bezons. He seemed glad to see me and made me sit between them. I complimented Bezons on his punctuality and asked what point they had reached. 'Still on the same subject,' said the prince, 'the same indecision.' I said that the time had come to put an end to all that, and I enlarged for some considerable time on the tragedy of a prince of his exalted rank being placed in such a situation. He did not interrupt me, save by fidgeting in his chair, for he was clearly very much displeased with himself. Just at that moment Mademoiselle[2] entered, followed by her governess Mme de Marey, my kinswoman and close friend, to whom I whispered that she must remove her pupil because we had urgent matters to discuss. She did not, however, have that trouble because after embracing his beloved daughter, M. le Duc d'Orléans dismissed her himself, and we all three once more sat down.

The interruption had presented me with a new weapon and the chance to appeal to his paternal love. I already knew from the prince's own lips that the King had mentioned Mademoiselle nearly two years earlier as a possible wife for M. le Duc de Berry. I asked him now what he proposed to do about it, for she had turned fourteen and had a figure more amply developed than is usual at that age,

---

[1] Saint-Simon's enemies, the cabal around Monseigneur.
[2] His eldest daughter, Marie Louise Elisabeth d'Orléans (1695-1719), later to become the Duchesse de Berry.

and it seemed to me that he must feel greatly concerned for her future. After the King's suggestion any other son-in-law would have been an anticlimax; yet he had placed himself in danger of having all his hopes shattered, and once again I saw no other remedy than a rupture with his mistress by the method I had suggested. M. le Duc d'Orléans, however, no longer complained of the method, only of the parting itself, and that more in sorrow than in anger. Thus I was encouraged to continue. I asked whether he would not first consult Mme de Maintenon. He was silent for a time and then said that if ever it came to action he must needs do so. I urged him in that case to use the same tone with her as I had advised with the King, but to be more expansive, in the confidence that she would well understand his unhappiness at the King's aversion. He should spread himself in expressing his love and gratitude, thus implanting the idea that only his hope of regaining the King's favour had persuaded him to make this sacrifice, and that for no other consideration would he have done so. The prince appeared to accept my counsel, and Bezons also; I therefore took the occasion to explain the small effect of a uniformly virtuous life upon Mme de Maintenon and the King, whose confirmed preference was for proselytes and converts. The world was full of men beyond reproach in the ways most dear to them, who had never yet managed to please them, and of others with reputations sullied by all manner of mean and shameful actions whom they had rewarded with gratifying, even spectacular, promotion, solely because repentance flattered their self-esteem. Ignorance in religion gave them a mistaken view of God's mercy to sinners; thus they could not see when ambition masqueraded as love of pleasure or turned licentiousness to a piety that would have passed unnoticed if sincere, but being called 'conversion' was usually well rewarded. M. le Duc d'Orléans's best hope was to follow that lead, and I implored him to see that there was no time to lose.

Bezons played his part nobly, but I was dismayed to perceive that the prince was not by half so low-spirited as when we had parted from him, and that he had fatally used the short respite to gather strength against us. I was at once convinced that if we did not carry the rupture by storm, so to speak, in this one interview, there would be no hope of later success, for he might escape us altogether, or, deciding during the night to lose all for love, silence us when we renewed the attack. Alternatively, he might take drastic action and be gone to Paris when we called on him next day. That thought struck me so forcibly as Bezons held forth on the advantages of consulting Mme de Maintenon that I resolved to brace myself for one last effort, one mighty struggle with no quarter given or received. While Bezons had his say I, therefore, considered how best to proceed, and in very truth I was shaking with fear. At last, after an interval of silence, I looked sadly at M. le Duc d'Orléans and said that however painful the battle with himself might be, he should realize that to us it was equally distressing. He had only love to contend with, and although I granted that for one so deeply smitten it must be a terrible moment, he should none the less spare a thought for the anguish of his devoted friends who were forced to break his heart, torment- ing him with cruel words and hurtful truths, behind which lay facts almost as unkind. How much more agonizing for us were the present circumstances, taking place not between equals, but with a friend so far our superior in rank, a prince whom we were accustomed to treat with vast respect, carefully avoiding anything even remotely likely to displease him—how infinitely more painful, since with our deep respect was mingled true affection. That was how he should value our struggle with him, believing that only vital necessity prompted us to engage in it. Let him not sink for ever into the abyss for want of the will to extricate himself, and leave us helpless to witness his ultimate destruction.

M. le Duc d'Orléans appeared to be convinced by this moving appeal. The only difficulty now remaining was to fortify a will so much weakened by immoderate passion. Unfortunately this clearly required still more harshness and plain-speaking, for he presently turned to Bezons, remarking that he must see his mistress to prepare her for the separation, if finally he did decide to leave her. At that point Bezons loudly exclaimed that he dared not take the risk, for it would certainly end in his yielding to her, and the only result would be a new, more shameful, and even more fatal attachment. The profound silence that followed this brisk interchange had a marked effect on M. le Duc d'Orléans, visibly increasing the resentful gloom which I had been so sorry to observe when I first suggested his consulting Mme de Maintenon. I thought I even detected a sense of defeat and became convinced that this was the moment for my final effort. Pulling myself together, I broke the silence by uttering such encouragements as I thought necessary to pave the way for my next assault. Then, when the time was ripe, taking a different tone, I declared that it was a monstrous shame to let his great gifts be wasted, since he was the only man of the royal blood who by his counsel (if he showed himself worthy of being consulted) and by his skill in war (if he recovered the authority to exercise it) could save the kingdom of his ances- tors. I could no longer refrain, I said, seeing that all other arguments were useless, from producing certain facts which I had hitherto been unwilling to disclose, even although I risked his anger. I should never rest, I added, if I held anything back and abandoned him to his fate from a false sense of respect.

I thereupon rose to my feet and, turning to him with a gesture, announced that I could no longer conceal the people's just anger. They had once had high hopes of him and had displayed enormous patience and indulgence; now, however, they had turned against him, some with scorn, others in a kind of rage, and the result was a great wave of indignation, as strong in the most dissolute as in men of purer habits. The public at long last had grown tired of his licentiousness, now become almost part of his nature, and had decided that neither age, nor learning, nor high responsibilities would ever change him. He not only had a concubine, but quite openly kept a separate establishment for her as his mistress Why should anyone tolerate in a Grandson of France, thirty-five years of age, what the justices and police would long ago have punished in one not sheltered by his exalted rank? He had moreover committed so many indiscretions of so dubious and rash a kind that the greatest crime of all was imputed to him. He might indeed be innocent of that wickedness; but it was unhappily true that one needed both to know his character and to feel well disposed towards him in order to believe it, and not take the sinister view that had permeated Society, beginning with the King, Monseigneur, and the whole of the royal family, producing an abhorrence that was rapidly turning to rage. I fixed my eyes on him as I spoke and could see that my vehemence made an impression; but I paused none the less, so as to give Bezons a chance to support me. He, however, had crumbled; he looked me up and down as though there were nothing in his head but the alarm engendered by my violence, and no courage left for words, apart from a few murmurs of assent. His obvious panic obliged me to be my own helper, and I turned again to M. le Duc d'Orléans, asking whether he would not seek an interview with Mme de Maintenon now. He hesitated a moment and then said that he could not persuade himself to act yet. That 'yet' gave me hope, and I looked at Bezons, entreating him to do some of the work, lest I become odious to the prince by pressing him too hard. He did speak then, but to very little effect, and soon ended by saying that he had nothing to add to my remarks. To do him justice, considering how frightened he was, I thought that he had done well in commending my words even as much as that. I then once more urged the prince to send a message, and feeling that he was weakening ever so little I decided that it was time to force him. I therefore rose, saying that he must let me have one final word.

M. le Duc d'Orléans, however, began to thank me in a voice so broken by emotion that I saw he was touched to the quick, and my observation was confirmed when he rose from his chair and reproached Bezons for fearing to speak out. Bezons made the excuse that I had left him nothing to say, to which I retorted sharply that my zeal had led me on when I perceived that he was speechless. This absurd interchange gave both of us the opportunity to produce fresh arguments; but meanwhile the prince had sat down again. At that I once more proposed sending a message to Mme de Maintenon; Bezons suggested calling one of the footmen, and I applauded that action as though it had already been performed, adding by way of encouragement something about the relief that one feels after a noble and painful effort. Bezons and I thus reasoned together, not daring to address the prince directly whilst he was still suffering from the effects of my tremendous onslaught, when we were amazed to see him suddenly rise, rush to the door, open it, and loudly shout for a servant. When one came running, he whispered something into the man's ear and then returned to fling himself down on a chair as though all the strength had been drained from him. Not knowing what had happened, I asked if he had sent the message. 'Alas! yes,' he replied with a broken-hearted look. I instantly made a leap towards him, thanking and congratulating him with all imaginable joy and satisfaction. He answered that he had not yet entirely made up his mind to speak; whereupon Bezons, who had also been congratulating him, changed to exhortations not to give way. I, meanwhile, tried to encourage him by reassuring Bezons; saying that the prince had not taken that crucial step only to retreat, that although his heart still quailed, mine was full of good cheer. We carried on in this way for some time, praising the prince's resolution, admiring his courage, pitying his distress, sympathizing with him in everything, urging him on, reflecting on the relief of finding peace and tranquillity after the storm, strengthening him by indirect methods instead of wearying him with admonitions. M. le Duc d'Orléans said little; but towards the end he repeated that Bezons had been too gentle with him and that he understood the need for home-truths, and he thanked me again for the force and frankness with which I had spoken.

Soon afterwards he asked the time, and since it was already nine o'clock in the evening he proposed going as usual to visit Monseigneur in Mme la Princesse de Conti's apartment. I asked permission to remain with Bezons in his *entresol*, for neither of us possessed a lodging or other place suitable for a private talk. He left us; I closed the door, and the maréchal and I once more seated ourselves to discuss the unexpected troubles which we had encountered. He thought that the prince was almost out of love, to which I agreed, although I still believed him deeply attached; on the whole, however, I thought that the final struggle would not be as hard as I had feared. We agreed that now, less than ever, ought he to be left for a single moment by himself; but at the same time we could not help lamenting our physical and mental exhaustion. Finally we agreed to meet again in the great gallery during the King's supper, and that afterwards Bezons should stay with M. le Duc d'Orléans to give him further encouragement when he had received Mme de Maintenon's reply.

Next day, which was Friday, 3 January, I could not find Bezons anywhere in the gallery or the State apartments. The King went to mass, with M. le Duc d'Orléans preceding him by eight or ten paces. In my anxiety to know whether or not he had seen Mme de Maintenon I approached him, and keeping my voice low and mentioning no names, I managed to inquire if he had yet had an interview.

He replied with so faint a 'yes' that I was seized with panic lest he had seen her and not spoken. After another 'yes' as weak as the first, my feelings overcame me. 'But did you tell all?' 'Yes, everything.' 'And are you satisfied?' 'No one could be more so,' said he, 'I was with her close on an hour and she was surprised and delighted.' Here he paused for a very long time, considering the shortness of the distance we still had to cover; then, after two or three false starts, he looked at me sadly, with a meaning glance, and said suddenly that there was something that troubled him; that he had best ask me straight to my face, and that he begged me for the sake of our friendship to tell him the truth. This staggered me but I promised to conceal nothing. 'Then here it is,' he burst out; 'that woman spoke exactly as you did; but what struck me most was that she said the selfsame things in identical terms, even down to the order of the sentences. Tell me, did she not consult you first? Were you not set to work on me?' 'Sir!' I replied, 'it is not my custom to take oaths, but I swear to you by Him whose house we now enter' (in other words, the chapel) 'and by all I hold most holy, that I spoke to you on my own initiative, and that no influences direct or indirect were brought to bear on me. As for that woman and the King, not only have they done nothing and said nothing, but they cannot possibly know anything of what has passed between us. After this solemn oath, which goes quite against my principles, I venture to say that you should know me well enough to believe my bare word.' He heaved a sigh of relief, and taking my hand said, 'Well, that is over, I do believe you, but I am glad you swore, for I must confess that such unanimity did seem remarkable to me.' 'Sir,' I continued, 'one last word to set your mind finally at rest. I swear to you once again that I have told you the complete and absolute truth.' 'That is all finished now,' he said, 'I no longer have the least suspicion.'

When I next saw Bezons I told him of the prince's extraordinary suspicions and of how he had made me swear. The maréchal was not in the least disturbed. He merely said with absolute assurance that I must tell M. le Duc d'Orléans quite simply that truth is one and indivisible, and thus came from Mme de Maintenon's lips in the same way as from mine. At that moment the King returned from the chapel, and we had time only to arrange to go separately to the prince's study, so as to avoid notice. I remained a short time chatting in the gallery, and then joined Bezons in M. le Duc d'Orléans's ante-room, for the prince did not return until half an hour later. I suggested going into the study while we waited, and so we did, shutting the door after us and sitting down to discuss all that had happened. As we were thus occupied, I reflected on the strange coincidence of my also being about to have an audience of the King, which in the circumstances might well re-awaken the prince's suspicions. After some thought, the personal pride and courtier's wariness that made me unwilling to mention my disgrace gave way before nicer considerations of honour and integrity, and although I had barely known Bezons before this affair, which was now less than twelve days old, I decided to consult him. I accordingly confided all my troubles to him and the fact that I was expecting an audience at any moment. I did not, however, tell him who had obtained one for me.[1] He appeared touched and gratified by my frankness, and advised me at once to tell M. le Duc d'Orléans, assuring me that no matter what he might once have suspected, he would now readily believe that my audience in no way concerned himself. Soon afterwards someone came for Bezons, and I was left alone.

M. le Duc d'Orléans returned, and at once led me into his inner study. He went and stood with his back to the fire, saying nothing, and looking quite bemused. After observing him for some time, I decided not to pester him at this crucial moment before he saw King Louis, and merely asked whether Mme de Maintenon seemed fully to have understood him. His 'yes' was so curt that I hastily inquired whether he would see the King before his dinner. His reply filled me with alarm, for it was an equally abrupt 'no'. 'What, Sir?' said I boldly, 'not going?' 'No,' he answered with a terrible moan, 'all is over.' 'All over?' I sharply retorted, 'all over because you have spoken to Mme de Maintenon?' 'No, indeed,' said he, 'I have also spoken to the King.' 'To the King!' I cried, 'You have told him all?' 'Yes, all. I could not trust myself to wait, for I have been in a turmoil ever since I saw Mme de Maintenon. I felt I must act at once, and I went with the King into his study after mass...' At that point, overcome with misery, he burst out weeping and sobbing and I retired to a corner of the room. A moment later, Bezons entered and was stunned by the scene that met his eyes. I quietly told him that the deed was done, which at first astounded him; but he soon sprang forward to thank and congratulate the prince. After that we said no more for a time, so as to give some respite to M. le Duc d'Orléans, who had thrown himself into an armchair and, now bemused, now violently agitated, was relieving his feelings in a stony silence punctuated by uncontrollable torrents of tears and sobs. We ourselves were deeply disturbed by the violence of his emotion, and therefore restrained our joy, scarcely daring to believe that the necessary rupture had at last been accomplished. Eventually we broke the silence, sympathizing with M. le Duc d'Orléans, praising his great effort, trying thus to calm his distress in some degree. We then summoned the courage for a small diversion, asking him what Mme de Maintenon had said, to which he replied, 'the same as you'; whereupon I felt that the time had come to speak of my coming audience of the King. He took the news wonderfully well, considering all things, even saying with what I thought surprising unselfishness that he hoped he had put the

[1] Saint-Simon's friend Maréchal, the King's surgeon, had with great difficulty persuaded Louis XIV to see him.

King into a good mood for me. Reverting to Mme de Maintenon, she had assured him that this would reinstate him in the King's favour, had promised to impress on King Louis the magnitude of the sacrifice, and ensure that Mme d'Argenton received the best possible treatment without *lettres de cachet* or other indignities, and permission to retire to a convent, country estate, or any town of her choice, without restrictions even as to travelling. That was exactly what I had proposed as being fair, always provided that she did not queen it at one of his inherited estates; the prince himself agreed with me regarding that.

At that point, my impatience got the better of me, and despite his tears and paroxysms of grief I asked how he had fared with the King. 'Very badly indeed,' he replied. This dismayed me beyond measure and I asked what had happened. He said he had followed the King into his study, and full of all that he had to impart had begged him to move to another room, where they might be alone. But the King was put out by that suggestion, having been taken unawares, and had demanded to know why, looking exceedingly vexed and haughty. M. le Duc d'Orléans had still insisted, and finally the King, looking like thunder, had taken him to the adjoining room. There the prince told him of his great decision, imploring him to order Mme d'Argenton out of Paris, but to spare her the humiliations of rough handling, a *lettre de cachet*, and banishment, for which she would certainly believe M. le Duc d'Orléans responsible. The King appeared surprised but not at all mollified. He coldly congratulated his nephew, adding that he should long ago have abandoned his dissolute life, but consented readily enough to expel his mistress from Paris without written orders. He then abruptly departed, as though fearing that the prince's confession might be only the prelude to some further request. I was truly disappointed; but I hoped that the King's coldness arose less from absolute dislike than from surprise and the ill-chosen moment, and that second thoughts on the greatness of the sacrifice might still restore the prince to his old footing. I therefore did my best to comfort and console him, and Bezons nobly supported me.

I then ventured to propose that he should inform his wife of a step that affected her so deeply. But at the first mention of her name he flew into a violent passion, vowing that he would not see her, at least not on that day, because her raptures would be unbearable. I replied rather hesitantly that she was more likely to sympathize than be tactless; but this he rejected with such haughtiness that I said no more. When I tried again he closed my lips by saying that he would discuss the matter with Mme de Maintenon, who understood his repugnance and strongly advised him not to see his wife that day for fear of finding her in a bad temper. He told Bezons and me later that he had settled an income of forty-five thousand livres upon Mme d'Argenton, almost the entire capital of which would go eventually to their son, who had been legitimized and accepted, and who has since become a grandee of Spain, Grand-prieur de France,[1] admiral of the galleys, and Abbot of Auvillé; all of which goes to prove that in France the best birth is to be born a bastard and so have none at all. In addition to all this wealth, Mme d'Argenton was allowed to keep more than four hundred thousand livres' worth of jewels, silver, and furniture, and M. le Duc d'Orléans took over all her debts so that she would not be harried by her creditors; that, too, cost him a pretty penny. He believed that this munificence would prevent even her from claiming more. All in all, the amount exceeded two millions, which I considered far too much; but I praised his generosity—I could not well do otherwise. Mighty prince though he was, such a disbursement should have taught him wisdom.

Just before we left, Bezons, spurred on by me, because I dared not mention her name again, made a third attempt on behalf of Mme la Duchesse d'Orléans which proved successful. M. le Duc d'Orléans finally consented to see her that day and tell her of the rupture, a kindness that relieved us considerably, for our haunting of the prince in the past three days had certainly aroused the suspicions of his servants, and we needed protection from the fury of Mme d'Argenton, Madame la Duchesse, and all that circle, who would rage at seeing him restored to favour, and would hold us responsible. It was now past noon. As we went away Bezons remarked that he had no strength left, and proposed lying concealed in the back regions of his Paris house until the first shock had worn off; thus hoping to escape from questioning and comments.

We parted in M. le Duc d'Orléans's gallery, and I went to call on the Duchesse de Villeroy, finding her alone at her dressing-table among her women. As soon as I entered I ask her to send them away, a liberty I often took with her. Directly they had gone I announced that the affair was finished. 'Finished, nonsense!' said she scornfully, knowing exactly what I meant although I had not seen her since our supper two evenings earlier. 'I'll never believe it until he has spoken to the King. He will promise anything, but he'll do nothing. You may be his friend, but I know him better.' 'Have you quite done?' I asked smiling, 'because there is no mistake about it. He spoke to Mme de Maintenon this morning, and later to the King. The whole affair is ended.' 'Wonderful!' said she tartly, 'he probably tells you that, but he will never do it.' 'But I can vouch for it myself,' I retorted. 'He has indeed spoken. I left him a moment ago.' 'Oh! is it really finished?' she cried in transports of delight, 'done, finished, finally ended?' 'Yes, truly,' I replied, 'it is all over and done with for good. I am not supposing or romancing; I am telling you for certain that they have parted.' Never have I seen a woman more joyful nor more incredulous. After a time she asked me to tell her all over again how it was accomplished; and I gave her the gist of it, and all the essentials as I have described them, together with certain names and details which are best

[1] The highest national rank conferred by the Order of the Knights of Malta.

omitted here; although they were necessary to the reconciliation which I hoped to effect between husband and wife. The Duc de Villeroy joined us at that point and shared our joy; but my words to him were continually interrupted by the duchess's exclamations of delighted astonishment.

She told me later that Mme la Duchesse d'Orléans had been saying that she was curious to know what had been happening in her husband's study; for she had learned of his tears and sobs, and that Bezons and I had been haunting him. Mme de Villeroy had repeated my remark when I left her after supper, and Mme la Duchesse d'Orléans had replied that if anyone could persuade him to leave his mistress it would be myself. She had gone on to say that she had made great efforts to draw me into her circle and win my friendship, but had been unsuccessful—all of which was perfectly true, for I never visited her except on formal occasions. She ended by saying that she had given up the attempt, glad enough that her husband should be intimate with a man of honour and intelligence from whom, unfriendly though he was, she felt she had nothing to fear. Becoming expansive, the Duchesse de Villeroy told me that Mme la Duchesse d'Orléans's joy was all the greater because she had been increasingly embarrassed and made miserable by Mme d'Argenton's insolence, and had foreseen no remedy. In desperation she had entreated the King and Mme de Maintenon to remove her, using every imaginable plea of conscience, pity and honour, but had made no impression on them. She had quite despaired of help ever coming from that quarter, or from her husband, who although his passion occasionally abated always returned more enamoured than before. To this I replied that it was most fortunate for the princess that she had failed and that the King's wisdom was greater than his paternal love. Had Mme d'Argenton been torn from M. le Duc d'Orléans's arms, love, and possibly wounded vanity, might well have driven him to extremes. He would never have believed his wife innocent, and once that idea had entered his head his marriage would have been destroyed and his wife the most wretched princess in all Europe.

At that point the Duchesse de Villeroy began to praise Mme la Duchesse d'Orléans for her wit, her prudence and strength of character, and her loyalty in friendship, saying that she would recognize her debt to me, and urging me to let myself become attached to her. I desired her to say that had I responded to the princess's gratifying approaches and done myself the honour of visiting her, my influence with the prince might have been much less effective. My caution had, indeed, proved doubly fortunate in that I had been able to enlighten M. le Duc d'Orléans regarding certain secrets not recorded here, for he might not have been so ready to trust me had I been on friendly terms with his duchess. Now, however, I no longer needed to remain neutral, and looked forward with pleasure to paying my court; none the less, there should be a certain interval. In the meantime I begged to convey, etc., etc.,—in other words, my compliments, and, above all, a strong recommendation to be secret, although that did not worry me unduly, for it was in her own interests and the subject was a delicate one.[1] I told her later how hugely I had been amused on the previous evening in Mme de Saint-Géran's drawing-room, by hearing Mme de Saint-Pierre[2] piteously lamenting over the sufferings of poor Mme la Duchesse d'Orléans under the insolence of Mme d'Argenton, and of the impossibility of aiding her, when all the time I knew that the affair was over and done with, and the news certain to break on the morrow.

It was by then nearing the hour of the King's dinner. I left Mme de Villeroy in order to go there and allow her time to dress before visiting Mme la Duchesse d'Orléans, to whom she was all agog to impart the good news at leisure. It was, as I have already mentioned, Friday, 3 January: the fourth Friday since the one on which I had first presented myself in hopes of an audience. I had begun to fear that nothing would come of it. The King was already at table. I went and stood with my back to the balustrade,[3] and towards the end of his dessert advanced to a corner of his armchair and begged him to be pleased to remember that he had allowed me to hope for a hearing. He turned and answered very courteously, 'Whenever you please. I would gladly hear you now, but I have business and there would scarcely be time.' A moment later he turned again and said, 'Tomorrow morning if you wish.' I replied that it was my duty to attend him at his own pleasure and convenience, and that I would do myself the honour of presenting myself next day. His answer seemed promising to me, for he had been affable, not in the least annoyed, and had shown his willingness to listen. Maréchal, the Chancellor, and Mme de Saint-Simon concurred in that opinion.

On my way back from the King I passed the outer door of Mme la Duchesse d'Orléans's apartment and was astonished to see Bezons emerge, for I imagined him to be in Paris, or well on his way thither. He was in the habit of paying her occasional visits; and he told me that she had sent for him, being anxious on account of what she had learned from the servants. He had told her all, and by so doing had vastly increased her joy. He said that he had given her the gist of our conversations, and described her as being in raptures and overflowing with gratitude to me, of which she had begged him to assure me. He none the less still dreaded the inevitable scandal and was more than ever eager to take refuge in Paris. He stayed only a few moments for fear that people should see us together, for all the

---

[1] This long account (greatly shortened—in the Pléiade edition it occupies forty-five pages) describes what Saint-Simon believed to be one of the finest actions of his life.

[2] A particular crony of the Duchesse d'Orléans. Her husband was Madame's master of the horse.

[3] The balustrade that fenced off the bed on the side opposite the windows. When the King dined à petit couvert, his table, with only one place laid, was put in front of the fireplace at right-angles to the balustrade.

world as though we were guilty conspirators. Since our main task was accomplished I let him go, for I had no further need to detain him.

On the following day, Saturday, 4 January, the last of those four days at the beginning of the year 1710 that were of such vital consequence to me, I made my appearance at the end of the King's *lever*, and watched him rise from his *prie-dieu* and enter his study without any sign to me. His *lever* was a court function which I rarely attended, and I therefore waited quietly while he went to mass and returned again to his study. Since his prolonged attack of gout he had taken to dressing lying on his bed,[1] and the attendant valets left little room for others. When the order was given, those with the study-entrée joined him, and the rest went to chat in the great gallery until his mass, leaving the captain of the guard alone in his bedroom. One of the blue pages[2] used to notify that officer when the King was ready to go to the chapel by the door leading out into the gallery, and the captain would then enter the study prepared to follow him.

I was thus the only person left in the bedroom besides the captain of the guard, who happened to be Harcourt.[3] He was surprised to see me lingering and asked what I wanted. Père Tellier was in the study with the King, but he did not stay long, and almost at once Nyert, the head valet on duty, came out, looked about him, and said that the King was asking for me. I immediately entered the study. The King was alone, leaning upon the lower end of the council table, as was his custom when he wished to speak to someone alone and intimately. As I approached I began to thank him for the favour which he had been pleased to grant me, and I spun out the compliment a little, so as to have leisure to observe his expression and readiness to listen. The former I thought severe, the latter complete. Then, since he still said nothing, I began. I said that I could no longer bear to live in disgrace (that word, however, I carefully avoided, replacing it by some longer phrase in order not to anger him. I employ it here only for the sake of brevity), and that I entreated him to tell me how I had offended. In case he should ask me what led me to imagine any change in his usual graciousness, I must answer that after having been included in every Marly for the past four years, my total exclusion now struck me as an unmistakable sign of disgrace, especially since it deprived me for long periods of the privilege of paying my court. The King's first words, looking vastly offended and haughty, were to say that this had no significance and indicated nothing whatsoever. But even had I not known the reason for my exclusion, his voice and expression would have confirmed that he did not speak the truth. Yet, since I had to accept his word,

---

[1] Only in bed was he free from the attentions of the various great nobles, whose privilege it was to dress him in the different articles of his attire. He always insisted on putting on his own underclothes in his bed.

[2] Blue was the colour of the royal liveries at Versailles and Marly.

[3] The Maréchal-Duc d'Harcourt.

I replied that what he had deigned to say relieved me considerably. None the less, since he was pleased to hear me, I begged him to let me unbosom myself—those were my very words—of many things that distressed me beyond measure and which others, as I well knew, had used against me.

It had all started, I continued, with rumours which I had scarcely dared to credit because of my youth and inexperience, but which were widely spread, to the effect that he had nominated me for the Rome embassy.[1] (As you will remember, these rumours were well-founded; but I spoke in this way because he had not mentioned the subject to me at that time [1706] or afterwards.) Since then, I had been a victim of envy and jealousy, for it was thought that if not stopped in time I might one day amount to something. Thus nothing I could do or say would prove my innocence to my enemies, even silence was accounted a crime in me, and M. d'Antin was for ever attacking me. 'D'Antin!'[2] exclaimed the King looking somewhat mollified, 'he has never so much as mentioned your name.' I said that this assurance gave me real joy, but that d'Antin had persecuted me in public on every possible occasion, and I could not but fear his having done me the same ill-service with His Majesty. By that time King Louis had begun to recover his composure and to appear more relaxed; he even showed a little graciousness, as though my concluding words had not displeased him.[3] I was just starting a new sentence with the words, 'There is, however, another man...', when he interrupted me, saying, 'But you too, Monsieur, you talk and you blame; that is why people speak against you.' I said that I took good care to speak no ill of anyone, and as for His Majesty, I would sooner die. Here I looked him straight in the eye with fire in my glance. Regarding others, although I kept a careful watch on my tongue, it was very hard not to speak one's mind on some occasions. 'But,' continued the King, 'you speak your mind on every subject, including affairs of State—our defeats, for instance, and with such rancour...' It was now my turn to interrupt, seeing that he spoke with ever-increasing kindness. I said that ordinarily I talked very little of State affairs, and then with great restraint; but that on one occasion, goaded by our disasters, my heart had overborne my head, and then something had occurred which to my intense astonishment had caused a scandal and done me much harm. I begged him to be my judge; to let me prove my innocence or humbly entreat his forgiveness.

I was well aware of the fact that my wager on Lille had been put to most wicked use; I had already resolved to tell the King the truth, and I grasped this opportunity which he so freely offered, making light of the whole matter in the

---

[1] See Vol. 1, pp. 287-291.

[2] The Marquis, later the Duc d'Antin (c. 1665-1736), the legitimate son of the Marquis and Marquise de Montespan. He was a great favourite with the King, and his was the only private house which King Louis regularly visited.

[3] Louis XIV on the whole preferred his courtiers to be on bad terms. He mistakenly believed that it helped his rule to keep them at loggerheads.

way he demanded from all who had dealings with him. I explained that during that siege, realizing as I did the vital need to hold the fortress and the unlikelihood of relief (seeing that three couriers had already gone in vain to the army with orders to march), I had been so much exasperated by those who persisted in saying that all was well that I had wagered four pistoles that Lille would fall unrelieved. 'Oh!' said King Louis, 'if you blamed and wagered only because you were anxious and distressed at the thought of defeat, there was no harm; on the contrary, you did well. But who was the other man of whom you wished to speak to me?' I replied that it was Monsieur le Duc, whereupon the King was silent, not saying, as he had done regarding d'Antin, that he had not mentioned my name. I then told him in as few words as possible, but omitting nothing essential, of Mme de Lussan's suit against me;[1] and, just as in the matter of Lille I had avoided mentioning Chamillart, Vendôme,[2] and Monseigneur, so now I carefully avoided naming his daughter Madame la Duchesse. I continued that the Chancellor and all the council, the premier président, and every member of the Parlement had found Mme de Lussan so unreasonable that they had rebuked her, and it appeared to me vastly strange that Monsieur le Duc should busy himself supporting his mother's lady-in-waiting when Monsieur le Prince, his father, had severely reprimanded her. I finally remarked that since His Majesty allowed subjects to bring suits against him every day of the week, it seemed a little odd that I might not defend myself against Mme de Lussan. Monsieur le Duc, however, had never forgiven me, as I had perceived on many occasions; but what was truly monstrous was that when I had gone as usual to La Ferté at Easter, quite unaware that Monsieur le Prince was dying, he should have told His Majesty that my absence was a pity because I could have set them all to rights in the matter of the length of mantles.[3]

The King, who had listened to all I had to say and was visibly impressed, said as though wishing to admonish me that I had a reputation for being very heated on matters concerning precedence, and that I was often meddlesome, inciting others and becoming a ring-leader. I replied that in the past I had done so, and believed that I had not thereby displeased him, begging him at the same time to recollect that since the matter of the collecting bag, seven years earlier, I had not been embroiled in any quarrel whatsoever. I reminded him briefly of what had happened then, and of how he had given me cause to believe him not

[1] A dispute (1707) over property left to Saint-Simon by his half-sister; Mme de Lussan was a relative of hers. The tale is a long and boring one. Saint-Simon says that he has omitted the *ennui inséparable de ce détail*, but the present translator has omitted still more of it.

[2] Chamillart, Saint-Simon's particular friend, who was dismissed from the ministry for war in 1709, and the great Duc de Vendôme (also disgraced), Saint-Simon's pet abomination because he was 'the fruit of royal bastardy', had filthy personal habits, and was lazy and negligent in his campaigns.

[3] The proper length of mourning mantles at funerals was a matter of rank and privilege that caused innumerable squabbles between the princes of the blood, the royal bastards, and the dukes. Saint-Simon had very strong ideas on this subject.

dissatisfied with my conduct. He admitted that this was so, and volunteered some further remarks, showing that he remembered perfectly. With that encouragement I did not hesitate to say that the Lorraines[1] had not forgiven me. Returning to the main issue, I added that it was hard after four years of not meddling that Monsieur le Duc should attack me in my absence, when I least expected it. The less formal tone which I had dared to take when speaking of the Lorraines and Monsieur le Duc, and the interest and unrestrained benevolence of the King's expression, emboldened me to declare that non-interference had plainly done me no good, since in my last absence I had been held responsible for the incident of the Duchess of Mantua, Mme de Montbazon, and their coaches.[2] Might I venture to ask what I could possibly do to escape such wholly undeserved and lying slanders, for I was far away at that time and totally unaware of any quarrel between those ladies? 'That,' said the King in a truly paternal tone, 'should teach you how Society regards you; and you must admit to having somewhat deserved your reputation. Had you never quarrelled, or at least not become so heated over questions of rank, no one would have thought to spread such rumours. You see now how carefully you should avoid such things, in order that the past may be forgotten, and your reputation retrieved by greater prudence and moderation before it utterly ruins you.' I replied that for the past four years I had striven with exactly that object, as I had just had the honour to inform him, and I should so continue in the future. But I implored him to see how little I had been concerned in these latest quarrels, and how I had none the less been blamed for them.

I said next that I wished to explain the truth about my not going to Guyenne after receiving his permission. The fact was that I had feared to become involved in a petty dispute that might have troubled him. The Maréchal de Montrevel had been encroaching outrageously on my authority as Governor of Blaye,[3] and I could not go there until the matter was settled. I had put my case to the Maréchal de Boufflers; he had given judgment in my favour, and I had fully expected M. de Montrevel to accept that judgment. He, however, had insisted that the King should decide, but rather than trouble him or, worse, fatigue him with a private dispute, I had preferred to allow M. de Montrevel to usurp my prerogative. King Louis so much relished these words of mine that he several times interrupted with approving exclamations, and afterwards praised me at some length. He did not, however, inquire into the rights and wrongs of the quarrel, for he detested

---

[1] The princely family of Lorraine, which Saint-Simon detested (although, in 1715, he was eager for his cousin to marry a Lorraine heiress and had nearly married one himself in 1695). He believed that they strove unceasingly to gain precedence over the dukes and peers.

[2] A most undignified brawl, when neither party would allow their horses to be reined back, so as to allow the other to go first through the second gate of the Palais Royal. See Vol. 1, p. 472.

[3] Any suggestion of tampering with his precious governorship of Blaye, which he had inherited from his father, was like showing a red rag to a bull.

any form of argument and vastly preferred to let everything fall into disorder, even against his own interests, rather than hear disputes debated or, above all, be asked to decide them. I then told him how I had been long absent in my misery at having, so I thought, displeased him; and I took this occasion to stress my love and devotion to his person and my earnest desire to please him in all things. I spoke almost familiarly, letting my heart guide me, because I could see from his face, voice, and words that I might do so with impunity. In point of fact he accepted my protestations with surprising graciousness, and left me convinced beyond all doubt that I had regained his good opinion. I even entreated him to notify me if he heard anything to my detriment, so that I might at once tell him the truth and beg him to forgive and admonish me, or alternatively see that I had not been at fault.

When he was quite certain that I had finished he got up from off the table. I asked him then to consider me for a lodging, so that I might pay my court with greater assiduity; but he said that none was vacant, and with a half-bow, still graciously smiling, he went to his other rooms. I, after making a very low bow indeed, went out by the door through which I had entered, having had more than half an hour's private audience, ending very favourably, indeed far beyond anything that I had dared to expect.[1] I called first on Maréchal, as was only right, to tell him what had passed and my consciousness that I owed it to him alone, which delighted him, for he thought the omens were good. Thence I went to the Chancellor, who was at leisure to listen to me because the King was at mass. We weighed each point with enormous care, and was much struck by the way in which the King had entered into every detail; his answers, interjections, and especially his admonishments. He afterwards declared that he did not know four men at the Court, no matter what their rank, whom the King would have treated thus. He exhorted me to be very prudent and to have good hope for the future. Knowing the King as he did, he assured me that I might be certain he no longer held anything against me, that no bad impression remained with him, and that I was fully reinstated in his regard. What, however, most surprised and delighted me was that M. de Beauvilliers whole-heartedly agreed with him. I can scarcely describe the joy of my friends, the way in which the Chancellor crowed over the matter of my retirement which, so he said, only his cleverness had prevented, or how hard I tried to express my thanks.

I then hurried to put Mme de Saint-Simon out of her anxiety, which was turned to great rejoicing. It was she who had set the Chancellor and my other friends at me, and by so doing had compelled me to essay that last chance, with

---

[1] Although the success of his audience may not immediately be apparent to the reader, Saint-Simon thought it had been a great success. It certainly impressed his friends, for it showed that he could defend himself against powerful enemies.

such success that the King ever afterwards treated me not only kindly but with a distinction remarkable towards a man of my age. Of my age, I repeat, because although thirty-five, which is not young, I still seemed very young compared with the King, especially since I held no office and thus had no occasion for intimacy with him. What a great treasure is a virtuous and sensible wife! Since nothing was more rare than for the King to grant an audience to those without official business, mine, especially because of its length, made a greater stir than I could have wished. I let people talk but remained silent, for one is not obliged to render an account of one's private affairs. Let us now return to M. le Duc d'Orléans with whom I spent the whole of that afternoon.

He had already told me that Mme de Maintenon had sent for the Duchesse de Ventadour and commissioned her to explain the situation to Mme d'Argenton; whereupon he and that duchess had arranged to summon Mlle de Chausseraye from her little house, the Château de Madrid.[1] He accordingly dispatched his post-chaise and that lady came immediately. The task seemed monstrously unpleasant to her, but the tears and pleas of her friend the duchess at last induced her to acquaint their mutual crony of the change in her circumstances. Mlle de Chausseraye was tall and stout, exceedingly clever and entirely given up to intrigue for the promotion of her own interests. She was of no account. Her real name was Le Petit de Verne, but because her father owned the miserable little estate of Chausseraye, in Poitou, she preferred to use that title. No woman was ever more cunning, more flattering without vulgarity, more feline or more false; no one more quickly took stock of her world and captured it. She had been one of Madame's maids of honour, but had long ago been superannuated;[2] indeed, it was in Madame's house that she had first met Mme d'Argenton, for she was intimate with all that circle and had gained much benefit from its members, including large sums of money from M. le Duc d'Orléans. It was incredible the number of affairs in which she had taken a hand. She was a great gambler on every possible occasion and lost literally millions. The King was good to her and more than once had retrieved her with very considerable sums. I was very well acquainted with her for she was excellent company and knew everything about everyone, thanks to her highly placed friends. At one time I was in the habit of visiting her regularly, but I soon perceived that the rupture between M. le Duc d'Orléans and his mistress had damned me in her eyes, and later, whenever she saw the opportunity, she was a dangerous enemy. There will be occasion to mention her again.

As I have said, Mlle de Chausseraye went straight to the Duchesse de Ventadour, and then on to Mme d'Argenton's house in Paris. That lady was out,

---

[1] In the Bois de Boulogne.
[2] In 1688. The maids of honour were always very young. This one was superannuated at the age of twenty-four.

but having learned that she was supping with the Princesse de Rohan and not expected back until late, Mlle de Chausseraye sent a message that she had important news and would await her return. When Mme d'Argenton showed no sign of returning she sent again demanding her presence. As soon as they were together she stated that she had something so grave to impart that with all her heart she wished someone else had been chosen. Thereafter she proceeded with such roundabout phrases, as though breaking the news of a death, that it was very long before Mme d'Argenton knew all. Tears, cries, lamentations re-echoed through the house, making the numerous servants aware that the end of her felicity had come, and with it the end of their own security. After a prolonged silence Mlle de Chausseraye uttered such consolation as she might, stressing the size of the endowment, the delicate attention of the omitted *lettre de cachet*, the freedom of the entire kingdom with the sole exception of Paris and the duke's hereditary estates. Gradually Mme d'Argenton grew calmer, and at last proposed retiring to the Abbaye de Gomerfontaine, in Picardy, where she had been educated and where her sister was a nun. They accordingly sent for M. le Duc d'Orléans's secretary, the Abbé de Thésut, and dispatched him to Versailles with a letter for the duke and another asking Mme de Ventadour to consult Mme de Maintenon as to this refuge

I was still chatting with M. le Duc d'Orléans and two or three members of his staff, endeavouring to the best of my ability to divert him, when the Abbé de Thésut entered and whispered a word in his ear. He changed colour, reflected a moment, rose, walked with the abbé to the farther end of his *entresol*, and signed to me to join them; whereat the rest left the room. He then said that Gomerfontaine had been forbidden, bursting into a perfect transport of rage and resentment, demanding to know whether I had ever known such cruelty, bitterly regretting that he had not escaped from Bezons and myself into the arms of his mistress on the night before the rupture. I let him storm awhile, and then said that before letting himself go entirely he had better discover the truth, and I asked the abbé what she was expected to do and why Gomerfontaine was banned. He said that Mme de Maintenon cherished a special love for the abbess and the entire community, which included several girls from Saint-Cyr, and that she had plans for its future which she did not wish Mme d'Argenton to spoil. I turned to the prince, who was still fuming, saying that he might be tormenting himself without cause, since I could imagine only two things capable of distressing him and injuring Mme d'Argenton, a written expulsion, which she had been spared, and a restriction on her liberty, which I did not find here. I had some trouble in persuading him to see reason, but eventually he consented to write to Mme de Maintenon although he fell back into his chair after the first words, exclaiming that he could not think, let alone write, and begging me to finish it for him; which I did, after excusing myself to the abbé.[1] They both approved of my suggestions, the abbé dictated, and the prince wrote and addressed the note with his own hand. It was then taken by his head-valet because the King was already closeted with Mme de Maintenon. The letter was given into her hands, but the King after asking from whom it came read it himself, which was exactly what we had intended. For the remainder of the evening I had to endure M. le Duc d'Orléans's complaints, and, since we were alone, the sight of his mistress's letters, for he had been in correspondence with her; I had the greatest difficulty in extracting his promise not to write again.

After supper the King told him that Mme de Maintenon's objections prevented the use of Gomerfontaine, but that apart from that one convent Mme d'Argenton had full liberty to go wherever she pleased for as long or as short a time as she chose; all of which was accompanied by expressions of affection, vastly different from those which the singularly ill-timed announcement had provoked. She remained only four days in Paris, and then went to her father's house near Pont-Sainte-Maxence. Her friends thought her expulsion abominable, but dared not protest against the rupture. The Duchesse de Ventadour, who was tender-hearted but could not protest because of her official post,[2] resorted to tears; the Duchesse de La Ferté and Mme de Bouillon both flew into a passion, and the dregs of Paris and the Palais Royal surpassed themselves in recriminations. The more reasonable and by far the greater number concealed neither their joy at the rupture nor their approval of the methods adopted, although two millions appeared to them excessively generous. To have left Mme d'Argenton in Paris courting the danger of a reunion, or at the very least of giving rise to fresh rumours, was clearly contrary to all good sense. They appreciated the impossibility of expelling her without the King's order, and therefore the absolute necessity of informing him first. As for the manner of securing her retirement, they thought it had been more than considerate.

On New Year's Day the King gave none of the gifts which his family were accustomed to receive from him annually, and he assigned the forty thousand pistoles which he usually took for himself to supply the needs of the Flemish frontier. This was against all precedent, but indeed supplies of every kind were most tragically lacking.

On Saturday, 15 February, the King was woken at seven o'clock, an hour before his usual time, because Mme la Duchesse de Bourgogne was in labour. He hurried to be dressed and go to her. She did not keep him long in suspense, for at precisely three minutes and three seconds after eight o'clock she brought into this world a Duc d'Anjou who is now the reigning

---

[1] Because the Abbé de Thésut was the Duc d'Orléans's secretary, and Saint-Simon had no wish to encroach on his duties.
[2] Madame's lady-in-waiting; she later became the governess of Louis XV.

King Louis XV. There was great rejoicing. The prince was immediately baptized by Cardinal de Janson in the room where he was born, and was then carried to his own apartments in the lap of the Duchesse de Ventadour, sitting in the King's chair, escorted by the Maréchal de Boufflers, with a detachment of the body-guard and their officers. Shortly afterwards La Vrillière took him the blue ribbon of the Order, in the presence of the entire Court. Both events vastly displeased his brother,[1] who made no attempt to conceal his feelings. Mme de Saint-Simon was in the Duchesse de Bourgogne's bedroom and thus happened to be one of the very first to see the new-born prince. The birth and afterbirth were most successfully accomplished.

I have spoken elsewhere of Courcillon,[2] a man like no other. He was witty and polished, an inexhaustible source of gaiety and fun, an unbridled libertine, with an impudence that knew no shame. He made grim jokes whilst they amputated his leg after the Battle of Malplaquet. Apparently they botched the operation, for it had to be repeated at about this time at Versailles, and so high that his life was endangered. Dangeau, that prudent and accomplished courtier, and his wife, greatly relished by Mme de Maintenon and always with the King, set to work on their son to persuade him to confess. He was bored. Knowing his father, he rid himself of that tedious subject by pretending to yield, saying that if he were so bad he would do things in style, and have Père de La Tour, general of the Oratory, and no other; let there be no argument. Dangeau shivered from top to toe, for he had witnessed the vast displeasure caused by that father's ministrations to the dying Monsieur le Prince de Conti and Monsieur le Prince,[3] and he dared not court that danger for himself or even for his son, if he survived. From that moment there was no further mention of confession; and Courcillon, whose sole aim had thus been achieved, was silent also, though he made a good story of it after his recovery.

Dangeau's brother was an abbé, an academician, grammarian, and pedant, a very good man but profoundly ridiculous. When Courcillon perceived that worthy father standing deeply distressed at the foot of his bed he burst into fits of laughter, imploring him to go and weep somewhere else because his grimaces were killing him. He went on to say that if he died the abbé would have to marry and continue the line, and he drew such an absurd picture of him in feathers and a cavalry uniform that everyone present laughed till they cried. His gaiety saved him, and he received the unique privilege of visiting the King and everyone else without his hat or sword because they impeded him, with his leg made almost entirely of wood, with which he never ceased to play pranks.

---

[1] The three-year-old Duc de Bretagne.

[2] Dangeau's son, Philippe Egon, Marquis de Courcillon (1687-1719).

[3] Saint-Simon claims that the Jesuits were furious at losing a 'royal confessional' to an Oratoire father. There had been a tremendous rumpus and those held responsible for introducing Père de La Tour had been punished.

There were many deaths about this time, and the first was that of the Duchesse de Foix, who was mourned by all, more especially by M. de Foix. She was Roquelaure's sister, and wrote to him on her deathbed asking him to forgive his daughter and the Prince de Léon,[1] which he accordingly did. Mme de Foix was the prettiest hunchback imaginable, tall, an exquisite dancer in former times, moving so gracefully that one could scarcely have wished her humpless. She seldom appeared at the Court, was much seen in Society and at the tables, and was extremely amusing without the slightest trace of malice. She never admitted to being more than fifteen, although she died childless at the age of fifty-five.

Another death, at the age of eighty-eight, was that of the Maréchale de La Meilleraye, the paternal aunt of Mme de Villeroy and of my brother-in-law the Duc de Brissac. She was marvellously vain and quite crazy on the subject of her ancestry. It was she who devised the princely coronet which she persuaded Brissac to add to his coat of arms, and which others, for no known reason, have since imitated. Equally unknown was the cause of her wild enthusiasm regarding her forebears. Her family was immensely distinguished in the reign of François I; but it does not do to trace them back much further than the 'Gros Brissac' of that epoch, who had been master of the royal bakehouse, master of the falcons, and Governor of Anjou and Maine. His father and grandfather were respectively Governor of the Château of Beaufort and Seneschal of Provence, but their wives were exceedingly common, and their forebears merely equerries in very small households, without connections, and no traceable ancestry before 1386, which does not add up to a very ancient line.

But to return to the Maréchale de La Meilleraye herself. There was talk in her presence one day of the death of the Chevalier de Savoie, brother of the famous Prince Eugene, who died young, and very suddenly, having been monstrously debauched but none the less exceedingly well provided with benefices, all of which occasioned a good deal of head-shaking. Mme de La Meilleraye, after listening for a time in silence, remarked with an air of absolute conviction, 'It is my considered opinion that where a man of that birth is concerned God would think twice before damning him.' Everyone burst out laughing but she could not be persuaded to change her views.

Her vanity was to suffer a cruel blow. She used to take every opportunity of apologizing for having married M. de la Meilleraye, whose second wife she was, and childless. Soon after his death, or even before it, she became enamoured of Saint-Ruth, formerly his page, and she nearly lost her *tabouret* when she announced her marriage to him. Saint-Ruth was a gentleman in a very small way, tall, well-built, known to everyone, but monstrously ugly, although whether it was marriage that made him so I cannot tell.

[1] They had eloped, causing a terrible scandal. See Vol. 1, pp. 357 et seq.

He was a gallant officer, had gained experience in the wars, and rose by sheer merit
to be lieutenant of the bodyguard and a lieutenant-general. He was also a brute,
and one day when the Maréchale had warmed his ears for him, he took his stick
to her and gave her a beating. This he repeated so often that that lady, unable
to endure it any longer, swallowed her pride and appealed for protection to the
King, who kindly undertook to put matters right. He summoned Saint-Ruth to
his study, called him to order, and forbade him in future to maltreat his wife. But
Saint-Ruth could not abstain. There were fresh appeals from the Maréchale, and
the King, growing angry, began to threaten. For a time Saint-Ruth restrained
himself, but the habit had grown on him and once more it gained the upper hand.
Once more the Maréchale complained, whereupon the King, seeing that Saint-
Ruth was incorrigible, kindly sent him to Guyenne on the excuse of a vacant
command for which there had been no other necessity than her pressing need to
be separated from him. The King afterwards sent him to Ireland, where he was
killed. He, also, died childless.

A third death shocked everyone and at the same time brought general relief.
Monsieur le Duc[1] had suffered attacks of some unrecognized disease accompanied by occasional fits, possibly of epilepsy or apoplexy. They were of short duration and he concealed them with immense care, even going so far as to dismiss
a member of his household for mentioning them to a fellow servant. He had
been afflicted with constant headaches, some of them very severe, for a long
time past, and ill-health had spoilt his pleasure in being free of a father who had
much obstructed him, and of a brother-in-law who was in many ways a sore trial
and often a source of real unhappiness.[2] Madame la Princesse, for whom he felt
some regard and affection, urged him to think of God and his health. After many
exhortations he promised to consider both, but not until after the carnival; for he
was determined to enjoy that to the full. He made Madame la Duchesse come
to Paris on Shrove Monday for the balls and receptions, and in the meantime
arranged to give two supper-parties for her and numerous ladies, and to take
them from ball to ball throughout the nights of the Monday and Shrove Tuesday.
On the Monday evening he went to the Hôtel de Bouillon and thence to his old
friend the Duc de Coislin, whose health was already failing. He had no torches
and only a solitary footman behind his coach. As they crossed the Pont Royal
returning from the Hôtel de Coislin he was taken so ill that he pulled the cord
and made the footman sit beside him, asking him to say whether his mouth was
crooked; but it was not. He then told the coachman to stop at the short flight of

[1] The last remaining prince of the blood of Saint-Simon's generation. The successors were too young to be considered.
Thereafter he was alone in his struggle to protect the rights of the dukes and peers against the encroachments of the
bastards, and the attacks of the Lorraines.
[2] Monsieur le Prince and M. le Prince de Conti. (Monsieur le Duc's eldest son was subsequently known as Monsieur le
Duc, although by tradition he should have been called Monsieur le Prince like his grandfather.)

steps leading up to his privy, so that he might enter by the back way and avoid the company assembled for supper at the Hôtel de Condé. He had lost his speech during the journey and for a time even was unconscious, but he managed to stammer out some last words before the footman and a cleaner, who happened to be on the spot, lifted him from his coach and carried him to the door of his privy, which was locked. They thereupon beat upon it so loud and long that everyone in the house heard them and came running. He was hurried into bed. Doctors and priests arrived with all speed, but their services were unavailing, for he showed no sign of life except for some horrible grimaces, and died at four o'clock in the morning of Shrove Tuesday.[1]

Madame la Duchesse, surrounded by masks and dominoes and a vast crowd of guests in carnival attire, was shocked by the suddenness and the fearful spectacle, but she firmly retained her presence of mind. She felt the need for M. du Maine, although they were not on good terms, and soon after Monsieur le Duc had been put to bed she summoned him from Versailles, together with M. le Comte de Toulouse and Mme la Princesse de Conti.[2] Mme la Duchesse d'Orléans she did not send for, because she had fallen out with her and could expect no good from her influence. Meanwhile she allowed herself to shed some tears. No one, however, supposed that she wept for Monsieur le Duc, but rather from a secret sorrow that had afflicted her these twelve months past[3] and because her deliverance came too late.

Monsieur le Duc was very considerably shorter than the shortest men,[4] and without being fat was thick throughout; his head was astonishingly thick, and his face was frightening. They say that one of Madame la Princesse's dwarfs was the cause. His skin was a livid yellow, his expression seldom free from anger and always so bold and so arrogant that it was hard to grow accustomed to him. He possessed wit and learning, the remains of a good education, and could when so disposed be civil, even gracious; but that was rare indeed. Unlike his forbears he was neither base nor greedy, but he had all their courage and displayed keenness and intelligence in war. He had also inherited their malevolence, and their skill in promoting themselves by artful encroachments; and was even bolder and fiercer in such attacks. His perverse morals he regarded as virtues, and the terrible vengeance which he more than once exacted, and which he would have thought most wrong in others, was to him a personal prerogative. He was always poised

---

[1] He is supposed to have died from the effects of his debauchery.

[2] Her two brothers and her half-sister, children of the King and Mme de Montespan. See list of the Royal Family in 1710.

[3] The death of M. le Prince de Conti, with whom she had been in love.

[4] All the Condés were short. Their grandfather (le Grand Condé) was a tall man; but their father was more than a foot shorter, and they were shorter still. The Duchesse du Maine was almost a midget. The Grand Condé once remarked bitterly that if the trend continued he would have to use a microscope to see his descendants.

to spring, so that people fled from him in fear; even his friends were not safe from cruel jests delivered to their faces, or songs made up on the spur of the moment that brought the house down and were never forgotten. They repaid him in the same coin and with even greater cruelty. Friends he had none, only close acquaintances, oddly selected, and most of them as insignificant as, apart from his rank, he was himself. These so-called friends fled from him; he pursued them to avoid being alone, and if he discovered that they received other company he would appear suddenly in their midst, rating them for not including him. I have seen such persons mightily discomfited.

A cruel streak drove him to maltreat everyone and to take such pleasure in it that there was no restraining him; and this was combined with the kind of insolence (if such a word may be applied to a prince of the blood) that makes a tyrant more hated than his tyranny. Domestic quarrels, wild outbursts of jealousy, and the bitter hurt of knowing them to be useless, ceaseless alternations of conjugal love and conjugal fury, the heartbreak of powerlessness in a nature so passionate and unrestrained, despair at his dread of the King, and at his father's evident preference for M. le Prince de Conti, rage at that prince's universal popularity compared with the general hatred of himself—such passions tormented him unceasingly, making him resemble certain wild beasts that seem made for the sole purpose of attacking and devouring the human race. Thus his only satisfaction lay in the insults and abuse that had become habitual with him because of his extraordinary arrogance; in them he did find some pleasure. Yet ferocious though he was to others, he was himself still more tormented. At the last States-General of Burgundy, which he held after his father's death, he made an effort to appear more approachable, and rendered justice with some semblance of kindness. He took an interest in the affairs of that province, and issued wise orders for keeping the peace; none the less he treated the Parlement itself with insolence, demanding rights which his father had never claimed, and securing them with many insults. To anyone who knew Monsieur le Duc this portrait would not seem exaggerated, for there was no one who did not regard his death as a personal deliverance.

I learned of his death when I was awakened at Versailles, where I was staying. I went to the King's mass and heard the full account and the arrangements for the funeral, and then visited M. le Duc d'Orléans who disposed as quickly as possible of some formal calls, and led me into a study where his duchess was waiting for their drawing-room to be free from visitors. There, when we three were alone, I learned what had happened between them and Madame la Duchesse during their visit of condolence that morning, and of what occurred later between the King and M. le Duc d'Orléans concerning the precedence of that prince's daughters and the princesses of the blood. As I have hitherto barely mentioned this affair, or referred to it merely in passing, I shall now explain it at some length, but still without all the details, which may be found in the documents, that is to say in the memoranda sent by both sides to the King, the correspondence with him and Mme de Maintenon, the records of his final ruling and of all the other reports and opinions. To tell all would mean too long a digression.

You must know that Mme la Duchesse d'Orléans was perhaps the proudest woman in the world and probably the most stubborn and tenacious in supporting her opinions and obtaining her desires. Born what she was, one might have expected her to have been content to rank so far above her sisters, who themselves were the first of their kind to marry princes of the blood.[1] But on the contrary, her higher rank as a Grandchild of France served only to encourage her to make further encroachments. She thought it intolerable that her children should rank merely as princes of the blood like their cousins, and she accordingly conceived for them the novel title of Great-grandchildren of France so as to give them precedence. M. le Duc d'Orléans considered the whole idea absurd from the beginning; but at that time he was entirely absorbed with Mme d'Argenton, with the result that he carelessly allowed the plot to grow until he had become thoroughly entangled.

Their son the Duc de Chartres[2] was still too young for any precedence to be claimed on his behalf, but their elder daughter had reached an age, and above all a physical development, that made her fit to be 'presented', as it was called, and launched into the worlds of the Court and Society. The first step in Mme la Duchesse d'Orléans's plan was to gain precedence for her over her aunts, Madame la Duchesse and Mme la Princesse de Conti. There was no trouble regarding the next generation because of the greater antiquity of the Orléans line; but with their mothers, the wife and widow of princes of the blood, it was different, for in France, among people of all conditions, married women always take precedence of the unmarried of similar rank, and so it had always been with princesses of the blood.

It appeared rash to reveal with undue suddenness this newly created title of Great-grandchild of France, and Mme la Duchesse d'Orléans thus thought it wiser to proceed by degrees, beginning by basing her daughter's precedence on the grounds of being of the senior branch. In the meantime she neither presented her nor allowed her to be seen in public; but as an opening gambit caused her to be addressed at the Palais Royal simply as 'Mademoiselle', there having been no one so named since the marriage of Mme de Lorraine.[3] That was readily accepted, for even the princes were not

---

[1] The Dowager-Princesse de Conti and Madame la Duchesse, the other two daughters of Louis XIV.

[2] Louis, Duc de Chartres, later Duc d'Orléans, who was aged seven in 1710.

[3] Elisabeth Charlotte d'Orléans (1676-1744), the Duc d'Orléans's sister, who had married the Duc de Lorraine in 1698.

averse to one of their number gaining a form of address that had heretofore been reserved for very close relatives of the monarch. It became the general mode of addressing her; the King did not object, and before long Mme la Duchesse d'Orléans would have shown herself deeply offended had anyone said differently. None the less, the delay in presenting her, and a certain rather rigid formality in the family circle (where it was not relished), aroused rumours. The princes of the blood were alerted and became vigilant; but nothing was said yet.

Soon afterwards, however, there happened to be marriage-contracts that required witnessing; Mademoiselle was of an age to sign; and it was then that the trouble arose. Mme la Duchesse d'Orléans desired her to sign before her aunts; those ladies violently objected; Mademoiselle to avoid defeat refused to sign at all, and her claim to precedence thus became public. There was a great rumpus, and much ill feeling between Mme la Duchesse d'Orléans and Madame la Duchesse, with their friends very imprudently taking sides. The claim was stated and had to be supported; old quarrels were remembered by both parties; remarks and repartee flew to and fro with extreme lack of restraint. The affair had reached this stage when Monsieur le Duc died, but the King had still not intervened, partly from an inborn dislike of giving judgment, partly to avoid angering the losing side.

This, however, was not the only quarrel between the Princesses. Mme la Duchesse du Maine[1] had kept the rank of princess of the blood after her marriage, but had not so far applied for a warrant, as the others had done when they married men who were not princes of the blood. Her hidden intention had been to support her husband's assumption of princely rank; later to claim that he held it by right, and in the course of time to change her own status to that of wife of a prince of the blood. Until then there had been little or no trouble with her sisters; but now that Mme la Duchesse had presented her daughters and introduced them to the Court and Society, her claim needed to be established. The witnessing of the marriage-contracts thus brought the matter to a head in her case also, and since she dared not refer publicly to M. du Maine's rank, she claimed that as a sister of Monsieur le Duc she had the right to sign before his daughters. When that claim was disallowed, she, too, refused to write her name. Her original demand was unprecedented, and doubly absurd because she had always signed before her husband, which she would not have done had he been born a prince of the blood.

All this had occurred before I was acquainted with Mme la Duchesse d'Orléans; and her husband had been so little interested that he had barely mentioned the affair to me. I therefore knew none of the details. He now told me that Monsieur

---

[1] The Duchesse du Maine was the daughter of Monsieur le Prince and thus ranked as a princess of the blood. M. du Maine had been granted all the privileges of a prince of the blood, but not yet the title.

le Duc's death had seemed to him a good time to settle the dispute and that he had spoken to the King that same morning, asking him to give his judgment at that moment when old quarrels were temporarily forgotten, and his ruling, whatever it might be, would be accepted meekly. The King had seemed to agree, but had warned him not to be too confident lest the judgment go against him; to which he had merely answered with a new appeal for a ruling. My comment was that nothing could be worse than the present situation, for Mademoiselle could appear nowhere in the company of her aunts since they refused to allow her precedence. I also thought (wherein I was much mistaken) that no matter what the King said, he would not decide against M. le Duc d'Orléans.

After mass that same morning the King visited Madame la Duchesse, lying beautifully dolorous upon her bed, and spoke seriously to her of ending her quarrel with Mme la Duchesse d'Orléans. He had been much troubled by their disputes, and he, also, believed that this was the right moment to end them. Full of such reflections, he went in the evening to call on Mme la Duchesse de Bourgogne, as he often did when she was confined, and contrary to his usual custom he dismissed the company after the first greetings. Only Mme de Maintenon, Monseigneur, and Mgr le Duc de Bourgogne remained, and they all gathered around the bed while M. le Duc de Berry was being summoned. The King then explained the affair to them and what M. le Duc d'Orléans had said; and all agreed that he should make a ruling. He proceeded to tell them to discuss the whole affair and to give their votes as they thought best, for in truth he cared very little which of his bastard daughters triumphed. Monseigneur, who hated M. le Duc d'Orléans and adored Madame la Duchesse, argued with all his might on behalf of the princes of the blood. Mgr le Duc de Bourgogne cast his vote likewise, but with better reason, and M. le Duc de Berry firmly agreed with him. A decision having thus been reached, the King sought some means of consoling Mme la Duchesse d'Orléans, and finally pronounced his verdict that Grand-daughters of France should be preceded only by Daughters of France or wives of Sons of France. Mme la Duchesse d'Orléans was thus assured of precedence over any future daughters of M. le Duc de Berry. On the other hand, the King ruled that the wives of princes of the blood should have precedence over all the daughters of Grandsons of France.

Next came the affair of the Duchesse du Maine, which the King wished to settle at the same time, and here the judgment went against her; for her claim to precede the daughters of the late Monsieur le Duc on the plea of being their aunt was defeated, and it was also ruled that princesses of the blood who married men of lower rank should, except by special warrant, lose their title. Thus her entire scheme for the advancement of M. du Maine fell to pieces, but the King said that he would at once send her a warrant in case she had not already applied for one. Thus all was settled, but the King imposed silence upon them until he had made the announcement after his supper. Here I must describe the ordinary arrangements so that you may understand how he proceeded on this occasion. When the King left the table[1] he was accustomed to stand for less than half a quarter of an hour with his back to the balustrade in his bedroom, where all the ladies who had attended him at supper stood waiting in a semicircle; all, that is, except those who had *tabourets*. The *tabouret*-ladies followed him from the supper-room behind the princes and princesses of the blood; stepped forward one by one to drop a very low curtsey, and then completed the half-circle of standing ladies, with the men standing behind them. The King amused himself for a little while admiring the dresses, faces, and graceful curtseys; said a word or two to the princes and princesses, and then, bowing right and left to the other ladies, and repeating this gesture once or twice with unexampled majesty, moved towards his outer study. He stayed there a moment to give his orders and then continued into the inner study.[2] There, with all the doors left wide open, he seated himself in an armchair, with Mme la Duchesse de Bourgogne, Madame, the three bastard Princesses, and Mme du Maine, when she was at Versailles, sitting on *tabourets* at either side and slightly behind him. Monseigneur, M. le Duc d'Orléans, the two bastards, the late Monsieur le Duc (as the husband of Madame la Duchesse), the two sons of M. du Maine, and d'Antin (after he was given charge of the buildings) all stood. M. d'O, lately governor of the Comte de Toulouse, the four head valets,[3] Monseigneur's head valets and those of his sons, the *concierge* of Versailles,[4] and the blue footmen all stationed themselves in the King's dog-room, which was adjacent to the one in which the King sat, and the door of that room too was left wide open. Thus everything that was said or done in the King's study could be heard and seen from the adjoining rooms. It was the same in all the palaces, except at Marly, where the ladies whom Mme la Duchesse de Bourgogne invited stood after supper with the maids of honour, and at Fontainebleau, where there was only one large drawing-room and all the ladies stayed with the King, maids of honour and duchesses sitting alongside the princesses, and the remainder standing, or sitting on the floor. Not one of them, not even the Maréchale de Rochefort, was ever given a hassock.

Such was the usual procedure; but on this particular evening the King called for M. and Mme la Duchesse d'Orléans when he entered his inner study, and instead of seating himself went to wait for them in a corner of the room, where he quietly gave them his judgment. M. le Duc d'Orléans was incapable of taking such things to heart; he had in any event been dragged into the affair by his duch-

[1] His supper-time was ten o'clock, and he spent precisely an hour at table.
[2] The two studies were made into one not very large room during the reign of Louis XV.
[3] Nyert, Blouin, Bontemps, and Quentin de Champcenetz.
[4] One of the King's thirty-two valets. His name was Michel de Bel.

ess, and was therefore not unduly dismayed, but his wife could not bring herself to speak. After that the King called the different members of his family one by one into another corner and announced to each only what concerned him or her personally. He then went to his armchair, and the remainder of the evening passed very drearily. Mme la Duchesse du Maine appeared especially mortified.

Next day I waited to see M. le Duc d'Orléans after he had been to the King's study and asked him what had occurred. 'The judgment went against us,' he said in a whisper, and then, taking me by the arm, 'Come and see the duchess,' which I had little desire to do since I expected her to be in a fury. He insisted, however, on dragging me after him, and we found her behind a coffee-table, in the alcove of her dark little boudoir overlooking the gallery. As soon as she saw me her tears, which had not completely dried, began to flow afresh and I therefore remained close to the door, hoping to slip quietly away; but she perceived my intentions and made me sit beside her. There we lamented together at some length, while she read me a letter in which she had confided her woes to Mme de Maintenon, begging that the announcement of Mademoiselle's betrothal to M. le Duc de Berry should be made soon, even if no more could be done for her at that time. Here M. le Duc d'Orléans interrupted us with the information that he had mentioned the subject to the King that very morning, explaining that the marriage would console them for other disappointments, to which the King had replied, 'So I should imagine,' with a mocking, bitter smile that had much distressed him.

Mme la Duchesse d'Orléans resolved to invent a migraine in order to avoid seeing anyone, excluding even Mademoiselle, whom she kept immured alone in her bedroom. On the following day she sought refuge at Saint-Cloud. Apart from the humiliation of the verdict and her pain at witnessing the triumph of Madame la Duchesse, she was forced to admit the failure of all her schemes to gain for her children the title of Great-grandchildren of France, and now saw them firmly placed on a level with other princes and princesses of the blood with no distinction of any kind. That was what had really maddened her, causing her to sulk and brood, and to keep her daughter more than ever private, in order, so she said, to compel the King to announce the betrothal. By that time it was already mid-Lent, when the King went three times a week to hear sermons in the chapel, accompanied by the princesses in order of precedence. Mme la Duchesse d'Orléans still refused to let Mademoiselle attend; and to bring matters to a head, went to Paris to console herself by holding court at the Palais Royal for the first time since Mme d'Argenton's expulsion. She succeeded there beyond her dearest hopes, reigning supreme over her husband's courtiers who, until then, had seemed scarcely to notice her, and filling her house continually with all the best in Society. In that brilliant situation, so novel for her, she often thanked me for what I had done;

and the impropriety of showing themselves at the Opéra so soon after Monsieur le Duc's death brought her increased pleasure: for she and her husband now sat close together in the little box he had constructed especially for Mme d'Argenton, and they often pressed me to accompany them.

A week was devoted to such grandeurs, after which they were obliged to return to Versailles, where their absence was not held against them. None the less, the duchess was no more amenable than before. The Duchesse de Villeroy failed to move her, and Mme la Duchesse de Bourgogne, who spoke to her with much wisdom, tact and kindness, was no more successful. The princess could see that such conduct was ruining all chance of a marriage between Mademoiselle and the Duc de Berry which she greatly desired for reasons that will appear in due course. Mme la Duchesse d'Orléans, however, persisted in saying that she would remain firm until Easter, after which the Princesses[1] would no longer be appearing in order of precedence. M. le Duc d'Orléans, fully realizing the danger of her behaviour in view of the projected marriage, spoke to her one day in my presence much more firmly than was his custom and eventually lost his temper, which again was unlike him, to the point of mentioning her birth in a manner distressing to her and vastly embarrassing to me. My response was to remain silent and to seize the first possible opportunity of removing myself into his study. He followed me, still raging, and I, raging also, ventured to give him a good dressing-down. I was obliged to call on Mme la Duchesse d'Orléans alone next morning in an attempt to bring her to reason; she reminded me of the scene with her husband, and I repeated all I had said to him. A few days later, M. de Beauvilliers stopped me in the gallery to say how necessary it was for Mademoiselle to appear. He had learned that Mme la Duchesse d'Orléans's obstinacy was being used maliciously against her with the King, that even Mme la Duchesse de Bourgogne was beginning to fear her pride, and that there was not a moment to lose. He was so insistent that she must be warned immediately, but without mentioning his name, that I forthwith obeyed him. Mme la Duchesse d'Orléans was alone. She listened to me, thanked me icily, and with an anger barely covered by politeness remarked that nothing I could say would move her.

Four days later Mme la Duchesse de Bourgogne sent for Mademoiselle herself, and warned her in a motherly way that she risked losing all because of her mother's foolish stubbornness, urging her to rack her brains for some means of obtaining leave to be seen at the Court. This must have had the desired effect, for I was quite dumbfounded to see her at the next sermon, in the full court dress befitting her rank. I went that same morning to visit her mother and found her lying in bed in floods of tears, in which state she remained all day, refusing even to look at Mademoiselle

[1] The King's three bastard daughters were known at the Court simply as 'the Princesses'.

in her full dress. She none the less agreed to present her to the royal family, and sent her afterwards to pay courtesy visits to the princesses of the blood. Madame la Duchesse was kind enough to smother her with kisses, and Mme la Princesse de Conti received her with most civil unconcern. After that Mademoiselle appeared on one or two other occasions in order to earn merit for obeying the King. Thus the judgment which the King was entreated to make for the sake of ending his daughters' quarrels served only to increase their jealousy—a jealousy which rivalry between the daughters of two of them for the hand of M. le Duc de Berry soon brought to a climax. Mme la Duchesse d'Orléans will henceforward appear so often that I have thought it best to describe these events at some length. They portray her better than any words.

When Monsieur le Duc's body was opened, they found in the head a kind of excrescence or foreign growth, which had increased to such proportions that it had killed him. The King decreed that his funeral should be attended by far fewer ceremonies than that of Monsieur le Prince, who had ranked as the senior prince of the blood. Thus there was neither memorial service nor oration; no one had cared enough to petition for the former, and regarding the latter, the subject was too difficult. The King appointed d'Antin governor to the new Monsieur le Duc to control his fortune and appointments, and he forbade the young duke ever to sleep away from his home without express permission. He was given the *entrée* to the study after the King's supper, as being the son of Madame la Duchesse, and d'Antin was also charged with controlling his conduct.

Madame la Duchesse fell into a fresh paroxysm of grief that took everyone completely by surprise. She told all her cronies that her husband's feeling for her had undergone a complete change towards the end; to less intimate friends she said, hoping it might be repeated, that she had lost Monsieur le Duc at a most unfortunate time as regarded her fortune and that of her daughters; that she did not know what would become of her, and that she was in fact destitute. She had received a million on her marriage and a vast amount of jewellery, as well as a dowry of twenty-five thousand livres. Yet she still said she had not enough to live on. By tears and appeals to his affection she extracted from the King, albeit late and unwillingly, a pension of thirty thousand écus. Monseigneur brought her this good news in great glee, and she thereupon dried her tears and quickly regained her spirits. She received visitors with immense ceremony, lying in bed, dressed in widow's weeds edged and lined with ermine, like those worn by widowed duch-esses, and like them wearing a head-kerchief. This is an outlandish head-dress made of cambric and entirely envelops the head. Nothing is worn on top of it; it falls in ample folds over the shoulders enveloping them also, and is exceedingly long, although far shorter than the ermine-bordered train of the dress worn beneath. Duchesses are the lowest rank allowed to wear either such head-dresses or such trains. The Queen's train measures eleven ells;[1] trains for Daughters of France nine ells, for Grand-daughters seven ells, for princesses of the blood five ells, and for duchesses three ells.

The new Monsieur le Duc,[2] wearing a mantle, received visits of condolence in the apartment of his late father. Piles of long mantles and other mourning garments were by the door, and no one was excused from wearing them. Those who brought their own, and others who took them from the door, men and women alike, wore them with the same irreverent air that had been noticeable after the death of Monsieur le Prince; but neither Monsieur le Duc nor Madame la Duchesse paid any heed. Monsieur le Duc received everyone standing, and punctiliously escorted to the outer door of his apartment all dukes and foreign princes,[3] including M. du Maine, who wore a mantle, and Mme du Maine in a mantilla. They also appeared to make light of the disrespect shown towards the mourning garments. The daughters of Madame la Duchesse, wearing mantillas, remained in her drawing room and escorted all the duchesses and foreign princesses to the door of the room, and Mme de Laigle, Madame la Duchesse's maid of honour, accompanied them to the door of the ante-room.

M. du Maine was much angered by the ruling for princesses of the blood, because it completely shattered the whole edifice so ably constructed by his wife in order to raise him to the level of a prince of the blood. He decided none the less to attempt to draw some advantage from the King's distress at giving him pain, and thought the time especially propitious because the board had been swept clear of opponents. The deaths of Monsieur le Prince de Conti, Monsieur le Prince, and Monsieur le Duc had left only minors (the eldest of whom was seventeen)[4] and M. le Duc d'Orléans—careless, negligent, ill-informed, until recently in bad odour with the King, and possessing a wife as whole-heartedly for the bastards as M. du Maine himself. Thus there was no one sufficiently high in rank or influence to go against him. As for the Sons of France, King Louis thought nothing of overriding their wishes; and not one of them, not Monseigneur himself, dared to say a word in protest. The courtiers counted for nothing, borne down, accustomed to servility of every kind, out-rivalling one another in flattery and self-abasement.

---

[1] An English ell was equal to 1 ⅓ yards, the Queen's train mst therefore have measured some 40 feet.
[2] Formerly called the Duc d'Enghien. In 1710, he reached the age of eighteen. He later became Louis XV's prime minister.
[3] The princes referred to were neither foreigners nor of royal blood. The size of their estates conferred upon them the title of prince, in all eyes save those of Saint-Simon. (For example, the Lorraines, Rohans, etc.)
[4] Minors in the Condé and Conti branches of the Bourbon family, in 1710. Condé: the new Monsieur le Duc, the Comte de Charolais, the Comte de Clermont, the Abbesse de Saint-Antoine, the Princesse de Conti, Mlle de Charolais, Mlle de Clermont, Mlle de Vermandois, and Mlle de Sens. Conti: the new Prince de Conti, Marie Anne (m. the Duc de Bourbon in 1713), Mlle de La Roche-sur-Yon.

M. du Maine thus considered the time perfectly ripe to secure for his children[1] at one blow the rank and dignities which he had obtained for himself only by continual encroachments, by verbal promises, by establishing precedents, and finally by the accomplished fact; for example, his appropriation of a seat in the Parlement. His firm supporter had always been his one-time governess Mme de Maintenon, to whom he had sacrificed his mother, and whom he ever afterwards treated with the most tender care, loving her more dearly than any sweetheart or ancient nurse, indeed wholly and without reserve. It was her influence that had raised him from the status of a complete nonentity to his present grandeur, a pinnacle which the former Mme Scarron, since become queen, thought marvellously fitting. From sentiments similar to his she now entered into all his plans for the ennobling of his descendants, and he had no trouble in persuading her that if the King showed himself even faintly willing they need fear neither the Sons of France nor M. le Duc d'Orléans.

Yet no matter how much King Louis may have loved his bastards, and especially this one; no matter how great his enjoyment of absolute power, it was most noteworthy that apart from royal marriages for his daughters, and governorships and other offices for his sons, all that he had done for them was meagre, gradual, without ceremony, and above all without anything in writing. Again and again he had suffered their encroachments, but on each occasion he had been driven beyond his first intentions; as, for example, when having allowed them to assume the outward dignities of the princes of the blood at his Court, he had found himself obliged to grant them similar honours in his armies, and was finally compelled to give them precedence over ambassadors. There, however, he did meet some opposition, especially from the nuncios who were cardinals.[2] No better proof of all this is needed than his aversion to M. du Maine's marriage, for the reasons which he stated at that time,[3] or his orders to the Maréchal de Tessé when he sent him to Italy to join M. de Vendôme at the head of an army.[4] All these events I have mentioned at the appropriate time, and I have said how grudgingly, almost as though against his will, he allowed his bastards to obtain fresh honours, and with them Vendôme, for their sake. On the present occasion, just as before, there was the same unwillingness, the same realization of the enormity asked of him, the same grudging surrender, the same absence of ceremony. The struggle

---

[1] The Prince de Dombes and the Prince d'Eu, aged ten and nine.
[2] Refers especially to Cardinal Delfini. Rome disapproved of cardinals who called on bastards as though they were legitimate princes. In 1700, Delfini had objected. The dispute continued for a month, after which time he expelled himself, without applying for the customary audience, and without the usual handsome present. The King was much annoyed.
[3] The King had said that it was not for such as him to found a line. See Vol. 1, p. 18.
[4] Tessé was ordered to make it appear as though Vendôme was the senior commander, even though his military rank was inferior. The Duc de Vendôme was never a Maréchal de France.

was not of long duration; it began only on 4 March, the date of Monsieur le
Duc's death and of the ruling on the rank of princesses of the blood; it ended
with a victory for M. du Maine on the sixteenth of that same month. When
all was settled between the King, Mme de Maintenon, and the duke himself,
there still remained the question of the announcement, which provided the most
shameful, yet most fascinating spectacle of all that long reign, for those who knew
the King and his pride in having absolute power.

At Versailles, on Saturday evening, 15 March, having supped and issued
his orders as usual, the King gravely entered his inner study, took up a position
near his armchair, and letting his gaze range slowly over the assembled company
announced to no one in particular that he was granting to M. du Maine's children
the same rank and privileges as those now enjoyed by their father. Then, without
a moment's pause, he signed to Monseigneur and Mgr le Duc de Bourgogne,
moving with them to the further end of his study, where for the first time in his life
that haughtiest of monarchs, that most severe and tyrannical of parents, humbled
himself to his son and grandson, begging them, since they must in turn reign after
him, to concede this new rank. He trusted, so he said, that for the love which he
believed they bore him they would protect M. du Maine and his children, whom
he also loved. He was growing old, he continued, and felt that death was near;
he therefore, and with all the urgency at his command, solemnly commended his
children to their care, trusting that after he was gone they would love them for his
sake. He pursued this touching theme for some considerable time, whilst the two
princes, somewhat moved, stood huddled together, quite petrified by his words
and request, and totally incapable of speech.

King Louis, who had clearly expected a more eager response, was still determined to have their promise. He now beckoned M. du Maine from the other end
of the room, where the entire company waited in deathly silence.[1] Taking him by
both shoulders and pressing him down to make the lowest possible reverence, he
presented him to both princes, saying once more that he must look to them for
protection after his death, and that he trusted in their love to carry out his wishes
after he was gone. He ended by asking them to give him their promise; at which
the two princes exchanged glances as though wondering whether they were awake
or asleep; but they said not a word until the King asked a second time, whereupon
they stammered something out, but not a definite assurance.

At that point M. du Maine, greatly discomfited by their evident embarrassment, and visibly disappointed at not having their firm promise, tried to kneel to
kiss their knees; but the King, his eyes full of tears, entreated them to embrace him,

---

[1] The inner study was a small room, crowded with members of the royal family and their ladies and gentlemen in
attendance. Everyone could hear plainly the King's words. It must have been a pathetic scene, giving a rare glimpse of
the gentler side of the King's nature.

so that he might be comforted by that token of their affection. He then continued to urge them to promise not to remove the rank he had granted; and the princes, more and more perplexed by that astounding scene, again mumbled some kind of an answer, but still gave no promise. I shall not at this time comment on that terrible error, nor on the worthlessness of a promise so extorted. Let it suffice that I have repeated word for word what I heard that same day from the Duc de Beauvilliers, who had learned all from the lips of Mgr le Duc de Bourgogne. The affair became known also through Monseigneur, who told all his friends, not concealing from them his horror at the newly bestowed rank. He had never loved M. du Maine, and all his life had suffered because of the King's greater affection for his bastards. When they were boys the Duc du Maine, although never actually disrespectful, had treated Monseigneur with scant consideration, in contrast to the Comte de Toulouse, who strove always to win his friendship. As for Mgr le Duc de Bourgogne, it was not long before I heard from his own lips his opinion of that novel and atrocious gesture, for neither he nor his father made any effort to hide their sentiments, which was another very big mistake.

After that last inaudible murmur from the two princes the King ceased to expect better, and returned to his chair showing no sign of chagrin; whereupon the study resumed its normal appearance. As soon as he was seated, he appeared to notice the prevailing melancholy and hastened to issue a further appeal, saying that it would much gratify him if everyone demonstrated their approval by congratulating the Duc du Maine; after which he was acclaimed by all and somewhat stiffly complimented by his brother the Comte de Toulouse, who, though he had received similar honours, appeared as much surprised as the rest of the company.

The difference of age and character gave the Duc du Maine a great advantage over his brother and tended to make them less than close friends. They rarely visited one another's homes, and although they observed the decencies affection was wanting between them and mutual trust entirely absent. M. du Maine worked for his own advantage and consequently for that of his brother without consulting him or even disclosing his plans. The Comte de Toulouse, on the other hand, strongly disapproved of the antics of the Duchesse du Maine, a fact which she did not fail to notice. She had in truth no liking for him and made no effort to win his regard, for she suspected him of urging the Duc du Maine to be firm with her. Indeed, M. du Maine's indulgence of his wife went beyond all bounds, although that in no way protected him from her tantrums.

On the following day, when the news became public, it was also learned that there would be no other proclamation beyond a note in the register of the master of ceremony, to this effect:

The King, being at Versailles, hereby decrees that the children of M. le Duc du Maine, as grandchildren of His Majesty, shall hereinafter enjoy the same honours, rank and privileges as those which M. du Maine at present enjoys. His Majesty has commanded me to make a note of this decree in my register.

That told all and nothing, and betokened nothing whatsoever, save in reference to the usual courtesies paid to the Duc du Maine. It did not mention the degree of rank, nor any justification of it, but merely stated the fact that they were His Majesty's grandchildren, without any qualification of that term. Never was an announcement more dolefully received. No one at the Court dared to object aloud, but everyone whispered and everyone deplored it. Society was not yet accustomed to the rank of M. du Maine, and now that same rank had devolved upon his children as well. It was abundantly clear, however, that expostulation would not only be useless, but would be considered a crime; and when it was known that the King wished M. du Maine to be congratulated no one dared to stand aloof. Some people had been so bold as to exclaim against the earlier rank; at this outrage no one had the courage to say a word; everyone paid his call with a glum face, and a perfunctory bow that looked far more like appeasement than a compliment.

I, myself, had only just been reconciled with the King. He had strongly exhorted me at my audience to be very moderate in all matters concerning rank. I was deeply wounded by the decree. I had never hitherto congratulated the bastards on any of the privileges which the King had allowed them to acquire. I now saw dukes, foreign princes, and all society without exception going to call on them, and I realized that to abstain would in no way lessen their grandeur or their joy, but only land me in worse disgrace than ever before. I therefore made myself swallow the bitter pill and called with the rest, but amongst the largest possible crowd. I made one very stiff bow to M. and Mme du Maine and turned sharp upon my heel. They had so many visitors and so many at a time that they scarcely knew whom to single out for notice, and whilst they were exchanging compliments with those nearest at hand the others, myself included, were able to make their escape.

Prudence and obedience made it advisable to call also on the Comte de Toulouse, and similar reflections led me to do this. He was not at home, but as I was returning through the small *cour de marbre*[1] I happened to meet d'O and asked him to inform M. le Comte de Toulouse that I had called to congratulate him. 'On what, Monsieur?' said he in his usual pompous manner. I said that what had been done for M. du Maine was supposed to benefit the Comte also. 'Indeed,' said he, 'are you referring to the fact that he will henceforth be expected to walk

---

[1] The hall with marble columns that had been the centre of the little château of Louis XIII.

behind M. du Maine's children?' Taken by surprise, I retorted that he appeared
to have gained so much for his descendants that he need not mind his nephews
preceding him. Thereupon d'O stepped closer to me, gazed at me fixedly like
one who is about to deliver a speech, and said, 'Sir, you may rest assured the
M. le Comte de Toulouse had no part in all this. M. le Comte de Toulouse has
no children at the present time and claims nothing for those he may have in the
future. He is perfectly satisfied with his present rank and desires no greater.' Much
surprised, I took my leave of d'O, a man with whom I had only slight acquaintance and seldom met; I knew his wife no better, and neither did Mme de Saint-
Simon. He was a supercilious pharisee, much given to monosyllabic utterances,
and appears to have leapt at an opportunity to explain something about which I
had not inquired and to give me that astonishing piece of news.

The fact of the matter, as I afterwards learned, was that the affair had caused
a marked coldness between the brothers. The Comte de Toulouse, when he first
learned of the scheme, had done his best to dissuade M. du Maine, either because
he disliked walking behind his nephews or because he thought the whole thing
so preposterous that it might endanger his actual rank. He was therefore quite
content to let his brother fall into the trap alone, and had no intention of doing
so himself, which, I imagined, had been the cause of d'O's remarkable outburst.
Through one person and another the sentiments of Monseigneur and Mgr le
Duc de Bourgogne had become known, and they added to their original mistake
by confirming what people were saying, until finally poor Mme la Duchesse de
Bourgogne so far forgot herself as to declare that Monseigneur would never
recognize that rank; still less would she and her husband when they came to
the throne. Until then the courtiers had been nearly bursting in their efforts
to keep silent; now, however, they began to murmur, and almost immediately
the lamentations became general, public, and most unseemly. The two heirs
having confirmed that everything about the affair was entirely objectionable,
extraordinary liberties were taken, for on account of the numbers involved no
one feared repercussions.

The King was too well informed to be unaware either of this flood
of complaint or of the disapproval of Monseigneur and Mgr le Duc de
Bourgogne, despite his unwonted appeal to their sentiments. He became
a prey to melancholy and remorse; which struck terror into both M. du
Maine and Mme de Maintenon, for they pictured him about to retract.
They therefore took bold steps to avert the danger by praising him to the
skies for securing obedience even within his family circle, stressing how
clearly this was shown by the general eagerness to applaud him, and the

raptures with which Society had greeted the new honours. By such means they made capital out of the compliments wrung from a servile Court, flattered the King at his weakest point, and left him uncertain what to believe.

Those months of March and April were a prosperous time for all the bastards, for Spain was once again urgently requesting the presence of M. de Vendôme, and he, seeing no prospect of employment in France and very lonely in retirement at Anet, longed for the King's consent, which Mme des Ursins continually sought on his behalf. In the meantime, the deaths of Monsieur le Prince and Monsieur le Duc seemed to remove all obstacles to his marriage to Mlle d'Enghien.[1] She was thirty-two, hideously ugly, and had spent her life hitherto in the back regions of the Hôtel de Condé in such straitened circumstances that she readily welcomed any marriage as a means of escape. The whole idea had originated in the minds of M. and Mme du Maine, who greatly desired a princess of the blood for Vendôme, so as to enhance the glories of bastardy. As for Vendôme himself, he had no inclination towards matrimony but was attracted at first by the honour of becoming Monsieur le Prince's son-in-law, and then piqued when disgrace made him less desirable. Now that the way was clear he was all agog to be wed.

M. du Maine undertook the negotiations; the King's consent was obtained, and the marriage was announced to take place on 26 April. Yet if ambition were needed to induce a man to wed Mlle d'Enghien, it took great courage for any woman to marry Vendôme, who was almost noseless and had twice been given up by the most expert doctors.[2] It seemed, however, that both parties were willing, she to gain riches and freedom, he for the glory of appearing still good enough for a princess of the blood, despite disgrace and disease. It took all his fortune to buy her, and it was settled in the contract for the money to remain hers if, as seemed probable, he died before her without issue, which did in fact occur. Madame la Princesse and Madame la Duchesse were informed of the alliance as something already arranged and in accordance with the King's wishes. Madame la Princesse burst into tears, invoking the little esteemed memory of her dead husband; but since there was nothing she could do to prevent the marriage, she surrendered and refused to hear it mentioned. Madame la Duchesse was haughty and lost her temper, but that was all, for she had no kind of influence over Mlle d'Enghien. M. du Maine took charge of everything, the contract, the publication of the banns, the ceremony itself; and the way in which the whole affair was managed displayed the extent of Vendôme's disgrace. He had enormous difficulty in obtaining permission to visit Versailles to ask the King's consent, and was then allowed to come

---

[1] Marie Anne de Bourbon-Condé, daughter of Monsieur le Prince; and sister of M. le Duc, the Princesse de Conti (not the dowager), and Mme du Maine. She was left badly scarred by smallpox.

[2] He had twice horrified and disgusted the Court by publicly announcing that he was taking a cure for syphilis.

only on condition that he kept to his own room and visited no one. Scarcely anyone called on him.

The audience was brief and unproductive, and he returned once more to Anet. He was not granted leave of absence even to witness the signing of the contract, which was presented for the King's signature by the Duc du Maine alone, unsupported by any member of the two families. Moreover, by the King's express desire, the wedding took place at Sceaux during one of the Marlys, without ceremonial or festivities of any kind, and in the greatest possible secrecy. King Louis firmly refused to hear of the betrothal being held in his study, and thus, the contract having been signed at Marly on 13 May, M. de Vendôme went straight from Anet to Sceaux on the morning of Thursday, the 15th, and that very same evening was betrothed, wed, and bedded with Mlle d'Enghien. Madame la Princesse, Monsieur le Duc, his brother M. le Comte de Charolais, Mme la Princesse de Conti with her son and daughters, M. and Mme du Maine and their children were present, and absolutely no one else at all. As soon as midnight mass had been said all the princes and princesses of the blood removed themselves and did not return. M. de Vendôme spent the following day alone with M. and Mme du Maine, their children and household, and his bride, leaving her there when he returned to Anet on the Saturday morning. Neither of them received any congratulations from the King or from any other member of the royal family. No one spoke of the marriage; it was as though it had not been. M. du Maine returned as soon as possible to the Court, and Mme de Vendôme to her mother until the Grand Prieur's house at the Temple, which was in great disorder, had been got ready to receive her, and the Grand Prieur himself was safely out of the country.[1] A few years earlier, how brilliant that wedding would have been! What a contrast to his triumphant returns from Italy! It was much remarked that although Vendôme had not previously met the younger princes of the blood, he did not pay his respects to them on that occasion. He conducted himself like a guest at someone else's wedding, and once back at Anet, appeared to forget that he had ceased to be a bachelor.

Mme la Duchesse de Bourgogne's confinement, followed as it was by Lent, kept the King for several months on end at Versailles, without excursions to Marly until the day after Low Sunday, when he went there from 28 April until Saturday, 17 May. I was on a visit to La Ferté at that time, but Mme de Saint-Simon asked for us,[2] and we went. I travelled there straight from La Ferté, and thenceforward never missed a Marly until the King's death, except once, not even those when Mme de Saint-Simon could not go. I noticed that the King spoke

[1] Philippe de Vendôme, brother of the Duc de Vendôme, and the Grand Prieur de France. He was a dissolute and quite unprincipled character.
[2] Courtiers did not wait to be invited to Marly. They said, 'Marly, Sire?', and were accepted or refused.

to me and distinguished me more than other men of my age who had neither office nor acquaintance with him. It was during that particular excursion that M. de Vendôme's marriage contract was signed, as I have described above. Thus re-established in my ordinary way of life, I had many conversations with my friends among the ministers and principal courtiers regarding the sorry state of our country's affairs, which they did not attempt to hide from me, and on which their views were similar to mine. A few days after our return to Versailles I went, as I often did, to spend the day at Vaucresson, where the Duc de Beauvilliers had made for himself the most delightful retreat imaginable. He usually spent the Thursday and Friday of each week there, and was inaccessible to all save his closest relatives and a few, at the most four or five, friends, whom he allowed to visit him. As we were walking alone together in the garden, our conversation gradually turned on Mgr le Duc de Bourgogne, and I told him all my thoughts. Although he had often been mentioned between us, we had never hitherto spoken of him at length, and M. de Beauvilliers had never before seemed so much impressed by my views. Our talk then moved on to other topics; and we left the garden, ending our long tête-à-tête only just in time to go in to dinner.

As we left the table, M. de Beauvilliers, who had been reflecting on our conversation, invited me to walk round his garden once more, and to repeat what I had been saying about Mgr le Duc de Bourgogne, adding whatever else might have struck me during the interval. I protested, thinking that he could scarcely have forgotten already, and because I considered that I had said enough. He urged me none the less, and I obeyed him. Our talk was an exceedingly long one; he rarely interrupted me, and when I had finished he asked me to write down my views regarding Mgr le Duc de Bourgogne's future conduct, together with the qualities which I considered he might with advantage correct or develop. This proposal took me completely by surprise. He pressed me, but I resisted him, asking what he proposed to do with the finished work. His answer was that such an essay might greatly benefit the prince, or at least be profitable to himself in advising him. I protested even more strongly, on the grounds that it was highly dangerous to let such people know one's opinion of them. He reassured me as best he could, stressing Mgr le Duc de Bourgogne's virtues and his manner of thinking; and we finally reached an agreement that I should write an essay but that he would make no use of it without my previous consent.

We then parted and rejoined the company indoors, I still amazed by his request but prepared none the less to obey him by writing an essay addressed ostensibly to Mgr le Duc de Bourgogne. A few days later I began. I composed almost half of it on the assumption that it would be shown to the prince, but my pen faltered at the need to include certain most essential matters. I decided then to let myself go, resolving to omit some passages if M. de Beauvilliers should wish the prince to read it, notwithstanding that I thought them indispensable. I kept a copy, and although it is rather long, I shall insert it here rather than put it with the rest of my papers because it will give you a better understanding of Mgr le Duc de Bourgogne. It is addressed to the Duc de Beauvilliers, the first words explain on what occasion. If it contains certain lines of argument and examples not to everyone's taste, this is because an essay intended to influence Mgr le Duc de Bourgogne had to be made acceptable to him and still more so to M. de Beauvilliers. Although the latter appeared more reliable and less bound by scruples than the prince at that time was, both were more likely to be impressed by arguments of this particular kind than by others better suited to the rest of the world.

Essay on Mgr le Duc de Bourgogne, 25 May 1710, addressed to M. le Duc de Beauvilliers, who desired me to write it.

[*This essay, although it is one of the most interesting passages in the Memoirs, and shows a great deal of most excellent common sense, covers more than twenty-five pages in the flowery style then calculated to impress royalty. It has therefore reluctantly been omitted. Fortunately Saint-Simon (who may have had the same appreciation of a reader's powers of endurance) added a shorter version, as follows:—*]

A short summary of my discourse may be of service for the sake of continuity. It must first be said that Mgr le Duc de Bourgogne was born with a temper truly alarming. In his rages he would try to break the clocks when they struck an hour calling him to some unloved task. He would even fly into a passion against the rain when it prevented him from doing as he wished. Opposition drove him to a frenzy, as I myself often observed in his early childhood. What is more, he had a preference for all things unlawful for mind and body. His banter was cruel because it was witty and pointed, exactly portraying a person's absurdities. All this was greatly exacerbated by an excitable, almost a violent nature that never in those early days allowed him to concentrate on any one thing. All pleasures he loved with boisterous enthusiasm, yet at the same time showed an arrogance and haughtiness that passed all description. He was, moreover, dangerously perceptive, able to lay his finger on the weakness in a chain of argument and to argue in his turn more keenly and exhaustively than his masters. Yet when his passion had abated, reason would return and finally prevail. He then saw his errors and admitted them with a desperation that sometimes recalled his previous rage. His mind, quick, vigorous, keen, struggled against these handicaps, and marvellous to relate overcame them entirely. As though by a miracle, in an amazingly short time religion and grace made a new man of him, changing his many serious defects to completely contrary virtues. You must therefore accept as the literal truth the praises of my discourse.

This prince, with a natural taste and aptitude for the abstract sciences, substituted them for pleasures that still held such a dangerous attraction for him that he shunned all diversions, even the most innocent, in terror. This, combined with abject slavery to the duty of loving one's neighbour, a constant fear of doing or saying something displeasing to God and a perpetual constraint in Society, which he thoroughly disliked, drove him more and more into solitude, where alone he felt free and could dispel his boredom by study, and devote a very large proportion of his time to prayer. The violence done to his feelings in overcoming so many and such compulsive faults, his yearning for perfection, his inexperience and fears, together with the bigotry that so often accompanies budding religious fervour, led him to adopt an exaggeratedly strict moral code, which made him appear frigid, and often (although this he did not realize) censorious. Thus he was driven further and further from Monseigneur, and even alienated the King. Let me give one example from a thousand which, though no doubt excellent in principle, had infuriated the King and set the entire Court against him only a few years earlier. We were spending Twelfth-night at Marly, and a ball was announced. Mgr le Duc de Bourgogne refused even to appear, and let this be known so long in advance that the King reasoned with him, jestingly at first, then tartly, and finally with extreme gravity, for he was much vexed by his grandson's disapproving attitude. Madame la Duchesse de Bourgogne and her ladies, even M. de Beauvilliers himself, tried to move him, but in vain. He would merely repeat that the King was master; that he did not venture to blame him; but the Epiphany being a triple feast, he would not himself profane it by curtailing the worship due on that so holy day for a spectacle only just permissible at ordinary times. Useless to urge that if he spent the morning and afternoon in church and the rest of the time at prayer in his study, he might well devote the evening to his duty as a subject and a son. All argument was vain. Except for the period of the King's supper he remained immured alone in his study. To add to this rigidity, his education had imposed on him a desire for literal exactness on every point, which greatly frustrated those who had dealings with him. It made him appear impatient, like a man with more important affairs to attend to, and no time to waste. At the other extreme he closely resembled those young seminarists who, after spending a day in the strict discipline of the cloister, relieve their pent-up feeling at recreation, by indulging in all the noisy, boyish pranks they can devise—other pleasures being forbidden them.[1]

The young prince fell passionately in love with his wife and abandoned himself to that delight like one who is strictly deprived of any other, playing with her and the young ladies of her household like a schoolmaster on holiday, while they in return treated him with girlish impudence. You will understand after this short explanation the cause of many of his oddities, and the reason that in my essay I laid so much stress on his religious fervour, which nothing would persuade him to reconsider, and no arguments abate, save those of religion itself. His first two campaigns went exceedingly well for him. Far from the objects of his fear and love, he was able to be more himself and less formal with other men. He was free also from the constraints of loving his neighbour;[2] the war and how to wage it being the one subject of every argument and conversation. Thus his intelligence, quick perception, and sincerity appeared, and he seemed to show real promise. His third campaign was a tragedy,[3] as I have already described, for during the course of it he began to realize with increasing clarity that he had an enemy who (monstrous but true) was more powerful even than he, at the Court and in Society, and that the imperious Vendôme, backed by his cabals, was taking advantage of the prince's failings to push audacity to its furthest limits. Those particular failings were misplaced diffidence, and the greatly excessive piety that so shamefully had changed an anvil to a hammer, and *vice versa*.

Such in brief was the gist of my discourse, in which, with well merited praise and other tributes scattered here and there to make the rest acceptable, I had tried to show the benefit which Mgr le Duc de Bourgogne stood to gain from the hours spent in his study, and the misuse to which he now put them, since nothing emerged from labours that were otherwise perfectly suitable to his rank and his personal edification. Then, after endeavouring to reveal what might be done with far less time than he was wont to spend, I turned to attacking his diffidence and, if the expression may be permitted, the wrong foot[4] on which he had placed himself with the King, Monseigneur, Society, and Mme de Maintenon, whose good opinion was of vital importance. I finally remonstrated against his endless private sessions with Mme la Duchesse de Bourgogne, both alone, which I sincerely commended, and with that mob

---

[1] 'It makes me shudder to see him still smothering flies in oil, abstractedly crushing grapepips, blowing-up toads with gunpowder, or playing battledore and shuttlecock in moments of crisis.' Had he lived to be king, he might well have disappointed Saint-Simon's expectations.

[2] Fénelon's influence had been all too strong.

[3] Vendôme, having lost the Battle of Oudenarde by his negligence, publicly insulted the prince during a council of war. The Duc de Bourgogne had been sufficiently restrained to say nothing. See Vol. I, p. 377.

[4] '*Sur le pied gauche.*'

of young women who took shameless advantage of his kindness, his fits of
abstraction, his fervour, and unseemly jollity that smacked so strongly of the
seminary. After stressing the improper behaviour of others, I turned to his
own conduct, and that was the moment when the pen twisted in my hand as
I reflected on the abominable use made in Flanders, and later everywhere, of
those particular failings to which continuance added tragic weight.[1] I none
the less dwelt as lightly as possible on that topic and so came to the major
theme of my discourse, the need for intercourse with other men. On that
theme I spread myself with a freedom that matched the need, entering into
detailed plans to lead the prince as it were by the hand, thus removing any
excuse he might make for not knowing how to proceed. At the same time,
I was only too well aware that what I urged so strongly went quite counter
to the methods of the King, and that ministers both past and present had
dreaded nothing half so much and with enormous care had frustrated any
move from the prince in that direction. Because of that I toned down this
part to the best of my ability, passing swiftly on to the apotheosis, by which
it may appear that I was not entirely convinced.

Thus far my essay had been within the compass of every member of
Society. Thereinafter the workings, so narrow, so precise, of Mgr le Duc
de Bourgogne's mind and the piety of the Duc de Beauvilliers, although
that was different and less bigoted, obliged me to deal with a matter which
few would relish, but without which neither the prince nor his old governor
would have stomached what went before. I felt it imperative to make some
mention of the slanders, so as to accustom the prince to argue with other
men; and of religion, in order to persuade him by monkish comparisons
to hear me on his conduct in Flanders, during his last campaign and
after his return, and thus convince him of the immensity of the harm inflicted
on him. Such preparation was completely essential before I dared to discuss
the impression which he gave of weighing and deciding every question
purely in religious terms, with the result that for him everything became
a matter of conscience. Everyone, for example, was convinced that he
left his opinion of the Spanish war to be formed by doctors of theology,
which explained why, when the King asked for his views at the Council, he
had been considerably surprised to learn that the prince had not given
the subject so much as a thought. This brought me of necessity to deal briefly
with the impropriety of long and frequent interviews with his confessor,[2]
and just as I had praised his former tutor to make more palatable what I

---

[1] He was said to have finished his game of battledore while couriers waited. Drake in similar circumstances was not criticized, but he went on to win.
[2] Le Père Isaac Martineau

afterwards wished to implant, so now I praised the confessor to avoid shocking the penitent and prepare the latter to consider and meditate well on the last Kings of Spain;[1] returning thence full circle to the disadvantage of his being unknown to his fellow men. My discourse ended as it had begun, with praise, the indispensable accompaniment of saying all that I wished; but God's grace, that had begun to work a miracle in him, completed its task so swiftly that he became a most admirable prince. His bigotry, his scruples, his failings all vanished, leaving him perfect in every way. Alas! such perfection was not for this world; we were not worthy of it. God showed it to us to demonstrate His goodness and power, and swiftly removed it to reward the prince's virtue and punish us for our sins.

That essay, of whose truths I was brimful, did not take long to write. I corrected nothing from the first stroke of the pen to the last, and I read it aloud to the Duc de Beauvilliers just as you read it here. I venture to say that it delighted him. He disputed only two assertions in the entire work, the too sedulous attendance in church on feast-days and Sundays (but he conceded that in the end), and the theatricals, on which I never got his agreement. He praised the entire passage on slander and piety, and was quite of my opinion regarding mixing with other men in the way that I proposed. He assented to all I had said of M. de Vendôme, whom I had avoided mentioning by name, and of Mgr le Duc de Bourgogne's conduct during and after his last campaign in Flanders. In a word, the whole essay met with his approval. He asked me to read it again, and I thereupon begged him to reconsider the part about the flies and toads, and other such pastimes, which I thought I might have overstressed. He agreed, but on the other hand he said that such matters required plain speaking, and would not consent to my omitting or even changing what I had written. I made him pay special heed to my remarks on the confessor; but he exclaimed approvingly of them.

After that we came to the best method of using it, and that was when there occurred the longest and most heated argument I ever had with him. He wished to show my essay to the prince, and to show it over my signature, of course telling him that he had asked me to write it. I expostulated because of the danger; but when after a long struggle he still had not gained my consent, and I had failed to make him give way, he finally suggested that we should consult the Duc de Chevreuse, but that nobleman was in Paris, and we were at Marly, on the excursion I mentioned earlier. I agreed to consulting a third person more in the hope of gaining time than with any thought of consenting to whatever M. de Chevreuse might advise. Mme de Saint-Simon was most distressed at my having undertaken such a task, for fear that I should lose possession of my essay once it was written. She was even more worried when she learned of the Duc de Beauvilliers's eagerness to show it; and she opposed him with all her strength. I was torn between her unhappiness and the wisdom which

---

[1] He was thinking of the doings of the Inquisition in Spain since the reign of Philip II.

she so often displayed, and my vast respect for M. de Beauvilliers, now much intensified by rather foolish vanity. We ended by agreeing between ourselves to take the advice of a great friend, a man who, because of his integrity, intelligence, knowledge of the world, and, above all, his knowledge of Mgr le Duc de Bourgogne, was eminently able to give us counsel. This friend was Cheverny, of whom I have already spoken.[1] I therefore read my essay aloud to him in my wife's presence. I received praise, Mme de Saint-Simon approbation. He agreed with her that it would be dangerous to show it to the prince for whom it was written, or to give him portions to read, even without mentioning my name; for the Duc de Beauvilliers could not possibly be suspected of having commissioned anyone else, in view of my ardent loyalty to Mgr le Duc de Bourgogne, my close friendship with himself, my well-known anger over Flanders and the calumnies thereafter, and my unique knowledge of the Court, which was apparent throughout the work. We therefore decided that no matter what the two dukes might say, I must refuse to allow my work to be shown to Mgr le Duc de Bourgogne who, saintly though he was, might well be vexed if not now certainly in the future at having been summed up so accurately by me, and, moreover, at having been found wanting in so many ways that he would not willingly change. This wise resolve once taken, I submitted my essay to the scrutiny of the Duc de Chevreuse, to whom I lent my copy so that he might have time to reflect. He much approved, but fortunately advised against showing, which got me out of my difficulty. At the same time he persuaded me to leave my copy with them, giving me his absolute promise that it should not leave their hands; and he did make me consent to their transmitting certain extracts to the prince, not mentioning my name, at various times and at long intervals, M. de Beauvilliers consented and so did I, after Cheverny and Mme de Saint-Simon had decided that by proceeding thus all danger would be averted. We left both dukes in ignorance of the fact that we had consulted Cheverny. It is sadly true that even the best of princes are willing to support the most fulsome and dangerous praise, but not the warnings, however salutary and moderate, of their most faithful servants.

It is now the moment to describe an epoch-making intrigue that split the Court in two. I shall need to retrace my steps, for it began several months earlier; and I shall continue until the end so as not to interrupt the narrative with the events of the campaign, in which some victories have to be recorded.

I did barely mention at the time of M. le Duc d'Orléans's rupture with Mme d'Argenton and the ruling regarding the princesses of the blood, that M. and Mme la Duchesse d'Orléans hoped to marry their daughter Mademoiselle to M. le Duc de Berry, and that Madame la Duchesse entertained a similar wish for her own

[1] See Vol. 1, p. 400.

daughter Mlle de Bourbon. I spoke also of Madame la Duchesse's hatred for Mme la Duchesse d'Orléans, who was herself on thoroughly bad terms with Mme la Duchesse de Bourgogne, and *vice versa*. These relationships I dealt with at some length at the time of the cabals, during the campaign when Lille was captured, and you must bear them in mind so as to understand what follows.

The obstacles to Mademoiselle's achieving this marriage were many and formidable. Generally speaking, we were engaged in a fierce and disastrous war; the kingdom was in dire need; it was hard enough to provide bare necessities, let alone the wherewithal for fresh endowments and the maintenance of yet another royal household. M. le Duc de Berry was not yet twenty-five years old and of a mild disposition. He was terrified of the King, and although he had made several overtures in affairs of the heart, he had never yet succeeded in bringing one to a conclusion. Thus there was no need for haste. Secondly, in the ordinary course of events, a foreign marriage would have seemed more advantageous, serving as a pretext for reconciliation with the Emperor, or even to neutralize Portugal, which at that time was a dangerous thorn in the side of Spain. The greatest personal objection, however, arose from the situation of M. le Duc d'Orléans himself, for he was not quite reconciled with the King, and Mme de Maintenon had not forgiven him for his vile jest in Spain. Moreover, the King of Spain still believed that he had conspired with the Allies to rob him of his throne. Public opinion in France and at the Court was not entirely convinced of his innocence, and those who were already shocked at seeing all the legitimate princes married to bastards would be far more dismayed by a mésalliance so near the throne. Finally, the bridegroom was the son, and, what is more, the favourite son of Monseigneur, who had never ceased to proclaim his hatred of M. le Duc d'Orléans in the most public fashion since the Spanish affair, and was completely dominated by the prince's most bitter enemies, who themselves had a rival candidate for the hand of M. le Duc de Berry.

All these objections both general and particular were apparent to M. and Mme la Duchesse d'Orléans; they saw no way of overcoming them, and remained in stony silence, a state of hopeless yearning that was the first obstacle for me to overcome, although I was fully aware of all the rest. Here I shall continue to explain my personal motives as truly as I do those of others. It was from self-interest of a most active kind that I passionately desired the marriage of Mademoiselle. I could see that Mlle de Bourbon had everything in her favour; but apart from the fact of her having been Monsieur le Duc's daughter, I could not forgive her mother for siding against me in my lawsuit with Mme de Lussan, and neither could she forgive me for my loyalty to those whom she and her cabal had most hated since the Flanders affair. Her power over Monseigneur already made me uneasy; how much more dangerous it might become if their children were married! Then her authority would be complete, and it was only too probable that she might succeed in what her cabal had already once attempted, namely the destruction of M. and Madame la Duchesse d'Orléans and my involvement in their ruin.

On the other hand I believed that if Mademoiselle were chosen, the influence of Madame la Duchesse and her wicked cabal would be greatly lessened in the next reign. I thus faced the dreadful alternative of imagining either my enemies or my closest friends at the height of power or plunged into ruin; with the consequent effects of either event upon my own future, not to mention the despair or triumph, and the part which I felt capable of playing to bring about the one or the other. Such considerations were more than enough to set in action a man of my strong feelings, a man well able to love and to hate, as I have done only too thoroughly throughout the entire course of my life. One thought only might have held me back, my strong preference for a foreign marriage which would have saved a prince so near in the line of succession from the defilement of bastardy, a state that filled me with horror. Whilst I thus hesitated, reflecting on all the possibilities, I perceived that Madame la Duchesse had managed to persuade the King that no foreign marriage was possible, since peace was too distant to delay indefinitely the marriage of a prince whose interest in women was already causing some concern. I then realized that while I thus marked time, Mlle de Bourbon was quietly gaining ground, and that, a family marriage having become inevitable, there was no avoiding bastardy. Once arrived at that point I carefully reviewed all possible objections to Mademoiselle, both the general and the personal, in the hope of devising some way of overcoming them. I thought that some of them might be removed by direct attack; others, more formidable, might be circumvented by infinite tact, and that, before attempting to convince others, even those whose futures lay in the balance, I must myself be reasonably sure of success.

The worst obstacle would have been a preference for a foreign marriage, but that, for the reasons already given, we did not have to face. The King would not consider such an alliance at that juncture, and we had nothing to fear from those who, for reasons of birth or office, might have had the right to advise him otherwise. With such persons he invariably preserved absolute silence on matters that concerned his family, disposing of these himself, and refusing to discuss them with anyone. The worst hindrances were M. and Mme la Duchesse d'Orléans themselves, who had exhausted their energies in fruitless lamentations, and were now ruining their chances by complete inertia. I depicted to them most vividly the personal interests of Madame la Duchesse; I ruthlessly portrayed their wretched situation in the present reign, and what might follow for them during the next, were she to succeed. I appealed to their pride, their jealous feelings, their indignation. Who could have believed that so much effort would be required to spur them into action? At last, however

after goading them with all the strongest arguments at my command, I managed
to convince them of their vital needs.

Mme la Duchesse d'Orléans, although by nature excessively idle, was the first
to be won over, less from selfish motives than from a great desire to outwit her
sister; and once having taken the first step she joined me in trying to bring pressure upon M. le Duc d'Orléans who, despite his intelligence and passionate love
of Mademoiselle, remained as stubborn as a mule, yielding, from start to finish,
only to our united efforts. I have often meditated on his extraordinary behaviour,
for I could not square such inertia with his ambition, self-interest, and the other
cogent reasons he had for taking action; nor could I comprehend why, after Mme
la Duchesse d'Orléans and I had repeatedly, at length, and most urgently pressed
on him the need for haste, he still used the slightest excuse to remain idle. I have
since suspected that knowing better than anyone what had really occurred in
Spain, he was convinced that the marriage was impossible but did not like to
confess why. It was his attitude that made my task so difficult, for I was obliged
continually to spur him on and not to allow myself to be discouraged by his blun-
ders that more than once nearly wrecked our plans.

The less support I received from him whose betterment was our chief
concern, the more I had to rely on others, and I therefore set out to form a powerful
faction that would diligently pursue my aims—diligently because from motives
of self-interest, the prime, nay the sole, instigator of every intrigue at the Court.
I made, for example, excellent use of Mme la Duchesse de Bourgogne, who had
many sound reasons for preferring Mademoiselle, quite apart from her dislike of
Madame la Duchesse. She perfectly understood the King's character and his love
of novelty, and was alive to the danger of a newcomer younger than herself, who
might charm him with a new form of the childish teasing that had served her so
well in the past, and which she still occasionally used to good effect. A Duchesse
de Berry ruled by Madame la Duchesse might prove to be a viper in her bosom,
turning her most innocent remarks to deadly poison. All this she realized clearly
enough; but she was young and gay, too much dazzled by the King's strong affection and the prospect of being queen, too much taken up with the daily round of
duties and pleasures to see the full gravity of the situation. I thus felt that I should
gain most from her by impressing her with the above reflections and from the
use to which she might put them with the King and Mme de Maintenon, both
of whom dearly loved her. Mme la Duchesse d'Orléans I judged to have neither
the charm nor the energy needed to guide her, more especially since she was
personally involved. I therefore cast about to find some other weapon and finally
fixed upon the Duchesse de Villeroy, whose blunt common-sense was often more
effective than tact; and my efforts in that quarter were highly satisfactory.

Mme de Levis[1] was of threefold use to me. First, she also was on bad terms with Madame la Duchesse, was attached to Mme la Duchesse d'Orléans and thus a partisan of Mademoiselle, and was devoted to Mme la Duchesse de Bourgogne, whose danger she clearly perceived. Secondly, despite her youth, she was hand in glove with Mme de Maintenon, and lastly, she was dearly loved and esteemed by her family and had considerable influence at their councils. She, indeed, with the Dukes of Chevreuse and Beauvilliers and their duchesses, proved to be my strongest support; we had many private consultations on matters that required delicate handling, and not always by the same individual. Yet another tool presented itself in the shape of Mme d'O, and although her passion for managing everyone and everything made her generally unreliable, she was useful enough when given work within her compass. Her husband in his frigid, pompous manner also assisted us, for he was attached to the Dukes of Chevreuse and Beauvilliers and much indebted to them, more especially because they had saved him from disgrace after the Lille campaign.[2] As for the Comte de Toulouse, he secretly preferred Mme la Duchesse d'Orléans to Madame la Duchesse; and M. du Maine was decidedly of the same opinion for, since the death of Monsieur le Prince, he had looked on Madame la Duchesse as his enemy.[3] Their quarrel was of immense assistance to Mme la Duchesse d'Orléans and M. d'O, for it enabled them to alarm him, and fear was by far his strongest emotion. They showed him all Hell opening beneath his feet if Mlle de Bourbon was chosen, the failure of his claim on Monsieur le Prince's inheritance, his future rank in jeopardy, and that of his children irretrievably lost, all through the malice of Madame la Duchesse. He felt as though his very salvation were at stake and set to work for us with a will. Such is the power of women, so influential at every court, so supremely important at ours! I now felt that I had enlisted sufficient numbers for our needs, and began to fear that secrecy, the very essence of all intrigue, might be endangered if any more were admitted. In retrospect, it seems incredible that I should have had to plan, supervise, and direct the endeavours of all these people, and that even with Mme la Duchesse d'Orléans herself I should have been forced to exert myself in order to overcome her lethargy.

I soon perceived that we must not miss the smallest opportunity, for M. le Duc de Berry was a fortress to be taken only by storm, and I therefore spoke very seriously to MM. de Chevreuse and de Beauvilliers and their duchesses of the rift at the Court; the certain ruin of Mgr le Duc de Bourgogne if Mlle de Bourbon were to be chosen, and the danger to the State if the royal brothers came to hate one another because of the enmity of their wives.

[1] Daughter of the Duc de Chevreuse.
[2] When he had been attached to the prince's staff and come in for much criticism.
[3] She had kept a firm grasp of the inheritance of Monsieur le Prince, despite the rival claims of the Duc du Maine as his son-in-law.

I also emphasized the danger to morality if M. le Duc de Berry remained much longer unwed. Such were the main threads of my discourse, but I did touch on the possibility of erasing the Spanish scandal and removing any chance of a revival, in even M. le Duc d'Orléans's mind, lest Mme la Duchesse grow too great, and he too much oppressed. Lastly I hinted at the prince's probable fate should the King of Spain's misfortunes lead to a return of Mme des Ursins, as then seemed only too likely. I well knew that I spoke to those who had no wish to see that lady at our Court, and thus I eventually persuaded them to act under my direction— no mean feat with persons so set in their ways, so prudent and scrupulous, so monklike vowed to neutrality and inaction, yet none the less occasionally remembering that they were not in fact so sworn.

Such were the instruments and groupings that my love for my friends, my loathing for Madame la Duchesse, and my own interest caused me to bring together and organize into a powerful and smooth-running machine that worked like leaven and was brought to perfection in that Lenten season. I knew all their actions, difficulties and triumphs, for they reported every detail to me, and every day I harmonized my plans with theirs. Before the end of Lent, Mme la Duchesse de Bourgogne had sounded the King and Mme de Maintenon and found them not unfavourably disposed. On one occasion she took Mademoiselle to visit the King in Mme de Maintenon's room when Monseigneur was present, and praised her to her face, remarking after her departure, with calculated carelessness, that she would make M. le Duc de Berry an admirable wife. Monseigneur had turned scarlet, retorting sharply that it would be a fine way to punish M. le Duc d'Orléans for his conduct in Spain; and thereupon he had left the room, leaving the company profoundly shaken by such a surprising show of feeling from one who was normally so calm and apathetic. Mme la Duchesse de Bourgogne's presence of mind did not desert her; 'Dear Aunt,' said she, casting a startled glance towards Mme de Maintenon, 'have I said something foolish?' But it was the King who answered with some heat that if Madame la Duchesse took that tone and worked upon Monseigneur she would have to reckon with himself; whereupon Mme de Maintenon skilfully took matters a step further, remarking that Madame la Duchesse was sure to continue since she had already gone so far. The subject was several times allowed to lapse and then was taken up again; the discussion ended with great indignation all round, and reflections that did Mademoiselle de Bourbon's cause far more harm than any good she might have gained from the affection between her mother and Monseigneur.

The scene was immediately conveyed to Mme la Duchesse d'Orléans and as swiftly transmitted by her to me. It confirmed my view that no time should be lost in convincing the King that Madame la Duchesse's influence was likely to make his son even harder to handle; that were their children to marry he might have to accede to demands from Monseigneur that originated from her, and that in his old age he might well lose control of his family and become a slave to both of them. By that time Holy Week was approaching, when I paid my usual visit to La Ferté, returning thence straight to Marly. I arrived to find everything in a turmoil; the King, ordinarily so serene in manner and countenance, seeming unable to suppress his vexation, and the Court quite convinced that some new disaster had occurred which no one dared to make public. Four or five days later the truth emerged. It appeared that the King had learned that the people of Paris and throughout the entire kingdom were grumbling bitterly because immense sums of money were being spent at Marly at a time when there was too little to furnish even the bare needs of the armies. He was far more displeased on that occasion than on many others when he had received similar warnings. Indeed, he was so angry that Mme de Maintenon had a hard task to prevent an immediate return to Versailles even although that particular Marly had been advertised to last three weeks.

His response after a few days was to announce with an air of sour satisfaction that he could no longer afford to feed the ladies at Marly. Henceforth, he said, he would be obliged to dine alone, as at Versailles, and sup every evening with his table laid only for the sixteen members of his family. The Princesses might each have a table for the ladies of their households, and Mmes Voysin and Desmaretz one each for such other ladies as did not wish to eat in their rooms. He added somewhat acidly that he proposed in future to do no work at Marly, except on minor details for his private amusement; thus he would spend no more money than at Versailles and might remain as long as he pleased without giving cause for complaint. He was wrong from start to finish. No one but the King could have been so much in error, unless, of course, his only mistake was in hoping to deceive the people. In the event, he found himself compelled to arrange tables for the persons of lower rank who had the privilege of eating at the Court, and had hitherto consumed leavings from the three tables set morning and evening for the King and the ladies. He had to make separate kitchens and other offices for the Princesses, and construct new buildings to house those who were dislodged and to accommodate the extra servants. The saving was nil; our enemies made rude jests about our so-called economies; the grumbling continued, and the delays, in dealing with State affairs, often of great urgency, were much prolonged because the King now felt able to absent himself longer and more frequently.

Madame la Duchesse, in her anxiety to keep a firm hold over Monseigneur, managed against all decency to obtain permission for Marly in the first two months of her widowhood. The King gave his consent reluctantly and only because he liked to see a full table; indeed, he had reduced the numbers for only a week. She benefited also from the retrenchments, for she brought her daughters with her, crying poverty against the cost of keeping a separate staff and table for them at

Versailles. There was another reason, too; she hoped that her girls, especially Mlle de Bourbon, would keep Monseigneur entertained during her time in mourning, and the King become accustomed to their presence, as would be bound to happen if they supped at his table. But no sooner was this decided than the King, who liked to keep the balance, suggested that Mademoiselle also should join the Marly excursions. That gave M. and Mme la Duchesse d'Orléans much food for thought; but after weighing all the pros and cons it was thought best to leave her at Versailles and endure the sight of Mlle de Bourbon spending whole days in the same room as M. le Duc de Berry, often at the same card table, and becoming known to the King. Such trifles, we believed, would not win the match for her. On the other hand, exposing Mademoiselle to the malice of the cabal and Monseigneur, under M. le Duc de Berry's very eyes, might ruin all her chances, and we therefore agreed to express gratitude, but not bring her out of seclusion.[1]

That was the moment when I first saw the need for haste and discovered that M. de Beauvilliers was of the same opinion. He came upstairs with me one day to Mme la Duchesse d'Orléans's room when she was slightly indisposed and, taking M. le Duc d'Orléans into a quiet corner, discussed the whole affair quite openly, which greatly pleased me, for I hoped that it might spur him into action. I felt, indeed, so much encouraged that after long consideration and assuring ourselves that our plans were progressing and Mme de Maintenon on our side, Mme la Duchesse d'Orléans and I together asked him to speak to the King. He flared up at first, but after being bombarded for a day and a half, and having no possible defence, since we had the approval of Mme la Duchesse de Bourgogne, Mme de Maintenon, M. de Beauvilliers, the Maréchal de Boufflers, and Père Tellier as well, he frankly admitted that he did not know how to go about it. Mme la Duchesse d'Orléans was astounded; as for me, I simply lost my temper, declaring that since he did such a vast number of foolish things every day with no ill results he might reasonably expect at least one of them to turn out well, and not refuse merely because his own interests might be served. I achieved nothing. He said that a royal marriage was absurd in war-time, and that of his daughter more senseless and inappropriate than any other; that he possessed neither the effrontery nor the courage to approach the King, and that in his present mood he would botch the whole affair. Faced with this flat statement, and seeing that Mme la Duchesse d'Orléans was still, as it were, petrified by surprise and disappointment, I produced my own solution, namely that M. le Duc d'Orléans, if

---

[1] 'Mademoiselle passionately longed for the marriage, but knew that the King disliked her because he thought her monstrously fat and unlikely to bear children. She had never loved denying herself, particularly not in eating, but she now resolved to be slim, no matter what the cost; and for an entire year she submitted to tight-lacing and only ate while running, never at mealtimes. This method succeeded, her figure improved and the marriage took place; but no sooner had she gained her purpose than she once more indulged her appetite, and in less than ten months had become immensely fat. It was commonly said that she indulged herself in other ways also. Indeed, it must be admitted that this princess was an outstanding example, in her period, of intemperance and profligacy.' *Memoirs of the Duc de Luynes*

he were determined not to speak, might consider writing a letter and putting it into the King's hand. That brought Mme la Duchesse d'Orléans back to life and speech, acclaiming this idea which had, in fact, originally been hers; but which I had rejected as being less effective than an interview. She had always thought that a letter which could be read aloud again and again to a circle of approving friends would do most good, and events proved her right. M. le Duc d'Orléans consented; but fearing second thoughts, I urged him to do it there and then. As he left the room, Mme la Duchesse d'Orléans said anxiously, 'You are not going to leave him, are you?', and then, 'Are you not writing as well?', meaning that she wanted me to write his letter for him. I accordingly followed him to his lodging on the ground-floor of the first pavilion on the chapel side of the *Perspective,* and found him, as usual, without pens, ink, or paper; but he had sent for them, and eventually some writing materials of very poor quality were brought. He then suggested that we should write together; but since he plagued me with questions after the opening lines I begged him to do his own work and leave me to mine, adding that he could then choose whichever he preferred, and add to or alter it as he wished. Whereupon I settled down to write. About midway I happened to look up as I was dipping my pen in the ink, and perceived that he had not written a single line but was calmly leaning back, watching me work. I spoke my opinion of him in a single word, and continued writing; and when he said, truly enough, that he could no more write than speak I did not contradict him.

That entire letter, which won us the marriage, I dashed off in one breath in M. le Duc d'Orléans's presence. It was not long, but I tried to include in it every-thing most likely to produce a quick decision in our favour—a touching opening, expressing respect and confidence, with a reminder that the King himself had made the first suggestion, proceeding to a list of the immense favours recently bestowed on Madame la Duchesse and M. du Maine, with a strong, yet tactful comparison with his own poverty; finally, another gentle reminder that the King had arranged his own marriage, delicately hinting at his august birth by comparison with his bride's, and saying that his only claim in asking was that his children were also the King's grandchildren, a piece of arrant flattery well calculated to sway King Louis. As soon as the letter was finished I read it to M. le Duc d'Orléans, who said that it was admirable, and would change nothing; although whether he really thought so or was merely lazy I could not decide. I had, however, written extremely fast in the minute handwriting which I used for my notes, and therefore, fearing his weak eyesight, I let him try to read it, which was a wise precaution because he found that he could not, and I accordingly took it to my own room to make a copy, promising to return with it later that evening. At this point two mishaps occurred; first, I was engaged to sup with Pontchartrain, whom I found already at table, and although I left immediately afterwards, he was, as always, abominably prying and inquisitive; yet there was nothing in my behaviour to put him on the track. Secondly, I learned that the King had retired early, and thus I did not visit Mme la Duchesse d'Orléans to read the letter as I had promised. I simply left it at her door because I did not wish to be seen calling on her so late. None the less my presence was remarked and everyone was curious. They got very little satisfaction from me.

M. le Duc d'Orléans allowed an entire week to pass with the letter still in his pocket, saying that extreme nervousness prevented him from delivering it. On Friday, 16 May, however, I learned from Maréchal that the King was feeling particularly well and had been joking at his first *lever;* that Mme de Maintenon was to be all day at Marly; that Père Tellier had come, as he always did on Fridays, and, best of all, that d'Antin was away in Paris. I found M. le Duc d'Orléans in the large drawing-room, waiting for the King's return from Mme de Maintenon's room, where he always went directly after mass when she was at Marly in the morning.[1] I gave him my news and asked how much longer he intended to procrastinate, adding that Mme la Duchesse de Bourgogne and Mme de Maintenon were both blaming him for his slowness. I said also that everyone was remarking on his look of dejection and my constant visits to Mme la Duchesse d'Orléans's lodging. He replied that he wished to act but dared not.

We spent a good three-quarters of an hour disputing in the drawing-room under the eyes of all the most important courtiers, I being all the while terrified lest we attract attention; but at last the King passed on his return and the large drawing-room emptied as the throng moved after him into the smaller one next his bedroom. I urged M. le Duc d'Orléans with all my might to follow and present his letter. He stepped forward a few paces and then turned back; but I, still exhorting, took him by the shoulder and pushed him in the right direction, stepping round him so as to place myself once more behind him, with the door in front. This performance was so often repeated that I was on tenterhooks lest the low-ranking persons still in the large drawing-room should notice, or the courtiers in the other room observe us through the double glass doors, revolving one around the other. In the end, I was so firm that, by dint of admonishing, pushing and turning, I managed to propel him into the next room and then, with enormous difficulty, through the wide-open doors of the King's bedroom, whence he could not return. Yet I still had to manœuvre him across the threshold. It now remained to be seen whether or not he would present his letter.

I followed him slowly, so as to avoid crossing the room by his side, and went to the window nearest the study, where room was made for me on one of the

---

[1] She usually spent the greater part of the day at Saint-Cyr, returning late in the afternoon, in time for the King's daily visit.

folding-stools in the recess. I sat next to the Maréchal de Boufflers while the King was changing his coat to walk in his gardens. I was not there longer than the time required for three or four *paters* before M. le Duc d'Orléans suddenly emerged, rushed through the room, and vanished from my sight. I rose with the rest and sat down again, much puzzled as to what could have occurred in so short a time. Some minutes later, the King appeared wearing walking-dress, and I followed him out-of-doors. I had been watching him carefully through the open doors when he was changing, and I continued to study him during the walk, for he must have been aware that everyone had seen the letter, and I wished to observe whether he would look cheerful, grave or meditative. I saw nothing whatsoever; in fact, he was so much as usual that I began to wonder what had happened to it. After a short stroll he stopped by the carp-pond beside Madame la Duchesse. M. le Duc d'Orléans made as if to join them but did not go too near. Soon afterwards the King turned to walk in another direction; but I held back, and M. le Duc d'Orléans also, for we were both eager to talk.

He said that he had presented his letter, and that the King had appeared surprised, asking what it was about; but when he explained that there was no complaint, only a matter on which he found it hard to speak, King Louis had relaxed somewhat, and had said that he would read it attentively. He had taken it with him into the adjoining room, and M. le Duc d'Orléans from his position near the door had seen him open it. After that we rejoined those who had followed the King, and went our respective ways. I was intensely relieved to hear that the deed was done; but I must admit to feeling somewhat alarmed lest my labours should prove unsuccessful. We did not have long to wait, for next day M. le Duc d'Orléans informed me that the King had read the letter twice over and was much better pleased than if he had spoken. He had even said that he, personally, was gratified by the request, but that Monseigneur might prove more difficult and that he must choose a good moment to speak to him.

A few days later we learned that Monseigneur had been induced to give his consent, and to fix an early date. In that happy situation I strongly advised M. and Mme la Duchesse d'Orléans not to appear over-eager, but on the contrary to be most prudent and discreet, keeping Madame la Duchesse and her allies serenely unconscious that a mine was laid beneath their feet, with a match already applied to the fuse. They agreed to be ruled by me. At our private meetings their rejoicing was unparalleled, and my joy equalled theirs, although it was not unalloyed.

One day, while we were still making plans, Mme la Duchesse d'Orléans had asked me with a meaning look, which I could not mistake, who, in my opinion, should be the lady-in-waiting. I fully understood, and replied immediately with the utmost coldness that she had better make sure of the marriage before concerning herself with the details. She had thereupon lapsed into silence; M. le Duc d'Orléans said nothing, and I quickly changed the subject. She did not mention the matter again until two days before I wrote the letter which I have already described, and then, in the midst of an important discussion, she suddenly gazed at me intently and said, 'If we succeed, it would give us great pleasure to have Mme de Saint-Simon for lady-in-waiting.' 'Madame,' said I, 'you are most kind, but she is too young and quite unsuited for such service.' 'But why?' she inquired, and fell to praising her in every way imaginable. After listening for a time, I interrupted, assuring her that my wife was not fit for that particular post, and suggesting other ladies of her acquaintance. It was quite useless, for she found some objection to all of them.

That second attack, so pressing, so unexpected, made both Mme de Saint-Simon and myself extremely uneasy. The very thought of a situation so far beneath persons of our birth and rank was abhorrent to us, and although we realized that regal vanity must needs be served by a seated lady,[1] we, ourselves, had no desire to suffer that indignity. We therefore resolved to take action in good time, I by consulting the Duc de Beauvilliers, and Mme de Saint-Simon by appealing to Mme la Duchesse de Bourgogne. Saying anything further to Mme la Duchesse d'Orléans would only have made her the more determined. I accordingly told M. de Beauvilliers all, stressing our extreme repugnance, and swearing that even though they appointed us we should still refuse. I besought him to turn the thoughts of those who had (or imagined that they had) the right to nominate in some other direction. He understood my feelings and promised to do his utmost. Mme de Saint-Simon contrived with the greatest discretion to obtain an audience of Mme la Duchesse de Bourgogne, her loyal friend for many years, and went to her at eleven in the morning just as she was stepping out of bed. She at once took my wife into her little sitting-room, and made her sit down beside her on a sofa. After the first compliments, Mme de Saint-Simon said that she came to her as to a never-failing refuge to beg a favour, confidently believing that it would not be refused her. She had hesitated long before coming, but now felt that she would reveal nothing secret, since it concerned a marriage of which the princess knew and approved. Here Mme la Duchesse de Bourgogne exclaimed, kissing her affectionately, 'You mean M. le Duc de Berry's marriage; you would like to be lady-in-waiting? I already had it in mind. The post is yours.' 'But, Madame,' said my wife, 'I came because I absolutely do not want it.' At that response Mme la Duchesse de Bourgogne's astonishment passed all bounds, and after a pause she inquired the reason for this violent aversion, whereat Mme de Saint-Simon replied that it might well seem strange to feel so deeply regarding a post for which she might never be

[1] One who had the right to sit on a *tabouret* in the King's presence.

chosen, but that from what I had said she believed that Mme la Duchesse d'Orléans had already decided. That was why she was entreating the princess to save her from a service which I did not much desire, and she still less. Her only wish, she continued, was to be one of Mme la Duchesse de Bourgogne's ladies, for with all her heart she loved and respected her. Should that be impossible she was content just to attend her court; to be employed elsewhere would be to her unbearable.

The princess was as kind as could be, insisting that she had been prompted solely by affection and Mme de Saint-Simon's best interests. She added that if Mademoiselle became her sister-in-law it would be largely by her doing; and that she hoped to spend much time with her and her lady-in-waiting, in whom she would need to have entire confidence. As for becoming one of her own ladies, that would scarcely be possible after serving Mme la Duchesse de Berry as her lady-in-waiting; but the Duchesse du Lude daily grew more infirm and was not immortal, and she cherished the hope that my wife might one day succeed her. Mme de Saint-Simon replied that to change from one employment to another might be difficult; to which the princess sharply retorted that she hoped everyone, especially the Duchesse de Berry, would know their duty well enough to sacrifice their ladies should she require them. My wife then protested that if she proved incapable she would be barred from other posts, and if successful there would be every reason to keep her where she was. She reverted once more to her inexperience, but Mme la Duchesse de Bourgogne would have none of that. The audience ended with expressions of mutual affection, the princess promising much against her will to do her best to avert the nomination. By that time it was half-past noon; Mme de Saint-Simon as she retired saw the princess's dressing-table already prepared in her bedroom, and several ladies waiting to pay their court, a sight that troubled her not a little since some of them were our close acquaintances.

Meanwhile preparations for the wedding were progressing too slowly for my liking, and although the King had said that he personally approved the marriage, he had as yet found no opportunity to speak to Monseigneur. On Monday, 26 May, he returned to Marly for the only visit which I missed after my audience. M. and Mme la Duchesse d'Orléans, who could ill spare me, often wrote to me, and several times made me join them for picnics at Saint-Cloud, where our meetings were less remarked. One such picnic was on Ascension Day, and I drove there during the afternoon with a coach and six. I found M. and Mme la Duchesse d'Orléans already at table with Mademoiselle and some of their ladies, at the prettiest little home-farm imaginable, adjoining the gate into the village, with its own delightful garden running alongside the avenue. I sat down with them to converse but, M. le Duc d'Orléans being vastly impatient, the meal was very cheerless and hurried.

After leaving the table Mme la Duchesse d'Orléans led me to another room, where we were alone until the prince joined us. I urged him to remind the King of his letter, if only in monosyllables, adding that such an air of discouragement ill-suited the present company and the presence of their servants. I then suggested going for a walk and conversing later; but, impulsive as ever, he swore that he cared nothing for the marriage, threatening to retire to his estates, which he declared were all falling into ruin. None of all this signified; it was merely his way of speaking when put out. Mme la Duchesse d'Orléans supported me stoutly, and at last he was very unwillingly persuaded to show me his farm, and afterwards to drive me round his gardens. Later that same evening we three walked together alone, I telling them not to let themselves be too much discouraged by the delay, remembering how unlikely victory had seemed at first. I warned them also with all the force at my command to try to conclude the affair during that Marly, as otherwise the marriage would certainly not be theirs. I prophesied that the King's readiness would decline; the difficulties with Monseigneur increase, and the effects of M. le Duc d'Orléans's letter be lost. Monseigneur, encouraged by Madame la Duchesse, would become, I said, more stubborn than ever, and the ever-postponed announcement would eventually die of sheer inanition.

They both responded to my vigorous words; Mme la Duchesse d'Orléans returned to the château, and her husband and I rejoined the rest of the company. The guests soon afterwards departed; he took Mademoiselle on one side and I remained with Mme de Fontaine-Martel, an old friend, and devoted to the whole Orléans family. She saw that something was amiss; guessed that it concerned the marriage and said as much, but I made no comment and showed no sign of embarrassment. She seized on the opportunity to tell me confidentially that M. le Duc d'Orléans would do well to hasten it by every possible means, since there were people ready to invent every kind of horror in order to prevent it, adding that already unspeakable things were being suggested regarding his passionate love for his daughter.[1] Hearing that, my hair stood up on end, for I realized as never before the kind of fiends with whom we had to contend.

As an immediate result, I reopened the subject with M. le Duc d'Orléans when we went for a stroll that same evening, urging him once more to reflect on his situation; the fact that without the marriage there was no future for him, and the vital need to have the announcement made during that Marly, failing which the entire project would fail. Perhaps my earnestness convinced him; at

---

[1] One source of the 'horrors' scandal was his obvious lack of enthusiasm for the wedding which would take his daughter from under his own roof.

any rate, he for once agreed with me, and I left him in a mood to take action. He then went in search of amusement indoors, while I took a few more turns round the garden with my kinswoman and childhood's friend Mme de Marey, Mademoiselle's governess. Before long, however, I received a message to the effect that Mme de Fontaine-Martel wished to speak to me, and returning to the château I was shown into a room where Mme la Duchesse d'Orléans was writing letters. It was she who had summoned me, having heard from Mme de Fontaine-Martel the horrible insinuation that had made my blood run cold. We lamented together at having to deal with such monsters; she protesting that there was no evidence of any passionate love whatsoever, and certainly none with his daughter, to whom he had been deeply attached since her second year, when he had nursed her day and night throughout a serious illness. We finally decided that it would not only be cruel to repeat this horror to M. le Duc d'Orléans, but also most unwise at a time when he needed to act speedily. Two days later, on Saturday, 31 May, M. le Duc d'Orléans tackled the King with a bluntness that did not always displease, provided it was not contradictive. As a result the King at last spoke to Monseigneur in his study, proposing the match in a paternal but none the less regal manner, with a benevolence that made acceptance easy, but invited no argument. Monseigneur hesitated and stammered; the King took advantage of his embarrassment to press him harder, and finally he surrendered. I can give no details because I learned nothing more. Having thus struck the fatal blow, the King sent for his nephew, giving him leave to tell Mme la Duchesse d'Orléans the joyful news, also Mme la Duchesse de Bourgogne and Mme de Maintenon, but no other person whatsoever. M. le Duc d'Orléans kissed the King's knee, for they were alone, begged permission to inform Mademoiselle of her approaching happiness, and returned to his wife, where behind locked doors they gave vent to their raptures.

On Monday, 2 June, Mme de Saint-Simon and I went to dine with Mme de Blanzac at Saint-Maur, a little château which she had on lease from the late Monsieur le Duc. She had taken it originally as a place to drink milk, but had made it her home for the past twenty years. We returned at seven in the evening to find a note from M. le Duc d'Orléans, delivered shortly after noon by a servant, as so often had happened during that Marly. I waited to open it until I was alone upstairs, with Mme de Saint-Simon. The envelope was addressed in his own hand, but the very brief contents were in the duchess's handwriting, beginning, '*Veni, vidi, vici!*', going on to say that as I might suppose her husband had dictated those words, but giving no details, simply swearing me to silence until after the announcement, at some future date. After my first delighted exclamations, in which Mme de Saint-Simon joined somewhat half-heartedly for she already had forebodings, I began to feel concerned at the delay; but while I was still considering, a footman appeared with a verbal message from Mademoiselle to the effect that her betrothal had been announced and that she was sending us the news by the same lackey who had brought it to her. My joy was then complete. I saw my friends secure and triumphant, my enemies surprised and outwitted; I felt proud at having played so important a part in that great victory, and rejoiced in my own situation, so different now, so hopeful for the future. Such considerations made me glad indeed.

I wrote at once to M. and Mme la Duchesse d'Orléans who had invited us to Saint-Cloud early next day. What a contrast to our last visit! We found the château seething with excitement, and a distinguished gathering eagerly expressing their joy. Everyone congratulated me; I was surrounded, indeed one might have almost imagined that I was the host. Most people spoke of the great alliance as having been my handiwork; but I turned a deaf ear to that. Encircled, embraced, passed from one to another, with Mme de Saint-Simon receiving her full share of the praise, I was propelled across that vast apartment towards the place where Mademoiselle stood with Mme la Princesse de Conti and her daughters, in a group of very eminent persons, who had come with all speed from Marly and Paris.

Mademoiselle exclaimed when she saw me, and came running to kiss me on both cheeks. She then took me by the hand and led me into the adjacent orangery. Once apart from the huge crowd which we could see only in the distance, she burst into such a flood of gratitude that I remained speechless with surprise. This she appeared to perceive, and in trying to mend matters she astounded me still more by enumerating my endeavours to procure her marriage, crowning all by informing me that her father had told her of every step. At that extraordinary revelation I could not help exclaiming at such lack of restraint on the part of M. le Duc d'Orléans. Yet her chatter was interspersed with words of sincere gratitude, spoken with a graciousness and dignity that surprised me no less, all mingled with a joyful agitation which she made no attempt to conceal.

Mme de Saint-Simon meanwhile was also surrounded and congratulated, people openly prophesying that she would be the lady-in-waiting, which she modestly disclaimed on the grounds of inexperience, youth, other commitments, and the large number of suitable ladies available. In so saying she let her personal preference appear so plainly that Mme de Châtillon[1] asked her if she really considered herself too young; to which she replied simply, 'Yes.' Mademoiselle, who hardly knew her, showered on her such a rain of caresses that the news of her probable nomination spread like wild-fire through the crowd of female courtiers, and she became the victim of such abject and pitiable flattery that her fears were greatly increased. She drove out in a carriage with one or two other ladies to meet M.

[1] Madame's lady-in-waiting.

and Mme la Duchesse d'Orléans on their return from Sceaux[1] to announce the
betrothal. It was a most happy encounter; the duke and duchess made room
for them in the coach and they all drove together into the courtyard, where the
entire company was assembled to greet them. When they saw me there were cries
of delight and, as they stepped down, repeated embraces and an exchange of
compliments. Madame and Mademoiselle came down the steps to receive them,
and they then drove out again, all of them together, to show themselves to the vast
crowds in the courtyards and gardens. As they stepped back into their coach they
desired me to wait until the numbers had somewhat diminished and we could
converse at leisure. I accordingly strolled among that great and noble company
awaiting their return.

As soon as they had taken leave of Madame, who returned to Marly, they sent
for me to join them in the orangery-garden, where directly I appeared they came
straight to meet me, leaving their other guests in order to tell me what had taken
place at Marly, just as I have recounted it here. They said afterwards that the King
would neither bestow any endowments on them nor give them a house until peace
had been signed, and that the young couple would eat meanwhile at Madame la
Duchesse de Bourgogne's table and use the King's officers and carriages. During
this conversation they had been leading me by imperceptible degrees towards
the other side of the garden, which was deserted; and at that point M. le Duc
d'Orléans suddenly turned round and rejoined the company, leaving me alone
with the duchess. She sat down on a nearby seat and invited me to sit beside her,
but that I would not do, for no matter what liberties I might take with them in
private, in public I never failed to show them respect. I am, indeed, persuaded
that however familiar such personages may encourage one to be, it is wiser and
more seemly to preserve the formalities; indeed one's self-respect demands it.
That is why, although I always sat as by right in their presence, I thought it best
not to sit alone with her on a garden-seat, especially not with everyone watching
us across the wide expanse of flower-beds. I therefore remained standing. She
continued the conversation for a moment and then abruptly stated that it was
time to decide on a lady-in-waiting, remarking that when I had appeared not to
welcome her first hint or her later more open suggestion of Mme de Saint-Simon,
she had not persisted. Now, however, she wished to say frankly that she wanted
no one else. I thanked her, but said that I quite sincerely believed my wife to be
unsuitable. She was too young, her health would not allow her so much fatigue,
she possessed neither the experience needed to guide a young princess, nor the
leisure, on account of our family and the situation with my mother.[2] I went on to
say that I was very sensible of Mme la Duchesse d'Orléans's desire to oblige us,

[1] They had been to visit the Duchesse du Maine.
[2] A dragon who ruled their lives.

but that I should do her wrong by being otherwise than frank. She replied that there were objections to every other lady and that she passionately and uniquely wished for Mme de Saint-Simon. I thereupon repeated once more all my arguments; but she continually interrupted me, saying, 'But it is for us to say whether we want her as she is; you have only to say that you will give her.'

After wrangling in this way for a good quarter of an hour, she vowing that my wife's integrity, virtue, and name for discretion made her all that could be desired, Mme la Duchesse d'Orléans promised that she should be asked to perform no duties that displeased her, and none which she felt unable to carry out. Nothing could have been more civil, and the princess's manner made her words all the more gracious. None the less, I stood firm, and after gazing sorrowfully at me for a few moments, she said, 'I see how it is; you do not care to take the second place,'[1] and her eyes filled with tears. She looked down, greatly discomfited; but I was less so than I might have been, for my mind was made up, and I could not say anything regarding the second place, since that was truly what held us back. I remained silent for the space of two *misereres,* and then spoke at random until Mme la Duchesse d'Orléans had recovered her composure, dried her tears, and made an effort to reply; after which she quickly rose, saying that it was time to go. Thereupon she walked silently to her carriage; curtseyed very politely to me, and was driven away.

Mme de Saint-Simon and I took our leave of Mademoiselle and returned to Paris. We both decided that this latest attack must have been planned in advance and that M. le Duc d'Orléans had reckoned that my more formal relationship with his wife would make me change my mind; we concluded, however, that no one could have refused more firmly or with greater respect. We congratulated ourselves on having gained the support of M. de Beauvilliers and Mme la Duchesse de Bourgogne; but I now recollect that in trying to be brief I have left out an essential part of my wife's audience. After reiterating the objections of her youth, inexperience, and devotion to the princess, without effect, my wife had fallen back on her delicate health, the management of our family, which I left entirely to her, and the age of my mother,[2] who very reasonably claimed from my wife an unremitting attention incompatible with the duties of a lady-in-waiting. That, however, had made Mme la Duchesse de Bourgogne no more amenable; she had simply replied that no one would expect more from Mme de Saint-Simon than she cared to undertake; that a tiring-woman was employed to bear without grumbling, or at least without support, all the tasks too fatiguing for a lady-in-waiting; that she should have all the leave that she required for family concerns, even for visits to La Ferté, and that as regarded my mother, the duty to her

[1] The first place was that of lady-in-waiting to the Duchesse de Bourgogne.
[2] Saint-Simon's mother was sixty-five in 1710.

should always come first; Mme la Duchesse de Bourgogne would personally guarantee that. Mme de Saint-Simon replied that all this was admirable in theory, but that in practice, as the princess herself must realize, it would not work, for it would set a bad example to the other ladies; to which Mme la Duchesse de Bourgogne's only response was to offer more and more highly gratifying exemptions. But she finally gave her promise, as I have already described, to prevent our being ruined by having to refuse a definite offer.

Our minds should now have been set at rest, since we had been careful to take our precautions in good time; but Mme de Saint-Simon, who rarely expects to have her wishes granted,[1] could not feel easy until an appointment had been made. That, however, was unlikely to be long-delayed, for the marriage had been announced and would take place as soon as the Pope's dispensation arrived.[2] We therefore began to consider whether or not to go to Versailles before the nomination, and we decided that it would look pointed to be absent when common courtesy would have indicated a visit to any private individual, and especially when the entire Court had assembled to pay their respects.

As we were dining on that same day, Wednesday, the Chancellor and his son, who had come to Paris because there were no councils on the Thursday, Friday, and Saturday before Pentecost, sent to invite us to call on them after dinner as they had something to tell us. This was it. On the evening after the announcement of the marriage there had been a discussion about the lady-in-waiting, in Mme de Maintenon's little sitting-room, between herself, the King, and Mme la Duchesse de Bourgogne. The King had at first suggested the Duchesse de Roquelaure because he was partial to her, which in itself was enough to make Mme de Maintenon hate her; but in truth she was an imperious, scheming woman, whose lordly airs enraged everyone, though at times she could be marvellously servile and flattering. Mme de Maintenon had seized the opportunity to say with a smile that if he wished to antagonize Society[3] he could scarcely do better; whereat he had appeared surprised and had turned to Mme la Duchesse de Bourgogne. When she thought the same, he said that they would not even consider her. He had then drawn from his pocket a list of the duchesses and picked out Mme de Lesdiguières, the niece of Mme de Montespan. She had a sweet disposition, was virtuous, capable, and extraordinarily witty, with that comical turn of phrase belonging to the Mortemarts;[4] but she had never in her life known the Court or Society, for she was poor, and lived in pious seclusion, seeing scarcely anyone. The King

---

[1] The present tense suggests that Mme de Saint-Simon was still living when he revised this part of his Memoirs.

[2] Necessary because they were cousins.

[3] An example of Mme de Maintenon's methods. She was not always successful.

[4] Saint-Simon often refers to this fascinating 'language' of the Mortemarts. It would appear that they said the most outrageous things in an innocently inquiring manner, as though butter would not melt in their mouths.

thought very highly of her, but finally said that she would not do on account of Jansenism, of which she had been suspected. There was no reply to that soliloquy.

My elevation following close after that of Lesdiguières, the King's eye fell on Mme de Saint-Simon's name. 'What do you think of her, Madame?' said he, addressing Mme de Maintenon, 'I hear nothing but good of her; it seems to me that she might do very well.' Mme de Maintenon agreed, adding that she was not personally acquainted with my wife but that everyone praised her, with never a word in disparagement. 'However,' she said, 'Mme la Duchesse de Bourgogne knows her well, and she can tell you more.' The princess praised her with faint enthusiasm, commended her virtue, but doubted her suitability. 'Why not?' asked the King, repeating the many excellent qualities for which she was known; to all of which the princess agreed, but still thought that she would not do. Whereupon the King, appearing more than a little surprised, had fallen to praising my wife's intelligence. Mme la Duchesse de Bourgogne allowed her that also, but concluded that it was relatively unimportant. Thereupon he became bored, saying that no one asked for perfection, and the princess then let slip that she doubted whether she would accept. That irritated him and he sharply retorted, 'Oh! as for refusing she'll not do that if properly asked and if she knows my wishes.' Mme la Duchesse de Bourgogne begged him at least to look again at the list, which he did, but immediately decided that no one except Mme de Saint-Simon was at all suitable.

We afterwards learned from Pontchartrain that right from the start people had said that Mme de Saint-Simon would be chosen, although no one believed her to desire the post. He also said that M. and Mme la Duchesse d'Orléans claimed to have written to me as soon as they were sure of the match, and made no secret of their desire to secure Mme de Saint-Simon. Pontchartrain had asked him whether he was aware of my sentiments, and knew that it would ruin me to be forced to refuse; but he had answered that although I did not want the post he felt sure of my accepting it if offered. Thereupon Pontchartrain, who loved to meddle, had urged our friends the palace-ladies to stir up Mme la Duchesse de Bourgogne; but she had told Mme de Nogaret that knowing what she did she hardly knew how to act. Pontchartrain now wished to remonstrate with her, but I quickly told him to mind his own business, saying that our silence should have been enough for M. le Duc d'Orléans, since Mme de Saint-Simon and I were fully old enough to see that a lady-in-waiting would be needed, and to have written to him and our other friends had we desired the post. Mme de Saint-Simon's tears were even more revealing; I never saw any man more amazed.

My wife then explained to the Chancellor all we had done to escape the nomination, and my three flat refusals to Mme la Duchesse d'Orléans; and I let fly against M. le Duc d'Orléans for trying to force me against my inclinations, and for saying that I should accept, when he very well knew that the contrary was true. The Chancellor allowed my anger to cool and my wife to dry her tears, and then said that things having come to such a pass he must change his mind, for he thought there was such fearful danger in refusing that he could not consent to our doing so. He showed me that the King was so little accustomed to being crossed that he would take it as a personal affront; that the crime would be unforgivable and constantly remembered; that we should find ourselves in deeper disgrace than ever, which the King would delight in bringing home to us at every opportunity; that as King Louis had himself proposed my wife he would be all the more inclined to show me favour also, and that since she was acclaimed by all the interested parties it would be very hard for him to produce a substitute. Two hours were spent consulting and arguing; but at last we resigned ourselves to staying the night at Versailles, resolved that if we could not avert the storm by fair means, we should at least avoid being destroyed by a refusal. We then left the Chancellor, and chancing to meet the Duc de Charost on his way back from Marly, we were stopped by him to hear news of much the same order, saying that our friends had bidden him warn us that there appeared no other alternatives than acceptance or ruin.

At that time we had no lodging in the château except the room lent us by the Chancellor, and we therefore spent the night with Mme de Lauzun.[1] Mme la Duchesse de Bourgogne happened to notice a man in our livery in the guard-room as she passed through on her return from Marly, and called to him, asking twice if Mme de Saint-Simon was expected; later, when she was playing cards with Monseigneur and Mme la Princesse de Conti, she saw him again speaking to Mme de Lauzun, and joyfully exclaimed that we must at last have arrived. The fact was that she had four times instructed Mme de Lauzun to write to my wife, as coming from herself, to be sure to come to Versailles on the evening of the King's return, and to impress on her that the post of lady-in-waiting would certainly be offered, and that a refusal would ruin us irretrievably. This letter never reached us, by the negligence or idleness of the servants. We learned that item of news from Mme de Lauzun herself, who was vastly surprised that we did not know it already. I shall not repeat the anger, the tears, the discussions that ensued. That same evening my wife was obliged to visit Mme la Duchesse de Bourgogne in Mme de Maintenon's room. As soon as she and her sister appeared they were surrounded. Mme la Duchesse de Bourgogne joined in the chorus of congratulation. Mme de Saint-Simon, somewhat embarrassed, said that they mocked her. Mme la Duchesse de Bourgogne reaffirmed that she was appointed. The

[1] Mme de Saint-Simon's sister.

King's supper produced other compliments, to avoid which I spent the entire evening in M. de Lauzun's study. I was so much annoyed by what Pontchartrain had said of M. le Duc d'Orléans that, in order to prevent myself from quarrelling with him, I needed time to remember our old friendship, his need of me, and the future when I should be thrown more and more into his company.

I saw him next morning as he walked before the King to mass. He joined me at once, and whispered into my ear the first words that he had ever spoken on the matter. 'Do you know that everyone is talking of your wife for us?' 'Yes, Monsieur,' I replied very gravely; 'and I am amazed at it, for nothing would become us less.' 'But why?' said he, somewhat embarrassed. 'Since you press me,' I retorted, 'the second place is something which we do not care to take.' 'You will not refuse us?' 'No,' I replied furiously, 'I am the King's subject and must obey him, but he must first command me, and I shall consent with the greatest possible reluctance, which the fact of your being the princess's father will do little to diminish, and nothing at all to appease our bitter resentment.' That dialogue took place as we walked to the chapel. Mgr le Duc de Bourgogne was all the while at our heels, craning forward to discover why I was so much vexed, and smiling to himself a little, for I happened to see him when I turned my head. M. le Duc d'Orléans did not speak again, and the entrance to the tribune brought that alarming conversation to an end.

It may seem hard to understand why the King and other royalty were neither put off by our reluctance, nor so deeply offended as to choose someone else. The plain fact is that they thought of themselves as a race apart, and were constantly encouraged to believe that agreeable fallacy by the eager homage, the near-worship, offered them by men and women ready to sacrifice all to minister to their pleasure, to study and forestall their every wish, and, against all reason, to pander to them with flattery and servility of every kind, and a total lack of restraint. It was indeed infinitely surprising to see those all-powerful personages stubbornly determined to drive us into accepting a post which every other courtier passionately longed for.

It was on Sunday, 15 June that the King decided to announce the appointment, and M. le Duc d'Orléans warned me towards the end of mass that he would do so. He told me also that when they were discussing the affair with Monseigneur in the study, the King had turned to him, exclaiming rather anxiously, 'I know your friend, how awkward he can be; he will not refuse me, will he?' Then, after reassurance, he had mentioned my hasty temper, not particularizing, indeed showing a certain respect for me, but very much concerned that I should be careful. All this he must have said in the hope that it would be repeated. M. le Duc d'Orléans had taken the opportunity to express his conviction that I had been slandered, especially in the matter of the Rome embassy, to which the King had replied airily that courtiers were like that.

On his return from mass the King called to me in the gallery, bidding me follow him to his study. He went to a little table against the wall, somewhat apart from the rest of the company, and near the door by which he had entered. There he informed me that he had chosen Mme de Saint-Simon to be the new Duchesse de Berry's lady-in-waiting; that it was a mark of great confidence to entrust a young princess so nearly related to himself to her charge at the age of thirty-two, and that it might also be taken as a mark of his belief in my expressed desire to be near him. I made a medium sort of bow, and replied that while I felt honoured by his trust in Mme de Saint-Simon, my greatest satisfaction lay in the knowledge that His Majesty was no longer displeased with me. That brief utterance, albeit spoken with great respect, allowed him to perceive my feelings, and he therefore proceeded to gratify my ears at some length with many civilities concerning my wife and myself—which no man knew better how to do, especially when there was an unpleasant dose to be administered. Then, looking more closely at me, and with a smile intended to be winning, he added, 'But you must guard your tongue,' in a friendly tone that seemed to ask for confirmation. I replied in the same tone that I had been most careful, more especially of late, and should continue to be so. He then gave me an even friendlier smile, as though he understood me and felt relieved at not meeting the expected opposition; indeed, almost as if my sacrifice had pleased him all the better because his ears were not wearied by argument.

He then faced the room and looking half towards me, and I towards him, he loudly proclaimed to the assembled company, 'Mme de Saint-Simon is lady-in-waiting to the future Duchesse de Berry.' There was a burst of applause as he went into the inner study. As is usual on such occasions I was immediately almost smothered by that vast assemblage, but I extricated myself politely and gravely, scorning to the last to simulate a gratification which I neither felt nor had expressed to the King. I sent at once to inform Mme de Saint-Simon that she was nominated and appointed. The news, though for so long expected, seemed almost to take her by surprise; she cried a little, but was obliged to make the effort to go and dress at Mme de Lauzun's apartment, where despite all precautions the doors were often forced open. The sisters then went to visit Mme la Duchesse de Bourgogne who was hurriedly arraying herself to dine at Meudon, where she had given Monseigneur some cause for complaining that she was always late. The general acclaim was as might have been expected; Madame la Duchesse de Bourgogne's welcome was astonishing; for she rose from the dressing-table, and taking my wife by the hand, walked hand in hand with her all the way to the chapel, only parting from her at the tribune. She said that although personally delighted, she wished my wife to know that she had tried her best to serve her, and at no small sacrifice, for by endeavouring to dissuade the King she had made him believe that she disliked her. In very truth, she added, she had been much perplexed, for loving Mme de Saint-Simon and the truth, as she did, she had scarcely known what to say in her disparagement. She had persevered none the less because one must serve one's friends in their own way and not as one would wish oneself. At the same time, she had foreseen that a refusal would mean total ruin, and thus was greatly relieved when we had consented to think again.

The long walk to the chapel was quite taken up with kind and loving speeches, the princess talking all the time and Mme de Saint-Simon finding it hard to get in a word of gratitude. She then went to M. and Mme la Duchesse d'Orléans's apartments, but they were with Mademoiselle and it was in her presence that she was greeted by them. Their delight changed to rapture when they caught sight of her, and Mademoiselle went so far as to say that the appointment had made her happiness complete. Yet, most surprisingly, Mme la Duchesse d'Orléans did not offer to present my wife to the King, and she therefore waited on him with her sister after the Council had risen. The King kept her in conversation for more than a quarter of an hour, commending her virtue and ability, and stressing the signal honour of receiving such an appointment at her age. He next praised her birth and rank, in a word said everything best calculated to please her. He ended by declaring that he had absolute confidence in her discretion, and thought the princess very lucky to have fallen into such excellent hands, always provided that she was capable of taking advice. Mme de Saint-Simon said very little, and that with modesty, taking good care, like myself, to show, albeit with great respect, that she was honoured, but felt grateful only for his trust.

In the evening, still accompanied by her sister, she called on Mme de Maintenon. Almost before she had time to speak, that lady addressed her with every imaginable civility, expressing her congratulations and praise, finally assert-ing that the King and Mme la Duchesse de Berry were really the ones who should be complimented for having secured a lady-in-waiting whose birth and rank shed lustre on the appointment. The visit was short, but the minutes were more crowded than I can well describe. I was astonished to find that Mme de Maintenon should even be aware that Mme de Saint-Simon conferred honour on the post, and still more so that she should exclaim at it. Moreover, as time passed, we were continually being surprised at learning that she repeated similar remarks both in and out of my wife's hearing, and more than once to Mme la Duchesse de Berry herself. Some truths are so self-evident that they must needs be accepted in even the most improbable surroundings.

I, myself, was most earnestly recommended to visit Mme de Maintenon that day. I had not set foot in her rooms since I paid my courtesy call with the rest of the Court, after the marriage of the Duchesse de Noailles.[1] Mme de Saint-Simon and I had no dealings with her, not even indirectly, and we never sought her company; indeed, I scarcely knew how her apartment was arranged.[2] On this occasion, however, I listened to advice and waited on her that same evening. I was admitted immediately, but was obliged to ask guidance of a lackey, and was propelled towards her bed in the alcove, in the manner of a blind man. She lay there surrounded by the Maréchale de Noailles, the Chancellor's wife, Mme de Saint-Géran, none of whom in the least intimidated me, and Mme de Caylus.[3] As soon as she clapped eyes on me she spared me the embarrassment of a compliment by speaking first, saying that it was she who should compliment me on the singular, nay unique blessing of a wife so full of merit that her appointment at thirty-two years old to be the lady-in-waiting of a princess of fifteen brought nothing but universal acclaim. Such praise was rare, she continued, and must be very sweet to a husband's ears; she could not sufficiently congratulate me. I replied that I could not sufficiently thank her for her kind words; then, looking about me at the company, I said less formally that the shortest visit often showed the greatest respect, and, making my bow, I at once departed.

The King provided us with every amenity calculated to sweeten the pill, and all without our having to ask or hint for anything whatsoever. He announced that so long as M. le Duc de Berry remained a grandson of the reigning monarch, the Duchesse du Lude and Mme de Saint-Simon should be treated as equal in every way, that is to say with a salary of twenty thousand livres, and another nine thousand in emoluments. He took a personal interest in constructing a most agreeable apartment for us at Versailles, and he dislodged d'Antin and the Duchess of Sforza so as to make a complete set of rooms for each of us, adding kitchens in the court below (an extreme rarity in the château), simply because we had always been in the habit of giving dinner parties and sometimes suppers as well, ever since we had first come to the Court.

On Sunday, 6 July, the marriage was celebrated at noon, in the chapel, by Cardinal de Janson, the Grand Almoner. Two of the King's almoners held the canopy. The King and the royal family, the princes and princesses of the blood, and the bastards were all present, with the duchesses of their households kneeling on hassocks and the dukes also. None of the foreign princes came, but some foreign princesses were among the duchesses, and they also had hassocks.

---

[1] The marriage of Mme de Maintenon's niece to the Duc de Noailles in 1698.
[2] Yet he was able to describe it in every detail. See Vol. I, p. 396.
[3] A cousin of Mme de Maintenon, and author of the charming *Souvenirs de Mme de Maintenon*.

The tribunes were filled to overflowing; but I placed myself there so as to gain a better view of the ceremony. Down below numerous ladies stood behind those who had hassocks, and behind them stood the men. After mass the curé of Versailles took the register to the King's prayer-stool for his signature; the royal family signed their names after his, but not the princes of the blood, with the sole exception of M. le Duc's children. That was the signal for Mme de Saint-Simon to rise from her hassock below the sanctuary-steps on the left-hand side, and to place herself behind Mme la Duchesse de Berry as she signed the register. That done, they all walked in procession out of the chapel.

There was a very pretty scene about precedence between Madame and Mme la Duchesse de Berry. The latter acquitted herself gracefully enough, until at last Madame took her by the shoulders and obliged her to walk in front.[1] On the following Wednesday, everyone went to Marly. The King gave a very inadequate present of jewellery to Mme la Duchesse de Berry, and nothing at all to her husband, with the result that he found himself too poor to play cards. Mme la Duchesse de Bourgogne told the King what was happening; but he, conscious of his own empty purse, said that he could give him only five hundred pistoles, blaming the country's misfortunes, and offering that small sum only because he was forced to realize that it was better to have a little than none at all.

That Marly was notable for Mme de Marey's resignation. She had been governess to all the children of M. le Duc d'Orléans, and was greatly respected by them. The King and Mme de Maintenon had hoped that she would have stayed with Mme la Duchesse de Berry, of whom she was fond (and the princess of her), as a woman of the bed-chamber, but nothing would move her; she insisted on retirement. We were not long in discovering the cause, for the more that young princess allowed her true nature to appear (and she made little attempt to conceal it), the more convinced we became that Mme de Marey was justified; and we marvelled at the care taken to keep it secret. We then realized how blind we had been in striving for this much desired marriage, and we deeply regretted a victory which, had I known the half, nay the thousandth part of what we were so tragically to witness, I should have done everything to prevent. No more at present! and in the future no more than it is impossible to hide.[2] I mention it here only because the many terrible events that took place later cast their first shadows on this Marly. Let us now return to where we digressed so that the record of this marriage might proceed without interruption.

[1] 'As they left the chapel Mme la Duchesse de Berry stepped in front of Madame, but she did have the civility to say, "Push me forward, Madame, I shall need pushing before I grow accustomed to walking before you. It will take me some time to get used to that honour.' " (*Memoirs of Dangeau*)

[2] In the *Souvenirs*, Mme de Caylus writes that not only was the bride still tipsy two days after the wedding, but that on the very next day she showed herself for what she was, another Queen of Navarre in her habits, with a taste for drink added, and ambition such as dissolute persons do not ordinarily possess.

The King made numerous promotions and re-appointed the same generals to the same armies. The Duc de Noailles left early for Roussillon. The Duc d'Harcourt was at Bourbon for the waters, and due to return in May to join the army of the Rhine. In the meantime he stayed at the Comte de Tavannes's château of Le Pailly[1] so as to avoid a long journey. Bezons received orders to report to him there and afterwards to take command of the army until his arrival.

Villars had been re-appointed to Flanders, but viewed his task with great disfavour. Having risen to unparalleled heights of favour, privilege, wealth and rank, he believed that for the first time in his life he might safely deliver a few unpalatable truths, since he had nothing to gain and risked only the loss of his command. He accordingly said a great deal to Desmaretz and Voysin about the desperate state of the fortresses, magazines, and garrisons, the pitiable condition of the men and officers, and the lack of supplies of every kind, including pay and allowances. Seeing that his words were falling on deaf ears, he ventured to state his complaints quite baldly to the King and Mme de Maintenon. He spoke with his papers spread before them on the table, giving them factual proofs which even they could not contest; but as he drew back that fatal curtain, the scene which he revealed appeared to them so terrible, so monstrously shocking that they found it easier to be angry than to accept such language from Villars, who had always been their comforter, constantly persuading them that all was in perfect order with preparations well in hand. The very frequency and brazenness of his lying had led them to regard him as their chief support, and to give him the supreme authority in every task; for he was the only one who never spoke discouragingly, but on the contrary made everything appear easy and filled them with good hope. Now that he voiced the unanimous opinion of all the rest of the army, their faith in him was shattered, along with his power to delude them in the hope of personal advantage. They saw him for the first time as he seemed to the world in general, absurd, crazy, impudent, lying, wholly irresponsible.[2] They reproached themselves for being so quick to raise him from nothingness to such towering heights, and at once avoided him, ignored him, let him perceive their altered feelings, and allowed others also to be aware of them.

Villars himself then took alarm. His intention had been to make his wounds, the deficiencies of the service, and the need for robust health in coping with them an excuse for enjoying his rewards in tranquillity, and avoiding the burdens of a calling from which he had nothing more to gain. He wished also to enjoy his fame and favour, and the reputation that led the King to consult him at every turn regarding the armies and generals. He became terrified as he realized the

[1] About 7½ miles south-east of Langres.
[2] Yet he had defeated Eugene and was the only one of the French generals to stand firm against Marlborough and stop him.

dangers to which he had exposed himself, and thought of what he might become without employment, family, or friends to shield him from his enemies and the anger of the public, whom he had consistently defied and outraged. He made a swift reappraisal, and just as shame had never restrained him in the past, so he felt none now in suddenly reverting to the language that had won him fame and fortune. Seizing a momentary lull before the appointment of a new commander for the difficult task in Flanders, he began again to lie and bluster, making light of present dangers, offering ready-made solutions, and pretending that no problem existed. This glaring reversal was plain to all, but it was sufficient to restore him to favour, and he received the command. That was not all; once back in authority he had the temerity to compare himself publicly to a Roman conqueror, ready after winning a great victory to sacrifice health, leisure, and all his comforts, and to fly once more to his country's aid at the behest of his emperor, despite wounds that made riding a torture. To such boasts he added a claim that he was renouncing all hope of curing his crippled leg by taking the waters, and went so far in that disgraceful vein that the Duc de Guiche, who had also intended taking the cure for a not so serious foot-wound received at Malplaquet, took his remarks personally and never forgave him.

Villars left for the frontier, travelling in his coach by easy stages so as to nurse his crippled leg. There then occurred an incident that might have seemed highly diverting had not the country's vital interests been at stake. The Maréchal de Montesquiou, his second-in-command, who was mustering the army near Cambrai, had never concealed from Villars the acute shortages; but he now sent the King a glowing account of the splendid condition of everything, which so pleased King Louis that he immediately forwarded the dispatch to Villars. As chance would have it, the courier reached Villars just two hours after a long screed from Montesquiou, full of bitter complaint and most disquieting details regarding the lack of bare necessities for the fortresses, magazines, and troops. Villars unhesitatingly returned the King's courier with the two reports by the self-same writer, dated on the same day, attaching only a note to say that the King and Voysin must decide for themselves which was nearer the truth. He then continued his journey, rejoicing at the lucky chance that had enabled him to confirm his unpalatable views at another's expense, and at the same moment to demonstrate the difficulty of the task that lay before him. The King gave no sign of having been affected by the contradictory reports; but Villars immediately published them both, although taking good care to conceal his action. The scandal was appalling. The two marshals did not argue the matter, but you may imagine the effect on their personal relations, and what the army thought of it; for the troops had little liking for either and made no attempt to reconcile them.

Prince Eugene and Marlborough did not want a peace. Their aim was to invade France itself, the former for the sake of glory and personal revenge upon the king,[1] the latter for wealth—a dominating passion with each of them. With that intent they resolved to make use of our weakness and the sorry plight of our troops and fortresses in order to push their conquests as far forward as possible. The King, on the other hand, mortified by continual defeats, passionately desired a victory that would frustrate the enemy's plans and give fresh impetus to the barren and humiliating peace talks at Gertruydemberg. The Allies meanwhile had taken up a very strong position. Villars missed an excellent chance of defeating them when he first arrived, a fact of which the whole army was aware, for he was warned in advance by many of the generals, including the Maréchal de Montesquiou, but had not trusted them, and dared not now risk an attack because the enemy's dispositions were complete. The army were grumbling at this major error, and Villars, feeling that they had just cause for anger, defended himself with impudent boasting, proclaiming that he preferred to destroy the enemy at leisure, whereas in reality he did not know even how best to attack.

In the midst of this crisis, which the ill feeling between the two marshals and the small respect felt for either rendered most serious, the King decided to send the Duke of Berwick to Flanders, partly to act as moderator, partly to raise morale, but with no authority other than his marshal's rank, and no settled command. He had orders to leave as soon as the armies joined in battle, or some other firm decision had been taken, and to attach himself to the army in Dauphiné, where the campaign opened later on account of snow and the mountains. This was a time when men would no longer work without rewards that far exceeded their service, or without some hope of personal advantage. It was a novelty equally pernicious to the State and to King Louis, who had created many giants in rank who in action proved to be pigmies, and were never afterwards considered fit for employment. We had now reached the golden age of the bastards. Berwick[2] was barely eighteen years old, when in 1688 he first came to France in the train of James II, during the English revolution. At twenty-two he rose at one step to lieutenant-general and served, in 1692, in Flanders. At thirty-three he commanded the French army in Spain, and at thirty-four was rewarded for his victory at Almanza by being made a grandee of Spain and a knight of the Golden Fleece. Since that time he had constantly commanded armies, and in February

---

[1] Prince Eugene was born in Paris, in 1663, the son of Prince Eugene Maurice of Savoy-Carignan and of the beautiful Olympe Mancini, a niece of Cardinal Mazarin. Louis XIV would not give him a commission in the French army because of his ugliness and frail physique, and forced him to enter the Church. He was known at that time as *le petit abbé*. After his father's death in 1673 and his mother's banishment from Louis XIV's Court, he renounced French nationality and, at the age of twenty, he entered the service of the Emperor Leopold. He is supposed to have sworn to return to France sword in hand. It is fascinating to think what might have happened had King Louis accepted him and he had fought against Marlborough.

[2] The illegitimate son of James II and Marlborough's sister Arabella Churchill.

1706 was made a Marshal of France, the only one under the age of thirty-six. Berwick's dukedom was English; but although foreign dukes do not rank in France, the King had exceptionally granted rank to the followers of King James, who had given Berwick the Garter during the revolution. That was great and swift promotion indeed, under a King who regarded all men of that age as children, save only the bastards who, to him, were as ageless as the gods.

In the previous year Berwick had asked for a peerage, being eager to accumulate all the honours and divide them among his children; but the King, who was so liberal with that dignity as to make it virtually worthless, had moments also of extreme parsimony. Berwick struck such a moment and was refused. At the time of which I speak, however, he must have known that they thought him indispensable, for he let it be understood that he must be rewarded and in that way received his peerage. He had had one son by a first marriage,[1] and several sons and daughters by the second.[2] His feelings for England were comparable to those of the Jews for their Messiah; and he continually deluded himself with false hope of a revolution to restore the Stuarts and give him back his lands and titles. He was the son of the sister of the Duke of Marlborough, who loved him dearly, and with whom he carried on a secret correspondence with the consent of the King and of the King of England. All three were duped; but the letters allowed Berwick to keep in touch with Englishmen and to lay plans for his own restoration, even under the government of that time. With that object in mind he extracted the unique favour of permission to choose his heir, and even to change as often as he pleased the inheritors of his various titles. Thus he had the temerity to request (and shameful to relate the request was granted) that his eldest son should be excluded from the inheritance of his French ducal-peerage, and the children of his second marriage be allowed to replace him. He desired to invest this eldest boy with the title of Duke of Berwick and with all his English estates; to make the second a Peer of France, and the third a Grandee of Spain. Three sons raised by inheritance to the highest rank in the three greatest countries of Europe! You must admit that this was no small thing to have achieved by the age of forty; not to mention all the rest that he had won. Yet England was his heart's desire. He had courted her ardently and in vain all through his life, flattering her governments, royally entertaining every distinguished English traveller, forming friendships with all her ambassadors.[3] Nothing, however, had served to reinstate

---

[1] That son was James Francis Fitzjames, later Duke of Liria. His mother was Lady Honora Sarsfield (née de Burke).
[2] Three: James, Duke of Fitzjames; Henrietta who married Clermont d'Amboise, and Francis, eventually Bishop of Soissons. Their mother was Anne Bulkely (m. 1700).
[3] Notably the Walpoles, Lord Stair, and Bolingbroke.

him. Thus, having deprived his eldest son of succession to rank in France, he was forced to fall back on a Spanish grandeeship for him, and further bound the boy to Spain by marrying him to a sister of the Duke of Veragua, who left her an income of more than a hundred thousand écus, with palaces, jewels, and furniture in profusion, together with very large estates. There will be more to tell of all this in the future.

There was a great scandal when the King consented to that special arrangement of allowing a younger son to inherit the highest rank in France, while the elder lived in hope of similar rank in England. That, however, was the supreme moment of the bastards. Berwick immediately purchased Warties, a mediocre estate near Clermont, and had it registered in the foreign and disgraceful name of Fitzjames, another shameful concession. Even the King was puzzled by that name and asked Berwick, in my presence, for an explanation, to which he replied without embarrassment, as follows. When an English king legitimizes his bastards, he gives them a name and arms, which are registered by Parliament and passed on to their descendants. These arms invariably contain those of England with certain distinguishing features. The names vary, for example Charles II's bastard the Duke of Richmond was surnamed Lennox, the Dukes of Cleveland and Grafton, Fitzroy, signifying the son of a king, and the Duke of St. Albans (another of that king's bastards) received the surname Beauclerk.[1] Lastly, the Duke of Berwick, King James II's illegitimate son, was named Fitzjames, or son of James; that will be the surname of all his descendants, and his French peerage is registered as the dukedom of Fitzjames. One cannot help laughing at the absurdity of such a name translated into the French language; it is scarcely surprising that it was thought scandalous to introduce it into France. The Parlement, however, either dared not or could not protest, and the name and rank were accepted without question.

Berwick waited until everything was signed and sealed and then left for Flanders, where he found the enemy so strongly entrenched that he quickly decided, like most of the other generals and the King himself, that Villars having missed his chance it was too late to attack. He carefully summed up the various opinions, noting that by unanimous agreement Villars had lost a fine opportunity, and having fulfilled his instructions returned to France after an absence of only three weeks. His report dismayed the King and those who had occasion to study it; soon afterwards letters from the army let everyone into the secret and turned public opinion altogether against that bombastic liar.

Berwick was less than twenty-four hours at the Court before leaving for Dauphiné, and for that reason was not received by the Parlement as a duke and peer until the eleventh day of the December following. That date is memorable

---

[1] He may have been named after Henry I of England (1068-1135), who was so-called because his scholarship was unusual in a king of that period.

also for two incidents which I shall now relate. First, the large number of us who attended his reception had the unpleasant experience of finding ourselves sitting completely surrounded by bastards, with bastards and sons of bastards ranged above us, and the English bastards below us all. This provided us with much food for reflection on the stability of the law in that island thanks to constant vigilance and firm protection, and the careless manner in which our French law may be set aside.

Berwick's friend the Duc de Tresmes, Governor of Paris, gave a banquet in his honour after the reception. Most of the dukes were present, together with other distinguished persons including Caumartin, counsellor of State and intendant of finances, who was invited everywhere by the Court and Society, and was an intimate friend of the Duc de Tresmes. Caumartin was very learned, yet pleasant in company, with a whole repertory of vastly entertaining anecdotes which he told well and wittily, albeit with fatuous pomposity. At heart, however, he was a good enough fellow and, in his own way, respectful of rank. I cannot think what possessed him at that moment to forget his surroundings, but while the dessert was still on the table he began a long history of some bastard's trial, at which he had been the judge, enlarging on the disadvantages of that kind of birth and the strictness of the law concerning it, holding forth at enormous length and with obvious enjoyment. Everyone looked into his plate and nudged his neighbour. A silence reigned which Caumartin mistook for attention and a tribute to his eloquence. M. de Tresmes more than once tried to stop him, but he still boomed on, pitching his voice even higher, deaf to all hints. The company at table almost choked in their efforts to chew and swallow; all were dying of thirst, yet no one dared to drink for fear of exploding, and for the same reason no one looked up. Caumartin, still engrossed in his tale and the pleasures of oratory, noticed nothing amiss. He frequently addressed himself to Berwick, as to the guest of honour, but the latter, seeing that he had totally forgotten his company, took not the least offence. On the other hand, poor Tresmes was in such a state that the sweat poured down his face.

Truly, the utter absurdity of the whole situation gave me enormous pleasure through my eyes and ears; also later, on reflection, as I thought of the contrast between that morning's ceremony and the subsequent banquet—the bastards triumphant followed by this grand parade of all their nothingness and disrepute.

The Maréchal de Villars found the army assembled under Cambrai. All told, it consisted of fifty-seven battalions, two hundred and sixty-three squadrons, and the garrisons of all the fortresses; but the numbers were not complete, not even in officers. For the past month the soldiers had been paid, and were receiving passable bread with small amounts of meat. Villars was involved in an absurd scandal that created a great stir at the Court and in the army. His wound, or the fuss he made about it, obliged him to ride with one leg resting on his horse's neck, rather as ladies ride. One day when he felt tired of appearing thus before the troops he let slip the remark that it bored him to have to ride like the whores in Mme la Duchesse de Bourgogne's retinue (all, incidentally, young ladies of the Court, including Madame la Duchesse's daughters). Such a remark in full hearing of the army by an unpopular general spread from one end of the camp to the other, and soon reached the Court and Paris. The ladies who rode on horseback were insulted, and the rest sided with them, Mme la Duchesse de Bourgogne felt obliged to appear offended and to complain. Not long afterwards Villars himself heard of this, and became greatly agitated at the sudden appearance of such a redoubtable band of enemies, who were particularly unwelcome in the middle of a campaign. In the end, the matter was settled in a peculiarly ignoble fashion by Albergotti, who swore that he had heard the maréchal speak thus of *vivandières* and other camp followers but never of Mme la Duchesse de Bourgogne's young ladies.

So much else went wrong for Villars in that campaign that he decided to return to his cure, and made such a to-do about his health that permission was finally given. Harcourt, who had only just arrived in Strasbourg after finishing a cure, received orders to rejoin the army immediately, with leave to make the journey by easy stages in his coach. He spent nearly a month in Paris on the way, and went from thence to Dourlens, where he had arranged to meet the Maréchal de Villars; after which, one commander continued on his road to the Flanders army and the other went straight to Bourbon, without visiting either Paris or the Court, which appeared rather extraordinary, not to say unamiable. Thus one lame man was replaced by another, and the incoming general was as little capable of support-ing fatigue as his predecessor. The new commander began with a cure at Bourbon, his forerunner finished with one, and Harcourt thus became saddled with Flanders which hitherto he had successfully managed to avoid. So ended a campaign, which proved to be the Duke of Marlborough's last. The army went first into forage-quarters and shortly afterwards into winter-quarters. M. d'Harcourt suffered a very slight attack of apoplexy with no after effects. The end of the campaign came at a good moment for him. Let us now turn to events elsewhere.

One incident which I shall touch on only lightly followed hard on the heels of others of a similar nature, and caused something of a scandal despite the efforts made to smother it. Mme la Duchesse de Bourgogne gave a supper-party at Saint-Cloud with Mme la Duchesse de Berry. Mme de Saint-Simon excused herself from attending. Mme la Duchesse de Berry and M. le Duc d'Orléans (but she far more than he) became so drunk that Mme la Duchesse de Bourgogne, Mme la Duchesse d'Orléans, and the rest of the company were shocked beyond measure. M. le Duc de Berry, who was also present, was given such comfort as was possible in the circumstances, and so were the great number of guests, whom their gracious hostess attempted with all her might to keep entertained. The after effects of the wine, both above and below, were embarrassing to witness but did not at all sober her, and the result was that she had to be returned to Versailles in a sottish condition. All the outdoor servants saw her, and they did not keep silence; but it was somehow concealed from the King, Monseigneur, and Mme de Maintenon.

Let us now return to events in Spain, which were of great importance in that year. I decided that it would be best to leave them until now, in order not to interrupt the narrative. I shall therefore take up the tale in the early months of that year and continue steadily on until the end. You will follow what happened more easily if you will bear in mind the failure of Torcy's mission to the Hague, and the unnatural and abominable clauses on which the humiliating peace negotiations of Gertruydemberg finally broke down, clauses inserted by men determined to destroy all hope of a peace and openly boasting that they could deprive France of everything by an invasion. You will then recollect the terrible danger facing Spain, since France, scarcely able to defend herself, was quite incapable of providing help, and, indeed, preferred to leave a loophole for peace by seeming to abandon Spain entirely, rather than submit to wholly unacceptable terms. That was why King Louis, to avoid the merest semblance of giving aid, had made such a display of recalling Mme des Ursins, and why that lady was conducting herself as though she were about to leave, and remaining for a few weeks longer only to settle her affairs.[1] In point of fact, I doubt whether any firm decision had been taken, and I am very sure that neither the Princesse des Ursins nor Their Catholic Majesties ever seriously considered her departure. It was a mere show of compliance, intended to be postponed and then forgotten altogether, as it very soon was, after the first announcement.

Meanwhile there were no French generals in Spain, a fact which M. de Vendôme turned to his advantage, correctly guessing that if the King of Spain were to ask for him, King Louis might be very glad to let him go. He had hinted as much to the Princesse des Ursins, who thought well of the idea, as showing the Allies that France still had vital interests south of the Pyrenees. In the event, the King's personal inclinations gave Vendôme his wish, although the probable effect upon the enemy delayed his departure until all hope of peace had vanished. King Philip made a second request for him in March, and towards the end of that month left Madrid and

---

[1] Mme de Maintenon to Villeroy, 8 October, 1711: 'Your friend in Madrid is writing me sad letters and miserably making plans in case she should be required to return to France. She feels very bitterly towards us. I have referred her to you to explain a situation which she cannot or will not understand. Princes as unfortunate as those to whom she is attached must be excused for a little injustice. My feelings for her will not change, but our correspondence has become exceedingly painful.'

placed himself at the head of his army in Aragon. Villadarias, one of their best and most experienced generals, who had long served in Flanders under the late King of Spain, was appointed second-in-command. King Philip shortly moved his headquarters from Saragossa to Lerida, where the troops and the townspeople greeted him with cheers. In June he was joined by troops from Flanders, and soon afterwards the army marched away in search of the enemy.

The Marquis of Bay, commanding a small army in Estremadura, took by assault the important fortress of Miranda-de-Duero, on the Portuguese frontier,[1] capturing the governor, the garrison, and the three hundred prisoners-of-war whom they were guarding. At this point, however, Starhemberg[2] recovered sooner than expected from an illness that had greatly assisted them and, swiftly mustering his forces, marched into the middle of the Spanish army. He captured some portions, defeated others, and compelled the remainder to retreat on Saragossa, whence the King of Spain sent a courier to King Louis, with still another urgent request for M. de Vendôme. All the blame fell on Villadarias, who was accused of negligence and rashness and immediately replaced by the Marquis of Bay. It was at the beginning of August that King Louis learned of the disaster and received the second appeal for Vendôme's presence. By that time the negotiations at Gertruydemberg had been broken off. Thus, the request was granted and Vendôme was at last given orders to leave for Spain. In the engagements just mentioned the Spaniards lost only about a thousand men, killed or captured, and a certain amount of baggage. They cost the enemy a number of officers, including one of the Princes of Nassau[3] and Lord Carpenter. Panic and disorder caused most of the damage.

The Duc de Vendôme, kept well posted from Spain by Mme des Ursins, and at home by M. du Maine, had secretly made his preparations and was ready to depart. A slight attack of gout and some private business delayed him a few days longer; but he made his farewell appearance at Versailles on the morning of 19 August. In the meantime M. du Maine had been in treaty with Mme de Maintenon to be allowed to take him to call on Mme la Duchesse de Bourgogne. The moment seemed propitious, since he was going at the request of the King of Spain and of the Queen, her sister, and thus not to visit her before leaving might have appeared disagreeably pointed. Accordingly, M. du Maine with Vendôme at his heels presented himself that same day while the princess was at her dressing-table.[4] It happened to be a Tuesday, the day for foreign ministers, and the room was crowded with ladies and gentlemen. Mme la Duchesse de Bourgogne rose to

---

[1] Near Braganza, which is in Portugal.
[2] Guidobaldo, Count von Starhemberg (1657-1737), commander of the Imperial army in Spain.
[3] Prince Francis of Nassau, who was illegitimate.
[4] The usual place for ladies to receive informal calls.

receive them, as she did for all princes, whether of the blood or otherwise, and also for dukes and duchesses, and then immediately sat down. After that unavoidable first greeting, she, who had been chattering and looking about her, very little concerned with her adornment and her mirror, now sat with her eyes riveted upon her reflection, saying nothing at all. M. du Maine, with M. de Vendôme glued to his side, was much discomfited, and although he was usually gay and bright in conversation he dared not utter. No one approached either of them. They remained thus for a good ten minutes in that crowded and completely silent room with everyone staring at them, and at last, when they could bear it no longer, they withdrew.

Such a reception was enough to prevent Vendôme from attempting a second, perhaps still more embarrassing leave-taking when, like the princes, and Marshals of France leaving or returning from their campaigns, he would have had to kiss her on the cheek. He may, indeed, have feared the unparalleled insult of a refusal. M. le Duc de Bourgogne, on the other hand, treated him civilly—which is to say far too well—and he received visits from Alba, Torcy, and Voysin. He paid his court to the King that same day in the customary manner, and on the following day, Wednesday, after the King's dinner, he took his leave and went thence to Paris. Since his wedding-day, he had only once gone there to see Madame la Princesse, and as Mme de Vendôme never visited Anet, where he habitually lived, husband and wife had had little chance of becoming better acquainted.

In Spain, in the meantime, Starhemberg had followed up his victory by attacking the Spanish forces under the walls of Saragossa and beating them soundly. Bay found them so stricken with terror when he took command that he almost despaired of them. Every infantry man (the infantry was little more than a militia) had thrown down his arms at the first assault. The Walloon guards and the few remaining regulars could not hold out unsupported and were defeated. The cavalry were routed; but they had acquitted themselves somewhat better. In short, all was lost—artillery, baggage, everything. The disaster was complete. King Philip removed from Saragossa, where he had witnessed the battle in very uncomfortable circumstances, and made straight for Madrid; whilst, unhampered by the enemy, Bay retired to Toledo with the remaining force of eighteen hundred men. M. de Vendôme received this bad news on the road to Spain; but as usual made no haste to restore the situation, preferring to allow the dust to settle before taking any action. He merely shrugged his shoulders and continued on his way to Bayonne.

After this victory the Archduke Charles held a council-of-war with Count Starhemberg, at which their next move was discussed with considerable heat and widely divergent opinions. Starhemberg was for attacking the small army

left by Bay on the Portuguese frontier—a sound plan that might have destroyed
King Philip's chances by cutting his communications with Portugal, the sea, and
France. Stanhope, on the other hand, was for marching straight to Madrid with
the Archduke, and having him at once proclaimed king, hoping to strike panic
throughout the kingdom by seizing the capital, and afterwards using Madrid
as a centre from which to spread out as need and opportunity arose. Starhemberg
saw the brilliance of this project, but considered it rash and unprofitable because
of the immense distances separating Madrid from the frontiers, the sea, and their
storehouses; for Madrid stood in barren country where there was neither food nor
fodder. Such arguments were prudent, but Stanhope, commanding the English
and Dutch forces that formed the greater part of this Allied army, declared that
he had received his queen's orders to march first to Madrid, unless events made
that impossible. The majority voted in support of him, the Archduke reluctantly
agreed, and preparations were hastily made for an advance that did indeed strike
terror throughout the whole of Spain, but none the less saved King Philip.

In Madrid itself the alarm was already considerable. It changed to terror
when the Archduke's arrival became a certainty, and there was general dismay
when the king decided to leave the indefensible city, taking with him the queen,
the baby prince, and his council. The nobles, with very few exceptions, expressed
their willingness to follow him no matter what might befall, and his departure took
place within twenty-four hours of its announcement. Before leaving, the queen
appeared on the balcony with the prince in her arms, and addressed the people
with so much eloquence, fortitude and courage, that she succeeded beyond all
expectations. Her words spread in the city and afterwards throughout the provinces; and thus, when the royal family left Madrid for the second time, they were
accompanied by cries and lamentations from the people who ran out of the town
and neighbouring suburbs to follow their king and queen. It took much firmness
and persuasion to induce them, for his sake, to return to their homes.

The Marquis of Mancera, more than a hundred years old and very highly
esteemed for his character and achievements, also made preparations to follow
the king and queen, but they sent word to him, accompanied by every imaginable token of love, that he was not to move. He returned his compliments, but
took the road none the less in his carrying chair, not daring to use other means
of transport for fear of armed bandits, the danger of the roads, or even of being
deserted. He travelled more than a league in this manner; but the king and queen
sent a second time, showing their appreciation of his zeal and rare devotion,
but giving him such firm orders to return that he was forced to obey. It was in
Valladolid that the unhappy court at last found refuge. But even in this terrible
crisis, the worst to which they had been subjected, their judgment and courage did

not fail. They faced their troubles united, and did everything possible to recover themselves. Thirty-three grandees signed a letter to Louis XIV, to be presented by the Duke of Alba, assuring him of their loyalty to King Philip, and begging for reinforcements.

Meanwhile the country as a whole displayed the finest and most shining example of loyalty and courage that the world has ever witnessed. Prelates and lower clergy, nobles and peasants, pensioners, townsfolk, whole communities, private persons, gentlemen, merchants, lawyers, artisans, all bled themselves white to equip fresh troops, fill the storehouses, and send provisions to the court in exile, and to those who had gone with the king. Each man gave much or little according to his means, but none held back. In brief, never has an entire nation made such great sacrifices untaxed and unsolicited, in a united effort that affected each district at one and the same moment. The queen sold her personal possessions and herself received small sums, as little as ten pistoles, honouring such devotion and expressing thanks for these gifts in the same loving spirit as that with which the money was offered, for these were great sums indeed to those who willingly gave their all. She often said to them that she wished she could ride her horse at the head of the army holding her baby son in her arms; her words and conduct won all hearts, and proved of immense value in that fearful emergency.

During the interval the Archduke had arrived at Madrid. He made a triumphal entry and was proclaimed king by force of arms, whilst his soldiers dragged the *corregidor*[1] trembling through the empty streets between barricaded houses; for most of the inhabitants had left, and the remainder were shut into back rooms. The soldiers dared not tear down the shutters for fear of increasing the general appearance of desolation, and, moreover, they hoped to win the people over by gentleness. The Archduke's triumphal entry was in fact as melancholy an occasion as his proclamation. There were a few very feeble cheers, so plainly forced that he was disagreeably affected and ordered them to cease. To cap all, he dared not risk the danger of lodging in the royal palace or near the centre of the town, but put up on the outskirts and stayed only three nights. He sent Stanhope to summon the old Marquis of Mancera for an audience, but the ancient lord excused himself on the plea of age, and Stanhope had therefore to return to him bearing the new oath of allegiance for his signature. The Marquis then said with admirable staunchness that he respected the Archduke's rank, but owed loyalty only to the king his master, whom nothing, so he said, would induce him to betray. He ended by very courteously asking Stanhope to leave, saying that he was tired and wished to go to bed. Nothing more was done, and he and his family did not suffer.

[1] The chief magistrate.

Madrid was little damaged, for Starhemberg maintained strict discipline, was inclined to be lenient, and displayed some consideration and respect for the inhabitants, hoping thus to appease them. His army meanwhile was perishing for lack of supplies. They could obtain nothing from the surrounding districts, and were without food for the men or fodder for the horses. They even lacked pay, since no money was forthcoming. Threats, entreaties, executions were useless, not one Castilian but would have thought himself dishonoured had he sold them anything or left behind anything worth their taking. By such means did this admirable nation, with no other resources than their courage and loyalty, maintain themselves in the midst of their enemies, and destroy the Allied army. At the same time, with unexampled industry, they succeeded in re-forming their own army, re-arming and re-equipping it to perfection, and replacing the crown on the head of their rightful king. How true it is that no power equals that which comes from the hearts of a people in the defence or restoration of their monarch![1]

Stanhope, although he must from the very beginning have seen the wisdom of Starhemberg's advice, appeared not the least put out by his failure. He was heard to say with consummate impudence that having seen the Archduke safely to Madrid, he had obeyed his queen's commands and accomplished his mission. It was now for Starhemberg, he said, to show his skill by a rescue; as for himself he cared little what happened to him. In the event, the Archduke's foothold in the capital was so precarious that after a stay of ten or twelve days he decided to remove to Toledo. There was very little looting, except for some tapestries belonging to the king, which Stanhope thought it no shame to steal. He was shamed later, however, when he was obliged to return them, even his fellow-countrymen having reproached him for that meanness.

On 20 September, Vendôme arrived at the king's headquarters, at Valladolid, almost simultaneously with the court. He had dallied on the way, amusing himself at Bayonne and elsewhere, on various pretexts of indisposition, hoping by that means to make his presence longed for, and better to foresee the probable course of events. He was astonished to find the court in such good spirits. As soon as the Archduke was known to be in Madrid, the queen had gone to Vittoria with the infant prince and the counsellors. She wished to be nearer the French frontier in order to ensure safe transit, should the need arise, and in the meantime she sent all her jewels to Paris, with instructions to the Duke of Alba to raise as much money on them as possible.

Soon after Vendôme's arrival, the king marched with him to Salamanca at the head of an army of twelve thousand men, all well equipped, armed

---

[1] When things looked very black, Saint-Simon sometimes contemplated becoming a Spaniard; but not after he had visited Spain.

and paid. Starhemberg was busy reconnoitring the country around Toledo, and the Archduke ordered the removal of all the ladies living on their estates whilst their husbands were with the king, on pain of forfeiting their furniture and other possessions. Starhemberg did not long remain at Toledo, but before he went he burned down the magnificent palace, named the Alcazar,[1] which Charles V had erected in the Moorish style. It was irreparably damaged. Starhemberg tried to pretend that the fire was accidental and moved on towards Aragon. There was now nothing to prevent King Philip from visiting his faithful subjects at Madrid, and he accordingly left the army for a short time and entered his capital on 2 December, to be greeted by vast crowds and unparalleled rejoicing. He alighted at Nuestra Señora de Atocha, which was held in particular veneration, and thenceforward the press was so great that it took him three hours to reach his palace. The town presented him with twenty thousand pistoles. During his three days' stay he did something almost unheard-of in Spain, for he visited the old Marquis of Mancera at his home, and by so doing nearly killed him with joy. The visit was accompanied by all the tokens of esteem, gratitude, and love so justly earned by the courage and loyalty of that aged and venerable man. King Philip sat with him alone for fully three hours, explaining the situation as it appeared at that moment and his future plans. He then presented the most distinguished members of his suite, not allowing the old man to rise for any of them. He embraced him before leaving and would not let him stir a single step beyond the door of his room to escort him to his coach. So far as I am aware, no other King of Spain has ever visited a subject since the time when Philip II visited the Duke of Alba on his deathbed who, when he saw his master, turned his face to the wall murmuring that it was too late, and refused to utter another word. On the fourth day, the King left Madrid to rejoin Vendôme and the army.

Thus that monarch who so recently had been facing almost certain ruin, a fugitive without money, troops, or supplies, now found himself at the head of a well equipped army, with ammunition and supplies in abundance, and a reserve of funds accumulated by the combined efforts of his loyal and industrious subjects. His enemies, on the other hand, were perishing for want of every necessity and retreating through a country up in arms against them, whose inhabitants vastly preferred to burn the crops than to sell them, and gave no quarter to stragglers, killing them within five hundred yards of their main body. Vendôme, astounded by this unlooked-for change, wished to make the most of it by uniting with the army which Bay had managed to maintain in Estremadura. Although too small to confront Starhemberg, it was strong enough to harry him and to make a thrust

---

[1] The name for the palaces of the Moorish kings. This one had been restored in 1535 for Charles V; it was again destroyed in 1936. The most famous Alcazars are in Seville, Cordoba and Segovia. The Emperor Charles V (1500-1558) was also Charles I of Spain.

to join the king. Starhemberg, now free of the Archduke's presence, made plans to frustrate Bay's move. He was already well acquainted with the Duc de Vendôme, having stolen many a march on him in his retreat from Tyrol, crossing five rivers ahead of him, and joining forces, despite all his efforts, with the Duke of Savoy. He accordingly devised a cunning trap to entice Vendôme into the centre of the Allied army, in such a position that his neck could be broken without hope of an escape. Stationing his troops in easily accessible quarters, sufficiently near to one another for reliefs to be made at short notice, he issued careful orders, more especially to Stanhope, whom he placed with his English and Dutch troops at Brihuega,[1] a small fortified town with a strong citadel, which he improved still more in the short time available. This little town stood at the head of all his army quarters, at the entrance to an open plain, which Bay's forces would be obliged to cross on their march to join the king.

Vendôme's army, daily increased by reinforcements sent by every noble, prelate, and township, as soon as the men were fit to serve, continued to march steadily towards Starhemberg, his sole purpose being to form a junction with Bay. Everywhere that Vendôme halted he found his lodgings, despite the rigours of winter, as comfortable as in summer, thanks to the zeal of those incomparable Spaniards. He soon learned of Starhemberg's dispositions, but construed them as Starhemberg desired; that is to say, he thought Stanhope dangerously exposed, too far from the main body to be quickly relieved, and thus very vulnerable to attack; all of which tempted him to risk his army for an easy victory so as to clear his path for the junction with Bay. That, at any rate, was the situation as seen by Vendôme. He therefore hastened his march, made his plans, and on the afternoon of 8 December arrived under Brihuega, calling on Stanhope to surrender. When Stanhope refused, Vendôme made ready to attack, and then discovered to his enormous chagrin that instead of a small garrison and weak defences he faced a large body of troops and was besieging a strong fortress. Vendôme had no desire to retreat, indeed could not safely have done so, and he therefore, as usual, proceeded to rage and storm, cursing and abusing everyone, blustering, bragging, doing the impossible to hearten his soldiers into making a conquest very different from what they had expected, yet most dangerous to relinquish. The magnitude of his mistake grew ever more apparent as the hours passed and fresh news was brought of the enemy's movements. It was then that Vendôme, two of whose assaults had already been repulsed, resolved to play at double or quits by ordering a third. But at that precise moment, just as the orders were being given, news arrived that Starhemberg was advancing against him with four or five thousand men—only half their full numbers.

[1] Fifty miles north-east of Madrid.

At this critical moment, Vendôme unhesitatingly risked the crown of Spain in a pure gamble. Hastening the attack by every means in his power, he took the King of Spain and all the cavalry into the hills through which the enemy were approaching, leaving all his infantry to attack Brihuega with their total strength and in unison. Every man-at-arms knew the dire peril in which he and his comrades stood, and all conducted themselves with such dash and courage that they captured the town in the face of most stubborn resistance, but with great losses. The enemy retired into the citadel and soon afterwards surrendered. In all, the whole garrison of eight battalions and eight squadrons gave themselves up with their commander-in-chief Stanhope, Lieutenant-generals Carpenter and Wills,[1] two brigadier-generals, and all their artillery. That was the moment when Stanhope, who had triumphed at Madrid, was forced to return the King's tapestries.

While the surrender was being negotiated, news of Starhemberg's advance continued to arrive. It required enormous vigilance to prevent those sent to parley from discovering that liberation was only a league and a half distant, for had they known, they might well have broken off the talks and returned to save the citadel. The night passed quietly enough, however; but on the morrow, the 11th, M. de Vendôme again found himself in trouble, for troops were needed both to encounter Starhemberg and to escort the captured garrison from Brihuega to Old Castile. In the end he decided to leave the regiments of Spanish and Walloon guards in Brihuega until the evacuation had been successfully completed; then, perceiving that a battle was imminent, he summoned them to join him, leaving no more than four hundred to guard the town.

Vendôme deployed his forces in battle array on a fairly level plain, although a number of low, loosely built stone walls made it exceedingly dangerous for horsemen to manœuvre. The cannon opened fire from both sides, and almost immediately afterwards the Spanish cavalry charged in two lines. It was already half-past three, but in Spain the winter days are longer than in France. At the start of the battle the cavalry of the Spanish right routed the enemy's left, and then fell upon and scattered some battalions of infantry, capturing a battery in the process. A moment later their left wing repeatedly charged the enemy's right, but with varying success. At last, they succeeded in driving the enemy back and uniting with their own right wing behind the lines of enemy infantry. At that precise moment, however, the Spanish centre began to waver, which M. de Vendôme thought so grave a matter that he decided to retreat on Torija, and at once gave orders to that effect. He then retired with the King of Spain and a large body of troops.

In the midst of that withdrawal, he suddenly learned that the Spanish cavalry had charged again and were masters of the battlefield, with large numbers of prisoners,

[1] Charles Wills (1666-1741). He became a member of George I's privy council.

and much artillery captured. Such agreeable and unexpected news induced him to return with the king to the heights above Brihuega, and to continue advancing until dawn, when they found themselves in a position to rejoin the victors on the field, where a body of Spanish cavalry had spent the night close to the enemy. Five or six enemy battalions had remained on the battlefield, uncertain how best to retire, leaving cannon, mortars, wounded, and wagons in all directions. Starhemberg himself had already made good his escape, taking advantage of the long night to gain a start. His baggage-wagons and most of his supplies and ammunition fell a prey to the victors.[1] In all, counting the garrison of Brihuega, they lost eleven thousand men, killed or captured, with all their ammunition, artillery, baggage, and a great many flags and standards. King Philip lost no more than two thousand men. They named it the Battle of Villaviciosa, after a neighbouring hamlet.[2] I should explain that Brihuega lies between Siguenza and Guadalajara, and rather nearer the latter, which is on the road to France, twenty-five leagues on this side of Madrid if one goes by Pamplona.

    When one thinks of the appalling risk which, had things turned out differently, might have meant the certain ruin of King Philip, it makes one shudder even today. The strength given him by the courage and devotion of his people after the defeat at Saragossa was a miracle not to be repeated. A second disaster would have meant even less hope of support coming from France, for our own exhaustion and losses would have prevented any attempt to restore him to his throne. Yet instead of husbanding that strength, so miraculously acquired, and trying to restore the situation without committing his entire army, M. de Vendôme flung it recklessly and totally into a carefully prepared trap. Moreover, such was his negligence that he did not trouble to inform himself of the strength of the place which he proposed to attack. Thus instead of a weak outpost he found himself confronted by a fortress; instead of a small advance guard, he found a strong garrison, commanded by the second-ranking but most powerful figure in the Allied army, and that army ready to fall upon him from the rear.

    Realizing at that point what he had undertaken, he saw the full danger of a double engagement—against Stanhope on the one hand, whom he had to defeat in one furious assault (two having failed); against Starhemberg on the other, whom he had first to intercept, then defeat, in the certain knowledge that if he failed, the Spanish crown and perhaps the king himself would pay the price of his folly. A miracle was granted, for Brihuega fell in his absence, and also in his absence the Battle of Villaviciosa was won. Another glaring mistake! That famous 'eye', so bragged of by his friends, seems to have betrayed him on this occasion. Blind to victory, all that he saw was

[1] Starhemberg, too, claimed the victory when he reported to the Archduke. After the battle he was left in possession of the field, and retired only after Brihuega's surrender. Stanhope was outnumbered by 5,000 men. The fortress does not seem to have been in very good repair, despite what Saint-Simon says. Stanhope did what he could. He sent Starhemberg a message to say that he could not hold out for more than twenty-four hours, but managed to resist until the evening of 9 December (a day and a half).

[2] The French and Portuguese had already won a battle there in 1665.

a slight wavering of the Spanish centre. Vendôme, that hero, who complained so loudly at the inevitable retreat after Oudenarde, now fled headlong with all the troops that he could muster. This was the same man who, at Cassano, thinking all was lost, hid in a distant blockhouse, where Albergotti eventually found him and informed him of victory, which he then claimed to have won. This so-called hero was in full flight to Torija when he heard the news. He returned to the battlefield at dawn and saw for himself all the signs of victory. Yet he appeared not at all ashamed of his faulty judgment, his monstrous errors in retreating, and in saving Starhemberg by removing so large a proportion of his army, regardless of the fate of the remainder. Not so! He once again played the victor with all the impudence of his earlier conduct in France and Italy; but in Spain this boasting served him no better. Such were the exploits of that mighty commander whom the Spaniards had petitioned for to save them. Truly he had shown them his quality even before his arrival.[1]

As soon as King Philip had been taken back to the battlefield by Vendôme and could no longer doubt his success, he sent a courier to the queen. In an instant her sorrows were turned to joy, and she walked out on foot into the streets of Vittoria, where the bells were ringing as they rang throughout the whole of Spain, especially in Madrid. Don Gaspardo de Zunigo, the Duke of Bejar's brother, was sent to Versailles with a letter to King Louis, saying that no one was better fitted to describe the battle than he, who had fought in it like a hero. He gave such an excellent report that the King and the entire Court exclaimed at his clarity, truth, and modesty. I found an opportunity to question him at leisure soon after he arrived. He had told the King everything, concealing nothing of what I have recounted of Vendôme; thus the cabal were quite unsuccessful when they attempted to triumph. Vendôme was unmasked and dishonoured, for the King's knowledge and opinion of him could not be disputed. Thus they dared not defend him at the Court, nor even in Society, but were obliged to make shift with boasting talk in the cafés of Paris, and in the provinces, where the details were as yet unknown.

The Allies cast all the blame for that unexpected reverse on Stanhope. He was not greatly outnumbered, had ammunition and food in abundance, and sufficient artillery; moreover the fortress was in excellent repair. Added to all this, he knew beforehand of Starhemberg's plans and why he was placed in Brihuega; and he must also have known that by holding out for seven or eight hours longer he might have ensured a victory and the destruction of the entire Spanish army. Starhemberg, indignant at this wholly unnecessary defeat, complained bitterly,

---

[1] Philip V, on the other hand, wrote to Louis XIV: 'Impossible to praise too highly the conduct and skill of the Duc de Vendôme, to whom we owe the capture of almost the entire enemy army and its defeat.' Saint-Simon in his blind hatred for Vendôme allows him no credit for defeating vastly superior forces. The Franco-Spanish victory produced for King Louis at that critical moment an incontrovertible claim—his grandson, not the Archduke, remained the King of Spain.

and many of his senior officers supported him. Stanhope, himself, who dared not disclaim the responsibility, was driven to apply for leave to return home and defend his conduct. He met with a very bad reception, was deprived of his military rank in England and Holland, and for some time after went in dread of forfeiting his life.

The Abbé de Pompadour died at this time not much regretted. A little gadabout even at the age of eighty-five or -six, he possessed a lackey almost as old as himself, to whom he paid supplementary wages to read his breviary for him, and who might often be seen mumbling it over in the corners of ante-rooms where his master visited. The Abbé de Pompadour appeared to believe that he thereby absolved himself from that duty, rather in the manner of canons when they pay their precentors to replace them in the choir.

The impossibility, only too disgracefully proved, of securing peace, and the exhausted state of the kingdom, caused the King acute anxiety and placed Desmaretz in a tragic predicament. The markets were saturated with bills of every kind; all were discredited to a greater or lesser extent, and there seemed no remedy for the resulting chaos. Treasury bills, paper money, bills issued by the receivers-general, bills for the *tailles*,[1] bills for the soldiers' pay and allowances were the ruin of those who had to accept them as payment from the King, and ruinous to the King also. The discount on them enriched the bankers and financiers at the public expense, and money ceased to circulate because the King made continual withdrawals and never repaid in gold. Such coin as escaped his grasp remained firmly locked up in the coffers of the tax-farmers. The capitation tax, doubled and trebled at will by provincial intendants, merchandise and produce assessed at four times their proper value, taxes on the well-to-do, taxes on every imaginable commodity, bore down on nobles and commoners, gentry and clergy alike, still without producing sufficient for the King, who bled his subjects white, squeezing the very marrow out of their bones, thereby enriching a great army of tax-farmers and revenue-clerks, in whose hands the greater part of the proceeds remained.

Desmaretz, to whom the King had at last been driven to entrust the finances, then conceived the idea of levying over and above the existing taxes that same King's tithe which Vauban had formerly proposed. His, however, was to have been one comprehensive tax, sufficient for all needs, paid directly into the King's coffers, with all other taxes abolished. You will recollect that the trembling financiers and angry ministers had contrived to have it rejected as anathema, and that this noble and devoted subject was finally disgraced. You should bear that well

---

[1] The *taille* took different forms. In most provinces it was reckoned on the estimated means of individual tax-payers; in others on the amount of land owned. In practice there were so many exemptions for noble rank, etc., that most of the burden fell on the peasants.

in mind, for Desmaretz, when he sought to revive Vauban's idea, regarded it in no way as being for relief or remedy (words abominable to financiers), but as an increase in the burden of taxation, which was exactly what he wanted. He quietly laid his plans, and when they were prepared offered them for scrutiny and final polishing to a committee formed by design of his two brothers-in-law, counsellors of State Bouville and Nointel, his brother Vaubourg, his confidential agent Harlay-Cély, a maître des requêtes, and three other financiers. These men, hand-picked for that special task, drew up the edict.

They laboured diligently to overcome the difficulties that beset them on all sides. They had first to extract from each individual an exact account of his wealth, possessions, assets and liabilities, demanding proofs and devising means to prevent cheating. These, however, were the only matters that caused them the slightest concern. They cared nothing for the crushing burden of such a tax on thousands of men of all sorts and conditions, nor for the suffering entailed by a compulsory disclosure of family circumstances. They disregarded the keeping up of appearances by many; the poverty disguised under honourable credit, whose cessation would inevitably bring ruin; the public gossip about each man's ability to pay; the family quarrels brought on by such revelations, the light thrown on many hidden shames. In very truth, the whole scheme savoured of those impious numberings that once provoked the Creator to lay a heavy hand on those who ordered them, and attracted condign punishment. Less than a month sufficed for the clever commissioners to produce a glowing report on this once benevolent measure for the cyclops who had given it them to examine. Desmaretz then joined with them in revising it, filling it with dire threats against possible delinquents, and completely disregarding the expenses which all land-owners must needs encounter. Once revised, the only remaining difficulty was to have the decree ratified.

At that point Desmaretz, who was adept at managing the King, showed him the proposal; but King Louis, although well accustomed to enormous taxes, could not quite stomach this one. For many years past he had heard from everywhere the cry of poverty, and the thought of this added burden visibly distressed him. The valets noticed his melancholy in his study, and Maréchal ventured to speak to him, fearing for his reason. The King then confessed that he was indeed troubled, and referred vaguely to the situation within the kingdom. After a week or ten days of depression, he seemed miraculously to recover his spirits. He sent for Maréchal, and as soon as they were alone together stated that he felt somewhat easier in his mind and would like to explain what had gone amiss. He then confided that extreme necessity had compelled him in the past to levy immensely high taxes; that in the present circumstances he was obliged to raise them very considerably, and that apart from feeling compassion, his conscience had cruelly tormented him at the thought of removing people's wealth. He had finally had recourse to Père Tellier who, after begging for a few days' reflection, had returned with the united opinion of the most learned doctors of the Sorbonne. One and all, they had given it as their firm opinion that every subject's wealth belonged to the King, and that thus, when he confiscated it, he took back only what was rightfully his own. King Louis added that this verdict had greatly comforted him, removing all his scruples and restoring his equanimity. Maréchal was too much astonished to utter a word; but fortunately the King left the room as soon as he had finished, and Maréchal remained where he was, completely dumbfounded. He told me this a few days later, when he had recovered somewhat from the shock. No comment is needed from me. It speaks for itself of what a king may become when he takes such a confessor, and turns to him alone for advice. It shows also what may become of a nation delivered into such hands.

Now is the moment to explain the conseil des finances and the work done by that body, which acted at that time exactly as it does today. The King held a meeting every Tuesday, and again on Saturdays, but never when he went to Marly. Apart from Monseigneur and Mgr le Duc de Bourgogne, who sat on all the councils, it was composed of the Chancellor, because he was once controller-general, the Duc de Beauvilliers, as chairman, and Desmaretz, the then controller-general, as well as two other counsellors of State who, at that time, were Peletier de Souzy and Daguesseau, father of the present Chancellor. Almost the entire time was spent by the King in signing bonds and documents, judging private quarrels that came within the sphere of finance, and hearing appeals regarding prize-money for captured enemy ships. Nothing else was ever discussed. Everything in the nature of finance, taxes, tariffs, statutes, the levying of new taxes, and the increasing of those already levied, was and is done by the controller-general, alone in his office, with an intendant acting as his clerk. If any matter of extreme importance should arise, the controller-general takes it up with the King when they are alone together, with the result that many of the decrees issued never appear outside the walls of the controller-general's office. Some of the most iniquitous are never even discussed elsewhere. The Secretary of State is forced to sign them and the Chancellor to seal them without reading, and the members of the finance council learn no more of them than the man in the street until after their publication. That is how things were managed in the old days, and how they still do them today. The capitation tax was no exception; it was proposed, seconded, and passed unexamined during the meeting, just as I have described, despite the unparalleled outrage of this, as it were, numbering of the people. Desmaretz went through the usual performance or, as one might well say, played the usual confidence-trick. The King, having been given free rein by Père Tellier, had convinced himself that all his subjects' goods were his own, and that what he did not take from them he left them purely out of generosity. Thereafter he felt no more compunction at taking whatsoever he pleased. He even relished the idea that the tithe would be levied over and above all the other taxes, duties, and occasional levies; and Desmaretz was given permission to make it law.

Thus, on Tuesday, 8 September, Desmaretz entered the finance council with the edict in his bag. For some days past everyone had known that a bomb-shell was about to burst and, trembling, clung to the kind of hopes that are based on wishes alone. The entire Court, and Paris also, waited dismally for news. People whispered, yet although the terms of the measure had deliberately been allowed to leak out, no one had dared to discuss it. The members of the council attended the meeting that day knowing as little as the general public, and, indeed, uncertain whether it was even on their agenda. When all were seated, Desmaretz drew out of his bag a very large file; the King announced that the impossibility of making peace and the extreme difficulty of waging war had caused Desmaretz to search for less conventional means of raising funds; that he had discovered this one, of which the King approved, and of which the members of his council would doubtless also approve when Desmaretz had explained it. Desmaretz then made a pathetic appeal, based on the stubborn ill will of the enemy and the weakness of the finances, ending by declaring that faced with the alternative of allowing France to be invaded or accepting this measure as a last resort, he thought that the latter would seem the lesser evil. The measure, he said, was the imposition of a tithe tax on every person without exception; but apart from the reasons afore-said, everyone would profit, because the levy—very small compared with what each individual received from the King in pensions and gifts (but apart from the flagrant injustice to such persons, how many others received nothing?)—would result in everyone's being paid regularly. Thus every individual would be better off financially, and the general public would benefit by the modest affluence caused by the freer circulation of money. He had tried, he added, to anticipate all the possible disadvantages to the King as well as to his subjects; but the gentlemen of his council would be better able to judge after hearing the edict read than by anything further that he could say. Thereupon, without waiting for comments, he read the edict aloud from start to finish and then fell silent. No one spoke.

The King asked for Daguesseau's opinion, he being the newest member of the council, with the privilege of speaking first. This worthy magistrate answered that the matter seemed to him of such great importance that he could form an opinion only after prolonged study of the measure, and he therefore begged the King to excuse him. The King promptly replied that Daguesseau was perfectly right; but that to study the edict was quite unnecessary, since no one could examine it more carefully than Desmaretz had done. The King fully concurred with his opinion, and there was thus no need to waste time with further argument. No one spoke except the Duc de Beauvilliers who, led astray by the teaching of Desmaretz Colbert's nephew, whom he regarded as an oracle in matters of finance, declared that although he fully recognized the disadvantages of this measure, he must accept it rather than see France invaded, and believed that even those who would most suffer by it stood to gain in the end.

Thus the bloody deed was done, signed, sealed, published and registered, amid smothered lamentations and most piteous complaints. Neither the levy itself nor its proceeds came up to the expectations aroused by that cannibalistic finance department. The King did not pay anyone a single halfpenny more than he had done hitherto. The modest affluence, the free circulation of money—the only balm offered in all Desmaretz's speech—turned out to be a mirage. I learned all that had happened on the very next day, from the Chancellor himself. A few days later, when the edict was published, a rumour was spread to the effect that he had vigorously opposed it at the council meeting. That would have done him much honour; but he was honourable indeed when he loudly denied that falsehood. When they questioned him he admitted openly that he had not spoken a word, saying, moreover, that he was glad of it because no matter what he might have said it would have made no difference. The decision had already been taken, and the reading of the edict was a mere matter of form, a ritual that in those circumstances was even surprising.

Some days after the publication, Monseigneur happened to go to dine at the ménagerie[1] with the princes, their wives, and some of the ladies—a most rare event for him. Mgr le Duc de Bourgogne, who appeared less constrained than usual, suddenly spoke out, expressing his indignation at the tithe and the multiplicity of the taxes, saying very bitter things against the bankers and tax-farmers, even against the administration, recalling by his just and holy anger memories of Saint Louis; Louis XII, the father of his people, and Louis the Just. Monseigneur was moved by this unwonted outburst to support, albeit somewhat tepidly, his son's protest against the cruel and profitless extortions, and the wicked rabble who so monstrously enriched themselves by sucking the blood of their fellow-countrymen. The few who were present were astounded, and a little comforted by the hope that in their time they might have some relief. It was not to be. The real successor of Louis XIV was this son of

---

[1] There was a menagerie for wild animals and birds at Versailles, but the word sometimes refers to a home-farm where the *animaux de ménage* were kept (for instance at Saint-Cloud) that supplied the château with eggs and milk.

a tax-farmer,[1] who, in his long and disastrous reign, has raised the existing taxes still further and invented others also.

I must now tell of another bomb-shell that burst upon my head, and describe at some length what I have hitherto only indicated—the incredible gullibility of Monseigneur. You will recollect du Mont, in whom Monseigneur trusted, and who had never forgotten my father's kindness. You will also remember that on Monday, 2 June, the King announced, at Marly, the betrothal of M. le Duc de Berry, and that on 15 June Mme de Saint-Simon was appointed lady-in-waiting. The marriage was celebrated at Versailles on Sunday, 6 July, and on the following Wednesday the King returned to Marly until Saturday, 2 August.

A few days after the beginning of that second Marly, as I was returning from mass with the King, du Mont tugged at my coat in the doorway of the little ante-room before the chapel. He had awaited me there so as to avoid notice. When I turned, he put his finger to his lips and pointed to the gardens below the cascade; I speak of that magnificent waterfall which Cardinal Fleury destroyed, and which used to face the back of the château. At the same time he whispered, 'Meet me at the arbours,'—a part of the gardens with a surrounding hedge that gave it privacy. This was the least frequented spot in all Marly, for it led nowhere. There was seldom anyone there, even in the afternoon and evening. Being extremely curious to know the reason for du Mont's extraordinary conduct, I went straight to the arbours and stood concealed behind the hedge, at a place from which I could watch for his coming through one of the openings. He made a furtive entry at the corner nearest the chapel. I stepped forward; but he asked me to return to the cascade, a spot still less frequented, and we accordingly stationed ourselves where the hedge was thickest, far enough from the openings to be completely out of sight.

These precautions surprised and somewhat alarmed me; but I was thoroughly frightened when I learned the reason for them. After a few words expressing grati-tude to my father and affection for me, du Mont explained that he was about to give me the surest possible proof of his love, but only on two conditions: first, that I should never afterwards betray, even by the smallest hint, my knowledge of what he was about to tell me; second, that I should take no action until he gave me leave. I promised on both counts. He then said that two days after M. le Duc de Berry's marriage he happened to go to Monseigneur's study towards the end of the morn-ing and found him alone and extremely vexed. He had followed him, still alone, through the gardens, which he entered by his study window, to the apartment of Mme la Princesse de Conti, entering that also by one of the windows opening on to the terrace of the Versailles orangery. The princess was alone at her writing-desk,

[1] Refers to Cardinal Fleury.

and Monseigneur had at once furiously exclaimed (which was most unusual) that she appeared remarkably serene, considering the circumstances. This alarmed her so much that she cried out to know the reason, whether there was bad news from Flanders or elsewhere. Monseigneur replied crossly that it was only that I had been heard to remark that now M. le Duc de Berry was safely married we must get rid of Mme la Princesse de Conti and her sister Madame la Duchesse, for then we should be able to manage the old fool (meaning himself) quite easily. She had therefore little cause to look so complacent.

Then quite suddenly he began smacking his thighs, as though whipping himself into a still more violent rage, voicing all the threats that such a remark might have deserved, had it ever been uttered, vowing to urge M. le Duc de Bourgogne to have me banished and ruined. Du Mont's long harangue continued for some time without my being able to discover Mme la Princesse de Conti's reply; but judging from his silence on that score and my knowledge of her circle, it cannot have been temperate. Alone with them both du Mont stood with his back to the wall, trembling, not daring to utter; and the scene ended only when the arrival of Sainte-Maure brought it abruptly to a close. No one can possibly imagine how du Mont's disclosures affected me, but of all my mixed feelings bewilderment was the uppermost. I gazed at him speechless, and then demanded to know how such a rumour could have arisen, how anyone could have dared to spread it, how anyone could believe it; and I begged him to tell me how I was supposed to act in inducing the King to banish his two daughters, princesses of the blood whom he dearly loved, and whether a man would not be stark, staring mad to conceive such a plot, madder still to boast of it, and downright wicked to use it to deceive a prince who had never openly, at least, been accused of lunacy. Du Mont conceded all this as being true and reasonable; but he none the less affirmed that the slander had been uttered and was believed. I dared not let myself go on the subject of Monseigneur's gullibility, but was glad to see by the way he shrugged his shoulders and some unguarded words that du Mont fully agreed with me.

After the first shock had worn off, I began to discern the pit that had been dug beneath my feet, and asked du Mont what was best to do. 'Nothing yet,' said he. 'I dared not warn you sooner because I was the only witness of that scene. Monseigneur has not acted. Wait until I say the word. I shall be on the watch.' 'But, Sir,' said I, 'how must I behave with Monseigneur raging against me, I who am in all the places, except Meudon, which he frequents? What am I to do in the salon? How can I pay him my respects? How avoid him whilst you are finding some way of making him see reason, despite the fiends who fill him with this slander which any child of six would disbelieve?' 'It is very hard for you,' said du Mont. 'Do not ask for Meudon. Do not go near him in the salon; but call on him now and then. Be careful to do that. If you conduct yourself so, he cannot harm you. There is nothing else I can advise at present.' He then besought me repeatedly not to forget my promise, let me thank him briefly, and hurried back by the way he had come, very fearful lest he should have been observed.

For a long time I walked up and down the arbours, reflecting on the extraordinary malice of those evil people, and their real opinion of the prince whom they had successfully deceived with such a tale. I miserably imagined our fate under such a king, ruled by those monsters and capable of believing such grossly false accusations. Recovering somewhat, I still could see no way of clearing myself of this slander, let alone defending myself from others which they might invent to destroy me. I returned home as unhappy as could be, and told only Mme de Saint-Simon, who was no less astounded and horrified. I obeyed du Mont's instructions to the letter, calling on Monseigneur from time to time at his apartment, avoiding him at other places, even at Marly, because the cabal around him contained those who most violently hated me.

I never learned—thank God for that!—who had induced Monseigneur to believe such a malicious and unlikely tale. Among all the men and women composing that cabal, I could not pin my suspicions on any one in particular. My disputes over precedence with the Lillebonne sisters and their uncle Vaudémont; my quarrel with d'Antin over Rome; my anger with the late Monsieur le Duc and Mme la Duchesse; above all, the events in Flanders, had made them all my enemies. Yet despite them I was reconciled with the King, and because I was not completely ruined they feared me. My intimacy with M. and Mme la Duchesse d'Orléans had increased their suspicions, and the marriage of M. le Duc de Berry was altogether too much for them, for although they did not know all the details, my part in it was only too obvious. My close friendship with the Chancellor and the Dukes of Chevreuse and Beauvilliers, both of whom they hated, as well as with many other important persons of either sex, alarmed them; but most of all, the attachment beginning to be formed between Mgr le Duc de Bourgogne and myself filled them with fear and made them determined to destroy me.

My situation appeared even worse because the future was more terrible to contemplate than the fears and anxieties of the present, although that was bad enough, and I therefore engaged du Mont in conversation one morning, towards the end of that same Marly. After remarking several times on the absurdity of the slander, intermingled with expressions of respect for Monseigneur, I begged him to inform the latter that I knew what was being said of me and that, regarding him as my future sovereign, I entreated him to grant me a quarter of an hour's audience. Should he refuse, I would ask him to see in my retirement to Guyenne a sacrifice to his unjust displeasure, until he consented to let me convince him of the untruth of this vile accusation. Du Mont could not but approve of my intentions and my expressions of respect for Monseigneur. He therefore promised to speak, but very unwillingly, because it still embarrassed him to have been the only witness of the scene mentioned above. He was timid and excessively cautious; everything alarmed and upset him. He began to say that the time was not ripe, that he would seize the first opportunity, and then fell to exhorting me all over again to be patient and secret. At that moment, however, Monseigneur, happening to cross the room, saw us in conversation, a fact that greatly pleased me, for I hoped he might inquire what was being said. The King's mass ended our talk. As I have already said, all this occurred during the second Marly after the wedding.

I had very little hope of du Mont's taking action, he being so feeble by nature; and thus Mme de Saint-Simon and I determined to seek other help as soon as I was freed from my promise. In the meantime, since what we wished to do could not be undertaken lightly on account of the vital importance given to etiquette at the Court, and since we were both exhausted and wished to be ready for instant action, Mme de Saint-Simon asked an audience of Mme la Duchesse de Bourgogne, a favour now no longer remarkable. She begged the princess to obtain the King's permission to go to La Ferté during the third Marly (a very short visit), promising to be at Versailles in time for his return. No difficulty about that, but much comment and envy of the favour, for no other lady-in-waiting, not even of the bastards, had leave to be absent even for two days. Such servitude was a custom that had become a rule. Mme de Saint-Simon used her privileges with discretion, but she did use them, and was the only one permitted so to do, which in itself was a great privilege.

We were thus able to go to La Ferté to rest and reflect, and it was there that we decided to act in the way I have described. I then returned to Versailles and accompanied the King on the third Marly since the wedding. Towards the middle of that visit du Mont once again tugged me by the coat as I returned from the King's mass, asking me to meet him in the arbours, to which I immediately went. He said that I might now safely speak to Monseigneur because sufficient time had elapsed to enable me to have heard the rumour from others, so that suspicion would not necessarily fall on him. He added after a long pause that he would not broach the subject himself, but that if Monseigneur spoke he would do marvels for me. I made him see how scrupulously I had kept my promise, and I did not say how feeble I thought him, because one must not extort more from people than they can give. Then, in order to be perfectly frank, I proposed asking Mme la Duchesse de Bourgogne to speak to Monseigneur on my behalf, which du Mont said was a happy thought. I promised to keep him fully informed, and we parted with expressions of mutual regard and his strong recommendation to continue as I had begun until Monseigneur was completely enlightened.

It was the impossibility of finding any friend who was also a member of Monseigneur's circle that had made us turn to Mme la Duchesse de Bourgogne. My wife begged a second audience of her and told her all, but without mentioning du Mont. The princess was indignant that a marriage sponsored by her should be so little regarded; she saw the danger to everyone, including Mgr le Duc de Bourgogne and herself, of Monseigneur's credulity; in short, she was thoroughly alarmed. She agreed with all that Mme de Saint-Simon said, graciously consented to speak to Monseigneur, and promised to choose a time when they were alone and not likely to be interrupted.

Two or three weeks later she kindly advised Mme de Saint-Simon to be patient, for although she had not yet found a suitable moment she would not fail us. Things continued in this way until after the fourth and last Marly, from which the King returned on Saturday, 15 November. On the following day, Sunday, Monseigneur paid a short visit to Meudon. He was back at Versailles on the Wednesday for the council of State, and afterwards returned once more to dine at Meudon, taking Mme la Duchesse de Bourgogne tête-à-tête in his coach. That was when she spoke. She began with Mme de Saint-Simon, who was also to dine at Meudon, with the royal princes and Mme la Duchesse de Berry. Monseigneur praised her enthusiastically, to which the princess promptly replied that he had none the less reduced her to near-despair. He appeared greatly surprised and asked how that might be, whereupon she bluntly repeated the slander. He flared up in anger. She let him vent his rage and then asked whether he believed it, continuing to say with consummate tact that although sincerely fond of my wife she had no special regard for me. The fact was, she said, that she could not endure to see him duped by such a glaring lie, for he must see that it would be impossible for anyone with the slightest knowledge of the Court, not to mention a man with the reputation of being a busybody, clever, experienced, and full of malice, to concoct so mad a scheme as that of expelling the two royal widows, whom both Monseigneur and the King their father deeply loved. Should I, in any event, have been likely to boast about it? No one with the smallest grain of sense would ever believe it. Nothing more was required to convince the unfortunate prince of the absurdity of the accusation which he had so readily swallowed. He honestly admitted having fallen into a trap; agreed with her every word, and confessed that he had been so furious that he had given himself no time to reflect.

She seized the opportunity to arouse his anger against those who dared to use him to suit their own purposes, reminding him that, being who he was, he could not be too much on his guard against lying reports and those who spread them. She dared not ask who had been responsible for this one, but she did warn him that all the members of his circle were my enemies, for reasons of rank or other causes. She then let him change the subject, which he was in great haste to do. When they arrived at Meudon she treated Mme de Saint-Simon as though nothing had happened; but that same evening she told her everything, and my wife expressed all the gratitude merited by this great service, rendered with such good grace, kindness and tact.

When I next saw du Mont, I told him without entering into details that Mme la Duchesse de Bourgogne had spoken to perfection, and had enlightened Monseigneur; at which he seemed vastly relieved. M. de Beauvilliers and the Chancellor had been much concerned to see me in that alarming situation; they were delighted to learn that I had escaped, and both of them strongly approved of my decision to keep Monseigneur at a distance, for I had all to lose and nothing to gain in his infernal surroundings.

At about this time, a Papal bull was issued settling once and for all the disputes concerning the missionaries and Jesuits in China and the rites of Confucius, ancestor-worship, etc.,[1] which were declared to be idolatrous practices. They were forbidden altogether; the Jesuits were censured for tolerating them; the actions of the late Cardinal de Tournon were praised, and his fortitude and death highly commended. This bull left the Jesuits more angry than ashamed. They ignored it at first, then openly made light of it; but so much has been written of this matter that I shall say no more, merely remark in passing that it was the beginning of the greater troubles that followed soon afterwards, with persecutions that still continue unabated, and even increase. I shall describe in due course this master-stroke of the devil, the Jesuits, and Père Tellier in particular.[2]

One result of the King's tithe was to increase by five men each company of infantry, and another was a tax on the usurers, who were making vast profits by dealing in the King's bills; that is to say, enriching themselves by impoverishing those who accepted them from the King. Such men were called 'jobbers', and their methods, varying according to the need of those who possessed the bills, consisted in paying, for example, three or four hundred livres (and most of that in kind), against a bill of say, a thousand francs. This process was known as *agiotage*,

---

[1] The Jesuits in China pretended to regard ancestor-worship and Confucianism as being not primarily religious, but acts of loyalty to the Emperor. On that understanding the Emperor allowed them to make converts and teach Christianity, provided that there was no incitement to rebellion. Cardinal de Tournon, the Papal legate, at once condemned the rites as idolatry, whereupon the Emperor put him in prison, where he died in all probability from torture. The legate's intervention destroyed the entire edifice which the missionaries had so carefully built up, and the dispute almost destroyed the Society of Jesus. It would have seemed primarily a matter for the Pope, but France was deeply involved, perhaps because the martyred cardinal had been a Frenchman by birth. Saint-Simon naturally sided with the Sorbonne against the Jesuits, whom he hated. He would have thought such indulgence to foreign rites as another of their 'new heresies'.

[2] Saint-Simon is speaking of the Bull *Unigenitus*, 1713.

and it was believed that as much as thirty millions were recovered by the levy.
Many people, on the other hand, made a fortune out of it, and I do not know
that the King's interests benefited in any way. Shortly after this the currency was
reminted, with great profit to the King and extreme hurt to private individuals
and commerce in general. In every period it has been considered a very grave
mistake—or even worse—to tamper with either corn or the currency. Under
Desmaretz the people first became accustomed to jugglery with the finances;
Monsieur le Duc and Cardinal Fleury later inured them to the same trickery with
corn, and even to famine deliberately created.

The inconvenience of M. and Mme la Duchesse de Berry having to borrow
the officers of the King's household and Mme la Duchesse de Bourgogne's footmen exhausted the patience of all concerned, and finally persuaded the King to
grant an establishment to his grandson without waiting for peace. Their pensions
were fixed on a par with those which Monsieur[1] and Madame had received,
but their establishment was on a vastly different scale. In Monsieur's time the
Queen-mother had been regent and had loved him dearly; thus he was not
stinted. Monseigneur's son met with quite other treatment. The revenue was not
sufficient for their ordinary household expenses; and nothing was allowed for
contingencies that are often unavoidable. They were given no furniture and no
house, either in town or in the country; and it was some considerable time later
that the Palais du Luxembourg was put at their disposal in Paris.

Berwick, overtaken by snow, was the first general to return. Harcourt came
home soon after, followed by Bezons; the officers of their various armies went into
winter-quarters. Villars also returned from drinking the waters of Bourbon.

On 16 December the Duchess of Mantua died in the flower of her youth[2]
and in a radiance of beauty that seemed to betoken perfect health. She had a long
illness, but succeeded in turning it to her own great advantage.[3] After her foreign
marriage she had little pleasure in life, for all Mme d'Elbeuf's grandiose schemes
and claims on her behalf came to nothing, and she lived very dismally after returning to Paris. She had had no children and nothing from her husband, who claimed
the honour of kinship with the King, who wore black mourning for a few days.

During the last days of that year a fraudulent alchemist[4] appeared, who claimed
to possess the magic formula for making gold. Boudin, Monseigneur's chief physician, took him to work at his own house so as to keep him under observation, and
under lock and key. As Boudin soon afterwards became very redoubtable and very
arrogant for one of his kind, it might be as well to portray him at this juncture.

[1] As the younger brother of the sovereign.
[2] She was not yet twenty-five.
[3] Meaning that she had tried to gain advantages for her family?
[4] He was a certain Jean Troin, a retired armourer from Fréjus.

His shape was as podgy as his name suggests; he was the son of one of the King's apothecaries who, in his day, had never excited notice. He had studied medicine, was methodical, intelligent, and well informed. Had he confined himself to hard work and serious study, he might have developed a sound, even an excellent understanding. What is more, he was learned in history and literature, and possessed an unaffectedly pleasant disposition. In conversation he was lively and agreeable, and so naïve that he diverted one continually without making the slightest effort. He so captivated M. Fagon, the tyrant of medicine and absolute master of all the doctors, that he could do as he pleased with him, and was admitted at all times to his room, which was kept locked and bolted against other callers. Fagon had a great dislike for the smell of snuff and went so far as to claim that it was poisonous. Boudin therefore wrote a paper against its use, and dedicated it to Fagon, reading it aloud in his presence, with his face all bespattered, his fingers stained, and a snuffbox never out of his hand. Had anyone else behaved in such a way Fagon would have called it outrageous; but he swallowed anything from Boudin. A man so agreeably disposed was bound to succeed at the Court, for he gave no one cause for jealousy. He was invited to the private suppers given by Monseigneur and M. le Prince de Conti. People of the highest rank fell over one another to invite him, and not all were sure of his accepting. The old asked him to dine, and the young to their suppers. He was rakish and debauched to an extreme degree, most delightfully greedy at table, and, best of all, with a frank and ready wit that charmed everyone.

They very soon spoiled him, for at bottom he was bold and impudent, incapable of restraint or of sparing people's feelings, so long as he feared no repercussions nor wanted for encouragement. He was first familiar, and then supremely insolent. Once received in the best Society, he became involved in its intrigues and before long was a party to some of the most secret and important schemes. One morning, the Maréchal de Villeroy, then at the very height of favour, teased him in Monseigneur's presence as that prince was taking physic. Boudin, angered by his haughty air, gave him a sharp answer, and when the maréchal persisted, made no bones about delivering such a snub that Villeroy was left speechless and the bystanders highly embarrassed. Monseigneur, who liked his doctor and much disliked the maréchal, did not intervene; but as soon as Villeroy had departed he burst into fits of laughter. There was a fearful scandal, but no one took any action.

Although Boudin at first showed interest in his calling, he soon grew rusty, and after a time quite ceased to visit the sick. Yet he never lost his curiosity concerning secret and outlandish remedies. In that respect he was completely genuine and openly attacked the Faculty for forbidding them, and for preferring to see people die, provided they did so according to the rules. He loved chemistry also, and was capable of understanding and practising that science; but he went still further by dabbling in alchemy, being convinced that the philosopher's stone would eventually be discovered and, for all his wit and learning, was duped a hundred times; thus he lost a mint of money, of which commodity he was inordinately fond. But to him no sums were too great for such a purpose, and he gladly left parties of pleasure and good company to return to his alembics and the scoundrels who cheated him. Deceived a thousand times, he allowed himself to be fooled again and again, laughing at his own foolishness, and also at his fears, for everything frightened him.

The gold-maker mentioned above captured his fancy, but like all the rest swindled him out of a deal of money. Nobles and ministers of State felt that he was a man to be reckoned with and treated him with care, as one who might become dangerous; but provided that he was not driven too hard, he knew his place and remembered it.

In the early days of December, the King announced that he wished there to be plays at Versailles and the usual *appartements*, even when Monseigneur was away at Meudon. He seemed to think that by keeping his Court rich in entertainment he could conceal from outsiders (and if possible from some of those within) the poverty and disorder in the kingdom. For similar reasons the carnival started sooner, and all through the winter balls of every kind were held at the Court. The wives of the ministers gave some that were very magnificent, and other entertainments as well for Mme la Duchesse de Bourgogne and Society in general. But Paris still remained sad and the provinces were not the less deeply wretched.

CHAPTER II

1711

*The Elector of Cologne celebrates mass before Mme la Duchesse de Bourgogne -
Prosperous marriage of Villefort and Mlle de Pincré - Death of Boileau-Despréaux
- Bitter blow for the Maréchal de Boufflers - Start of dispute leading to the Bull
Unigenitus - Illness of Monseigneur - Death of Monseigneur - Death of the
Duchesse de Villeroy - Changes at the Court - Pontchartrain betrays my friend-
ship, deceives and supplants me - I break with him - I save him from ruin - I have
an audience of the Dauphin - Future prospects - My second audience - Mme la
Dauphine surprises us - I reconcile M. le Duc d'Orléans with the Dauphin - M. le
Duc d'Orléans abuses my confidence - The King's hard-heartedness to his family - I
reconcile M. de Beauvilliers with the Chancellor - Death of the Duc de Lesdiguières
- Death of the Princess von Fürstenberg - Death of the Maréchal de Boufflers -
The Campaign in Flanders - Fearful risk taken by Marlborough - The Princesse
des Ursins plans to gain a kingdom - Secret disgrace of the Duc de Noailles - The
Jesuits' vile plot against Cardinal de Noailles*

THE ELECTOR OF COLOGNE[1] arrived in Paris at the beginning of the new year
and was at once granted an audience *incognito* of the King. Mme la Duchesse de
Bourgogne also received him *incognito* in the presence of Mgr le Duc de Bourgogne.
He amused himself for some weeks in Paris and then paid a visit to Meudon.
Monseigneur made no difference for him; but sat at dinner in his armchair at
his usual place, with a pleated napkin beneath his plate and du Mont to hold his
tazza. The Elector sat opposite among the courtiers, on a straight-backed chair
similar to theirs, not at all as is customary for princes of the blood. He was given
no napkin under his plate, no silver, and no *tazza*, but was in every way treated
like an ordinary courtier. Monseigneur then took him over the house, but showed
him no respect, unhesitatingly stepping before him through the narrow doorways,
whilst the Elector deferentially drew back, addressing him always as Monseigneur,
a form become habitual because the King never used any other, except on rare
occasions when he referred to 'my son'; but the words 'Monsieur le Dauphin'
never passed his lips.

---

[1] The same who took Holy Orders of porter, exorcist, reader, and acolyte; was ordained priest and finally consecrated
bishop all in five consecutive days. Vol. I, p. 321.

Two days later the King received the Elector in his study, after which the latter proceeded to the chapel to celebrate mass before Mme la Duchesse de Bourgogne; for he greatly relished saying mass, both the high and the low, and officiating at every other kind of religious ceremony. He had often begged Mme la Duchesse de Bourgogne to hear him; and he now celebrated at the high altar of the chapel like any other bishop. Mme la Duchesse de Bourgogne sat above in the tribune, partly so as to avoid having to kiss the corporal-cloth[1] which is brought to her by the priest when she sits below; but also to make it seem that there was nothing strange about this mass. None the less, the Elector made her a very low bow as he came and went from the altar, and bent his knee like any ordinary chaplain at the *dominus vobiscum* and the benediction. Mme la Duchesse de Bourgogne stood to acknowledge his low obeisances and curtsied to the ground. Madame was scandalized by the whole affair and took great care to be absent, and indeed the Elector might well have dispensed with it; but not only had he proposed the mass, he had pressed for it, and had let it be understood that he would think Mme la Duchesse de Bourgogne vastly uncivil if she did hear him. He usually claimed the privilege of wearing cardinal's robes as an arch-chancellor of the Empire; but on this visit he wore a short black coat with a red, or sometimes a black, *calotte,* and stockings to match. He was fair-complexioned and had an unusually large and somewhat long wig; he was also painfully ugly with a huge hump behind and a smaller one in front; but he seemed not in the least disturbed on that account. On his previous visit the King had given him an extremely fine diamond cross which he wore round his neck on a flame-coloured ribbon.

There was no priestly function that he did not delight in—not even that of preaching; but you shall hear how he distinguished himself in that capacity. At Valenciennes,[2] on 1 April, he summoned everyone to be present in church to listen to his sermon and there was a great congregation. He mounted up into the pulpit, gazed down at the congregation below, and cried at the top of his voice, 'April Fool! April Fool!'; whereat his entire orchestra accompanied by trumpets and kettle-drums echoed a response. Meanwhile he had ducked down and disappeared. That is a typical German joke, and a princely one; but the congregation, although they laughed heartily at the time, were none the less vastly shocked. When the Elector took his leave of the King he was given an exceedingly large present of money and left the Court very well satisfied.

At this time a marriage took place of so little moment that it would not be worth mentioning were not the circumstances so extraordinary. I refer to the marriage of Villefort and Jeannette.[3] It appeared to offer so little and produced

---

[1] Used in Roman Catholic churches to cover the material elements of the Eucharist.

[2] He was living in exile there. Louis XIV felt that he owed him a debt of gratitude because he had been turned out of his electorate while fighting on the side of France.

[3] Etienne Joseph d'Izarn de Villefort de Montjeu, Marquis d'Haussy, and Jeanne Thérèse de Launay de Penchrec'h.

so much. Let me explain the persons involved. Villefort's mother, beautiful, well-bred, well-formed, lost her husband who commanded some fortress the name of which I cannot now recall. She had no relatives except her children, and nothing, or precious little, to share with them. A woman of spirit and adventurous, but virtuous and innocent of all flightiness, she had a personal introduction to Mme de Maintenon that gained her an audience. Now no one in the world was more susceptible to a pretty face than that lady and King Louis. This particular countenance, so modest, sad, and afflicted, touched both their hearts. Mme de Villefort was given a pension, taken under their special protection, discovered to be intelligent, and continued in favour because of her beauty. Her husband had been a gentleman; she herself was of good family. Mme de Maintenon referred to her as her 'lovely widow', and appointed her to be one of the two assistant-governesses of the Children of France. So much for the bridegroom's antecedents.

The bride, Jeannette, was a lady of Brittany, surnamed Pincré. Her father was dead, and had left his widow penniless with a swarm of children,[1] all very young. Thus reduced to beggary, the poor woman made her way with them all as best she could to Versailles, and flung herself upon her knees by the door of Mme de Maintenon's coach as she stepped in to drive to Saint-Cyr. Mme de Maintenon was charitable; she made inquiries concerning that unhappy family, gave them money, found places for the children, as befitted their ages, and took one little girl, a tiny child, into her own household, handing her over to the care of her maids until such time as she had shown her quality and was old enough to enter Saint-Cyr. The child was very pretty; she diverted Mme de Maintenon's women with her prattle, and amused their mistress also. The King sometimes encountered her as they were dismissing her. He caressed her. She did not fear him in the least, and he was charmed to find a delightful child whom he did not alarm. He grew into the habit of playing with her, and when the time came for her to enter Saint-Cyr, he would not hear of it.

She became still more amusing and even prettier, showing signs of budding wit, personality, and a freedom that was never ill-timed and never tedious. She spoke to the King on matters of every kind, asking questions, joking with him, teasing him when she found him in the mood, even playing with his papers when he worked, but always with discretion and restraint. She behaved in the same way with Mme de Maintenon; indeed, the entire household became fond of her. In the end, even Mme la Duchesse de Bourgogne treated her with respect, and feared her too, suspecting that she carried tales to the King; yet, in fact, she never harmed anyone. At last Mme de Maintenon herself came to think her altogether too clever and discerning, and dreaded lest the King should come to care for her overmuch. Thus it was a mixture of fear and jealousy that made her wish to be rid of her by way of an honourable marriage.

[1] Eight children altogether.

She many times suggested this; but the King would have none of it. Finally, however, she succeeded in making a match for her with Villefort, son of her 'lovely widow'; and the King, who had already given Jeannette several presents of money, now gave her still more as a dowry. To her husband he gave the governorship of Guérande, in Brittany, and the promise of the next colonelcy to fall vacant in an infantry regiment.

Mme de Maintenon thus thought herself safely delivered of her presence, but not so at all, for when all the arrangements had been made, the King firmly declared that he would refuse his consent unless Jeannette returned to live in Mme de Maintenon's household exactly as before. Who would have believed that only a year later[1] she was to become their sole resource in leisure hours and so remained until the King's death. Mme Voysin gave the wedding breakfast, the pair were bedded at Mme de Villefort's, and Mme la Duchesse de Bourgogne presented the nightgown. In later years the husband was appointed a *gentilhomme de la manche* of the present king, and advanced himself still further during the wars.

The death occurred about this time of Boileau-Despréaux, so famous for his wit, his writings, and above all for his satires. One might almost say that he was super-excellent in that last style, despite the fact that he was the best-natured man imaginable. He was commissioned to write the King's History; but was found to have done almost no work upon it.[2]

A few days later, the Maréchal de Boufflers suffered a most cruel blow. His elder son, aged fourteen, handsome, well-built, full of promise, had been wonderfully well received when he was presented formally to the King to thank for the reversion of his father's governorships in Flanders, more especially for that of Lille. The boy had then returned to the Jesuit college where he was a boarder.[3] I do not know what boyish prank he played with Argenson's two sons; but the Jesuits whipped him for it, wishing to show that they neither favoured nor feared anyone; yet they well knew that they had nothing to fear from the Maréchal de Boufflers. Very prudently they abstained from touching the two other boys who were equally to blame, because they had daily dealings with Argenson, the lieutenant of police, on the subject of proscribed books, Jansenists and many other matters of vital interest to them. Young Boufflers was a lad of high spirit; he had done no worse than the others; he became so desperate that he took ill that very day. They carried him to the Maréchal's house; but could not save his life. His heart was broken, and his blood also must have been poisoned, for the purples[4] had already appeared. Four days later

---

[1] After the deaths of Mgr and Mme la Duchesse de Bourgogne.
[2] Nicolas Boileau (called Boileau-Despréaux) (1636-1711), the poet. He was appointed Historiographer Royal conjointly with Racine. What remains of their work is in Racine's hand. The larger portion was destroyed in a fire, which may explain why Saint-Simon thought his contribution such a small one.
[3] Louis-le-Grand.
[4] A condition of the blood when it escapes from the veins and makes purple blotches on the skin.

he was dead. Picture the state of his mother and father! The King was much
moved; he would not let them ask for an audience or be in attendance, but simply
sent one of his gentlemen to convey his sympathy and to tell them that he would
grant the same reversions to their second son. As for the Jesuits, the scandal was
prodigious, but no action was taken against them.

In that same month of March there appeared the first glimmer of the beginning of the quarrel that produced the Bull *Unigenitus*,[1] so fatal to Church and State,
so tragic for religion in general, so profitable to Jesuits, Sulpicians and Vaticanists,
to the riff-raff and the worthless—indeed, to rogues and knaves of every category.
This Bull, purposely designed to produce an effect similar to that of the Edict
of Nantes, has everywhere led to riots, fraud, bewilderment and chaos, accompanied by violence that still rages throughout the kingdom and, even after more
than thirty years of the most cruel persecution, is felt in every trade and profession as a burden that daily becomes more onerous.

I shall take care not to embark upon a history of religion, not even on one
limited to facts and deeds, for that alone would fill volumes. It were better by far
that the public had received less instruction on doctrines, endlessly repeated and
multiplied, and had learned more of the true origins and progress of the whole
monstrous affair, the conduct and proceedings of the opposing sides, the vast
fortunes (even for laymen) that were made from it, the riches lost, and all the far-
reaching and hideous consequences of breaking open that Pandora's box. The
results have been much in excess of the hopes of some and the fears of others. It
has been used to suppress laws, tribunals, and principles, and to put in their stead
a military inquisition that deluges France with *lettres de cachet* and annihilates all
justice. I shall therefore confine myself to describing only that small part which
came under my own eyes, and sometimes through my hands, treating this great
matter as I have endeavoured to treat all the rest, and leaving to more scholarly,
worthier, and less idle pens what I neither saw nor learned from the participants.

In order that you may understand what little I shall say now and again
of an affair that was the chief preoccupation of the remainder of the reign of
Louis XIV, the minority of Louis XV, and the entire period of Cardinal Fleury's
influence, you must recall many events that lie scattered throughout these memoirs.
It would be tedious to repeat them here; but I shall give a list of them so that you
may the more easily discover them in the places where they are described. You
should first remember the storm that broke out over Quietism; the disgrace of

---

[1] The Bull *Unigenitus*, published 1713, in which Pope Clement XI condemned Jansenism. Many of the French clergy
refused to accept it. There resulted a furious quarrel between the Jansenists in the Church and the Parlement on one side,
and the Jesuits on the other. Jansenism was a reaction against the orthodox Catholic dogma of *sufficient grace*. Jansenists
believed in the extreme difficulty of obtaining salvation, and the need for the elect to live apart from ordinary men who
were probably damned.

M. de Cambrai;[1] the great danger that threatened the Dukes of Chevreuse and Beauvilliers and bound them still closer to that prelate; the triumvirate[2] formed against him; the behaviour of the Jesuits, who preached against but did not harm him, and who, in the secrecy of their inner council, supported him with all their might; the union that emerged from all this; what has been said of Saint-Sulpice, of Bissy, Bishop of Toul (later of Meaux and subsequently elevated to the cardinalate), of Père Tellier and the sorry state of the episcopate, which had been filled deliberately with men of no repute or learning, many of them without honour or conscience, and some quite openly devoted to self-interest and the party best able to promote them; finally the Chinese affair, the unhappy situation of the Jesuits on that account and their hatred (particularly that of Père Tellier) for Cardinal de Noailles, against whom they discovered a most useful weapon in Jansenism; last of all, the character of Cardinal de Noailles himself, and all that may have been learned of the natures of the King and of Mme de Maintenon.

With all this in mind, it should not be too hard to credit Père Tellier with a burning desire to rescue his Society from public disfavour and at the same time to strike a blow at Cardinal de Noailles. For such a tremendous undertaking he needed an affair of vast importance affecting the vital interests of Rome, and one in which he would be the Vatican's only champion. He sought tirelessly to discover a suitable issue and form the connection. The Chinese scandal forced him to act quickly. He took as his sole advisers (excluding all others, even the Jesuits) Pères Lallemant and Doucin, men as cunning, false, and subtle as himself, and equally rabid against Cardinal de Noailles who, for some excess, had deprived the last-named father of a Church pension, extracted from Harlay, Archbishop of Paris, at a moment of weakness in his latter days. Pères Lallemant and Doucin lived in Paris at their professed house where Père Tellier also resided, and all three were secretly feared by the other Jesuits for their malice and fanaticism, even by those most dedicated to the views and interests of the Society.

At this moment the omens appeared favourable to Père Tellier. Through Monsieur de Cambrai he had the Dukes of Chevreuse and Beauvilliers on his side, also Pontchartrain (but not his father)[3] and Argenson. By the two last named he could be sure of conveying to the King's ear any matters in which he did not wish to appear in person. The friendship and alliance between Cardinal de Noailles and Mme de Maintenon had ceased to trouble him; for it had already worn threadbare in her inconstant mind. Three men now filled the place of the

---

[1] Fénelon.

[2] The triumvirate against Fénelon: Cardinal de Noailles, Bossuet, Bishop of Meaux, and Godet des Marais, Bishop of Chartres. Of these three only Cardinal de Noailles was alive in 1711.

[3] Pontchartrain's father Louis II Phélypeaux, Comte de Pontchartrain, Chancellor of France.

late Monsieur de Chartres in her heart:[1] his successor and nephew[2] because Saint-Cyr lay in his diocese, although at twenty-seven or twenty-eight he was still, as it were, young enough to be given sugar-plums; her confessor La Chétardie, Curé of Saint-Sulpice (but you already know his total imbecility),[3] and Bissy, Bishop of Meaux, whom the late Monsieur de Chartres had bequeathed to her as his Elisha. She had received him in that spirit, never perceiving that he was given body and soul to the Jesuits for the sake of advancement—and more especially to Père Tellier and his accomplices. That was the result of his secret bargaining with Rome to gain the crimson robe when he was still only Bishop of Toul. Since his translation to Meaux he and the Jesuits had come still closer; for Mme de Maintenon's avowed faith in him made him of great service to them, and they to him. None the less, old acquaintance and Cardinal de Noailles's episcopal rank made it impossible for her to refuse him some consideration and an occasional private audience, a fact that vastly disturbed the Bishop of Meaux who was as eager as Père Tellier to see him discarded altogether.

At this point you must recollect that despite the aversion felt by the clergy of Saint-Sulpice for the Jesuits, and the hatred and jealousy of the latter for them, they were both united in loathing Jansenism and worshipping Rome. Thus the Jesuits were able to lead the Sulpicians in this matter and to use them in any way that appeared serviceable. The plans having been prepared and the final arrangements made, it was decided to take the first step by proxy, so to speak, and to allow the storm to break over a book, entitled *Réflexions Morales sur le Nouveau Testament*, by Père Quesnel,[4] in the edition which Cardinal de Noailles had recommended when he was Bishop of Châlons. No need to speak further of Père Quesnel who has been mentioned more than once in these memoirs, and who in any case is universally known. His book had already received the approval of Vialart, Cardinal de Noailles's predecessor at Châlons, and for more than forty years had edified the entire Church without evoking the least breath of criticism. Cardinal Bissy himself had commended it in a pastoral letter to his diocese of Toul, advising his clergy to obtain a copy, and adding that if poverty prevented their owning many books, this one alone would supply the wherewithal to give their flocks the necessary doctrinal and religious instruction. Père de La Chaise used to keep it on his table, and when someone expressed surprise at the name of the author, he would answer that he loved the good wherever he found it; that this book was a veritable gold-mine of most excellent instruction, and that therefore he kept it always close at hand for his own edification.

[1] Godet des Marais had been her spiritual director.
[2] Charles François de Moustiers de Mérinville, Bishop of Chartres since 1709.
[3] Who read Mme de Maintenon's private letters aloud to the nuns of the Convent of the Visitation. See Vol. 1, p. 490.
[4] Père Pasquier Quesnel (1634-1719), the celebrated Jansenist theologian.

A book with a world-wide reputation, its excellence and sound doctrine guaranteed on the title-page by many famous authorities, might well have been thought proof against attack; but the precedent of the successful assault on *La Fréquente Communion,* the great work of M. Arnauld, a writer even more highly considered than Père Quesnel, freed Père Tellier from any such qualms. He convinced himself that an attack might safely be launched both against the book and against Cardinal de Noailles for recommending it, and he employed for this bold enterprise two persons who were entirely unknown, isolated, and commonplace, for the very reason that this made them all the harder to confront and altogether dependent on his protection. One of them, Champflour, Bishop of La Rochelle, was the very image of ill breeding, even of vulgarity, and with no more sense than the modicum required to be a fanatical papist. He had, in fact, been exiled for that very crime in 1682; but Saint-Sulpice had united with the Jesuits to save this martyr to their favourite cause, and had finally pitchforked him into La Rochelle.[1] Père Tellier's other tool was Valderies de Lescure, less plebeian than Champflour, but quite as vulgar and as papist, and equally devoted to the Jesuits, who had made him Bishop of Luçon. Ardent, impetuous, by nature a very firebrand, he was poor but, in a very minor way, a gentleman; the other was of the dregs, and both were sunk in the most complete obscurity, knowing no one of the slightest importance. In order to train them in what they were required to do a priest was sent to them. By name Chalmet, he had been a pupil at Saint-Sulpice, was finished at Cambrai, and had been well instructed by the great Fénelon who eagerly awaited his return, hoping to gain much from the overthrow of the last of his three conquerors and the support of Père Tellier, himself supported by Fénelon's old friends, but unable to speak out on his behalf.[2]

Chalmet was a man of parts, with the hard, steely vigour of the pedant, wholly committed to the Vaticanism of Saint-Sulpice, devoted to Monsieur de Cambrai, yielding in everything to the Jesuits and more especially to Père Tellier. He went secretly to Saintonge,[3] going backwards and forwards between La Rochelle and Luçon, working very quietly to bring the two chosen vessels together for private indoctrination, but treating them all the while with a lofty arrogance that made them complain of his tyranny. Indeed, they have often since been heard to grumble at him, with scant regard for discretion or their own self-respect. Chalmet none the less persuaded them to collaborate in drafting a pastoral letter containing a condemnation of *Réflexions Morales sur le Nouveau Testament,* by Père Quesnel, in the edition which Cardinal de Noailles had recommended when he was the

---

[1] Many historians take a different view of this prelate.
[2] As the King's confessor, Père Tellier did not wish to seem to interfere.
[3] Saintonge, the ancient province of France, capital Saintes, now forms part of the department of Charente-Maritime.

Count-bishop of Châlons, with a reproach so clearly directed at that prelate that no one could have been deceived, attacking him quite ruthlessly and in the most savage terms for spreading a heresy. The intention of this letter was to sound a general alarm, and not by any means to let it lie hidden in the dioceses of Luçon and La Rochelle. Paris was flooded with copies which, against all the rules of the Church and police, were posted on the doors of the churches and even on that of the archiepiscopal palace, which was how Cardinal de Noailles first learned of its existence.

The Bishops of Luçon and La Rochelle each had a nephew at the seminary of Saint-Sulpice. They were remarkably stupid boys and no more capable than their uncles of taking any action on their own initiative, especially not this bold and ingenious method of advertisement which had obviously been the work of many hands. Cardinal de Noailles, finding himself thus violently and impudently assaulted by two country bishops, made the fatal mistake of the dog that attacks a stone, forgetting that an arm has thrown it. He immediately summoned the superior of Saint-Sulpice[1] to his presence and demanded the expulsion of the two schoolboys. The superior tried to warn him of the scandal of such abrupt expulsions, pleading the boys' excellent qualities and the harm done to their reputations, but all to no purpose. La Chétardie, Curé of Saint-Sulpice, then decided to intervene, thinking that his influence would prevail; pious and simple though he was, he was deceived by the glory of possessing Mme de Maintenon's full confidence and the awe with which people regarded him in consequence. Thus he hastened full of zeal to the archiepiscopal palace; but returned highly indignant, having discovered his mistake. The expulsions were not revoked.

In the meantime Mme de Maintenon took offence at the scant consideration given to her dear confessor. Bissy, Bishop of Meaux, knew well how to make capital out of that. The expulsions provoked an outcry. Cardinal de Noailles complained to the King, who heard him with sympathy, but reminded him that he had brought much of the trouble upon himself. After this there was an interval, owing to the Cardinal's natural inertia, until the time came for his next weekly audience, which he had not thought it prudent to anticipate. His enemies, however, used it to work upon the King who had still done nothing, much though he liked and respected Cardinal de Noailles. Père Tellier speaking to him face to face, and Bissy working through Mme de Maintenon, managed to keep him inactive, and the cardinal did not press King Louis, being firmly convinced that in the end he would have justice.

At that point a letter intended for the King's eye was sent to the bishops for their signature and afterwards forwarded to Père Tellier, who showed it to

[1] François Leschassier (1641-1725).

King Louis during the ordinary course of his duty as minister for the Church's affairs. That letter, which was soon afterwards published, was strongly and most cunningly worded; it was plain to see that those mitred asses could have had no part in it, except to append their signatures, and that the real author was some polished and subtle courtier, most evilly inclined.[1] After lauding the King to the skies, comparing him in his love and defence of the Church to Constantine and Theodosius, the bishops implored his protection, not for themselves abject at his feet, nor yet for their expelled nephews, but for the very life of the Church, the episcopate, and sound doctrine. They appealed for justice also against Cardinal de Noailles (who, they claimed, had attacked them and acted oppressively), citing the example of their nephews to show the probable fate of those whom he even suspected of defending the right; for he had no proof, since the boys did not stand convicted of distributing or posting up the original pastoral letter.

After a lengthy and powerful preface condemning Père Quesnel and his *Réflexions Morales sur le Nouveau Testament*, as approved by Cardinal de Noailles, they pictured that prelate as an enemy of the Church, the Pope, and the King, exactly resembling those bishops of Rome who became tyrants under Constantine and his immediate successors, and trampled beneath their feet the more orthodox clergy. That portrait, so totally unlike the life and character of Cardinal de Noailles, unmasked the entire plot by its cruelty and by the very style of its composition; for it demonstrated beyond all doubt that nothing so bold, subtle, and powerful could have emanated from either La Rochelle or Luçon. The whole intention was clearly to cover that first wanton attack by an unseemly and most harmful scandal, with the aim of using the boys' expulsion to arouse the King's anger at a supposed encroachment on his supreme authority. Thus the tables would neatly be turned, and Cardinal de Noailles himself would be put on the defensive. That indeed is exactly what happened. The Cardinal's original complaint had been received with sympathy; the expulsions were mentioned, but not in reproach. At his next audience, however, when he tried to complain of the letter, King Louis, who had been worked upon in the interval, returned to the nephews with a harsh rebuke to him for daring to take justice into his own hands. Yet although the King had swallowed part of the bait, he remained shocked by the bishops' impudence, and allowed the cardinal to see that he thought their sudden attack quite uncalled for, and believed it to be personal.

Another very serious error made by Cardinal de Noailles was not to bring with him a copy either of the pastoral or of the subsequent letter. Had he been able to read aloud some of the more vicious and subtly hurtful passages, skilfully

---

[1] There is some evidence to support the theory that Fénelon wrote or at least inspired this letter. Another theory is that Père Tellier was the author.

paraphrasing them, taking full advantage of the King's credulity; had he persuaded King Louis of the existence of a plot and of the desire to create a scandal, and shown him that two stolid country bishops could never unaided have devised so subtle an intrigue, let alone sustained it with such artful boldness, he might have induced the King to end the affair there and then. But the cardinal was slow in thought, gentle, not bred for courts and intrigue; his conscience was clear; he had faith in himself and in his high standing with the King, and he therefore rested content with having restored the situation to what it had been before the letter, never doubting but that King Louis, as he had earlier promised, would give him justice.

It was now the turn of Père Tellier to have an audience. He spurred the King on to resent the supposed encroachment on his authority, representing that it was his duty to protect the humbler and more obscure prelates against persecution for upholding good doctrine; and at the same time, Bissy, Bishop of Meaux, laboured to similar effect on Mme de Maintenon. As a result of their efforts, when Cardinal de Noailles returned to the King a week later, he was astounded to be told to hold his tongue since he had taken justice into his own hands, and to find his own way out of his difficulties. The two bishops were now exactly in the situation for which Père Tellier had planned. Their complaint had been intended simply to distract attention from the injury which they had inflicted, and thus protect them from its consequences. As it had now turned out, after publicly attacking a cardinal on a question of faith, they found themselves, despite the enormous difference of rank, treated as his equals. Cardinal de Noailles in this situation spoke to the King, saying that since His Majesty left him alone to face a totally undeserved campaign of slander and insult, he begged to be allowed to defend himself. The reply was a cold permission to act as he thought fit.

Two days later he published a strong but brief pastoral letter, purporting to expose various errors in that by the two bishops, treating it as a slander, perpetrated in their names, and adding somewhat unnecessarily that he did not believe them capable of having written it themselves. He further protested at the general agitation over doctrine, and at the manner in which certain of the bishops chose to meddle with the research of others, forbidding on pain of his displeasure the reading of their letter, which he rebuked in various other ways. It may well seem that he had every right to treat them in this way, considering that the King, after at first abandoning him, had given him leave to act; and that he had, moreover, acted with great restraint in view of the nature of the offence. Be that as it may, his letter was counted against him as yet another crime, and brought down upon him a ban against appearing at the Court without a summons.

The two bishops, or rather those who urged them on, seized this as an opportunity to write a second pastoral letter, which evoked an admirable reply from Hébert, Bishop of Agen, in the same ecclesiastical province. Hébert had won a great reputation as Curé of Versailles, and Cardinal de Noailles had influenced his promotion; what he now wrote was excellent—scholarly, forceful, pious, representing to them with episcopal modesty and restraint the great wrong which they did by troubling the Church and personally attacking the Cardinal.

Meantime the Cardinal's enemies were not idle, but on the contrary busily engaged in inspiring other slanderous documents. Shortly afterwards there appeared a pastoral letter by Berger de Malissoles, Bishop of Gap, an attack less crude, but quite as spiteful as the others, and Cardinal de Noailles forbade the reading of that also. He then drafted a most excellent letter addressed to Bishop Hébert, giving a résumé of all that had occurred, framed with great moderation and a humility so noble in the circumstances that the document was everywhere regarded as his manifesto and widely distributed. The whole affair, by this time, was arousing the indignation of those who were neither devoted to the Jesuits and the hope of personal advantage, nor blind to the wicked use being made of supposed Jansenism in order to discredit and ruin innocent persons. The manifesto convinced all who still remained neutral, and made such a sensation that the aggressors took fright and sought to devise other means of reaping benefit from this rich field. Enough for the present. It is now time to return to other matters.

In Spain, as I have already said, there was little activity during this year. Her unexampled endeavours had left her too much exhausted for fresh victories, and her enemies, defeated after their very brief triumph, were in no condition to attack.

Throughout all Holy Week, M. du Maine's children appeared triumphant in the ranks of the princes of the blood. Their parents' joy was great indeed, and the King was much pleased. The scandal was enormous. In that year Easter Day fell on 5 April. On the following Wednesday, after the Council had risen, Monseigneur went to dine at Meudon taking with him Mme la Duchesse de Bourgogne, tête-à-tête in his coach. Courtiers customarily applied for invitations to the Meudon visits; and this one was billed to last a week, until the Marly on the following Wednesday. I however had absented myself since the Monday of Holy Week, intending to appear at Marly on the same day as the King. Meudon excursions had become increasingly burdensome to me since the incident of Monseigneur's inconceivable credulity, which I have already described; and despite the fact that Mme la Duchesse de Bourgogne had shamed and disabused him, I did not care to risk going there. The house to me was a haunt of devils, all of whom were my personal enemies. I therefore avoided it, which caused me some embarrassment with Monseigneur and his circle; but had I gone there I should have fared much worse.

Although that situation was causing me grave anxiety, other considerations were still more disquieting. Each day the prospect drew nearer of a future when Monseigneur would reign surrounded by the enemies who desired my ruin. They had only to express the wish. For lack of other comfort I lived on my courage, telling myself that one never experiences all the good or all the evil one has reason to expect. Thus, hoping against hope, I put my trust in the uncertainty of all earthly things and shrugged off the future; although I remained in terrible anxiety regarding Meudon and the present.

That was why I made the decision to spend the Easter fortnight resting far from Society and the Court; although at that time every prospect save that of Monseigneur was pleasing. For this ill there appeared to be no remedy and it was causing me acute distress until, quite suddenly, at the moment least expected, God chose to deliver me. I was alone at La Ferté save for M. de Saint-Louis, an old cavalry officer, highly esteemed by the King and M. de Turenne, who for many years past had been living in retirement at La Trappe, and a gentleman from Normandy, a former captain of my regiment who was much attached to me. On Saturday the 11th, I spent the morning walking with them and was alone in my study shortly before dinner when a messenger from Mme de Saint-Simon was announced: he brought the news that Monseigneur had been taken ill.

That prince, as I have said, had driven to Meudon on the day after the Easter festival. As he was passing through Chaville he had chanced to see a priest taking Our Lord to a sick person, and with Mme la Duchesse de Bourgogne he had stepped down from his coach to kneel in prayer. He asked to whom they were going, and learned that it was to one dying of smallpox, which was very prevalent at that time. He had had it only lightly and fleetingly in early childhood and was mortally afraid of it. He was therefore much alarmed, and remarked that same evening to Boudin, his chief physician, that he should not be surprised if he developed it. The rest of that day was without incident. Next morning he rose to go hunting, but weakness overcame him as he was dressing and he fell out of his chair. Boudin had him put back to bed. The state of his pulse gave great cause for anxiety all that day; but Fagon told the King in such a casual way that he thought nothing of it and went to Marly after his dinner, where he several times received news from Meudon. Mgr and Mme la Duchesse de Bourgogne stayed there for dinner, and did not leave Monseigneur's side for a single moment. The princess enhanced the duties of a daughter-in-law by her natural grace and charm, and gave everything to Monseigneur with her own hands. Her heart cannot have been deeply troubled by what her mind must have told her was possible; but her care and devotion never flagged and she behaved with feeling and without affectation. Mgr le Duc de Bourgogne, so simple, so saintly, always so concerned to do his duty, did it now in full measure; and although there was grave suspicion of small-pox, which he had not had, he refused to leave Monseigneur's bedside, and did so at last only in time to attend the King at supper.

When the King heard their news he sent such clear orders to Meudon that they told him as soon as he wakened of Monseigneur's grave danger. He had already announced when he returned to Marly on the previous evening that he would go to Meudon next day and remain there throughout the illness, no matter what it might turn out to be, and he drove there immediately after his mass. Just before leaving he forbade his children to follow him; he also issued a general inter-diction covering all who had not had the smallpox, which was kind and consider-ate of him; and he gave permission for those who had already had it to pay their court to him at Meudon, or to stay away if they felt nervous.

I shall continue to speak of myself with the same frankness which I have used in speaking of others, and relate what happened as truthfully as I am able. In the situation in which I then was with Monseigneur and his circle, you may easily imagine how the news affected me; for I realized from what I had learned of Monseigneur's condition that for better or worse the issue would soon be decided. I was, however, very comfort-able at La Ferté, and I therefore resolved to wait for further news, returning Mme de Saint-Simon's courier, and asking her to dispatch another next day. The rest of that day I spent in a state of flux, gaining and losing ground alternately as I strove to guard the Christian against the courtier; for at this critical moment my mind was invaded by a host of unsuitable thoughts, bidding me hope for a sudden and unexpected deliv-erance with the happiest omens for the future. Thus I eagerly awaited the courier's return, which occurred on the afternoon of the following day, Low Sunday. From him I learned that smallpox had declared itself, but that otherwise things were as well as could be expected. This seemed fully confirmed by the news that Mme de Maintenon, who never left her room when she stayed at Meudon, had gone to Versailles early that morning to dine with Mme de Caylus, and appeared in no hurry to return. I thus concluded that Monseigneur was saved, and determined to stay at my home. After listening to advice, however, as all my life I have done and been the better for it, I regretfully gave orders to depart on the next day, and did so early in the morning. At La Queue, fourteen leagues from La Ferté and six from Versailles, a certain banker named La Fontaine came to the door of my coach as I was changing horses. He had just come from Paris and Versailles where he had seen some of Mme la Duchesse de Bourgogne's servants who had told him that Monseigneur was better, giving details that seemed to prove him out of danger. There thus appeared to be no further cause for alarm, save in the treacherous nature of such an illness in a stout man of fifty.

The King held his council and worked as usual with his ministers during the evening. He saw Monseigneur night and morning, and often after dinner as well; and sat for a long time in the *ruelle*[1] beside his bed. On the Monday, the day of my return, he had dined early and had driven out to Marly, where Mme la Duchesse de Bourgogne had gone to meet him. As he passed through the gardens of Versailles he saw his grandsons who were waiting for him. He would not let them come near, but simply called out 'Good-day' as he went past. Mme la Duchesse de Bourgogne had already had smallpox; but it had not marked her. When I arrived at Versailles I sent a note to M. le Duc de Beauvilliers, at Meudon, asking him to tell the King that I had returned as soon as I learned of Monseigneur's illness, and should now be at Meudon, save that I felt myself to be covered by the general interdiction. He sent me word that my gesture was appreciated, and repeated on behalf of the King that neither Mme de Saint-Simon (who, like me, had not had smallpox) nor myself should go to Meudon. This exclusion did not much distress me. Mme la Duchesse de Berry (who had had the sickness) was also deprived of the privilege of seeing the King, unlike Mme la Duchesse de Bourgogne; neither of their husbands had had it. For the same reason M. le Duc d'Orléans was prohibited, but Mme la Duchesse d'Orléans, who was not in that category, was permitted to see the King, although she took scant advantage of the permission. Madame did not see him at all, though there was no reason for excluding her. The ban very rightly covered the King's two grandsons, but he did as he pleased regarding other members of his family.

Versailles presented a very changed appearance, Mgr and Mme la Duchesse de Bourgogne openly held their court; it was like the dawn of a new day. All the courtiers were congregated there; all Paris flocked to attend them and, since tact and prudence are not typically French virtues, all Meudon came too, and were believed when they swore they had not entered Monseigneur's bedroom. The times to pay one's court were at the *levers* and *couchers*, while dining and supping with the ladies, in general conversation after meals, or when walking in the garden. The state apartments were not large enough for the crowds. Couriers arrived every quarter of an hour bringing news of Monseigneur. The illness was taking its course. There was every reason for hope and confidence, a general eagerness to please at the new Court, majesty and sober good cheer on the part of the young prince and princess, who had a gracious welcome for all comers and took particular care to greet everyone. The crowd was amiable; there was satisfaction all round, with the Duc and Duchesse de Berry seeming mere nonentities. Five days passed in this way, everyone thinking of the future and trying to adapt his conduct to suit any eventuality.

On Tuesday, 14 April, the day after my return, the King, who found Meudon very dull, held the usual Conseil des Finances in the morning and followed it,

[1] The space between the bed and the wall, where visitors sat to talk.

against his usual custom, with a Conseil des Dépêches in the afternoon. I saw the Chancellor afterwards, and he assured me that Monseigneur's general condition was good, Fagon actually having stated that all was as well as could be wished and beyond what they had dared to hope. The Chancellor appeared full of confidence, and I believed him all the more readily because he knew Monseigneur and did not dismiss all cause for anxiety, although he expressed none beyond what was reasonable. Monseigneur's old friends the fishwives of Paris, who had once before appeared when an acute attack of indigestion was mistaken for apoplexy, again called attention to themselves by arriving at Meudon in hired coaches. Monseigneur had insisted on having them admitted to the bedroom; whereupon they flung themselves down at the foot of the bed, kissing it again and again. Then, overcome with delight at the better report, they swore to make the whole town glad by *Te Deums* in every church. Monseigneur, never insensible to popular support, at once gave orders for them to be shown the house, entertained to dinner, and sent away with a present of money.

Meantime, as I was returning from the Chancellor and crossing one of the courtyards at Versailles in order to reach my own apartment, I saw Mme la Duchesse d'Orléans walking on the terrace of the new wing. She called out to me, but as Mme de Montauban was with her I pretended not to hear and continued on my way.[1] Our apartment was on the first floor of the new wing, almost adjacent to those of M. and Mme la Duchesse de Berry; they were giving a supper-party for M. and Mme la Duchesse d'Orléans and a few of their ladies, including Mme de Saint-Simon, but she had sent her excuses, pleading a slight indisposition. I had been in my study only a short time when they announced Mme la Duchesse d'Orléans, who looked in for an hour's gossip before supper. I received her in Mme de Saint-Simon's room; she herself was not there at first, but soon afterwards she entered to make a third in the conversation. The princess and I had been itching to see one another and discuss the whole situation, regarding which we were in entire agreement. She had arrived from Meudon only an hour earlier and had seen the King. It was now eight o'clock.

In speaking to me she used the very same words which Fagon had used to the Chancellor, describing the cheerfulness at Meudon, praising the care and skill of the doctors, who neglected nothing, not even those little homely remedies that are so often despised. She enlarged on the success of their treatments and, to be frank, albeit to our shame, we both lamented the fact that Monseigneur at his age and size might still escape from that dangerous disease. She sadly reflected in the wittily languishing manner of the Mortemarts that after so much purging he was

---

[1] Mme de Montauban was 'humpbacked, lopsided, hideous, raddled with paint and covered with patches, debauched, avaricious, wicked, a kind of monster', and rarely came to the Court because no one would speak to her there.

unlikely to harbour even the least little likelihood of apoplexy, and that the chance of indigestion was irretrievably lost now that he had at last taken fright and handed himself over to the doctors. Even more gloomily, we concluded that we had best resign ourselves to the expectation of his living and reigning a very long time; and thence we came to predicting the fatal consequences of his reign and the vanity of trusting in even the most ominous symptoms, for his health, which had seemed at such a low ebb, had found renewal and recovery in the very jaws of death. In short, we fairly let ourselves go, although not without certain scruples occasionally intervening to check our fascinating talk which, notwithstanding, Mme la Duchesse d'Orléans in her droll manner always brought back to the point of departure. Mme de Saint-Simon, all goodness, tried in vain to check our more outrageous utterances, but the brakes were off and there ensued the most fearful struggle between the expression of sentiments that, humanly speaking, were quite natural, and the sensation that they were not altogether Christian. Two hours passed in this way, very quickly as it seemed to us, and then we were interrupted by supper-time. Mme la Duchesse went to her daughter, and Mme de Saint-Simon and I to my own room where company had assembled and we all sat down to eat.

While everything at Versailles and even at Meudon was in appearance tranquil, a change was actually taking place. During the day, the King had several times seen Monseigneur, who greatly relished such tokens of affection and kindness; but at the after-dinner visit he had noticed a great swelling of the face and head, which so much shocked him that he stayed only for a moment and shed tears as he left the room. Everything possible was done to reassure him, and after the meeting of the council he walked in his gardens. None the less, Monseigneur had failed to recognize Mme la Princesse de Conti, and Boudin was alarmed. Monseigneur himself had never ceased to be so. His courtiers had seen him one after another; some of those closest to him had not left his room, and he continually inquired of them whether his sensations were usual in that illness. At the times when he believed their reassurances he had high hopes of recovery. At one moment he told Mme la Princesse de Conti that he had been feeling unwell for some time past but had not liked to admit it, and that on Holy Thursday he had been hard put to it to hold his prayer book.

At about four in the afternoon he grew so much worse that Boudin suggested to Fagon that they should send to Paris for other advice since, as Court physicians, they never saw infectious fevers and had no experience in treating them. Fagon thereupon flew into a rage, refusing to send for anyone or listen to reason, asserting that nothing would be gained by arguments and conflicting opinions, and that they would do as well, if not better, without interference from outside. Thus although

Monseigneur's condition hourly worsened, it was agreed to keep the truth a secret. By seven o'clock even the courtiers had noticed a deterioration, but because they were terrified of Fagon no one dared to warn the King and Mme de Maintenon. Mme la Princesse de Conti and Mme la Duchesse de Bourgogne felt equally helpless and tried to comfort one another. What was altogether extraordinary was that they decided to let the King sit down to his supper before disturbing him with talk of desperate remedies, and he finished his meal without receiving any kind of warning. Indeed, from Fagon's reports and the general silence he imagined Monseigneur to be at any rate no worse, although on account of the swelling he had been anxious about him earlier in the day.

While the King was thus calmly at his supper, panic had broken out in Monseigneur's bedroom. Fagon and the other doctors had tried one remedy after another without waiting for any to take effect. The curé of Meudon, who called every evening to inquire, found the doors wide open and the footmen distracted. He entered the room, and when he perceived the truth so belatedly recognized, ran to the bed and, taking Monseigneur's hand, spoke to him of God; then, observing that though almost bereft of speech he was still conscious, he extracted some sort of a confession (which no one had thought of) and proposed certain acts of contrition. The wretched prince managed to utter a few words distinctly and to mumble others, touched his breast, clasped the curé's hand, appeared imbued with the proper sentiments, and received absolution with apparent eagerness and repentance.

By this time the King had risen from table. He nearly fell over backwards with astonishment when Fagon appeared before him utterly distraught, crying out that all was lost. You may imagine the horror that seized everyone in this sudden transition from absolute confidence to the last degree of despair. The King had hardly recovered himself before he at once started towards Monseigneur's apartments, cutting short the tactless efforts made to prevent him, and saying that he wished to make sure that no remedy was neglected. As he was crossing the threshold, however, Mme la Princesse de Conti, who had flown to Monseigneur's side in the short interval since the end of supper, tried to prevent his entering. She even went so far as to press him back with her hands, saying that he must now think only of himself.

After that, the King, almost fainting from this sudden and complete reversal, sank down upon a sofa near the door of the ante-room. He asked for news from all who came out of the bedroom, but few had courage to answer him. On his way to Monseigneur he sent for Père Tellier, who had already gone to bed but hastily dressed again and was soon in Monseigneur's bedroom. By that time, however, it was too late—at least so all the servants said; but that Jesuit, perhaps to give the King reassurance, maintained that he had found good and sufficient grounds for giving absolution. Mme de Maintenon had hastened to the King and was sitting down beside him on the sofa, attempting to weep. She made an effort to take him away, for the coaches were ready in the courtyard; but could by no means induce him to leave until after Monseigneur had expired. The coma lasted for nearly an hour after the King entered the ante-room. Madame la Duchesse and Mme la Princesse de Conti divided their attention between the dying man and the King, to whose side they often returned. As for the rest, the doctors were bewildered, the servants distraught, the courtiers whispering. They all jostled one another continually so that there was constant movement but scarcely any change of position. At last the dreadful moment came. Fagon left, a signal that made it generally known.

The King had been profoundly distressed and shocked at the absence of a proper confession, and he lashed out at Fagon before he allowed Mme de Maintenon and the two princesses to lead him away. The apartment was on the ground floor, level with the courtyard. As he went out to step into a carriage he noticed that the first one was Monseigneur's own *berline,* and he signed for another to be brought because the sight of this vehicle distressed him. Yet he was not too much overcome to notice Pontchartrain; and he called out, telling him to warn his father and the other ministers to come later than usual to Marly next day, for the Wednesday meeting of the council of State. I shall not comment on his extraordinary self-control, but merely say that those who witnessed it were astounded, and so were all who heard of it later. Pontchartrain replied that since the agenda concerned only current affairs, the meeting might well be postponed until the King was less harassed. To this he consented. He got with difficulty into the coach, supported on either side. Mme de Maintenon stepped in after him, followed by Mme la Princesse de Conti who sat in front. A crowd of officers belonging to Monseigneur's household had flung themselves down upon their knees, lining the whole length of the courtyard on both sides of the King's way, imploring him with terrible cries to have compassion on them, for they had lost their master and would die of hunger.

While Meudon thus provided a scene of horror, everything at Versailles was tranquil and serene. We had finished supper, our guests had retired a little later, and I was chatting with Mme de Saint-Simon as she undressed before going to bed. Suddenly a former footman of ours, whom she had given to Mme la Duchesse de Berry to serve her at table, entered in a state of great distress. He said that there must be bad news from Meudon, because Mgr le Duc de Bourgogne had whispered to M. le Duc de Berry and his eyes were full of tears. He had left the table precipitately, and when a second message came the entire company rose and went into the drawing-room. Surprised by this sudden change, I went quickly to Mme la Duchesse de Berry's apartment, but found no one there. They had gone in a body to Mme la Duchesse de Bourgogne's room and I followed them in great haste.

All Versailles was assembled there; the ladies in undress, for most of them were ready for bed, the doors wide open, and everything in a turmoil. I soon learned that Monseigneur had received Extreme Unction and was now unconscious, and that his condition was regarded as hopeless. I also learned that the King had sent Mme la Duchesse de Bourgogne a message to the effect that he was on his way to Marly and that she was to wait for him in the avenue between the stables as he wished to see her when he drove that way.

Amid all the thoughts and emotions that came crowding upon me I concentrated what attention I could spare upon the scene before my eyes. The two princes and the princesses were in the little ante-room behind the alcove, where the accessories had been laid out for the *coucher* of Mme la Duchesse de Bourgogne. She, herself, went backwards and forwards between the two rooms, filling in the time until she had to meet the King. She bore herself graciously as ever, but there was a look of compassion and strain about her, which many people mistook for grief. When people spoke to her as she passed, she answered their inquiries or said a few brief words. The expressions on the faces of the bystanders were truly eloquent; one needed only to have eyes and not the least knowledge of the Court to read the desires of some, while the countenances of those who had nothing to gain remained perfectly blank. Some were self-possessed; others seemed cruelly affected, or else were very grave, careful to reveal nothing of their joy and relief. My first action was to question several persons, but I did not place much reliance on their words, nor on the spectacle before me, for I feared lest there might be all too little cause for so much excitement. I then brought myself to reflect on the common lot of man, and that I, too, should one day find myself at the gates of death. None the less, my joy kept breaking through these passing thoughts of religion and common humanity, by which I strove to remember the proprieties. My own deliverance seemed so tremendous, so unlooked for, that from evidence which boded better than the reality, I believed that the State had everything to gain from this death. Among such reflections, however, I could not help but fear that the patient might still recover, and then I did feel mortally ashamed of myself.

Deeply immersed as I was in my own thoughts, I did not forget to send word to Mme de Saint-Simon that she had better come, nor to keep a secret watch on every face, appearance and action. Thus I indulged my eager curiosity, confirmed my first impressions (they have never been proved wrong) of every noteworthy person present, and drew the proper conclusions from those first impulsive movements that are rarely controlled and are therefore sure signs, for those who know the Court and their fellow men, of attachments and sentiments that are invisible at calmer moments.

I saw Mme la Duchesse d'Orléans arrive, but her set, dignified expression told me nothing. She entered the little ante-room, but soon afterwards returned with M. le Duc d'Orléans, whose manner, agitated and confused, reflected the general excitement rather than any personal emotion. They left together. A few moments later, I noticed Mgr le Duc de Bourgogne in the distance, near the door of the ante-room. He appeared profoundly moved and distressed, but the searching glance which I shot at him could detect no tender feelings, only the intense preoccupation of a man absorbed in his own thoughts. The footmen and valets were already crying noisily, their affliction showing how much such kinds of people stood to lose. At about half-past midnight news was received from the King, and I saw Mme la Duchesse de Bourgogne come out of the little ante-room with her husband, who now seemed even more deeply affected and immediately returned. The princess took her shawl and hood from the dressing-table; then, erect, purposeful, and almost dry-eyed, she crossed the room, her inner turmoil betrayed only by the furtively questioning glances which she cast to right and left. Followed only by her ladies, she went down the grand staircase to her coach.

Soon after she left I took the opportunity to go to Mme la Duchesse d'Orléans's room, for I was longing to be with her; but as soon as I entered I learned that they had gone to Madame's apartment, and I pushed my way through the crowd in pursuit of them. I met her as she was returning and she asked me very gravely to accompany her. M. le Duc d'Orléans was still with his mother. Having regained her room, she sat down, and the Duchesse de Villeroy, the Maréchale de Rochefort, and five or six other ladies of her circle gathered round her. I was twitching with impatience at finding so great a company, and Mme la Duchesse d'Orléans, no less exasperated, took a candle and stepped into the back of the room. I then tried to say something into the ear of the Duchesse de Villeroy, for we thought alike in the present circumstances, but she gave me a gentle push and urged me in a whisper to control myself. It nearly choked me to have to keep silence amid the ladies' conventional expressions of pity and surprise; but at that moment M. le Duc d'Orléans appeared at the door of his study and called to me to enter.

I followed him downstairs to his inner study, that led into the great gallery, he almost swooning, and I with my legs trembling because of all that was happening around and within me. By chance we sat down facing one another, and I observed with intense astonishment that tears were falling from his eyes. 'Monsieur!' I exclaimed, rising to my feet. He understood at once and answered in a broke voice, now weeping in earnest, 'You may well be surprised, indeed so am I; but such scenes are moving.

He was a good man and I have known him all my life; when they let him alone he treated me well and was kind to me. I know that my grief will be short, and that in a few days' time I shall see every reason to console myself, considering the bad feeling which they created between us. At present, kinship, pity, humanity, are all involved, and one does feel moved.' I praised his sentiments but expressed my intense astonishment on account of his bad relations with Monseigneur. At this he rose, put his head in a corner, nose to the wall, and began to weep and sob most bitterly, something I never would have believed had I not seen it with my own eyes. After a short silence, I urged him to compose himself, saying that he would soon have to return to Mme la Duchesse de Bourgogne's apartment, and that if he were seen with red eyes everyone would ridicule him for a piece of arrant humbug, for the entire Court knew on what sort of terms he had been with Monseigneur. He then did what he could to patch up his eyes, and was still at that work when word came that Mme la Duchesse de Bourgogne had returned and that Mme la Duchesse d'Orléans was about to go to her. He also went to join her and I followed.

Mme la Duchesse de Bourgogne had waited only a short time in the avenue before the King drove up. She stepped down from her coach to greet him at his carriage door, but Mme de Maintenon who was sitting on that side called out, 'What are you thinking of, Madame? Do not come near us, we are pest-ridden!' I never learned what gesture the King made to her, but I know that he did not kiss her, on account of the contagion. The princess immediately stepped back into her coach and returned to the château. The fearful secrecy with which Fagon had concealed Monseigneur's true condition deceived everyone so completely that the Duc de Beauvilliers, who had slept at Meudon throughout the illness, actually returned to Versailles after the Conseil des Dépêches. He usually retired about ten o'clock because he was an early riser, and that night he had gone to bed without the least anxiety. It was not long afterwards that a messenger arrived summoning him to Mme la Duchesse de Bourgogne's apartment, where he found the two princes and Mme la Duchesse de Berry waiting in the ante-room. When the first embraces were over, after Mme la Duchesse de Bourgogne's return, which in itself told all, M. de Beauvilliers observed that it was stifling in that small room, and persuaded them to go through the bedroom into the drawing-room that separates it from the great gallery. The windows were then opened and the two princes, each with his princess beside him, sat down on a sofa that stood near the windows with its back to the gallery. The whole company in this room was dispersed, standing and sitting in no kind of order, the ladies of the intimate circle sitting on the floor near the foot of the princes' sofa.

From then onwards in that room, and indeed in the whole apartment, countenances might be read like open books. Monseigneur was dead. Everyone knew it, everyone spoke of it, no one now held back out of deference; those first moments revealed first impulses in a true light, and for once free of the constraint of good manners. Yet everyone behaved discreetly amid the anxiety, excitement, shock, overcrowding, and general chaos of that eventful night. In the outer rooms smothered groans might be heard from servants in despair at losing a master who suited them to perfection, and dreading the thought of serving another (the King) whom they greatly feared. Among them were strangers, the more intelligent footmen of the chief personages at the Court, who had hurried to hear the news, and clearly showed by their manner to which clique their masters belonged.

Farther away were crowds of courtiers of all descriptions, the greater number, fools that they were, drawing sighs from their very heels, while with dry eyes and roving glances they praised Monseigneur with one voice and for one virtue only—his kindness, pitying the King for losing so excellent a son. The cleverer or more astute among them pretended to be anxious for the King's health, congratulating themselves on remaining cool amid so much confusion, and leaving no one in doubt of it by constant repetition. Others seemed truly afflicted, and the members of the stricken cabal[1] wept bitterly, or controlled their tears with an effort as obvious as any sobbing. The hardest or most cunning kept their eyes on the ground, or meditated in distant corners on the probable outcome of this totally unexpected event, and still more on their own futures. There was little or no conversation among those variously affected, although every now and then someone would let fall a remark which was echoed by his neighbours, words dropping at the rate of one every quarter of an hour. Faces were sad or haggard, gestures more frequent than intended, and for the rest there was almost absolute stillness. Those who were merely curious or indifferent remained impassive; only the fools chattered and asked questions, adding to the sorrow of the mourners and being an embarrassment to the rest. Those who were glad tried in vain to increase their appearance of gravity by looking sad or stern; yet all that they could achieve was a thin veil, through which keen eyes might discover their real feelings. Such people stood as motionless as those most afflicted, on their guard against public opinion, curiosity in others, complacency in themselves or impulsiveness; but nevertheless the excitement in their eyes made up for their bodies' lack of motion. A change of position, as of men sitting uncomfortably or tired of standing, a particular care to avoid one another's glance or even to prevent eyes from meeting, tiny incidents arising from such encounters, an indescribable hint of release in the whole deportment of these people, shone through their efforts to be calm and controlled. A liveliness,

[1] The circle around Monseigneur, who had been relying on his accession to make them powerful.

a kind of glitter distinguished them from the rest, making them conspicuous in spite of all their efforts to the contrary.

The two princes with their princesses sitting beside them and trying to comfort them were exposed to every eye. Mgr le Duc de Bourgogne wept in all sincerity, quietly shedding tears of compassion, piety, and prolonged strain. M. le Duc de Berry was equally sincere, but he might have been weeping tears of blood, so bitterly he cried. Indeed, it was not merely sobs that came from him, but shrieks and howls, even bellowings. Sometimes he was quiet, but only because he was choking, and then his cries would break out again, so loud, so monstrously loud, that they resembled the uncontrollable trumpetings of deep despair. Many others joined in these heart-rending outbursts, goaded thereto by emotion or a sense of the proprieties. At last he drove himself into such a paroxysm that they were forced to undress him then and there, to have remedies prepared and the doctors summoned. Mme la Duchesse de Berry was beside herself; you shall soon discover why. The bitterness of despair was imprinted on her face. You could see as plainly as though it were written a perfect frenzy of uncontrollable woe, not from grief or affection, but from pure selfishness. There were intervals when she was dry-eyed, but sullen looking and angry. Then came torrents of tears and gestures, involuntary yet restrained, betraying the deep anguish that resulted from her preceding meditations. Her husband's cries sometimes interrupted her, and then she was quick to support and embrace him or offer him smelling-salts; you could see her eagerness to minister to him. Then, just as swiftly, she would relapse again into her own thoughts, followed by a storm of weeping that helped her a little to stifle her sobs. Mme la Duchesse de Bourgogne also comforted her husband, finding that easier than to show any sign of needing consolation herself. She paraded no false emotions, yet one could see she did her utmost to produce the tears which she felt that decency required, and which often will not come when they are most needed. A frequent use of her handkerchief reflected the sobs of her princely brother-in-law, and a few tears occasioned by the scene around her, and carefully husbanded, were encouraged by artful rubbing to smudge her cheeks and make her eyes red and swollen; but all the time her furtive glances wandered over the bystanders and scanned the face of each one in turn.

The Duc de Beauvilliers stood beside them, looking as cool and detached as though nothing had happened and the scene were an everyday occurrence. He quietly attended to the princes, giving orders to allow only a few to enter, notwithstanding that the doors stood open, and sending for all that was needed without any fuss or misjudgment, behaving, in fact, as though he were at an ordinary *lever* or *petit couvert*. His composure was unruffled, for since his conscience forbade him either to be glad or to conceal how little grief he felt, he was able to preserve a truthful appearance to the end. Madame, attired again in fall court-dress, arrived shriek-ing, not rightly knowing the cause for either.[1] She drowned with her tears all whom she embraced and made the château re-echo with her cries, presenting the remarkable spectacle of a princess wearing formal attire in the middle of the night, and coming to weep among a crowd of women in dishabille or what resembled fancy-dress.

Mme la Duchesse d'Orléans had left the princes and was sitting near the fireplace with her back to the gallery, among a group of ladies; but she was very silent and they gradually moved farther off, which pleased her very much. Only the Duchess of Sforza, the Duchesse de Villeroy, Mme de Castries, and Mme de Saint-Simon remained, who were thankful to be left alone and drew into a little knot beside one of the camp-beds. They pulled the curtains together, and as all were of the same mind regarding the event that had led that great company to assemble, they began to talk freely in low voices. For reasons of security, a number of these camp-beds were set up every night for the use of the Swiss Guard and floor-polishers in all the state apartments, and they had been put there as usual before the bad news came from Meudon. In the middle of the conversa-tion, Mme de Castries, who was touching the bed, felt something stir, which terrified her, because she was nervous of everything although she had plenty of courage. The next moment a great bare arm pulled the curtains apart, and the ladies saw a huge Swiss Guardsman between the sheets, only half-awake, yawning and staring hard at the people round him, whom he was very slow to recognize. Then, obviously thinking it unsuitable to get out of bed in such exalted company, he buried himself once more between the sheets and pulled his curtains. The fellow had apparently gone to bed before the news arrived, and had slept so soundly that he had only just wakened. The most ludicrous incidents do sometimes happen to relieve the most solemn spectacle, and this one made several of the ladies laugh, although Mme la Duchesse d'Orléans feared lest they might have been overheard. On reflection, however, they were reas-sured by the man's sleepiness and evident stupidity.

As for me, I endeavoured to keep an open mind. Although everything seemed to prove what had happened, I refused to believe it until I had found some respon-sible person to confirm the news; I then chanced to see M. d'O, who told me the facts, over which, when I knew them, I tried not to rejoice openly. How well I succeeded I do not know, but one thing certain is that neither joy nor sorrow abated my curiosity, and while I was careful to preserve the decencies, I did not think it necessary to pretend to any grief. I no longer feared repercussions from

---

[1] Madame wrote next day, 16 April, to her aunt the Electress of Hanover: 'Those who imagined that they were harming me by alienating Monseigneur le Dauphin's affections may perhaps have saved my life, for had we been on the same terms as before Monsieur's death I might have died from fear or grief or have remained inconsolable; whereas at present I can support the affliction patiently and grieve only for the King.'

Meudon, nor persecution by its relentless garrison, and since the King was at Marly, I felt unconstrained and could study the crowd at my ease, allowing my eyes to dwell on those who from various motives were much or little affected. Thus I followed the movements of certain personages and endeavoured stealthily to penetrate their inmost thoughts; for indeed, to one who knows the inner life of a Court, these first moments after some tremendous event are intensely gratifying. Each face reminds one of the cares and intrigues, the laborious efforts to advance a private fortune or form and strengthen a cabal, the cunning devices designed and executed for such purposes, the attachments at varying degrees of intimacy, the estrangements, dislikes, and hatreds, the unkind turns played and the favours granted, the tricks, petty shifts, and baseness of some individuals, the dashing of the hopes of some in mid-career, the stupefaction of others at the summit who had thought their ambitions fulfilled. By the same blow a new importance was given to their adversaries in the opposing cabals; the force of the recoil at that same moment brought the affairs of some (notably myself) to a successful conclusion and consequently to extreme and unlooked-for joy, while fury was displayed on the faces of the rest, in spite of all their concern to hide it. At such times one's glances fly from face to face, trying to penetrate the very soul. In those first moments of shocked surprise and sudden upheaval those interested may take stock of all that they observe, realizing their astonishment at not finding expected qualities in some for want of intelligence or courage, and in others seeing more than they had dared to hope. Such an amalgamation of ambitious people and momentous events is a delight to those who understand, and ephemeral though it may be, it provides one of the greatest pleasures to be enjoyed at courts.

To that pursuit I therefore devoted myself, and with all the more alacrity because, while I myself had been accorded a very real deliverance by this death, I was closely bound up and engaged with the illustrious personages who could not force the tears to their eyes. Thus I rejoiced in the unalloyed gain to them, and their gratification increased my own, raising my hopes and promising me the peace of mind of which, before this sad event, I had had so little prospect, for I had never ceased to distrust the future. On the other hand, as an opponent of the cabals and almost a personal enemy of their leaders, I realized at my first keen glance and with inexpressible delight, all that was slipping from their grasp and all the troubles that would crush them. I knew so well the affairs of the different cabals, their leaders and the varying degrees of their leadership, their ramifications and sub-divisions, that several days of meditation would not have told me these things half so clearly as that first sight of faces which reminded me of others, not then seen, but none the less delectable morsels for my mind to feed upon.

I stayed for a little while longer to consider the scene in that vast and now chaotic chain of state apartments. The tumult had lasted for fully an hour, yet the Duchesse du Lude, who was in bed with the gout, had still made no appearance. Thus, finally, it was the Duc de Beauvilliers who decided that it was time to deliver the two princes from their distressingly public situation. He suggested that M. and Mme la Duchesse de Berry should retire to their own rooms and allow the Court to leave those of Mme la Duchesse de Bourgogne. His advice was at once accepted. M. le Duc de Berry moved slowly forward, partly unsupported, partly leaning on his wife. Mme de Saint-Simon, with a handful of officers from their household, attended on them. I followed, but at a distance, so that my curiosity should not be observed. The prince wished to sleep in his own room, but Mme la Duchesse de Berry refused to leave him. Indeed, he appeared so much congested, and she also, that a complete faculty of doctors, all furnished and equipped, was asked to remain with them. They spent the whole of that night in weeping and sobbing. From time to time M. le Duc de Berry asked for news from Meudon, being apparently incapable of understanding the reason for the King's departure. Sometimes he inquired whether there was no longer any ground for hope, and then wished to send for further news. Only much later in the morning was the tragic veil drawn from his eyes, so hard is it for nature and self-interest to accept the final truth. I cannot describe his state when at last realization came. The condition of Mme la Duchesse de Berry was not much better, but that did not prevent her from taking all possible care of him.

The night passed more quietly for Mgr and Mme la Duchesse de Bourgogne, and they went to bed reasonably peaceful. Mme de Levis whispered to her that since she had no cause to be afflicted it would be dreadful to see her pretending. To which she replied quite sincerely that without making any pretence she was moved by compassion and by the scenes she had witnessed, and was restrained by a sense of decency, no more. They asked some of the palace ladies to spend the remainder of the night in armchairs in their apartment. The curtains were not drawn, and before very long the room had become the temple of Morpheus. The prince and princess were soon asleep, and though they woke once or twice it was only for an instant. They rose early and without ceremony. The fountains had dried up within them; from then onwards they wept seldom and quietly, and only when the occasion demanded. The ladies who had watched and slept in their room told their friends what had occurred. No one was surprised, and since Monseigneur was no more no one was scandalized. Mme de Saint-Simon and I spent two hours alone together. At last it was common sense rather than any desire for sleep that sent us to our beds, and we slept so little that I was up and dressed by seven next morning. Nevertheless, some insomnia is sweet, and such awakenings are a delight.

Meanwhile, at Meudon, horror reigned. When the King had departed such attendants as had remained with him followed, piling themselves into whatever vehicles came to hand. In a moment Meudon became a desert; and Mlle de Lillebonne and Mlle de Melun went to Mlle Choin[1] who, isolated in her garret, was just beginning to feel the first transports of despair. She knew nothing, for no one had thought to bring her the bad news, and she realized her misfortune only when she heard the sound of lamentations. Her two friends bundled her into a hired coach that happened to be available and took her with them to Paris.

A crowd of officers and servants of Monseigneur's household, and many others besides, spent that night wandering about in the gardens. Some of the courtiers slipped away singly and on foot. There was a complete dispersal. One or two, at the most, of his valets stayed with the body, which was a most laudable action; and La Vallière,[2] the only courtier who did not abandon him living, remained with him in death. He had great difficulty in finding anyone to send for the Capuchins to pray beside the body. Decomposition set in so rapidly and so violently that it was not enough to open wide the doors and windows on to the terrace; La Vallière, the Capuchins, and the few remaining valets were forced to spend the night out of doors.

Everything earlier had been so quiet that no one had dreamed of the King's going to Marly that night. Nothing was ready for him; the keys had been mislaid; there were only a few nightlights, and no candles at all.[3] In those circumstances the King and Mme de Maintenon were obliged to sit for more than an hour in the ante-room to her apartment, with Madame la Duchesse, Mme la Princesse de Conti, and Mmes de Dangeau and Caylus, the last named having hurried from Versailles to be with her cousin.[4] She and Mme de Dangeau stood modestly in various parts of the ante-room, but for short periods only. Other ladies who arrived later remained in the salon despite all the confusion, for they did not know where else to go. For a long time they were forced to grope about in the dark without even a candle, and when the servants did at last find the keys they were so distraught that they mixed them up. Gradually, however, the bolder spirits began to show their faces in the ante-room, and then all made their appearance, partly out of curiosity, partly from a desire to show zeal. The King sat in a far corner between Mme de Maintenon and the Princesses, weeping for long stretches at a time; but at last they unlocked Mme de Maintenon's door and he was relieved from that uncomfortable situation. He entered the room alone with her and they

---

[1] Mlle Choin: Monseigneur's official mistress, a woman of no birth who never appeared in public. He was thought to have married her because she always slept with him in the State bed at Meudon.
[2] The nephew of Louis XIV's mistress.
[3] Candles in the royal residences were always new. Used ones were a perquisite of the major-domo and were removed every night. So it was in Buckingham Palace before the Prince Consort's reforms.
[4] Mme de Maintenon.

remained alone together for another hour. He then went to bed—it was nearly four o'clock—and left her a breathing space in which to recover. After his departure the rest of the party were free to find accommodation for themselves, and Blouin announced that anyone who wished to lodge at Marly should tell him, so that he might inform the King and notify those he selected.

To sum up the character of Monseigneur: it would appear that he was without vice, virtue, knowledge or understanding, and quite incapable of acquiring any such qualities. He was infinitely lazy, with no imagination or personality, no taste, no resolution, no discernment, capable only of being bored and of affecting others by his ennui. Nature fashioned him like a ball to be rolled hither and thither at the will of others. Stubborn, and in all things excessively mean, incredibly gullible and easy to prejudice, a prey to most pernicious influences, unable either to escape from them or to realize their vileness, drowning in fat and gloom, he would, albeit with no desire to do ill, have made a most abominable king.

The purples and smallpox of which he died, and the sudden infection that followed, made them think it useless as well as dangerous to open his body. He was prepared for burial, some say by the grey sisters, others by the floor-polishers of the château, or perhaps by the workmen who made the coffin, over which they threw an ancient pall belonging to the Meudon parish church. There was no other retinue than the few who had remained with him, that is to say La Vallière, some junior officers, and the Capuchins of Meudon, who took it by turns to pray over the coffin, without funeral hangings, and without lights, save a few candles. He died about midnight, between Tuesday and Wednesday. On the Thursday he was taken to Saint-Denis in one of the royal coaches, undraped and with the front window removed to allow room for the foot of the coffin. The Curé of Meudon and the chaplain-in-residence rode in the same coach, which was followed by another, also undraped, containing the Duc de La Trémoïlle his first gentleman, and M. de Metz his high-almoner, on the back seat. In front were Dreux the grand master of ceremonies, and the Abbé de Brancas who later became Bishop of Lisieux. These two coaches, accompanied by footmen and twenty-four royal pages carrying torches, formed the whole of the very short procession that left Meudon at six or seven in the evening, crossed the bridge at Sèvres and the Bois de Boulogne, and arrived at Saint-Denis by way of the Saint-Ouen plain. The body was then lowered into the royal vault without any kind of ceremony.[1]

Such was the end of a prince who for nearly fifty years allowed others to plan for him, while he, standing upon the steps of the throne, led the life of a private, not to say an obscure, individual; so much so indeed that nothing in it was

---

[1] In fact, the King asked Cardinal de Noailles for three thousand masses to be sung, and two hundred from the *Quinze-Vingts* (the famous hospital for the blind of Paris, founded by Louis IX in 1260), not to mention public prayers.

remarkable except his estate at Meudon and all that he did to beautify it. A hunter, but not for pleasure, a near-voluptuary, but without discrimination, at one time a great gambler, but only for the sake of winning, after he began to build he would stand whistling through his teeth in a corner of the salon at Marly, drumming with his fingers on the lid of his snuffbox, staring vacantly round him, observing almost nothing, without conversation or diversions, I almost feel inclined to say without either thoughts or feelings. Yet because of his high rank he was the head and centre, the soul, the very life of one of the strangest, most sinister, most secret and, despite its ramifications, most united cabals that have emerged since the Peace of the Pyrenees ended the revolt of the King's minority. I have dwelt too long on this prince, whose character almost defies description because only the surface of it was known. It would take volumes to describe even that. None the less, the subject was sufficiently interesting to warrant my enlarging on this little known Dauphin,[1] who was nothing himself, who counted for nothing in his long, vain wait for the crown, and with whose death, at last, the cord was broken on which depended so many hopes and fears and schemes.

After what has been said at various times of Monseigneur, you may easily imagine the emotions aroused within the royal family, the Court, and the public by the death of a prince whose merit lay all in his birth, and his substance all in his body. I could never discover what had endeared him to the fishwives and the rabble of Paris, unless it was his unwarranted reputation for kindness. If Mme de Maintenon had felt relieved by the death of Monsieur, she was infinitely more so after the death of Monseigneur, for his intimate circle had always aroused her worst suspicions. They had never felt for one another less than aversion; he was crushed by her presence; she was very wary of him and watched him continually, trying to discover his secret thoughts, or rather the thoughts of those who ruled him. Since the Lille campaign she had become very friendly with Mgr le Duc de Bourgogne, and her relationship with Mme la Duchesse de Bourgogne was most truly that of a wise and loving mother with the best and most affectionate of daughters. She regarded their new elevation as the guarantee of her own position, and an assurance of her future peace and comfort, no matter what might befall.

As for the King, no man was ever more prone to shed tears, less often made sad, more swiftly restored to equanimity. He must have been deeply moved by the death of a son who in his eyes had never passed the age of six, although in fact he was past fifty. Exhausted by that miserable night he slept late. When he woke, Mme la Duchesse de Bourgogne and Mme de Maintenon visited him together. He then rose, as usual, and went into his study where, taking the

---

[1] 'The Dauphin...grew up to be a merely genealogical incident at his father's court' (extract from the *Encyclopaedia Britannica*, 13th edition, article on Bossuet).

Duc de Beauvilliers and the Chancellor into the recess of one of the windows, he arranged for the rank and title of Dauphin to pass from that moment to Mgr and Mme la Duchesse de Bourgogne, to whom I shall henceforward refer in no other way. On the Thursday, he busied himself with lists for Marly, and ordered d'Antin to visit Mlle Choin to assure her of his protection and a pension of ten thousand livres, unasked; for she had not even begged to be remembered by him. Mgr and Mme la Dauphine sent her kind messages and each of them wrote to her personally. Her grief was less prolonged and less violent than might have been expected, which astonished everyone, and made them think that she was not so important as had generally been supposed.

On that same Thursday, the King received an informal visit from the Queen of England who drove from Versailles after calling on the sons of Monseigneur, accompanied by the Princess of England who made it abundantly evident by her curtsey that she gave precedence to the Dauphine only because the Dauphin was now the heir-apparent, whereas she herself still remained heiress-presumptive. The princess sat in her coach during all that Marly visit because of the foul air, on account of which the King of England had preferred to remain at Saint-Germain. On Friday the King went shooting in the park. On Saturday he held the finance council and reviewed his light cavalry on the high ground above Marly. He worked that evening with Voysin in Mme de Maintenon's room, whence he issued most shocking orders to the effect that although the Court must wear mourning for an entire year, he himself should not do so; that princes of the blood, dukes, and foreign princes, officers of the crown and other high officials should dress as though in mourning for himself; but that he should dress as usual because he had not worn mourning for Mme la Dauphine de Bavière.[1] I have now followed the King's movements until the Sunday, when Marly again became populated. It may be of no less interest to see what had happened meanwhile at Versailles.

As you may imagine, no one slept on that first night. Mgr and Madame la Dauphine attended mass together very early next morning. I arrived towards the end and followed them back to their apartments. There were very few courtiers, for no one had expected them so early; but the princess wished to be at Marly before the King was awake. They were surprisingly dry-eyed, and one could see that they thought less of Monseigneur's death than of their new status. A smile that escaped them when they were very close to me and talking very low showed this plainly enough. Yet since they scrupulously observed the decencies no one could blame them nor wish it otherwise, having regard to all the circumstances.

Their first concern was to strengthen the ties that bound them to M. le Duc de Berry, to revive his old affection for Mme la Dauphine, and strive by every gentle

---

[1] Monseigneur's late wife, the Dauphine Marie Anne Christine Victoire of Bavaria, who had died in 1690.

means to persuade Mme la Duchesse de Berry to forget her past bad behaviour, and make easy the new difference in rank. In that pleasant frame of mind nothing was too much trouble. They called on Mme la Duchesse de Berry in bed as soon as they were dressed, which was very early indeed, and Madame la Dauphine returned to her after dinner. M. le Duc de Berry, whose attachment to his brother had never been shaken, was despite his grief much moved by these loving advances, so promptly made, so unsuited to the new difference in their rank. Most of all he was moved by Madame la Dauphine's gesture, for he had rightly been feeling for some time past that he had ceased to merit so much kindness.

Mme la Duchesse de Berry repaid them with tears, embraces, and soft words. Her royal heart, always supposing that she had one, was very conscious of the past and she was shaken to the core by this display of generous kindness. Energy, uncontrolled and tending towards violence, over which religion had no power, left no outlet for her emotions except anger. She had deluded herself into believing that provided she restrained herself in every way in order to secure her brilliant marriage she would be able afterwards to do as she pleased, a state of affairs of which she was perfectly convinced. Having absolute ascendancy over M. le Duc d'Orléans and over a husband in the first raptures of his passion, she had no difficulty in shrugging off a mother too wise to meddle in an all too familiar situation. With Madame, her grandmother, good for nothing except formal appearances at the Court on state occasions or at family reunions, she had no one who could act as a mother-in-law. Her lady-in-waiting greatly disliked serving her, and had been coerced into accepting the post on condition of being required only for ceremonial duties, never for those of a governess. The whole responsibility for her conduct thus fell on Mme la Duchesse de Bourgogne. It had at first amused her to act as chaperone; and she was the more inclined to make a pet of the bride because she herself had raised her to her high position. Disillusionment soon followed. A thousand stories might be told on that subject, but as time went on they lost their significance because the full gravity of the situation became revealed. Suffice it to say that Mme la Duchesse de Bourgogne, so gentle and kind, was perhaps too much so to be capable of using the curb, while Mme la Duchesse de Berry was so intractable that she would not endure even the mildest rebuke. Resentful at finding herself part of someone else's court; rebellious at ceremonial, irked by the fixed routine, the tedious duties, the demands, especially that of showing gratitude, she was not assisted by her lack of discipline in childhood, her depravity, her tantrums or, as they called it, her temperament, which was still further aggravated by the reading of pernicious books.

Thus when the King made of them two separate households both ladies were

thankful to be released from the obligation of dining together, and the King's
servants were vastly relieved at no longer having to wait on the bride. One story
out of many will serve as an illustration. One morning a newly appointed usher
of the King's bedchamber was attending her while she finished dressing, when
Mme la Duchesse d'Orléans suddenly arrived to make some necessary adjustment.
This usher, from carelessness or inexperience, opened both sides of the double door
to let her enter; whereupon Mme la Duchesse de Berry flushed crimson, trembled
with rage, and proceeded to welcome her mother with remarkably little warmth.
As soon as she had gone, the princess summoned Mme de Saint-Simon, asked furiously if she had witnessed the man's insolence, and bade her have him immediately
suspended. Mme de Saint-Simon recognized his offence, promised that it should
not occur again, and that in future the double doors be opened only for the King's
children. As for suspending one of his gentlemen, only lent to her for her service,
because he had shown too much honour to her lady-mother, she might think it
best to confine herself to a reproof. Mme la Duchesse de Berry insisted, wept,
flew into a passion. My wife allowed her to vent her rage, then quietly rebuked
the usher and taught him his duty.

Sunday, 18 April, saw the end of the King's retirement. The royal family and
those selected from among the applicants for lodgings repopulated Marly, which
for four days had been a desert. It was announced that the King would stay three
months, so as to escape from the foul air of Versailles, and that on Monday, 19
April, he would receive the silent condolence of the Court, everyone wearing
mourning mantles and mantillas. M. du Maine, as you have already seen, had
lost no time in acquiring rank as princes of the blood for his sons after the deaths
of the only princes strong enough to oppose him.[1] He felt far more secure now
that Monseigneur too was dead. Only Mgr le Duc de Bourgogne remained, and
although this should have been more than enough to check him, he perhaps dared
to hope for his death also, since he had witnessed that of his father. In the meantime
he sought to further his ambitions. He well knew M. le Duc d'Orléans's weakness
and lethargy; he knew M. le Duc de Berry's nature; he thus believed that with the
aid of Mme de Maintenon he had nothing to fear in the present and might safely
allow the future to take care of itself. It so happened that the Duc de Tresmes was in
waiting that year, which was a stroke of luck for M. du Maine; for although a man
of the utmost integrity he had not the smallest knowledge of the Court and Society,
and in many other ways was abysmally ignorant. What is more, he was as servile
as any lackey and more eager than the dullest country bumpkin to pay his court.
That being so, he was at M. du Maine's command. Now it was part of de Tresmes's
duty to announce the procedure for these visits of condolence. He raised with

[1] The late Prince de Conti, the late Monsieur le Prince, and the late Monsieur le Duc.

the King the question of whether the bastards should stand in the line to receive the visitors on the pretext of having been Monseigneur's brothers and sisters. King Louis thought it preposterous, but uttered no flat prohibition, which was all that M. du Maine had dared to hope. Nothing was settled, but it was already much not to have met with a firm refusal, and Mme de Maintenon was wise enough to leave well alone. So the affair stood until the Monday morning; but between the meeting of the council and the King's dinner M. du Maine gained his point and the Duc de Tresmes announced the orders accordingly. So great was the amazement that most people asked for them to be repeated. The moment had been well chosen because the King had just sat down to table; all the rest were either at dinner or on their way to dine, and the visits were fixed to begin immediately after two o'clock. There was no time to argue, much less to object. Everyone obeyed with a blind, unwilling obedience that had become all too familiar. Thus by a sly trick the bastards stood, and were accepted, on a level with the Children of France, with results which the King did not live long enough to discover.

At half-past two the King ordered the doors of his two studies to be flung open. One entered through his bedroom. He was wearing ordinary morning dress but held his hat under his arm, and stood with his right hand resting on the table, in the study nearest to the door of his bedroom. Mgr and Mme la Dauphine, M. and Mme la Duchesse de Berry, M. and Mme la Duchesse d'Orléans, Madame la Princesse, Madame la Duchesse with two sons and two daughters, M. du Maine, and the Comte de Toulouse entered in procession and formed a wide semi-circle before the King. All wore long mantles and mantillas with the exception of the widows, who wore only short veils. The Dowager Mme la Princesse de Conti was ill in bed, the other Princesse de Conti[1] and her children had remained in Paris on account of the bad air from the smallpox, and Mme du Maine and her family were absent at Sceaux for the same reason. All Society, dressed as for a funeral, and all Marly crowded into the drawing-rooms and the King's bedroom. Twelve or fifteen duchesses entered first in line, then ladies, titled or untitled, in no particular order, with among them some of the foreign princesses who, contrary to their usual custom, had not taken care to arrive early. After the ladies came the Archbishop of Rheims, followed by about fifteen dukes in order of rank, and after them the men, titled and untitled, with foreign princes and prelates mingling with them haphazard. Four or five fathers and sons of the Rohan family formed themselves up in order of seniority towards the middle of the line, but some gentlemen who perceived this contrivance stepped between them, and in the end they, too, were out of order when they entered the study. Each person walked straight up to the King, and when still at some distance made a very low bow, which he returned

---

[1] The Princesse de Conti referred to here is Marie Thérèse de Bourbon-Condé (1666-1732), widow of the Prince de Conti who died in 1709, not her sister-in-law, called the Dowager, who was his elder brother's widow.

with marked courtesy to every titled person, man or woman, but not to anyone else at all. Once one had made one's bow, one went slowly into the adjoining study and then out by the little anteroom before the chapel.

Mantillas and long mantles used to be the prerogative of people of a certain rank, but that distinction has disappeared with so many others; thus many passed before the King whom neither he nor anyone in the royal circle recognized, and not even members of the Court could say who they were. Men of the gown[1] were also among them, which looked most unseemly. It would be hard to credit that this multitude of strange faces, and their complicated vestments, produced no absurdity to upset the gravity of that solemn occasion. They did so indeed, and the King was often hard put to it to conceal a smile, and at one moment succumbed entirely, together with all the company present, when some nonentity filed past him having lost most of his mourning garments. When after a very long time all was over in the King's study, those who were entitled to be visited returned to their own rooms to receive callers. The Sons and Daughters of France received, and the male and female bastards; also, and this did seem rather comical, M. le Duc d'Orléans, as Mme la Duchesse d'Orléans's husband. Juniors in rank or age called on their seniors, who did not return their calls. The sole exception was Madame, because of her position as the widow of Madame la Dauphine's grandfather,[2] and the grandmother of Mme la Duchesse de Berry. She was visited by all the Sons and Daughters of France, but not by M. and Mme la Duchesse d'Orléans. One made one's way as best one could on this round of visits, entering and leaving in no settled order, simply passing through, in by one door and out by another, wherever it seemed least congested. That was how, owing to the crush and Madame la Princesse's sly ruse, the following incident was possible. When one left Madame la Duchesse, a gap having appeared in the doorway of her boudoir, one suddenly found oneself in the presence of Madame la Princesse, all prepared to acknowledge bows and curtseys that were neither hers by right nor ordered for her. Many people were taken by surprise; others pretended not to notice her.

The Duc du Maine and the Comte de Toulouse received their visitors standing together in M. du Maine's room, which one entered from the garden. Having gained their point they were determined to seem modest and considerate by not obliging people to visit them each separately. M. du Maine nearly fell over backwards making excuses for the trouble they were giving, and half-killed himself escorting titled persons to the door and paying them compliments. M. le Comte de Toulouse also escorted certain visitors to the door with sufficient courtesy but

---

[1] Members of the Parlement and the Palais de Justice, whose black academic gowns stood out in sharp contrast to the gay scarlets and blues of the courtiers and soldiers.
[2] The Dauphine was Monsieur's granddaughter by his first wife, Henrietta of England.

less ostentation. I forgot to mention Mme de Vendôme, who had also filed past the King. She was not visited because the bastardy in her husband's family was not so recent, but she did not lie in ambush like her mother Madame la Princesse. Neither the King nor any of the princes sat to receive their callers. Had one sat down with them as one had the right to do, there would have been no end to the visits and many a somersault over empty chairs, on account of the crush and the small size of the rooms.

On the following day, Tuesday, 21 April, Mgr and Madame la Dauphine, M. and Mme la Duchesse de Berry, Madame, and M. and Mme la Duchesse d'Orléans went in one coach after dinner to call at Saint-Germain, all wearing mantillas and long mantles. They first went to visit the King of England, but did not sit; afterwards they visited the queen and sat in six armchairs. M. and Mme la Duchesse d'Orléans were given only folding stools. Monsieur du Maine was present, but only for the honour, and to be treated on a par with a Grandson of France. The Queen of England excused herself for not wearing a mantilla to receive them; that is to say, she wore only a short veil because, in France at least, widows never wore mantillas. She added that the King had expressly forbidden it in her case. That excuse was considered to be the very height of courtesy. King Louis, who was always most careful to protect the English queen from ever feeling her unhappy situation, would never have allowed her to wear a mantilla, nor the King of England a mantle, when receiving State visits of condolence for a Dauphin who had not reigned. As the party was leaving they expressed a wish to visit the Princess of England; but that the queen would not permit, and sent to summon her instead. She appeared highly gratified that such a courtesy had been proposed. From that time onward no one sat. The princess, like her mother, wore no mantilla; she could not sit in an armchair in her mother's presence, and the Children of France could neither be without armchairs when the queen was seated, nor retain them when the Princess of England had only a stool. Next day, the King went to Versailles at eleven in the morning to receive the condolences of the foreign ambassadors and afterwards the members of the various religious orders. Then, after dining in private, he listened to harangues by the Parlement, the Chambre des Comptes and the Cour des Aides. He returned that same evening to Marly.

At this time I lost a friend whom I most deeply mourned, namely the Duchesse de Villeroy who has been mentioned more than once in the course of these memoirs. Honest, unaffected, frank, loyal and secret; despite her little wit, she succeeded in making herself redoubted at the Court, and ruled both her husband and her father-in-law. She was proud in every conceivable way, especially of her rank; yet at the same time was so arrogantly and publicly conscious of her birth,[1] even compared with her husband's, that it sometimes embarrassed him. Her temper was uneven; I myself never fell a victim to it, but she was subject to moods and was brusque and harsh in her manner—a characteristic of all her family. She was a great crony of Mme la Duchesse d'Orléans, and had been so for many years past, she also enjoyed the entire confidence of Madame la Dauphine; both of them were fond of her and feared her not a little. She had many friends of both sexes and deserved them. In friendship she was kind, loyal, ardent, very ready to break the ice. In her later years she became something of a personage; people felt that they dared not ignore her. Her appearance was truly remarkable; for while the lower part of her face was most disagreeable, more especially when she smiled, it was truly charming above her mouth. She was tall, stately, and splendidly attired; no one at the Court had a nobler air, and although her hips were too high and her shoulders also, no one better graced the balls and entertainments. No beauty, not even women far handsomer than she, could hold a candle to her. A few months before her death, when she was still in radiant health, she told Mme de Saint-Simon that she had been altogether too fortunate in her life, for whichever way she turned her happiness was complete. She said that this alarmed her, for such an enviable condition could not endure and she feared either some un-looked for disaster or approaching death. It was the second that overtook her.

Her husband was in residence as captain of the guard, replacing the Maréchal de Boufflers, who was in Paris on account of his son's death. She, herself, greatly feared smallpox, having never suffered an attack. She none the less insisted on Mme la Dauphine's taking her to Marly in the first days of the King's retreat, on the pretext that she must see her husband. Nothing would dissuade her, so avid do people become for petty distinctions at the Court. Yet all the time she was mortally afraid; immediately afterwards contracted the disease, and died of it at Versailles. The Abbé de Louvois and the Duc de Villeroy went into quarantine with her. The former remained inconsolable, the latter was not so for long, for he soon enjoyed the sensation of being his own master. He was, however, not born to be that, and all too soon his father had him once more in leading strings.

The Emperor[2] also died at this time and of the same malady; but few lamented him. He was a prince with a most violent temper, below the average in wit and capability; showed little esteem for his mother the late Empress,[3] no tenderness for his wife,[4] and scant respect or affection for his brother the Archduke.

---

[1] She was born Le Tellier, a daughter of Louvois.
[2] Joseph I (1678-1711), Holy Roman Emperor from 1705.
[3] His mother was the Empress Eleonora Madeleine Theresa, Countess Palatine of Neuburg, third wife of the Emperor Leopold I.
[4] His wife was Wilhelmina Amalia of Brunswick-Lüneburg (later Hanover).

His court was a dangerous place where even the greatest could not feel secure. Prince Eugene may have been the only loser by his death, for he had enjoyed his confidence and was on abominably bad terms with the Archduke, who blamed the prince for assisting him so little at Vienna and could not forgive him for refusing to go to Spain. Their quarrel had of necessity been smoothed over; but Prince Eugene never became reconciled with him. For France, the Emperor's death was a great event and a piece of unexpected good fortune that finally led to a peace and the preservation of the Spanish monarchy. I shall not pause here to relate the important consequences that eventually led to the signing of the peace treaty, first at Utrecht, then by the new Emperor. It were better to read of these events in the documents, rather than as recounted by me, for there they are written by a master hand. Suffice it merely to say that Torcy immediately visited the Elector of Bavaria and spent an entire day with him.

Never were changes so complete as those which were caused at the Court by the death of Monseigneur. You have already seen the difference in the new Dauphin and his wife, in M. le Duc de Berry's sentiments and in those of his duchess, in the position of M. and Mme la Duchesse d'Orléans, and in the heart of Mme de Maintenon, who was relieved of all cares in the present and of all anxiety for the future. M. du Maine readily shared his old governess's feelings, for he had never been on good terms with Monseigneur, and had been shaken by the latter's objections to his various elevations. With the new Dauphin and Mme la Dauphine he was far from feeling secure, but there the situation was different. M. le Duc d'Orléans's easy-going nature appeared to the Duc du Maine more of an advantage than a hindrance. He was beginning to enjoy an unaccustomed tranquillity when, at Marly, a few nights later, he was seized by a fearful illness. His valet heard him gasping for breath, and found him unconscious. He cried for help. Mme la Duchesse d'Orléans rushed weeping to her brother's side, Madame la Duchesse and her daughters came for the sake of propriety, and many others appeared to pay their court, hoping that the King would learn of their zeal. M. du Maine was bled and deluged with remedies because none proved immediately successful. Fagon, who took all of two hours to dress by slow degrees, arrived four hours late on account of his nightly sweats. It was he who was most in demand on this occasion, because he knew the disease by personal experience, though he had never suffered so extreme an attack. He grumbled loudly at the bleeding and other remedies. They discussed whether or not to tell the King, but the majority were against disturbing him. King Louis thus learned at his *petit lever* of the alarms and excursions in the night; by that time there had already been a marked improvement. As soon as he was dressed he went to see this cherished son, and visited him twice a day until he was well again. All this time Mme du

Maine had remained in her pleasure-palace at Sceaux, saying that it would certainly kill her to see M. du Maine in such a state. He, having grown accustomed to approve servilely of all her doings, greatly praised her conduct, and went to visit her as soon as he was able to walk.

At Versailles, few personalities emerged at a first glance, and even these few were hard to perceive, so carefully did they conceal themselves. None the less, as you may well believe, there was a scramble to rally behind the new powers and the great men about to receive recognition. You will easily understand the feelings of the Duc de Beauvilliers, the only man for whom Monseigneur conceived so strong an aversion that he could by no means hide it. Beauvilliers now watched the elevation of a pupil who loved to consider himself still in the same status, and publicly showed that nothing had changed between them. A great lover of his country, most sincere in his desire to promote religious truth, he now saw himself on the threshold of doing useful service to both, above all of preparing for the return of his beloved Fénelon, and afterwards of becoming his collaborator in everything. Amid his simplicity and truly saintly piety, some remnant of human weakness made him suddenly light of heart, lending him fresh courage for the worthy plans for which, until then, he had had little zest—a kind of inspiration seized him, all the more delightful to behold because it came to him so seldom. Chevreuse, his inseparable companion, rejoiced with him and for the same reasons. Both their families and their friends were gladdened by this consolidation of their fortunes and by the prospect of fame that would not be long in coming. The man, however, above all others affected by Monseigneur's death was Fénelon, Archbishop of Cambrai.

That prelate, confined for the past twelve years to his diocese, was, as the years passed uneventfully by for him, growing old beneath the weight of disappointed hopes. He was still anathema to the King, even worse hated by Mme de Maintenon because he had once been her man, and remained the chief target for the abuse of that evil cabal that had ruled Monseigneur. Thus he was left with no other support than the unswerving devotion of his former pupil, himself a victim of that odious cabal and, by the laws of nature, likely for a long time to remain so—for too long, at least, to give his old tutor any hope of escaping from his death in life. Now, in the twinkling of an eye, his pupil had become the Dauphin, enjoying, as we have seen, a kind of foretaste of his coming reign. What a transformation for an ambitious man! I have described Fénelon as he was before his downfall; *Télémaque,*[1] the famous work that served most of all to plunge him deeper in disfavour and render him unforgivable, portrays him to the life. None the less, and although you are now better acquainted with that prelate who was regarded with awe even in the deepest

[1] *Les Aventures de Télémaque,* 1699, Fénelon's epic-novel written for the education of the Duc de Bourgogne.

disgrace and exile, and was, in himself, a most remarkable character, it may be as well to add something further at this point.

With all his social graces and his appearance of worldliness, Fénelon, in exile, fulfilled all his duties as bishop as though he had no other cares to distract him. He visited hospitals, gave alms generously but judiciously, attended to his clergy and religious houses. Nothing escaped his eye. He said mass every day in his chapel, often officiated at church services, performed all his episcopal functions without needing to be reminded of them, and often preached. He found time for everything yet never seemed busy. His open house and generous table gave the impression of the residence of a governor of Flanders;[1] yet in every way it was becoming to the Church. Always there were famous generals lodging with him, and many other officers, healthy, sick or wounded, all supplied and cared for as though each was his only guest; and he was usually present at consultations with the doctors and surgeons, behaving like the kindest of chaplains, going often to the hospitals and alms-houses, never neglectful, never grudging, always gentle and open-handed. He was loved by all and sundry. Yet that benign image was not the whole picture; for it must also be said that he deliberately sought out those who were capable of restoring his fortunes and bringing him to the seat of power. He was intimately bound up with that section of the Jesuits, headed by Père Tellier, which, never deserting him, had even gone out of their way to give him support. Latterly he had written much calculated to strengthen their union and at the same time, as he hoped, to please the King. To be kept silent in the councils of the Church was the natural fate of a bishop whose doctrine was formally condemned; he had too much intelligence to resent that, and was too ambitious to heed the voices raised against him in the Church, not to mention those others who assailed him for reasons which the enlightened could readily comprehend. He steadily persisted, never shifting his aim, giving his friends occasion to speak of him, flattering Rome that had so ill-used him, persuading the entire Society of Jesus to regard him as capable of rendering the highest kind of service—a prelate for whom no effort should be spared. In the end he had managed to make friends even with La Chétardie, the imbecile director, nay the master, of Mme de Maintenon's conscience.

In the current pen-battles Fénelon had invariably been gentle of word. His passionate desire for popularity had prevented his joining in a war of action. The Low Countries teemed with Jansenists, and with those reputed so to be; his own diocese and the town of Cambrai were full of them, and such people regarded both as havens of peace and refuge. Happy in finding security with one of their

---

[1] Fénelon's arch-diocese of Cambrai included the dioceses of Arras and Saint-Omer, in France, and Tournai and Namur, in the Spanish Netherlands.

pen-enemies, they took nothing amiss that Fénelon either did or wrote, and although he much disapproved of their doctrine he left them alone. Their blows were aimed at other prelates, and nothing that they said tended to lessen the general devotion to Fénelon himself. He thus, with enormous skill, had managed to preserve his reputation as a quiet, peace-loving Man of God, without losing that of an archbishop with great capabilities, whom it was in the Church's best interests to support.

Such was the Archbishop of Cambrai's situation when he learned of Monseigneur's death, the sudden elevation of his former pupil, and the new importance of his greatest friends. No bond was ever stronger or more solid than that which united the Little Flock, based, as it was, on loyal and profound mutual trust, similar in its essence, so they believed, to the love of God and of his Church. Nearly all of them, great and small, were persons of exceptional merit, save for one or two who merely presented that appearance and were accepted by the rest in good faith. They had one aim, which no amount of disgrace could deflect; they advanced steadily towards one goal, the return to power of Fénelon, their leader. Until that time they lived and breathed for him alone, thinking and acting in everything according to his teaching, receiving his word on all subjects as though he were the very mouthpiece of God. What may not such charm effect when it captures the hearts of excellent and highly intelligent persons, more especially when they are convinced that it is of divine inspiration, containing in its essence, piety, virtue, the worship of God, the protection of His Church, and the salvation of souls? You will now readily understand the powerful influence exerted by the Archbishop of Cambrai over the Dukes of Chevreuse and Beauvilliers and their wives, who were one with them in everything. It was probably only out of consideration for Fénelon that the Duc de Beauvilliers did not go into complete retirement after the death of his sons. M. de Chevreuse and he both longed for seclusion, and that longing had latterly become so intense that their private lives were totally unsuited to their high employments. Only a genuine desire to work for the glory of God, the Church, and their own salvation kept them still in office, for they sincerely thought it their duty to remain where they might grasp some opportunity to bring about the return of their spiritual father. The sudden change effected by Monseigneur's death seemed to them an act of Providence specially designed for the benefit of Monsieur de Cambrai, something for which they had patiently waited, with no prospect of its ever coming to pass—the reward of the righteous who live by faith, never giving up hope, and are delivered at last.

It is true that I never heard them speak in this way, but to those who like myself belonged to their intimate circle, the pattern of their lives and sentiments was so consistent that to understand them was more a matter of observation than practical evidence. In matters of religion they were extraordinarily secretive, discussing them only with other devotees of proven loyalty and discretion, admitting no new converts for fear of making mistakes, and at ease only within their own close circle—an environment so dear to them that they preferred it to any other. It was thus that the more than brotherly love of the Dukes and Duchesses of Chevreuse and Beauvilliers for one another had first arisen; it was the cause of their private retreats to Vaucresson at every weekend, accompanied by a very small group of humble and most carefully selected disciples. It was the reason for their almost cloistral seclusion at the Court and their extreme devotion to the new Dauphin, whom they had carefully trained to share their beliefs, and whom they regarded as a second Ezra, rebuilder of the Temple and guardian of the Chosen People after their captivity.

Amid the Little Flock was a member from earlier days, one who had been given her first instruction by M. Bertau,[1] at his classes in the Abbaye de Montmartre, to which she had gone every week in company with M. de Noailles, who was shrewd enough to extricate himself in time. This lady was the Duchesse de Béthune, who had daily increased in piety until she became Mme Guyon's best pupil. She was regarded by them all as a very saint, revered even by M. de Cambrai, and venerating him only out of humility and the consciousness that hers was the weaker sex. In that group she became the dear friend of both duchesses and of their husbands, and was treated by them with immense respect. The Duc de Béthune, her husband, was a mere kitchen-brother,[2] tolerated only for his wife's sake; but their son the Duc de Charost reaped all the benefit of his mother's saintliness. He was upright and honourable, with every additional merit to be won by feats of arms, and an entire devotion to M. de Cambrai formed the basis of his character. Moreover, he was exceedingly ambitious, jealous in proportion, and a lover of the highest Society, which he perfectly adorned. He was cut out for the world of fashion, not at all for that of affairs, since he had had no kind of education, not even in religion, save of the variety peculiar to the Little Flock. He was loyal and very capable of true friendship, for he was amazingly secret despite an almost intolerable verbosity inherited from his father. He was perhaps the only man to combine successfully a professed and lifelong devotion to religion with the boon companionship of the worst libertines of his day, and real friendship with some of them. But indeed, they all sought his friendship and included him in every adventure except debauches, not only without mocking him for his austerity but (I speak here of the best and gayest Society of the Court and the army) freely accepting him and restraining themselves for his sake. He was truly most excellent company, brave and gay, with ideas and turns of speech that were a constant pleasure. M. de Beauvilliers had long wished M. de Charost to be my friend,

---

[1] A priest of the Oratory; his was the chief responsibility for starting Mme Guyon on her perilous career.
[2] *Frère Coupe-choux* (Brother Cut-cabbage), the lowest form of life in a religious order.

and once we had become acquainted we did develop a close and lasting friendship. I never knew Monsieur de Cambrai, for at the time when he lost favour I had scarcely entered Society, and I never exposed myself to the mysteries of the Little Flock; thus in the estimation of the Dukes of Chevreuse and Beauvilliers I rated in merit much below the Duc de Charost. None the less, he knew them only as an initiate of their beliefs, whereas to me they gave their entire confidence in matters concerning State affairs, the Court, and the guidance of the new Dauphin. They never spoke to me of religion, although they were quite open regarding their love and admiration of Monsieur de Cambrai and their plans for his return. It was not until some years later that I perceived they did not give Charost their confidence to the same extent; indeed, he often complained to me of their secretiveness. I was of course most careful not to let him know that they were less guarded with me, but, surprised at their different treatment of a man much older than myself[1] and their intimate friend, I began to seek for a cause. Charost's energy was all physical. He was far better known in Society than I, but had very little understanding of State affairs, or of what was afoot in the secret and powerful cabals. He was therefore quite ignorant of the workings of the Court, which I learned of through my links with the principal personages of both sexes and my passion for discovering, unravelling, and generally keeping up to date with intrigues that were always fascinating, and which it was often useful, and sometimes highly advantageous, to know. Mme de Saint-Simon also was fully trusted by MM. and Mmes de Chevreuse and de Beauvilliers, who held a very high opinion of her virtue, conduct, character and intelligence. I was thus able to discuss everything with them, and especially those matters in which the Duc de Chevreuse did not shine. Lastly, as you already know, I had had occasion to warn them in advance of affairs, not clearly visible at the time but of vital importance later, which they found hard to believe even when they happened exactly as I had foretold.[2] That had set the seal on their confidence in me, for they had received many proofs of my true and disinterested friendship. It was thus an immense satisfaction for me to be the one person at the Court held in entire confidence and affection by those who were bound to be the most powerful influences with the new Dauphin who would set the tone in all things. The more my intimate connection with these persons became apparent, the more careful I was not to show gratification or appear self-important, but above all to conduct myself exactly as I had done before. From all these revolutionary changes at the Court I concluded that two men, the Dukes of Beauvilliers and Chevreuse, stood to gain immediately, and

[1] In 1711, Saint-Simon was thirty-six years old, the Duc de Béthune-Charost was forty-eight.
[2] Referring to his prophecy that the Duc de Bourgogne's service with Vendôme in Flanders, in 1708, would be disastrous for his reputation and make him a victim of calumny.

that a third, the Archbishop of Cambrai, was likely to benefit in the more distant future.

The dukes' first piece of advice to the Dauphin was to be more prudent than ever, and to adopt a still more submissive air in the King's presence, so as to disarm the jealousy which his grandfather had allowed himself to show on more than one occasion. Magnificently reinforced by his clever wife, he redoubled his attentions to Mme de Maintenon, who was so much gratified to find a Dauphin on whom she could rely in the place of one who had hated her that she surrendered to him completely, and in so doing won for him the King's affection also. In the very first fortnight after Monseigneur's death, the company at Marly perceived an extraordinary change come over the King, who was used to being cold and formal with his legitimate descendants. Encouraged by his advances, the Dauphin began to show more confidence in Society, which he had feared in his father's lifetime because, despite his august rank, gibes against him were received with applause. That had been one cause of his extreme shyness, and his habit of shutting himself into his study, where alone he could feel safe and at ease.

Fully accepted by the King, with Society respectfully eager to serve him and the insolent cabal dispersed, this prince hitherto so timid, dour, and constrained might be seen joining in social activities, becoming increasingly self-confident, dignified, grave and affable. One saw him acting host in the salon at Marly, and during recreation, like a god in his temple, presiding over a circle of adoring courtiers, graciously receiving their tributes and acknowledging them with quiet courtesy. Hunting ceased to be his only topic of conversation; he began to delight the more serious with his pleasant, edifying talks on current affairs, and left the rest all admiration. Anecdotes of a suitable nature when the occasion offered, happy similes, always discreet and inserted without contrivance, interludes of relaxation, even of amusement, sometimes, but very rarely, interspersed with learned quotations appearing like sudden flashes from a richly stocked mind, opened all eyes and ears and hearts to give him welcome.

Gracious to all, he none the less paid proper attention to the claims of rank, birth, age, and experience (qualities for too long dishonoured by the baser elements at the Court), rendering to each his due with a courtesy greatly enhanced by dignity. Amid the general rejoicing, no one dared to hold back; people wondered that it could be the same man, that it was not all a dream. From the Court to Paris, from Paris to the most distant provinces, reports of the change flew so fast that those few who had always loved him could scarcely believe their ears.

This would be the right moment to explain my own situation with the Dauphin, and the great trust reposed in me in preparing for a future, in which the Duc de Beauvilliers, the Dauphin, and the Duc de Chevreuse all wished me to play a part. The circumstances are vitally interesting, but I must first sweep some litter from the path—a task I would gladly avoid did it not form an essential prelude to what follows.

You will recollect the Marquis de Montrevel's continual encroachments on my authority at Blaye, as a result of which I was unable to visit my governorship. By 1709, I had become so discouraged that I resolved to leave the Court for ever; yet by the end of that year I was more firmly established than ever before. When Chamillart handed over the finances to Desmaretz he issued a decree concerning the coastguard officers, whose military and inherited commissions, like everything else emanating from the finance department, were made to seem more attractive by rights and privileges artfully calculated to extract purchase money from foolish young Frenchmen who never tire of chasing after such trifles. This disgraceful piece of chicanery was then given to Pontchartrain so that he might extract profit for the navy, and he, ever anxious to extend his power, acted immediately. First he raised the price of the commissions; then he changed the wording of the order to suit his own interests, and lastly inserted a clause whereby coastguard officers became answerable not to local governors as heretofore, but to admirals and the navy office.

[*There now ensued a violent quarrel with Pontchartrain for tampering with Saint-Simon's authority in his precious governorship, which he had inherited from his father, and regarded much as Naboth must have done his vineyard. The hour-by-hour description of his feud with the 'black-hearted, deceitful, ungrateful and wantonly spiteful' Pontchartrain occupies eleven furious pages of the Pléiade edition, and appears now very like a storm in a teacup. In the end, Mme de Saint-Simon and the Chancellor managed between them to calm him, and he was persuaded to purchase for himself and his descendants the Blaye captaincy. So the matter ended. But never afterwards did he willingly speak to Pontchartrain.*]

On 8 May, *lansquenet* and other games were again played at Marly, which had become sadly depopulated after Monseigneur's death put an end to such diversions. Mme la Dauphine had been reduced to snakes and ladders[1] in her bedroom, for want of better entertainment; for she did not play cards in the salon until another week had passed. Thereafter Marly returned to normal. The King spent his Whitsun there for the first time, because smallpox was still raging at Versailles. There was no ceremony of the Order.[2]

The Duc de Beauvilliers gloried in his pupil's elevation. No longer afraid of Monseigneur's court, he dared to speak more frankly to the King, especially now that, with Mme de Maintenon's encouragement, King Louis had decided to trust

---

[1] *L'Oie* (goose), an early form of the game. The board was covered with goose-feathers pointing either up or down.
[2] Near this place in the manuscript is what appears to be a circle of teardrops surrounding a cross, and it is supposed that his wife's death interrupted his revision at that point. One may well imagine his grief. He did not work again for six months.

his grandson. M. de Beauvilliers now walked with head erect, showing the weight of his years less plainly; his manner was less formal, his moments of relaxation longer and more frequent; in conversation he seemed at ease, quite unlike his old self. An extraordinary change came over him; he was firm, brisk, vigorous, driving straight to the point, brushing objections aside. Together we passed the entire Court under review without his once exclaiming at my frankness or disputing my assertions. It seemed as though he remembered my candour on other occasions and how often I was better informed than himself as to the true nature of certain individuals, which charity and distance had concealed from him. I discovered that he, too, had a rooted aversion for Pontchartrain, which might have gratified me had I not been alarmed for the Chancellor and his wife, whom I truly loved and esteemed, and for the children of Pontchartrain's first wife,[1] so nearly related to my own. I dreaded misfortune coming to them, for I already imagined the Chancellor dismissed, or resigning broken-hearted at his own request.

I had told no one of my own feelings, especially not M. de Beauvilliers, knowing him to be on bad terms with the Chancellor; but he spoke very frankly to me of them both—in fact unbosomed himself completely. The difference in our ages[2] made no barrier now; our candour on every subject was reciprocal and constant. He was sure of my discretion and, I may also say, of my integrity; my devotion and loyalty to himself without fear or favour he could never have doubted, for he had been my intimate friend ever since I first arrived at the Court at the age of sixteen, when my great desire to marry his daughter had brought us together. Our review of the entire Court, which I have already mentioned, led us to discuss those whom it would be wise to bring near or keep far from the Dauphin. Paris then became our subject; we spoke of the men of the gown, not considering how to place persons whose rank made that unimportant, but to agree concerning their merits, in order to praise some and disparage others in the Dauphin's hearing. Four or five long conversations at short intervals, tête-à-tête (a fact which I mention especially because the Duc de Chevreuse was never present), brought us to an end of these important matters, and another discussion followed soon after in which we dealt with all those who took part in the affairs of State.

I had warned M. de Beauvilliers some time earlier that a close attachment was being formed between d'Antin and Torcy, encouraged by the latter's sister Mme de Bouzols, a hideous creature but still charming, a past mistress in intrigue, and a lifelong crony of Madame la Duchesse. Nothing, except d'Antin himself, was more respulsive to the Duc de Beauvilliers than the cabal of Madame

[1] Pontchartrain's wife Eléonore de La Rochefoucauld-Roye (Mlle Chefboutonne) was Mme de Saint-Simon's first cousin, her mother the Comtesse de Roye having been the Maréchal de Lorges's sister. She died in 1708.
[2] Saint-Simon was thirty-six, Beauvilliers sixty-three.

la Duchesse. He cared as little for Torcy, but like the wise and moderate men that they were they preserved the decencies. You already know of M. de Beauvilliers's extraordinary piety, and of his passion for Mme Guyon, and especially for Monsieur de Cambrai and his Little Flock, a devotion that more than once had nearly ruined him, but was none the less strong on that account. As a result he also favoured the Jesuits and the clergy of Saint Sulpice, who never at any time had deserted that prelate. Thus he was blind to all concerning Rome, and in regard to Jansenism was both blind and deaf. The King grew more credulous as he aged. Hearing no other views on Church affairs, of which he was supremely ignorant, he fell a prey to the Jesuits and the directors of Mme de Maintenon's conscience, speaking through her lips. Thus Rome and the Jesuits gained ground continually, encouraged at every turn by M. de Beauvilliers. Torcy thought differently; he attached immense importance to defending the rights of the Crown and the freedoms of the Gallican Church, and was fully alive to Jesuitical trickery and the vulgarity of Saint-Sulpice. Thus at the Council he often opposed the Duc de Beauvilliers. Torcy was exceedingly well informed, a man of wit, honour, integrity, and learning. He spoke quietly, with restraint, almost modestly, saying only what was required, but saying it well because he had a gift for both oratory and writing. Most often reason was on his side.

M. de Beauvilliers came last but one in the order of voting. It was almost more than he could endure to have to listen to Torcy, and he found it still worse to be obliged to differ from him, especially since his opinion was usually that of the other ministers. Worst of all was that this brought him under fire from the Chancellor, who spoke after him and never spared him, sometimes to the point of downright rudeness. Beauvilliers thus came to think of his colleagues as being united in religious matters, with the Chancellor providing ammunition for Torcy and reinforcing him with all the might of his wit, independence, and authority. M. de Beauvilliers called this Jansenism, and to his mind Jansenists were only slightly less abominable and dangerous than Protestants. Torcy, moreover, was guilty in M. de Beauvilliers's eyes of two other crimes; firstly he had never been a follower of Monsieur de Cambrai; secondly he was the husband of Mme de Torcy who exercised a very strong influence over his mind, reaching it by way of his heart. She also had an excellent brain and was well-informed; furthermore she was independent and incapable of hiding sentiments that conformed perfectly with her maiden name.[1] Not that she was imprudent, still less did she display her convictions, but people were none the less aware of them. Thus to M. de Beauvilliers's way of thinking she was a kind of heretic who had perverted her husband and

---

[1] Mme de Torcy was an Arnauld, of the same family as Antoine, Le Grand Arnauld (1612-1694), who championed the Jansenists against the Jesuits; and of Angélique (1591-1661) and Agnès Arnauld (1593-1671) both of whom had been Abbesses of Port-Royal.

kept him on so tight a rein that no re-conversion was possible. M. de Chevreuse, despite his renunciation of Port-Royal, where he had been educated, was less bigoted than his brother-in-law. He was a strange mixture; for he had been fully as much enthralled by Mme Guyon as had M. de Beauvilliers, even more so by Monsieur de Cambrai, and was quite of their persuasion, yet he retained a profound aversion for the Jesuits as a result of his upbringing. This he took care to conceal, but once or twice he let slip an indication which, after we became friends, he did not contradict. He was therefore always upon his guard, and being more worldly-wise than M. de Beauvilliers he was less easily deceived concerning the plots of Rome. The monks of Port-Royal still enjoyed his affection and respect—he admitted as much to me; yet if his sentiments were the same as theirs his practice was quite otherwise. All this may be hard for you to credit, but it is the truth. This being so, he was not as violently opposed to Torcy as was the Duc de Beauvilliers, and strove hard to keep up appearances for want of any chance of coming to a better understanding. I, who knew all the inner history of the situation, was not unduly surprised when M. de Beauvilliers in our review of the ministers mentioned Torcy as the first to be dismissed.

We had some argument over Desmaretz. The duke had reached the point of being totally unable to hold any discussion with him; thus he was not in a position to deny his rigid obstinacy and extreme ingratitude. But those faults were unconnected with religion; no suspicion of Jansenism rested on him; what is more, he had been still in exile at the time of the Archbishop of Cambrai's disgrace. Innocent on those two counts, which M. de Beauvilliers considered vital, he had other qualities which served to whitewash him. He was Colbert's nephew and trained in his principles; he had the reputation of being the most able of the bankers, and finally, M. de Beauvilliers had himself restored him to favour after an enormous expenditure of time and effort, and could not bring himself to destroy his own handiwork. Nothing that I said had the slightest effect. No one better was found to take his place, and thus it was decided to retain him.

We had no difficulty in reaching a decision on Voysin, for we instantly agreed that he must be dismissed—no ability, a courtier's honour, no connections, hardhearted, uncouth, and Mme de Maintenon's man through and through. I tried to sound the duke on Chamillart and was pleasantly surprised, even moved, by his reply. He said they had been friends for forty years and that he himself had strengthened the bonds by marrying his niece to Chamillart's son. He recognized Chamillart's absolute integrity and agreed that his understanding was far greater than was generally allowed; he feared, however, that the Dauphin would be violently opposed to his return. He added that, in any event, he possessed a weakness incompatible with the welfare of the kingdom; that he knew him to be incorrigible in that respect, and would therefore be very loath to see him reinstated. That weakness was Chamillart's intransigent stubbornness; and he proceeded to tell me things that astonished me, even though I myself had had some experience of his rigidity and knew of people whom he firmly refused to forgive, despite the serious danger of their rancour. All this greatly distressed me, more especially as I was obliged to agree with him, and thus I sadly bid farewell to all hope of seeing my friend once more in the saddle.

As for Pontchartrain, M. de Beauvilliers had the worst possible opinion of him, which could not but flatter my confidence in my own judgment, although I trembled when I thought of his father, of whom the duke now spoke with complete freedom, and even more so than before, for he now told all. Rome, Jansenism, above all views totally opposed to those of Monsieur de Cambrai and his doctrine, had raised a barrier between them that first became apparent when the Chancellor took charge of the finances. Their bickering at the Council was almost continual, and to make matters worse the Chancellor frequently allowed himself a certain injudicious levity that brought the laugh on to his side. He some-times went so far as to let slip indecorous, indeed mildly shocking remarks, very upsetting to a gravity that in affairs of lesser importance was often out of place. In other surroundings the Chancellor made as little effort to restrain himself, and there were times when Beauvilliers and he ceased to be on visiting terms. At this particular juncture they had not quite reached that stage, but they were very far from amicable. In truth the wounds which they inflicted upon one another were so deep and continual that neither could forgive the other, and their animosity was public knowledge, even though the Chancellor still remained on good terms with the Duc de Chevreuse.

Although Pontchartrain was always at loggerheads with his father and deeply respectful in his manner to the Duc de Beauvilliers, he was no better liked for that. The sad result of the raid on Scotland, which I described earlier,[1] was rightly attributed to him, and was considered unforgivable by the Dukes of Chevreuse and Beauvilliers who had originated the plan. You have already seen how badly the Dauphine treated him, and that the King, usually so ready to defend his ministers, did not trouble to intervene. None the less, it will be as well for you to know him better, and since he has long been dead to the world although still above ground, I shall speak of him living as though he no longer existed.[2]

He was of average height, his face long, with sagging cheeks and monstrous thick lips, was altogether disgusting, and deformed as well, since smallpox had removed one of his eyes. The glass-eye that replaced it was perpetually a-weep,

---

[1] The raid on Scotland, Vol. 1, pp. 345-369.
[2] Saint-Simon was writing in 1743. Pontchartrain did not die until 1747.

making his appearance alarming at first glance, but not nearly as frightening as it should have been. He had a sense of honour, but perverted; he was studious, well schooled in the work of his department, tolerably industrious and ever anxious to appear more so. His perversity, which no one had curbed or checked, permeated all that he did. He loved to hurt for hurting's sake, and took uncommon pleasure in it. If he ever did a kind action he boasted of it to such an extent that it sounded like a reproach. What is more, he made the recipient pay dearly for the favour, refusing it at first, and then producing the endless complications with which he liked to hedge himself about. To cap all, he was mean and treacherous, and prided himself on being so. He was a skilful investigator, prying, informing, injuring, as crabbed and meticulous as any schoolmaster, with all the failings and meannesses of one born to government service and pampered in it to excess. It was impossible to deal with him on account of his bullying manner and continual queries. No one had rights except himself, and he demanded every one of them with the arrogance of a most cruel tyrant. Setting himself up to be the judge of everyone's actions, he pretended to have the right to call all men to account. Woe betide him who through poverty or cowardice fell into that coil for it was broken only by a quarrel.

Over and above his natural ill nature he was actively malignant, and if he bore a man a grudge would pursue him to the very gates of Hell. His speeches were in perfect conformity with the complications behind which he entrenched himself, for he divided them under three headings, continually inquiring with immense self-satisfaction whether he had not made his point. No matter who spoke with him, he monopolized the talk, constantly interrupting, questioning, setting the tone and the subject with an affected giggle that was enough to make one weep. He spoke hesitantly, gruffly, always repeating himself, with an air of superiority that made one want to vomit and to knock him down all at the same moment. Ever eager to know all the details of family histories and intrigues, he was jealous and envious of all, behaving towards the navy like an overseer of galley-slaves. No officer, no admiral even, was safe from his taunts at public audiences, no man or woman escaped his dictatorial glance. He relished saying unkind things and issued severe reprimands like a schoolmaster, on the pretext of being a friend and offering advice. His chief pleasure was to lay traps, for he delighted in doing a disservice, and was at daggers drawn with his parents and their friends, thus more than proof against their requests for trifling favours or pleasures. Indeed, he took such a particular pride in not obliging them that the Chancellor and his wife had made it a rule never to ask him for anything nor to recommend anyone to his notice, saying openly that he was sure to refuse. Being of consequence was his vanity of vanities, and the thought of ceasing one day to be a minister his devouring canker.

In other respects, too, he was unfit for Society, pleasures, or amicable converse. Ever obsessed by his responsibilities, he insisted that everyone, men and women alike, no matter what their rank, should suit themselves to his moods and convenience. You have seen how rudely he treated the Comte de Toulouse, d'O, and the Maréchal d'Estrées, and how the wives of the two last had ruined his chances with Mme la Dauphine and Mme de Maintenon who, though she liked and respected his mother, could never abide him. His only hold over the King was the entertainment he provided with the malicious gossip he got from his informants in Paris, which lay within his department. The Jesuits and Sulpicians hated him for his disobligingness, and imputed his merciless hunt after Jansenists solely to a general delight in cruelty. With all his baseness and arrogance, he was amazingly frank regarding his birth, and although he did not tell all, he candidly admitted that he came of obscure bourgeois stock from Montfort l'Aumaury. On the other hand, in his functions as a secretary of State he was arrogance personified.

The Duc de Beauvilliers unburdened himself of all these complaints during that one talk, and I felt the truth of all his imputations. It was indeed a most violent attack, and any attempt that I made to moderate it was brushed aside. As soon as I perceived that he was not to be shaken I decided not to anger him by expostulating. I simply listened and did my best to let something be left unsaid as an excuse for reopening the subject later. At last the conversation turned to other topics and Pontchartrain was not mentioned again. Several days afterwards the duke took me aside during one of the King's outings and immediately returned to Pontchartrain. I saw at once that he had something important to tell me. I was quite prepared, and he was ready to overcome me with a host of arguments, all of them unanswerable. I let him have his say. He pressed me closely about many of Pontchartrain's actions and his general conduct, his atrocious temper, his malice, his unwillingness to oblige, his pleasure in doing an injury, his mania for extending his authority, his habit of humiliating all and sundry, his infamous behaviour towards innumerable persons, many of them of high rank. None of all this was new to me, especially not the last accusation, from which I had so recently and damnably suffered. It was therefore not without inner conflict that I made ready to oppose M. de Beauvilliers.

When he had finished, I replied that I had no desire, even had I the power, to obstruct him in anything that concerned Pontchartrain himself, but that I could not wholly abandon the Chancellor's son, faulty, and worse, though he might be. I spoke with feeling of my love for the Chancellor and his grandsons, and this manner of opposing a man so naturally kind and well intentioned as M. de Beauvilliers caused him to reflect. I could see that my bluntness and reasoning half-annoyed, half-pleased him. He none the less persisted; but I answered him as before, not vexing him with contradiction, only asking whether he thought Pontchartrain

quite irredeemable. He did not answer; I said no more; he appeared to meditate. At last he told me that at that very moment Pontchartrain was in extreme
danger; that for my sake, since I appeared to wish to save him, he would add that
the Dauphine and Mme de Maintenon had sworn to destroy him; that the King
alone was on his side but unlikely to put up a strong resistance if those powerful
batteries opened fire. As for himself, were he vengeful I might well imagine how
he would think and act; but vengeance apart, which his religion forbade, he was
persuaded that Pontchartrain's dismissal would be for the good of the State, and
that it would certainly take place unless he changed completely. That being the
case, it was for Pontchartrain to reform, if he so pleased, after which his future
might be reconsidered. I asked whether he was predicting a remote possibility or
a storm about to burst. He said that he most emphatically meant the second. I
shuddered but, not daring to press for further details, I merely begged him to wait
a little before destroying a man who understood at least the navy, lest his successor
should give those who had displaced him cause for repentance. I never learned
the name of the intended successor, but I have reason to think it was Desmaretz.

At that point M. de Beauvilliers gave me permission to warn Pontchartrain
to control his temper at his public audiences, to be less malicious in conversation with the King and less harsh in his reports to the Conseil des Dépêches.
He also bade me give him the names of certain persons whom his rudeness had
particularly offended, but forbade me to tell him whence I had my information. I
thanked him for his great kindness and again begged him to hold his fire until he
saw the result of my labours. He promised nothing, but I could see that he hated
seeming to enjoy his vengeance and on that ground was inclined to listen to me.

Needless to say I had ample food for reflection, for besides what I have already
said of the terrible consequences for the Chancellor and his grandsons, I knew that
even were this blow averted there was no lasting security for them. Pontchartrain
being what he was would not long restrain himself, and any backsliding might
be fatal considering his unpopularity and the coolness, to say no worse, existing
between his father and the Duc de Beauvilliers. All my life I had longed to see
those two reconciled, but only as one longs for the impossible. They were totally
dissimilar, excepting in their love for the State. There was no basis for a mutual
understanding. In their friendships, views, temperaments and feelings they were as
contrary as they possibly could be, and the different attitude of these excellent men
towards religion was in itself a most potent cause of their disharmony. Considering
the changes taking place at the Court, it was plain to me that if the Chancellor
and his son were dismissed without being reconciled with M. de Beauvilliers
they would have no place in the new order. I therefore resolved to attempt the
impossible, no matter how hopeless the task might appear for, truly, in my present

rosy situation there was only this one thorn—the fact that my two greatest friends were so much out of sympathy that they seemed bent on destroying one another. Only stark necessity prevented my thinking the effort sheer lunacy.

That same evening I called on Pontchartrain after his supper guests had departed. Since I very seldom visited him, my arrival at that unaccustomed hour must have surprised him all the more. I began without preamble, looking very grave and very formal, saying that it had never been my custom to offer him advice, and that I felt less than ever disposed to do so at this particular time. There were, however, certain things which I felt obliged to say. He must not ask my reasons or the names of my informants, simply mark my words and act upon them without delay. I then said everything in one breath, like a lesson learned by heart. He heard me throughout with the attention demanded by my open-ing words, for he was quick to perceive that my terrible accusations came from a higher source. He then tried to excuse himself for some of his faults and to blame others on his quick temper. I replied that that was all one to me; his business was to profit from what he now learned; mine was to go to bed. Thereupon I left him as suddenly as I had come. Next day I repeated all to the Duc de Beauvilliers, who alarmed me still more by stressing the imminence of the coming storm, but none the less consented to await the result of my efforts.

A few days later, I was walking in the gardens after midnight alone with the Dauphin and the Abbé de Polignac, when their conversation turned to the government of Holland, the toleration there of different religious sects, and thence before long to Jansenism. The Abbé seized the occasion to say everything calculated to please. The Dauphin then gave me the chance to have my say, and I expressed my opinions very frankly. The walk was longer than usual because the weather was so delightful, and I left the Dauphin only when he re-entered the château. I shall later explain my views on these matters because they concern much of what follows and, more especially, my relations with the Dauphin. On the very next morning M. de Beauvilliers took me on one side in the salon, in order to tell me that the Dauphin had been much pleased by my words because they had convinced him that I was far removed from Jansenism. He went on to say that he had set the prince's mind quite at rest on that score, and that as a result he had conceived a much higher opinion of me in other ways also.

M. de Beauvilliers continued that the Dauphin had grave doubts of Pontchartrain in regard to Jansenism—of Pontchartrain who regularly paid his court to the King by zealously persecuting them! On that particular point M. de Beauvilliers's scruples were so strong that although, as he himself said, the Jesuits imputed Pontchartrain's conduct to sheer malevolence, he would be convinced only if I vouched for him. What had given rise to the rumour was Pontchartrain's habit, after the death of his wife, of frequenting Père de La Tour, but I was able to assure M. de Beauvilliers that in a very short time he had dropped him like a dirty rag, and had not been heard to mention him since. Later that same evening we met again. During the interval the duke had reassured the Dauphin on the subject of Pontchartrain, and that was the first service that he rendered him. One thing, however, that he completely failed to understand was why the Jesuits should be so violent against him; and then of his own volition he advised me to warn him of their ill will, which might do him more harm than he realized.

Towards midnight, I paid Pontchartrain another visit in exactly the same form as before. The time and manner of it caused him no less astonishment, and what I had to say far more. On the first occasion he may have wondered who had sent me; this time he was in no doubt. Although he bore the palm for discourtesy when he was not afraid, in alarm or necessity he could crawl with the humblest. Thus you may well imagine the kind of messages which he gave me to deliver to M. de Beauvilliers, and the proposals for his future conduct with the Jesuits. The duke was so well satisfied that he gave me leave to warn him, as though coming from myself, of the fearful danger threatening him from the Dauphin, and to suggest various means by which he might retrieve himself, all of them quite alien to his character and usual behaviour. M. de Beauvilliers went so far as to desire me to say that he would find some occasion for Pontchartrain to work with the Dauphin and would advise him then how he should comport himself.

I therefore called on him for the third time. Never have I seen a man so transported, for he experienced ruin and rescue all in one breath and his protestations, addressed as much to M. de Beauvilliers as to myself, were endless. As for me, I knew how little they were to be relied on for it was barely three weeks since he had sent d'Aubenton to me, and I therefore received his promises with icy disdain, showing him very plainly that personal liking played no part in the unhoped-for salvation that I offered him. Be that as it may, thus warned, he became very prudent, and as M. de Beauvilliers was unwilling to appear directly in the matter I myself was obliged to act as go-between, under the seal of strictest secrecy. Pontchartrain did work with the Dauphin, for the duke so arranged matters, and the prince was pleased with him. This state of affairs lasted for the remainder of that Marly, after which we went directly to Fontainebleau without returning to Versailles, on account of the foulness of the air.

During the course of these memoirs it will have become apparent that the friendship and confidence between the Dukes of Chevreuse and Beauvilliers and their duchesses had greatly increased. They lived in love and friendship with Mme de Saint-Simon and, perhaps uniquely with persons so stiff and reserved, on terms of complete trust and intimacy with her, based on respect for her virtues and long experience of her wise, benevolent mind and firm principles, and increased (supposing that to have been possible by) their knowledge of all that she was to me and I to her. You will thus understand that we six formed a group without secrets from one another who discussed everything. We met continually, not only once but several times a day when we were together, and we were rarely long apart because their house at Vaucresson was near at hand and my wife and I seldom left the Court. This association, formed so long ago, became ever more closely knit as time passed, and was already firmly established at the time of Monseigneur's death. That being so, it was only natural that M. de Beauvilliers should wish to inspire his pupil with feelings of esteem and friendship for me also. He hoped that he might gradually learn to trust me, but was most anxious not to appear to exert an influence.

The Duc de Beauvilliers was the most prudent and cautious of men. Mme de Maintenon's aversion and the various shocks received from the King had increased his natural diffidence. He feared lest he be suspected of imposing on the prince; and he feared also to arouse jealousy of me, remembering the piercing glances which had been aimed in my direction after my nomination for the Roman embassy. He had therefore laid down strict rules for my conduct towards the prince and for his towards me. I was to visit him only at the hours when he held court, and then only briefly and rarely, often enough for my visits not to appear unusual, not so often as to create any suspicion of favour. If anything, I was to err on the side of neglect. For similar reasons the Dauphin was to take little notice of me in public and to show no more courtesy to me than to others of my rank. None the less, every so often the Dauphin gave me an expressive look, a stealthy smile that told me all I wished to know. Apart from M. de Beauvilliers's strong influence, everything that the prince could discover of my life and character was well calculated to please him. He liked people who led quiet and busy lives; he liked happy marriages; he admired loyal friendships, and in all such things I had, as you know, been most fortunate. Nothing in my past could shock or disgust him; my attachments were all to persons of whom he approved; my hatreds had been kept for his enemies, and this without ulterior motives or contrivance. I had all my life kept on good terms with the Jesuits, many of whom, for example Père Tellier, counted me as a friend, and in particular Godet, Bishop of Chartres, who was truly attached to me. They were sufficient guarantee against any suspicion of Jansenism, and our talk in the garden at Marly had made him doubly certain on that count. As to my private sentiments, they will appear so often in what follows that they may need some explanation, for which this would seem a suitable moment.

The famous Abbot of La Trappe had been my guide in this as in so many other matters of which I would like to have had practical as well as theoretical knowledge. I regard all sects as being pernicious to the Church and the State. There is one sect only, that of Jesus Christ. I regard as heretical the five notorious propositions and all the books that contain them; but I know also that some people honestly believe them to be sound and true and for that reason have banded together to form a sect. Thus in no way am I a Jansenist. On the other hand, I hold most dear (and this far more as a matter of conscience than of policy) what are so wrongly termed the liberties of the Gallican Church—these mis-named liberties being neither privileges, concessions, nor usurped rights, not traditional, nor merely tolerated, but the constant practice of the Church universal. They are liberties which the Church of France has most zealously defended against attacks and encroachments by the Vatican which has defeated and subjugated all the rest and, by its unjust demands, done infinite harm to the Christian religion. I use the term Vatican out of respect for the Bishop of Rome who alone retains the title of Pope and is in faith believed to be the head of the Church, the successor of Saint Peter, the first bishop, with superiority and jurisdiction by divine right over all other bishops whomsoever they may be: on whom alone devolves the care and protection of all the Christian Churches—he being the first vicar of Christ, that is to say the first of all His vicars who are bishops.

I should add that I regard the Church of Rome as being the mother and mistress of all the Churches with whom we are in communion—mistress, *magistra*, but most certainly not *domina*, and that I do not accept as an act of faith that the Pope is either the sole bishop, or the bishop universal, ordinary and diocesan of every other see; or that he alone possesses the episcopal power from which emanates the authority of all other bishops, as the Inquisition, which I hold to be abominable in the sight of God and most odious to man, would have us believe. I hold that the signing of the famous Formula was a most obnoxious measure, barely permissible even when administered in the strictest terms of the Peace of Clement IX, and otherwise completely illegal. I am thus very far from believing that the Pope is in any sense infallible or supreme, or even on a par with the oecumenical councils that alone have the right to establish articles of faith, and are incapable of error.

Regarding Port-Royal, my sentiments are exactly those of the King when he said to Maréchal with a sigh that all the most saintly, scholarly, noble, and enlightened pronouncements of the last two centuries have emanated from there. I think that the terms Jansenist and Jansenism are like pitch, used as a convenient method of blackening people's characters, and that out of a thousand so dubbed, perhaps less than two merit the name. Not to believe all that the Vatican chooses to lay down on matters spiritual or even temporal, to lead a quiet, hard-working, and secluded life, or to be attached to those who do so, is enough to be credited with the taint of Jansenism; and this widespread and wholly unjustifiable net of suspicion, so serviceable to those who use and profit by it, is most harmful to religion, Society, and the State. I am sure that the Jesuits fulfil an admirable purpose when they restrict themselves to what Saint Ignatius laid down for them. The Society is too numerous not to contain many saintly men, some of whom I have known, but it also contains very many who are exactly the reverse. Their policy and their jealousy still cause much harm; their piety and devotion to the instruction of the young, their wide learning and enlightenment do much good. That is already enough for a man of my condition; to go further into details would be to speak out of my place and beyond the scope of these memoirs. This explanation will displease those who claim that Jansenism and Jansenists are heretical, and will certainly be even less welcome to those who from caution, ignorance, or self-interest see Jansenists wherever they look for them. What continually amazed me was that M. de Beauvilliers, whose caution ranged him with those described above, ever allowed himself to put up with me in the way that throughout his life he did, without the smallest cloud ever darkening our friendship, especially considering my absolute frankness with him on that as on all other topics.

In many parts of these memoirs you have seen how firmly Mme de Saint-Simon could rely on the continued kindness of Mme la Duchesse de Bourgogne, and how determined that princess had been to make her lady-in-waiting after the Duchesse du Lude's retirement. Her temporary situation with Mme la Duchesse de Berry, which she had been forced to accept, had brought her closer to every member of the royal family. The more they saw of her the more they liked her and, if I may be allowed to say so of such august persons, they all, even the King and Mme de Maintenon, honoured and esteemed her. Mme la Duchesse de Berry's disgraceful conduct only increased their sense of my wife's prudence and excellent principles, and of the wisdom, modesty and virtue of her way of living. She was, indeed, perfectly virtuous, but although very strict with herself she was all kindness and gentleness with others, so that instead of flying from her disapproval people of all ages came to her for sympathy, seeking her advice again and again in the dangers and troubles into which their errors had led them. The Dauphin who, especially since M. le Duc de Berry's marriage, often saw her in his apartments, grew to like and even to trust her, which gave me still another ally in his intimate circle—one, moreover, whom the Duc de Beauvilliers strongly supported because he loved her and had the highest possible opinion of her character. Thus everything tended towards my also winning the Dauphin's trust and friendship.

There had already been some talk of my becoming more closely attached to him. M. de Beauvilliers had first suggested it; but he had warned me that any change must be made with the utmost caution, in order that people might come gradually to accept it and not be alarmed. He reminded me that at various times I had narrowly escaped from the vilest slander; that everyone would therefore be against me if I gave them the slightest cause for jealousy, and that my only chance was to hide my hopes. He urged me to move with extreme caution, step by step, as the prince's power to protect me increased—in other words, as he gained the King's entire confidence, and greater authority in the affairs of the State and Society. I thought none the less that it would do no harm to take some soundings, even in those early days, and I therefore joined the Dauphin one evening in the Marly gardens, when he had only a small following. Emboldened by his gracious smile I whispered into his ear that events of which he already knew had hitherto kept me from him, but that I now hoped to show my devotion more openly, trusting that that would not displease him. He replied in an equally low voice that there had indeed been obstacles, but that he believed they no longer existed; that he knew my feelings for him and looked forward with pleasure to seeing me more often. I quote his exact words because his ending was so particularly gracious. Thereafter I joined him more often in his walks, unless the people surrounding him were those whom I had cause to fear, and I began to speak my mind more freely. Nevertheless I was still unwilling to be seen with him in Society, and only approached him in the salon when a suitable occasion presented itself.

I already knew his views on the administration of the kingdom and on other matters of that kind. They coincided with my own and were also the opinions of the Dukes of Chevreuse and Beauvilliers, who had kept me well informed. Such agreement was too fortunate to be wasted, and I began to look for an opportunity of broaching the subject. This was not long in coming. A few days later, the Dauphin and Dauphine entered the salon deep in conversation. I approached sufficiently near to hear their final words, which led me to inquire if anything were the matter, not impudently, but with the friendly and respectful air which I had begun to adopt towards them. The Dauphin replied that they were going to call at Saint-Germain for the first time since his succession—the first time, in other words, since the State visit in mourning garments—and that this would necessitate a complete change in precedence concerning the Princess of England. He explained the difficulty, eagerly stressing the need to protect all his hereditary rights. 'How it rejoices me to hear you speak like that!' I exclaimed, 'how right to insist on ceremony, for when it is neglected nothing else is honoured!' He agreed enthusiastically, and I seized that perfect moment to say that if he in all his glory, with his rank so firmly secured, felt it necessary to take precautions, how much more did we dukes, whose rights were so often questioned and even usurped, have reason to mourn our losses and strive in future to protect ourselves. He concurred so heartily that he might have been an advocate pleading our cause, and he ended by declaring that he regarded our reinstatement as an act of justice essential for the good of the realm. He added that he knew me to be well versed in all these matters and would like one day to discuss them with me. At that point he rejoined the Dauphine and they went together to Saint-Germain. The matter that gave rise to this short but important conversation was that in Monseigneur's lifetime Mme la Duchesse de Bourgogne had given precedence to the Princess of England; now she was the Dauphine, wife of the heir-apparent, she would walk first everywhere.

A few days later, the Dauphin sent for me. I entered by the privies, where du Chesne his first valet, a most upright and secret man in whom he trusted, was waiting to conduct me to his study. He was alone. My thanks were not unmingled with references to my conduct past and present, and my joy in his new situation. His reply showed that he was less afraid of frankness than of appearing vain of his present glory. He said that hitherto he had not attempted to do more than listen and study, thinking it no part of his duty to express an opinion. Now, however, the King had ordered him to inform himself regarding the affairs of State, to work with the ministers, and to assist him personally. Thus he felt that all his time belonged to the State and the public good; that it would be like stealing to waste it with other things, and that in future he would seek diversion only when tired or in need of recreation, so as to return to work refreshed.

He went on to speak of the King with much gratitude and affection, saying that he felt it was his bounden duty to relieve him as much as possible of his burdens, seeing that King Louis had confided in him and asked for assistance. While I thoroughly approved of these excellent sentiments I feared lest gratitude degenerate into blind admiration, and I therefore remarked that the King was ignorant of many things that would certainly disturb him deeply because he made it impossible for people to converse with him. That chord, struck ever so lightly, plainly made a deep impression. The prince, after a few words to the effect that he knew from M. de Beauvilliers that I could be trusted, admitted the truth of what I had said, and immediately began to attack the ministers. He enlarged on the boundless authority which they had usurped or wrung from the King, the dangerous uses to which they might put it, and the impossibility of bringing anything to the King's attention excepting through them. Then, mentioning no names, he allowed me clearly to understand that this kind of government was quite contrary to his liking and principles.

Returning affectionately to the King, he blamed his bad upbringing and the pernicious hands into which he had successively fallen, as a result of which, on pretexts of policy or delegation, all the authority and all the benefits of power had gone to the ministers. The King's mind, naturally so good and just, had been led astray until habit had firmly established him in practices that brought much unhappiness to the country. He then once more spoke of himself with humility, giving me cause to admire him greatly. After that he returned to the conduct of the ministers, and I took the opportunity to mention their encroachments on the powers of the dukes and on those of persons of the highest birth. At this he exclaimed in indignation, becoming heated on the subject of the title 'Monseigneur', which they denied to us, but insisted on receiving from all untitled people. I can scarcely express how much scandalized he was by this piece of insolence, this ludicrous misuse of a designation that raised the bourgeoisie above the highest nobility. I let him have his say, as much for the joy of hearing these admirable sentiments from the lips of him who would soon make our laws and rulings as to discover how far his indignation would carry him. I then traced for him the origins of this complete reversal of the established order, and mentioned that by the purest chance I had preserved three of M. Colbert's letters to my father, in all of which he had addressed him as *Monseigneur*. That information appeared to give the Dauphin as much pleasure as though he were personally concerned. He instructed me to send for the letters, and expressed his amazement at the revolutionary change. He prolonged the discussion because he liked to go deeply into every subject, and at the end it had lasted more than an hour. His final words were to bid me tell him when the letters had arrived, because he would have other matters to discuss with me at our next session.

It is hard to describe my feelings as I left the Dauphin. I had seen a prince, pious, tolerant, just, enlightened, ever striving to improve his mind; best of all, unattracted by the tittle-tattle that more often than not is the prime interest of such exalted persons. Another marvellous difference which I perceived in him was that, once having given his regard and friendship, he was proof against absence or even long separation. I rejoiced exceedingly at having gained his confidence so completely during our very first conversation, and on a subject of such vital importance. I already foresaw the destruction of those hammers of the State, those all-powerful enemies of the nobility whom they had trampled underfoot, but whom the life-giving breath of this prince, soon to be King, would restore to their rightful position. This general longing for the restoration of rank and order was my heart's desire, far outweighing any thought of personal advancement. I savoured all the joys of this prospect, and of deliverance from a servitude that was secretly so intolerable that, despite all my endeavours, my exasperation sometimes became apparent.

I could not deny myself the pleasure of comparing anticipation of the reign of Monseigneur, which I had so greatly dreaded, with all its possible horrors in general and in particular, and the solid blessings of this his son's pre-reign, so soon to be followed by the reign itself, which he had prefaced by baring his heart to me in friendship. At the same time he had opened the road to everything to which a man of my rank could legitimately aspire whose only wish was for order, justice, toleration, the good of the State and its people by honourable means in which honesty and truth would shine out.

A brilliant and not too distant future unfolded before my eyes. Yet I resolved still to be very careful lest this favour should cause people to fear and band against me. I determined to cherish my hopes in secret and to use my discretion when asking for audiences in which I had so much to learn, so much gently to implant, so much to give me strength. I should, however, have thought it both thankless and disloyal not to show my gratitude to the one person to whom all this was due; and, knowing that the Duc de Beauvilliers held the key to the Dauphin's heart and mind, I felt it no treachery to go to him immediately and tell him all.

My second audience with the Dauphin took place a few days later; and here let me say once and for all that it was usually du Chesne his head valet who informed me of the appointed time, and if it was I who desired the audience I requested it through him. At Versailles, Fontainebleau, or Marly, wherever we happened to be, I invariably entered his apartments secretly through the privies. Thus no one observed me, except on one occasion the Dauphine, as I shall shortly describe. I gave the prince M. Colbert's three letters. He took them, examined them closely, read them all, and exclaimed at the happy chance of their having been preserved despite the trivial contents. He looked once more at the dates, exclaiming again at the abominable impertinence of the ministers (he did not mince his words) and the injustice to the old nobility. My chief desire was to sound him on his feelings regarding all that concerned our status as dukes, and I therefore gently turned the conversation to that subject. I found him on the whole marvellously well informed about the origin of our rank[1] and its position in relation to the State and the Crown, and deeply conscious of the vital need for the Kings of France to restore and uphold this the highest distinction in the kingdom. I spoke to him again of the difficulties of his first visit to Saint-Germain after Monseigneur's death,[2] and reminded him of the disgraceful innovation regarding the precedence of the Elector of Bavaria travelling *incognito*; how at Meudon he had dared to take even Monseigneur by the hand, well knowing that no objection would come from that quarter. I asked him to consider the ill effect upon the King's majesty and the Crown of the toleration of such abuses, and the serious consequences if their glory were debased. That allowed me to contrast the position of the grandees of Spain with that of the dukes and peers of France, and gave

---

[1] As the supporters and defenders of the Crown. At the coronation of French kings in early times the Crown of Charlemagne was held over the king's head by the dukes and peers of France. Surrounded by dukes, he advanced to his throne. Thus at one moment it appeared to onlookers as though the king vanished behind a protective hedge of dukes.

[2] The mourning visit to Saint-Germain, where everyone had been obliged to stand because Princess Louise, who should have given precedence to the new Dauphine by sitting on a stool in her presence, had made no attempt to do so. As no one had liked to insist, they had all remained standing.

me an opportunity of describing the policy of the Spanish king Charles V, who not only raised the status of grandees in his kingdom but sent them abroad to foreign courts where, as his representatives, they were granted the highest privileges, thus shedding lustre on his crown far beyond the borders of Spain.[1] I passed thence to England and the kingdoms of the north, finding no difficulty in demonstrating that none of these countries permitted its nobility to be treated in such a manner as France tolerated.

The Dauphin was keenly interested; he appreciated all my reasoning, often finished my sentences for me, and gladly accepted what I said as being the truth. We had a most agreeably instructive talk, during which to my intense delight he himself exploded at the bare mention of the princes of the blood, talking eagerly of the iniquity of their pretensions and the wickedness of the novel rank of the bastards. 'It is a great misfortune,' said he, 'to have children of that kind. God in his mercy has saved me hitherto from that; but who is to say what I may not do in the future? I shall fall into many kinds of temptation. Pray God He may deliver me! But even should I have bastards, I do not think that I should ever thus elevate, or even legitimize, them. None the less, only by God's grace do I have this feeling, and since I may not count on deserving its continuance I must learn to curb myself lest I succumb to the danger of such evils.' These excellent sentiments, so humble and so wise, enchanted me, and I praised him to the skies.

You will easily imagine my joy after those two audiences. The welfare and good government of France and thereafter the restoration of our rights was my heart's desire. In the Dauphin I recognized the same longings, seeing myself capable of assisting him in that great work and at the same time of gaining advancement, provided I exercised restraint in my enjoyment of those precious hopes. Thereafter I saw him often in private, and always immediately after went to tell all to the Duc de Beauvilliers, and obtain his advice, which I later repeated to the prince. Neither his pride nor his kindness was offended by anything that I said, and he not only freely discussed persons and events with me, but encouraged me to speak frankly of everything concerning them. He took notes during our talks and afterwards gave them to me, and I returned them to him later, annotated as he had desired, and gave him also notes I had made, which he kept for a time and later gave back to me after discussing them.

My pockets were always crammed with notes when I went to see him. Indeed, it often made me chuckle as I crossed the salon, to observe those onlookers whose

---

[1] Sometimes, when affairs were going badly for the dukes, Saint-Simon thought seriously of becoming a Spaniard because they managed things so much better in that country. He changed his mind after visiting Spain in 1721. The king referred to was in fact the Emperor Charles V, who was also Charles I of Spain.

characters were hidden under my coat, and who were very far from imagining the important conversations that were taking place about them. At Marly, the Dauphin now used one of the four great apartments on the same floor as the salon. In the bedroom, the bed was placed with the foot towards the windows, and in the *ruelle* on the hearth-side was the door to a dark little privy through which I habitually entered. A small portable writing-desk stood between the chimney-piece and one of the two windows; and facing the entrance and behind the writing-table and chair was another door leading into the Dauphine's rooms. A chest of drawers containing nothing but his papers stood between the windows. There was always a short discussion on general events before the Dauphin seated himself at his desk and invited me to sit facing and very near him. On one such occasion after I had become more intimate with him I took the liberty of advising him to draw the bolt across the door behind him; but this he refused to do, saying that the Dauphine was most unlikely to appear since it was not her usual time. I replied that I was not so much afraid of the Dauphine as of the crowd of courtiers who followed her everywhere. He was adamant, however, and I dared not press him. We had a long session, and after it was over spent a great while sorting our papers. He gave me his notes, took mine, placed some of them in the chest of drawers but did not lock it, and left the remainder on top of the desk. He then began to converse, standing with his back to the fireplace, papers in one hand and keys in the other. I was at the desk with one hand full of papers, and with the other sorting them, when suddenly the door opposite me opened and the Dauphine entered. The first exchange of glances between the three of us (for thank God she was alone) will stick in my memory for ever. Our eyes glazed, our bodies remained as immobile as statues, our silence, our utter consternation lasted fully the time of a slow *pater.* The princess was the first to speak. Turning to the prince, she said in a quavering voice that she had not expected to find him in such good company and smiled, first at him, then at me. I had just sufficient time to return her smile and to lower my eyes, before the Dauphin, smiling also, replied, 'Well, Madame, since you do find me so well occupied, you will perhaps have the goodness to leave me.' She looked at him a moment longer smiling rather more broadly; gave me another glance, and with a really gay smile turned on her heel and closed the door behind her, for she had not quite crossed the threshold. Never have I seen a woman more surprised; never, to tell the truth, was any man half so frightened as myself, although I did somewhat recover myself when I saw that she was alone.

'Well, Sir!' said I to the Dauphin. 'Suppose that you had consented to bolt the door?' 'You were right and I was wrong,' he replied; 'but there was no danger since she was alone. I can vouch for her secrecy.' 'Indeed, I do not doubt it,'

I said, although in fact I was none too sure,[1] 'but it was a miracle that she was not followed. Had she been, for you there might have been a gentle reprimand, but for me it would have meant ruin.' He once more admitted his mistake and promised to be more careful in future. The Dauphine had not only found us alone together, which would have been enough to astonish anyone, but she had caught us in the act—red-handed, as they say. I did not think that she would willingly betray the Dauphin, but I did fear her love of gossip, lest she be lured into telling our secret. In the event, she appeared to have told no one, or only trusty persons who guarded the secret well, for nothing ever transpired regarding it. I had no more to say, and our business concluded with my putting some papers into my pocket and the prince locking up the remainder. I then withdrew by my usual route through the privy.

After that the Dauphine often smiled at me as though to remind me of this occurrence, and began to look at me with particular interest. She had always been fond of Mme de Saint-Simon, but she never mentioned the incident to her. Me she more or less distrusted because she was mortally afraid of the Dukes of Chevreuse and Beauvilliers, whose ways were not hers, and was aware of my close friendship with them. Their sober lives and influence over her husband were a menace to her in many ways; Mme de Maintenon's dislike of them did nothing to reassure her, while the fact that they were in the King's confidence was positively alarming to one of her timid nature. She was particularly afraid of them, more especially of M. de Beauvilliers, on account of that matter most dangerous for her in relation to her husband, and perhaps also to the King.[2] She little knew, and no one could tell her, that the other party concerned was equally alarmed and had taken all possible precautions to prevent discovery. As for me, whom she had no reason to fear in that quarter, I had never been her friend. To be that, one needed to play cards, and I did not gamble. Any other means of communication was fraught with difficulty and I had never made the effort. This did not mean that there was any ill feeling between us, for I was a very dear friend of the ladies in whom she trusted, the Duchesse de Villeroy, for example, Mme la Duchesse d'Orléans, Mme de Nogaret, and others. She was essentially frivolous, and any serious aversion for me would have upset her cherished plan to replace the Duchesse du Lude,[3] after her retirement, by Mme de Saint-Simon.

I have already said that Mme de Maintenon detested me, although at that time I only half-suspected this. After the King's death, I learned from Chamillart,

---

[1] Saint-Simon may not have known for certain that she spied for her father Victor Amadeus II, Duke of Savoy, even though he was at war with France. The King knew (see footnote 2, p. 256, Vol. 1). Mme de Maintenon, although she loved her, said that her early death was perhaps a good thing for France.

[2] Alluding to her love-affair with the Marquis de Nangis (see index, Vol. 1).

[3] The Duchesse de Lude had been her lady-in-waiting ever since she first came to France as a little girl, in 1696. The princess had never cared for her and, according to the Venetian ambassador, was most unkind, mimicking and teasing her abominably.

who had carefully concealed it from me until then, that he had far less trouble in persuading the King to replace my name on the regular list for Marly than in appeasing Mme de Maintenon, and that he had had veritable tussles with her, hard ones, too, in vain attempts to overcome her aversion for me, or at least to make her explain its cause.[1] I had no friends in her circle and I had made no effort to become acquainted with her. She was, in any event, incredibly difficult to approach. What she was, and much of what she did, made me dislike her extremely.

Despite so many matters, both public and personal, to occupy my mind, I was also busily concerned in effecting a reconciliation between M. le Duc d'Orléans and the Dauphin; and in order to achieve that aim I wished first to improve relations between him and the Duc de Beauvilliers. Everything would have been easy save for his own conduct and that of his daughter—incredible though this might seem in a man who, convinced of the need for reconciliation, very greatly desired it. The strong and intimate bond of his daughter's splendid alliance, the close friendship between his wife and the Dauphin, his fondness for the Duc de Chevreuse, and his publicly avowed devotion to the Archbishop of Cambrai and the Society of Jesus all favoured the endeavour. The only but very great obstacle was M. le Duc d'Orléans's way of life, his affectation of boasting about his debauchery and godlessness, with ill timed jests about religion that alienated the Dauphin and shocked the Duc de Beauvilliers to the core of his being. The King, moreover, kept a close watch on him, for he found his nephew's conduct execrable in more ways than one, and in one way especially, as I shall shortly explain. His suspicions were fortified by Mme de Maintenon's hatred, on which the marriage of M. le Duc d'Orléans's daughter, although arranged by herself, had had no mollifying effect.

That alliance which should have reunited the entire royal family proved to be nothing but a source of discord. I have already mentioned Mme la Duchesse de Berry's appalling character; of which her public and most unsuitably promiscuous love-affairs were by no means the worst feature. The elevation of the Dauphin and Dauphine, to whom she owed so much, aroused in her nothing but envy and malice; and the fact that she still needed their protection added to her fury. Brought up to hate her mother and despise her for the defilement of her adulterous birth, she showed her feelings quite openly after marriage. Even though she owed her present position to the very fact of her mother's birth and influence; although she had received from her nothing but kindness, her loathing and contempt frequently exploded into most shocking scenes, which

---

[1] Mme de Maintenon's dislike for Saint-Simon was not surprising in view of his opinion that she had risen from the gutter (which was not true) and that her life before, during, and immediately after her marriage with the crippled poet Scarron had been disreputable.

Mme la Duchesse d'Orléans did her best to ignore, but which often brought down upon Mme la Duchesse de Berry a just and severe rebuke from the King.

Worse even than that; possessing a strong and violent nature, she enjoyed using her power over her husband and her father. M. le Duc de Berry, mild, easy-going, and virtuous, was deeply in love with her, and besides being blinded by his passion lived in terror of her tantrums. M. le Duc d'Orléans was weakness and evasion personified. He had doted on this child since her babyhood, preferring her to all his other children and loving her increasingly as time went on. He also feared her; and she, perceiving the double advantage she held over both of them, constantly misused her power. M. le Duc de Berry, who was honest and straightforward as well as passionately in love, proved to be no match for her in witty sallies and repartee; and he often allowed himself to be led beyond his better judgment and good principles, for when he dared to contradict her he brought down upon himself the whole violence of her wrath. As for M. le Duc d'Orléans, he usually disapproved of her conduct and said so, to Madame la Duchesse among others, and even to M. le Duc de Berry himself. In his daughter's presence, however, he was no stronger than the rest, and if he attempted to make her see reason it was not rudeness alone that he received. She treated him like a negro slave until she had reduced him to pacifying her by asking her pardon, for which she made him pay very dear.

I have already described how abominably the world misconstrued his paternal affection; but indeed, no one would have imagined such a thing had it not been for that vile cabal. Their jealousy, which had been aroused by the splendid marriage they had been unable to prevent, had now turned to an attempt to ruin it, and the continual presence in her drawing-room of an, alas!, bone-idle father, who found endless entertainment in his daughter's witty chatter, gave free rein to their devilish tongues. The slanderous rumours finally reached M. le Duc de Berry's ears and greatly increased his dislike of having to compete with his father-in-law for his wife's company and attention. For him it was the last straw. All of this, coming to the knowledge of Mme de Saint-Simon and myself, made us determine at all costs to prevent an open quarrel on so false and shocking a pretext. I had already vainly endeavoured to discourage M. le Duc d'Orléans from continually visiting his daughter, on the grounds that it fatigued M. le Duc de Berry. I had then spoken more frankly, and, after a suitable prelude, had shown him how necessary it was that I should continue. He had appeared astounded, exclaiming at the wickedness of the accusations and the treachery of bringing them to the notice of M. le Duc de Berry. He also thanked me for my warning, saying that I was the only one who would have dared to enlighten him. I left him to draw the conclusion that he had no one but himself to blame.

That conversation took place at Versailles about four o'clock one afternoon. Excepting for Mme de Saint-Simon, only Mme la Duchesse d'Orléans had known of my intention, and she had strongly urged me to intervene. Yet the morning after, Mme de Saint-Simon informed me that on returning from the King's study with Mme la Duchesse de Berry, the princess had gone straight to her privy and had demanded her presence. There, looking furious and haughty, she had declared herself to be astounded at my apparent desire to spoil her relations with her father; and when Mme de Saint-Simon looked surprised, she had added that no doubt I would like to separate them, but that I should never succeed in doing so. She had then repeated the very words which I had used to M. le Duc d'Orléans, which he had been pleased within the hour to repeat to her. Mme de Saint-Simon heard her out; remarked that the horrid rumour was indeed the current gossip, and pointed out that no matter how false it might be she could not altogether discount the appalling consequences. Surely it were best for M. le Duc d'Orléans to know the truth, and surely, in telling him, I had given such strong proof of my loyalty and desire for their happiness as to disarm all suspicions to the contrary. My wife then made her curtsey, turned on her heel, and left the princess to go to bed.

Such conduct from M. le Duc d'Orléans appeared entirely unforgivable to me, and I accordingly went straight after dinner to Mme la Duchesse d'Orléans to make a complaint, saying to her shortly that after one such experience with her husband I should take good care to see him so rarely that there would be no chance of a repetition. As for Mme la Duchesse de Berry, in future I should take her opinion of me for granted. Mme la Duchesse d'Orléans was horror-stricken. She tried to say everything suitable in the circumstances and at the same time to plead paternal affection, imploring me not to abandon him, for I was the only one who dared to tell him the truth; she used all her powers of persuasion, which were not small, to make my love for him condone this lapse, great though it had been. Despite her endeavours I did not prolong my visit. I made no haste to call on her again, and I entirely ceased to see M. le Duc d'Orléans, which distressed them both. They both pleaded with Mme de Saint-Simon. Mme la Duchesse de Berry, having apparently been scolded by her father, tried rather ungraciously to be reconciled with her. Mme la Duchesse d'Orléans begged me, in the most eloquent terms, to visit her daughter. M. le Duc d'Orléans came to see me uninvited, profuse with apologies, blandishments, and everything best calculated to make me relent. For a considerable time I remained icily silent, formal, and respectful. Then I lost my temper and spoke with absolute frankness, which he seemed rather to prefer, for he redoubled his excuses, prayers, promises of loyalty, and vowed never again to abuse my confidence. I therefore pinned my faith on the sharpness of the lesson and so we were reconciled, with a firm resolve on my part to let him do as he pleased with his daughter, and in future to be very careful in any matter that concerned her.

The light of sweet reason and piety that shone on M. le Duc d'Orléans after his rupture with Mme d'Argenton had not been of long duration, although from motives of policy, perhaps, it lasted until after Mme la Duchesse de Berry's marriage, six months later. Boredom, old bad habits, the low company which he frequented in Paris, combined to drag him down, and he sank once more into a life of debauchery and godlessness, albeit with no official mistress, and without quarrelling with his wife, except on the subject of his daughter. Father and daughter vied with one another in witty jests against morality and religion, often in the presence of M. le Duc de Berry, although he was attached to them both and found their merriment in vilely bad taste. The King was fully aware of his nephew's conduct, and was deeply shocked by his return to lechery and drunkenness. Thus there had come about yet another estrangement between uncle and nephew, less perhaps on account of M. le Duc d'Orléans's own behaviour than because of Mme la Duchesse de Berry; all of which was well known to M. de Beauvilliers, who was consequently not at all eager to come to terms with him.

I none the less strongly urged the Duc de Beauvilliers not to lose interest in him, stressing the great need to preserve what had been the main purpose of Mme la Duchesse de Berry's marriage—the inner harmony of the royal family. I represented the good influence which he might bring to bear on M. le Duc d'Orléans who, under his guidance and that of the Dauphin, might change for the better and become as great an asset to family unity as he was now a hindrance to it. I supported my arguments with M. de Chevreuse's good opinion, and did not forget to remind him of M. le Duc d'Orléans's sentiments regarding the Archbishop of Cambrai. Lastly, I stressed the prince's interest in history and the arts and sciences, on which subjects the Dauphin also loved to converse, and of which M. le Duc d'Orléans was a master, able to discuss them clearly and convincingly. They might well become subjects of mutual interest, equally pleasing to both parties. M. de Beauvilliers was impressed by my opening remarks, but raised the objection that the unseemly jests which M. le Duc d'Orléans occasionally let fall in the Dauphin's presence, to the latter's great annoyance, might prove an insuperable barrier to friendship. I saw the truth of that too well to deny it, but at last persuaded him that even this obstacle might be removed. I said no more then, well knowing that everything depended on a change of heart which it must be my first endeavour to procure; but because of M. le Duc d'Orléans's flightiness and his regrettable habit of advertising his impiety, which, in truth, was more affected than real, I dared make no promises, not even to myself.

I lost no time in tackling him, and without too much difficulty made him concede the solid advantages of friendship with the Dauphin and, which was one and the same, with the Duc de Beauvilliers. After that admission, I easily persuaded him to desire such friendship, and therefore to remove an impediment caused, as he himself admitted, by his own conduct. When I saw that I had made him uncomfortable to the point where I might safely offer him a solution, I remarked that I should not lecture him on his bad habits, or on opinions wrong in themselves and not really held by him, for he already knew my views, and my arguments would therefore have no effect. The means were in his own hands and victory easy, provided there was no backsliding. I entreated him first of all to avoid any, even faintly irreligious remarks in the Dauphin's presence, or anywhere else from whence they might reach his ears; secondly, to go less often to Paris and, if he must indulge in debauchery, to do so at least in private, and to exercise sufficient restraint to prevent the after-effects from being visible next day. He grasped thankfully at a plan that did not entirely forbid him his pleasures, and swore to abide by my advice, more especially with regard to his words in the Dauphin's presence. I informed M. de Beauvilliers of what I had done, and before long even the Dauphin had begun to notice a change and to remark on it, which M. de Beauvilliers reported in due course to me. A friendship did gradually develop, but because M. de Beauvilliers disliked all innovations and was not accustomed to seeing M. le Duc d'Orléans, the arrangements at the beginning were all made through me. Thus after that Marly, during which the Duc de Chevreuse had been absent, everything was done through him or else through me, one or other of us.

The King had been at Marly ever since the death of Monseigneur. He had gone there straight from Meudon the night of the 14-15 April, and had remained there afterwards on account of the foul air at Versailles, and for the sake of the princes his grandsons. He stayed exactly three months; left on Wednesday, 15 July, after holding his council and dining, drove thence to Versailles, where he spent a short time in his study and, after sleeping a night at Petit-Bourg,[1] went on next day to Fontainebleau, remaining there until 14 September. One trifling incident of that journey I should not think worth recounting, did it not so well portray the King.

Mme la Duchesse de Berry was for the first time pregnant, nearly three months gone, greatly incommoded, not a little feverish. M. Fagon thought it much better for her to postpone the journey for a few days. Neither she nor M. le Duc d'Orléans dared make the suggestion. M. le Duc de Berry timidly put in a word but was firmly snubbed. Mme la Duchesse d'Orléans, more nervous still, appealed to Mme de Maintenon who, albeit she had little love for Mme la Duchesse de Berry, thought the journey so unwise that with Fagon's support she spoke to the

---

[1] The country house of the Duc d'Antin. Louis XIV hated to be anywhere else but in his own home. D'Antin's house, Petit-Bourg, was the only private house in which he would consent to spend a night. See Vol. 1, pp. 338 f.

King. Useless. She did not give up, however, and the argument continued for four days. At last, the King lost his temper, but consented to her going by boat instead of in his coach; he would concede nothing else. They had even greater difficulty in obtaining permission for her to leave Marly on the 13th, so that she might rest at the Palais Royal on that night and on the 14th, and embark next day for Petit-Bourg where the King was to spend the night, continuing the journey by water, and arriving at Fontainebleau on the 16th on the same day as himself.

M. le Duc de Berry received permission to travel with his wife, but both were told angrily not to leave the Palais Royal, not even to go to the opera, although for that they need not have set foot out of doors but could have walked there on the level all the way, through the apartments of M. le Duc d'Orléans, which had direct access to the boxes. This command was repeated to them on the 14th, on the pretext of an inquiry regarding their healths, and it was also given to M. and Mme la Duchesse d'Orléans, who had been placed under the same ban before leaving Marly. Mme de Saint-Simon had strict orders never to let the princess out of her sight, and a second message to that effect was sent to her in Paris. You may well imagine how carefully these orders were obeyed. Mme de Saint-Simon was obliged to sleep at the Palais Royal, but was given the queen-mother's apartments. They had a hard task in persuading M. le Duc de Berry to endure the restrictions.

The task of procuring boats for the journey was given to the provost of the merchants; but he had so little warning that he made a bad selection. Mme la Duchesse de Berry, with the fever still on her, did not arrive at Petit-Bourg until ten in the evening; the King, however, was vastly pleased because she had obeyed him to the letter. Mme la Dauphine watched them re-embark on the following day. Melun bridge nearly finished them, for the princess's boat struck it and was almost overturned, bursting apart with a tearing sound. They were indeed in very great peril; but they managed to escape with nothing worse than a bad fright and some delay, eventually disembarking at Valvin where carriages were waiting for them. It was two hours after midnight when they arrived at Fontainebleau. Mme la Duchesse de Berry was immediately put to bed. She had done herself an injury, and miscarried of a daughter at six o'clock on the morning of Tuesday, 21 July. Mme de Saint-Simon informed the King at his first waking, before the *grandes entrées* were announced. He did not seem unduly affected, although his commands had been responsible for the mishap. The Duchesse de Beauvilliers and the Marquise de Châtillon had the task of escorting the embryo to Saint-Denis. Because it had been female, everyone was soon consoled. Mme la Duchesse de Berry suffered no ill effects.

M. le Comte de Toulouse had been suffering acutely from pain in the bladder for the last two months of that Marly. By the end of the excursion he was receiving almost no visitors. The King had more than once been to see him, but none the less insisted on his travelling to Fontainebleau with the rest of the Court, although riding in a coach was agony, and riding on horseback even more so. He, too, made the journey by water, but was confined to his room for almost the whole time that the Court was at Fontainebleau, except for once or twice when he visited the King. All this goes to prove that no excuses for absence were accepted on such journeys, and that the King liked to make his family continually aware of the fact that he was their master. Soon after their arrival he paid the Dauphine the extraordinary compliment of sending his musicians to play at her mass, as he had been wont to do for Monseigneur. The Dauphin did not want them, for he usually heard mass early and felt that they might disturb his meditations, greatly though he enjoyed their music. The Dauphine had not asked for this favour and it moved her deeply. It also served to show the Court how highly the King prized her.

When we were settled at Fontainebleau, I began to consider how best to reconcile M. de Beauvilliers with the Chancellor. I had continued to speak to him of Pontchartrain, not mentioning his father, but stressing the change in him and his implicit obedience to the instructions relayed to him by me. M. de Beauvilliers appeared so truly gratified that I resolved to test him, in order to discover whether Pontchartrain would be allowed to retain his office; for although hopeful on that score I was not as sure as I could have wished. I accordingly arranged to meet M. de Beauvilliers alone in the Galerie des Cerfs,[1] to which he had the key. The entry was at the foot of the private staircase, and it was the place he chose to talk in private, walking up and down, safe from eavesdroppers. After a few preliminary words concerning Pontchartrain's conduct, I extracted a firm promise from M. de Beauvilliers that, provided he remained as tractable, he would be left in office. I thanked him, and having thus made sure that Pontchartrain was out of danger, I felt that the time had come for the bold stroke which I had been preparing. At the same time, I fully realized that if I did manage to effect a reconciliation between him and the Chancellor it would be by force, so to speak, and against the inclinations of both. M. de Beauvilliers was too much offended and too conscious of his new power to listen to any praise of the Chancellor from me; and the Chancellor was too envious of the duke's rise in influence to endure the thought of humbling himself by making any advances.

Full of these plans, I went one afternoon to the Chancellery, where the Chancellor had a lodging, at a time when he was likely to be alone. There was a small private garden running the entire length of his room and on

---

[1] Made by Henri IV on the ground-floor of Fontainebleau, and so-called from the stag-hunting scenes in the decorations.

the same level. He used to call it his 'Chartreuse'; indeed it was very like,[1] and he loved to walk there alone, or sometimes with me. He led me into this little garden as soon as I arrived, for he was all agog to talk after our long separation during the Marly. After a brief exchange, touching first on one topic then on another, as old friends do when they have much to say, I inquired concerning the ministers' work with the Dauphin and the new authority of the Duc de Beauvilliers, which appeared greatly to disturb him. I asked if he knew what had happened at Marly. He replied that he had heard nothing of any particular interest; and at that point, looking him straight in the face, I asked whether truly he had heard nothing to affect him personally. He said, 'No,' and showed a lively curiosity to know my meaning. 'Well, Sir!' said I, 'that is what comes of spending every Marly at your home at Pontchartrain. It may show you the danger of such a habit, for your son has been within an ace of dismissal.' 'Alas!' he replied, shrugging his shoulders, 'his general conduct and foolish actions have long led me to expect that calamity.' Then turning to face me and looking much disturbed, 'Tell me everything; what has he been doing?' I told him all, with everything most calculated to alarm him, but carefully not describing the manner of the Duc de Beauvilliers's intervention, leaving him rather to imagine its probable effect in view of their quarrels and the duke's new powers, at which he more than once angrily exclaimed. I kept him on tenterhooks for several minutes, though he was impatient to learn his son's fate; and I purposely tormented him until he was ready to die of fright. Only then did I relieve his mind by saying that Pontchartrain was saved, and that I believed he might be upheld by his rescuer.

Picture the Chancellor gasping, embracing me, eagerly asking the name of the generous friend to whom he owed his son's salvation. I was very slow in replying, being most anxious to excite him still further. When at last I spoke, it was only to remind him of the imminence of the danger and the apparent hopelessness of Pontchartrain's situation; and despite his urgent questioning I went on to stress the enormous debt of gratitude owed to his saviour by the entire Pontchartrain family. The Chancellor thereupon asked whether I proposed ever to tell his name. At that I looked him in the eye with a glance of the utmost severity, which it was scarcely becoming for me to adopt to a man of his standing, but I felt that on this one occasion I might justly do so. 'How surprised, how ashamed you will feel when you hear the name of the man to whom you should humble yourself in gratitude! It is none other than he whom you have hated without cause, and continually persecuted wherever you encountered him. None other than M. de Beauvilliers himself.' Then, raising my voice and giving him a look full of fire,

---

[1] Saint-Simon may have been thinking of some of the Carthusian and Carmelite monasteries like the one at Marlagne which so much delighted him in 1692 (Vol. I, p. 7). The monks had cells each with a chapel and a small garden and 'the most delicious spring-water in their park that I have ever tasted'.

'M. de Beauvilliers who had only to keep silent to have your son dismissed; but who has saved him and re-established him in office. What say you now? Believe me, you should hang your head in shame.' 'What can I say?' replied the Chancellor, his voice breaking with emotion. 'Only that I am his servant for ever and ready to do anything to prove it.' Then gazing at me, he embraced me, saying with a catch of his breath, 'This is your doing; I know your touch. Ah! how well I know it! But truly, what a noble gesture for a man in M. de Beauvilliers's position, considering the terms on which we have been. I beg you, go to him and tell him that I am at his feet; I kiss his knee; I am his slave for ever. But before you go, tell me everything all over again, with any details that you may have omitted.' Now I made no objection, but spoke at such length that I have been obliged here to give only a shortened version, and in so doing I made no attempt to keep anything secret regarding M. de Beauvilliers.

The Chancellor continued to thank me for this great service to him and to his son, whom at that moment I had small reason to love, assuring me of his eternal gratitude and his desire to be guided by me in future. I replied that where he was concerned I only paid my debts, and that all his thanks should be given to the Duc de Beauvilliers, who hitherto had received nothing but annoyance from both him and his son. I entreated him, however, to do nothing until I had warned M. de Beauvilliers that his secret was out and (although I did not say this) until I had persuaded him to receive the Chancellor and be reconciled. I then went straight to M. de Beauvilliers and told him all. He turned red with anger, demanding with more than a little irritation why I had taken it upon myself to interfere. I said it had always been my dearest wish, nay my firm purpose to mend matters between him and the Chancellor, whose perilous situation was causing me acute anxiety. That so far mollified him, that he consented to allow me a little credit, not for good deeds, but for good intentions. After that I had no trouble in persuading him that without any encouragement his generosity had put the Chancellor and his son in his debt for life; but that if he would agree to be friends with the elder I would vouch for his being an endless source of comfort and support, and for both of them rendering valuable service to the State. M. de Beauvilliers, now quite appeased, charged me to convey a rather chilly compliment to the Chancellor, to the effect that he was ready to show both him and his son how sadly they had misjudged him; that at the Council all should speak freely and only bitterness and ill-temper be restrained, and that for his part he would always endeavour to support such measures as were agreeable to the Chancellor.

I took care not to tell the latter how coldly I had been received at first; but I informed him of all the rest. He was very eager to go immediately to seal the grand reconciliation, but for some reason M. de Beauvilliers insisted on putting off their meeting for ten days or a fortnight. I afterwards suspected that having been taken unawares, almost forced, he needed time to control himself, in order not to seem ungracious when they met. The Chancellor at last begged me to ask him as a particular favour to go to the Council on the next occasion by the long dark passage that is bounded on one side by the first valet's bedroom, and on the other by a vast wardrobe. It was the only means of getting from the ante-room into the King's bedroom. There, walking almost by his side, he could take the duke's hand, squeeze it, and thus tell him in silent language all that he was not yet allowed to speak. M. de Beauvilliers consented to this arrangement, and the scene took place as I have described. Ten days later M. de Beauvilliers bade me inform the Chancellor that he was to dine on the following day with the Duc de Chevreuse and would gladly converse with him then. Much to my surprise he refused to let me say anything whatsoever to M. de Chevreuse, although he generally told him all; moreover, he would not allow me to be present at the dinner. The meal went quite smoothly, with only a slight improvement of the usual frigid atmosphere; but afterwards M. de Beauvilliers asked the Duc de Chevreuse to leave them alone together. There ensued a spate of thanks from the one side, followed by embraces and promises of friendship from both parties. To be brief, they repeated to one another all that I had said to each of them in private, and by mutual agreement resolved to keep their reconciliation a secret, so as to disarm gossip. For some considerable time Society was kept in ignorance of what had taken place; but their changed conduct at the Council gradually opened the eyes of their fellow ministers, and thereafter, somewhat belatedly, those of the courtiers. All this occurred during the first fortnight at Fontainebleau.

The Duc de Lesdiguières died in Paris at the age of eighty-five. He had no children and the peerage thus became extinct. He was an imbecile courtier, and a brother of the Duc and the Maréchal de Créquy who were the very reverse of him in character. His wife, an inheritor of the wit of the Mortemarts, was foolish enough to be seen weeping for him, and was much ridiculed in consequence. 'What else would you have me do?' she said, 'I respected him like a father and loved him as though he were my son.' But when this made them laugh still more she was obliged to dry her eyes. She had spent the greater part of her life in strict retirement with Mme de Montespan. Her husband had been something of an encumbrance at that time; but despite all her wit she found her freedom an embarrassment.

The Princess von Fürstenberg died about this same time. She was the only, and immensely wealthy, daughter of Ligny, the maître des requêtes; her mother was a sister of old Mme de Tamponneau.[1] In her youth she had been enchantingly pretty, a perfect picture, and although born with a limp which she made no

[1] Mme de Tamponneau: who had the gift of attracting Society without providing any refreshments. See Vol. 1, p. 92.

effort to disguise was one of the finest dancers of her time. She was the sweetest woman imaginable, perfectly amiable, and charmingly naïve. The Duchesse de Foix was her friend and shared a lodging with her at Versailles. One evening that lady, returning home late after playing cards at Monsieur le Grand's house, found the Princess von Fürstenberg gone to bed and most piteously lamenting that she was dying and that all was over as far as she was concerned. Mme de Foix asked what ailed her. The princess replied that for the past two hours she had lain in bed with a splitting headache, throbbing arteries, and in a perfect bath of perspiration. Truly!, she said, she did feel very ill and thought that her heart had begun to fail. Picture Mme de Foix most deeply distressed but, with no other bed to go to, having to go round to the farther *ruelle* and stretch herself out on the extreme edge. As she inserted herself with great care so as not to disturb her friend, her leg touched something scorching, whereat she fell to screaming until the maid came running in with a candle. The object was a bed-warmer,[1] left forgotten in the bed, the heat of which was causing all the princess's discomfort. Mme de Foix teased her unmercifully, and so next day did all the Court.

I cannot imagine how a German so well born as her husband ever came to marry her; he left her a few years later established at the Court and returned to Germany, where he became first minister to the Elector of Saxony. His wife never had a *tabouret* and never even asked for that privilege, but her husband's uncle Cardinal von Fürstenberg eventually requested it on her behalf. He pretended that his nephew had sent for her, and made her begin her packing and start a round of farewell visits; although she took a very long time to complete them. When she was all ready to depart, the cardinal told King Louis a sad tale of his nephew's situation in Germany, not daring to set up house with his wife because of the misalliance, unable to visit her on account of the pressure of State affairs; becoming desperate lest his line should be extinguished. He was now driven to send for her, no matter what the consequences; but he would take it as a great personal favour, and it would ensure for her a warmer welcome, if the King would honour her by allowing her to be seated at his supper-table before she left France for ever—just on one occasion. The King, who never liked to refuse a man who had served him well, granted the request. Thus she sat; but she was extremely careful not to take leave of him, and very soon afterwards postponed her journey. Monseigneur, who liked her, suggested that to discontinue the *tabouret* would be worse than to have refused it in the first place. Cardinal von Fürstenberg argued that once having had that privilege she could not appear at the Court without it; and that her husband might think that her absence meant banishment. In the end she kept her *tabouret;* but her return to Germany receded into the distance

[1] *Un moine*: a heated log put in the bed.

and in the end no more was heard of it. She spent the remainder of her life as a seated-lady at our Court.[1]

The Maréchal de Boufflers died at Fontainebleau in his sixty-eighth year. He has figured so often in these memoirs that little remains to be said of him. When his last illness seized him he had just returned from a visit to Paris. In four or five days it led him to the gates of death. A quack produced a remedy that almost saved him by inducing him to perspire, and strictly forbade any kind of purge. Next day, the Faculty, astounded to find him in such good trim, ordered him to take physic:[2] it killed him within the day, the symptoms clearly showing that it had been poison on top of the earlier remedy. Little credit reflected on the doctors responsible. He was universally mourned, and everyone praised him, despite the fact that he had quite fallen out of favour. The King praised him also, but not much, and was greatly relieved by his death. His widow was taken to the house of the Duchesse de Guiche, where the Dauphin and Dauphine visited her. Immediately afterwards, however, she returned to Paris and would allow no favours to be asked on her behalf. Indeed, she indignantly refused all such suggestions. She was none the less in very straitened circumstances,[3] and a few days later was persuaded to allow the King to grant her a pension of twelve thousand francs.

The armies of the Rhine and the Alps spent the time of the campaign observing and subsisting. Bezons, acting in support of Harcourt, fed his troops at the enemy's expense on the farther side of the Rhine, while Harcourt himself remained with the bulk of our forces in our lines at Wissembourg. The campaign proceeded uneventfully until the middle of October; and then Harcourt, having nothing more to fear, left his army in forage-quarters and went to drink the waters of Bourbon.

In Flanders, Marlborough and Prince Eugene, united as ever, were content for a long time to subsist on the King's territory and to keep his army confined within its lines.[4] Compared with their earlier campaigns, this was letting us off lightly; but it was none the less humiliating. To the Allies, however, such advantages, though real enough, were unworthy of their past achievements. Marlborough, at the very height of such glory as is permitted to generals of his nation, faced serious trouble at home which he needed to offset by a sensational victory. Prince Eugene, on bad terms with the new Emperor, was much hampered

---

[1] From the *Sourches Memoirs*: 'A few days later the King gave the honours of the Louvre *(droit de cousin, droit de carosse, de chaise, de livrée)* to the Princess von Fürstenberg, who had been allowed a *tabouret* for one day only at the time of her marriage. It may have been part of the bargain for her estate at Grignoles, which the King bought for three hundred and sixty thousand livres to give to Mme de Maintenon, who greatly desired it because it bordered on her own property.'

[2] Physic always meant purging.

[3] Boufflers spent royally and left huge debts.

[4] The French lines of defence, ninety-nine miles in all, from Namur to the south of Boulogne. Villars was so proud of this enormous work of fortification that when Marlborough sported a new scarlet coat, labelled *Ne plus ultra* by his tailor, Villars applied the same inscription to the lines, even going so far as to write to the King that he had enticed Marlborough to the *Ne plus ultra*.

by the government at Vienna. Their interests were thus identical. It was to both
men's advantage to continue the war, on which all their power and glory rested, and which daily increased their wealth (especially that of Marlborough
who was as grasping as he was greedy). Such pressing needs persuaded them
to undertake an adventure clearly of a most dangerous kind, which, thanks to
their good fortune, daring, and the incomprehensible conduct of the Maréchal
de Villars, succeeded perfectly.

Villars was covering the town of Bouchain. Apart from the fact that
very few fortresses still remained to us on that sorely tried frontier, Bouchain
was of the greatest importance, guarding as it did the headwaters of the
rivers, and being the key to a wide stretch of country. In order to besiege it,
Marlborough was obliged to make a wide detour, skirting around our army
and the fortress itself, during which time he was forced to expose himself
to appalling risk at the crossing of the River Scheldt.[1] That risk, however, the two enemy commanders willingly undertook, despite the danger
of being attacked when their armies were only half-way across, or scram-
bling up the farther bank. Villars gleaned information from every possible
source, but paid his spies so badly that he received their warnings too late.
He proceeded to follow the enemy. Had he made sufficient haste he might
have overtaken them at the Scheldt; but having shown his desire to retrieve
his earlier mistake, which he could not disguise, and having arrived well in
time on a broad expanse of plain, he decided to encamp. Many of the generals,
including the Maréchal de Montesquiou, brought him news that the enemy were
very close and in extremely poor shape. They all assumed that he would attack
at once in order to make up for lost time. The army, however, was astounded to find him slow, indifferent, full of contradictions, for the news of the
enemy's miserable condition had spread through the ranks, giving rise to
an eagerness reminiscent of the old days of France's glory. Exhortations
to action were repeatedly pressed upon him, far beyond what was seemly. Villars remained unmoved. He proclaimed his personal courage, which
no one doubted, and bragged of what he would do on the following day.
The army, furious, lay all that night in battle order, and after repeated delays did not finally march until half the morning had gone. They
marched in vain. The enemy were now far ahead of them, having owed
their salvation to the extraordinary slowness of the Maréchal de Villars,

---

[1] It was indeed an appalling risk to take; but Marlborough managed to give Villars an entirely false idea of his intentions.
Many of his contemporaries considered it to have been his finest stratagem and manœuvre. It was on this occasion that he
gave his famous order: 'The Duke desires the infantry will step out'; and so they did.

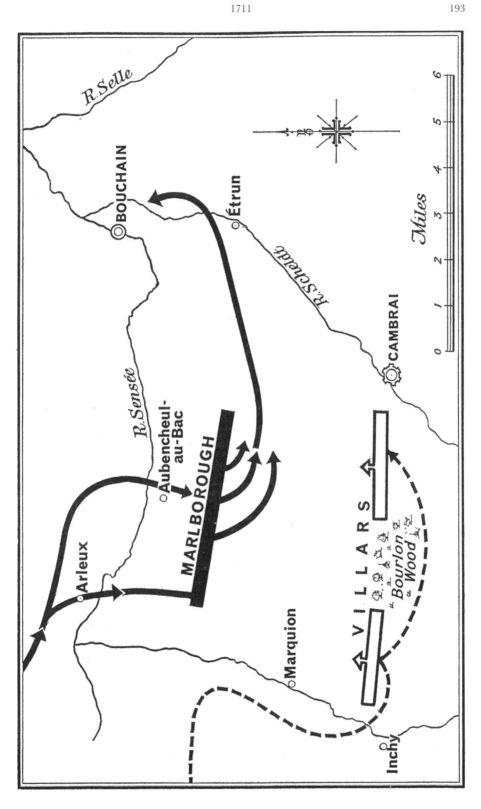

whose motives for remaining inactive are a complete mystery,[1] since it was generally agreed that he was bound to have been victorious.

[In 1709 the (Whig) Duchess of Marlborough had been replaced in Queen Anne's confidence by her cousin, the (Tory) Abigail Hill (Mrs Masham), with serious effects on the standing of Marlborough himself in the Queen's regard; and in 1711, the Duke, accused of misappropriating public moneys, was deprived of all his offices. When, on 31 December, 1711, Queen Anne wrote to Marlborough relieving him of his command, Louis XIV remarked, 'That will do for us everything that we desire!']

Villars sent his letter by courier to the Court, which had been kept four days in the most acute anxiety. When at last the man arrived at Fontainebleau he was brought by Voysin to the King, who had just said good-night. The Dauphin was already undressing, but he hurriedly put on his clothes, and with everyone else hastened to the King to learn the result of the battle and the names of the dead and wounded. The ante-room was crowded with people who imagined that Voysin was reading the list to the King. They waited with the utmost impatience for him to emerge, and then learned from him that no battle had been fought. But to return to the army. When Villars saw that the enemy had escaped him he burst into a fury of reproaches; whereupon the generals gazed at one another in complete astonishment. Finally Albergotti and one other spoke out, reminding him that had he listened to them he would have marched sooner. Montesquiou, who felt most injured, and more secure than others on account of his marshal's baton, spoke more frankly than they. An absolute denial, a flat, curt contradiction, without with your leave or by your leave, repaid him for those home-truths; whereupon, trembling with rage, he clapped his hand to his sword-hilt and abruptly departed. Villars took this as a triumph for himself, the only one in a campaign during which he had missed two splendid chances one after the other. Thereafter he behaved with even greater arrogance, more especially since after that shameful scene with Montesquiou he no longer ran any danger of being openly contradicted. Yet the facts were against him and the entire army knew it, for although Montesquiou was very little liked he was visited by crowds of officers. In the end Villars was brought somewhat to his senses and began to feel highly embarrassed. He took steps to make up the quarrel. Armies no less than Courts contain meddlesome busybodies, and there were many only too glad to make mischief between the two marshals. Montesquiou would have been hard put to it to defend such an atrocious and public insult as he had offered to a superior officer, and thus he was not unwilling, for the sake of the public good, to let matters rest. To sum up this shameful affair; there was no question of explanation, which would have been impossible, nor of excuses, which would only have made things worse.

---

[1] What Saint-Simon did not know was that Villars was obeying Louis XIV's explicit orders to remain on the defensive while peace negotiations were secretly going on with Queen Anne.

Forgetfulness, or the pretence that nothing had happened, was the only course left.

Never in all his life had Marlborough taken such an appalling risk. He publicly congratulated himself on his escape and turned his attention to the siege of Bouchain, for which he had been willing to endanger his whole army. Villars at first hoped to save the fortress by maintaining free access to it across the marshes.[1] The garrison was a strong one, commanded by Ravignan,[2] who came over to consult with the marshals. His presence was something of an embarrassment, for he had been taken prisoner with the Tournai garrison[3] and sent home on parole, the problem of an exchange preventing him from further active service. He had explained his unhappy circumstances to the Duke of Marlborough who most generously gave him leave to serve, but warned him that this permission extended only to serving against the English, not the Imperial or the Dutch armies. That proviso did not, however, stop Ravignan, who was a man with vast ambitions only attainable in the wars. He enjoyed soldiering, was an excellent officer, and belonged to the same family as Président de Mesmes[4] who took a great interest in him. He was also known to the King, whose page he had been, and who had often laughed at his boyish pranks out hunting. He had never hesitated to serve as an inspector-general (which was his rank) whenever he had the chance, but had not been in command of an army because his English permit did not allow that. When a clever man was needed to command at Bouchain during that summer, he was sent there because no one imagined there would be a siege. When the siege began the problem was to decide whether or not to let him remain. To leave him there would be a direct infringement of his parole, in the eyes of the Imperials and the Dutch. Moreover there was a great difference between serving in the line with a crowd of other officers, and organizing the defence of a beleaguered fortress; even Marlborough might have considered it an abuse of his clemency. According to all the rules of war, Ravignan was firmly excluded from any terms of surrender and would be hanged on the spot. Not even Marlborough, however well disposed, could prevent that.

When Ravignan appeared at headquarters, the whole question was considered at some length, and it was finally decided that neither his honour nor the rules of war should be put to the test. There was even talk of sending another general to replace him that same evening. Ravignan, on the other hand, valued his honour and his given promise less than the shame of abandoning his command in full view of the enemy. He asked Villars's permission to stay, and pressed so hard that that marshal, already provoked by a siege brought about by his own tardiness,

---

[1] Across the marshes surrounding Bouchain were narrow paths which the French protected with parapets of long faggots bound together with willows and rushes.

[2] Joseph de Mesmes, Marquis de Ravignan (1670-1742).

[3] In 1709.

[4] Jean Antoine III de Mesmes became Premier Président of the Parlement at the beginning of 1712.

with consequences that might well prove disastrous in the next campaign, was not
unwilling to leave in place a good officer whose resistance might be strengthened by
the prospect of death by hanging. Thus against the general opinion Villars took it
upon himself to allow the return of Ravignan, who did not need telling twice.

The communications with the fortress, protected with so much skill and
hard labour, proved impossible to maintain. Albergotti, who guarded them, was
driven back, and that reverse was considered to be decisive so far as the fortress
was concerned. This gave cause for bitter recriminations between Albergotti and
Villars; and these were pressed very far indeed. Villars continued to show every
sign of wishing to fight and defend the fortress, but it is far from certain that he
had any such intention. Be that as it may, his thundering did not last long, for he
was soon compelled to withdraw in order to subsist. After a month's defence a
parley was sounded for; the garrison were declared prisoners of war and were
marched to Tournai. The enemy generals with great magnanimity pretended to
know nothing of Ravignan. They spent another month in repairing the fortress,
by which time it was mid-October. Marlborough was eager to cross the Channel
to rescue his defeated party and mend his fallen fortunes. Prince Eugene, although
bound to him by their mutual interests, was not without his own troubles at home.
Thus private reasons and the lateness of the season induced them to terminate
the campaign. Villars was not ill-received when he returned, since there was no one
to replace him for the next season. Montesquiou spent the winter on the frontier,
and was not best pleased by a short visit which he paid to the Court.

Chalais[1] took leave of the King, at Fontainebleau, before taking up his
commission in the King of Spain's bodyguard—the Walloon company, of
which M. de Bournonville was captain. Mme des Ursins always retained a lively
affection for the name and relatives of her first husband,[2] whose nephew Chalais
was, he being the only son of M. de Talleyrand's elder brother[3] who resided
permanently on his estates. Young Chalais had thus never experienced the life of
the Court or the King's service; and although his father was not best pleased with
the appointment, the boy himself was only too thankful to be given a chance. For
other reasons besides family affection, Mme des Ursins was glad to have someone who, for want of better, would be loyal to her alone, and who was equally
unknown in France and in Spain.

That lady, not content with reigning supreme in Spain, had begun to think
of ruling a kingdom of her own. She had therefore seized the opportunity,
when the King of Spain had presented the Elector of Bavaria with his subject
provinces in the Low Countries, to have a clause inserted in the deeds to the

[1] Mme des Ursins' nephew, Louis Jean de Talleyrand, Prince de Chalais (1680-1757).
[2] Her first husband, Adrien Blaise de Talleyrand, self-styled Prince de Chalais (d. 1670).
[3] Her husband's elder brother Jean de Talleyrand, Marquis d'Excideuil, later known as the Prince de Chalais.

effect that the Elector must provide her with estates producing an income of a hundred thousand livres, and full sovereign powers over them during her lifetime. It was soon agreed that her capital should be La Roche-en-Ardenne.[1] You shall see how this kingdom of hers took various forms, changed its location, and in the end completely evaporated. But in the early stages, the Princesse des Ursins felt so sure of it that she concocted a most ambitious scheme, namely to barter it with King Louis for the independent sovereignty of Touraine and Amboise— a kingdom to be hers for her life, and afterwards to revert to the Crown of France. That having been arranged, she proposed to leave Spain and establish herself in France for her remaining years.

With all this in mind, she sent her favourite d'Aubigny,[2] whom I have already mentioned, with orders to build her a sumptuous residence in France and prepare everything for her occupation. He accordingly bought a large field between Tours and Amboise, but rather nearer Amboise, without the surrounding acres or the manorial rights, which would not be needed since she proposed to become sovereign lady of the entire province. D'Aubigny began at once to build a vast, solid, and most magnificent palace, with courtyards and out-buildings, and all the requisites for gardens of an enormous size, which the appointments of the residence matched in splendour.[3] The whole province, the neighbouring districts, Paris, even the Court itself were amazed. No one could understand such an immense expenditure on what was a mere villa; for a house set in the middle of a field, without estates, revenues, or manorial rights, could not rightly be called otherwise. Still less could people comprehend the erection of this great and splendid cage in order to house the bird that built it. For a long time it remained a complete mystery, and this folly of Mme des Ursins became, as you shall see, one of the chief reasons for her downfall.

Let us not pursue the story of her disappointment, but see what became of that great palace, which was complete in every detail, fully furnished and equipped, at the very time when she finally despaired of ever possessing a kingdom. No one seriously imagined that d'Aubigny, for all the wealth he had amassed, would have dared to construct this huge palace for his own habitation; but enlightenment regarding the real owner came slowly as the rumour spread that the Princesse des Ursins was behind it all. It was at first thought that she was tired, or tired of Spain, anxious to end her days in her own country, yet unwilling to be a mere appendage of our Court after having queened it so absolutely elsewhere. But a palatial residence without land was utterly incomprehensible. Only when the news of her incredible claim to sovereign status became public were all eyes

[1] In [Belgian] Luxembourg.
[2] Jean Bouteroue d'Aubigny, whom Saint-Simon called Mme des Ursins' confidential agent. See Vol. 1, pp. 234, 236, 254.
[3] The Château de Chanteloup, near Amboise. Nothing now remains of it.

opened to the truth about Chanteloup, as the house was named. The down-fall of this ambitious woman, as will be seen in due course, prevented her from enjoying her royal residence. It remained the property of d'Aubigny, who played host there in grand style to many curious neighbours and distinguished travellers, but did not conceal the fact that it was not for himself nor with his money that the great house had been erected. In the end he lived there permanently and was well liked and respected in the district. It was there also that his wife died, leaving him with a daughter of tender years, who subsequently married the Marquis d'Armentières.[1]

The campaign in Spain had come to nothing; there had been only trifling encounters. The Archduke had been too weak to undertake anything at the beginning; later, as soon as his brother the Emperor Joseph was dead, his only thought was to leave, and he had only money enough to pay for his journey. M. de Vendôme also lacked money, and therefore did everything to persuade the two courts that he should besiege Barcelona, for which enterprise he was amassing armaments. The King and Queen of Spain spent the winter at Saragossa and the summer very uselessly at Corella.[2] The Duc de Noailles,[3] having nothing to do in Catalonia, had been assigned to M. de Vendôme's command. He had joined the Spanish court early in March; M. de Vendôme, himself, rarely made an appear-ance, on the pretext of preparing for the siege. The constraint of court-life did not suit him; he preferred to reign and live free at his own headquarters. Thus the summer and autumn had passed, and just before winter set in the Spanish court returned to Madrid.

On Monday, 14 September, the King returned from Fontainebleau by way of Petit-Bourg, and arrived at Versailles on the 15th. Cardinal de Noailles had been summoned to appear on that same day. He was at the coach-door when the King stepped down. He immediately had a rather long audience of the King, and a still longer one of the Dauphin. The prince had done much work concern-ing this affair while he was at Fontainebleau, and I had day after day received reports of his progress from the Bishop of Bordeaux.[4] There were two essential questions: the personal quarrel between Cardinal de Noailles and the Bishops of La Rochelle and Luçon, into which the Bishop of Gap had intruded himself like the devil into miracles; and Père Quesnel's book, that is to say the doctrinal dispute, wherein the said bishops had acted merely as shoehorns to insert the argument. They felt all the odium of their transitory status; that it could not long endure, and that it would end by their being pulled down in the same way

---

[1] Adélaïde Jeanne Françoise Bouteroue d'Aubigny (1717-1746). She married the Marquis d'Armentières in 1733.
[2] In Navarre.
[3] The Duc de Noailles, formerly the Comte d'Ayen, who had married Mme de Maintenon's only niece Mlle d'Aubigné. Saint-Simon was very jealous; Noailles's opportunities were just what he had longed for for himself.
[4] Saint-Simon's friend Armand Bazin de Bezons (1655-1721), Bishop of Bordeaux, made Archbishop of Rouen 1719.

through the quarrel on doctrine, unless more help[1] than that of the three aggressors materialised. Père Le Tellier, who ruled the Bishop of Meaux and through him had complicated the Dauphin's labours, had used the interval to make every bishop under his influence write a letter to the King, expressing horror at the doctrine contained in Père Quesnel's book and condemning it. The servants of the Jesuits—the weak ones who dared not break with the busy confessor, the greedy ones, and the ambitious—made an impressive total. Cardinal de Noailles got wind of these operations, all of which pointed to the Jesuits of the Rue Saint-Antoine,[2] and in particular to the Fathers Lallemant, Doucin, and Tournemine. Certain highly indiscreet and vastly impertinent threats escaped them; and other bigwigs of the Society echoed their menaces. Cardinal de Noailles removed from these clerics the right to confess or preach, and thus created a fresh disturbance.

Such was the situation at the time of the return from Fontainebleau. The bishops' letters were about to descend on the King, because it had taken some considerable time to compose them all on the same theme but in different styles, to send them to the various dioceses for signature, and to have them re-dispatched. Monsieur de Meaux had introduced all manner of difficulties, he could now invent no others, and Monsieur le Dauphin was all the more anxious to end the affair when he saw that the petitions of this small group of Jesuits would stir up still more enmity. The King, although prepared by Père Tellier, heard Cardinal de Noailles's arguments regarding the petitions, and would not permit the latter to bias the Dauphin, who gave his judgment that very day to the cardinal—by whom it was gladly accepted. Voysin had already received the consent of the three bishops who, hoping the cardinal would raise an objection that would bring him once more into disfavour, had greatly praised the judgment and given the Dauphin their replies within the week.

The judgment ruled that the three bishops should together compose a new pastoral letter in atonement for the previous ones; that before seeking to publish it they should send it to Paris for examination by the Dauphin's nominees; that it should then be shown to the cardinal himself, and, only if he approved it, published; finally, that the King should then send to him a letter (which the King already had in his possession) from the three bishops, as further reparation for all that they had previously written, and that in neither letter should Père Quesnel's book be mentioned. The Dauphin, in sublime ignorance of the subtlety of the Jesuits and the ambitions of the Bishop of Meaux, believed that all was now well, and that the rumpus over the book would subside with the personal quarrel in which he had intervened. If there were truly a foundation for the novel complaints about a book for so long highly prized and

[1] Pères Le Tellier, Doucin and Lallemant, see p. 121.
[2] Saint-Louis, in the Rue Saint-Antoine, was the Jesuits' professed house.

universally accepted, he hoped that the question would be discussed in peace and amity by reconciled prelates. Yet it was not hard to discern a plot. The business of writing a pastoral letter and submitting it for examination might well be spun out, and any number of difficulties might arise, and the specially imposed silence would allow complete freedom to raise the question again after the reconciliation, on the noble pretext of purifying doctrine. The Dauphin, however, could never have believed so ill of his neighbour. How little did he imagine the dozens of letters being composed at that very time, or the astounding chance that revealed the whole knavish plot and handed it down to posterity!

On the day following the return from Fontainebleau, the Duc de Noailles returned from Spain and, obeying the King's express orders, presented himself immediately in Mme de Maintenon's room. I have already mentioned that weakness and lack of supplies of every kind had kept the armies inactive, apart from a few minor engagements, too trifling to interrupt the Duc de Noailles's assiduous attendance on the King of Spain at Saragossa and Corella. A lust for power, encouraged by the favour shown him as Mme de Maintenon's nephew, and the lustre gained by commanding an army, had led the Duc de Noailles to embark on an enterprise so foolhardy that it meant certain ruin. At Saragossa he had become acquainted with the Marquis of Aguilar, captain of the king's bodyguard, and a friendship had sprung up between them, owing to their similar tastes and ambitions. I do not know which of them first conceived the idea, but they adopted it with equal fervour, and devoted all their energies to promoting what they fondly hoped would make them masters of the Spanish court and kingdom.

The Queen of Spain already showed symptoms of the scrofula that caused her death.[1] She no longer accompanied the king on his endless hunting expeditions, but was obliged to keep to her apartments, living a much more private life, and wearing a hood that covered her head and throat and also part of her face. The conspirators knew that the King could not be without a woman, and was accustomed to let the queen rule him. They deluded themselves that the Princesse des Ursins' power depended entirely on the queen, and that if the queen lost her influence, her duenna would fall also. Moreover, judging the king by themselves, they believed that the queen's illness might be used to turn him against her. That once achieved, they proposed to give him a mistress, in the conviction that marital fidelity would soon succumb to physical needs. With such a mistress, who must needs look to them alone for council and support, they reckoned to supplant the queen and become themselves what the Princesse des Ursins then was to the court

---

[1] Scrofula, tuberculosis, the King's evil, which it was believed could be cured by the King's touch, on his return from taking the Sacraments. Suppurating glands on her neck may have been the cause of the hood, but in the early eighteenth century many other afflictions of the head and eyes were confused with scrofula.

and the State. This squalid intrigue did little credit to the brains that conceived it, and particularly ill became a foreigner so nobly, agreeably, and newly established in Spain as the Duc de Noailles.

Be that as it may, they immediately set to work, taking every opportunity to become intimate with the king. Both of them, Aguilar because he had once been war minister, Noailles by reason of his late command, had plenty of excuses for long and serious conversation. Both were in high favour with the queen and Mme des Ursins, whom they courted with increasing ardour for fear lest their plot be discovered. So matters stood during the entire time that the court remained at Saragossa.

The king's removal to Corella, which entailed a separation from his wife, seemed to them a suitable moment for the first move. They attacked him boldly on the subject of his health (always a tender spot as they well knew), filling him with apprehensions, and suggesting that he was in danger of contracting the queen's illness if he continued to eat and sleep with her. Their tender solicitude was so graciously received that they felt hopeful. When they pressed on, their hopes increased. They condoled with him on his physical discomfort; they urged on him the need to satisfy his desires. Finally they proposed the mistress. Until then all had gone beyond their best expectations, but at the word 'mistress' the king was profoundly shocked. He withdrew into himself; refused to speak to them except on general topics, and rebuffed their advances. His stiff embarrassment was a fatal portent which they were quite unable to overcome.

They were indeed undone, for no sooner was the king with the queen and Mme des Ursins than he revealed the smooth, deceitful proposal made to him by two men whom those ladies were continually praising for their single-minded loyalty and discretion. Picture the commotion! Yet it was decided to say nothing for the time being, lest they be cheated of their vengeance. The queen wrote indignantly to her sister the Dauphine. Mme des Ursins, with all the art of which she was so superb a mistress, wrote to Mme de Maintenon; and however angry that lady and King Louis may have felt with the princess for abusing her power (more of that anon), this revelation shocked them to the core. The King's anger was on the grounds of immorality, ambition, and insolence. Mme de Maintenon was wounded where it most hurt her—her absolute rule of Spain through the medium of the Princesse des Ursins. Both were revolted by the ingratitude— black treachery was the Dauphine's word—of one who, having been loaded with wealth, rank, appointments and privileges and, most of all, honoured with their confidence, had now impudently abused it. Mme de Maintenon, who had treated her niece's husband as a son, and sometimes as an adviser, was the more especially distressed. She showed little outwardly, but in her heart she never forgave him. The Dauphine had looked on him as a friend and was deeply hurt for the sake of the queen her sister. She felt infinitely grateful to Mme de Maintenon for so hotly pressing an affair that involved her own nephew, and for defending her sister's cause with so much ardour.

In Spain, Aguilar was banished to his estates. The Duc de Noailles, in the short time allowed him for packing, found all doors locked against him and all faces frozen. He arrived, as I have said, on the day after the Court's return from Fontainebleau, and reported to the King in Mme de Maintenon's room. Everything was made to appear as usual, but the interview was ominously short.

It was not long before the Court perceived by the King's icy manner and the Duc de Noailles's discomfort in the presence of the Dauphin, and especially of the Dauphine, that something very grave had occurred. No one knew what, for his recall had not yet been announced, and its cause was not even suspected. The ladies of the inner circle observed that he was rarely with Mme de Maintenon, whose coldness and constraint were more than obvious, in great contrast to her previous solicitude. M. de Noailles, endeavouring on the one hand to conceal his unhappy plight, and on the other to find some means of reinstating himself, was in a most alarming predicament. His family were furious with him and would do nothing to help him. His wife, a perfect simpleton for all that she was Mme de Maintenon's niece, had become very wearisome to that lady, scarcely dared to speak to her, and rarely saw her except to receive a scolding. His uncle the cardinal was on the worst possible terms with Mme de Maintenon and scarcely better with the King. As for the ministers, Noailles had committed a crime unpardonable in the eyes of such men as the Dukes of Chevreuse and Beauvilliers; and to make matters worse, he was his father's son.[1] He was out of favour also with M. and Mme la Duchesse d'Orléans, having sided against that lady in her many quarrels with Madame la Duchesse. I do not imagine that in his palmy days he would have let this disturb him, but at such moments even trifles assume great importance.

I was known to be a close friend of M. and Mme la Duchesse d'Orléans, and believed also to be the friend and confidant of the Dukes of Chevreuse and Beauvilliers. My private audiences with the Dauphin had not yet been discovered, but something was suspected because of the prince's manner to me, and his frequent conversations with Mme de Saint-Simon at Marly, or at his own receptions, to which we were now always bidden. The princess's desire that my wife should succeed the Duchesse du Lude was well known. The King and Society treated her with particular consideration, and the King looked on me also with kindness. In view of all this, M.

[1] The Maréchal de Noailles (the duke's father) had done his best to oust the Duc de Beauvilliers who had never forgiven him.

de Noailles decided that I was the man for him, and a fortnight had not elapsed before he trained his batteries on me.

He is now a Marshal of France, commander-in-chief of the first army, and a minister of State, and will figure henceforth in these memoirs in so many different guises that, although he is alive, healthy, and three months my junior, I think it highly desirable to describe him. He is the kind of man who would inevitably have acquired an immense fortune, even had he not found one ready-made. He is sufficiently tall, but stocky in build, with a firm and heavy tread. His dress, plain, or at best an officer's uniform, aims at a show of unpretentious honesty, which he supports with a hail-fellow-well-met air. It is rare to find a man with more, or more varied, talents, or one better skilled in tuning his mind to the moods of others, persuading them, if he so pleases, that he is fired with the same ambitions and loyalties, and active in the same causes. Kind and affable when he chooses, never appearing bored, no matter how much he may be so in reality, full of banter, with a salty wit that never offends, bubbling over with exquisite sallies and repartee, he is excellent company and a fine musician, possessing a gift for saying whatever he pleases with perfect control, even after an entire day spent in the salon at Marly during one of the unhappiest and most anxious periods of his life. I speak from having watched him time and again, knowing his situation from his own lips, and asking him later how he contrived to appear so gay, so cultivated, so well informed. That side of him, however, is the merest husk, for if one probes, one quickly discovers him to be the master of nothing but grandiose language. None the less, he tells a tale charmingly, and has a talent for finding amusing nothings that brighten even the dingiest and most thorny discussions, and all apparently without the smallest contrivance. Those are indeed fine qualities in a courtier. Unhappily he has another side.

All his amiability, all his protestations of friendship and esteem conceal the kind of barbarity which poets attribute to the Tartars. He is a very sink of iniquity, false-hearted and treacherous, making use of everyone. Scorning the commoner virtues, and serving only his own advantage, he is the most abandoned libertine and a bare-faced and unwavering hypocrite. He lends himself to any mean trick, and if caught red-handed appears unashamed, and continues in the same way with even less concealment. An adept at lies and slander, if he is cornered he twists snakelike, spitting venom, using the most abject shifts to entice one back and crush one in his coils. He has behaved thus without due offence or cause to friends who trusted him, even to those to whom he admits being greatly indebted. At the root of his villainy is a boundless ambition that leads him into most foul intrigues. Yet his roving and undisciplined mind constantly betrays him, at one moment tempting him to be reckless, at another holding him back in fear. He is then hesitant and fearful, not knowing how to act, until in the end he cannot protect himself from the effects of his evil-doing. His mind becomes confused, which is the cause of that useless marching and countermarching that so much fatigues his soldiers, those conflicting orders issued six, eight, or even ten times in rapid succession to the same troops in the space of a single hour, for no apparent reason. Similarly, in affairs of State he adopts a plan, pursues it hotly for a week or two, abandons everything for its sake, and then forgets it to take up a second plan, which he pursues with equal ardour until a third presents itself, and so it continues.

A man who appears so frank and amiable but whose mind is dark and secret, ready to stick at nothing, taking treachery and crime in its stride, is, thank God, a rarity, for he is a real danger, luring men to their doom like the siren in the poem. My own temper, honest, frank, liberal, and far too simple, was of the very kind to fall to his charm. He showed me only his more attractive side. I willingly accepted his husks for grain. I did not know him then, nor did I guess that he wore a mask; I did not even know why he had returned from Spain. I did not, to be sure, delude myself that he made advances to me for my own sake. I thought rather that he saw behind me M. le Duc d'Orléans and the Duc de Beauvilliers, and, guessing at the Dauphin, wished for my friendship so as to be on the safe side. I was enchanted by this past-master in the art of pleasing. I responded to him, and gradually warmed to his confidences; but I gave him none in return, for I sensed somehow that he was over-eager.

Spain and his campaigns served as an introduction. Certain revelations concerning the King's private life, that had eluded me because its centre was Mme de Maintenon's room, led me to trust him, and when that trust was better established there followed talk of the present and the future. He then struck two melodious chords that had the desired effect on me. The first was our much abused rank, the second, the sad plight of his uncle the cardinal. Thus I believed that we were united on these two subjects. He introduced them only after smoothing the way in other directions, but soon began to use them to increase my confidence and so serve his own ends.

His next move was to reveal his unhappy relations with M. and Mme la Duchesse d'Orléans, of which I was well aware. He admitted to feeling embarrassed, and frankly said that he would be obliged if I could set matters right for him. This I was all the more willing to do because being unaware of his true situation with the King, I imagined that Mme de Maintenon would soon restore him to favour. Thus believing, I felt that d'Orléans would gain most from a reconciliation, and might find in him a useful source of information and a warning voice. Mme la Duchesse d'Orléans expressed modified pleasure; her husband proved more difficult because he could not forgive the Spanish plot. I none the less besieged him for four or five days, and in the end conquered him, so that they agreed to receive the Duc de Noailles after dark, without further explanation, in fact, on the old friendly footing. This they did, and I afterwards learned that the meeting was successful and that others had followed, although at long intervals.

At that point M. de Noailles began to fear lest I discover the truth about Spain—which by that time I knew, though I thought it best to say nothing. He had been dismayed by its effect on the Dauphin, and hoped to persuade me to speak to M. de Beauvilliers on his behalf, for that nobleman appeared to offer the only means of reconciliation with the prince, and through him with the Dauphine. Thereafter he could use his sisters to soften the princess, and thus gradually melt the icefield surrounding Mme de Maintenon. That at least was what I gathered from his cryptic utterances, following a long description of the mischief done to him in Spain where, so he said, he had been ruined for the sole purpose of destroying Aguilar, why he did not know, except that some Spaniards were jealous of an honest man and glad to harm him. The disgrace, he added, had rebounded upon him at our Court, where they were as unwilling to hear his side as had been the King of Spain. He continued these complaints for several days on end before eventually disclosing his wishes regarding the Duc de Beauvilliers, whom he greatly praised, saying how deeply he had always been impressed by his virtues, and ending by showing a strong desire to meet him, in the hope that better might follow. He was infinitely tactful, appearing anxious not to cause me embarrassment and, since he loved to talk, I let him continue while I considered how best to act. What brought me at last to consent was the conviction that he would eventually return to the favour of his doting aunt, and thereafter of the King and the Dauphine, who was shallow, incapable of true friendship or lasting emnity, and, moreover, was surrounded by his near relations. I also concluded that so gifted a man, senior captain of the Guard, and brother of three palace-ladies, would be very close to the Dauphin after his accession. The prince might well find him agreeable, and it would therefore be best to have him on our side and not bearing us a grudge for rebuffing his advances. Thus, when he pressed me, I readily consented and set about to effect a reconcilation between him and M. de Beauvilliers.

I first approached M. de Chevreuse, believing that his natural amiability would incline him to support me, whereas M. de Beauvilliers's profound aversion for one who was the nephew both of Mme de Maintenon and Cardinal de Noailles might well make him refuse even to listen. I was not mistaken. M. de Beauvilliers's manner was frigid in the extreme, but when I pointed out that nothing was required of him beyond ordinary civility, a few kind words, and a brief exchange on matters of general interest, he asked for a few days to think it over. He then allowed me to return with an answer that went a little beyond bare politeness. M. de Chevreuse was more forthcoming.

I delivered these replies with great care for accuracy. M. de Noailles's gratification was not at all diminished by my very moderate success, and his thanks were
effusive. A meeting was arranged. MM. de Chevreuse and de Beauvilliers were
delighted with him and thanked me for my trouble. As for de Noailles, he was in
the seventh heaven, for he saw himself well on the road to friendship with the
Dauphin. Thereafter his impatience knew no bounds, and he boldly asked me,
although declaring that it was too soon to expect favours, if I would do my best
for him in that quarter also. I took soundings, and after discovering that the two
noblemen did genuinely like him, I managed to persuade them that granting him
a favour swiftly and unasked would greatly increase his gratitude. They conceded
that this was true, and shortly afterwards a distinct change could be observed in
the Dauphin's manner to the Duc de Noailles, who came to me in raptures, covering me with thanks, and vowing that M. de Beauvilliers had been his saviour, the
open-sesame to his future prospects. Alas for all concerned! No use saying more!
Let us return for a moment to Cardinal de Noailles.[1]

On account of the difference of age and rank, he was a man with whom I
had had little previous acquaintance. His deplorable weakness at the time of the
destruction of Port-Royal-des-Champs[2] had turned me somewhat against him,
but the cynical hypocrisy of the trap set for him by the two bishops, the manifest
innocence of their wretched victim, and his patience and quiet confidence in the
rightness of his cause had stung me to anger with the whole wicked conspiracy. I
was intimate with many of his friends who had disclosed to me the whole truth,
and although Père Tellier did his best to deceive me, he was not clever enough to
conceal his knavery. He was also credited with having engineered the banishment
from the Court of M. de Noailles, which so disgusted me that I went one morning
to pay my respects to that prelate towards the end of one of his public audiences, so
as to let people see whose side I was on. My visit moved him deeply, more especially
because I had displayed so little caution; and he showed his appreciation by explaining the affair to me at some length. That was how a friendship sprang up between
us that grew continually and ended only with his death. A few days later the King
gave him an audience, after which his case was turned over to the Dauphin.

The Court had scarcely returned from Fontainebleau before the bomb
exploded with the deadly effect planned by its fiendish contrivers. The King

---

[1] It is very important to differentiate between Cardinal de Noailles, whom Saint-Simon thought almost a saint, and the
duke whom he thought little better than a devil.
[2] See Vol. 1, p. 495 f.

received the deluge of letters from hypocritical bishops trembling for the true faith, and compelled, so they said, by Cardinal de Noailles's extreme danger, the dictates of their conscience, and their sacred office (for which they stood accountable to God) to throw themselves at the feet of the Church's eldest son, suppressor of heresies, entreating him to protect, as always, the right doctrine. This pathetic appeal with variations was given substance by the spurious image of the two poor and unknown bishops who had found themselves in duty bound to attack the Archbishop of the Metropolis in all his Roman carmine, supported by his noble friends and relatives, his favour and his great reputation. The scandal was appalling. The King, beset at all hours by Père Tellier his hands overflowing with suitably annotated letters, was as much disturbed as though the Faith itself had been about to succumb. Many other letters were received by Mme de Maintenon also, and Bissy, Bishop of Meaux, made her savour them to the full, so that she, too, added to the King's alarm.

At the very moment of victory, however, something occurred that might well have undermined the entire plot if only Cardinal de Noailles had brought himself to act. Let me repeat that I shall not enlarge on an affair that already fills many volumes; I shall tell only what came to my own knowledge, and leave the whys and wherefores to the documents. It so happened that Père Tellier's first letter to the Bishop of Clermont, bidding him write to the King, and explaining just how to compose his letter, so that in effect he had only to copy, sign, and address it, together with a model of a companion letter to Père Tellier, and the original of a letter from that priest to his nephew the Abbé Bochart de Saron, treasurer of the Sainte-Chapelle, at Vincennes, all fell into the hands of Cardinal de Noailles. These missives so blatantly revealed the plot that nothing afterwards could have re-buried it. The cardinal had only to take them to the King, show them to him, and without dispossessing himself of these vital documents explain the full abomination, plead for justice, and particularly for the banishment of Père Tellier to some distant spot whence nothing more would be heard of him. He should next have gone to Mme de Maintenon and told her all.

Père Tellier would then have been ruined irretrievably, the letter-writing bishops silenced, and Cardinal de Noailles once more returned to favour with his reputation greatly enhanced. But instead of taking that wise and easy course, the cardinal felt so sure of his prey that he talked, and postponed action until the day of his weekly audience. The truth by that time was out, and Père Tellier had been informed. The extreme peril of that priest lent him the wings and the courage required to prepare the King, who was so partial to his confessor that he believed him. Thus at his audience the cardinal found that he had been forestalled. Amazed and indignant at the King's apparent imperviousness to a blatant deception, he was so much bewildered that he did not see that King Louis had none the less been shaken. That was the moment when he should have summoned all his strength in order to convince him; instead of which he waited until his next weekly audience, by which time the King's mind had been made up, and the confessor had still further misled him. Cardinal de Noailles's only weapons were gentleness and compassion; thus he had no chance of success. Père Tellier, despite his bold front, had secretly been dreading the effect of the Cardinal's audience; when none appeared his relief was enormous at having escaped with the biggest fright that he and his fellow-conspirators were ever to experience in the entire course of their lives.

The Dauphin, however, was not so easily gulled. He and the Dauphine spoke their minds freely in this matter, for he told me and others also that by rights Père Tellier should have been dismissed. It was immediately after the Court's return from Fontainebleau that the King had placed the entire affair in his hands. He gave too much weight to the theological aspect, but I thought that I detected in him the beginning of a deep distrust of the Jesuits, borne out by the above remark that concerned not only Père Tellier, but also the Bishop of Meaux. What made me doubly sure was that on the last occasion of my working with him, two days before the Court returned from Marly to Versailles, and five or six days before the Dauphine's fatal illness, he suddenly began to speak of Cardinal de Noailles as we were sorting our papers, and made a most illuminating remark. After praising the cardinal for his piety, sincerity, and sweet temper, he said, 'No one will ever persuade me that he is a Jansenist', and thereafter advanced many arguments to support that statement. The conversation ended by his commanding me to go deeply into everything relating to the Gallican liberties and the affair of Cardinal de Noailles. He then told me that the King had entrusted him with the whole matter and that he was anxious with my assistance to settle it once and for all. He several times bade me go to Paris to consult those whom I thought likely to be best informed, and to consult the best books about Rome and our freedoms because he wished to study those two aspects in particular. The Dauphin had never before given me the slightest inkling that he was thinking along those lines; I can only suppose that he decided to act when dreadful suspicions were aroused in him by the discovery of the Abbé de Saron's batch of letters. He made me promise to start work at once and not to delay a moment because, he said, the affair had dragged on far too long. As a matter of fact, I was just about to spend several days in Paris for that very purpose when I was delayed at first by the Dauphine's illness and then entirely prevented by the worst disaster that had ever befallen France.

CHAPTER III

1712

Président de Mesmes appointed Premier Président of the Parlement of Paris - Our plenipotentiaries go to Utrecht - Marlborough wishes to leave England - The Dauphine's wardrobe removed from the Comtesse de Mailly and then grudgingly returned to her - Row between Mme la Duchesse de Berry and Mme la Duchesse d'Orléans - The King dines privately with Mme de Maintenon - Death of Gondrin, La Vallière's humorous remark - Monsieur le Duc loses an eye - Mysterious disappearance of a snuffbox - Death of the Dauphine - Death of the Dauphin - The Archbishop of Rheims's terrible suspicion of the Duc de Noailles - Obsequies of the Dauphin and Dauphine - Death of the little Dauphin - I find myself in grave danger - Cause of their deaths - Suspicion falls on M. le Duc d'Orléans - Character of that prince - The Princesse des Ursins and the Duc de Vendôme become highnesses - Entertainments at Marly - I spend a month at La Ferté, and my reason for doing so - Death of the Duc de Vendôme - The Battle of Denain - Death of M. de Soubise - Death of Reffuge - Peace negotiations between France and England - I compose a memorandum on the renunciations - Death of the Duc de Chevreuse - Death of the Duc de Mazarin - The King is bored - Return of the Maréchal de Villeroy

THE YEAR opened with the appointment of a new premier président of the Paris Parlement. Peletier, a very mediocre magistrate to be holding after-dinner audiences in the lordly manner of his predecessors, had succeeded Harlay solely on the reputation of his father, whom the King had liked and esteemed even after his retirement. His son,[1] however, was most notably lacking in any of the qualities required for that high office, and after his accident, when the floor had fallen in beneath his chair as he sat at table,[2] he was so much weakened by the fright (not withstanding that no one was hurt) or possibly by a disturbance of his brain, that he could no longer do his work. Thereafter he lagged behind in his duties, and

---

[1] Louis le Peletier. His father Claude had in the first instance been a protégé of Godet des Marais, Bishop of Chartres, and Mme de Maintenon.

[2] The accident happened on 18 December, 1707. Saint-Simon says, 'He was dining at home at the Palais de Justice with his family and one or two counsellors when the floor suddenly subsided and they all fell into the cellar. A pile of firewood stopped them from falling the whole distance, or even from being injured. Only the children's tutor was hurt. The premier président's wife was the only one so placed that she did not fall. They were all severely shocked; the premier président so much so that he was never afterwards the same.'

remained in office only because his father kept him there. He was already a rich man and could hope for no further advancement, but his father still persisted. As soon as his father was dead, Peletier's only thought was to send his resignation to the King, which he accordingly did on the last day of the old year.

Five days later, M. du Maine offered the post to Président de Mesmes; it being the King's express desire that his beloved son should make that nomination because in time to come he might need to have the premier président wholly on his side. Those Mesmes were of peasant stock from Mont-de-Marsan; many of them, even today, remain in the lowest category of those who still pay the *taille*. That is the absolute truth, notwithstanding the family tree concocted, published, and advertised by such of them as have become wealthy, thus successfully hood-winking Society, despite the fact that one cannot deny marriages or entirely disguise the humbler occupations of the pen and gown beneath calligraphical flourishes and ornaments.

The new premier président's father had three sons and two daughters. The eldest became premier président, as I have described; the second, a certain Abbé de Mesmes, was monstrously debauched; the third, a Knight of Malta, was scarcely less so, but was none the less loaded with benefices and commanderies by his brother's influence, and later became our ambassador to Malta. Of one daughter, Mme de Fontenilles,[1] I shall speak later; the other was an Ursuline nun. After this necessary preamble, let us turn to the man himself.

During his father's lifetime be was known as the Sieur de Neufchâtel. He was tall and very portly, with a colossal countenance, much pitted by smallpox; but from the face down, his whole figure and his bearing also were exceedingly graceful, and in his old age became almost majestic. His aim was to ingratiate himself with Society, and he so far succeeded that he was allowed to mix freely with the best and gayest company at the Court. In all other respects he was ill-bred, and so grossly licentious that his father conceived a violent aversion to him, and to such an extent that he scarcely dared to approach the old man, for fear of blows being rained upon him, or plates thrown at his head at the dinner-table, even in respectable company, who often intervened and sometimes managed to reconcile them. Young Mesmes was, however, incorrigible, with no thought in his head except for his pleasures and the spending of money. His youthful debauches made him acquainted with young men of high rank, whom he assiduously cultivated, avoiding as much as possible the company of the other lawyers of the Palais de Justice.

Promotion to président-à-mortier at the death of his father did not at all moderate him for, deciding that he was now a member of the nobility, he

---

[1] Louise Marie Thérèse de Mesmes, Marquise de Fontenilles (1668-1755). She and Saint-Simon became friends in the reign of Louis XV.

proceeded to keep open house in the grand manner. The distinguished company that had frequented his father's house, and his close connection by marriage with M. de La Trémoïlle,[1] M. d'Elbeuf, and the children of Mme de Vivonne, who still lived and remained a link, persuaded him (so greatly had they spoiled him) that he was of their quality. He took pains also to attach himself to every courtier, including d'Antin,[2] who came within his reach, and he thus rose by degrees to acquaintance with M. and Mme du Maine, who needed men well placed in the Parlement and were not at all averse to cultivating présidents-à-mortier. De Mesmes, enchanted by his reception, determined to gain a powerful protector in the King's favourite son, and for that purpose, with a total disregard for his dignity, gladly lent himself to all the caprices of Mme du Maine. He introduced his brother the Knight of Malta, and together they attended all the pleasure-parties at Sceaux, and the night-long feasts as well.[3] The knight thought it not unbecoming in him to act in the charades, whilst the president danced in the amateur ballets amidst a crowd of twenty or more of her servants. Indeed, so much her slave did he become that he never dared to absent himself, nor refuse to be painted in costume as a pictorial record of their diversions, in among a group of her footmen, with a Swiss Guard beside him dressed in her livery. That last absurdity made him appear vastly foolish in Society, and much displeased the Parlement.

As he rose in seniority, he understood the need to be rather more regular in his attendance at the Palais de Justice, and decided that it might not come amiss if he somewhat softened his manner towards the more eminent of the advocates, prose-cutors, and clerks, albeit without endangering his status as a member of the Court and Society whose air and modes he adopted. Moreover, he made some attempt to supplement his ignorance by familiarizing himself with the life of the Palais, and learning the foibles of those magistrates who were renowned and sought after in their chambers. He possessed a ready wit, great presence of mind, and a gift for public speaking that made him pleasant to hear. He was also perceptive, quick and apt in repartee, bold to the point of insolence, without heart, honour, or decency. All was for show—principles, religion, conduct; he was well skilled in setting traps and bringing down others by ridicule. Friends and promises counted for little with him, but he could keep both when it served his interests. In all other ways he was delightful company, charming at table, with excellent taste in furniture, jewels, diversions, and entertainments—in everything, in short, that the world most admires. He was a great one for buying and selling, a spendthrift quite unashamed

---

[1] The Duc de La Trémoïlle's wife was a niece of the Maréchale de Vivonne, who had been Antoinette de Mesmes.

[2] D'Antin was a cousin of the Vivonnes. Their father the Maréchal was his uncle, the brother of his mother Mme de Montespan.

[3] There were once fourteen in succession. The Duchesse du Maine suffered from insomnia, which was why her parties lasted all night. The Knights of Malta were a religious order, not usually to be seen acting and dancing.

of his extravagance but at the same time on the alert to make a bargain and very ingenious at procuring one. Civil, affable, gracious with discrimination, and supremely arrogant, he was none the less respectful in his bearing to the true nobility, and toadied abjectly to ministers and to those who had influence at the Court. His innate absurdity was never better portrayed than in a charade performed one Christmas to mock certain courtiers and members of Society, who were seen appearing one after another in front of the Crib. I forget the verses, save that the first line went 'I am M. de Mesmes', and that they ended, 'I come to ask the Babe to sup with me in Lent.'[1] Let that suffice for the present concerning a magistrate who was bent at all times on being taken for a courtier and a man of quality, and who in the process made himself appear vastly absurd to all who were the genuine article.

Passports for our plenipotentiaries arrived on New Year's day. They each had a private audience with the King, and left for Utrecht one after the other in the first week of the year. At this same time M. de Vendôme attempted to besiege Cardona, but was very promptly obliged to raise the siege at some considerable cost. The Archduke had sent five or six thousand troops to Catalonia, in the expectation that the English would not remain there long. He had received the Imperial crown at Frankfort and had gone from thence to Vienna, after writing a furious letter to the States-General, exhorting them not to conclude a peace. He had seen that everything in England tended that way, and that the Duke of Marlborough, who felt insecure, had obtained permission from Queen Anne to take his duchess overseas as soon as they had relinquished their posts at the Court and in the army. The Duke of Ormonde[2] was appointed to replace him in command of the queen's army in Flanders, and shortly afterwards the Duke of Argyll,[3] commanding the English troops in Catalonia, received orders to bring them back to England by sea.

A most unhappy disgrace came to Mme de Mailly, who was mistress of Mme la Dauphine's wardrobe. The expenses had risen to more than double those of the late queen, and yet the princess sadly lacked for anything new, fashionable, or ornamental in her attire. There had been a public outcry, and her ladies daily lent her their tippets, muffs, ribbons, and other feminine adornments. Mme de Mailly,

---

[1] The verses went somewhat as follows:

> Alone, in no royal following, appears M. de Mesmes,
> For fear lest in among a crowd some might not note his name.
> He says to good Joseph, fal, lal,
> 'I am M. de Mesmes'.
> Then bending down he asks the Babe
> To sup one night, in Lent.

In Lent, when there were no dinner-parties! It was the time to invite poor relations, country-cousins, and the dull and worthy.

[2] James Butler, 2nd Duke of Ormonde (1665-1745).
[3] John Campbell, 2nd Duke of Argyll (1678-1743).

in her indolence, had left all to one of the waiting-women, who imagined that she herself was Mme de Maintenon's niece because her mistress had that relationship.[1] Desmaretz, now firmly in the saddle, had scene after scene with the mistress of the wardrobe on the subject of such huge expenses, and the bills with which she haughtily presented him. His patience was at last exhausted; he spoke to Mme de Maintenon and to the King, and together they spoke to Mme la Dauphine. She, too, despite her gentleness, had had enough, after suffering in silence for years on end. The result was that the care of her wardrobe was removed from Mme de Mailly and given to Mme Quentin the head tiring-woman, and Mme de Mailly's maid was dismissed for enriching herself to the detriment of the wardrobe and the merchants. Mme de Mailly wept, screamed, vowed that her honour was smirched, and altogether created such a rumpus that at the end of a fortnight Mme de Maintenon produced some kind of a face-saver for her; but the post itself, and the real authority over the wardrobe, she never recaptured. No one pitied her, for her excessive pride and vanity had alienated all her friends, and in any case, people had been shocked to see the Dauphine so ill dressed.

Those first days of the new year produced another family quarrel. Mme la Duchesse de Berry, who ruled her father and her husband, and did everything imaginable to vex the princess her mother, was herself governed by one of her waiting-women, a girl of spirit, but extremely mischievous. Her name was Vienne. She was the daughter of M. le Duc d'Orléans's old nurse, and having once found her greatly to his liking, he still had a regard for her. The late Monsieur[2] had inherited from the Queen-mother a pearl necklace of such beauty and rarity that it passed for being unique. Mme la Duchesse d'Orléans doted on and wore it very often, which in itself was enough to make Mme la Duchesse de Berry determine to take it from her; and to vex her still more, she demanded it, well knowing that she would be refused. She then said that she would have it none the less, since it belonged not to her mother but to M. le Duc d'Orléans, from whom she managed to extract it. The row was appalling. Mme la Duchesse de Berry made a show of publicly wearing the necklace and displaying it to everyone. The quarrel grew so heated that eventually Madame herself felt obliged to see the King in his study, where she did not confine herself to the affair of the pearls alone. The ensuing rumpus and the rift between mother and daughter became generally apparent, for Mme la Duchesse de Berry, unable to support the King's anger, took to her bed, where the Dauphine went more than once to bring her to reason. M. le Duc de Berry was too much in love to remain neutral, and M. le Duc d'Orléans, torn

---

[1] The Comtesse de Mailly was, in fact, Mme de Maintenon's first cousin once removed.
[2] Philippe I, Duc d'Orléans (1640-1701), brother of Louis XIV.

between them, did not know what to do for the best. He had more trouble on his hands than just the pearls, for the King had ordered the waiting-woman to be dismissed, and had lashed out at the Duc de Berry when he dared to plead on her behalf. That command was the last straw. Mme la Duchesse de Berry took it as a personal affront which her vanity could not brook on top of all the other humiliations of defeat. It was, however, useless to weep, scream, howl, or hurl abuse at her father and her husband for their weakness; she was compelled to obey, dismiss her maid, ask forgiveness of her mother (whom she never forgave) and return the necklace to her. Mme la Duchesse d'Orléans, having achieved her main object, did everything possible to soften the blow, promised to put matters right with the King, and herself led Mme la Duchesse de Berry to his study after supper when, two days later, he wished to impress upon her her disgrace. He spoke to her like a father, but also like a king, and thus her humiliation was complete, except in her own mind. In a few days she was appearing in public at the King's supper, looking much as usual, but concealing with infinite difficulty the rage that consumed her.

Mme de Saint-Simon, who avoided as much as possible a household where she could do nothing to assist and had everything to lose, took no part in this affair, except as the unwilling witness of the tears and furious outbursts. I behaved as usual to M. and Mme la Duchesse d'Orléans. Ever since the event which I earlier described, when M. le Duc d'Orléans repeated some words of mine to his daughter and she turned on me with the utmost viciousness, I had scarcely set foot in her house, and had not mentioned her to her father (nor had he dared to speak of her to me), but never in my life have I seen a man more discomfited. He gave the waiting-woman a pension, and some time later arranged a marriage for her in the provinces. One might write volumes on all that happened in the household of Mme la Duchesse de Berry; the tales would certainly be surprising, but they would scarcely be edifying, and thus I shall do no more than recount such matters as became publicly known, or were otherwise of particular interest.

At the beginning of the year the King began once or twice a week to have his dinner served in Mme de Maintenon's room. He had never done such a thing before, but he continued in that way for the remainder of his life, except that in high summer he more often than not ate his dinner at Trianon or Marly, but without sleeping there. The numbers were kept very small, and the company was always the same: the Dauphine, but alas! only for the first few occasions, Mme de Maintenon, Mmes de Dangeau, de Levis, d'O, and de Caylus—the only one who was not a palace-lady. No one else was present, not even the major-domo. The King's valets carried the dishes and plates as far as the door, and Mme de Maintenon's people served them. The King stayed only a short while afterwards and returned later at his accustomed time. When the weather was very bad, he would sometimes play *brelan* or *reversis*[1] with the same ladies for very small stakes and sometimes also on Friday evenings, when he did not see his ministers. All this lent immense prestige to the ladies in question, but brought them no special privileges, not even the freedom to risk speaking to the King of themselves or their families. The dinners were occasionally followed by music, for which the King returned after spending half-an-hour in his own apartments. The concerts lasted until six o'clock precisely, and occurred only when the weather was exceptionally bad. They were sometimes given in the evening instead of in the afternoon but, as with the dinners, no other persons were admitted. At about this time several men and women were expelled from Paris after being caught cheating at *faro*,[2] a game very properly banned, which disappeared altogether after that punishment.

On Monday, 18 January, the King went to Marly, an excursion which I take particular care to note. They had scarcely arrived before Boudin, the Dauphine's chief physician whom she greatly liked, as I have already mentioned, warned her to take precautions because he had it on good authority that someone meant to poison her and the Dauphin as well, to whom he spoke in similar terms. Not content with that alarm, he blurted the whole matter out in the crowded drawing-room, looking so wild that everyone was terrified. The King saw him privately, but he continued to affirm that his information was well-founded, although he did not know whence it had originated. He stood firm on that contradiction; but if he was ignorant of the source, how could he have been so certain of its accuracy?

His friends had quickly put a stop to his preliminary outburst, but the declaration was made in public and it was repeated. What was most strange was that about twenty-four hours later the Dauphin received a similar warning from the King of Spain, couched in vague terms, not giving any names, but purporting to be quite reliable. In this second warning only the Dauphin was explicitly mentioned, but there were dark hints concerning the Dauphine. That, at least, was what the Dauphin said to me, and I never heard that he said anything different to others. The royal family made light of these rumours, arising no one knew where, but the intimate circle were none the less impressed, and there was a gravity, silence, and dismay about the Court that permeated all their usual occupations and amusements.

At about this same time occurred the death of Gondrin,[3] d'Antin's eldest son,

---

[1] Reversis was played with counters, red on one side, black on the other. The object was to turn all the counters on the board to show the reverse colour. The players, playing in turn, could reverse a whole line by enclosing them at either end with counters of the opposite colour. One counter was played at a time.

[2] Faro: a betting game on the turn-up of the cards.

[3] Louis de Pardaillon, Marquis de Gondrin. He was only twenty-three.

who left issue by one of the Duc de Noailles's sisters,[1] who later married the Comte de Toulouse. Grief affected the widow to such a degree that she fell gravely ill and the Last Sacraments were administered. The whole family gathered round the bed, and her mother the Maréchale de Noailles, who loved her to distraction, burst into sobs, crying aloud to God in her anguish, offering her life as a sacrifice together with the lives of all her other children, if only this one might be spared. Thereupon La Vallière, who had been kneeling at some distance but had distinctly heard what she said, rose quietly from his knees and went to her, saying out loud and very piteously, 'Sons-in-law included, Madame?' No one who was present could help joining in the great burst of laughter that overtook them all, even the Maréchale herself. All of which provided a most absurd scandal at the Court. Very shortly afterwards the sick woman recovered, which gave them all the more reason to laugh.

I have already mentioned Maréchal Catinat,[2] his wisdom, modesty and altruism, his superior sentiments, and great talents as a commander. It now only remains for me to record his death at an advanced age, in his little house, Saint-Gratien, near Saint-Denis. His simplicity and frugality, his contempt for the world, his inner peace and steady conduct put one constantly in mind of those great Roman generals who returned quietly to their private lives after well-deserved triumphs, full of love for their country, and undisturbed by the ingratitude of Rome, which they had served so well.

Catinat turned his philosophical mind to even better account by sincere piety. He had wit, good sense, and the ability to think. He never forgot his lowly origins. His dress, coaches, furniture and house, were as simple as could be. So also were his manners and his whole appearance. He was tall, spare, dark-complexioned, seemingly pensive, sometimes even slow, looking perhaps a little commonplace, but with fine, bright eyes. He deplored the monstrous errors that followed one upon another, the steady suppression of all rivalry, the luxury, the ignorance, the mingling of ranks, the inquisitions replacing police inquiries. All these signs of disorder he observed, saying that only when the confusion had led to a dangerous crisis would the kingdom be brought back to order.

On Saturday, 30 January, the Dauphin and M. le Duc de Berry, in company with Monsieur le Duc, went to shoot driven game. The ground was frozen hard. As chance would have it, M. le Duc de Berry took his stand at the edge of a long and very wide pond, and Monsieur le Duc stood on the other side a great distance away, opposite to him. M. le Duc de Berry fired. A pellet ricocheting off the ice hit Monsieur le Duc, blinding him in one eye. The King heard the news as he

---

[1] Marie Victoire Sophie, Marquise de Gondrin (1688-1766). In 1723 she married the Comte de Toulouse.
[2] Maréchal Catinat (1637-1712), Maréchal 1693. See Vol 1, p. 92.

was walking in his gardens. On the following day, Sunday, M. le Duc de Berry went to Madame la Duchesse and fell on his knees before her; he had not dared to see her the previous evening, nor even to visit Monsieur le Duc, who was bearing his injury with great patience. The King visited him on the Sunday, as also did the Dauphin and Dauphine, who had already seen him the evening before. They all went to him again on Monday, 1 February. The King visited Madame la Duchesse also, and thereafter returned to Versailles. Madame la Princesse,[1] all her family, and several of Madame la Duchesse's female friends then established themselves at Marly. M. le Duc de Berry was most deeply affected. Monsieur le Duc was ill for some considerable time, and then immediately afterwards, while they were still at Marly, developed measles;[2] after a brief convalescence at Saint-Maur, he again fell ill, this time with smallpox.

On Friday, 5 February, the Duc de Noailles gave the Dauphine a very beautiful snuffbox filled with fine Spanish snuff, which she tried and found excellent. This occurred towards midday, and she afterwards placed the box on a table in her private drawing-room which no one else ever entered. That same evening she contracted a feverish chill, retired to bed, and did not rise again, not even to go to the King's study after supper. She slept badly, but rose at her accustomed hour and went about her life as usual. That evening the fever returned. She was unwell the whole of that night, but felt slightly better on the Sunday. At six o'clock that evening she was seized with a sudden pain below the temples, in area not much greater than a sixpenny piece, but so violent that she implored the King not to enter when he came to visit her. This agonizing pain continued without intermission until Monday the 8th, and was not relieved by smoking or chewing tobacco, nor by quantities of opium and two bleedings from the arm. When the pain abated the fever increased. She said that she suffered more even than in child-bearing.

The sudden violence of the attack gave rise to rumours about the snuffbox given her by the Duc de Noailles, for she had mentioned it to her ladies when she went to bed on the first day of her illness, and had praised both the box and its contents; but when Mme de Levis went to fetch it from the table in her boudoir it was not there, and, to make a long story short, it was never seen again. The disappearance seemed strange enough when it was first discovered, but the long and fruitless search, followed by such sudden and dreadful happenings, aroused the darkest suspicions.[3] They did not point directly to the giver of the box, or else where so carefully disguised that they did not reach his knowledge. The rumours,

---

[1] Madame la Princesse, the widow of Monsieur le Prince, was M. le Duc's grandmother. If she brought all the family, children and grandchildren, they would have been a party of twelve.

[2] It is worth noting, in view of what follows, that the royal party had been in contact with at least one case of measles.

[3] Saint-Simon appears seriously to have believed that the royal family were poisoned. It seems far more likely that the Dauphin and Dauphine and their elder son died of measles, greatly assisted by exhausting bleedings and purgings by the royal doctors.

indeed, were made light of, even in the intimate circle where so many hopes were fixed on that adored princess, on whose life depended the fortunes of her little group of intimates. The fact that she took snuff was unknown to the King (although Mme de Maintenon knew). Had he ever discovered this habit of hers there would have been a terrible to do, which was why no one had mentioned the snuffbox and its strange disappearance.

On the Monday night the Dauphine was very drowsy. All that day, during which the King came often to her bedside, she was in a high fever with short periods of delirium. Spots began to appear on her skin, which made the doctors hope that the disease might be measles, for it was prevalent at that time, many people having developed it both at Versailles and in Paris. The Tuesday night was harder to endure because by that time the hope of measles had faded. Early on the following morning the King went to see her and found that she had been given an emetic; but although the result was all they could desire it had brought her no relief. At this point they persuaded the Dauphin, who had never left her side, to go out into the garden for fresh air; but he was so anxious that he returned almost at once. Towards nightfall she grew worse, and about eleven the fever increased. It was a very bad night. The King went to her at nine o'clock on the morning of 11 February, and Mme de Maintenon was with her all the while, except during his visits. By this time the princess was so bad that they decided to speak to her of the Sacraments; but although so weak, she seemed surprised and questioned them about her condition. They reassured her as best they might, but continued gently to press her, urging her not to delay. She thanked them for their frankness and said that she would prepare herself.

A little later, fearing lest there be a sudden change, her confessor Père de La Rue,[1] a Jesuit whom she had always appeared to like, came to the bed and urged her to wait no longer. She looked at him, answered that she perfectly understood him, but did no more, and when La Rue offered to hear her then and there she did not reply. Being a man of some intelligence, he realized that something was amiss and tactfully changed his method of approach. Suggesting that she might have some personal reason for not wishing to confess to him, he bade her not to be afraid but to name a priest, saying that he would fetch him himself and bear all the responsibility. She then admitted that she would prefer M. Bailly, a priest of the mission of the parish of Versailles, a man with a high reputation, who confessed the more orthodox members of the Court and was not free of all suspicion of Jansenism, although that was rare among those missioners. Unfortunately Bailly was in Paris. The Dauphine seemed distressed when she heard this news and wished to wait until his return, but Père de La Rue told her that she had best not waste precious time

[1] Charles de La Rue, one of the most fashionable preachers of that day.

which the doctors might put to good use after she had received the Sacraments. She then asked for a Franciscan friar named Père Noël, and Père de La Rue went immediately to fetch him and brought him to her.

You may imagine the scandal caused by this sudden change of confessor at that awful moment, and all the rumours that it aroused. I shall return later to that subject, for I must not interrupt a tale of such tragic interest. The Dauphin was by this time quite overcome by grief. He had hidden his distress as long as possible in order to stay by her bedside, but when the fever could no longer be concealed the doctors wished to spare him the agonizing scenes which they foresaw. With the King's approval, they therefore did everything to persuade him to remain in his own room, and sustained him with lying reports of his wife's condition.

The Dauphine made a very long confession; immediately afterwards Extreme Unction was administered and she received the Last Sacraments, which the King went to salute at the foot of the grand staircase. An hour later she asked for the prayers for the dying, but they told her that that moment had not yet come and, comforting her, urged her to try to sleep. During all this time the King and Mme de Maintenon remained in the drawing-room, to which the doctors were summoned to confer in their presence. There were seven doctors altogether, some of them attached to the Court, others brought from Paris. They unanimously recommended that she should be bled from the foot before the fever returned, and that an emetic should be given in the early hours of the morning if the bleeding produced no good results. When the fever returned it was less violent than before, but the night was cruel. Next morning the King came very early and the Dauphine was given the emetic at nine o'clock; but it had no effect. As the day wore on fresh symptoms appeared, each one more distressing than the last. She was conscious only at rare intervals. Towards evening her servants became so distraught that they admitted several strangers to the room, even though the King was there. He left her only a few moments before she died, and stepping into his carriage at the foot of the grand staircase was driven away to Marly with Mme de Maintenon and Mme de Caylus. They were both so deeply afflicted that they could not summon sufficient strength even to visit the Dauphin.

No princess coming so young to a foreign Court was ever better trained or better instructed. Her prudent father was acquainted with the modes of our Court and had explained them perfectly to her, teaching her the only way in which she could be happy with us. He was greatly assisted in his task by her natural quickness and intelligence, in addition to which she possessed many amiable qualities that won the people's love. Her personal relationships with her husband, the King, and Mme de Maintenon caused her to be regarded with respect and approval by men with ambitions. From the first moment of her arrival she strove to achieve that end, and throughout her entire life she persisted in that worthy endeavour, from which she reaped continual benefit. Gentle, shy, but shrewd also, she was so kind that she dreaded causing the least pain to anyone, and although she was lively and pleasure-loving, she was capable of forming her own opinions and of acting upon them consistently and for long periods. The constraints of Court life, that were often near torture to her, bore down upon her most heavily, but they did not seem to affect her. Kindness came naturally to her, and she showed it to all, even to her own household.[1]

In appearance she was plain, with sagging cheeks, a brow too prominent for beauty, a shapeless nose, and thick sensual lips; but the line of her chestnut hair and eyebrows was well marked, and she had the prettiest, most eloquent eyes in all the world. Her few remaining teeth were badly decayed, which she was the first to remark on and laugh at. She had, none the less, a fair complexion, a beautiful skin, a small but admirable bust, and a long neck with just the suspicion of a goitre that was not unbecoming. The carriage of her head was noble, she was stately and gracious in her manner and in the expression of her eyes, and she had the sweetest smile imaginable. Her waist was long, slender without being bony, and very supple. Altogether, she had a perfect figure and she walked like a goddess on the clouds. Her charm defies description; it showed in her impulsive ways and gestures, and coloured her most ordinary remarks. She was always natural and unaffected, sometimes, perhaps, a little childish, but with a spice of wit. She delighted all who met her because, by her own graciousness, she had the knack of putting everyone else at ease.

She loved to be pleasant, even with the most ordinary and low-born persons; but seemingly made no effort to be popular. When one was with her it was easy to believe that she was wholly and solely one's friend. The entire Court was enlivened by her youth and high spirits; she flitted hither and thither like a nymph, like a summer breeze, seeming to have the gift of being in many places at once, and bringing life and gaiety wherever she passed. Every diversion was made more amusing by her presence; she was the life and soul of every ball and play and fête, as well as enchanting everyone by the grace and elegance of her dancing.

Cards she loved, even for low stakes, for she was easily entertained, but she preferred to play high. She was very quick and clear-headed, the finest gambler imaginable, and could see through her opponent's strategy in a moment. But she was as cheerful and as much pleased to spend an afternoon in quiet reading and sewing, or in conversation with her 'serious ladies', as she called the elder palace-ladies. She never spared herself, not even for her health's sake, and never forgot the least little thing likely to please Mme de Maintenon and, through her, the King. In that respect

[1] Others took a less charitable view of her nature. In 1698 the Venetian ambassador wrote, 'The little Duchesse de Bourgogne is sly and spiteful. She fawns most abjectly on Mme de Maintenon, and in private calls her "Grandmamma".'

her versatility was amazing; it never for a moment flagged, although she tempered it with a caution learned by long experience, for she knew exactly when to be discreet and when bold. Her personal wishes, her pleasures, even, I repeat, her health she sacrificed to them, and she thus became familiar with them in a way that none of the King's children, not even his bastards, was able to approach.

Her public manner was serious, reserved, reverential to the King, and shyly formal with Mme de Maintenon, whom she called 'Aunt', with a pretty mingling of affection and respect. In private with them she chattered, skipped and frolicked, sometimes perching on the arm of their chairs, sometimes on their knees. She had a habit of flinging her arms round their necks, kissing and hugging them, rumpling them and taking hold of them by the chin. She would rifle their desks, rummaging among the papers, unsealing their letters, and sometimes, when she saw that it would amuse them, insist on reading them aloud and commenting on what she read. The King's private rooms were open to her at all times, even when couriers came with important dispatches and during the meetings of the council, and she was always ready to oblige, to assist by smoothing away difficulties, or to do a kindness, except for someone for whom she had conceived a violent antipathy, as she had for Pontchartrain, whom she sometimes called 'your one-eyed villain' when speaking of him to the King. She was so daring that one evening when the King and Mme de Maintenon were talking affectionately of the English Court—it was at a time when they hoped to make peace with Queen Anne—she said, 'You say, Aunt, that the English queens are better than the kings, but do you know why?', and dancing all about the room, she continued, 'It is because under kings the women rule, but with a queen the men do so.' The wonder of it was that they both burst out laughing and agreed that she was perfectly right.

I have already said enough of her disapproval of Monseigneur and of the members of his intimate circle. I shall not say more, save that she took great care to hide her feelings from the Court in general, masking them under an appearance of being on pleasant terms with him and perfectly serene among them all when she was at Meudon. None the less, the situation was deeply embarrassing to her and she swore to be revenged after Monseigneur's death. One evening at Fontainebleau when the princesses and their ladies were with the King in the drawing-room after supper and she had been diverting him by pretending to chatter in half a dozen different languages and other such nonsense, she suddenly noticed that Madame la Duchesse and Mme la Princesse de Conti were eyeing one another and scornfully shrugging their shoulders. As soon as the King had risen and moved to his inner study to feed his dogs, the Dauphine seized Mme de Saint-Simon and Mme de Levis by the hand, and pointing to those princesses, only a few feet away, cried: 'Did you see them? Did you see them? I know as well as they do that I behave absurdly and must seem very silly; but he needs to have a bustle about him and that kind of thing amuses him.' Then, swinging on their arms, she began to laugh and sing, 'Ha-ha! it makes me laugh, Ha-ha! I can laugh at them, because I shall be their queen. I need not mind them now or ever, but they will have to reckon with me, for I shall be their queen,' and she shouted and sang and hopped and laughed as high and as loud as she dared. Mme de Saint-Simon and Mme de Levis whispered to her to be quiet lest the princesses should hear her, and the entire company think that she had taken leave of her senses, but she only skipped and sang the more, 'What do I care for them? I'm going to be their queen!', and so she continued until the King's return. Alas! sweet princess, she believed what she said, and who could have thought otherwise? But for our sins it pleased God very shortly after to arrange matters differently. So far, indeed, was she from imagining her approaching end that on Candlemas Day, when she was alone with Mme de Saint-Simon in her bedroom, the other ladies having gone before her to the chapel, she began to speak of the many people of the Court whom she had known and who were now dead, of what she would do when she, too, grew old, and of how no one but Mme de Saint-Simon and Mme de Lauzun would remain from the days of her girlhood; and she had run on in this way until it was time to go to hear the sermon.[1]

In spite of these many good and amiable qualities, she had another side to her nature, both as a princess and as a woman; not indeed where the keeping of secrets or loyalty to friends was concerned, for there she was like a deep well, nor in her discretion concerning the interests of others; but she had certain small human failings that marred her perfection. She gave her friendship to mere acquaintances whom she saw often, if they amused her, or if she happened to need them (indeed, so far as I am aware, Mme de Saint-Simon was the sole exception), and she admitted to this dangerous weakness with a grace and candour that made it seem almost agreeable in her. As I have said, she liked to please, and thus she could hardly be blamed if some pleased her in return. When she first came to the Court she was kept strictly apart, and then surrounded with elderly gallants, whose romantic inclinations were no whit reduced because decrepitude forbade their enjoyment of them. As time went on she came more into the world and chose companions of her own age, but less for their virtues than for their good looks. She was naturally sociable and ready to like those whom she saw every day, although (and this was never sufficiently encouraged) she took as much pleasure in serious reading and conversation with the elder ladies of her household as in the lighter, more scandalous gossip of the rest, who often led her further than she wished—for shyness and some remnants of modesty still restrained her. None the less, she did go to very great

---

[1] For other stories of the Dauphine, see *Saint-Simon at Versailles*.

lengths, and a princess less lovable and less beloved might on many occasions have found herself in serious trouble. The manner of her death revealed some of these mysteries, and also showed the extreme tyranny which the King exercised over the members of his family. Both he and the Court received a shock when, in those awful moments when the present vanishes and only the future is feared, she desired to change her confessor and repudiated the entire Order to which he belonged, before she would receive the Last Sacraments.

With her death all joy vanished, all pleasures, diversions and delights were overcast, and darkness covered the Court. She was its light and its life. She was everywhere at once; she was its centre; her presence permeated its inner life, and if, after her death, the Court continued to subsist, it merely lingered on. No princess was ever more sincerely mourned, none more worthy of regret. Indeed, mourning for her has never ceased, a secret involuntary sadness remains, a terrible void which nothing can ever fill.

The King and Mme de Maintenon were penetrated with the most violent grief, the only real grief which he ever experienced. Immediately after reaching Marly he went straight to Mme de Maintenon's room, then supped alone in his bedroom, and stayed only a short time afterwards in the study with his natural children and M. le Duc d'Orléans. M. le Duc de Berry, immersed in his own deep affliction, and feeling even more deeply for Monseigneur his brother, remained at Versailles with Mme la Duchesse de Berry, who for her part was overjoyed to be thus unexpectedly delivered from one greater and better loved than herself, and to whom she owed everything. She forced her mind to govern her impulses, however, at least so far as she was able, and managed to keep up appearances. On the following morning they both arrived at Marly in time for the King's *lever*. The Dauphin, ill as he was, and stricken with the most bitter personal sorrow, did not leave his room at Versailles, and refused to see anyone except M. le Duc de Berry, his confessor, and the Duc de Beauvilliers. The last named had been lying ill at his town house for the past week, but he made the effort to leave his bed and go to his pupil, and was thus able to admire the great qualities with which God had endowed him; for never did the Dauphin appear so noble as in that last terrible day, and throughout those that followed until his own death. This was the last occasion on which they were to meet in this world.

On the morning of 13 February, they managed to persuade the Dauphin to go to Marly, in order to spare him the anguish of hearing noises in the room above where the Dauphine had died. He left at seven in the morning by the back door of his apartments, flinging himself into a blue chair,[1] in which they bore him to his coach. A few courtiers, more tactless than inquisitive, were standing by it,

---

[1] There was a fleet of blue sedan-chairs at the service of the courtiers at Versailles.

and he courteously returned their bows. When he reached Marly, he stopped first at the chapel to hear mass, and was then carried to a window, through which he entered his apartments. Mme de Maintenon went to him at once. You may imagine the agony of that encounter; it was more than she could long endure, and she very soon returned to her own room. The Dauphin was obliged to receive the princes and princesses also, but they respected his feelings and stayed only a few moments. Even Mme la Duchesse de Berry visited him, attended by Mme de Saint-Simon, to whom he directed a glance expressive of sorrow shared. He afterwards remained alone with M. le Duc de Berry for a long time.

By then it was almost the time of the King's *réveil,* and when the three pages came to make the announcement I ventured to enter with them, and the Dauphin allowed me to perceive that he had seen me, turning upon me so kind and loving a look that I was deeply moved. None the less, his appearance horrified me; his eyes were wild and glazed, his face had changed colour and there were spots on it, but livid rather than red. I noticed that there were a great number of them, and that others in the room had perceived them also. He was standing. Shortly afterwards they came to inform him that the King was awake. The tears which he had for so long held back came brimming over his eyelids. He turned away at the announcement but did not otherwise move. The only people with him were the three pages, du Chesne, and myself; they more than once asked him to go to the King, but he neither moved nor spoke. Then I approached him and signed to him to go, and I spoke to him too in a low voice; but seeing that he still made no move, I dared to take him by the arm, saying that he must sooner or later see the King, who was waiting for him and must be longing to embrace him, and that it would therefore be kind not to delay. Then, gently urging him to start, I took the liberty of giving him a little push. He gave me such a look as nearly broke my heart and immediately left the room. I followed him a little way and then went to recover myself. I never saw him again. God grant that I may meet him in that eternal life to which His mercy will surely have called him.

The company at Marly (very small on that occasion) were assembled in the large drawing-room, and the princes and princesses and those who had the *grandes entrées* were in the smaller room between the King's apartments and those of Mme de Maintenon. She was in her bedroom, but when they announced the King's *réveil* she had gone in to him alone, passing through the small room and all the people there assembled, who then followed her. The Dauphin, entering by way of the offices, found all this crowd in the King's bedroom, but the King none the less called to him as soon as he observed him, and embraced him lovingly and repeatedly for a long time. Those first moments of emotion were interspersed with broken sentences, tears and sobs.

After an interval, during which the King had time to look closely at the Dauphin, he too was alarmed by the symptoms which we had earlier observed, and all those present were equally dismayed, most of all the doctors. The King desired them to take his pulse, which was very weak, or so they afterwards said—at the time they merely remarked that it was not quite normal, but that all would be well if he went to bed. The King thereupon embraced him again, telling him very lovingly to take good care of himself and bidding him go to bed, which he did, never to rise again. By that time it was late. The King had spent a wretched night and his head ached. When he was at dinner he greeted the few great nobles who presented themselves, and afterwards went to visit the Dauphin, who had developed a fever and whose pulse was weaker than before. He then went to Mme de Maintenon, supped in his bedroom, and spent only a short time in the study with those who were accustomed to be with him. From this moment the Dauphin saw no one but his pages and the doctors, his brother for short periods, his confessor for rather longer, and M. de Cheverny for a very little while. His days were spent in prayer and the reading of sacred books. The list for Marly was drawn up on the spot and the company were notified, as had been done at the time of Monseigneur's death so shortly before.

The next day, which was Sunday, the King spent as he had the previous Saturday. Anxiety for the Dauphin increased. He had not disguised from Boudin, in the presence of du Chesne and M. de Cheverny, that he did not expect to recover and that by his sensations he felt that Boudin's warning had been correct. He repeated this more than once with the greatest unconcern, showing contempt for the vanities of this world and an inestimable love and fear of God. Impossible to describe the general alarm! On Monday the 15th, the King was bled, and the Dauphin was no better. The King and Mme de Maintenon saw him separately more than once. No one else was admitted except M. le Duc de Berry for a few moments, his pages scarcely at all, M. de Cheverny very rarely. He continued to read and pray. On Tuesday the 16th he was worse, complaining of a consuming fire that did not correspond with the exterior appearance of the fever, although his pulse was hard to find, highly abnormal, and most alarming. As the day wore on, there was a general deterioration as well as great disappointment because the spots had spread from his face all over his body and were mistaken for measles, which gave some cause for hope; but the doctors and the more thoughtful members of the Court remembered that a similar rash had appeared on the body of the Dauphine, although that was not publicly known until after her death.

By Wednesday the 17th the illness had worsened considerably. I received news continually through Cheverny and also through a certain Boulduc, who came to speak to me whenever it was possible for him to leave the bedroom. This

Boulduc was an excellent apothecary in the King's service; after the death of his father he had become our apothecary also and was devoted to us all. He was quite as capable as the best of the doctors, as we had proved for ourselves, and moreover possessed great courage, honour, discretion, and wisdom. He spoke freely to Mme de Saint-Simon and myself; had already told us his suspicions regarding the Dauphine, and had said as much to me very frankly from the second day of her illness. Thus I no longer had any hope; but some people, it would appear, will continue to hope until the end, and against all reason.

The pains like a consuming fire increased during that day, becoming more and more agonizing. Later in the evening the Dauphin sent to ask the King's leave to take communion very early next morning, without ceremony or spectators at the mass, which would be said in his bedroom. No one knew of this at the time; it was made public only on the following morning. That same Wednesday evening I had gone late to visit the Duc and Duchesse de Chevreuse, whose lodging was in the first pavilion. We were lodged in the second, both on the side of Marly village, and by that time I was in a state of utter misery. I had seen the King only once a day, and had gone out solely to hear the news, and then only to M. and Mme de Chevreuse, for thus I could be sure of seeing none but those as deeply affected as myself, people with whom I could be perfectly frank. Mme de Chevreuse was as hopeless as I, but M. de Chevreuse, always calm and over-confident, always seeing life through rose-tinted spectacles, tried to prove to us with much talk of good constitutions and remedies that there was more reason to hope than fear, all with a serenity that exasperated me and caused me to round upon him somewhat discourteously; but it was a relief for Mme de Chevreuse and the few who thought as we did. I then returned and spent a very miserable night.

Early on the morning of Thursday, 18 February, I learned that the Dauphin had been impatient for midnight to come, had received the Sacraments immediately afterwards, had spent two hours in close communion with God, and that his head was now much confused. Mme de Saint-Simon told me later that he had received Extreme Unction, and had died at half-past eight o'clock. These memoirs were never intended to record my personal sentiments; if ever, long after my death, they should come to be published, readers will understand only too well what my feelings were and the state to which I was reduced, and Mme de Saint-Simon likewise. Suffice it here to say that we could scarcely bring ourselves to appear in public even for a moment during those first days; that I wished to give everything up and retire from the Court and Society, and that it was only the wisdom and good guidance of Mme de Saint-Simon which prevented me from so doing. Even so she had a hard task.

The prince, first heir presumptive and then heir apparent to the throne, was born with a violent temper and in his early youth had been terrifying. Hard and choleric to the last degree, subject to transports of rage even against inanimate objects, furiously impetuous, unable to brook the slightest opposition, even from time or the weather, without flying into a passion that seemed likely to destroy his entire body, he was stubborn beyond measure, mad for all kinds of amusement, a woman-lover and at the same time, which is rare, with an equally strong propensity in another direction. He loved wine and good eating just as much, was passionately fond of hunting, and listened to music in a kind of ecstasy. Cards delighted him, but he so hated to lose that it was dangerous to play against him. In sum, he was a prey to all the passions and loved all pleasures. Often tyrannical and naturally inclined to cruelty, he was ruthless in sarcasm and exposed fools with devastating truth. From his celestial height he thought of other men, no matter who they might be, as of little atomies bearing no comparison with himself, and although he and his brothers were supposed to have been brought up as perfect equals, he regarded them at best as go-betweens twixt himself and the human race. He was extremely intelligent and quick-witted; even in his rages his retorts were marvellously apt, for at his most furious his arguments were always reasonable and well-founded. Acquiring abstract knowledge was mere child's play to him, but his interests were so keen and varied that they prevented him from concentrating on any one subject, and thus he never became competent. They were obliged to let him draw at his studies, otherwise he would not learn; but although he had considerable talent and aptitude, and although without it his lessons would have borne no fruit, the practice may well have contributed to ruining his figure.

He was short rather than tall, with a long, dark-complexioned face the upper part of which was exceedingly handsome, and with the finest eyes imaginable. His glance was keen, melancholy, striking, awe-inspiring, at most times gentle, always piercing; his expression agreeable, noble, sensitive, so humorous that it encouraged wit in others. The lower part of his face was less good, for it was too pointed, and his nose, long, high-bridged, but not shapely, did not become him. His chestnut hair was too thick and curled so tightly that it frizzed. His mouth and lips were pleasant enough when he was not speaking, and his teeth were not decayed, but his upper jaw protruded so far that it almost enclosed the lower, producing a most unhappy effect. Apart from the King himself, he had the finest legs and feet that I have ever seen, but both they and his thighs were too long in proportion to the rest of his body.

When he had left the nursery his back was straight, but it was soon noticed that it had begun to curve, and they made a collar and cross of iron, which he wore at all times in his apartments even when there was company, and they neglected none of the games and exercises likely to straighten such a deformity. Nature, however, proved stronger; he grew hump-backed, and so much more so on one shoulder that he limped, not because of any inequality of his legs and thighs but because when his shoulder dropped there was not the same distance between his hips and the ground, which caused him to lean towards one side instead of standing upright. He walked no less easily for that, nor less far, nor less quickly and enjoyably, for he continued to like walking and riding, although he rode very ill. What was surprising was that for all his intelligence and perceptiveness, and despite all the virtues which he later acquired and his true and notable piety, the prince never learned to see his body as it really was, and would never acknowledge his deformity. This failing caused great anxiety to others lest they be tactless or indiscreet, and was hard for his valets when they dressed him and arranged his hair, for they had to try to conceal the defect as much as possible and yet be very careful not to appear to see what was visible to all. From this we must conclude that it is given to no man to reach perfection here below.

The prince never completely fulfilled his intellectual capacity; but like the bee, gathered his honey from the finest and sweetest blossoms. He endeavoured to meet men of learning and to extract from them the knowledge and ideas he sought. Occasionally he would confer with some of them, but as it were casually, and on some special topic, or, more rarely, he would see them in private to obtain necessary information; but such interviews were never repeated nor habitual with him. I have never heard, and it surely would not have escaped me, that he ever worked continuously with any one person, excepting with the ministers, including by that term the Duc de Chevreuse and certain prelates. Apart from them, I was the only person to have free and frequent access to him, either at my request or his command; and on such occasions he spoke his mind about the present and the future confidently, with restraint and discretion. He would enlarge on the plans he thought beneficial and on general topics, but was more reserved about private matters and individuals. At the same time, he would try to learn all he could from me. I adroitly gave him the opportunity for such outpourings, and often successfully, for he came to feel more and more confidence in me.

An entire volume would scarcely suffice to recount all the conversations that took place between the prince and myself. What love of goodness he had! What unselfishness! What learning! What excellent ideas! What pure intentions! Dare I say it? what a clear reflection of the Divinity appeared in his pure soul, so strong, so simple, retaining in as high a degree as is permitted here below the image of its Creator! In him one saw the shining example of a laborious, active, virtuous, wise and Christian education on a brilliant pupil who was born to rule.

The degradation of the nobility was odious to him, and the idea that all were equal within its ranks wholly abominable. That latest innovation, applying to all save holders of office, and in other ways confusing nobles with gentlefolk, and vice versa, appeared to him as the final stroke of injustice, and the resulting loss of rank an immediate danger to a military kingdom. He remembered that in times of greatest peril France had owed her salvation to the old nobility, who knew their rank and acknowledged its various degrees. They were thus able and willing to march to their country's defence by companies and provinces, no one overstepping his place or refusing to obey men greater than himself. The prince saw that this strong defence had been destroyed, for there is no man now who does not claim equality with all the rest, and thus co-operation, authority, and obedience have ceased to exist. He was, indeed, profoundly moved by the decline of the old nobility, and was shocked by the steps already taken, and still continuing, for the purpose of ruining them and keeping them under. He had observed the decay of courage, morals, and humanity, brought about by poverty and mixed marriages; for such base marriages have become increasingly necessary in order to avoid actual starvation. It enraged him to see the French nobility, once so illustrious, reduced to a level almost indistinguishable from that of the common herd. Truly, the only remaining difference is that commoners have the right to work in all the professions, including that of arms, whereas the nobles must choose between a deadly, stultifying idleness that renders them unfit for anything, the mock and scorn of all, and death in the wars after exposure to the insults of under-secretaries of State and secretaries of intendants. Even the greatest lords, whose birth and rank alone should place them above the rest, cannot avoid unemployment or, when serving with the armies, humiliation by the quill-drivers. Above all, the prince could not stomach the crimes against the profession of arms, on which this kingdom was founded and sustained; for example the wickedness of a man's retiring honourable and famous, perhaps with a pension, a veteran several times wounded, a lieutenant-general, maybe, and having, unless he be of the nobility, to pay the same taxes as the peasants of his parish[1] and being classed in every other way on the same level. This I have seen happen to elderly Knight-captains of Saint-Louis, pensioners, who were without hope of any exemptions, whereas exemptions are granted by the score to the lowest grades of pettifogging bank clerks.

The noble and most Christian precept that kings are made for their peoples, not peoples for their kings, was so firmly implanted in his heart that splendour and war were hateful to him. It thus happened that he sometimes argued too forcibly against war; he was carried away by truths too hard for the ears of worldly men, and on that account people often said maliciously that he was afraid to fight. His justice was blindfolded with all the thoroughness that safety requires. He carefully studied every case that came to the King for judgment at the various councils,

---

[1] Saint-Simon held that a soldier or sailor who offered his life in defence of his country and could not promote his private interests when away at the war, should not be asked to pay taxes at the same rate as those who stayed at home and tilled their fields in peace.

and if any great matter were involved, he worked with the experts, consulting their opinions, but not slavishly adopting them. At least every fortnight he took Communion with notable reverence and serenity, and he always wore the collar of the Order, with the mantle and bands. He saw his Jesuit confessor once or twice each week, sometimes for long sessions; but latterly, although he went more frequently to Communion, he did not prolong those audiences. He perfectly understood the King, respected him always, and, towards the end, loved him as a son should do. He paid him homage as his subject, but always retained a proper sense of his own rank. Mme de Maintenon he treated with the civility that their respective situations demanded. When Monseigneur was alive, he was careful to render him his due, but one could feel his constraint; and his absolute disapproval of the internal life of Meudon was evident. I have so often described the cause of his embarrassment that I shall not dwell on it now.[1] He loved his brothers tenderly and his wife with passion. His grief at losing her broke his heart, and only by a most prodigious effort did his religion survive the blow. It was a sacrifice which he offered without reserves and it killed him; yet in his terrible affliction he showed nothing mean nor common, nothing unworthy. Spectators saw a man driven frantic by grief, wringing from himself the strength to preserve a calm front, but dying in the struggle. It was this struggle that brought his life to a premature close.

It was the same in his last illness, for he never believed that he would recover; he maintained that opinion in spite of his doctors, and did not conceal from them the reasons on which he based it. Indeed, from first to last his sufferings confirmed his suspicions. What an appalling thing to have had that conviction regarding his wife's death and his own! But Great Heavens! what an example to us all. The most personal, most sublime secrets may not yet be revealed; thus God alone knows the price he had to pay! How fine an imitation he gave of Jesus Christ upon the Cross! I refer not only to his death and suffering, but also to his gentle, patient spirit, his supreme selflessness! Such thankfulness he expressed that he was not required to reign and render an account of kingship! How humble, how excellent he was! How truly he loved God! How clearly he saw his own sins and unworthiness! How modest his hopes! How peaceful his mind! How marvellous his understanding of God's mercy! How holy his fears! How long he read and prayed; how eagerly received the Last Sacraments! How deep his self-questioning! How invincible his patience; how kind, how considerate he was to all who approached him! In his death France suffered her final punishment, when God disclosed to her the prince whom she did not deserve. Earth was not worthy of him; he was already ripe for the joys of Paradise.

---

[1] The cause was Mlle Choin, the Grand Dauphin's official mistress, whom he was believed to have married secretly because she slept in the state bed and had an armchair in Monseigneur's presence, whereas everyone else, even including the Duchesse de Bourgogne, had to be content with a tabouret.

Consternation was deep and general and spread to other lands and courts. The people wept for one who had thought only of their deliverance; all France mourned a prince whose sole desire had been for her happiness and welfare; the sovereigns of Europe publicly mourned for one whom already they had taken as their model, and whose great merit might one day have made him an arbiter between the nations. The Pope was so profoundly moved that, unasked, he set the Roman tradition aside, and with universal approval held a special consistory at which he mourned the incalculable loss suffered by Christendom and the Church, announcing at the same time that he would himself officiate at a solemn requiem in the Vatican chapel.

The sequence of tragic events compels me to retrace my steps. The Dauphine, as I have already mentioned, died at Versailles on Friday, 12 February, between eight and nine in the evening. I returned brokenhearted to my room, where Mailly, Archbishop of Rheims, who was in the habit of visiting me at unusual hours, found me alone. He also was deeply affected as, indeed, was everyone else, and he was all the more distressed because his dear sister-in-law, the Comtesse de Mailly, would lose her post as lady-in-waiting. She had already told him of the incident regarding the snuffbox. The archbishop now related that he had been in the unhappy princess's bedroom during all the King's visit and for some considerable time beforehand, and he further said that the Duc de Noailles, as captain of the guard on duty, had entered in advance of the King, looking strangely preoccupied, as though he had some purpose in mind and was in no doubt of achieving it. He had, indeed, appeared unusually alert and composed. He had stayed only a short time in the room, and had then departed to return escorting the King, after which, despite his still evident preoccupation, he bore an undoubted look of satisfaction.[1] The archbishop spoke as though the entire tragedy had been of his making; and, indeed, said so firmly and distinctly.

It should, however, be borne in mind that the Maillys could none of them endure the Noailles. They were consumed with jealousy because Mme de Maintenon favoured that family, and it was their particular folly to have taken offence because the Comtesse de Mailly, who was merely the daughter of her first cousin, had not been treated in the matter of dowry on terms of perfect equality with her brother's only child. What is more, apart from the general quarrel, the archbishop nurtured a private grievance, dating from the time when, as a mere abbé, deputizing at a Church assembly, he had dared to contradict the president Cardinal de Noailles, at that time at the very height of favour. That prelate tried at first to reason with him, then, vexed by continued insolence from

---

[1] This sentence is more obscure than at first appears. Saint-Simon can scarcely mean that the Duc de Noailles felt calm and satisfied at the knowledge of the Dauphine's imminent death.

a subordinate, had spoken in a manner which the other never could forgive.

M. de Mailly told me of this event at the time when it happened and there-after several times repeated that he should never forget it. I therefore reminded him of this ancient grudge, hoping to make him question his motives, but he only grew heated in an endeavour to convince me. I then declared that no one else would ever believe that the Duc de Noailles had committed that abominable crime, especially not since he stood to lose all by the Dauphine's death, and greatly depended on the favour of Mme de Maintenon, who at her advanced age[1] might never recover from the shock. Thereafter I produced every possible argument, but without making the slightest impression on him. He stood firm on the affair of the snuffbox, which, indeed, remains a mystery even today. I begged him at all events to maintain an impenetrable silence, which he did; but when he died many years later, he was still of the same conviction. That, however, was all one to me; others who had heard the rumour were as little affected by it, and no one at all suspected the Duc de Noailles. I, myself, regarded it so little that our personal relations remained unchanged, for we were very good friends at that time and until after the King's death; but somehow or other neither of us ever referred to the matter of the snuffbox.

Immediately after leaving the Dauphine, her confessor Père de La Rue went to the King's study requesting an audience. He was straightway admitted, and over-coming his embarrassment as best he might, he informed the King of her desire to confess elsewhere. Nothing could more have alarmed King Louis![2] A thousand terrible suspicions rose to his mind. Whether religious scruples caused any part of his fears I do not know, but they must have disquieted him. His anger was curbed because of the tragic circumstances but he allowed free rein to his displeasure. La Rue made good use of the argument that there was not a moment to lose, and thus managed to terminate what had been a most awkward interview.

The body of the Dauphine was left upon her bed throughout the whole of Saturday the 13th, with the face uncovered. At eleven o'clock that same night it was opened in the presence of the entire Faculty, the lady-in-waiting, and a woman-of-the-bedchamber. On Sunday the 14th, it was placed in a coffin on a dais three steps high, and on the day following it was taken into her state drawing-room, where altars had been set up, and where masses were read continually throughout the morning. Four bishops seated on the right-hand side, wearing copes and rochets,[3] were relieved at regular intervals, and alerted by officers of the Church. They had demanded chairs with backs, hassocks, and sprinklers; but the first two were refused them and they were offered instead folding stools with-

---

[1] Mme de Maintenon was seventy-seven in 1712.
[2] The King's alarm was due to his anti-Jansenism. For he believed that the Jansenists were revolutionaries at heart.
[3] A rochet is a close-fitting kind of surplice worn by bishops and abbots.

out hassocks. They should not by rights have had sprinklers, but after making a great rumpus they succeeded in obtaining them.

To understand the ritual, which I have not yet needed to explain, you must know that in the presence of a dead prince those in attendance are allowed only such privileges as they had enjoyed in the prince's living presence. In church, people sit on folding stools; and the rule remains the same regarding both the seating and the kind of seat given. Hassocks are given in church only to members of the royal family, bastards, dukes, duchesses, and those who rank as 'foreign royalty', or who have been granted grace and favour *tabourets*. Thus, only to such persons do the heralds, who stand at the four corners of the coffin, offer hassocks for the short prayer that follows the sprinkling with Holy Water, and they remove the hassocks when such persons rise from their knees. The heralds also present sprinklers to these persons, who return them after use. They give sprinklers also to Officers of the Crown and to their wives; among Officers of the Court, only those first gentlemen of the King's bedchamber who are not dukes, their wives, the lady-in-waiting, the maid-of-honour, the groom-in-waiting and his wife receive sprinklers. All these persons kneel without hassocks during the short prayer. The rest, no matter who, male or female, even though they be wearing mantles and mantillas, take sprinklers from the font and afterwards replace them, the heralds making no movement to assist them. The heralds know when to offer sprinklers by hearing the names announced loudly by the usher at the door; no other persons are announced in that way.

Six ladies wearing mantillas sit opposite the bishops, and are relieved in a body at regular intervals during the day, each one having been notified of the time of her watch by a letter from the head of protocol. The ladies who compose these watches are two duchesses or princesses (provided with hassocks), two palace-ladies who are not duchesses, and two gentlewomen of sufficient standing to have eaten with the princess and ridden in her coach. The King himself nominates the two titled ladies of the first watch.

On the morning of Friday the 19th, the body of Monseigneur le Dauphin was opened, a little more than twenty-four hours after his death, in the presence of the entire Faculty, some of his boyhood companions, and the Duc d'Aumont, representing the King. The heart was taken at once to Val-de-Grâce, in Paris. Chamillart, Bishop of Senlis, Madame la Dauphine's first almoner, rode in the first coach on the right-hand back seat, bearing the two hearts. Madame la Princesse sat beside him on the left, Mme de Vendôme and the Princesse de Conti in front, with the Duchesse du Lude beside one of the doors, and the Duc du Maine by the other. The Duc d'Aumont, as first gentleman-of-the-bedchamber, followed in one of Monseigneur le Dauphin's coaches; then came Madame la Dauphine's coach filled with palace-ladies, two of whom remained as watchers. This procession reached Val-de-Grâce after midnight, and all was over before two o'clock. For the return there was no ceremony, and those who wished spent the night in Paris. When the procession had left Versailles Monseigneur le Dauphin's body was brought from Marly without ceremony, and was placed on the same dais to the right of that of Madame la Dauphine. On the following Saturday the King informed the Duchesse de Ventadour that he wished Mgr le Duc de Bretagne to adopt the name and rank of Dauphin, and that same evening he invited Madame into his study after his supper, with the other princes and princesses who ordinarily remained with him until his *coucher.* Thenceforward she joined their party every evening.

On Tuesday, 23 February, both bodies were taken from Versailles to Saint-Denis in one hearse. In that procession, which started at six o'clock in the evening, almoners on horseback, wearing rochets, supported the corners of the pall. The gentleman-in-waiting and the master of the horse rode one on either side. The hearse was preceded by three coaches, in the second of which rode M. le Duc d'Orléans with the Duc d'Aumont, and d'Antin in front. In the third coach, nearest to the hearse, were four bishops in rochets and copes, a King's almoner in a rochet, and the curé of Versailles wearing a stole. Three coaches followed; the first, which was one of the King's coaches, contained the four princesses and the Duchesse du Lude, the second contained Madame la Dauphine's ladies, and the third, which was Madame la Duchesse's coach, contained the princesses' maids-of-honour. This procession entered Paris by the Porte Saint-Honoré two hours after midnight, and left by the Porte Saint-Denis at four o'clock, arriving at Saint-Denis between seven and eight in the morning. There was absolute quiet in Paris and no incidents.

On Saturday, 27 February, the King returned to Versailles from Marly. He had eaten alone in his bedroom morning and evening during all that excursion and with little ceremony. He chose not to receive the Court's formal condolences, as after Monseigneur's death; but sent word to say that he would see them all together immediately after his return to Versailles. The princes and princesses of the blood and the bastards were there awaiting him in his study. The Duchesse du Lude and Madame la Dauphine's ladies, her groom-in-waiting and other senior Court officials stood by the study door; the other ladies waited in the King's bedroom, and the men stood in the ante-chamber and in all the other rooms as far as the door to Mme de Maintenon's apartments. All wore mantillas and long mantles. The King arrived at four o'clock and went straight to his study by the little private staircase. He then, in order to see everyone present, walked slowly through all the rooms to Mme de Maintenon's door. The Duchesse du Lude was the only one whom he embraced, saying that he was in no state to speak to her at that moment but would do so before long. Half an hour later, Mme de Maintenon desired her to come to her room with Madame la Dauphine's ladies. They had removed their mantillas. The King spoke courteously to one and all, and detained the Duchesse du Lude, inviting her to be seated, and talking privately with her and Mme de Maintenon for some considerable time. Thereafter he saw her many times in that same way, but hardly ever in public, except at Marly, when her health permitted her to go there. All at Versailles, wearing mantles and mantillas, formed in line to visit the princes and princesses, beginning with M. and Madame la Duchesse de Berry, and ending with the Comte de Toulouse.

On Tuesday, 1 March, the King saw the foreign ministers in his study before mass, all of them wearing long mantles. On the following Saturday, he heard the orations of the Parlement, the Chambre des Comptes, the Cour des Aides, and the Cour des Monnaies; the orations were spoken by the various presidents. The President of the city council of Paris spoke last, and the best of all was the speech by the provost of the merchants. All this was before mass. Next day, Sunday, the Council of State appeared to make an oration, and they were immediately followed by the Académie Française.

On that very day, the two infant Sons of France, who had been ailing for some time past, were taken seriously ill with the same symptoms of measles that had appeared on Monseigneur le Dauphin and Mme la Dauphine. Both had received private baptism at birth. The King now instructed the Duchesse de Ventadour to arrange for a christening ceremony; to appoint whomever she thought fit as sponsors, and to name both children Louis. On the following day, Tuesday, 8 March, the court physicians summoned five others from Paris. The King continued to hold the finance council, went shooting after his dinner, and worked with Voysin each evening, in Mme de Maintenon's room. Bleedings and purges did not avail to save the little Dauphin. He died that same day, shortly before midnight. He was five years and a few months old, strong and tall for his age. He showed great promise on account of his high courage and good sense, but was also causing some anxiety because of his obstinacy and self-will, not to mention his excessive arrogance. M. le Duc d'Anjou had not yet been weaned. The Duchesse de Ventadour, assisted by women of the bedchamber, kidnapped him and stubbornly refused to let him be bled or given physic.[1] The Countess of Verua, when she was poisoned at Turin and very near death, had been saved

---

[1] Madame wrote: 'When the little Dauphin became quite red with the smallpox and sweated, the doctors opened a vein, and in consequence of this operation the poor child died....His little brother had exactly the same illness. While the doctors were busy with the elder child, the nurses locked themselves in with the younger prince. Yesterday, the 9th, the doctors wanted to open a vein because the child had severe fever; but the governess, Mme de Ventadour, and her deputy, strongly opposed this, and steadfastly refused to permit it, simply keeping him nice and warm. So this child was saved'—and eventually became Louis XV.

by an antidote belonging to the Duke of Savoy,[1] and had brought a little back
with her to France. The Duchesse de Ventadour sent to ask her for it, and was
able to give it to M. le Duc d'Anjou because he had not been bled. It is a remedy
that cannot be given after bleeding. He was most gravely ill; but he recovered,
and is our King today. They afterwards told him what had happened, and ever
since he has shown marked attention to the Countess of Verua and to all her
relations. Thus, in less than a year, three Dauphins had died, one of them still a
young child; and, in the space of twenty-four days, the father, mother, and elder
son were all dead.

On Wednesday, 9 March, the body of the little Dauphin was opened, and
during the night his heart was taken without ceremony of any kind to Val-de-Grâce,
and his body to Saint-Denis, where it was laid on the dais between the bodies of
his father and mother, Monseigneur le Dauphin and Mme le Dauphine. M. le Duc
d'Anjou, now the sole survivor, succeeded to the rank and title of Dauphin.

I shall omit what happened at the King's *réveil* after the death of Monseigneur le
Dauphin because in all respects it was similar to that which occurred after Madame
la Dauphine's death. The King repeatedly embraced M. le Duc de Berry with great
tenderness, saying, 'Now I have only you!' The prince burst into tears; no one could
have been longer or more deeply afflicted. Mme la Duchesse de Berry was obliged
to stay in the room; she kept her countenance with sufficient decorum, but in truth
she was enraptured to see herself and her husband ranking above all others. In
Spain, the grief and horror at these successive calamities were beyond belief.

For some unknown reason the King, who, after Monseigneur's death had
insisted on everyone draping[2] who normally did so when he draped (although he
himself did not wear mourning), would allow no one to drape for Monseigneur
and Mme la Dauphine, excepting only M. and Mme la Duchesse de Berry. Since
members of their households necessarily draped when they did so, a question
arose regarding Mme de Saint-Simon who claimed the right not to, against
their wishes, offering as examples the Duchesses de Ventadour and de Brancas
in the household of Madame. We argued that those ladies were separated from
their husbands and had their own settlements and coaches, whereas Mme de
Saint-Simon and I lived together and she used her husband's equipages. A
tremendous controversy then ensued, for they made this question of draping a
point of honour. M. and Mme la Duchesse de Berry begged us so insistently, for
the sake of friendship, as something on which they set great store, that in the end

---

[1] No other historian seems to have mentioned an antidote to poison. This terrible succession of blows stupefied
France and shocked all other countries. As messenger after messenger brought the news the rumour spread that they
had all been poisoned by the Duc d'Orléans, although there was never any kind of proof offered. It is almost certain that
their deaths were due to smallpox or measles and their treatment by the doctors.

[2] Draping involved wearing mourning black, with black hangings over the coaches and the walls of drawing-
and dining-rooms.

we were obliged to consent. As a result, our household was parti-coloured; every-thing of mine or ours was in colours, and everything of Mme de Saint-Simon's was black, which appeared vastly absurd.

M. de Beauvilliers, who had been ill in bed at Versailles, went for greater quiet to his house at the lower end of the Rue de l'Orangerie. You will find it hard to conceive his agonies of grief, and the noble piety, resignation, and cour-age with which he endured them. I know nothing so hard to describe, so impos-sible to imitate, so incomparably admirable. On the day of the death of our Dauphin, I locked myself into my lodging and left it only for a moment to join the King on his outing in the gardens, when he passed near my window after his dinner. Curiosity was partly the reason; but wretchedness at seeing him look almost as usual drove me indoors again very quickly. This was at the precise moment when they were removing the Dauphin's body. I saw something occur-ring in the distance, and fled back to my room, from which I scarcely re-emerged during the whole of that excursion, save to spend the afternoons closeted alone with the Duc de Beauvilliers, for he admitted almost no one else. I must confess that I made a detour between the canal and the gardens of Versailles, in order to reach his house by the Orangery gate, and so spare myself the sight of the funeral procession, which no amount of duty could have made me join. I admit that it was weak of me! I had neither the invincible piety of the Duc de Beauvilliers to sustain me, nor even that of Mme de Saint-Simon, who was suffering as keenly as I. The truth is that I was in despair. To those who understand my plight, my state of mind will seem less extraordinary than my ability to support that shattering disaster. It struck me at precisely the age at which my father had lost Louis XIII;[1] but my father had, at least, been given great joy; whereas I, *gustavi paululum mellis, et ecce morior!* Yet even that was not the whole of it.

Locked in the Dauphin's desk were the various memoranda which he had asked me to prepare for him. I had written them confident of absolute secrecy. He had kept them in the same spirit. My work was thus clearly recognizable; there was even a long document in my own hand, which alone would have sufficed to ruin me irretrievably with the King. One cannot foresee such catastrophes. The King knew my writing. He was not so familiar with my way of thinking, but he had a shrewd idea of my convictions. I had sometimes spoken too freely, and kind friends at Court had not hesitated to fill in the gaps. This danger applied also to the Duc de Beauvilliers, and at a further remove to the Duc de Chevreuse. The King having recognized me in these memoranda, would also have discovered the free, almost perfect trust existing between the Dauphin and myself, on matters so highly important and so very little to his liking. He was as yet completely unaware

[1] Saint-Simon's father was thirty-seven at the death of Louis XIII.

that I had been closer to his grandson than any other courtier. Knowing me to be an intimate friend of the Duc de Beauvilliers, he would never have believed that this intimacy with the Dauphin, these secret meetings on highly confidential affairs, could have taken place without M. de Beauvilliers's connivance. Yet it was M. de Beauvilliers's personal duty to take the Dauphin's locked desk to the King, to whom du Chesne had surrendered the key immediately after his death. The suspense was agonizing; for it was one chance in a million that I should not be ruined and banished for the remainder of the reign. What a contrast between the clear skies under which I had recently lived so confidently, and the abyss that had suddenly opened beneath my feet! At that moment I perceived the vanity of all earthly success, with a pang that showed me how much I still clung to it.

Fear of the opening of the desk scarcely troubled me; I had to force myself to think of it from time to time. Sorrow at my own loss, but far, far more at the thought of all that France was losing by the death of that incomparable Dauphin, pierced me to the heart and numbed my senses. At first I could think only of retiring from the world, never again to fall a victim to its false promises. Even when at last I resolved to stay, my friendships with M. le Duc de Berry and M. le Duc d'Orléans (which, in view of the King's age, many greater than myself would have paid dearly to possess) had not the slightest savour for me. Grief made me dead to comfort or reason, and I freely displayed all that, from prudence or politics, I had hitherto kept so private. Mme de Saint-Simon, no less stricken, equally incapable of deceit, but stronger than I, and with more faith in God, had the good sense to live in mortal dread of these documents. The Dukes and Duchesses of Beauvilliers and Chevreuse alone knew the secret, and they were the only ones whom we consulted. We decided that M. de Beauvilliers should keep possession of the writing-desk until he had recovered sufficiently to take it himself to the King; and that then, under his very nose, he should make an attempt by some means or other to extract the vital papers from among all the rest. It would not be an easy task, for he had no idea of their whereabouts; but it was our only hope. We were kept in suspense for more than a fortnight.

On the last Monday of February, for the first time, the King saw M. de Beauvilliers in his study at five o'clock in the evening. My lodging was not far from his, on the same floor, opening on to the central corridor of the new wing, on the same level also as the King's own apartments. On his return, the duke called on us to tell us that the King had bidden him bring the Dauphin's box of documents to Mme de Maintenon's room on the following evening. He said again that he dared promise nothing, but would do his utmost to conceal my work from the King. He also said that he would return next day and tell us all. You may imagine our state of mind as we waited, and how firmly we kept our door closed. He

came, as promised, and before sitting down let us know that all was well. He then
related that, most fortunately for us, the whole top-layer of papers in the box,
to some considerable depth, consisted of a mass of documents concerning the
finances. These he read aloud in their entirety, hoping thus to fatigue the King,
and he succeeded so well that before long King Louis was glad to hear only the
headings. Becoming at last convinced that the bottom layer contained nothing of
greater interest, he bade M. de Beauvilliers throw the entire contents on the fire.
The duke said that he did not wait to be told twice, especially since he had caught
a glimpse of my writing and had promptly covered it. He stuffed all the papers
back into the box, and shook them out into the fire, with the King and Mme de
Maintenon on either side of him, taking great care meanwhile to hold them well
down with the tongs, and to see that all were completely burned before he stepped
back from the hearth. We three embraced with a relief that was comparable only
to the danger from which we had escaped.

Horrors no longer postponable paralyse my fingers. I would suppress them
were it not for the truth I serve in writing; the fresh horrors that followed, their
publicity[1] in all Europe, and their momentous consequences compel me to
disclose them as forming an integral part of all that I witnessed at the Court.
The Dauphine's illness, so sudden, so unfamiliar to the doctors, so terribly rapid,
kindled imaginations already shaken by the warning given to Boudin and reiterated
by the King of Spain. King Louis's anger at the change of confessor, which, had
she lived, would have been vented on the princess, gave place to grief at his loss
of her, or, more truly speaking, at the loss to him of all pleasures and amusement.
Anxiety led him to wish to discover the cause of the immense calamity, in order to
avoid any repetition of it and to restore his peace of mind. He therefore gave the
Faculty precise instructions from his own lips how they should proceed.

The autopsy brought no comfort. There was no sign of any natural cause;
but within the head they found other signs, near the spot where she had suffered
such intolerable pain. Fagon and Boudin were in no doubt as to poison, and said
as much to the King in Mme de Maintenon's presence. Boulduc told me that he
also had been convinced, and the few other witnesses whom the King consulted
signified their agreement by miserable silence. Maréchal alone maintained that
nothing suggested poison, except for a few extremely ambiguous symptoms which
he had seen in other bodies where there had been absolutely no grounds for
suspicion. He said the same to me—to me, from whom he concealed nothing. He
added, although he would not swear to it, that these atrocious suspicions were killing the King by inches, for they would allow him no peace of mind for the rest of
his life. Indeed, they did have that effect for a long time to come. King Louis was

---

[1] Saint-Simon is supposed to have invented this word.

outraged. So determined was he to discover the originators of the infernal plot that he would not listen to Maréchal's arguments; although Maréchal himself disputed hotly with Fagon and Boudin, they stuck to their first opinions and never afterwards departed from them. Boudin, who was in a perfect frenzy at losing his post, a princess who had shown him much kindness and even trust, and all the personal ambitions that had perished with her, wildly advertised the certainty of poison, while the other witnesses whispered the suspicion to their friends. In less than twenty-four hours the entire Court and Paris were full of it. The first grief for the death of an adored princess changed to indignation, rapidly followed by fear and curiosity, soon monstrously increased by the Dauphin's illness.

The very nature of that illness, what everyone knew he had believed about it, the care he had taken to persuade the King to take precautions, the suddenness and the manner of his death, intensified the horror and desolation, and brought peremptory orders from the King for an autopsy. This was carried out in the Dauphin's bedroom at Versailles, as I have already described. The result was appalling. The 'noble portions'[1] were decomposing; the heart disintegrated when the Duc d'Aumont took it to place it in the urn, and flowed from his fingers on to the ground. The blood had putrefied. An intolerable stench filled all that vast chamber. The King and Mme de Maintenon impatiently awaited the report. It was given them that same evening, no detail omitted.

Fagon, Boudin and a few others reported having discovered the violent effects of a most subtle, most acute poison that had consumed the whole interior of the body, except for the head, like a raging fire. The head itself had not been so attacked, but had been affected in a manner very similar to that of the Dauphine. Maréchal, who had opened the body, stubbornly held to his opinion, despite Fagon and the rest, stoutly maintaining that there was no sure sign of any poison, that he had opened other bodies in much the same condition when there had been no thought of foul play, that the poison which had attacked them both and killed the young Dauphin also was a natural infection caused by the putrefaction of the blood inflamed by a raging fever, so deep-seated that few signs of it had outwardly appeared. That was the true cause of the rotting of the various organs. No need, he said, to seek any further, for that, in itself, was enough to have caused a perfectly natural death, such as he had witnessed in a number of bodies, although rarely to such a wide extent. It was, however, a question of the degree, not of the nature, of the disease. Fagon and Boudin contradicted Maréchal's opinion, and both were violently acrimonious. At last Maréchal himself grew heated, and ended the argument by informing the King and Mme de Maintenon before all the assembled doctors that he spoke the simple truth as he saw it and as he believed it, and

[1] The head, lungs, liver and brain.

that to say otherwise was mere guesswork, most liable to make the King's life a misery, oppressed by mistrust and profitless surmises, which was the shortest way to poison him as well. He then exhorted King Louis, for the sake of his health and peace of mind, to put aside these terrible fancies, for in Maréchal's view they were wholly unreasonable. Finally, he rounded angrily on those who were seeking to spread false alarms.

Maréchal recounted this incident to me later, and at the same time said that, although he considered that the deaths might well have been natural, he had some doubts, on account of all the unusual symptoms. He said that he had persisted mainly out of pity for the King, and in indignation because he had sensed a plot to throw all the guilt upon M. le Duc d'Orléans. He warned me of this as a friend of us both; for although a man of his word, and truth and goodness personified, he was a rough-spoken fellow who never minced his words. Yet he was always perfectly respectful and never forgot his place.

Despite my seclusion, it was not long before I learned what was being averred regarding M. le Duc d'Orléans. The ugly whispers did not long remain secret. The speed at which they travelled through the Court to Paris and the provinces, to the remoter monasteries, and finally to all the peoples of Europe, reminded me of how swiftly the news had flown at the time of the wicked Flemish plot against the very prince who now was so deeply regretted.[1] The cabal then so well organized had been destroyed, as I have described, and its detestable leader[2] reduced to playing the hero in Spain. Broken the cabal had been, but although rendered powerless and discouraged by all the changes, it was not entirely disbanded. Vaudémont, his d'Espinay niece, and the other relics of Meudon still survived. They hoped against hope, and braced themselves against adversity. They now seized on this tragic episode to breathe again and, under Mme de Maintenon's guidance, what heights might they not hope to reach! How high, indeed, did they succeed in climbing!

You already know, not the Dauphin's intentions regarding the bastards, for that was a secret, but the strong disapproval of their aggrandisement which he and his wife had displayed, even under the King's eye. The Duc du Maine had had so little hope of becoming reconciled with them that he had made no advances, either personally or through Mme de Maintenon, the wretched and embarrassed witness of his disfavour, or even through the King, who after so much humiliation in his efforts at appeasement had not dared to attempt anything further. As for his duchess, who was if possible even more eager for rank, she never budged from Sceaux, where she played the goddess and pretended to despise the Court.

M. du Maine, the biggest coward and the busiest schemer imaginable, had

---

[1] For the slandering of the Duc de Bourgogne, see Vol. I, p. 382.
[2] Vendôme, then in Spain, was the 'detestable leader' of the cabal.

been living in mortal terror for his rank and dignities, and was too intelligent not also to fear for the vast wealth that was unlikely to remain his if his self-made throne were destroyed. His children were growing up;[1] the King was ageing rapidly; he had trembled at the thought of the not distant future, the prospect of which his fears brought even closer. He had no friends on whom he could rely in the circle of the Dauphin and Dauphine. He had seen no escape anywhere. Their deaths had been to him as much a deliverance as to France they were the most overwhelming catastrophe. What an ill wind! What a stroke of luck for him! What a transition from dread of suffering the fate of Enceladus to sanguine hopes of a career like Phaeton's, with sound expectation of its longer duration![2] Amid the general mourning he thus rose with renewed strength; but being a master of the most sinister arts—I shall not say the very blackest, for no suggestion of them has come to me[3]—he thought it would benefit him to fasten suspicion on someone else, and it killed two, nay a hundred birds with the same stone to let that someone be M. le Duc d'Orléans.

The slow rehabilitation of that prince with the King, and the deaths of every other royal prince old enough to voice an objection, had gained for the Duc du Maine his latest and most monstrous step in rank. By damning M. le Duc d'Orléans with this outrageous calumny, and persuading the King and Society that it was true, he reckoned to discredit him for ever in the most vile and humiliating manner. Should fortune, which had so happily rid him of his most redoubtable opponent, treat him less kindly in the person of the Duc de Berry, he might well believe that that prince would let himself be guided by the King and public opinion, and that his grief would soon change to fear and loathing of his brother's murderer. Thereafter, or so M. du Maine calculated, the means would not be wanting to outwit a prince so weak, and so easily influenced.

The princes of the blood were all too young to be of any account. The Duc de Chartres, born in 1703, was still under parental control; Monsieur le Duc was twenty; the Comte de Charolais not yet twelve; the Comte de Clermont five, and the Prince de Conti seventeen. Only Monsieur le Duc amounted to anything; but the King completely ignored him, and neither he nor his mother dared so much as to breathe in the royal presence. Madame la Princesse, lacking the sense or the spirit for anything except her prayers,[4] lived in terror of her daughter the Duchesse du Maine; her other daughter the Princesse de Conti spent her

---

[1] The Duc du Maine's two sons were fifteen and fourteen years old.

[2] Enceladus was a giant who rebelled against Jupiter and was imprisoned under Mount Etna. Phaeton came to grief in driving the chariot of his father Helios, god of the sun.

[3] Does Saint-Simon mean that he had no notion what they were, or that he had no sure proof?

[4] Saint-Simon says elsewhere that she was equally hideous, virtuous, and silly.

life in Paris occupied with family concerns, and never ventured to approach the King. As for Mme de Vendôme, in the King's eyes she simply did not exist. Thus the field was free for M. du Maine. He was well able to take advantage of that!

Mme de Maintenon had eyes only for him, and since the death of her adored Dauphine had centred on him all her affection. She loathed M. le Duc d'Orléans; you already know why. Her most favoured nursling had thus little trouble in persuading her of something that seemed to justify her hatred and at the same time furthered his own interests; or, if not herself entirely convinced, she was ready to delude the King and influence Society. No one could have mistaken the prime mover and seconder in this dreadful accusation, for neither of them made the slightest pretence of concealment in the King's presence. Mme de Maintenon rounded on Maréchal in front of him, going so far as to say that everyone knew the culprit's name, and mentioning M. le Duc d'Orléans. The King assented in horror, as though there were no doubts, and both of them appeared to think that Maréchal took a liberty when he expostulated.[1] Fagon nodded agreement, and Boudin was mad enough to say that the facts were beyond question, and tossed his head insolently when Maréchal reproved him. All this occurred at the reading of the report on the autopsy. Thereafter, in the King's study the Duc du Maine returned again and again to the subject; and although he took some heed of the attendant valets, more than one overheard him and spread the rumour from mouth to ear. Blouin, and those who took their tone from him, did not scruple to retail the frightful accusation as something which both the King and Mme de Maintenon believed; and Fagon lent them his authority by continued silence, which combined with Boudin's virulence to suppress any objections from the Faculty.

The entire Court was similarly struck with terror when they saw those closest to Mme de Maintenon making charges that were all the more convincing because spoken with a show of horror and reluctance. The small group that still clung to the Duc and Duchesse du Maine, and all their circle at Sceaux down to the lowest servants, not only spoke, but screamed for vengeance against M. le Duc d'Orléans. The more ambitious courtiers, and those who made it their chief aim to please, adopted the same tone. Thus there was a repetition in a different way of the same kind of gossip and expressions of opinion that were so prevalent during the Lille campaign against the prince whom everyone now mourned, with the

---

[1] Madame wrote: 'As though I had not sufficient sorrow by the deaths of Madame la Dauphine and Monsieur le Dauphin...another and still more poignant grief cuts me to the heart. Certain wicked people are spreading a rumour that my son poisoned them. I am convinced of his innocence—I would stick my hand in the fire for it. I thought at first it must be a joke, for I could not imagine such a thing being said seriously. That, however, was how they reported it to the King, but he spoke kindly to my son and promised him that he did not believe it.' In another letter of the same date (8 April, 1712) she accused the Duc du Maine, d'Antin, and Madame la Duchesse of having originated the slander.

same overwhelming terror suppressing contradiction and reducing defenders to silence. Maréchal, who very prudently had told me only the half when he warned me of the approaching storm, now told me every detail of what had passed in Mme de Maintenon's room, just as I have recounted it here.

M. le Duc d'Orléans had openly shed tears at the deaths. His personal interests were in direct contrast to those of M. du Maine. Indeed, had he been a very fiend vomited from Hell, his master-plan might have been to kill the King and thus rid himself of his implacable enemy, Mme de Maintenon. The time is not yet come for a full description of this prince; a sketch will suffice to depict his unhappy situation and the abominable nature of the accusation, so wickedly devised, so widely spread, so ably and spitefully sustained. In very truth, the malice was little less horrible than the imputed crime, and M. du Maine gained by it advantages far exceeding his best hopes. He might well have set the kingdom in revolt had he been less bankrupt in heart and courage, and with a reputation less utterly discredited.

The Dauphin had always liked M. le Duc d'Orléans. The Duc de Chevreuse had strongly recommended him in boyhood, because the Duc de Montfort, his eldest son, was one of the prince's intimates, and thus M. de Chevreuse saw him frequently and greatly enjoyed conversing with him on history, but more especially on science, and sometimes on religion, hoping to reclaim him. The Archbishop of Cambrai saw him also and greatly enjoyed his company; and conversely M. le Duc d'Orléans grew fond of him and held him in such high esteem that he stoutly defended him at the time of his disgrace, and never afterwards changed towards him. That, despite the contrast in their ways of living, had won him the regard of the Little Flock, and the influence of that circle over the Dauphin needs no comment. Apart from their support, the two princes often met in the King's apartments, and almost every evening in the Princesse de Conti's salon, where they would settle down in a corner to discuss the sciences, on which no one could speak more agreeably or more clearly than M. le Duc d'Orléans. Theirs was a long-standing friendship; they had always been glad to meet, and were as much at ease in one another's company as the differences in their rank and ages would permit. The Dauphin's marriage and the closer family bond further cemented their mutual liking.[1]

The Dauphine had been deeply attached to her father and mother, the Duke and Duchess of Savoy. In France she had found her grandfather, Monsieur, who

---

[1] The Dauphine's mother was Anne Marie d'Orléans, daughter of Monsieur (Philippe I, Duc d'Orléans) by his first wife, Henrietta of England. The Dauphine's grandmother was thus an Englishwoman, another example of the mixed relationships in the European royal families. The Duc d'Orléans, Monsieur's son by his second wife, was the Dauphine's uncle.

was the father both of Mme de Savoie and of M. le Duc d'Orléans. As you already know, she and Monsieur became truly fond of one another, and this fondness passed to her uncle, whom she made a point of defending, even when he was most in disgrace with the King and Mme de Maintenon. In the same way, M. le Duc d'Orléans, whom I had kept fully informed of the plot during the Lille campaign, staunchly defended the prince from the moment of his return from Spain. Shortly afterwards, when the Spanish affair[1] placed M. le Duc d'Orléans in great danger, he found a firm ally in Mgr le Duc de Bourgogne at the council, and a loyal defender in his wife, although she must have known that she acted against the wishes of the King and Mme de Maintenon. Later, when she had become Dauphine, she won that lady over, and through her the King, to agree to the marriage of Mme la Duchesse de Berry, and when she and Mme la Duchesse d'Orléans became close friends, her affection for M. le Duc d'Orléans increased.

I note the above events merely as reminders. All of them may be found described in various parts of these memoirs. Altogether, they serve to show that M. le Duc d'Orléans had every bit as much to hope from the reign of the Dauphin and Dauphine as the Duc du Maine had cause for fear. The contrast is a glaring one.

Only compare the position of M. le Duc d'Orléans, whose rank and estates were in no danger, and the precarious situation of M. du Maine, and then search for the poisoner.[2] That is not all. Remember how ill M. le Duc d'Orléans was treated by Monseigneur, who was demanding his head,[3] and then recollect how I found him weeping in a corner of one of the outer rooms on the night of his death; how shocked I was at this demonstration; how I tried to make him feel ashamed, and how he then answered me.[4] Great heavens! What a contrast between this grief at the death of an enemy, and the jesting of M. du Maine and his intimates in a corner of the study, when he left the King almost *in extremis,* after committing him to the care of an ignorant peasant,[5] whom he proceeded to mimic, so that great gales of laughter were heard at the farther end of the gallery, to the horror of those who passed through. This is a known fact, very characteristic of M. du Maine, as I shall show in detail at the proper time, provided I am spared to continue these memoirs until the death of the King.

Most unfortunately, outward appearances well served the interests of M. du Maine, who made use of them with all the arts of which he was such a master.

---

[1] See Vol. 1, p. 462 et seq. In 1708, when commanding the French army in Spain, the Duc d'Orléans was accused of plotting to dethrone Philip V, in order to take his place.

[2] Although, almost certainly, no such poisoner existed, it seems strange that the rumours did not point to the Duchesse de Berry, who had a very bad character, and far more to gain than the Duc d'Orléans.

[3] Monseigneur wanted to have the Duc d'Orléans tried for treason. See Vol. I, p. 465.

[4] He said that he had always been fond of Monseigneur, who had invariably been kind to him. See Vol. II, p. 136.

[5] Saint-Simon is casting forward to the time of Louis XIV's death.

M. le Duc d'Orléans, forced into a marriage[1] which his mother and the public outcry showed him to be disgraceful, was immediately afterwards launched into Society. Reacting swiftly against the severe restraints of his boyhood, he at once plunged into debauchery, choosing the most abandoned rakes as his boon companions. Everything was forgiven him because of his rank and youth. He believed that by despising his wife and living a dissolute life he would regain in the eyes of Society all that his marriage appeared to have lost him. Soon afterwards, a caprice for irreligion and the inordinate vanity that made him advertise his opinions; intense boredom with every pleasure not positively licentious; complete idleness at the Court, where he was forced to spend many hours away from his boon companions; an inability to attract other friends, and perpetual brawls with his wife and her circle, drove him to seek for solitude; but being accustomed to live in a crowd, he could not endure it for long.

Thus he came to study the sciences and to make experiments in alchemy, not attempting to manufacture gold (he was always scornful of that pursuit), but amusing himself with the curious processes of chemistry. He engaged a chemist named Homberg,[2] a man with as good a reputation for honour and integrity as for his calling; watched him performing experiments, and worked beside him, all quite openly, being ready to discuss these activities with men of science at the Court and in Paris, and often inviting them to watch him and Homberg at their labours. At one time he boasted of having tried to raise the devil, admittedly without success; but after he fell in love with Mme d'Argenton and lived with her he found other interests only too similar,[3] and liable to be given a more sinister interpretation. He was present, for example, on an occasion when they looked into glasses of water to see the present and the future, and I have recounted other strange happenings which he related to me before leaving for Italy.[4] It is enough to mention in passing these unfortunate diversions, for he had no evil intentions whatsoever. The Spanish affair, from which his reputation never fully recovered; the atrocious rumours concerning his relations with his daughter, which almost prevented her betrothal to M. le Duc de Berry; the public outcry to which he paid all too little heed; finally the horrible suspicions directed at Monsieur at the time of his first wife's death,[5] and the fact that M. le Duc d'Orléans was his son, formed a weight of evidence that served to bewilder the King and deceive the public.

As I have already said, the rumours were so readily believed that on 17

---

[1] The Duc d'Orléans, aged seventeen, had almost literally been compelled by the King to marry the youngest of his bastard daughters by Mme de Montespan. See Vol, I, p. 12.

[2] The Dutch scientist William Homberg (1652-1714), famous for his work on phosphates.

[3] Similar to devil-raising.

[4] The Duc d'Orléans was shown a vision of himself wearing an unusual kind of crown, 'with four hoops and nothing on the top'. See Saint-Simon at Versailles, p. 121.

[5] Monsieur had been suspected of poisoning his first wife Henrietta of England.

February, when he went with Madame to give Holy Water to the Dauphine, the bystanders all along the way made the most offensive remarks out loud. Both he and Madame heard them distinctly without daring to seem to notice; but you may imagine their indignation and embarrassment. He had cause to fear even worse from a credulous and excited crowd when he went alone, on 22 February, to give Holy Water to the Dauphin. Indeed, he was subjected as he passed to most abominable threats from the rabble, whom no one restrained; they shouted abuse and remarks at him, pointed with their thumbs, and used such filthy epithets that he was fortunate to escape being torn to pieces. There was a repetition of the same scene during the funeral procession. Precautions had been taken to prevent a riot, but at times the crowd's anger was alarming. They made threatening gestures, cat-calls, and every imaginable calumny levelled at M. le Duc d'Orléans. Near the Palais Royal, when the procession passed that way, the din was so loud that for several minutes he had very real cause to fear.

You may imagine the use to which M. du Maine put the public rage, the rumours in the Paris cafés, the gossip in the salon at Marly, the talk at the Parlement, where the premier président most virtuously paid his first instalment,[1] and among those who came hurrying back from the provinces and abroad. A man sows in order to reap, and M. du Maine's harvest surpassed all his hopes. The death of the little Dauphin and the report of the autopsy gave fresh impetus to the anger and intemperance, which allowed the bastard, Blouin, their followers at the Court, and Mme de Maintenon to go to even greater lengths, and the King to sink into despondency, fear, hatred, and perpetual anxiety. That was the condition in which they desired to keep him, so as to render him more compliant and easier to control.

When the rumour first broke upon Marly and the world in general, everyone began, not just to avoid M. le Duc d'Orléans, but positively to desert him in the King's study and the drawing-room. If he approached a group of courtiers, they all, without the least compunction, turned sharp around to right or left, and met again behind him. He was shunned with most marked discourtesy. Even the ladies for a while deserted Mme la Duchesse d'Orléans, and some never returned to her. He could do nothing but wait for the storm to pass; but this storm was too carefully organized, and his isolation continued until the last Marly of the King's life, when that monarch openly threatened to destroy him. Whenever the rumours seemed likely to die down in Paris and the provinces, fresh means were found to revive them, and this lasted until long after the King's death. I was the only person—the only one, I repeat—who continued to see M. le Duc d'Orléans as usual, visiting him at his house, approaching him in the King's room, sitting

[1] M. de Mesmes, by spreading the slanders, was making his first payment for being made premier président.

with him in a corner of the drawing-room, where we certainly had no cause to
fear interruption, and walking with him in the garden, under the very windows
of the King and Mme de Maintenon. At Versailles, I saw him every day, exactly
as I had been used to do.

It came to his ears shortly afterwards that La Feuillade was spreading abominable lies about him in Paris. He became blind with anger, and I had all the
trouble in the world to prevent his sending one of his household to insult La
Feuillade by giving him a sound thrashing. That was the only occasion on which
I ever saw M. le Duc d'Orléans lose his temper or go to such extremes. During
all this time, the Chancellor, M. de Beauvilliers, and my various other friends,
male and female, persistently warned me that I took a very grave risk in going
so contrary to the rest of the world and the feelings of the King and Mme de
Maintenon regarding M. le Duc d'Orléans. They told me that not to break nor
to cease from all intercourse with him was honourable and would be understood;
but to be so constantly in his company in public, in the garden at Marly under the
King's very eye, and before the entire Court, was pure folly, of no service to M. le
Duc d'Orléans, and so displeasing as to bring me to certain ruin.

I stood firm. It appeared to me, indeed, that a time of such absolute disaster
was not the moment to desert a friend if one believed him to be innocent; but
that, contrariwise, one should draw closer to him than ever, for the sake of one's
own self-esteem, for the comfort one might give him, which he received from
no one else, and in order to show one's indignation at the slander. My friends
broached the subject very often. They said that the King thought ill enough of me
already, that Mme de Maintenon was vexed—indeed, everything best calculated
to make me nervous. I remained unmoved, however, and continued to see M. le
Duc d'Orléans as usual, often for three or four hours at a time. I shall revert again
to this matter. At present we must return to the other happenings of that year.

There were two trifling events in Flanders during the month of March.
The enemy bombarded Arras to burn our stores of forage, but caused hardly
any damage. The Maréchal de Montesquiou learned that they had placed eight
hundred men in the village of Sluys.[1] Broglio, today a Marshal of France and a
duke, received orders to attack. He encountered a force of three hundred cavalry
retiring under cover of cannon fire from the Château of Sluys. He compelled them
to retreat into the château, which he took, together with the village and the entire
position, killing or capturing all eight hundred and the three hundred cavalry also.
We were so little accustomed to successes that this one was much talked of.

A very much better piece of news was the arrival of Ducasse at Corunna,
with richly laden galleys which he had brought back from America. They had

---

[1] Not the port in Dutch Flanders, but a village near Douai.

been expected with great impatience for some time past, and it was feared they might be captured on their return. They were of valuable assistance to Spain, which stood in great need of them, a considerable encouragement to trade, and a vexation to the English and the Dutch, who had been searching for them for a long time at great waste of labour and expense. The King of Spain was so glad that he made Ducasse a Knight of the Golden Fleece, to everyone's amazement and disgust. No matter how great the service he had rendered, that was not the coin in which he should have been paid. Ducasse was well known to be the son of a humble pork-butcher selling hams at Bayonne. He was valiant and well made. He embarked on a warship at Bayonne, crossed over to America and became a pirate. Thus he acquired a fortune and was made the chief of those adventurers; he then joined the King's navy, and rendered him distinguished service. Eventually he became a lieutenant-general[1] and might well have been a Marshal of France, had his age and length of service allowed; but he travelled so far that he was already old when he arrived. He was an excellent citizen and one of the best and most generous men that I have ever known, who without the least servility never stepped out of his place. When his rank and reputation brought him within range of the Court and Society, everyone respected him.

There died at this time a man of better birth, but whose talents would have kept him selling hams all through his life, had his father done so before him. This was the Comte de Brionne,[2] brought low by a long series of apoplectic fits. He was made a Chevalier of the Order in 1688, and was considered the best dancer of his day, although not very tall, and on the stout side. He was a decent sort of man on the whole, but duller and stupider than you can well conceive; one never saw him at the Court, except in the public rooms, and no one ever went to his house. His family ignored him, and so did everyone at the royal stables. Monsieur le Grand, never a loving father, said that his son drank all his best wine and was altogether unbearable; he thus had little difficulty in consoling himself.

Two very eminent Spanish grandees became priests at this time; one of them was the Count of Monterey, the other the Marquis de los Balbases. The privileges of the clergy in Spain are such that an individual's entry into the priesthood guarantees his wife against all investigation, because he retains his rights in the division of their lands and wealth, which makes inquiries extremely difficult, and almost always fruitless. The clergy are also protected from civil law, and thus it is impossible to punish them. Such considerations, much more than piety, or even the desire of great nobles to become cardinals, prompt those who fall into disgrace after high employment to enter the priesthood.

---

[1] Naval and military ranks bore similar names in Louis XIV's France.
[2] Henri de Lorraine-Armagnac (1661-1712), son of the Grand Ecuyer de France (the King's master of the horse) the Comte d'Armagnac, called Monsieur le Grand.

Spain, as well as France, had its Titans who stood to gain as much by the Dauphin's death, and moved at even greater speed to profit from it. The Princesse des Ursins, who already thought herself a sovereign, was impatient to let Spain feel the weight of her new dignity, of which it was as yet unaware. She dared not move without the consent of France, but she well knew how to set about obtaining this, and also how to gain support for her inconceivable ambitions, which she must have realized would raise a public outcry. She accordingly joined the interests of the Duc de Vendôme to her own, in order to secure for her higher rank the support of Mme de Maintenon and M. du Maine.[1] Once certain of their approval, she extracted from the King of Spain an order to the grandees, and consequently to the whole of Spain, to address her in future as 'Your Highness', and the Duc de Vendôme also, to whom letters patent were sent, giving him all the ranks, honours, and privileges once enjoyed by the two Don Johns. This innovation produced such an appalling scandal, and caused so much horror and dismay, that some explanation is needed.

You must know that the rank of a Grandee of Spain is equal to that of all heads of States who are not kings; that it yields to no one in that respect, and that although the Dukes of Savoy were given, in Spain, very slight precedence on very rare occasions, such as the marriage of the famous Charles Emmanuel with the Infanta, it was more a matter of degree than of rank. No need to mention what happened during the visit of Charles I of England when he was Prince of Wales, because the heir presumptive of the throne of Great Britain is above all parity. You know also that, since the reunion of the various Spanish possessions by the marriage of Ferdinand and Isabella, only two younger sons of Spain have grown to manhood—Ferdinand, brother of Charles V (who was also Charles I of Spain), King and Emperor, who founded the imperial branch; and Ferdinand, son of Philip III, born in 1609, who without taking Holy Orders became Archbishop of Toledo, and Governor of the Low Countries, where he died in 1641. Thus there were no descendants and no princes of the Spanish royal house. There were, however, two legitimized bastards, both named Don John of Austria. Both distinguished themselves, especially the first, a son of Charles V.[2] He is famous for winning the Battle of Lepanto, and nearly always acted as commander-in-chief of the Spanish forces on land and sea. He died unmarried in 1578, at the age of thirty-three. The second Don John, son of Philip IV by an actress,[3] and born in 1629, died unmarried, aged fifty, in 1679. He was Grand Prior of Castile, an honour that carries with it grandeeship, an

---

[1] Vendôme being the grandson of Henri IV's bastard, any royal honours granted to him set a precedent for the Duc du Maine.

[2] Born at Ratisbon, 1545, died 1578, son of the Emperor Charles V (Charles I of Spain) and Barbara Blomberg, a native of Ratisbon.

[3] Maria Calderón.

income of a hundred thousand écus, and the rank of general in the Spanish armies.

You will recollect that when I spoke of the Grandees of Spain,[1] I said that the bastards of unmarried persons inherited in almost the same way as legitimate children, so long as none such existed from a subsequent marriage, and even succeeded to the title of Grandee of Spain, always provided that there were no family impediments such as legitimate uncles, aunts, or first cousins. Indeed, in Spain, bastards of this category differ very little from legitimate sons. Bastards of married men and unmarried women suffer more formalities and restrictions; but they also inherit, and succeed to grandeeships. Both Don Johns were bastards of this second category; and thus their right to inherit the throne brought them promotion to be Highnesses and of superior rank. It was on that precedent that Mme des Ursins aspired to elevate the Duc de Vendôme, thus paying her court to the Duc du Maine by setting a precedent for him in France. By such a move she hoped to please the King and Mme de Maintenon where they were most susceptible to flattery, and, under the wing of M. de Vendôme's 'Highness', gain acceptance for her own, after which she would have no compunction in preventing his further rise, on the pretext of not pushing public resentment too far. The anger in Spain was extreme; Don John was forgotten; no one remembered seeing him, or remembered his 'Highness'; M. de Vendôme was not the bastard of their late king; he had no right to the throne of Spain; no parity with Don John; yet he and Mme des Ursins were apparently to be treated exactly as though they were royal princes on a level with the Prince of the Asturias. So intolerable did this appear that many people abandoned the court and the king's service rather than address them as highnesses. In France, the indignation was equally great, and Mme de Maintenon and M. du Maine, although secretly in raptures, were obliged to appear unmoved. Even the King kept very quiet about it. They well knew how to prime him with useful reflections on the benefits to be gained.

The King went to Marly on Wednesday, 6 April, and, notwithstanding that the Dauphin and Dauphine were as yet unburied, he resumed the usual parlour-games in Mme de Maintenon's room on the Friday, and desired that the drawing-room should be as usual, with M. and Mme la Duchesse de Berry having tables for *lansquenet,* and other card tables set up for the rest of the Court. It was not long before he was once again dining twice a week with Mme de Maintenon and listening to concerts with her and the same small circle of ladies.

The King of England contracted smallpox at Saint-Germain. He was made to take the Last Sacraments. No one knows why he followed Madame la Dauphine's example in refusing a Jesuit confessor. He sent instead for the curé of the parish and confessed to him. His mother the queen shut herself in with him

---

[1] A very long digression which has not been included in this shortened version of the Memoirs.

and took every care to protect the princess[1] against foul airs. It was all in vain. She took the smallpox none the less, and died on the seventh day, Monday, 18 April. It was a great grief for the queen, who had the sad prospect of being separated from her son by the terms of the peace treaty, and of uncertainty regarding his future. The body of the English princess was borne without ceremony to the convent of the Daughters of Sainte Marie de Chaillot, where her mother had made several retreats. On account of the smallpox, the queen received no visits of condolence.

Mme de Villacerf, widow of that Villacerf who had charge of the royal buildings and was always high in favour with the King, died at a great age from being bled after a slight attack of fever. They severed one of her arteries by mistake.

Mme Bouchu, widow of the counsellor of State and mother of the Comtesse de Tessé, was more fortunate. She for a long time concealed a cancer, having told her secret to only one waiting-woman. With equal secrecy she put her affairs in order, dined out, had her breast removed next morning, and did not inform her family or anyone else until several hours later. She made a perfect recovery. After displaying so much wisdom and courage, she should have had more sense than to marry, many years later, the Duc de Châtillon, a legless cripple, for the joy of being a duchess and for his vast riches, and then long afterwards to die of pneumonia, brought on by persistence in flaunting her *tabouret* at Versailles in bitter cold weather.

Père Tellier considered that Père de La Rue needed some mark of esteem after what had happened to him at the death of Madame la Dauphine. The King accordingly appointed him M. le Duc de Berry's confessor, announcing at the same time that he was reserving for the little Dauphin Père Martineau, who had been the confessor of him for whom all Europe mourned.

Let us now return to Marly, where the diversions had started afresh, even before France was buried at Saint-Denis. You already know how much my friends were disquieted by the total nonconformity of my conduct towards M. le Duc d'Orléans. It became more marked as the days passed. I could not bring myself to take their advice, which I at first mistook for worldly weakness. At last the concordance of their opinions, although for the most part they could not act in concert, made me reconsider. I by no means underrated the threat of the King's anger and the indignation of Mme de Maintenon, which I believed to be what they described; but I could not persuade myself that my being more or less often with M. le Duc d'Orléans, whom everyone else shunned with most noticeable discourtesy, would make him appear less deserted or less guilty in the sight of the world. Yet that was where my crime lay, and the cause for the alarm of the

[1] Louisa Maria Theresa (1692-1712).

Dukes of Beauvilliers and Chevreuse, the Chancellor, and my other friends both male and female. I had received several warnings that the King was displeased at having watched me from his windows walking in the gardens with his nephew, and that Mme de Maintenon had expressed surprise that I, alone, should visit and talk with him. She and M. du Maine liked such remarks to come to my ears, hoping to disturb me and to make me change towards M. le Duc d'Orléans.

All this occurred between the two Marly excursions, and greatly increased in the course of the second, during which the burial at Saint-Denis took place to the accompaniment of hostility and insults from the crowds. Marly, moreover, is so arranged that everyone could see me each day in his company. Things at last went so far that, a few days after the interment and towards the end of the excursion, M. de Beauvilliers urged me to go to La Ferté, even before the Court returned to Versailles, and so put a safe distance between myself and the storm which he saw gathering over me. I waited a few days longer; but he called on Mme de Saint-Simon one morning when I was at the King's mass, and said that he knew for certain that Mme de Maintenon was about to explode, and that with no reason given I should be expelled unless I absented myself for a time of my own accord. He then promised to keep me informed of anything that might concern me, and to tell me when I could safely return. He also advised Mme de Saint-Simon to concoct some kind of code, but not with numerals, so that she might pass on to me his instructions during my absence, and entreated her to do it that same day, and to make me leave on the following, as though I had urgent business at La Ferté. He would, he said, speak himself to the King and obtain his consent to my leaving Marly four or five days before the end.

M. de Beauvilliers was still with her when I returned to our lodging. His increased alarm was less impressive than his stern voice and the decision and urgency with which he spoke, all quite out of his character, and such as he had not used with me for years past. Other people's secrets were impenetrably safe with him; but his tone and expression showed me what he did not say, namely that he knew of an order[1] which he was not at liberty to divulge. Mme de Saint-Simon and I no longer argued. I spent the remainder of that day discreetly spreading the news that urgent business summoned me to La Ferté, paying my court as usual, calling on M. and Mme la Duchesse d'Orléans, and making preparations to leave next morning. Never did I see anyone's face change so swiftly from extreme sternness to smiles as that of M. de Beauvilliers when he heard that I was about to leave. He never told me any more, but I feel convinced that the King and Mme de Maintenon had warned him that I should be expelled unless I followed his advice to leave of my own free will. My departure passed unnoticed; no one's suspicions

---

[1] In other words, a *lettre de cachet*.

were aroused. I was kept fully informed; but still learned nothing of what my situation then was or would be on my return. Similarly, I never knew what occasioned my return, the desirability of which was conveyed to me in the same way. I was absent for four or five weeks and went straight back to the Court, where I lived in M. le Duc d'Orléans's company exactly as I had been wont to do.

Tragic events are often accompanied by unexpectedly ludicrous incidents that divert the public when they least expect it. The Duc de Tresmes's household furnished one such, which caused a tremendous stir and much amusement. He had married his eldest son to Mlle Mascranny.[1] She was the only daughter of a maître des requêtes, immensely wealthy, an orphan and, when her marriage took place, under the guardianship of her uncle the Abbé Mascranny. She was no child at that time. With so much wealth she felt sure of happiness; for she was unaware that that was not the usual lot of Potier wives.[2] Mme de Revel, an impecunious and childless widow, sister of the Duc de Tresmes, went to live with him in order to chaperon his daughter-in-law, who was as unwilling to be governed as the aunt was unfitted to guide her. Discontent changed to ill-temper, then to complaining, then to quarrels and lawyers, and finally to discovering a means to gain her freedom. The young lady had more spirit than her in-laws. She managed to enlist her entire family in the quarrel, even distant relations like the Caumartins, who finally broke with the Gesvres. She then took refuge with her maternal grandmother, old Mme de Verthamon, who idolized her and had brought her up, and from that safe retreat she issued appeals for an annulment on the pretext of impotence. Documents piled up on either side; statements of the facts flew hither and thither. You may well imagine their content and the kind of jokes which they provoked. The case was brought before the bishops. The Marquis de Gesvres swore that he was not impotent, and since this required proof, surgeons were ordered to visit him, and midwives were appointed by the Church to examine her, which was done, and a report submitted. It is hard to describe adequately the scenes occasioned by this affair. Well known, even distinguished persons attended the trial purely for entertainment. They were there from early morning, and their descriptions were the talk of the town. The poor Gesvres nearly expired from shame and embarrassment, and bitterly repented that they had ever entered such a contest. The trial continued for some considerable time, always producing fresh absurdities, and ended only with the death of the Marquise de Gesvres. It was said, somewhat spitefully, that the blame was not all hers, and her husband appeared to confirm this view by not remarrying during the next thirty years.

---

[1] The bride was Marie Madeleine Emilie Mascranny. She was twenty-eight when they were married in 1709.
[2] The family name of the Duc de Tresmes was Potier de Gesvres.

The generals in command left for their armies, with their lieutenant-generals and the other officers serving under them. Villars was posted to Flanders, Harcourt and Bezons to the Rhine, Berwick to Dauphiné and the Alps; and Fiennes, a lieutenant-general, replaced the Duc de Noailles in Catalonia, for no one wished to give that nobleman further employment.

Two men of vast bulk, excellent wit, moderate learning, worth and honour, both of them much in Society, and both more than ordinarily debauched, died at this time, leaving a void in good company. Cominges was one; La Fare the other. Cominges was the great-nephew and son respectively of Guitaut and Cominges, both of them governors of Saumur and captains of the Queen-mother's Guard, and both made Chevaliers of the Order in 1661; they were government spies and were employed on missions of the utmost delicacy.[1] Guitaut died suddenly at the Louvre, in 1663, aged eighty-two, unmarried. Cominges, his nephew and reversioner, the father of the Cominges I am dealing with here, was a man of some importance throughout his life. He finally became ambassador to Portugal and England, and died at the age of fifty-seven, in March 1670. He married the daughter of Amalby, counsellor of the Bordeaux parlement. His mother was even more commonplace, as were all but a very few of the Cominges wives. They bore the full name and arms of the Cominges, and claimed to be descended from the Counts of that name, but never at any time were they able to prove relationship or connection, and no one knows what they were before 1440. The Cominges of whom we are speaking never served except as a volunteer, and then always as aide-de-camp to the King who, despite Cominges's morals[2] and his idleness, never saw him without greeting him, treating him always with friendliness and esteem, on account of his connection with the Queen-mother. During the King's campaigns, the courtiers jokingly called the biggest bombs and mortars 'Cominges', and the name has stuck to them ever since; Cominges, himself, thought the jest misplaced and never grew accustomed to it. He was indeed a very bulky man; but handsome.

La Fare[3] was the other grossly fat man. He was captain of M. le Duc d'Orléans's Guard; had held the same post under Monsieur, and with good reason felt proud of his career. What would he have said had he seen his children today, one of them with the Fleece and the Order, and the other a most unworthy Bishop of Laon? He had too much good taste not to have been ashamed. He was a man whom every one liked, save only Louvois, whose discourtesy forced him out of the

---

[1] Guitaut and Cominges: François de Cominges, Comte de Guitaut (d. 1663), and his nephew Gaston Jean Baptiste (1613-1670). Some of the delicate missions were the arrests of princes and nobles at the time of the Fronde.

[2] It appears that he was scandalously connected with the Marquis d'Effiat.

[3] Charles Auguste, Marquis de La Fare. Mme de Maintenon wrote to the Princesse des Ursins: 'La Fare is now out of his death-agony, and is displaying as much piety as he was previously free-thinking. He says that he always believed, but out of snobbishness had pretended not to' (16 November, 1711). A volume of his poems was published in 1755.

service. La Fare used to say that he owed his weak digestion entirely to Louvois; but, all said and done, he was a dreadful glutton, and so stuffed himself with cod after a serious illness that he died of it. He turned out pretty verses, but never, either in prose or verse, did he write against anyone. In his latter years he was apt to fall asleep wherever he happened to be; but what was most surprising was that he could wake up and continue the conversation exactly where he had left it.

On 6 June news came from Spain that the queen was delivered of a prince, whom they named Don Philip, and that on 22 May the Emperor had been crowned King of Hungary, at Pressburg, with great pomp and splendour.

Vendôme triumphed in Spain, not over the enemies of that kingdom, but over the Spaniards themselves, and on account of our tragedies. Considering his age and the ages of those whom we mourned, he had expected to be exiled for life. Their deaths gave him a fair hope of returning to our Court and of once again becoming a personage of importance. His 'Highness' was the gratifying first fruit of his sudden deliverance. The equalizing of his rank with that of the two Don Johns had given him cause for rejoicing in the tears of France where, raised to that unparalleled height, he envisaged playing for all it was worth the part of a prince of the blood royal, leaving the Spaniards in a state of hopeless despair. His idleness, lewdness, and love of debauchery had prolonged his stay on the frontier, where he found it easier to satisfy his lusts than at Madrid; for there, although he made few efforts to restrain himself, he could not avoid some formality, nor the duty of appearing occasionally at the court.

He returned to the capital to profit by the self-interested generosity of the Princesse des Ursins; but, as I previously remarked, he had to be content with their mutual 'Highness', and received nothing more. She made all haste in dispatching their necessary business concerning the army, and sent him straight back to the frontier. He on his part, overloaded with honours which he would never have dared to claim for himself; embarrassed by the rancour of the grandees and nobles whom his promotion had degraded, and tempted by idleness and unmentionable pleasures, was very glad to leave. There was nothing for him to do; the Austrians, surprised and weakened by the departure of the English,[1] were unlikely to begin an offensive. Vendôme, enjoying his astounding change of fortune, had the pleasant prospect of contemplating it at leisure, with the excuse that his army was not yet ready for action. For greater independence, he parted company with his staff; and with two or three intimates, and the valets who were his boon companions, established himself at Viñaroz, a remote, almost deserted

---

[1] After the defeat of Philip V the British troops had been repatriated. Their purpose had been to prevent the union of France and Spain. They could not reasonably have been expected to fight for the union of Spain with Austria.

little village, by the seaside, in the kingdom of Valencia, where he could gorge on fish to his heart's content. That he did with immense enjoyment for more than a month. He then fell ill. They easily believed that dieting would restore him, but the disorder, after being quiescent for a longish period, suddenly increased with such alarming symptoms that those few who were with him suspected poison and sent in all directions to get help. The illness, however, refused to wait for that. He grew violently worse, with most dreadful effects. When his will was placed before him he could neither sign it, nor word a letter to the King pleading for his brother's[1] return to the Court. His friends then abandoned him with all speed, leaving him to the mercies of two or three of the lowest servants, whilst the remainder before they departed stole all that they could lay hands on. He spent his last days without benefit of clergy—not that there was ever any question of a priest for him—and without assistance, save for one lone barber-surgeon. When his few remaining valets saw that he was *in extremis* they seized on what possessions he still retained and, for want of more valuable loot, pulled the blanket and mattress away from under him. He cried out most piteously, entreating them not to leave him to die naked on the straw; but I do not know that he obtained even that grace.

So died on Wednesday, 10 June that most vainglorious and (to say no more, having necessarily already said so much) most fortunate of men. He was fifty-eight years old. Yet blind, unlimited favour could do no more than make him a hero of intrigue, a commander who was a very bad general, a subject who proved most treacherous, and a man whose vices in every kind were a disgrace to humanity. His death brought renewed life and joy throughout the whole of Spain. Aguilar,[2] the Duc de Noailles's friend, had returned from exile to serve under him, and was strongly suspected of having poisoned him; but since no inquiry was thought necessary, he took no pains to defend himself. The Princesse des Ursins, who for her own personal advantage had used him in life, profited also by his death. She felt well rid of a new Don John at the head of the armies of Spain, no longer a refugee in exile and of necessity her willing tool, but delivered from those who had condemned him, swiftly recovering his old influence in France, whence he would soon receive complete protection. Thus she was not at all disturbed by the undisguised rejoicing and frank criticisms of the court, Madrid, the army, and even of the king and queen, who made no pretence of grief. None the less, in order to protect herself and pay her court cheaply to M. du Maine, she arranged for the body of this most hideous monster to be taken to the Escorial, and thus topped the heap of his undeserved honours. He did not die in battle; moreover,

[1] Philippe de Vendôme (1655-1727), Grand Prieur de France 1687-1719, exiled for his depravity.
[2] Iñigo-de-La-Croix Manrique de Lara, Count of Aguilar (1673-1735). Vendôme's lick-spittling secretary Alberoni was also a suspect. It was he who engineered the second marriage of Philip V. Alberoni was made a cardinal in 1717, and will henceforth figure largely in the Memoirs.

no private persons are buried at the Escorial, whereas in France several lie at
Saint-Denis. This last honour was therefore in recognition of his birthright, and
M. du Maine was so jubilant that he could scarcely contain himself.

Pending the time when I shall describe my own visit to the Escorial (if strength
is given me to continue these memoirs until the death of M. le Duc d'Orléans), I
must explain that famous place of burial.

In the Pantheon are laid only the bodies of the kings, and of the queens who
had issue. In another chamber, arranged like a library, close by but not on the
same level, are stowed the queens without issue and the legitimate daughters and
younger legitimate sons of the king. A third chamber, as it were the ante-room of
the above, is correctly named the decay-chamber, although the second chamber
is improperly sometimes called that. Nothing is to be seen there beyond the four
white walls, and a long, bare table in the centre. The walls are enormously thick.
Niches are carved in them, and the corpses are placed each in a niche, which is
subsequently walled up so that nothing remains visible. When it is thought that
sufficient time has elapsed for all to be decayed and free from odour, the wall is
re-opened and the corpse removed. It is then laid in a coffin through the foot
of which something may be seen. The coffin is covered with rich material and
carried into the burial-chamber adjacent. The body of the Duc de Vendôme was
still walled-up when I visited the Escorial some nine years later. They showed me
the place where he was stowed, and it was bare, like the rest of the four walls,
without a mark of any kind. I gently asked the monks assigned to me as guides
how soon he would be moved to the neighbouring chamber. They avoided a
direct answer, looked indignant, and did not scruple to let it be understood that
since so much trouble had been taken to wall him up, he might as well remain
there for ever.

I do not know what M. du Maine did with the unsigned will, for which he
took the responsibility; but he could not persuade the King to make any show
of grief for M. de Vendôme, nor to forgive the Grand Prieur, who remained in
exile at Lyons until after the King's death. But King Louis did none the less wear
black for a few days. Mme de Vendôme received all the great riches and estates
settled on her by her marriage-contract; after her death Mme du Maine inherited
both Anet and Dreux; the rest of his lands went to other heirs of the Duchesse
de Vendôme. The King, however, immediately reclaimed the estate of Vendôme,
and all other crown property. Vendôme's creditors were gradually repaid, and
his valets served their own interests as well as possible. The Grand Prieur
claimed nothing for himself and received nothing—he being unable to inherit

because of his vows as a Knight of Malta. It is not yet time to recount what happened to Alberoni.

At this point a trifling incident must be recorded because it shows how tightly the King kept his ministers in check, believing that he did best by keeping them down. On 21 June, the Duc d'Uzès arrived at Marly with letters from the King of Spain. Torcy took him to the King, who after they had left the study went to Mme de Maintenon's room and worked there with Voysin and Desmaretz, both together. It was a rare event for him to be with two ministers at the same time. While they were working, an anxiously awaited courier arrived from England. Torcy took the dispatches to the King. Voysin and Desmaretz left and waited with the courtiers until Torcy also left. Yet all three were ministers. Torcy undoubtedly made a detailed report of those particular dispatches on the following morning, in their presence; it appears that he read them aloud from beginning to end because they were so extremely important. Voysin and Desmaretz then gave their counsel, as did the Duc de Beauvilliers, the Chancellor, and Torcy, himself. It may well be that when they went to take leave of the King after Torcy's departure, he himself had informed them of their contents; but he did not detain them, and the courtiers waiting in the drawing-room witnessed that lack of formality.

On 17 July a truce was announced in Flanders between France and England, by the commanders of both nations. A month earlier Prince Eugene had sent a raiding party of two thousand cavalry into Champagne, and had nearly captured the Archbishop of Rheims, on his pastoral visits. They burned a suburb of Vervins, passed close by Sainte-Menehould, caused disturbances in Champagne and around Metz, crossed the Meuse at Saint-Mihiel, and the Moselle near Pont-à-Mousson, took a number of hostages, and had withdrawn to Trarbach before either Saint-Frémond or Coigny, who were sent to intercept them, could join battle.

[*On 29 January, 1712, the plenipotentiaries of the Tory Government of England began peace negotiations with the French at Utrecht, without keeping their allies fully informed of the conditions. When the French terms were published, the Dutch and Austrians accused the English of deserting them by accepting a French demand that Philip V should remain King of Spain and the Indies. None the less, a peace seemed imminent. In February, however, there suddenly occurred the sequence of deaths in the French royal family, which left only a sickly two-year-old child, not expected to live, as security against the union of France and Spain under Philip V, who was next in the natural order of succession to the throne of France. Fear of this very event had been the chief cause of the War of the Spanish Succession. The English proposed that Philip should*]

renounce the throne of France then and there, but the French declared that this would be illegal.
Louis XIV then agreed (28 May) to a proposal that, on succeeding to the French throne, Philip
V should renounce the throne of Spain. This Philip refused to do; and the Allies demanded a
renewal of the war.[1] *The Tory government had replaced Marlborough (a Whig) by the Duke*
of Ormonde, who was ordered to take the British forces to join the allied armies assembling in
Flanders. He reached The Hague on 9 April, where with many civil excuses the Dutch and
Austrians explained that they had given Prince Eugene the supreme command. On 21 June a
truce was declared between France and England, and in mid-July 12,000 British troops were
withdrawn from Flanders.]

On the night of 20-21 June, Prince Eugene cut the trench in front of Le
Quesnoy, despite the armistice which preceded our truce with the English. Jarnac
brought the surrender to the King at Marly on 8 July. La Badie,[2] who was in
command and had been taken prisoner with the entire garrison, was fiercely
attacked by Villars and the army in general for his poor defence. Prince Eugene
granted him permission to return and justify his actions at the Court, but no
sooner did he arrive in Paris than he was thrown into the Bastille. Broglio, on
the other hand, defeated eighteen hundred enemy horse, and killed or captured
nearly all of them. Such trifles heartened us.

The King left Marly on 13 July after the council of State, spent an hour or two
at Versailles, slept at Petit-Bourg, and went to Fontainebleau on the following day.

Prince Eugene invested Landrecies. The King, much incensed that he should
continue to take risks although deserted by the English,[3] wished to profit by their
absence and thought very ill of Villars for allowing the fortresses on the last frontier to be besieged and taken without a fight to defend them. Villars repeatedly
received orders to that effect. He replied by boasting; he even boasted publicly;
but did no more than take soundings and still retreated, missing more than one
occasion for coming to grips with Prince Eugene. Some, indeed, were so obvious and appeared so advantageous that the soldiers openly grumbled. He said
that he was seeking some means of relieving Landrecies;[4] and with the utmost
impatience the King every day awaited couriers from Flanders. But Montesquiou

---

[1] Louis XIV is supposed to have said, 'If the war is to continue, I would rather fight my enemies than my
grandchildren.'

[2] Charles d'Espalungue de La Badie, governor of Lille.

[3] The British troops when they made their retreat were watched in icy silence by their allies. The fortresses of Tournai
and Mons which they had helped to capture shut the gates in their faces, although it is said that food was handed to them
over the walls. They were made to feel most bitterly humiliated. Stern discipline held them until the end of the march, but
then there were violent scenes when the men broke their muskets and cursed Queen Anne.

[4] Although Villars proceeded to win the Battle of Denain—the only battle which France had won in the Low Countries
since the wars of William III—Saint-Simon could not bring himself to give him the credit. Voltaire said that the Battle of
Denain was more essential to the safety of France than the Peace of Utrecht, and that Villars should have been called the
saviour of his country. Napoleon said Denain saved France; yet Saint-Simon still disparages Villars. Perhaps he could not
bear such a bounder to have glory when the noblesse de l'épée like the Duc de Noailles were failures.

saw an excellent opportunity for a battle. He was well known to the King because he had for a long time been adjutant of the Guards regiment, then inspector, and finally general-in-charge of infantry, but most of all because of his intimate attachments to the principal indoor valets. He secretly sent a courier to the King with his plan, noting that Villars was sure not to approve, and urging the need to seize the chance when it came. A quick answer was returned. He was ordered to put his plan into effect even despite Villars, but to use sufficient tact in dealing with him.[1] Eugene's utter contempt for Villars led him to commit a fatal error by dangerously increasing the distance that separated him from Marchienne, and also from Denain,[2] a fortified camp in which he left eighteen battalions and some cavalry and where his principal magazines were established.[3] Acting on that information, Montesquiou persuaded Villars to march. During the march, he advanced with a vanguard, four lieutenant-generals and four brigadier-generals, and sent Broglio, later a Marshal of France, forward with the reserve to capture five hundred bread-wagons on their way to the enemy. This Broglio did with conspicuous success, well before the attack on Denain.

Montesquiou and his vanguard arrived at top speed before Denain, quickly made his dispositions, and immediately attacked the trenches. Villars marched on at a slow pace with the main body. His anger with Montesquiou for having advanced without orders increased beyond measure when he heard the cannon-fire. He sent order after order forbidding him to attack, commanding him to wait, yet not at all speeding his own progress because he was determined not to fight. Montesquiou returned his aides-de-camp, saying that the battle had already begun and that they must face the consequences, and he pressed his attacks so hard that he took the trenches, entered Denain, seized possession of it and of all the stores and artillery, and killed great numbers, for very many were drowned in trying to escape,[4] including Count de Dohna,[5] who was in command and in an excellent position to defend himself had Prince Eugene decided to attack us there. That prince arriving with his army on the farther side of the river, watched us dispatch our business, gathered up the fugitives, and halted because he did not think himself strong enough to relieve a captured Denain. In the meanwhile,

---

[1] No doubt Eugene also heard those words.

[2] The plan at the end of 1711 had been to carry the war into the heart of France. Prince Eugene may have been so much exasperated by the English defection that he was led to take unwarranted risks in order to stick to the original plan.

[3] At Marchienne were 'more than a hundred bilanders [huge barges], a hundred pieces of cannon, three hundred wagons with their harnesses, the hospital of the army, and, in the storehouses and bilanders, a prodigious quantity of bombs, grenades, bullets, musket-balls, powder, corn, meal, hams, bacon, cheese, butter, beer, wine, brandy, merchandise, ladders, hatchets, bills, planks, matches, flints—in a word, all sorts of provisions necessary for two sieges—and there were likewise a good number of horses'.

[4] The losses were so great because there was only one pontoon bridge by which to withdraw from Denain, and it was very soon broken under the weight of the wagons. The river was very deep and thus enormous numbers were drowned when they were driven back into it by the French.

[5] Jean Frédéric, Count de Dohna (1664-1712). One of Marlborough's veterans, defeated by Berwick at the Battle of Almanza, in 1707. See Vol. 1, p. 332.

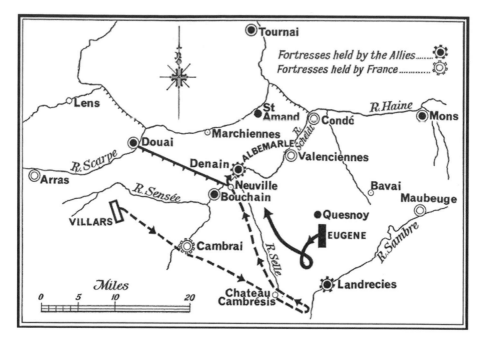

The Battle of Denain

[*Villars's sudden change of direction on the night of 22 July foxed Eugene who believed that he intended to relieve Landrecies. Eugene was left on the other side of the river, unable to catch up with the French in time, and unable to cross over because there was only one bridge.*]

Tingry,[1] later Maréchal de Montmorency, having been warned by Montesquiou, moved from Valenciennes, and by successfully defending a bridge on Prince Eugene's shortest road to attack Montesquiou, forced him to make a long detour on the eastern side of the Scheldt, so that he arrived on the scene too late.

When Villars appeared with the remainder of the army, all was over. He crammed on his hat[2] and made warlike speeches to the dead and the enemy across the river, and sent Nangis, who was one of the four brigadier-generals leading the attack, to the King. Voysin received him and took him to King Louis on Tuesday, 26 July, at eight o'clock in the morning. He was given lavish praise and twelve thousand livres for his trouble. The enemy's losses were very great, and those of the Maréchal de Montesquiou very small. The only son of the Maréchal de Tourville was killed at the head of his regiment, which was a thousand pities, and left his sister an heiress. She has since married M. de Brassac, and

---

[1] The Prince de Tingry, Christian Louis de Montmorency, Chevalier de Luxembourg. He was the fourth son of the Maréchal de Luxembourg, made a Marshal of France in 1734; died 1746, aged seventy-one.

[2] 'Gentlemen, settle your hats! Charge!' was a French cavalry command of the seventeenth and eighteenth centuries.

became one of Mme la Duchesse de Berry's ladies, when that princess was allowed to have them.

Villars, completely bewildered by a battle fought and won despite him, wished to stay where he was; but Montesquiou, who by that time was sure of the King, did not heed him, and on the very evening of the battle, which was on Sunday, 24 July, detached Broglio with twelve battalions to attack Marchienne, where the remaining and larger part of the enemy's magazines were established. He then followed in person, with eighteen other battalions and some cavalry, and Villars dared not absolutely forbid him, after all that had happened. He took Saint-Amand on the way, where there were eight hundred men, and the Abbey of Hasnon, with another two hundred. Villars,[1] assistant surgeon-general of the army, arrived at Fontainebleau on the last day of July with quantities of flags, and it was learned through him that Overkerque,[2] a general greatly esteemed by the Dutch, had been killed at Denain. On Monday, 1 August, Artagnan arrived at Fontainebleau, an hour before noon, sent by his uncle Montesquiou to inform the King that he had taken Marchienne and captured all the troops there. In the fortress there were six battalions, a detachment of five hundred men of the garrison of Douai, and an entire regiment of Waldeck cavalry (on their way to join Prince Eugene's army, but prevented from leaving when the fortress was invested), sixty pieces of cannon, besides magazines full of war materials and provisions, five hundred bilanders lying loaded on the river, six of them containing two hundred thousand kegs of powder—and all this captured with hardly a man lost. Montesquiou was given all the credit by the Court and the army for these two successful operations which, as it were, broke the spell that for so long had kept us most wretchedly bound. They truly appeared like miracles of Providence, and marked the end of all our disasters.

Montesquiou had the wisdom to be prudent and modest, to let Villars brag until people made fun of him, to pay heed to Mme de Maintenon's too obvious shielding, and to remain content with the glory which no one denied him. At Fontainebleau there was such overwhelming joy that the King was gratified, and for the first time in his life thanked his courtiers. Prince Eugene, lacking food and supplies of all other kinds, raised the siege of Landrecies immediately afterwards; vast numbers deserted him.

The Duke of Württemberg, commander of the Emperor's Rhine army, had received orders to attack our lines at Wissembourg; he advanced and battered them with cannon-fire for two days on end without doing any damage, suffered a

---

[1] No relation to the Maréchal. Charles de Villars-Chandieu, a Swiss by birth.
[2] Count Cornelius van Nassau, the third son of Count Hendrik who died in 1708. He was drowned in the Scheldt.

fairly large number of casualties, and retired; after which we burned their batteries. That was the only exploit on either side during the campaign in Germany.

M. de Soubise[1] did not long enjoy seeing his son clothed in the Roman carmine. He died in Paris on 24 August, aged somewhat over eighty, a prince with an income of more than four hundred thousand livres, as he occasionally divulged to his closest friends, in an ecstasy of delight at his prodigious wealth. It was the fruit of discretion such as few would care to imitate, of contempt for conventions to which long tradition has given increasing strength, of heeding the lesson learned from the example of M. de Montespan, of choosing to swallow a humiliating, only half-concealed affront in return for the colossal fortune gained by the beauty of his second wife,[2] his secret understanding with her, the marvellous skill with which she managed to retain her ascendancy long after the time for winning it had passed, and the way in which both of them attuned their conduct to that one end. I have already said so much in other parts of these memoirs of the immense estates, residences, and honours which they thus acquired, that little more is needed to depict M. de Soubise, except to say that he was the handsomest of life-guardsmen, and one of the best-proportioned men of his day in face and figure, even in extreme old age, and one who cared not a rap that he had laid himself open to the deadliest insult one Spaniard can use to another, and that even among their rabble is never forgiven.

I well remember how, when I was in Madrid, the Marquis de Saint-Simon,[3] who was learning Spanish, lost his temper with one of my coachmen and called him....,[4] meaning something quite different. Instantly, the man pulled up, got down from his box, threw his whip in the face of the young man in the coach and left us, refusing to drive us any farther. It took five or six days to convince him that there had been a mistake, due to ignorance of his language and of the meaning of the word; only then did we manage to appease him. I do believe, however, that M. de Soubise, who so well merited that name, would never have allowed anyone to call him so to his face, for he was exceedingly brave and a good lieutenant-general.

He was a son of the second Duc de Montbazon by his second wife the lovely Duchesse de Montbazon, who was an Avaugour, of the bastards of Brittany, also

---

[1] François de Rohan-Montbazon, Prince de Soubise (1631-1712), son of Hercule de Rohan, Duc de Montbazon and Marie d'Avaugour-Bretagne, his second wife, and husband of that Mme de Soubise who had such a brilliant and reward-ing career as the King's mistress. Their son was made a cardinal in 1712. See Vol. 1, p. 412.

[2] Mme de Soubise, who died in 1709, was Anne de Rohan-Chabot, second wife of François de Rohan-Montbazon, who was made Prince de Soubise on his marriage with her. Saint-Simon says of her, 'Happy beauty was the best dowry of all at the Court of Louis XIV.'

[3] Henri, Marquis de Saint-Simon (1703-1739).

[4] A blank is left in the manuscript, although the word is plain enough from what follows. Saint-Simon's discretion here regarding a word no more indecent than many which he uses elsewhere is on a par with his extreme hesitation in calling spades by their name in the preceding sentences.

known by the names Goëllo and Vertus,[1] and her mother was a Fouquet de La Varenne, daughter of that famous La Varenne who, starting from scullion, became cook, then dresser to Henri IV, and his Mercury in amorous adventures, later meddling in affairs of State so as to become a personage of importance, procuring the reinstatement of the Jesuits in France and sharing La Flèche[2] with them. The Jesuits thus owed the government of this rich and splendid college entirely to La Varenne's patronage. He later grew immensely wealthy and retired to La Flèche after the death of Henri IV. There he was stricken with madness when a magpie flew out of a tree exclaiming repeatedly, 'Pander! Pander!' (*maquereau*), for no one could persuade him that it was merely a tame magpie, escaped from a village where it had learned to talk. He mistook it for a miracle on the lines of Balaam's ass, designed to rebuke him for his life and the sins by which he had made his fortune. He left the shooting-party and took to his bed; a fever then developed, and he was dead in two or three days. It was from such shameful and almost immediate ancestry that Mme de Soubise rose by skill and influence even as I have recounted, posing not as a Fouquet de La Varenne, but as a La Varenne of the very good Anjou family of that name, which has been extinct for more than a century. M. de Soubise was the brother of the second wife of the Duc de Luynes who married his maternal aunt, by whom he had the Comte d'Albert, Mme de Verua, and a number of other children. He was the paternal uncle of the Duc de Montbazon who died a confined lunatic in 1699, and of the Chevalier de Rohan who was decapitated before the Bastille, in Paris, on 27 November, 1674.[3] After the death of M. de Soubise they dared not attempt what he had successfully achieved at the death of his wife, namely, to have her taken straight to Notre Dame de la Merci on the pretext that the entrance of that church was opposite his own front door.[4] His body, like that of any ordinary person, was taken first to the parish church, and thence to the Merci, where they wished to have him buried. Cardinal de Noailles had issued an order that effectually prevented any repetition of that kind of surprise attack.

At that same time I lost the Marquis de Saint-Simon,[5] the oldest member of my family. His father and brother had quietly run through an income of more than forty thousand livres without ever leaving their estates. His younger son for want of anything better, had joined the Guards regiment, in which he had risen by seniority to be captain and then brigadier-general, and was much liked and

---

[1] A small district of Brittany.
[2] The military school of La Flèche for the sons of soldiers.
[3] Louis de Rohan, born c. 1636. He was accused of conspiring to invade Holland.
[4] See Vol. 1, p. 413.
[5] Eustache Titus, Marquis de Saint-Simon (1654-1712). His father and brother were Claude de Rouvroy-Saint-Simon, Comte de Vaux-sur-Meulan (1626-1709), and Nicolas, so-called Comte de Saint-Simon (1651-1710).

esteemed. The old man had dined with me at Fontainebleau only four or five days before his death. I took this opportunity to present my son, still a boy in the King's estimation, for he had not yet joined the service. The King at once gave him a lieutenancy in the Guards.

Reffuge[1] died at this time also. He was a very decent, worthy man, a man of parts, and of great courage, eminently capable in war. A retired lieutenant-general, he was governor of Charlemont, and had commanded Metz. He knew more of all kinds of genealogies in every country than any other man in Europe, from the histories of crowned heads down to those of ordinary citizens, and possessed such a memory that he never made mistakes regarding names, rank, branches, dates, or alliances, nor on the subsequent life story of each individual. He was extremely reticent on such matters; but perfectly sincere when he did speak of them. His memory, one might say, was truly alarming. For example, he received at Metz a courier from one of the German princes of the Rhine, and nearly bowled him over by saying as he returned his dispatches, 'I have the honour of knowing your master', and immediately recited in the greatest detail his entire genealogy. He was highly respectable, and sober, but vastly absent-minded. His valets sometimes took advantage of that fact to bring him at one time seven or eight glasses of wine, none of which he had ordered, and he would swallow all of them without thinking. Thus he was frequently drunk, and when he came to his senses could never imagine how it had happened. He was old, and left a daughter[2] married to the only son of the Comte du Luc, and an only son,[3] unmarried, as virtuous and as brave as his father, and now serving as a general-officer with an excellent reputation; but although equally modest, he is not so good a genealogist.

The Abbé Servien[4] was expelled from Paris, and sent I forget where. He was the brother of Sablé and of the late Duchesse de Sully, all three of them children of the Surintendant des finances.[5] Nothing could exceed the obscurity and the dissipation of the lives of those two brothers; both were excellent company, and both were immensely witty. One night the Abbé was at the Opera when they sang during the prologue an immoderately fulsome refrain in praise of the King, and repeated it several times. The Abbé, growing bored with so much servility, very comically reversed the sense of the song and sang back his own version most lustily, looking vastly absurd, which made the audience laugh and applaud him and silenced the actors. His exile was not for long; he feigned illness, and since the intention had been merely to show scorn of him, he was soon permitted to

---

[1] Pompone, Marquis de Reffuge.
[2] His daughter Marie Charlotte (1688-1756) had married the Marquis du Luc.
[3] Henri Pompone, Marquis de Reffuge (1686-1766).
[4] Augustin, Abbé de Servien (d. 1716).
[5] Abel Servien, Surintendant des finances in 1654, member of the French Academy: he died in 1659.

return. He never appeared at Court, and rarely in Paris among good company. His tastes did not lie in those directions, although his wit was urbane—a subtle, original fount of humour that never appeared contrived. He died as he had lived, in a sorry fashion, in the rooms of a ballet dancer, where he was caught unawares. None the less, he read his breviary punctually, as did Cardinal de Bouillon.

At this time a superfluity of wolves was causing much trouble in the province of Orléans. The King's wolfhounds were sent there, and the peasants were authorized to take arms and hold a number of wolf-drives.

Peace negotiations between France and England were almost at a standstill, while England essayed to gain acceptance by her allies of the proposed terms. As I have already said, I shall omit this great event because it is described by a master hand in the documents,[1] from Torcy's journey to The Hague until the signing of the peace at Utrecht. I only add that our domestic and repeated tragedies[2] produced a difficulty that held up the treaty, which had already been drafted in London, and much delayed the signing of it. Queen Anne and her council were prevented by considerations of the King of Spain's right to ascend the throne of France, if the august and precious link[3] that alone excluded him should come to be broken. Neither England nor her allies could possibly consent to allow the two most powerful crowns in Europe to rest on the same head. Their difficulty was voiced. King Louis was in no condition to refuse his compliance, and it therefore became a matter of solving the problem in such a way that the event would never come to pass, and that all the powers might be secured permanently against its happening.[4]

From the very beginning, the question was discussed by the Dukes of Chevreuse, Beauvilliers and myself. The Duc d'Humières was later included in our conversations, and the Duc de Noailles, who had taken infinite pains to retain their good opinion since I had reconciled them, was admitted as a fifth. He prided himself on his wide reading, on his acquaintance with eminent historians, and on being himself no mean historian, and truly, it was hard not to be dazzled by his wit, smooth tongue, and superficial brilliance; but among all these five persons, the only one with any real knowledge was M. de Chevreuse. M. de Beauvilliers had never found time to give the matter any deep consideration; indeed, for years past he had had no time even to read, on account of his many official functions. I am not so bold, nor so foolish as to speak of my own qualifications; I would

---

[1] *Les Pièces.* These documents are the copies which Saint-Simon made of Torcy's memoranda on the negotiations at Gertruydemberg and Utrecht, now kept at the Dépôt des Affaires Etrangères.

[2] The deaths of the three Dauphins.

[3] The 'link' grew up to be Louis XV.

[4] The difficulty was finally resolved by Philip V signing an act of renunciation of the French throne. Saint-Simon was intensely busy at this time, preparing memoranda for the Ducs de Beauvilliers, Chevreuse, and Noailles on the exact forms desirable for such an act.

frankly prefer to let them be judged by my work on the documents.[1] Let me none the less say that we had no difficulty in agreeing to my general proposals, which were approved and seconded by the Duc de Chevreuse; but thereafter we were obliged to go into the details, and that work was ill-suited to M. de Chevreuse's leisure moments, for as we have already seen, he was a minister *incognito*.[2] Neither M. de Beauvilliers nor M d'Humières was capable of it, and I myself had not the strength. Thus when the Duc de Noailles offered to produce an exhaustive memorandum embracing the whole affair, giving reasons and proofs to put the renunciations on a permanent and legal basis such as the English could agree to, we accepted his offer. He promised the Dukes of Chevreuse and Beauvilliers in our presence to write and present it to us before the Court left for Fontainebleau. It was during that interval that the Duc de Charost was admitted to our councils.

From time to time I asked the Duc de Noailles for news of his labours, and the others also inquired of him. He always assured us that he was progressing and would keep his word. There still remained, however, the greatest difficulty of all, namely, how to bring the King to consent to the terms, and MM. de Chevreuse and de Beauvilliers, whose particular task that was to be, were greatly troubled.[3] None the less, after concluding that only they of all the ministers could work on the King with any hope of success, and that he himself had expressly desired them to handle the question, they believed that he might be persuaded that his authority was safe, and that having such dire need to gain peace and the consent of the English, he would eventually resign himself to the giving of legal stability to the renunciations.

In these circumstances I was continually under pressure from M. le Duc de Berry and M. le Duc d'Orléans.[4] The latter thought me thoroughly well versed in the forms needed to make the renunciations valid, and had so persuaded M. le Duc de Berry. He had been shunned and isolated since the affair of the poisonings, and had only myself to talk to, and M. le Duc de Berry, living in terror of the King's harshness and jealousy, dared not speak to anyone. Thus I was the only person with whom they either could or would discuss these matters. Both of them had the strongest reasons for not renouncing the crown of Spain in a manner that was legal and binding according to the laws of France, unless every precaution was taken at the same time to secure the crown of France by equally firm renunciations on the part of the King of Spain and his descendants.

[1] He probably means his *mémoire* on the renunciations.
[2] See Vol. I, p. 344.
[3] Saint-Simon remarks that 'the English, accustomed to their Parliament, believed that ours had similar authority, and wished to support the renunciations by the strongest legal power in France (the Parlement), upheld by all the King's authority. Louis XIV, on the other hand, wrote in his *Mémoires*: 'It is perfectly certain that the obligation to accept the rulings of subjects is the final calamity for men of our rank.'
[4] The Dukes of Berry and Orléans were vitally concerned, because if the little Dauphin (Louis XV) died, as appeared probable, they would come first and second in the line of succession after Philip V.

That was the matter on which they consulted me. I temporized as long as possible, but when the Duc de Noailles undertook to produce his memorandum I felt that I could put them off no longer, and I accordingly gave my opinion to M. le Duc d'Orléans, who was himself well informed concerning our history. M. le Duc de Berry I saw very rarely and never in private. Since he knew almost nothing it would have required many long conversations to brief him, and as I was anxious not to appear personally, M. le Duc d'Orléans agreed to tell him of my proposals.

The affair was at that stage just before we went to Fontainebleau. M. de Noailles had not yet produced his memorandum, but was excusing himself on account of the importance of the work and the great number of subjects to be dealt with and arranged in order. He assured us, however, that he would be ready to show us his manuscript as soon as the King arrived, or very soon after. The delays continued, until we became aware that he was keeping unknown persons hidden on the very top floor of his lodging in that part of the Galerie de Diane which gives on to the garden; that he was employing them in research; that he was continually remodelling his work, and that thus he would never finish it. We frankly said as much to him; and although profoundly embarrassed, he could not but admit that we were right.

M. de Beauvilliers, hard pressed by continual demands from the English, decided to wait no longer. He asked me to write the report. I defended myself against the suggestion as best I could, and indeed, I had brought very few books to Fontainebleau, and no one capable of assisting me in a work which I certainly had never expected. Useless to object even for the best of reasons! I was obliged to yield to M. de Beauvilliers's authority. I therefore set about the task in a place where I had no help and no leisure to write. I still had to appear at my usual times with the other courtiers, and to eat in company—at Fontainebleau especially people dined and supped continually with one another. Above all, I was obliged to mingle as usual with Society and my ordinary acquaintance, for fear lest I be suspected of some serious intrigue. Thus my labour was always being interrupted, which was most detrimental to good results, especially in matters of that kind. I was often driven to work at night. I do not know why I was more spied on than usual at that period; but I was always watched. Mme de Saint-Simon had been unable to come to Fontainebleau that year since she was recovering from measles. We wrote to one another every day, and although we sent nothing in any way confidential through the post, neither of us received a single letter on which the seal had not visibly been broken. That was what made me extra careful to avoid appearing to seek seclusion, and caused my work to be interrupted, making it much more difficult. M. de Beauvilliers lodged in the Galerie de Diane, opposite to the Duc de Noailles, in rooms that were permanently theirs.

Mine were at the other end of the château, above part of the queen-mother's apartment, and my windows overlooked the fountain court. Every evening M. de Beauvilliers crossed that wide space alone, without lackeys or torches, or anyone accompanying him, groped his way up my short staircase and, during the King's supper, made me read over what I had written that day. He stayed with me about an hour, and returned alone as he had come. Of us five, only the Duc de Noailles was unaware that I also was at work, and only the Duc de Beauvilliers saw my manuscript before it was finished. He was pleased with it, and said as much to the other three. Meanwhile, the Duc de Noailles was making his unknown helpers sweat in their garret, and finally emerged with a shortish memorandum just at the moment when mine was nearing completion. I shall not attempt here to analyse either work; but I must frankly say that, style apart, the Duc de Noailles's was extremely feeble to say the least, and that nothing but the style was his own. In principle, his work and mine agreed well enough. Mine may be found among the documents. I entitled it *'Concise Memorandum of the Formalities required in order to provide that the Renunciation of the King of Spain, for himself and his descendants, shall be legally and permanently binding in France'*. The amount of material and the need to produce proofs so led me on that although I had intended to be concise, I did, in fact, compile a substantial work. You must see and study it among the documents in order to comprehend the dispute that followed. Thus I shall take it for granted that my reader has already seen my Memorandum (so-called concise) on the Formalities, etc., which may be found among the documents.

[*Saint-Simon proceeds to cover sixteen pages (in the* Pléiade *Edition) describing in great detail his dispute with the Duc de Noailles. It was chiefly concerned with Saint-Simon's insistence that only the ducal-peers could properly figure as guarantors in the Parlement, whereas de Noailles wished to include governors of provinces and knights of the Order. 'From which,' says Saint-Simon, 'it was only too plain that he wished to curry favour.' Everyone, including Orléans and Berry, became extremely upset, but most of all the Duc de Beauvilliers, when he was asked to decide the issue. Saint-Simon retreated into history as far back as 1329 in order to establish precedents; and so passed the whole of their time at Fontainebleau. Finally, Nancré (see Vol. I, p. 315), just before the Court returned to Versailles, discovered what was afoot, and made all public.*]

I was thus occupied when, right at the end of the Fontainebleau visit, I received warning of a blow which at that particular moment I least deserved. Nancré had been sniffing around, and had picked up tag-ends of conversations between M. le Duc d'Orléans and myself, when he had interrupted us unexpectedly. He had obtained, through Mme d'Argenton, the captaincy of the prince's Swiss Guard, although Mme la Duchesse d'Orléans had always desired that post for

Saint-Pierre whom, out of pique, she subsequently made her first equerry, much against M. le Duc d'Orléans's will, which had caused many quarrels. Nancré was a citizen of Paris, Dreux by name, of the same family as Chamillart's son-in-law; but his father had been in the service; had risen to be a general with a good reputation and the governorship of Arras, and had married as his second wife one of La Bazinière's daughters, who was sister of the mother of Premier Président de Mesmes, and lived in friendship with them all. Nancré was a man of great intelligence who had grown bored with being lieutenant-colonel of some regiment, which one I have forgotten, but he had achieved that rank by seniority. He lived on the closest terms possible with his stepmother, elderly, beautiful, moving in the best Parisian Society. She lodged with him at the Palais Royal and queened it there. He elbowed himself into Society, wherever he could find a way; for he had what was needed to please, and no scruples restrained him. He wished to rise in the world and did not much mind how. He now sought to be empowered to treat with M. le Duc d'Orléans concerning the forms for the renunciations. In his chagrin at Torcy's refusing him that honour, he went to tell him that it was I, with my mania for the peerage, who was confusing the prince's mind, and delaying the peace. Torcy, with whom I had not the slightest acquaintance, and who was a friend of many who were no friends of mine, reported to the King what Nancré had said. King Louis spoke angrily to M. le Duc de Berry and mentioned his informants. M. le Duc de Berry himself put me on the alert. That made me beg him not to summon me in future, so as to give the King no further cause for anger, and to conduct all our intercourse through Mme de Saint-Simon and M. le Duc d'Orléans. I could not take the same line with that prince without its becoming noticeable, so I steeled myself to expect the worst. The King, however, made no sign, and since I had persuaded both princes to let the registrations be made in the presence of the peers, Nancré's knavish trick had no repercussions. I therefore let the matter rest, thinking that I had no reason to do or say anything with regard to the King.

Despite the unwillingness of the Allies and the various obstacles raised by them, the peace negotiations with England were so far advanced that the Duc d'Aumont was appointed ambassador to London while the Duke of Hamilton was nominated ambassador to France. M. d'Aumont was at that time in close liaison with the Duc de Noailles and myself. I shall have occasion to speak of him later.[1] He was given a salary of eighty thousand écus, eighty thousand livres in compensation for the loss on the exchange, and fifty-four thousand for his expenses, with three months' payment in advance. He was also made a Chevalier

[1] At the time of the affair of the Bonnet.

of the Order in quite exceptional circumstances, at a low mass, just before his departure. The Duke of Hamilton was a youngish man, very much of the queen's party,[1] and very highly esteemed. The party that opposed the queen, furious at being unable to prevent a peace, used every shift to do him harm. Shortly before these events he had won a lawsuit in the House of Lords against Lord Mohun, who was a Whig. The Whigs so worked on Mohun that almost against his will he was forced into a duel with Hamilton, and was killed on the spot. A certain Macartney, acting as his second, thereupon stabbed the Duke of Hamilton in the back and fled the country.[2] Queen Anne in great distress and indignation then appointed the Duke of Shrewsbury, one of her most trusted ministers, as ambassador to France.

At the beginning of October, the King spent a week at Rambouillet with M. le Comte de Toulouse, accompanied by a very small retinue. Except for the cost of the King's own table, M. le Comte de Toulouse bore all the expenses. That was when we first learned of the death of Godolphin,[3] who had been Lord Treasurer and chief minister of England, and the leader of the Whigs. His son was married to the eldest daughter of the Duke of Marlborough, in whose country residence he died of a stone, for they were the closest of friends. His death came as a great relief to Queen Anne and her new ministry, was a terrible disaster for the opposing party, and the final blow for the Duke of Marlborough.

The death of the Duc de Chevreuse, which took place in Paris, on Saturday, 5 November, between seven and eight in the morning, gives me an opportunity to enlarge on one who has figured prominently and often in these memoirs, and with whom I lived on terms of close friendship for very many years. Although I have already said much of him, there is much more that I could tell if space allowed, some of it vastly diverting and perhaps even more of it profitable. He was born with an excellent wit, a pleasant nature, and a taste for learning, especially for the arts and sciences, and he received an admirable education from masters who gave him their love and applied all their great gifts to his upbringing.

His father the Duc de Luynes, equally intelligent, and fully as skilled as his son in the arts of oratory and writing, had become devoted to the monks of Port-Royal-des-Champs, which was in close proximity to his estate of Dampierre, and after the death of his first wife, mother of the Duc de Chevreuse, retired there to live. He shared their austerities and to some extent in their works, and he entrusted to them the education of his son who, having been born on 7 October,

---

[1] The Tories.

[2] Because General Macartney was Marlborough's loyal officer, the Tories believed that Marlborough was responsible for Hamilton's death. Swift wrote, however, that he had been stabbed by the dying Mohun. Macartney returned and gave himself up for trial after the accession of George I. He was acquitted.

[3] Sidney Godolphin, 1st Earl of Godolphin (1645-1712). His son Francis married, 1698, Henrietta Churchill, Marlborough's eldest daughter.

1646, was only seven years old at the time of his mother's death. The gentlemen of Port-Royal turned their whole minds to the instruction of the little boy, partly from affection for his father, partly because they found much to cultivate in the character and talents of their pupil.

M. de Chevreuse grew up to be well-built, sufficiently tall, with a noble and agreeable countenance, but very ill endowed in the way of riches. He acquired vast wealth by his marriage, in 1667, to the eldest and beloved daughter of M. Colbert. Apart from her dowry and repeated presents of immense sums from his father-in-law, he gained the elevation of Chevreuse to a dukedom confirmed in his favour,[1] inheritance of the fortune of the Duc de Chaulnes, his father's first cousin, the post of Captain of the light cavalry of the Guard, and lastly the governorship of Guyenne.

Mme de Chevreuse[2] his wife was a brunette, and a most delightful woman, tall, and with a particularly good figure. The King at once made her a lady of the Queen's household, wherein she managed to please everyone, was on excellent terms with the King's mistresses, on even better ones with Mme de Maintenon and, despite her inclinations, very much a part of the King's private life, for he grew to dislike her absence. All this she contrived to be, despite mediocre wit, with frank and remarkable integrity, and most admirable virtue which never failed her in any predicament. I have already mentioned the harmony of their marriage, and of the unity existing between her and her sister the Duchesse de Beauvilliers, and between the two dukes, who were thus brothers-in-law. I have told how M. de Chevreuse travelled in Italy and Germany, and of the rank he enjoyed there; of the part they all four played in the storm over Quietism, because of which Mme de Maintenon became their implacable enemy; of their devotion to the Archbishop of Cambrai, from which nothing could deflect them; of the responsible ministerial post which M. de Chevreuse held *incognito* until his death, and of many other matters, especially regarding Mgr le Duc de Bourgogne, M. le Duc d'Orléans, and M. le Prince de Conti.

At other times I have mentioned his peculiar mentality, his dangerous method of reasoning, his excellent heart, and how he sometimes persuaded himself to believe the most arrant nonsense in all sincerity, and attempted to make others believe it also, but always with a gentle and most charming courtesy that never forsook him. He was, indeed, the complete opposite of anything resembling over-bearingness or arrogance of any kind. Specious arguments, varying conclusions

---

[1] The estate of Chevreuse had before been only a brevet-dukedom, granted for life, but not registered and sealed as hereditary.

[2] The Duchesse de Chevreuse (1652-1743) was Jeanne Marie Colbert, eldest daughter of the minister. She was not, in fact, made a palace-lady of the Queen until 1674.

from them, a characteristically rapid leap to deductions which he could never see were mistaken, such were typical of his mind and methods.[1] He marshalled his arguments so clearly, and pressed them with so much skill, that one was lost if one did not stop him at the outset. After one or two propositions that appeared comparatively reasonable, and to develop out of one another, he would press on to a final conclusion which, however staggeringly wrong one might feel it to be, seemed to present no obvious loophole for contradiction. By nature he was addicted to indirect methods, although always perfectly sincere, and thus he was slow to abandon his devotion to the doctrines of Port-Royal, for he could persuade his mind to accept the strangest oppositions without losing his love of truth. It was this same inclination to false reasoning that led him to fall a lifelong victim to the charms of Mme Guyon and to M. de Cambrai's eloquence. His love for his father helped to ruin him, for he set up all his half-sisters in establishments,[2] and also provided his half-brothers with certain smaller gifts: without his generosity, they would have had nothing. In the end it was his timber-merchants who made him bankrupt, for he owned the forests of Chevreuse and Saint-Léger, and others adjacent, and conceived a passion for constructing paved paths by which to transport his timber, but was no better off when the work was finished. He then made a canal in order to float his logs down to the Seine, but when two-thirds of it had been dug he discovered that not a drop of water would ever pass through it. The requisitions, compensations, and general expenses had been enormous. He was overwhelmed with debts and worries, and at last was forced to sell the forest of Saint-Léger to the Comte de Toulouse, who added it to his estate of Rambouillet, leaving Dampierre landless. Indeed, when the governorship of Guyenne suddenly descended on him as a windfall from God and the King, he was almost at the end of his resources.

He mismanaged his health just as badly. He had suffered from gout from the age of nineteen, although he had done nothing to deserve it, it having come to him by inheritance. He feared to be crippled like his father, who had not deserved it either, or like his brothers, who later became even worse disabled. He therefore took to a diet that kept down the gout, which he had only rarely and slightly, and preserved him from other infirmities; but he carried this regimen to excess and it finally killed him. M. de Vendôme, who dined with him on occasions at Marly, in the early days, when the King liked people to go to the grand-master's table, once said that M. de Chevreuse poisoned his stomach with chicory-water throughout

[1] Saint-Simon named him *grand artisan de quintessence*. Fénelon wrote to him in 1699: 'Allow me to tell you that without realizing it you often have a great inclination to argue and be absorbed by details. It is a lifelong habit; you do it instinctively, without reflection, and almost all the time. Your rank increases the subtle temptation and the great variety of your affairs urges you always to hurry. I have often noticed how you rush from one occupation to another, and are carried away by them each in turn. The trouble is that you indulge your passion for dissecting and entering into details.'
[2] There were five half-sisters and two half-brothers.

the entire course of the meal, just for the sake of drinking a bumper of wine with sugar and nutmeg at the end. And truly, that was his usual custom, for in health as in business he never learned to let well alone.

Never did a man so 'possess his soul in patience', as the Psalmist puts it. Neither the disorder in his affairs, nor his disgrace at the time of the storm over Quietism, nor the deaths of his children, nor even that of his sublime Dauphin, succeeded in upsetting his calm, or changing his kind and loving heart. He offered all such afflictions to God, whom he never forsook, and towards whom his whole life and all his actions were directed. He was gentle, modest and courteous, even to his servants; with his friends and near relations he was gay and excellent company, without trace of stiffness or formality, for he loved pleasure and diversions. But he lived secluded, despising the social round, and so loving to study that it was well nigh impossible to drag him into Society; indeed, very many people at the Court were unaware that he kept a most excellent and lavish table. He never appeared at meals until the second course was served; that he would hastily devour a shoulder of rabbit or a grill, whatever was least acid, and for dessert, a few sweetmeats, which he thought were good for the digestion, with a weighed portion of bread from which the crust had been removed. He liked to leave the table in such a condition that he returned to work as comfortable as when he broke off; and usually he went to his study very soon after the meal was over. Towards midnight he would eat some kind of an egg dish, or fish cooked in water or oil, and he kept to this diet even on feast-days. He did everything late and rather slowly. Times and seasons meant nothing to him, and accidents used to occur on that account which caused us much amusement in the family circle, and gave M. de Beauvilliers the opportunity to tease him unmercifully, despite the respect with which he always treated him.

M. de Chevreuse used sometimes to keep his horses standing harnessed for twelve or fifteen hours at a time. One morning, at Vaucresson, he had decided to dine at Dampierre. The coachman first, then the postillion, grew tired holding the horses' heads. This was in the summer. By six in the evening, even the horses were bored. There ensued a tremendous noise that set the house shaking. Everyone rushed out. They found the coach in fragments, the great door of the house splintered, the garden gate that enclosed one side of the courtyard battered down, in short, complete destruction which it took a very long time to repair. M. de Chevreuse, quite oblivious of all the commotion, was much surprised when he learned what had happened, and M. de Beauvilliers persecuted him for months afterwards by continually asking the amount of the damage.

The Chancellor used to say that the brothers-in-law were one in heart and soul, and it is true that what one thought the other believed also. But, despite that similarity, M. de Beauvilliers had a good angel who prevented him from acting quite in the same way as M. de Chevreuse. This is the exact truth, as you will realize when I come to describe M. de Beauvilliers. It seems strange that two men, who in action were so much the opposite of each other, could have spent their lives together without ever being separated, in a close and constant unity that never failed them for a single moment. They lived in the same neighbour-hood, lodged together at Marly, and very near to each other at Versailles, ate together every day, and never let a day go by without meeting two, three, or even four times.

M. de Chevreuse wrote readily and agreeably, in an admirably clear style and handwriting—which last is exceedingly rare. His family not merely loved but adored him, and with them he was always the same, gentle, gracious, and helpful. To those who did not know him, he appeared stiff, composed, somewhat pedantic, and people were thus kept at a distance, for he was little known in Society. During the stay at Fontainebleau that year, he and Mme de Chevreuse suggested an expedition to Courcelles. I met them at their house, and being on such intimate terms with them I walked unannounced into his room, where I surprised him standing in front of a cupboard, secretly imbibing a glass of quinine. He blushed, and asked me as a favour not to tell anyone. I promised, but warned him that if he constantly took quinine on an empty stomach it would kill him. He agreed, but when I pressed him, he confessed to having done so for several months past for the sake of his digestion. I noticed then, and, indeed, I had known for a long time, that he was eating less than ever. The worst of it was that he had gradually adopted Cornero's[1] regime, which greatly benefited that Venetian, but killed many other people, including M. de Lionne, the famous secretary of State.[2] He did not last long after that; but fell ill in Paris, bearing acute pain with great fortitude, and dying quietly and at peace, surrounded by his family and friends. When they opened his body, they found that his stomach had been perforated.

The Duc de Mazarin died at his country house, where he had lived in retire-ment for the past thirty years. He was more than eighty years old, and no loss to anyone, for eccentricity carried beyond a certain point ruins the finest character. I have heard his contemporaries say that there was never a man cleverer or more agreeable; that he was the best company in the world, very well read, generous, with excellent discrimination, in every way a sound man, and an intimate friend of the King who continued to remember him kindly, notwithstanding that he did everything possible and impossible to make himself forgotten. He had inherited

[1] Louis Cornero, who was a member of a famous Venetian family.
[2] The Marquis de Lionne (1611-1671). Minister for foreign affairs, 1663.

vast riches from his father the Maréchal de La Meilleraye,[1] a very able general, continuously in favour, from whom he had the governorships of Nantes, Brest, Port-Louis, and Saint-Malo. The maréchal did his best to dissuade Cardinal de Mazarin, his close friend, from fixing upon his son, who was already the richest eligible bachelor in France, as husband for his niece and inheritor of his wealth and title. The maréchal said that the thought of so much wealth frightened him, for its very size would overwhelm his son and be the ruin of the entire family. He was none the less forced to yield. During a lawsuit that later ensued between the Duc de Mazarin and his own son, it was proved in open court that his wife had brought him twenty-eight millions, and that he had the governorships of Alsace, Brisach, and Belfort besides the bailiwick of Haguenau, which alone produced an income of thirty thousand livres. The King admitted him to all his councils, gave him the *entrées* of a first gentleman of the bedchamber, and showed him every distinction. I nearly forgot that he was also governor of Vincennes.

Piety, generally so salutary, and so becoming to men of talent, poisoned all the gifts that had been showered upon the Duc de Mazarin by nature and fortune. To begin with, he insisted on his wife's gadding about with him everywhere, to everyone's great indignation. He then made himself wholly ridiculous and quite intolerable to the King, because he would insist on telling him his dreams concerning King Louis's private life with his mistresses.[2] After that episode he retired to his estates, where he fell a prey to monks and holy hypocrites, who took advantage of him and made holes in his millions. He took to mutilating beautiful works of art, and held lotteries for his servants' places; with the result that his cook became steward, and his floor-polisher his secretary. He believed that by drawing lots the will of God was revealed. The Château de Mazarin caught fire; everyone rushed to extinguish the flames, but he ran to chase away the scoundrels who were frustrating God's purpose. He loved to have lawsuits brought against him; if he lost them, he ceased to own what was not rightfully his, if he won, he kept his land with a clear conscience. He drove his agents demented because he demanded so many details, and required them to do such absurd things. For example, he forbade women and girls to milk the cows on his estates, because, he said, such an occupation might give them nasty ideas. An account of all his follies would be never-ending. He wanted his daughters to have their front teeth drawn out because they were pretty girls and might become vain. He travelled continually from one of his estates to another, and for many years dragged the corpse of Mme de Mazarin about with him. By means such as these he frittered

---

[1] Charles II de La Porte (1602-1664), Maréchal de France, 1642. His second wife was a cousin of Richelieu, which may have accounted for some of his wealth.
[2] On that occasion King Louis said, 'Have you quite finished? I have been thinking for a long time that you were touched here,' putting his hand to his forehead.

away the greater part of his millions, and in the end all that was left to him were the governorships of Alsace and of two or three other places.

On 28 November, the King sent Berwick to join his command. Two days earlier the King had seen Chamillart, in his study, for the first time since his disgrace. Blouin introduced him by the back way after the King's return from Marly. King Louis received him with kindness and gave him permission to visit him from time to time. I like to recount that for a long time past the King had desired to see him, and had more than once sent him word to that effect. Chamillart was deeply moved by this mildly expressed wish for his presence, which was far from agreeable to Mme de Maintenon. The audience was only for a quarter of an hour, but they were alone. He left also by the back way, allowed himself to be seen by very few, and at once returned to Paris, where he lived surrounded by the best and gayest company of all the Court and town. On the few occasions when I went to Paris, I supped with him nearly every evening.

The King grew bored in Mme de Maintenon's room, in the intervals of working with his ministers. The Dauphine's death had left a gap that was not filled by the games of the very few ladies who were sometimes admitted. Concerts were more frequent, and for that very reason had become tedious. Somebody then had the idea of enlivening the evenings with scenes from Molière's plays, performed by the King's musicians in costume. Mme de Maintenon brought the Maréchal de Villeroy home by water[1] to amuse the King with reminiscences of their boyhood. She introduced him alone to that small circle, hoping that his gossip might animate it somewhat. He made himself useful to her by breaking the ice around certain topics outside the ministers' spheres which she wanted the King to discuss with her afterwards: thus giving her an opportunity to press these matters with more tact and security than if she were herself to raise them. The deaths of the princes of the blood without adult issue, those of the Dauphin and Dauphine, the worse than ruin into which black treachery and intrigue had thrown M. le Duc d'Orléans, and the terror of M. le Duc de Berry in the King's presence, opened new horizons for the boundless ambitions of M. du Maine, supported by his all-powerful governess. The Maréchal de Villeroy was a servile courtier—no more; no other instrument would have aided better, and Mme de Maintenon made sure of his being close at hand in case of need.

[1] Because his wound made riding or bumping about in a coach excruciatingly painful.

CHAPTER IV

1713

King James leaves France for ever - The Abbé de Polignac is made a cardinal - Death of Mme de Mailly - Brissac's prank - Death of the Archbishop of Auch - The Duchess of Shrewsbury changes the hair-style of French ladies - The King gives a ruling for the Governors of Guyenne and Blaye - Pontchartrain's black treachery - Acts of Renunciation - Comical interlude at the session of the Parlement - Peace is signed - Père Tellier's monstrous plans - Pontchartrain's second marriage - The Bull Unigenitus *is published in Rome - Momentous conversations with Père Tellier - Death of the Chevalier de Grignan*

DURING THE early part of that year, the diversions in Mme de Maintenon's room became more and more frequent. There were dinners, concerts, scenes from operas, lotteries with only black tickets,[1] dinner-parties even at Marly, and sometimes also at Trianon, still with the same restricted numbers and the same ladies. The Maréchal de Villeroy was always present at the plays and concerts, very occasionally the Comte de Toulouse who loved music, hardly ever M. du Maine, and no other men at all, save for the captain of the guard when he came to announce the King's supper if a concert was not over.

The Pope had reserved *in petto*[2] four cardinals' hats (the sovereigns' nominations) from his 1712 promotions. Three of these were for Spaniards; the fourth was for King James's candidate, the Abbé de Polignac. The Archduke had violently protested against any nominations being accepted from King Philip who, he declared, was no longer King of Spain, and had produced his own nominee in Benedict Sala, Bishop of Barcelona, with fearful threats should he be refused. King Philip had insisted on his rights, and there had been angry exchanges.

The Abbé de Polignac's name had gone unchallenged; but his ambassadorial rôle at Utrecht being incompatible with a cardinalate, King James had asked for his hat also to remain *in petto*, for the time being. Peace was on the point of being signed by France, King Philip, and the English; only the Emperor refused because, although chosen and crowned

---

King of Spain by the Allies, he was still treated merely as Archduke by France
and the Spaniards. The Pope, attacked on all sides, and foreseeing that sooner or later the Archduke would rule Italy, thought that King Philip would be
content if his nominations were accepted along with that of Sala. Only the details
remained to be settled at Utrecht, and he therefore notified King Louis that he
would announce Polignac's promotion.

It was indeed an extraordinary situation for a cardinal *in petto*, a nominee of
King James, to be working against that prince, and dealing him a mortal blow
by consenting to his exile from France, under any conditions that the English
cared to make. Polignac's formal visit to return thanks at Saint-Germain ought to
have embarrassed him considerably; but nothing upsets a cardinal. Polignac, in
any event, had only the queen to fear for, with the consent of the English, King
James, using the title of Chevalier de Saint-Georges, had already departed to Bar
with a very small retinue. M. de Lorraine refurnished the château for him, and
visited him there. The king then went to Lunéville as the guest of M. and Mme
de Lorraine,[1] and afterwards visited M. de Vaudémont, at Commercy, making a
long stay with each of them in turn.

Louis XIV, who never entirely threw off the veneration which Cardinal Mazarin
had implanted in him for prelates of that rank, settled with Cardinals de Rohan and
Polignac the places that they should occupy during the sermons in chapel. He gave
the matter long, personal consideration, and went so far as to mark them out on
paper, in their presence, and to their entire satisfaction. Nothing, until then, had ever
been written down. The King afterwards gave Cardinal Polignac an audience for
Utrecht, and spent nearly two hours with him, tête-à-tête.

Old Mme de Mailly[2] died at this time, aged eighty-five or -six; her head
and health were as good as though she were still only forty. Her long face and
pointed nose had inspired her nickname 'the snipe'. She was a Montcavrel, and
long after her marriage became the family heiress; whereupon by hard work,
constant attention, skill, and lawsuits, she brought herself and her husband
from extreme poverty to great wealth and power as landowners. She ruled her
children with a rod of iron, and flung one of them into the Abbey of Saint-
Victor, a fate he would gladly have avoided. None the less he became its prior,
and later Bishop of Lavaur, a benefice of some importance. She forced another son into the priesthood, for which he never forgave her, and left him to rot
penniless, at Saint-Victor, until the alliance of yet another of her sons with a
cousin[3] of Mme de Maintenon, turned that Abbé de Mailly into an archbishop,

---

[1] M. and Mme de Lorraine: Leopold, Duc de Lorraine (1679-1729), the husband of 'Mademoiselle', and Elisabeth
Charlotte d'Orléans (1676-1744), the Regent's sister.
[2] Jeanne de Monchy-Montcavrel, Marquise de Mailly (1628-1713).
[3] Marie Anne Françoise de Saint-Hermine, who married Comte Louis de Mailly in 1678. She was widowed in 1699.

first of Arles, later of Rheims, and finally brought him a cardinalate, as you shall in due course discover. As for her daughters, one escaped her and married the head of the Mailly family; the other, whom she compelled to be a nun,[1] made a virtue of necessity and was a very good one, becoming a most excellent Abbess of Poissy, loved and respected by all that vast community. It was not noticeable that God blessed Mme de Mailly for her labours on His behalf, considering all that has since happened in that family.

Old Brissac,[2] who for several years had been living in retirement, was another who died very old. He was a lieutenant-general, Governor of Guise, and had been adjutant of the King's bodyguard for a long time. A gentleman in a very small way, he had risen from the ranks by attracting the King's notice because of his keenness, his care for detail, and his devotion to the King alone. He gained such a reputation for knowing all about the bodyguard that even the captains, all great nobles and general officers, felt that he must be handled with tact and consideration. The junior officers stood greatly in awe of him. To speak plainly, he was a coarse, common sort of man, exceedingly disagreeable and abominably spoilt by the King; but he was a man of honour and good principles, honest and decent, and respected as such. At the same time many people disliked him, and everyone, including the courtiers, even the greatest among them, dreaded having to deal with him, for he could be dangerous. He was the only man who ever dared to attack Fagon on the subject of medicine, and barked at him before the King in a way that put Fagon into a rage, and made the King and the spectators laugh until their sides ached. Fagon, himself a man of no little wit and short-tempered, gave back as good as he got and thereby caused much merriment; but at the same time, he could not endure to see Brissac, or even to hear him mentioned, without losing his temper.

One anecdote about this adjutant of the bodyguard will give a sidelight on the Court. Every evening at Versailles there were public prayers followed by evening service, and on Sundays and Thursdays there was also benediction. In winter the service was at six o'clock; but in summer it was at five, so as to allow time to go out of doors afterwards. The King always attended on Sundays, and during the winter rarely missed on Thursdays. At the end of the prayers, a blue footman on duty in the tribune would run to warn him, so that he was able to appear a moment before the benediction. But whether or not he was expected, the service always began at the proper time, and guards were always posted in the tribune where he stood. The ladies made a point of filling the bays between the tribunes,

---

[1] Jeanne Charlotte Rose, Abbess of Poissy. There were, in fact, three daughters, the two others being Marie Louise who became Abbess of Lavaur, and Anne Marie Madeleine who, in 1687, married her cousin René V, Marquis de Mailly, who died in 1698.

[2] Albert de Grillet, Marquis de Brissac (1627-1713).

and in the winter they took care to make themselves seen by holding up the little candles they carried to light their prayer-books in such a way that the beam fell full upon their faces. Regular attendance was accounted a merit. Thus all the ladies, young and old alike, did their utmost to be observed by the King and Mme de Maintenon.

Brissac grew tired of seeing so many ladies who had not the reputation for desiring to hear benediction, and one day he laid a plot with other officers of the bodyguard. Towards the end of prayers he entered the royal tribune, rapped with his staff, and cried out in a loud voice, 'Gardes du Corps, you may dismiss! The King will not come to benediction.' Everyone obeyed his order; the guards removed themselves, and Brissac hid behind one of the pillars. Then a soft whispering was heard among the ladies filling the other tribunes and, a moment after, each one had snuffed out her candle and vanished, leaving only Mme de Dangeau and two others of no great standing.

All of this occurred in the old chapel. The officers, having been forewarned, posted the guards on the staircase to Blouin's room and in the back passages, where they were out of sight, and when Brissac had given the ladies ample time to go out of earshot, they reappeared. It was all timed to perfection, so that the King arrived and benediction started only a moment afterwards. He always ran his eye around the tribunes to see who was there, and being used to seeing them filled to capacity he was extremely surprised to discover no one but Mme de Dangeau and two other ladies. When he came away he mentioned the matter and expressed his astonishment. Then Brissac, who always walked near to him, began to laugh and told the whole story of the prank which he had played on those pseudo-saints, because he was heartily tired of seeing the King deceived. The King was much amused and his courtiers still more so. It was soon discovered which ladies had blown out their candles when they heard that the King was not coming, and some of them were so furious that they would have liked to scratch out Brissac's eyes. Indeed, he almost deserved that fate because of the scathing remarks he made about them.

Another death, which I would omit had his character been less strange, was that of the Bishop of Viviers.[1] He was the brother of Chambonas, a member of M. du Maine's household, and thanks, no doubt, to that support he was able to live for ten years in succession in furnished lodgings near my house in the Rue Saint-Dominique. He wrote letters most of every night, wearing out several secretaries in the process, and beginning again in the early hours of the morning. His self-imposed business was to keep all the diocesan bishops informed regarding the movements of the Languedoc fanatics, and he constantly sent news of that province to Bâville[2] the intendant, who was himself in residence at Montpellier, but

---

[1] He was Antoine de La Garde de Chambonas, and had been Bishop of Viviers since 1690.
[2] For Intendant Bâville and the Fanatics, see Vol. I, p. 213.

could do nothing to stop the flow from Paris, which included long memoranda and instructions. This bishop had an income of fifty thousand livres from his bishopric, and another stipend from an abbey. He left six hundred thousand livres; which reminds me of an eccentric of another kind, the Archbishop of Auch, Desmaretz's brother, who spent his entire life in Parisian furnished lodgings, never out of his dressing-gown, seeing no one, opening no letters, simply allowing them to accumulate in heaps. The King wearied of him at last, and told Desmaretz to return him to his diocese. But it had become almost impossible to move him. For years past he had been living on borrowed money and by other dubious shifts, and no one was found willing to pay for his journey. His secretary, continually badgered by creditors, in desperation suggested attacking the monstrous mountain of letters and packages, to see whether there might not be a banknote contained in one of them. Being at the end of his resources, the archbishop unwillingly consented, and together they set to work, to find no less than a hundred and fifty thousand livres, in bills of exchange of varying amounts, for want of which they had been starving. He then departed, having no further difficulties in paying his journey.

The Duke and Duchess of Shrewsbury[1] had already been living in France for some time past. He had his first audience as the English ambassador in the customary manner; but since there was neither a queen nor a dauphine, his duchess paid her respects to King Louis in his study, between the council and his dinner-time. The Duchesse d'Aumont presented her, accompanied by the Baron de Breteuil, as the head of protocol. She had her *tabouret* that same evening at the King's supper. The English are great travellers. Shrewsbury, then an Earl, carried the sword of State at King James II's coronation in 1685, and was his trusted High Chamberlain. He, however, deserted him in 1688 and was one of the 'seven eminent persons' who invited the Prince of Orange to come to England. He then went to Italy and married, in Rome, the daughter of the Marchese Paleotti and of Catherine Dudley, who was herself a daughter of the Duke of Northumberland by Marie Madeleine Gouffier de Brazeux. What a parentage! Although she was Italian by birth, her religion proved no bar to the Duchess of Shrewsbury's marriage. She followed her lord to England, where the Prince of Orange gave him a dukedom and the Garter. He also became a secretary of State.

She was a tall, stout creature, who grew mannish in her old age. Once handsome, and still aspiring to be thought so, she wore a low *décolletage*, arranged her hair behind her ears, in ringlets,[2] and covered herself with rouge and patches and other such aids to beauty. She had no sooner arrived than she began to make herself felt, speaking very loud and very volubly in excruciating French, and ready to eat

[1] The Duchess of Shrewsbury was Adelaide Paleotti, who married Charles Talbot, Duke of Shrewsbury (1660-1718).
[2] With a bandeau, the hair in curl-papers and bows of ribbon.

from any man's hand. Altogether she behaved like a lunatic, but her gambling, her table, her magnificence, even her desire to be friendly made her the fashion, and it was not long before she had pronounced the ladies' style of hairdressing to be perfectly ridiculous—as indeed it was, for they then wore erections of wire, ribbons, and false hair, supplemented with all manner of gewgaws, rising to a height of more than two feet. When they moved, the entire edifice trembled and the discomfort was extreme. The King, so autocratic in small details, detested this fashion, but despite his wishes it continued to be worn for more than a decade.

What the monarch could not command, the taste and example of an eccentric old foreigner achieved with surprising speed. From those exaggerated heights the ladies suddenly descended to an extremity of flatness, and the new style, so much simpler, more practical, and infinitely more becoming, has lasted to the present day. Sensible folk now long for some other mad foreigner to come and relieve our women of the enormous round hoops[1] that are in every way inconvenient for the ladies themselves and for others as well.

This is a good moment to speak of a ruling which I obtained at this time for my governorship of Blaye. The matter in itself would not have been of much consequence if the outcome had not been so disturbing. You have seen earlier that all my efforts had failed to prevent the encroachments of the Marquis de Montrevel;[2] you have also seen that this had kept me from going to Guyenne when the alarming effects of my wager on Lille made me wish to retire from the Court.[3] Wearied at last by his continued insolence, I decided to separate my governorship from that of Guyenne. La Vrillière put the matter to the King, who received it so well that I had good hope of success; but when, shortly afterwards, the Guyenne governorship was given to M. du Maine's second son, I saw that no more could be achieved in that quarter. None the less, I so much wanted to be done with the whole affair that I resolved to call upon M. du Maine and, after telling him of Montrevel's various affronts, ask him to judge between my rights and those of his son and then beg the King to make a permanent settlement. I should thus be able to put from my mind the thought of what had been stolen from me, and enjoy in peace and comfort whatever remained.

M. du Maine who, despite my conduct towards him, had all his life sought my friendship, now overwhelmed me with thanks and civilities and agreed to my proposal. Montrevel was summoned. He dared not question M. du Maine's judgment, but was so angry at being brought to book that he took to greeting me carelessly, with most marked want of respect, whenever we chanced to meet. At

---

[1] The fashion for wearing hoops came to France from England in 1718.
[2] The Maréchal-Marquis de Montrevel was the general commanding in Guyenne from 1704 until 1716. See Vol. I, p. 453.
[3] See Vol. I, p. 501.

Marly his behaviour was so outrageous that after a time I looked him straight in the eye and refused to bow at all. Picture him then in a positive fury, going off to call upon M. du Maine, vowing that I had insulted him, and complaining bitterly. A few days later when I also visited M. du Maine, he spoke to me of the maréchal, asking what had happened between us. I told him all, adding that, since I always moved in the highest Society, I need not fear accusations of discourtesy; but neither was I accustomed to people putting on airs, and Montrevel's manner required that I show my contempt for fops and bullies, and make quite sure of there being no misunderstanding. M. du Maine tried to reason with me, in view of our situation and the trouble that might result from quarrelling with a man whom I was liable to encounter at any moment. He said also that some insults were best ignored or laughed at. I replied that I did laugh; but that enduring perpetual insults was something to which I was not accustomed, and that the maréchal was the last man in the world to persuade me to accept them. I said that I understood him very well and knew him to be mad; that I realized his tendency to explode; but that I felt fully capable of making him eat his words, and believed that the King was too fair-minded not to blame the aggressor and exonerate the sufferer who had merely retaliated. In a word, Montrevel might count on my not changing in my conduct towards him, until he changed his own, absolutely and completely. In the meanwhile, if he felt aggrieved, he had only to accept my cards.[1] I thereupon quitted M. du Maine, leaving him far from displeased but wishing that my answer had been different.

I never learned what he said to Montrevel; but two days afterwards I was astonished to see the latter, who had been avoiding me and might have continued so to do, wait until I was well within his range, and then, before the entire company, deliver in my direction the deepest, most impressive, and most respectful bow imaginable. I returned the salutation with immense courtesy, and from then onwards proper civilities were resumed between us.

I continued to press M. du Maine—and at last, on Sunday, 19 March, after the sermon, a new ruling was made by the King, in his study, alone with M. du Maine and La Vrillière. I won all, with the exception of one article in the new statute, namely that the Governor-general of Guyenne might be escorted by his uniformed guards with shouldered carbines whenever he came to Blaye, whether or not the Governor of Blaye was in residence. The article clearly laid down that the Governor-general of Guyenne and the Governor of Blaye, both being officers of the Crown, should keep to their official rank when in their governorships. Thus, not only did Montrevel have to accept my superior authority in my own territory, but he was

---

[1] *'Prendre des cartes'*: according to the *Encyclopaedia Britannica*, visiting cards originated at the Court of Louis XIV; but there is evidence to suggest that they were used even earlier. Would Saint-Simon really have fought a duel to defend his governorship?

forced to give me precedence everywhere else. He was furious, outraged, and for the first day or two quite unable to contain himself. I never learned what made him realize his folly; how deeply he might displease the King and M. du Maine; how much cause he gave me to mock him; but soon he could no longer endure to see me, and at the end of a week returned suddenly to Guyenne. Never after that did he interfere in any way with my governorship of Blaye.

All this would have made me perfectly content, had it not been for Pontchartrain's black treachery. You already know that, although I had every reason to further his disgrace and was no longer his friend, I had gone to the opposite extreme and had saved him. Moreover, I had effected a reconciliation between his father and the Duc de Beauvilliers, and had afterwards resumed friendly relations with Pontchartrain himself, for which he never ceased to thank me, with protestations of eternal gratitude. He never discussed the Blaye militia with me, and I, for my part, said nothing because I was waiting on events.

At Marly I had visited M. du Maine rather more often than usual, for I was not normally in the habit of seeing him except on formal occasions. Marly is so arranged that everyone notices one's movements, especially to the pavilions and on the *Perspective*, where M. du Maine had his permanent lodging. Pontchartrain was inquisitive, even in trivial matters; he saw that I visited M. du Maine frequently, and was all the more astonished because he well knew, from the old days, my feeling regarding the bastards. He questioned me. I replied only that I did indeed see M. du Maine now and then. That answer fired his curiosity. He discovered the facts, although I never learned through whom. He then took the matter of the coast-guards to the King, with the result that though the ruling was already established, and the Blaye militia placed under the control and nomination of the Governor, King Louis added the words 'without prejudice to the sense of the edict affecting the appointment of coastguard captains', which meant that having won all my claims against the governor and military commandant of Guyenne, I had entirely lost the battle against Pontchartrain and the coastguard captains. That ruling was made at Versailles, and it was there that I discovered Pontchartrain's treachery.

Those who recollect past events will easily comprehend my outraged feelings. I sought out La Chapelle,[1] one of Pontchartrain's high officers and his confidant, who had been involved in our quarrels and knew how I had benefited him and his father also. To La Chapelle I described what had happened, immediately adding that I well knew the difference between the power and importance of a secretary of State and my own; but I was also aware that if a man sets his entire mind on achieving something he usually succeeds, and that most surely I would sacrifice everything, wealth, position, favour, lands, and all that I held most enjoyable in

[1] Henri Besset de La Chapelle. He was the son of one of Louvois's head clerks, and was disgraced in 1715.

life, to bring about Pontchartrain's total ruin and disgrace. Nothing, I said, would make me slacken my ceaseless efforts towards that one end; on no consideration whatsoever would I relent, and my persevering, untiring efforts would undoubtedly in the end prove successful. Useless for La Chapelle to reason with me; to all his talk I replied that I should not again discuss the matter; that Pontchartrain might possess my militia unhindered, and that in the meanwhile I should be working with all my mind and strength to ruin him and bring him down. So saying I left the room, which was on the top floor of Pontchartrain's apartment at the château.

La Chapelle, who had been terrified by the venom with which I had uttered that plain threat, at once descended to tell all to the Chancellor, and I had not been in my room for more than half an hour when one of his servants arrived begging me to go to him immediately. I went. He was pacing up and down his study, looking exceedingly sad and greatly disturbed. As soon as he saw me he exclaimed, 'What is this I hear from La Chapelle? Can it be true?' 'That, Sir,' I replied, 'depends on what he chose to tell you.' The Chancellor then repeated word for word all that I had said to La Chapelle; not a word was changed. I said that to destroy Pontchartrain was my firm intention, from which nothing would ever divert me; that I regretted La Chapelle's indiscretion, but since he had told all, I was too honest to deny it. Nothing that the Chancellor could say would have the power to move me. I reminded him of events at Marly and at Fontainebleau, and of all that had previously taken place between his son and myself. I enlarged upon his black ingratitude. The Chancellor agreed that it was infamous; but he still tried to melt me for the sake of himself, his wife, and his grandsons. I said that this did not prevent his son from being a monster of depravity, as hateful as he was hated, who had placed me in a position where I must risk all to gain justice, and if I lost have no hope of redress. Let Pontchartrain enjoy his triumph, I said; I should not try to obstruct him; but let there be no talk of forgiveness. I preferred to lose my governorship altogether rather than owe my rights to his bounty, grace, and favour; and so far as it lay within my power I should repay him for his treachery on every possible occasion. There was mortal enmity between us. It would be a fight to the finish.

Never have I seen a man more confounded. He had no words with which to answer me. He knew me down to the very marrow of my bones, and realized that I should keep my promise no matter how powerful his son might be. The Chancellor was my closest friend after the Duc de Beauvilliers; he saw that the King had grown old; he was aware of the good terms on which I stood with M. le Duc de Berry, and of what I might later be to M. le Duc d'Orléans, having regard to our long friendship and the services I had rendered him. He trembled for his son, but knew not what to say or do. A lengthy silence followed. Now and again a speaking look directed at me told of his shame and loving affection. Together we paced his study. I said that I thought him too fair-minded to cease to love me because I had been stabbed by his villainous son for worse than no reason; that I sincerely pitied him for having fathered such an offspring; that I should do all in my power to make him forget, if possible, the just and unchangeable determination which he had forced me to disclose.

He embraced me. He said that even had he so wished he could not have ceased to love me, for that was impossible, but that I was plainly too angry for him to say more at that time. He would none the less continue to trust in my love for him, the effects of time, and my own second thoughts. We embraced once more; I said nothing—and so we parted. On the following day there was a similar interview with his wife, with whom I was no less frank, firm, and restrained. Both parents understood their son's character; but his mother, although he showed her even less consideration, bore him a tender love which her husband did not share. She could not condone his wicked behaviour, nor his black ingratitude, but she continually harped on forgiveness. I dealt with her by expressing all possible respect and personal affection, but not weakening in the slightest degree. It was then the turn of Mme de Saint-Simon, her piety, sweetness, and wisdom making her more restrained in her utterances, but in no way lessening her sense of dignity. All that she did was to echo their distress.

I ceased altogether from seeing Pontchartrain, never approaching or speaking to him in public; and in the King's apartments at Marly I barely greeted him. He appeared greatly embarrassed whenever he saw me, and bowed to me several times. I visited the Chancellor and his wife even more frequently than before, and sat with them in conversation. They hoped eventually to pacify me, and so things continued between us. In the meanwhile, I showed no sign of resentment at the restriction in the new ruling; and I thanked the King for doing me justice; but when I thanked M. du Maine, I spoke my mind regarding Pontchartrain, and he appeared to be equally indignant, to know him as well as I did, and to detest him quite as much. You shall see from what follows that Pontchartrain's black treachery was to cost him dear.[1]

The time had come for the renunciations. The peace was delayed. The King's vital interests required that it should be signed without further postponement, and the English court was no less eager to consummate this great work and enjoy the triumph of imposing it upon the other powers, than to secure a respite from her own internal troubles. The King of Spain had already given them satisfaction on this vital issue, with the accompaniment of the solemn rites, ceremonies, and oaths required by Spanish law and traditions. It was time for France to follow suit.

---

[1] When, under the Regent, Saint-Simon had Jérôme de Pontchartrain dismissed, he clearly did not do so without sufficient cause.

[*Philip V of Spain was Louis XIV's elder living grandson. If he were to die childless, his successor would normally be the Duc de Berry and his descendants, or, failing him, the Duc d'Orléans and his. Failing both, the Spanish throne mould go to the princes of the blood (Monsieur le Duc and his brother the Comte de Charolais) in order of seniority. Philip V of Spain and the same princes were next in line of succession to the throne of France, should Prince Louis (later Louis XV) die without an heir. The War of the Spanish Succession was fought in order to prevent such a possible conjunction of the thrones of France and Spain, lest France become too powerful in Europe.*]

I have already said all that is needful on this matter, and the subject is dealt with fully in the documents. It would therefore be redundant to explain at length the uselessness of a French prince of an elder line renouncing his rightful claim to a succession, unless France also consented by a new law, laid down with all the formalities required to give it permanence. Also needed was the renunciation by France of the claim of her own two royal princes and their descendants, and of the two princes of the blood next in line, in order of seniority. These royal princes, subjects of the most autocratic and jealous monarch that ever reigned (the grandfather of one, uncle and father-in-law of the other, and grandfather after a certain fashion[1] of the two princes of the blood), were forced, together with the peers of France, to witness the registration of this act by the Parlement, without publication of its contents, without previous debate, and without their opinions being asked—not that any of them would have dared to speak, except in approval. Thus was executed the ratification of that solemn act of the Parlement, designed to establish a new order of succession against all precedent in France. Its purpose was to give Europe the security not attained after the formal renunciations at the time of the Peace of the Pyrenees, or by the marriage contracts of Louis XIII and XIV, all of which had duly been enregistered in the Parlement. The treaty itself, with the renunciations most explicitly stated, was signed and sealed, on the frontier, by the first ministers of France and Spain, and the sovereigns of both countries in the presence of their courts solemnly swore to abide by it. The radical difference between what then took place and the events which I am about to describe will be only too obvious.

The blind worship of his absolute authority, of which the King was so inordinately jealous that it had become the chief concern of his life, was unshaken by the novelty of such an act, its supreme importance within and without his kingdom, its effect upon his line and his immediate family, or even by the fact that the idol to whom he sacrificed all would soon desert him, leaving him as naked before his maker as the meanest of his subjects. The most he would do to solemnize the enregistration was to provide for the presence of the peers, and even then his vanity was so overwhelming that he made only a general announce-

---

[1] Their mothers were legitimized bastard daughters of Louis XIV.

ment desiring their attendance at the Parlement to witness the ratifying of the Acts of Renunciation.

This I learned only four days before the event. I spoke to several of my fellow peers, and then informed M. le Duc d'Orléans that, if the King relied only on that one announcement, he could not reckon on the attendance of the peers, for unless they received his summons in the proper manner through the grand master of ceremonies they would not be present. That firm statement, which would have been followed by the deed, as in the case of Monseigneur's funeral, had its effect. M. le Duc d'Orléans and M. le Duc de Berry spoke seriously to the King, and at the last moment Dreux[1] called personally on all the peers who were lodged in the Château de Versailles, and left for those who were not at home a note to the effect that M. le Duc de So-and-So was thereby informed that the King proposed to treat matters of high importance at the Parlement, on a certain day, and desired his attendance. The notes were signed 'Dreux', and were dated. To the peers living in Paris, he merely sent cards, but was obliged to go himself to call on the princes of the blood and the legitimized princes, and they were thus not sent any note. When at last the English realized that no more could be extorted from us, and being, as I have said, in great haste to conclude a peace, they decided to be content with what they had gained. This is what finally occurred.

That great session of the Parlement was scheduled to begin with a formal address by Premier Président de Mesmes to M. le Duc de Berry, who was to make a reply. The thought of that reply troubled the prince exceedingly. Mme de Saint-Simon, to whom he confided his fears, managed to procure a copy of the premier président's speech, and gave it to M. le Duc de Berry to help him in composing his answer. The task, however, proved too hard for him. He admitted as much to Mme de Saint-Simon, declaring that he had no notion what to say. She suggested handing it over to me, an idea of which he vastly approved. I wrote his reply on my ordinary writing-paper, in my ordinary hand.[2] M. le Duc de Berry pronounced it excellent, but too long to learn by heart. I made it shorter. He wished it to be shorter still; in the end it filled only three-quarters of a page. He had then to learn it; and that accomplished on the evening before the session, he recited it to Mme de Saint-Simon, with her hearty encouragement, alone in his study.

On Wednesday, 15 March, I called on M. le Duc de Berry, dressed for the Parlement;[1] and shortly afterwards M. le Duc d'Orléans, dressed likewise, appeared at the head of a large suite. At about half-past six both princes stepped into M. le Duc de Berry's coach, the Duc de Saint-Aignan and I sitting in front.

---

[1] Thomas II de Dreux, Marquis de Brézé, a friend of Chamillart's. His son Thomas III married Chamillart's nicest daughter.

[2] Saint-Simon's ordinary hand was several times larger than the minute writing that he used for the memoirs.

He also wore parliamentary dress, and was M. le Duc de Berry's first gentleman of the bedchamber. By the door on his side sat the captain of the Duc de Berry's guard, holding his bâton, and on the other side M. le Duc d'Orléans's first gentleman. Several other coaches followed, containing the suites, and the princes' coach was escorted by a large body of M. le Duc de Berry's guard, with its officers. He was very silent during the entire drive. Sitting opposite him, I thought that he was worried by the consideration of what he had to do, and of his reply. M. le Duc d'Orléans, on the other hand, was remarkably cheerful, telling us tales of his nocturnal adventures on foot in Paris which had taught him to know the streets. In this leisurely fashion we arrived at the Porte de La Conférence[2] (a gate which has since been destroyed), at the end of the terrace and the quay of the Tuileries gardens, where the trumpets and kettledrums of M. le Duc de Berry's guard had been posted. They made a tremendous din all the rest of the route, which was taken at the speed of a slow march as far as the Palais de Justice.

When we arrived, we proceeded at once to the steps of the Sainte-Chapelle, at the entrance to which the Abbé de Champigny, as treasurer, received them, in accordance with the custom for the Sons of France. The rails in front of the two choir-stalls nearest the altar on the epistle side had been covered with a foot-cloth, and there were hassocks for the two princes. I purposely left the third stall empty, and removed the hassock from the fourth. M. de Saint-Aignan knelt on the hassock in the fifth stall.[3] No other hassocks had been provided, and no one else sat in the high stall on either side of us. The chief officers of the princes' households took their places in the lower stalls on both sides of the altar, leaving empty those immediately below the princes. The body of the chapel was full of people, including many persons of quality who had come in the princes' retinues, but not in the royal coaches, which were reserved for the suites. When low mass at the high altar was over, we left the chapel, by the door of which two présidents-à-mortier were stationed with two counsellors of the great chamber to greet the princes.

After a short address, we set out once more, the two presidents, one on either side of M. le Duc de Berry, and the captain of his guard walking behind him with his bâton. M. le Duc d'Orléans walked in the procession in front of him, between the two counsellors; I walked alone before M. le Duc d'Orléans, and M. de Saint-Aignan, also alone, preceded me. The chief officers of both households and many other persons of quality walked in no particular order both behind and in front, and M. le Duc de Berry's guards, with shouldered muskets, had great difficulty in clearing a passage for

---

[1] Parliamentary dress was either black or some dark colour, with a short cloak to match, a sword, and the hat with the white plume proper to the peers.

[2] The Porte de la Conférence, named after the *Conférence de Suresnes* (1593), between representatives of King Henry IV and of the *Ligue*.

[3] Saint-Simon removed the hassock in order to make a gap between the princes and the dukes. The Duc de Saint-Aignan was a junior, acting as the heir of his brother the Duc de Beauvilliers, whose two sons had died in 1705.

him. The crowd was so large from the Sainte-Chapelle to the high chamber that you could not have dropped a pin to the ground amongst the people who clambered over one another on every side.

The chamber was in full session when M. le Duc de Berry arrived. That is to say, there were present the princes of the blood, legitimate and legitimized, and the rest of the peers, all the members of the Parlement, and of the *tournelles*, *enquêtes*, and *requêtes*[1] were in their places, together with the counsellors of honour, the honorary counsellors, and four former maîtres des requêtes. All those in session sat below; above and behind were seats decorated with the *fleur-de-lis* for such members as could not find room on the ground floor, where scarcely any seats remained, except for the peers. The session was held below because the business in hand was supposed to be treated *in camera;* but the whole chamber was in confusion, with all sorts of people standing in the crowd. Room was found at the back for as many courtiers and other persons of quality as possible.

The two princes followed by the présidents-à-mortier crossed the floor to go to their seats; the Duc de Saint-Aignan and I took our places, entering the chamber immediately in front of them. The two counsellors, who had waited behind at the entrance, found seats where best they could. The entire chamber rose and uncovered at the entry of the princes, and as soon as the princes were seated and covered put their hats on also. The Duke of Shrewsbury, with the head of protocol and some other members of the English embassy, was seated high up in the gallery, on the side of the fireplace, in a seat especially prepared for him, as an essential witness on behalf of England. I shall now proceed to record the names of the peers who were present, and to list beside them the absentees, most of whom had not yet reached an age to be received into the Parlement. This will give you a knowledge of all the ducal-peers of France, at that time.

Peers in Session	*Peers Absent*
M. le Duc de Berry	Cardinal de Janson,
M. le Duc d'Orléans	Evêque-Comté de Beauvais.
M. le Duc de Bourbon	(He was dying, but in any event
M. le Prince de Conti	cardinal-peers do not attend the
M. le Duc du Maine	Parlement, because they rank only
M. le Comte de Toulouse	according to their own peerages.)

---

[1] The law courts under the *ancien régime* in the Paris Parlement: *La Tournelle Criminelle* and *La Tournelle Civile*. *Les Enquêtes* and *Les Requêtes* were the courts of inquiry and appeal.

Peers in Session	*Peers Absent*
Archevêque-Duc de Rheims, Mailly (later cardinal)	Duc d'Uzès (was in Languedoc)
	Duc d'Elbœuf
Evêque-Duc de Laon, Clermont-Chaste	Duc de Ventadour (neither of them
Evêque-Duc de Langres,	had troubled to be received into the
Clermont-Tonnerre	Parlement)
Evêque-Comte de Chalons, Noailles	Duc de Montbazon (ill)
Evêque-Comte de Noyon,[1] Châteauneuf	Duc de Luynes
de Rochebonne	Duc de Brissac[2]
Duc de La Trémoïlle	Duc de Fronsac (none of these last three
Duc de Sully	was of an age to be received)
Duc de Richelieu	Duc de La Rochefoucauld (blind)
Duc de Saint-Simon	Duc de Valentinois[3] (at Monaco)
Duc de La Force	Duc de Bouillon (ill)
Duc de Rohan-Chabot	Duc d'Albret (not received)
Duc d'Estrées	Duc de Luxembourg (at his governorship,
Duc de La Meilleraye et Mazarin	in Normandy)
Duc de Villeroy (Jnr)	Duc de Villeroy, Maréchal de France
Duc de Saint-Aignan	(resigned)
Duc de Foix	Brevet-Duc de Gramont
Duc de Tresmes	B-Duc de Guiche (both of these two,
Duc de Coislin, Evêque de Metz	resigned)
Duc de Charost	B-Duc de Louvigny (not received)
Duc de Villars, Maréchal de France	Duc de Mortemart (not received)
Duc de Berwick, Maréchal de France	Duc de Beauvilliers (resigned)
Duc d'Antin	Duc de Noailles (on duty as captain of the
Duc de Chaulnes	guard)
	Duc d'Aumont (Ambassador, in England)
	Duc de Béthune (resigned)
	Cardinal de Noailles, Archevêque de Paris
	Duc de Boufflers[4] (not received)
	Duc d'Harcourt, Maréchal de France (ill
	at his house in Normandy)

The session thus comprised one Son and one Grandson of France, two princes of the blood, two bastards, five ecclesiastical peers, and eighteen lay peers. Absent were the two infant princes of the blood, two cardinal peers, and ten other peers, either away or ill, nine peers not received (most of them being too young), and six who, having resigned in favour of their sons or brothers,

---

[1] Charles François de Châteauneuf de Rochebonne (1671-1740), Count-Bishop of Noyon, 1707.
[2] The Duc de Brissac had inherited his ducal-peerage in 1709, and was the Grand Panetier de France (the Lord High Baker), in charge of the bread and other victuals.
[3] The Duc de Valentinois was also Prince of Monaco.
[4] Joseph Marie, Duc de Boufflers (1706-1747), inherited 1711. He was the younger son of the Maréchal de Boufflers.

no longer attended the Parlement. Altogether there were, at that time, seven ecclesiastical peerages, seven archbishop or bishop peerages, and thirty-seven lay ducal-
peerages, not counting the bastards. Twenty-five were absent for various reasons,
and therefore, including M. le Duc de Berry, there were twenty-nine of us in session.
It would have served the Chancellor's interests well had he taken the chair; but
he did not care for ceremonial. He had not attended the Parlement since he was
appointed Chancellor, and the session about to take place seemed to him highly
irregular. The King, very reluctantly, had agreed to allow some pomp beyond that
which normally attended the enregistration of any act; but he did not require the
presence of the Chancellor, who was far from eager to receive any such order.

When M. le Duc de Berry was at last seated, there was some difficulty in
obtaining silence; but as soon as he could make himself heard, the premier président gave his address. After he had finished, it was time for the prince to reply. M.
le Duc de Berry half-raised his hat, replaced it immediately, looked at the premier
président, and said, 'Monsieur!' A moment later he repeated the word 'Monsieur!'
He then gazed at the assembly and once more said, 'Monsieur!' He turned first
towards M. le Duc d'Orléans, both of them by this time scarlet in the face, then
to the premier président, and ceased altogether, being quite incapable of uttering any other word than 'Monsieur'. I was sitting opposite the fourth président-
à-mortier, and could plainly perceive the prince's discomfiture. It made me feel
positively ill; but there was nothing that I could do. At last, the premier président
put an end to the sorry spectacle by raising his cap to M. le Duc de Berry, bowing
with great respect as though the reply had been made, and at once calling on the
King's representative to speak. You may picture the embarrassment of the courtiers present, and the dismay created in the magistrature. The King's advocate then
explained the business in hand, with long digressions into flowery oratory. What
had to be done was to extract from the records of the Parlement the letters patent
in which King Philip, before he went to Spain, had retained the right to succeed
to the throne of France, for himself and his descendants; to read his renunciation,
for himself and for all his line, of the succession to the French throne, and those
on behalf of M. le Duc de Berry and M. le Duc d'Orléans to the throne of Spain.
The premier président declared the King's will. Joly de Fleury, the avocat-général,
acted as spokesman for the Parlement and made the requisitions; the case for the
procureur-général was also made; we assented by raising our hats. All this took an
immensely long time.

The presidents and all the magistrature then rose, making low bows to M.
le Duc de Berry, who uncovered without rising. The presidents, followed by the
judges, retired to the refreshment room. M. le Duc d'Orléans likewise remained
seated, both for the bows and for the withdrawal, and following his example, the

two princes of the blood and the two bastards (who normally always rise for présidents-à-mortier when the latter rise for them) remained firmly planted, and the peers (who never rise, either for the présidents-à-mortier or for the premier président because they do not stir for them) remained in their seats also. We thus remained seated until all the officials had left the chamber; after which we moved closer to the princes and to one another, and the courtiers and other persons of quality left their benches and moved out on to the floor, where the princes and everyone else stood and chatted in no kind of order. At the end of a quarter of an hour, M. le Duc d'Orléans singled me out in the great crowd to ask me whether we ought not to resume our seats before the presidents returned. I replied that might be so, but it would be sufficient if we sat down a moment before they appeared, or even took our seats as they came in. He thought that might be soon, since they had only to put on their long red gowns with the *épitoges*, and take their *mortiers*[1] in their hands, and they would not wish to keep M. le Duc de Berry waiting. He desired me to tell the peers that M. le Duc de Berry and he were about to go up to their seats. I did this a moment later, and the floor was cleared. All those present were trying to find places from which to see and hear.

I do not know what the princes said to each other when they were again seated, for although I, too, sat on the bench against the wall, I was a long way from them and fifteenth in the line, because, although at a *lit de justice*[2] the ecclesiastical peers are placed on the high seats on the left of the King's corner, at an ordinary session, such as this one was, they sit on the right. Soon after we had taken our places, my name was passed down the line of peers above me, bidding me go and speak to M. le Duc de Berry and M. le Duc d'Orléans, who were asking for me. I went to them where they sat near the King's corner, and since no one but ourselves was yet seated, neither they, nor the peers before whom I passed, rose for me. At other times, in an ordinary session, the Sons of France, princes of the blood, and other peers always stand when a peer arrives and only sit when he does. M. le Duc d'Orléans made me stand between him and the Duc de Berry, and they both asked me if they should rise when the premier président and the rest re-entered the chamber and filed along the benches to their places. I said no, that they should put their hats on then and there, so as to be already covered when the presidents arrived. Then, when the presidents bowed before being seated, they should incline their bodies slightly, and make no other motion. That one gesture should suffice, if they let their eyes travel down the entire length

---

[1] The *épitoge* was a kind of hood, as on a graduate's gown. The *mortier* was a round cap of black velvet edged with gold braid. Full parliamentary dress for lawyers consisted of a scarlet gown, and a cloak lined with the same colour for the presidents. Counsellors wore a red gown with black trimmings and a square cap.

[2] A *Lit de Justice:* a session of the Parlement at which a King of France imposed his will in person, with the proclamation 'Le Roi le veult'.

of the row. The princes appeared satisfied and said no more. M. le Duc, who had overheard this exchange, stopped me as I went back to my seat to ask whether he ought to rise. I smiled, saying that I did not know how much respect he, personally, felt that he owed those gentry, but that M. le Duc de Berry and M. le Duc d'Orléans would neither of them rise nor to make the least appearance of so doing, because they felt under no such obligation, and neither would the peers budge, and with that I continued to my seat.

Presidential arrogance did not fail to grasp at this perfect opportunity to humble the Sons of France. They took more than three-quarters of an hour to change their dress, and people were grumbling so loudly at the delay that we could hear them from the high seats. At last they appeared. I noticed that the premier président and the two or three who followed next after him flushed scarlet when they saw that M. le Duc de Berry and M. le Duc d'Orléans remained firmly seated, that the two princes of the blood and the two bastards copied them, and the peers also. Thus they received no more than slight inclinations of the head (such as I had proposed) from anyone. When all were seated, which took a very long time, the ushers called for silence.

Because of the pretence that the earlier session had been held *in camera*, a second session was needed in order to make known what had taken place. The premier président therefore ordered all the doors to be opened, notwithstanding that they had not been closed for an instant during the whole of that interminable morning, and although the chamber was already so full that no one else could have entered it. When the noise had somewhat abated, the King's representatives began to read and argue all over again the entire matter as it had been treated before, but in different language so as to display their powers of oratory. Thus the boredom was extreme.

The most solemn events, sometimes even the most tragic, occasionally have their ludicrous side. I cannot resist describing two such incidents of which I was a very close witness during these ceremonies. During the first session, my rank had placed me between the Dukes of Richelieu and La Force—they had already been present a longish time, awaiting the arrival of M. le Duc de Berry. Soon after I took my seat, I observed that old Richelieu was fidgeting, and he asked me whether I thought that we should be long. I said that I feared so, from the number of the readings and the displays of oratory by the King's advocates. He then started to grumble and complain, giving me no rest from his questions and wrigglings, and at last said that he was dying to go to the closet, and absolutely must leave his seat. I tried to show him how improper it would be for him to quit the session, in full view of the assembled company as he crossed the floor of the hall. That, however, did not quell him, and I soon had to endure a fresh attack. I knew the man I was dealing with from an experience which I described earlier[1] because it was indeed most peculiar, I knew also that he was in the habit of taking senna every evening, and frequently a *lavement* during the morning, which he carried with him for four or five hours, and rendered up wherever he happened to be, as and when the occasion demanded. I began to tremble for his breeches, and even more for my own nose. I looked everywhere to find some means of ridding myself of my dangerous neighbour, and saw to my chagrin that the crowd made any movement impossible. To be brief, his demands to be let out, coupled with threats of an explosion, occupied the entire session, and grew so insistent towards the end that I more than once thought myself lost. At last it was over, and I begged the Abbé Robert, clerk of the great chamber,[2] who was sitting directly behind me and had overheard all, to take M. de Richelieu out, which he had the utmost difficulty in doing, even with the aid of the ushers. M. de Richelieu did not return for the second part of the session.

The other absurdity was not so alarming for me. Monsieur de Metz[3] was sitting with his back against my knees, on the bench immediately below me. Soon after the session began, I saw him growing more and more impatient, remarking on the uselessness of the long speeches, asking whether those fellows meant to keep us all night at the Palais de Justice, fidgeting, and saying finally that he was bursting to piss. He was exceedingly funny about it; for he was naturally humorous and ready to enliven the most serious affairs. I advised him to piss straight forward over the ears of the counsellors below on the lower benches. He shook his head, but cursed the avocat-général audibly, between his clenched teeth, jigging about to such an extent that the Dukes of Tresmes and Charost, his neighbours on either side, had to tell him to sit still, as though he were a child. We were all in fits of laughter. He wished to retire; he saw that this was impossible; he swore that never again would he attend that sort of gathering; he protested that no matter who suffered he was going to relieve himself, and he entertained us in this way throughout the entire session. I never saw a happier man, when all was over.

It was by then very late. The session rose, the princes left by the little staircase in the King's corner; the two presidents, and the two counsellors who had received M. le Duc de Berry at the Sainte-Chapelle, escorted him on his return. The remaining presidents left by way of the gallery near the refreshment room, and the peers, walking two by two preceded by an usher, went out through the other gallery. M. de Saint-Aignan and I separated from them as we quitted the

---

[1] For the other misadventure of M. de Richelieu, see Vol. I, p. 52.

[2] The Abbé François Robert, a doctor of the Sorbonne and a very learned jurist (d. 1722).

[3] The Duke-Bishop of Metz, Henri Charles du Cambout, Duc de Coislin, member of the French Academy; became duke and peer in 1710, inheriting from his elder brother. His family all enjoyed a joke, mostly of the bathroom variety. (See *Saint-Simon at Versailles*, p. 53.)

great chamber, and went to rejoin M. le Duc de Berry and M. le Duc d'Orléans, in order to drive with them in their coach. They returned to the Palais Royal in state, as they had come. The conversation was grave in the extreme because M. le Duc de Berry appeared much upset, embarrassed, and greatly discomfited. On arrival they changed into their ordinary dress, and M. de Saint-Aignan and I changed also. M. le Duc d'Orléans, during the interval between the two sessions, had invited many of the peers and persons of quality to dine with him, and he asked me to invite others whom he could not immediately observe. We circulated the State-apartments of the Palais Royal, which M. le Duc d'Orléans had re-decorated most splendidly, until all the company was assembled. We were then served with a vast and sumptuous meal, most lavish and delicious, yet all of it Lenten fare. M. le Duc de Berry sat in the midst, in an armchair, M. le Duc d'Orléans presented the napkin to him, and he alone was given a drinking-bowl, and another napkin beneath his plate. They had, however, given him no *cadenas*.[1] M. le Duc d'Orléans took his seat on M. le Duc de Berry's right, in a chair similar to those provided for the rest of the company. His gentlemen did the honours, and M. le Duc d'Orléans supervised them, most gracious and relaxed, but none the less dignified and restrained. It was a lengthy meal because there was much to eat and all was delicious; what is more, we were dying of hunger. The crowd of onlookers, the great number of guests, and the large assortment of dishes did not prevent the service from being remarkably quick and orderly. Everyone was attended to as though there were no more than five or six at table; but M. le Duc de Berry's deep and gloomy silence effectually prevented any gaiety. We talked to our neighbours, however, and the excellence of the food kept us well entertained. The two princes of the blood and the two bastards were not invited, and neither was the English ambassador.

Later, the princes drove in state to the Porte Saint-Honoré, thence returning to Versailles. When they arrived, they found a messenger waiting. The Duchesse de Tallard, married on the previous evening, was receiving calls in the Duchesse de Ventadour's bed, and the latter duchess had sent to beg the princes to honour her grand-daughter by a visit before they returned to their apartments. The reception was over, and the bride was only waiting to see them before rising from the bed. They went at once, and were greeted by, among others, the Princesse de Montauban who, not knowing what had occurred, began in her usual fulsome manner to pester M. le Duc de Berry with congratulations on his affable, gracious, and most dignified address to the Parlement, adding thereto all the flattery which she thought most likely to please. M. le Duc de Berry blushed scarlet and advanced straight towards the bed, whereupon she praised him more than ever, admiring the modesty that caused him to blush and say

[1] A *cadenas* was a case containing a special spoon and fork.

nothing, never drawing breath until they had reached the bride. The prince stood for a moment or two, and then returned to his own apartments, where he found Mme la Duchesse de Berry entertaining friends. He spoke scarcely a word, even to her; seized hold of Mme de Saint-Simon, and led her alone into his study.

Flinging himself into an armchair, he burst into tears, crying out that he had disgraced himself, and then, between weeping and sobbing, he told my wife how he had been struck dumb and shamed before all that great company, how everyone would be talking of it and calling him a fool and a simpleton. He then let fly at Mme de Montauban for her silly compliments, saying that she must have known and must have intended to mock him, and thereafter, in the extremity of his rage, calling her every bad name imaginable. Mme de Saint-Simon did everything possible to soothe him on both counts. Nothing availed, however, for he suddenly began to attack the Duc de Beauvilliers and the King for his lack of education. 'Their only thought,' said he, 'was to keep me back and stifle any talents I might possess. I was the youngest; they feared lest I become a rival to my brother, and they destroyed me. I was taught nothing except how to hunt and gamble. They have turned me into a fool, good for nothing, the mock and scorn of all.' Mme de Saint-Simon was full of compassion for him, and did her utmost to raise his spirits.

That alarming conversation lasted for nearly two hours, and then it was time to go to the King's supper. There was another similar conversation on the following day, but it was rather less charged with emotion, and Mme de Saint-Simon was able gradually to console him, although still not entirely. As for Mme la Duchesse de Berry, she hardly dared say a word, and M. le Duc d'Orléans even less. But as a matter of fact no one afterwards dared to mention the subject either in or out of his hearing, and nothing was ever said of that session of the Parlement or any part of the princes' excursion to Paris. That same day, after leaving the Palais de Justice, the Duke of Shrewsbury sent couriers to England and Utrecht, and soon afterwards a peace was signed with all the great powers, save only the Emperor.

It was on Good Friday, 14 April that Torcy entered Mme de Maintenon's room with the Chevalier de Beringhem, now master of the horse, bringing the longed-for news that peace had at last been signed, late at night on the previous Monday, by England, Holland, Portugal, and the two new Kings of Sicily and Prussia. To tell all shortly, the ratifications were received on 14 May, and on the 22nd peace was proclaimed with great solemnity in Paris. M. and Mme du Maine, who were now thinking seriously of their popularity, came from Sceaux to the Duc de Rohan's house in order to witness the ceremony in the Place Royale. They appeared on a balcony and threw money into the crowd. Such generosity would have been less kindly regarded by the King had others indulged in it. That evening there were bonfires in front of the houses, several of which were illuminated. On 25 May a *Te Deum* was sung in Notre-Dame, and that same evening there were magnificent displays of fireworks on the banks of the Seine, followed by a splendid banquet given by the Duc de Tresmes, governor of Paris, at his own expense, at the Hôtel de Ville, for the ambassadors and vast numbers of other distinguished people of the Court and Paris, of both sexes, with the King's twenty-four violinists[1] playing throughout the entire meal.

Mme la Duchesse de Berry had been delivered, at about four o'clock on the morning of Sunday, 26 March, of a prince whom they called the Duc d'Alençon. He came at seven months, and such was the adulation that almost the entire court discovered that they had either been born, or had had children thus prematurely. The rejoicings were short-lived; his delicate health provoked many alarms, and he died at midnight, on Saturday, 25 April. The King appointed the Duc de Saint-Aignan and the Marquis de Pompadour to escort the body to Saint-Denis. They left Versailles after dinner on Monday, 27 April, with the guards, pages, and coaches of M. le Duc de Berry. The Bishop of Séez[2] was carrying the heart, and for that reason took the place of honour, and M. de Saint-Aignan, as a duke, took the second place at the back of the coach. M. and Mme de Pompadour sat in front, she as governess, and the little body was placed between them. As soon as they were through the courtyards and a little way down the avenue, M. de Saint-Aignan politely made Mme de Pompadour change places with him. From Saint-Denis they bore the heart to Val-de-Grâce. M. and Mme la Duchesse de Berry were deeply affected.

The Emperor's stubbornness in holding fast to the Empire for the sake of his selfish interests obliged us to send all our armies to the Rhine and the Moselle. Villars was appointed to the Moselle, and Harcourt to the Rhine. Soon after, however, Villars excused himself on account of his wound, and asked permission to go to Barèges. Bezons took his place, and 12 and 15 May were the dates fixed for the departure of the commanders of the two armies. Harcourt then had another fit of apoplexy and, being unable to serve, he resigned. That event cancelled the journey to Barèges, for the Maréchal de Villars now accepted the Rhine army. The King gave him a hundred thousand francs for his military needs; but he had done nothing about them on the assumption that he would not serve. He left at once; so also did Bezons.

Père Tellier[3] was advancing with giant strides towards the goal of his life's ambition, for which he laboured ceaselessly in the privacy of his study, and which

[1] The violinists of the King's private orchestra.
[2] Dominique Barnabé Turgot (1667-1727); he had been Bishop of Séez since 1710.
[3] Le Père Michel Le Tellier (1643-1719), Jesuit; appointed the King's confessor in 1709. He also confessed Monseigneur on his deathbed. After the King's death he was expelled from the Court, and died at the Jesuit College of La Flèche, on the Loire, in the modern département of Sarthe. See also Vol. I, p. 499.

high office and prodigious influence enabled him to view with good hope of success. You already know the abominable nature of that Jesuit. All the omens seemed to favour him. He had to deal with a monarch who, by his own admission, was abysmally ignorant, having been raised by the queen his mother in the firm conviction that those who were called Jansenists formed a republican party within the Church and State, and were sworn enemies of his absolute rule, which was the idol he worshipped. He had throughout his life made himself inaccessible to all, save those who opposed them. He had, moreover, been brought up to yield in all things to the Vatican; to use his absolute power to oppress the Parlement, and to exile, or even to imprison, such scholars as displeased Rome by protesting against her encroachments on the rights of the Gallican Church and State. He had been carefully guided to hold fast to such views by his confessors (who were always Jesuits), and also by Mme de Maintenon, who was trained by M. de Chartres, her late director, to hold similar opinions. He had bequeathed her on his death-bed to the care of La Chétardie, and of Bissy, then Bishop of Meaux, who scarcely ever let her out of his sight.

That Bissy, whose soul was devoured by ambition beneath the pharisaical exterior of a shabby Sulpician seminarist, was permanently attached to the Jesuits, on whom he relied to make his fortune, and without whom, having no family, friends or influence, he could not hope for advancement. Bissy was too worldly not to be aware of Mme de Maintenon's dislike of Jesuits, but far too astute to leave his powerful patrons for the sake of an old woman who might die at any moment. He therefore kept concealed from her, whose daily routine made her blind to anything more distant than the tip of her nose, and who was marvellously trustful with those whom she favoured, his long and intimate connection with the Society, and allowed her to believe that he associated with Père Tellier solely for the sake of harmony within the Church and the protection of its doctrine—in other words, against Cardinal de Noailles. Indeed, he played his cards so well that Mme de Maintenon, who was gradually becoming obsessed with the affair, was glad to hear of Père Tellier's machinations with the King; for she imagined that she could work in concert with, and, as she imagined, direct him; although she showed no inclination to see or speak to him, or even to have him told more than the bare necessity required. She intended to conduct operations through Bissy, whom she firmly believed to be of one mind with herself. Père Tellier, for his part, intended to use Mme de Maintenon's influence with the King through the medium of Bissy, yet without appearing to consider her existence.

By such underhand methods they managed to gull King Louis, who accepted all their advice, and whose minister for the Church was Voysin, Mme de Maintenon's willing tool, entirely dependent on her for advancement, and as ignorant and as corrupt as anyone could desire. It was by this iniquitous intrigue that Bissy's nomination to the cardinalate was engineered. Mme de Maintenon and Père Tellier, acting separately but with equal ardour, procured it for him, and Rome gladly welcomed him as one from whom much advantage might be reaped, and who, for Rome's sake, would willingly trample on anyone or anything. For Père Tellier, Bissy's promotion offered great benefit; none the less, with so much work to be done, he felt the need for additional support.

His prime object, as I have said, was to give the Pope some hold over France, with affairs in our country that would oblige him to forgive the Jesuits and forget the matter of the Chinese ceremonies,[1] which, in their estimation, had reduced them to a pitiable condition. His secondary desire was to be revenged upon Cardinal de Noailles who, against the Jesuits' wishes, had risen to the see of Paris, with influence and credit far outweighing theirs in the distribution of benefices. Père Tellier knew the Cardinal's weakness (which the whole world later recognized when he allowed the King, without opposition, to destroy Port-Royal-des Champs); had managed to draw away from him many of his adherents, had so far embroiled him with Mme de Maintenon that she had become his worst enemy, and thereafter had put the King against him in the matter of Père Quesnel's book, the *Réflexions Morales*. Tellier hoped great things from the fact that de Noailles's salt had begun to lose its savour. What is more, the general interdiction against the Jesuits from holding any pulpit or confessional in Paris, save only that of the King, had redoubled their enmity against the archbishop; and Cardinal de Noailles had been imprudent in separating himself from those bishops, chapters, schools, clergy, and congregations who should have been his greatest support, both within and without the Church.

Père Tellier's aim was to create such disorder and schism in the affair of Archbishop de Noailles and Père Quesnel's book, that the intervention of Rome would be requested, against all the laws of the Gallican Church, all our traditions, all common sense. For it has been the established custom for all such disputes to be judged in the districts where they occur, except when an appeal is made to the Pope who, through his legates, reviews and amends the preliminary verdict, or else confirms it. Now such inquiries have always been conducted by a council, before whom the author of a disputed book defends his doctrine, and the words and meaning of challenged statements. That, however, was not Père Tellier's intention at this moment. He well knew what the result would be if the work of Père Quesnel were to be judged in that way. What he desired was to have the book suppressed by law, and afterwards to make it a matter for persecution, so as to regularize the doctrine of the Society of Jesus, which, until that time, had been merely tolerated by the Church of France. His true purpose in engineering an appeal to the Pope was to extract from him a judgment

---

[1] For the affair of the Chinese ceremonies, see Vol. I, p. 407 and Vol. II, p. 112.

in the form of a bull which, by condemning a vast number of the propositions contained in Père Quesnel's book, would by contrast honour the school of Molina[1] and turn its tenets into absolute dogma, thus destroying every other group that had hitherto enjoyed freedom within the Catholic Church. Since he could scarcely hope to have each separate group branded as anathema, he desired to gain a condemnation of them all *in globo*, so that, none being completely acquitted, all would be equally condemned. The very vagueness of the edict would allow it to be interpreted as desired, even to the condemnation of the challenged propositions in Père Quesnel's book, which were, in fact, no more than extracts from Saint Paul and other portions of the Scriptures, or else taken from the works of Saint Augustine, Saint Thomas, and the early Fathers. This was the first occasion on which anyone had dared to draw such inferences in favour of Molina, for the purpose of establishing the supremacy of his school (which is fundamentally opposed to all others), and by so doing forbid all that until then had been freely allowed by the Church.

To draw up such a bull or constitution, great skill and cunning, as well as boldness, were needed in order to save it from the cardinals and theologians of Rome and, more especially, from the followers of Saints Augustine and Thomas; to flatter Rome and the Pope with vast ultramontane claims, and yet not be so blatant as to shock the King or risk defeat in the Parlements. It had also to be worded in such a way that the Pope would feel bound to support condemnations so unwarrantable that he would be quite unable to explain them if the French bishops requested enlightenment. Pride in so-called papal infallibility would forbid his allowing others to interpret them, and he would thus be forced to demand unquestioning acceptance. With Rome and the Pope on their side and equally concerned for their interests and their difficulties; with the King of France already inclined to ask for a judgment and too much enamoured of his absolute authority not to use it to the full, the Jesuits were in a position to gain supremacy for their school at the cost of the total ruin of all the others. Supported by both King and Pope, they would then be able to impose on the ignorance or weakness of certain bishops, attract others from motives of ambition, oblige the theologians to declare themselves for one side or the other, greatly strengthen their Society, and find opportunities for destroying their opponents by persecuting all who distrusted absolute power in either King or Pope. That, unhappily, is the situation in which we now find ourselves.

Discord having thus cleverly been sown among the French bishops meeting in their councils to debate the question of Père Quesnel's book, the opinion that only Rome could give judgment was arrived at unanimously. The King accordingly wrote to the Pope asking urgently for a decision, and for one strongly weighted against Père Quesnel.[1] The Pope referred him to the previous condemnation; the

---

[1] Not Molinos (1628-1696), the Quietist, but Luis Molina (1536-1600), the Spanish Jesuit, whose doctrine, opposed to that of Jansen, played so great a part in the disputes over Grace.

King continued to press. Père Tellier, in order to place both in such a position that they could not retreat, then induced King Louis to give his royal word that any bull would be received without argument, no matter what its contents.

For Père Tellier the situation in Rome was as favourable as it appeared in France. Père Daubenton,[2] of whom I shall have further occasion to speak, the most learned and urbane of scholars, finished with the life of Society and the Court, but no less convinced a Jesuit than Père Tellier, had been dismissed from his post as confessor of the King of Spain through the intrigues of Mme des Ursins, his reputation and manœuvrings having annoyed her. He had removed himself to Rome, where he was at that time the French assistant to the General of the Jesuits, and only second to the latter in importance in the eyes of the great nation concerned. Like many other prominent members of that Society, he lived on terms of close intimacy and mutual trust with Cardinal Fabroni. I do not know whether he was one of those persons (including many most eminent, as well as the humble) whom the Jesuits by means of presents and pensions had managed to win to their side in Rome—the pensions, etc., being proportionate to the services rendered. Such methods were not new to the Jesuits, and have served them well on all occasions. Indeed, such is their usual practice; but neither those who are bribed, nor those who bribe them, are much in the habit of boasting about it. As regards Fabroni, his meagre private fortune, the open support afforded him by the Jesuits throughout his life, the diligent, sometimes passionate way in which he fought their battles and defended their interests, give one reason to suspect that he did not lend them his services for nothing. Moreover, it is widely known (he has made no effort to deny it) that he has been more ardent in the Jesuit cause than the most rabid of their party, not excluding Père Tellier himself. Fabroni was a mediocre citizen of Pistoia, but came to Rome well-equipped with brains, energy, a theological training, a readiness to labour industriously at the most unrewarding tasks, and the determination to make a name for himself at any price. Cardinal Albani,[3] at that time young and outstandingly able, sought his assistance at the Registry of Briefs;[4] made excellent use of him, and grew so accustomed to his advice that he fell under the domination of that proud and passionate character. When Albani became Pope, he made Fabroni a cardinal, thereby further strengthening the bonds of his own servitude. Thus it came about that Fabroni and Daubenton were together commissioned to draft the bull in question, by the Pope's particular wish. The King had asked for it to be composed in consultation with Cardinal de La Trémoïlle, having regard not only to the content, but also so as to avoid jeopardizing the maxims of the Gallican Church. The affair made

[1] For the origins of the Bull *Unigenitus*, see Vol. I, p. 77.
[2] Le Père Guillaume Daubenton (also spelled d'Aubenton) (1648-1721).
[3] Giovanni Francesco Albani (1649-1721). Cardinal 1690; became Pope Clement XI in 1700.
[4] Registry from which minor papal briefs were issued.

much stir. A ruling on dogma, for France, in the first instance, aroused the courts of the Vatican. The Sacred College demanded to be consulted; many of the older and more eminent of the cardinals spoke to the Pope, who decided that it would be right to seek their counsel, and promised that the bull should not be issued until they all had had time to examine it, and then only with the approval of the majority. The Pope made a similar promise to Cardinal de La Trémoïlle, whom he looked on as being in charge of the King's business. The affair had reached this point when Cardinal de Janson died, and Bissy was nominated to the cardinalate.

It was now five years since Pontchartrain had lost a wife who was in every way enchanting, perhaps the only woman who could ever have had enough goodness, sense, self-control, and patience to have endured him as a husband, and whose high reputation had supported him and kept him in office. He soon grew tired of play-acting at grief;[1] and although he already had two sons, he determined to marry again. His face, so excessively hideous and revolting (but it was agreeable and even delightful, compared with the rest of him), did not prevent his high office from making him a desirable match. Mlle de Verderonne, who was rich and an Aubespine like my mother, but only a very distant connection, was pleased to accept him.

The Chancellor, who had observed with increasing distress my conduct towards his son, took it into his head to patch up the public quarrel by insisting that I should attend the wedding. I exclaimed at the very idea. He none the less continued to press me. I appealed to his wife. She, more open to reason, tried to persuade him to let me be; but he begged, urged, became angry, spoke with the voice of authority, which he occasionally used towards me. At last I gave in. I said that it was tyrannical of him thus to force my consent; that I would never alter in my behaviour, intentions, or plans regarding his son, and would even repeat what they were; that I could not imagine what he thought to gain by dragging me to a wedding which the memory of his first daughter-in-law[2] was bound to make distressing; and that, after what had passed, I could not but think that his son would be as much embarrassed by my presence as I should be afflicted by his. I do not know what the Chancellor intended, but he was willing to acquit me of everything else, provided only that I went to the wedding and consented to notice M. de Pontchartrain now and then; in other words that I should no longer make a display of not seeing him, and of turning my back on him whenever we chanced to meet. Be that as it may, I could hold out no longer. He dared not approach Mme de Saint-Simon with a similar request. The memory of her dear cousin was still too close to her heart to allow her to attend such a ceremony without intolerable pain. She could not have brought herself to respond to the bride's eager advances, for the place that she

[1] For Pontchartrain's exaggerated grief, see Vol. I, p. 364.
[2] Mme de Saint-Simon's first cousin and great friend.

was taking hurt her too much. She said so frankly, and almost never visited her. As for me; I went to that wedding as one goes to execution. It took place at Pontchartrain before very few witnesses. The Bishop of Chartres (the diocesan) officiated. The Chancellor and his wife never ceased to weep for their first daughter-in-law, and did not attempt to conceal their tears. Their friends and relations were only a little more restrained. The entire domestic staff wept continuously. Those who supported Mlle de Verderonne remained plunged in a gloom which the sullenness of the bridegroom did nothing to dispel. I never knew two days to pass more slowly.

The evening entertainments in Mme de Maintenon's room became ever more frequent, for nothing filled the gap caused by the death of the poor Dauphine. The Duc de Noailles who, as we have seen, was now a rarity in the royal circle, attempted to ingratiate himself with an oratorio on the subject of the peace, the words by Longepierre,[1] and the music by Lande,[2] master of the chapel-music. It was several times sung before the King. This was at Marly, to which the excursion was very long.

The Duke of Shrewsbury was in some haste to return to England. He obtained a privilege never before granted to any ambassador or foreign envoy, and he regarded it as an extraordinary favour. He came alone to Marly, without a retinue and unaccompanied by the chief of protocol, to dine with Torcy, who gave him, on the King's behalf, the portrait of King Louis set in sixty thousand livres' worth of diamonds. He saw the King when he arrived, and took leave of him alone in the study. His wife arrived on the same day to dine with Mme la Princesse de Conti, and in the afternoon she also took her leave of the King in his study, after which both of them returned to Paris that same evening, and left for England without other good-byes.

The Queen of Spain was confined for the last time, giving birth to a fourth prince.[3] He was given for godparents the King and Queen of Sicily, his maternal grandparents,[4] and was named Ferdinand. By the deaths of his elder brothers he later became Prince of the Asturias. He has since married the King of Portugal's daughter by a sister of the Emperors Joseph and Charles, the last princes of the House of Austria; but has had no children by her.[1] He was born at Madrid on 23 September, 1713, and was proclaimed and sworn at the Cortés of 1724, as heir to the Spanish kingdoms.

---

[1] Hilaire Bernard de Requeleyne, so called Le Baron de Longepierre (1650-1721). He had been the Comte de Toulouse's tutor.

[2] Michel Richard de La Lande (1657-1726). One of the four masters of the chapel music.

[3] Ferdinand (1713-1759), proclaimed Prince of the Asturias in 1724, when his brother Louis Philippe de Bourbon succeeded for a few months to the Spanish throne on the (temporary) abdication of Philip V, on whose death in 1746 he became Ferdinand VI of Spain.

[4] Victor Amadeus, Duke of Savoy, and Anne Marie d'Orléans (daughter of Monsieur and his first wife Henrietta of England), King and Queen of Sicily, 1713-1720.

Daubenton and Fabroni had meanwhile ended their sinister labours with-out the knowledge of any other person, except for a general impression that they were working on a constitution to settle the French question. The document was brought with similar secrecy to the state of completion which Père Tellier had demanded. Everything about it was made abundantly clear—except the truth. Skill and cunning were the governing factors, and all the secret intentions were most completely fulfilled. Its skill could not have been greater; its audacity far surpassed anything attempted in earlier centuries because it went so far as to condemn in appropriate terms texts straight from Saint Paul, which at all times since Jesus Christ had been regarded as utterances of the Holy Ghost. Some heretics had indeed attempted to distort certain passages of the Scriptures by giving them incor-rect and far-fetched meanings; but until then, no one had ever dared to reject them outright, or to condemn them. That is where this constitution exceeded all previous attempts. Where it resembled them was in the scorn it poured on Saint Augustine and the other Fathers, whose doctrine had always been accepted by the Popes, the general councils, and the entire Church. It was indeed a hard morsel to swallow, but quite indispensable for the purpose in view. The two compilers well understood the difficulty; they could scarcely hope to pass the cardinals, to whom the terri-fying innovations would appear immensely shocking. Nor would Cardinal de La Trémoïlle accept the ultramontane principle, which was entirely necessary to win Rome's consent.

Daubenton had hitherto provided the skill; it was now for Fabroni to supply the effrontery. They clapped the printers under lock and key; drew off as many proofs as they needed; kept both type-blocks and men confined until there was no more reason for concealment; went to the Pope, and read him the document at speed. They were none the less not speedy enough to prevent Clement from being alarmed by such condemnations of Saints Paul and Augustine. He protested. Fabroni insist-ed on his hearing the whole, which Daubenton continued quietly to read. The Pope desired to keep the document in order to read it at leisure and make corrections. Fabroni proceeded to treat him as in earlier years, first bewildering him, and then bullying. Pope Clement then tried to alter course, pointing out the danger of expos-ing before the cardinals a positive condemnation of Saint Paul. Fabroni, however, would not be stopped. He stated that it was absurd to offer his work to editors, and that he would never submit to cross-questioning, nor yet should the Pope, in whose name the work was done, and whose function it was to pronounce upon it and make his own decision. Clement pleaded the promise he had given (more especially to Cardinal de La Trémoïlle) to make no pronouncement without prior consultation, and that other promise to the Sacred College that no constitution

[1] Ferdinand's wife was Marie Madeleine Josephe Thérèse Barbe of Braganza (1711-1758).

should be published until after it had been examined by sub-committees, and then only with the approval of the majority. At that point Fabroni lost his temper, telling the Pope that he behaved like a child and a weakling; presenting him with the constitution once and for all, as it stood, and adding that if the Pope had been so foolish as to give his word, he need not make matters worse by sticking to it. He then departed, leaving that pontiff utterly confused, and immediately proceeded to have his document advertised in all the places where new bulls and constitutions were customarily displayed.

This outrageous action caused considerable disturbance among the cardinals, who felt that they had been mocked and cheated. They met in small groups at one another's residences, and very soon reached a decision regarding their strongest objections. The heads of the three orders,[1] and the more eminent among the rest, went in parties of eight, ten, or six, to interview the Pope, expressing their dismay at the breaking of a solemn promise, and their indignation at seeing a doctrinal bull issued in Rome, without the prior consultation that their rights, their carmine and their office as his assessors and counsellors required. The Pope could find no answer. He protested that the document had been published without his knowledge, and tried to fob them off with compliments, excuses, and the tears that, with him, were always close at hand. That, however, did not appease them. The cardinals retired for a further examination, and to maintain their wounded dignity. Casoni, Davia, and other eminent scholars with experience in such questions, found the contents even more scandalous than the method of procedure. They returned to the Pope, declaring that his new constitution went contrary to the doctrine which the Church had upheld century after century, namely that of Saint Augustine and the other Fathers, accepted by the general councils and by every Pope except himself; that not even the heretics had dared to refute texts from the Scriptures, and that he would be the first since Jesus Christ to shake the very foundations of religion, if he condemned the actual words of Saint Paul.

What kind of fate would this bull have met in France; what would have become of Père Tellier's well-laid plans, had it been destroyed at Rome, almost before its birth? It was by a master-stroke of skill, bribery, and intrigue that the Jesuits and their adherents succeeded in warding off the death-blow. Cardinal Albani[2] and the Pope's other adherents busied themselves suggesting compromises which they had no intention of carrying out, and thus parried the first attacks. Then the advantages of remaining united with the Pope, the benefits conferred on the cardinals by his infallibility, and the increase in power which they would gain from the ultramontane maxims, persuaded the baser and more

[1] The three orders: of bishops, priests, and deacons.
[2] Not Giovanni Francesco but Annibalo Albani, made cardinal in 1711. He was the nephew of Pope Clement XI.

cautious of those prelates to give their consent. Thereafter they acted as a curb on the Sacred College, the bishops and the regular clergy, whose consciences warned them to oppose the bull, but who were at last reduced to loathing it in silence.

On the day that the bull was published in Rome, it was sent to Père Tellier by a special courier who outstripped by several days the one who brought it to the Nuncio. He received it at Fontainebleau, on Monday, 2 October, and next morning presented it to the King in private audience in the study. The Nuncio delivered it with a flowery speech in Italian, which His Majesty understood and, having been well primed by Père Tellier, replied in the most gracious manner imaginable. It was further observed that a long drive around the canal, arranged for that afternoon, was cancelled in order to allow the King to work on the document alone with Voysin, until six o'clock in the evening. In the meanwhile Père Tellier had released one or two copies, in order to test reactions. He had done this even before the Nuncio presented it to the King, and had summoned the premier président and the deputies, who were so much alarmed by the ultramontane maxims that they had sent a memorandum to the King on the previous day, 1 October.

In France, the bull had the same unfavourable reception as in Rome. There was a general outcry. Cardinal de Rohan declared that it was unacceptable; even Bissy protested. Some prelates were outraged at its having been hatched in such complete obscurity; others were horrified by the proposition on excommunication, by which the Pope became the virtual master of every crowned head; others again were scandalized by the condemnation of doctrine and texts from Saint Augustine; all were appalled by the refutation of Saint Paul's own words. Everyone in the first week was of the same mind. Cardinal de La Trémoïlle to whom, in particular, the Pope had broken his word, and who was quite unmoved by papal tears, sent a courier merely to justify himself for permitting the publication of a constitution that went against the very principles of the Gallican Church. All the ministers were roused, with the exception of the Duc de Beauvilliers. As the contents of the bull became more generally known, the Court, Paris, and the provinces rose against it. Père Tellier alone stood firm, shaking a warning finger at Bissy, as at a man still only on probation, whose hat might well not materialize if word were sent to Rome. He dealt firmly also with Rohan, and then took steps to intimidate every bishop, so far as he was able, leaving none of them unassailed.

The constitution had to be accepted, but the manner of its reception presented a problem, because of the opposition with which it had been greeted. Père Tellier, who still cultivated my society, had often tried to discuss the affair with me both before and after the appeal to Rome. I did my best to avoid such discussions, but I could scarcely bar my door against him, and particularly not at Fontainebleau,

where he was always in residence. In the end, I had answered him so firmly and
frankly, according to the truth and my personal opinions, that Mme de Saint-
Simon had reproached me, saying that I might soon find myself exiled or in the
Bastille. When the constitution arrived in France, Père Tellier asked for an interview in order to discuss it with me. I thought that he meant to show it me, for as
yet no one had seen it, and the Nuncio had not yet taken it to the King. When we
were alone together, I therefore asked to see it; but he replied that he had only the
one copy, on which he was working. He promised, however, to send me another as
soon as possible, assuring me meanwhile that the contents were good and proper,
and such as I might approve. The object of his visit, so he said, was to consult me
as to the best method of securing its acceptance. I could not help smiling at his
coming to me for advice in a matter of which he had far better knowledge, and on
which he had probably already decided. He none the less launched into a lengthy
dissertation, partly complimentary, partly on the awkwardness of the situation,
on account of the original alarm that was beginning to spread. He pressed me so
hard for advice that I said at last that he appeared to me to have a precedent to
follow in the manner by which the King had made M. de Cambrai's condemnation accepted,[1] for he had done that legally, without dispute, and according to the
proper ecclesiastical forms. I had scarcely finished before he interrupted me with
an innocent, confiding air that still astounds me, saying that he dared not take
the risk; that the method was too dangerous, and that he should be very wary of
giving the constitution into the hands of the provincial Church assemblies, under
the rule of bishops who were away from Paris and not under his eye.

I then realized that he intended to use force, and that made me argue with
him, pointing out the irregularity of acceptance only by such bishops as happened
to be in Paris. 'Happened, indeed!' said he, 'I have no thought of leaving it to
chance. What I mean to do is to summon from the provinces all the bishops who
will serve my purpose, and prevent those from coming who seem likely to cause
difficulties. What is more, since I cannot easily stop those who are now in Paris
from attending the required assembly, and since some of them may oppose me,
I shall pack the meeting with bishops *in partibus*[2] and even include some who are
nominated, but not yet in receipt of their bulls. In this way I can be sure of having
sufficient strength to drown any dissent.' I shuddered at his language, remarking
that the practice was known as trimming and selecting. 'Quite!' he exclaimed angrily, 'that is my purpose. I have no idea of submitting to any deputations.' 'But,' I
retorted, 'how can the bishops who are in Paris by chance, and those summoned
from the provinces, accept for their absent colleagues unless they are given powers

[1] In 1699.
[2] *In partibus infidelium:* in unbelieving countries; this term once applied to bishops of countries where there was no catholic
hierarchy.

of proxy?' 'That I will grant them,' said the confessor, 'because, confronted by two dangers, one must avoid the greater, and in this instance the greater lies in trusting to luck and taking no precautions. Provided that they accept the bull in the assembly, I care little for the others; and after that support, we shall see who dares to go against the Pope and the King. The bull's defects will weigh nothing in comparison with the authorities that sanction it; it will be received as it stands, which is what we require.' We continued to argue and discuss for some time longer, less, for my part, with any hope of convincing him, than from a desire to hear more. For I silently marvelled at this barefaced swindle, this ruthless trampling on every rule, and the unbelievable ingenuousness of his bland self-exposure. His frankness was something which I could never comprehend, in a man so false, so artful, so subtle; moreover, I could never see what he hoped to gain by it. He left me appalled, both by himself and by the consequences which I already foresaw.

We arranged for another session to discuss the contents of the bull, after I had received a copy, and we accordingly forgathered a few days later, while the Court was still at Fontainebleau. I thought that he looked triumphant. He had reduced Bissy and Cardinal de Rohan to obedience, and had received excellent news from his spies in Paris. I did not attempt to make truth and reason prevail with one who so obviously cared for neither, because I dared not quarrel with this dangerous man who appeared to place in me such rash confidence. I said therefore that, despite my having heard much discussion of the doctrines in the constitution, I was, like everyone else, deeply shocked by many of the propositions which it contained, and especially horrified by the direct condemnation of the words of Saint Paul. Moreover I found nothing edifying in a doctrinal bull that veiled its true meaning in obscure language, instead of enlightening men's minds with clarity and precision. I was not sufficiently learned, I continued, to discuss with him questions of theology, but regarding the claims of Rome, especially in the proposition concerning excommunication, I should make so bold as to tell him that this part of the constitution was wholly unacceptable, and ought never to be received.

He replied that we could return to that later, and at once proceeded to give me a long lecture on doctrine, whilst I, realizing the futility of argument, listened almost in silence. So went the greater part of that interview. Returning finally to the excommunications, he became evasive, well knowing that his replies were not sound. He added, however, that he would like to have one more talk with me in my lodging at Versailles, on the Friday next after the first Friday of the King's being in residence, because until then he could not leave Fontainebleau. He next informed me, with such apparent ingenuousness that I could scarcely believe my ears, of the number of bishops whom he had summoned from the provinces, and of the other measures which he had taken—divulging all with unbelievable candour. He then left me, promising to visit me again, in my lodging, on the day appointed.[1]

So that you may have a better understanding of what followed, and, more especially, of what occurred to me, I shall describe my lodging at Versailles. On one side, and on the same floor, it led into the gallery of the New Wing,[2] which is on the same level as the tribune of the chapel. On the other side, one step higher, it filled half of the wide corridor opposite the great staircase that connects the lower to the upper gallery. First there came a *demi-double*,[3] opening on to the corridor which gave light to the privies and exits. There was then an ante-room with doors to right and left, on either side of which was a bedroom with two doors, and beyond that a drawing-room with one. All these five rooms had fireplaces, and so had the first dark ante-room. The whole of this dark *demi-double* was cut by *entresols*, beneath which both drawing-rooms had small back-studies. These back rooms were lower than the drawing-rooms, through which they received their only light. All the rooms were panelled, and the back rooms had doors and windows that completely disappeared into the panelling, so that, when they were shut, the rooms themselves were invisible. In the back room on my side, I had a writing-table, my chairs and books and everything else that I needed. The few close friends who knew of its existence used to call it my den, and indeed that was not a bad name for it.

Père Tellier did not fail to come at the appointed time. I had to tell him, however, that he chose a bad moment, because M. le Duc and Mme la Duchesse de Berry had invited themselves to partake of a collation with Mme de Saint-Simon. We expected them immediately, and since they were apt to perambulate the entire apartment, I could not be sure of privacy in either my bedroom or my study. He appeared so much put out, and pressed me so hard to find a place inaccessible to visitors, that I finally admitted that there was just one possibility, and I asked him to send away Frère Vatbled,[4] so as to avoid his being seen in the ante-room. I then showed him to my den, saying that we could send for candles so as to be independent of the light from my study, and also be safe from visitors, provided we stopped talking as soon as anyone entered. He thought this an excellent expedient, and dismissed his companion. We locked ourselves in, sitting nose to nose, on either side of my writing-table, between two lighted candles standing upon

---

[1] Having been with the King every day at Fontainebleau, Père Tellier did not need to follow him to Versailles for the weekly examination of the royal conscience, which occurred on Fridays.

[2] It is now called the North Wing, situated between the entrance to the tribune of the chapel and the Salle du Théâtre.

[3] *Le double:* signified a room on the side away from the façade (in the lining).

[4] This Frère Louis Vatbled (d. 1735) held the post of Keeper of the King's Confessors, with the duty of accompanying them everywhere they went. He was attached to Père de La Chaise before Père Tellier, and later to Père de Linières, the confessor of Louis XV.

it. There he proceeded to give me a résumé of the virtues of the Bull *Unigenitus*, having brought with him a copy, which he placed on the table. I interrupted, in order to bring him to the proposition on excommunication. This we discussed with vast politeness, but very little harmony. The condemned proposition, as everyone knows, reads as follows: '*That unjust excommunication must never debar a man from doing his duty.*' As a result of the condemnation, it would now read: '*Unjust excommunication debars a man from doing his duty,*'[1] and the enormity of that premise strikes one still more forcibly than the simple truth of the original statement. The concealment of that truth is what makes it obvious. The frightful possibilities and consequences of such a condemnation must surely be plain to all.

I shall not attempt to give you the whole of our conversation. It was too long, and too animated. I explained briefly that being, as they were, at the opposite extremes of life, the King might die, and the Dauphin also; that in the event of this double disaster (for when arguing one must foresee everything, especially such events as are natural and therefore probable) the crown, by right of seniority, would pass first to the King of Spain, and then, because of the renunciations, to M. le Duc de Berry and his descendants. If the brothers should then happen to quarrel, each would find armies and allies in France to support them. In that case, supposing the constitution to have been accepted as it stood, the Pope, by excommunicating the one prince, would be free to give the crown to the other, if he so pleased. For in the light of the condemnation, no matter how just the claim of the excommunicated prince, no matter how clear his duty to stand by his followers, he would be forced to abandon them once it was accepted that unjust excommunication debars a man from doing his duty. From that moment, the Pope would be master of all the crowns of his communion, with power to remove them from their rightful owners and to dispose of them as he pleased.

This argument, so simple, to the point, and unanswerable, left Père Tellier in a state of complete bewilderment. He flushed scarlet, and began to rant and rave. After a time, however, he gathered himself together and, with a smile that seemed to promise finality, he announced, 'See! I can blow your argument to pieces in one short sentence. Now listen to me! In the event you mention, which alas! is only too probable, if the Pope sided with one or other of the contestants and excommunicated the other together with all his followers, that excommunication would be of a different kind from the one which the Pope intends by this bull. Not only would it be unjust, but absolutely wrong. Now note the difference and accept it, for the Pope, in that particular eventuality, would have no possible reason to excommunicate either prince. It has never been suggested that wrongful excommunication

---

[1] The Papal condemnation seemed to imply that there could be no such thing as unjust excommunication—in other words that the Pope was infallible.

either could or should prevent a man from doing his duty. Consequently, such a condemnation, resting on false premises, would neither advantage the one prince nor disadvantage the other, who would continue to act as though no excommunication had been pronounced.'

'Brilliantly spoken, Father!' said I. 'A fine and most subtle distinction, and one for which I must admit I was unprepared. None the less, pray allow me a few objections. Would the Ultramontanes agree on the invalidity of such an excommunication, and if unjust, would it not immediately become invalid? How could the Pope order a wrong, and, moreover, order it under pain of excommunication? If he can excommunicate unjustly, and impose obedience to his proclamation, how shall such boundless power be limited? What shall prevent his wrongful excommunications from being honoured and obeyed in the same way as are his just ones? Lastly, if this bull comes to be accepted by the bishops and parlements throughout the entire kingdom, and consequently by every preacher, confessor, and director, it will be drilled into the heads of all sorts and conditions of men that wrongful excommunication must prevent a man from doing his duty. If there should then come to pass the events which I have mentioned, do you suppose that it will be easy to persuade the peasants, soldiers, citizens, officers, lords, ladies, and the world in general of the subtle difference? Will they be able to perceive this difference in a bull fulminated by the Pope? Could you explain it to them calmly at a moment when they are taking up arms? These, Father, are very strong objections, and, between ourselves, I can see no greater reason for non-acceptance than that of preventing the Pope from taking upon himself this new authority to dethrone monarchs, release their subjects from their oaths of loyalty, and dispose elsewhere of their thrones, all of which would be contrary to the words of Jesus Christ and the Holy Scriptures.'[1]

My short exposition infuriated the Jesuit because it uncovered all his trickery and empty sophistry. He still avoided the personal issue, but he raged; and the more he restrained himself on my account, the less he could defend the question in hand. At last, as though to compensate for his moderation towards myself, he let himself go entirely regarding the methods which he proposed to use in order to force the entire kingdom to accept the bull, without modifying it in any way. In his passion, for he had lost all control, he let slip many things which I am sure he would have paid dearly could he have unsaid them. Indeed, he told me so much of his real intentions, and of his determination to use force, so much that was shocking, abominable, horrifying, all uttered with such extreme violence, that I literally felt I should faint. I gazed at his face, opposite mine between the two candles, and only separated from me by the width of the table. I have elsewhere

---

[1] Saint-Simon was thinking of the 'divine right'.

described his vile countenance.[1] In that moment, dizzy with the sound and sight of him, I was seized as he spoke with a sudden appreciation of what that Jesuit in reality was—a man who by his personal and avowed nullity had nothing to hope for, either for himself or his family, who might not have so much as an apple or a glass of wine more than his fellows, who was approaching the time when he must settle his reckoning with God, and whose deliberate purpose, plotted with extraordinary skill, was to set fire to the State and its religion, and open the door to most fearful persecutions. All this he was willing to do not for himself, but solely for the glory of the sect of Molina. The intensity, the violence which he displayed, absolutely transported me, so that I found myself suddenly interrupting him to ask, 'Father, what age are you?' His utter amazement, for I was gazing at him intently and could see it written on his face, brought me to my senses, and his reply finally restored me. 'What?' said he. 'Why should you wish to know that?' The very effort which I had to make in extricating myself after that extraordinary question, of which I fully realized the alarming import, gave me my answer. 'The fact is,' I replied, 'I have never looked at you so long and continuously until this conversation between these two candles, and, despite all your labours, the goodness and healthiness of your face is so amazing, that it truly astounds me.' He seemed to swallow this, or else put up so good a showing that I never afterwards perceived the least difference, for he had private conversations with me very often, and almost always on his visits to Versailles, and was as candid as ever, although I should have welcomed anything but that. He said he was seventy-four years of age, that his health was indeed excellent, and that he was used to leading a hard and laborious life. We then returned to the point at which I had interrupted him.

Shortly afterwards we were reduced to complete silence, and scarcely dared to move because we heard company entering my study. Happily they did not remain long, and Mme de Saint-Simon, who was aware of our plight, helped to remove them. More than two hours then elapsed; he brazenly defending himself with childish sophistry, and supporting the use of force with a mixture of arrogance and boastfulness. I, never shifting my ground, except over trifles, for I was firmly convinced that the most desperate and savage decisions were already made and decreed. We then separated, each of us still of the same mind. He left me, saying many civil things regarding my brilliance; but averring that I was mistaken, that I did not fully comprehend the matter, that my prime objection was specious and unimportant, that he was surprised but begged me to give myself more time for reflection. I firmly retorted that I had made up my mind and had no ability to do more. On the whole, however, he appeared to be extremely pleased with me,

[1] For Père Tellier's alarming appearance, see Vol. I, pp. 408-9

although he had extracted nothing solid. I, for my part, took good care to seem delighted with him.

I let him out by the little door behind my study, so as to escape notice, and when I was once more alone and locked in I flung myself exhausted into a chair and remained for a long time contemplating my extraordinary trance and the horrors that had caused it. The first effects were observable immediately after the assembly of the bishops, in Paris. That, however, belongs to the history of the bull, and there I shall leave it, returning only when I need to describe the parts that went through my hands, or in an equally curious manner under my eyes or through my ears.

The year ended with the death of the Duke of Medina-Sidonia.[1] It happened suddenly at Madrid, just as he was about to enter the King of Spain's coach, in his capacity of Master of the Horse and Knight of the Order. He was one of the greatest of the Spanish nobles, very old, and most deeply devoted to King Philip. He left a son, who also had descendants, and was head of the great and ancient House of Guzman, and premier duke of Spain; but grandeeship means everything in that country and, although his title was one of the most ancient, I have already remarked that there is no seniority among grandees. I shall have occasion to speak of him again at the time of my embassy extraordinary to Spain. I shall also mention his high office as president of the council of Castile. Ronquillo[2] held that same office at one time, and in his official capacity refused to give his hand to M. de Vendôme at a reception, despite that unwarrantable 'Highness', and the rank which Mme des Ursins had secured for M. de Vendôme, for the sole purpose of gaining similar rank for herself.

The Duc d'Aumont returned from his embassy to England, and had a long audience of the King in his study. One noticed that he affected all kinds of English fashions, even down to attaching his cross to the blue ribbon, in the way a Knight of the Garter wears his star. His return was not greeted with loud applause, but the money which he had managed to extract from that country may somewhat have consoled him.

The Elector of Bavaria arrived in Paris, on Monday, 18 December, from Compiègne. He went to Versailles on Wednesday the 20th, saw the King after dinner, and was shown up through the back offices in the usual way. They were closeted together for half an hour. The Elector then returned to Paris, where he saw very few people, being vastly disappointed at no longer having any expectation of becoming King of Sardinia.

---

[1] Juan Claros Alfonzo Perez de Guzman-el-Bueno (1642-1713). He was the eleventh duke.
[2] Francis Ronquillo, governor of the council of Castile from 1705 to 1713 (d. 1719). His son Pedro was killed in 1710 at the Battle of Villaviciosa.

CHAPTER V

1714

The King gives no presents for the New Year - The Bull Unigenitus, *persecutions begin - Mortal illness of the Queen of England - Death of the Queen of Spain - Philip V retires to the Medina-Celi Palace - Death of Mme de Moissens - Death of Charmel, the King's unkindness to him - Death and Character of the Maréchale de La Ferté and her sister the Comtesse d'Olonne - The Princesse des Ursins is disappointed of her kingdom - Her intrigue to take the place of the late queen - She contrives the marriage of King Philip to the Princess of Parma - Visits of the Marquis de Brancas and Cardinal del Giudice to the Court - Death of the Chancellor's wife - The Duc de Berry ill from poisoning - Death of the Duc de Berry - Death of the Maréchale d'Estrées - Death of the Duchesse de Lorges - Spain signs a peace treaty - The King of Spain tardily announces his approaching marriage - The King's cryptic word regarding Mme des Ursins - Retirement of the Chancellor - I become acquainted with Maisons - The bastards pronounced capable of the succession - Death of Queen Anne - The King makes a will - Trouble over the Bull* Unigenitus *- M. le Duc d'Orléans is taken poorly - The monstrous affair of the bonnet - Black treachery of M. du Maine - The bastards triumphant - I speak my mind*

ON THE first day of this year, 1714, neither the grand nor the first almoner happened to be present at the high mass of the Order. Thus there was some difficulty in deciding whether the almoner on duty, or Cardinal de Polignac, who did not have the Order but was standing by the prayer-stool, should present the Gospel for the King to kiss. The King chose Polignac. He gave no presents that year. The only people concerned were Mme la Duchesse de Berry, with whom he was displeased, and Madame, whose pension he had recently very greatly increased. As for M. le Duc de Berry he did not need to consider him, for only a year earlier his pensions had been augmented by four hundred thousand livres. A few days later, the King desired him to attend the finance council, but to be present at several meetings before expressing an opinion, just as he had remained mute at the meetings of the Conseil des Dépêches before becoming a full member. The King had followed this same procedure with Monseigneur and with Mgr le Duc de Bourgogne.

That winter was rich in Court balls. There were several, both in full dress and in masks, at the apartments of M. le Duc de Berry and Monsieur le Duc,[1] and elsewhere. There were balls also in Paris and at Sceaux, where Mme du Maine gave numerous banquets and nightlong dances,[2] and acted in plays. Everyone from Paris and the Court attended, and M. du Maine did the honours. Mme la Duchesse de Berry was pregnant and attended no balls, except those given in her own house. On account of her pregnancy, the King allowed her to come to his supper in her dressing-gown. In similar circumstances, only the two Dauphines had had that privilege.

The Abbé Servien, whom I have already mentioned,[3] could not endure the lengthy praises of the King in the prologue at the Opera. He suddenly emitted out loud the most outrageous parody; but so apt and so comical that the entire audience echoed it and applauded him. Two days later, he was seized and taken to Vincennes *incommunicado*, with no servant to wait on him. Seals were placed on his papers, for form's sake; but he was not the kind of man to possess any documents fit for a better purpose than to light the fire. Indeed, even at the age of sixty-five, which he then was, he was most monstrously depraved.

We now come to the firing of the first volleys in defence of the constitution, and the beginning of that persecution which has created thousands of confessors and a few martyrs, depopulated the schools and colleges, encouraged ignorance, fanaticism, and vice, rewarded wickedness, put all religious communities into utter confusion, made disorder everywhere, established the most tyrannous and cruel inquisition, and all the horrors that have increased continually during the past thirty years. Let that sentence suffice; I shall not further blacken these memoirs, for apart from the actions which we every day observe, many writers have concerned themselves with the affair and are still so concerned. That is not the way of the teaching of Jesus Christ; but of Reverend Fathers[4] and their ambitious adherents.

The Queen of England fell gravely ill at Saint-Germain, and received the Last Sacraments. The doctors gave her up, and she was glad of it. Life had held nothing for her for many years past, but she had put her unhappiness to most

---

[1] On 9 July, 1713, Monsieur le Duc had married Mlle de Conti (Marie Anne de Conti, 1689-1720), and on the same day, the Prince de Conti had married Mlle de Bourbon (1693-1775). Mme de Maintenon, writing to the Princesse des Ursins on 10 July, said, 'Our weddings are over. I cannot say to the extreme happiness of all the parties concerned, for Mlle de Conti wept yesterday during mass. She fell on returning from the offertory and felt ill. I think that very high heels and very tight stays may have contributed. They say that Monsieur le Duc notices all her faults, but likes her for her docility; everyone speaks well of her.' Later, on 17 July, 'The two princes are with the armies. They say that the Prince de Conti is madly in love, and that Monsieur le Duc is very fond of Madame la Duchesse.'

[2] She suffered from insomnia and loved her parties to go on all night. She once gave fourteen in succession.

[3] Augustin Servien (d. 1716). Saint-Simon says of him that, although monstrously debauched, he had a pretty wit, and was vastly cultivated and agreeable.

[4] Meaning the Jesuits.

pious use. The King paid her the greatest possible attention during her last sickness, and Mme de Maintenon did likewise.

The Queen of Spain had for a long time suffered severe attacks of scrofula around her face and throat. She was now *in extremis*. Unable to obtain any help from her doctors, she desired to have Helvétius,[1] and begged the King, by a special courier, to send him to her. Helvétius, who felt highly embarrassed and knew the hopelessness of the queen's condition, was most loath to go; but the King gave him peremptory orders. He left forthwith in a post-chaise, followed, lest there should be an accident, by one containing Orry's son.[2] Who but a prophet could then have foretold that this Orry would become controleur-général in France, with enormous powers and for a very long time, and a minister of State as well? We might have dispensed with his services as easily as Spain could have done with his father's, who, at that time, lived in a splendid apartment at the royal palace, and whose favour and administration displeased the Spaniards more and more. Helvétius arrived at Madrid on 11 February. He saw at a first glance that only a miracle could save the queen. She had a Jesuit confessor, but followed the example of her sister Madame la Dauphine. When the time came for the Last Sacraments and for serious thoughts of death, she thanked him, and sent for a Dominican instead. The King of Spain continued to sleep in her bed until the 9th. She died on Wednesday the 14th, displaying great wisdom, fortitude, and piety.

The king immediately left the palace, and established himself at the other side of Madrid, in the palace of the Duke of Medina-Celi. It was not far from Buen-Retiro,[3] where the princes of Spain were soon afterwards taken. There was mourning throughout the whole country, for the queen had been most truly loved. Not a family living in the provinces but wept at her death, and no one in Spain has yet recovered from their loss. I shall speak of this again at the time of my Spanish embassy. The King of Spain was much moved, but somewhat in the royal manner. They persuaded him to go out hunting and shooting, so as to breathe the fresh air. On one of these excursions, he found himself within sight of the procession that bore the queen's body to the Escorial. He gazed after it; followed it with his eyes, and went back to his hunting. Princes, are they human?[4]

King Louis greatly lamented the death of the Queen of Spain. He wore violet mourning for six weeks. M. le Duc de Berry draped also. Mme de

[1] Adrien Helvétius (1661-1727), son of a doctor, father of the encyclopaedist. He had been Monsieur's physician, had continued in the service of the Duc d'Orléans, and had been made inspector-general of the Flemish hospitals in 1710. See also Vol. I, pp. 150-1.

[2] Philibert, Comte de Vignory (1689-1747). He was made contrôleur-général des finances in 1730, and a minister of State in 1736. He was the son of Jean Orry (1652-1719).

[3] Buen-Retiro was a holiday palace built by Philip IV at the gates of Madrid.

[4] M. de Brancas, however, wrote to Torcy on 13 February, 'I am most surprised at the little grief displayed by the court and the townspeople at the death of the queen, especially having seen how generally her subjects adored her.'

Saint-Simon did not wish to drape; she said, very reasonably, that she was not separated from her husband as were the Duchesses of Ventadour and Brancas; that her coaches were mine, and that I was not draping. They argued for several days, but in the end M. and Mme la Duchesse de Berry made it a point of honour, and begged so hard that we were obliged to comply. Thus we found ourselves parti-coloured in our private lives, with some of our coaches and liveries black, and others coloured.

Mme de Moissens died at this time, aged seventy-eight, in a fine self-contained lodging, lent her by the King, at the farm of the Luxembourg Palace. He afterwards gave it to Mme de Caylus. Mme de Moissens was as good a woman as her younger sister Mme d'Heudicourt was bad. She had very little in the way of wealth and seldom appeared at the Court. She was excessively thin, with a figure that was alarming because of its gigantic height. Her eyes blazed, her face was scarlet, and she had long, white teeth that projected monstrously; altogether, she looked very like a witch. She lived a secluded and pious life, and had no children by her husband who was killed in 1672, in a duel with Saint-Léger Corbon.

You have read, in its appropriate place, of the Comte du Charmel's devotion to Mlle Rose;[1] how he went into voluntary exile, and stubbornly refused ever again to see the King. King Louis's resentment against those who retired to their estates and never came to see him was the chief reason for his disgrace. His grudge against Le Charmel did not lessen; it rather degenerated into a terrible callousness, to say the least. Le Charmel, suffering from a stone, begged leave to come to Paris to be cut. Permission was firmly refused.[2] The need was pressing; he was obliged to have the operation at Le Charmel. It was so severe, or perhaps so badly done, that he died in three days, having displayed the most noble sentiments of piety and repentance. It is rare indeed to carry devotion so far, and to sustain it with the fervour and exactitude which Le Charmel practised, in an infinity of good works and other religious exercises. He had hardly any book-learning, and no polish or wit, except such as remained to him from having lived in the best Society.

The Maréchale de La Ferté died in Paris at this same time, aged over eighty. She was the mother both of the Duc de La Ferté and of the Jesuit Père de La Ferté, and was the elder sister of the Comtesse d'Olonne[3] who was enormously rich, and childless, whereas the maréchale herself was extremely poor. Mme d'Olonne was the widow of a cadet of the Trémoïlle family, who all his life had made a gaming- and bawdy-house of his home. The two sisters had been born

---

[1] See Vol. I, pp. 149-150.
[2] It was the suspicion of Jansenism that made the King so cruel to him.
[3] The sisters were Madeleine d'Angennes (1629-1714), widow of the Maréchal-Duc de La Ferté, and Catherine Henriette d'Angennes, Comtesse d'Olonne (1634-1714). Mme d'Olonne had been the mistress of the Prince de Condé. Her husband was Louis de La Trémoïlle-Royan, Comte d'Olonne (1626-1686).

d'Angennes, of a junior branch that became extinct with them. Their beauty and debauchery had caused a great scandal. No woman, not even those most notorious for their love affairs, had dared to see or be seen with them anywhere. So it was in the old days; things now are very different. When they were old and people still would have nothing to do with them, they tried to turn to religion. They lodged together, and, on one Ash Wednesday, they went to hear the Lenten sermon. This sermon was on fasting and the absolute need for penitence. It gave them a thorough fright. 'Sister,' remarked one to the other after they had returned to their home, 'this is become serious; it is no laughing matter; if we do not do our penance, we shall be damned. Sister, what must we do?' There was a long pause. 'My dear,' replied Mme d'Olonne, 'this is what we must do. We must let the servants fast.' She was indeed a monstrously greedy woman and, despite all her intelligence, of which she had much, she fully believed that she had devised an excellent solution. None the less, she did in the end, in all sincerity, turn to piety and repentance, and died three months after her sister the maréchale. Although the maréchal's husband had been a hot-tempered man, he was perpetually gulled by her, or else he put up an excellent show of so being. No one can ever forget that it was she who made it easy to legitimize a bastard without mentioning the mother's name; for on her example (which I have mentioned)[1] was based the legitimization of the King's children by Mme de Montespan.

The Duke of Berwick was appointed by the King to convey his compliments and condolences to the King of Spain. There was also the matter of the siege of Barcelona, and the surrender of the Catalans, who still held out there despite the peace, and were receiving secret assistance. Mme des Ursins relished that supple courtier Tessé too much to desire a change of general, and had, through King Philip, asked for his recall from Italy. But Tessé had nothing further to gain at Madrid, and did not at all wish to be landed with that burdensome mission. The King and Mme de Maintenon, for their part, and for reasons that will appear, preferred the Duke of Berwick to any other candidate. Quite apart from his ability, keenness, and knowledge of Spain, Berwick was on exceedingly bad terms with Orry, having treated him on several occasions as he deserved. Thus he was little to Mme des Ursins' taste, for she found him honest, stubborn, and stiff as a ramrod, all qualities which she least liked to encounter, especially in the commander of an army. The King allowed the Duke of Berwick fifteen battalions, and Ducasse was appointed to command the naval squadron that supplied all the needs of the siege; but illness, and later contrary winds, somewhat delayed his departure.

You must now recall all that had happened regarding that royal status which Mme des Ursins had planned to gain by the peace treaty so long and so

[1] See Vol. I, p. 47, referring to the legitimization of the bastard son of Charles Paris, Duc de Longueville, and the Maréchale de La Ferté. He had been known as Charles Louis d'Orléans.

scandalously delayed by the King of Spain; how she had counted on obtaining a kingdom and exchanging it later with King Louis for Touraine and the districts around Amboise; how she had commissioned her faithful d'Aubigny to build her a splendid palace there, and how it was almost completed by the time that all her hopes were blighted.

To Mme de Maintenon, the thought of royal rank for herself was so far beyond her wildest dreams that she received a most unpleasant shock. It hurt her pride to feel the differences in birth and breeding that had rendered the Princesse des Ursins' ambitions not wholly beyond the range of possibility. She felt jealous because the all-powerful influence that had borne the other lady so high was largely her doing and the result of her support. She thought it disgraceful in the princess to wish to rise above her protectress, and to flaunt regal state beneath that lady's very nose. The King himself considered such ambitions wholly unwarranted, and was much vexed to find the peace delayed for such a reason. He had greatly disliked being obliged to use persuasion, and, when that had failed, having to speak to his grandson as a parent and a master, and to conclude the peace despite him; for King Philip had refused to comply, and in the end had yielded only because of the impossibility of continuing the war without the aid of France, and for so absurd a reason.

You may well picture the fury of Mme des Ursins who, after pressing her claim with such extravagant tenacity, now found herself the laughing-stock of Europe, having reaped nothing but scorn from her daring intrigue. There had thus arisen a barrier between the two supreme directresses of France and Spain, which was one of the reasons that had made the King prefer Berwick to Tessé. After the princess's attempt to secure royal rank, things were never the same again between her and Mme de Maintenon;[1] but Mme des Ursins had reached such heights in Spain that she felt well able to dispense with her former protector. You already know how artfully she had contrived to isolate King Philip, how she had kept him immured with the queen and inaccessible, not only to the courtiers, but also to his great officers of State, and even to most of his staff, so that in the end he was served by three or four valets, all of them French, and all devoted only to Mme des Ursins. On the pretext that he was mourning the loss of his queen, his solitude was prolonged, and the privacy of the Medina-Celi was preferred to Buen-Retiro, where his courtiers might have assembled and their access to him have been harder to prevent. Mme des Ursins filled the queen's place, and, as an excuse for remaining with him during his retirement, appointed herself governess to his children. Moreover, to avoid its becoming known how much they

[1] Mme de Maintenon's letter to the Princesse des Ursins, 19 July, 1714: 'Our letters would certainly be far from dull were we to say what we really thought. I might expect to hear very little praise for us, and you would hear much blame for the manner in which you keep His Catholic Majesty to yourself, thus excluding him from an entire nation that has never appeared to lack merit. But what purpose would be served by our disputing?'

were together, she ordered the construction of a wooden corridor to connect the King's study with the apartments of his children, where she lodged. By this means they were able to visit one another at all times, un-watched, and without having to traverse a long series of vast rooms crowded with courtiers. It was thus impossible to discover whether the king was by himself or with Mme des Ursins, which of them was visiting the other, or how much time they spent together. This wooden 'lean-to', roofed, and with windows, was put up in such haste that even on holy days and Saints' festivals the work continued, which the court found very shocking, as did those who directed the workmen. The controller of the king's buildings, who first received the order to make the men work on such days, asked Père Robinet[1] the king's confessor (and the only good one he ever had) whether the men should not rest on the Sunday and Monday of the Ascension. Robinet replied that the king had said nothing to him, and made the same answer a second time. At the third attempt he said that he must wait for the king to speak first. At the fourth, he lost patience, and answered that if it were a question of destroying the work already accomplished he thought that such labour, even on Easterday, might be forgiven; but to finish that particular passage he believed that work on holy days and Saints' days was certainly not necessary. The entire court applauded him; but his words reached the ears of Mme des Ursins, and she was far from pleased.

It was thought that she aspired to be something more to King Philip than his sole companion, and the rumour spread with alarming speed. It was hinted that the king having no need for offspring, since he already had so many, desired only to have a wife who would educate them; that Mme des Ursins, not content with spending the entire day with him, and, like the late queen, being present when he worked with his ministers, reckoned that it would be wisest to secure her grip by gaining access to him at all hours of the day and night. He was used to fresh air, and had begun to need it the more for having been so long confined during the queen's last illness and in the days following her death. Mme des Ursins appointed four or five gentlemen to go with him, excluding all others, even those high officers of State, whose company he most needed. Chalais, Masseran, Robecq,[2] and one or two others surrounded the king whenever he took the air. They became known as the king's *recreadores* (men chosen to keep him amused). These precautions and sieges, together with hints deliberately dropped in conversation, finally convinced everyone that what she intended was to marry him. There was general dismay. His grandfather was thoroughly alarmed, and Mme de Maintenon who, although twice on the very verge of it had never been proclaimed queen, grew

[1] Le Père Pierre Robinet, Jesuit (b. 1656). He had been appointed confessor to Philip V in 1705, and was disgraced in 1715.
[2] Mme des Ursins' nephew, Jean Louis de Talleyrand; the Marquis de Crèvecœur (1687-1743), who became Prince de Masseran in 1720; and Charles de Montmorency, Prince de Robecq (d. 1716).

green with envy. But if Mme des Ursins ever seriously entertained such high hopes, she did not do so for long. The King of Spain, hungry for news of his native France, used often to question his confessor, the only person other than herself to whom Mme des Ursins allowed him to speak privately. Robinet was as anxious as any courtier to foresee the end of a plot whose existence no one at the courts of France or Spain doubted for a moment. With extraordinary skill and courage, he allowed himself to be drawn into a window recess and plied with questions, putting on meanwhile such an air of mystery and reserve that the king's curiosity was roused. When the desired effect had been achieved, Robinet said that if the king insisted on an answer, he must confess that the gossip in France was the same as at Madrid, namely that the king was about to honour the Princesse des Ursins by making her his wife. Thereupon the king had flushed, sharply retorting, 'Oh! no, certainly not that!'; and had immediately quitted him.

Whether or not Mme des Ursins learned of that blunt answer, or whether she already despaired of success I do not know, but she turned about-face and, realizing that his state of suspension in the Medina-Celi Palace could not last for ever, resolved to keep the king by some other means. A queen, so she imagined, who owed her spendid situation to herself and had no other support, would be bound to seek refuge in her arms, out of gratitude and from necessity. She accordingly summoned Alberoni, who since the Duc de Vendôme's death had been acting as chargé d'affaires for the Duke of Parma, and proposed a marriage with the Princess of Parma,[1] daughter of the late Duke and of the Duchess of Parma, and niece of the ruling duke, who had married his brother's widow. Such a disproportionate alliance appeared to Alberoni so impossible that he saw no hope of ever gaining the consent of France, nor had he the least idea that they would dare to proceed without it. For plainly, a young person, the issue of double bastardy, by a Pope on her father's side and by an illegitimate daughter of Charles V on her mother's, and herself the daughter of an insignificant Duke of Parma, was scarcely the stuff from which to make a Queen of Spain.

The Princesse des Ursins, however, was deterred by no such scruples. Ruling, as she did, the King of Spain, and knowing that the feelings of the King and Mme de Maintenon had changed towards her irrevocably, she actually determined to defy them; by hook or by crook to force this marriage which held so much promise for her, and then to use the new queen as she had used the old. King Philip was pious; he needed a wife; the princess, herself, had reached an age when all her charms required artful assistance. She therefore set Alberoni to work, and you may well believe that in Parma no difficulties were raised, once it was

---

[1] Elizabeth Farnese (1692-1766), Princess of Parma, Queen of Spain. Married Philip V as his second wife on 4 September, 1714.

discovered that she meant business. Orry, still working by her side, and through her influence all-powerful, was her sole confidant in this mighty intrigue.

At that time the Marquis de Brancas was, as I have already mentioned, the French ambassador to Spain. He had expected to be made a grandee when King Philip left Gerona, and had been very close to becoming one; but he firmly believed that Mme des Ursins had reduced that honour to a Fleece, and he had never forgiven her. He was Mme de Maintenon's ally, and therefore highly suspect in the eyes of the princess who, in any case, knew that he bore her a grudge for his lost honour. She therefore allowed him no access to the king and kept watch on him everywhere else. Brancas, however, was aware of all that was happening, for the king's confessor confided to him, as a fellow Jesuit, all his anxieties, and the leading figures of that unhappy court unburdened themselves also, believing that only France could rescue them. Brancas saw all the dangers, but remembering the fate of the Abbé d'Estrées,[1] and fearing even for his couriers, he begged the King to summon him for two weeks to Versailles, on urgent business too dangerous to commit to paper. An answer came with the King's consent, but instructing him to wait at some place on the road to France, where he might meet and confer with the Duke of Berwick, on his way to the siege of Barcelona.

Mme des Ursins, who always contrived to know everything, learned before-hand, not only of Brancas's return to France, but also of his intended meeting with Berwick. She took fright, and pressed so hard through the King of Spain for the maréchal's presence that such a meeting became impossible. She then posted sixteen relays of mules along the road to Bayonne, and sent Cardinal del Giudice, the Grand Inquisitor and a minister of State, post-haste to France, making him leave on Holy Thursday—he being base enough to truckle to her. By that means she killed two birds with the same stone, for although Giudice was then her slave, she thought that a cardinal, Grand Inquisitor and minister of State might at any moment become an embarrassment. Thus she rid herself of him for the time being, and meanwhile charged him with a mission, trusting in the authority of his robes and his high offices in Spain. She had also gained a start on Brancas, which at our Court was no small advantage.

Brancas, seeing the need for haste, followed on Good Friday and made such speed that he overtook Giudice at Bayonne on the night when he slept there. As he drove through that town, he bade the commandant entertain and delay the cardinal for as long as possible on the following day, and meanwhile pressed on, arriving at Bordeaux escorted by twenty-eight led post-horses, having collected them along the way in order to deprive Giudice of their use. He thus reached Paris two days in advance; went

---

[1] When the Abbé d'Estrées was ambassador to Spain, Mme des Ursins intercepted and read his letters to Louis XIV. See Vol. I, p. 236.

straight thence to Marly, and reported at once to the King. He was granted a very long audience, with Torcy present, and was given a lodging for the remainder of his stay. The cardinal, on the other hand, rested four or five days in Paris, and then called on Torcy, who presented him to the King after his *lever.* He was closeted with them for a full hour, after which Torcy gave him dinner, and soon after that he returned to Paris. According to what Torcy told me later, Giudice was somewhat at a loss to explain why he had come. He had no official business to transact; indeed his entire mission was to praise Mme des Ursins and complain of the Marquis de Brancas. His praises were of necessity rather vaguely worded, for the princess had not trusted him sufficiently to reveal her true situation at our Court, and had given him no other instructions. Thus his business with the King concerning her was soon finished. As for the Marquis de Brancas, there was no specific crime of which to accuse him; his guilt was only in having been too clear-sighted and insufficiently devoted to the princess.[1]

Cardinal Giudice was a man of parts, a courtier, statesman, and intriguer, who felt all the indignity of so trifling a mission for a man of his rank and importance. He was agreeable in conversation, affable, waiving differences of rank and office, and making himself much relished and sought after in good Society. He waited assiduously on the King, not importuning him for audiences which his mission did not justify, but showing by his behaviour that he was unaware of Mme des Ursins' decline in favour. His presence appeared to be due to his desire to gain esteem and trust, so as to enlist the support of the King in his hope of becoming Spain's first minister; but as we shall see in due course, this ultramontane goose-chase ended in destroying all his hopes. His sole achievement lay in preventing the return of Brancas to Spain; but there, although he did not know it, Brancas was more than half of the same mind, for he had nothing to gain at the Spanish court while his relations with Mme des Ursins were so bad, and he was not a man knowingly to waste his time. It was necessary to follow the course of this affair so far. Let us now retrace our steps.

For a long time past, Mme de Pontchartrain,[2] the wife of the Chancellor, had been threatened with dropsy of the chest, after almost a lifetime of asthma. She was the daughter of Maupéou, president of one of the courts of law, and had not been wealthy; but she was a good match for Pontchartrain who, at the time of his marriage, had had even less. It would be impossible to imagine an uglier woman; but she was stout, well-shaped and fresh-complexioned, with an imposing air and something of refinement. No other minister's wife, no other lady, for that matter, ran her

---

[1] The cardinal's real business was to try to secure some modifications of the 'renunciations' of Philip V, which Saint-Simon would surely have known from the Duc d'Orléans. It is strange that he does not mention this.

[2] Mme de Pontchartrain was Marie de Maupéou, who married Louis Phélypeaux de Pontchartrain in 1668. Her father was Pierre III de Maupéou, Seigneur de Monceau.

house half so well, combining comfort with grandeur, and avoiding mishaps
with infinite tact and foresight, and no appearance of embarrassment. She was
exceedingly dignified, with that exquisite politeness that measures and discrimi-
nates between degrees of age and rank, and thus puts everyone at ease. She
had also much wit, though she always tried to conceal that fact, and a pleasant
and resourceful mind. Thus she could adapt herself to suit her company, but
was never insincere; indeed, when occasion offered, she displayed a gaiety, quite
astonishing; but combined it with admirable good sense and an ability to sum
people up such as few men of her day possessed. It was indeed surprising that a
woman of the professional class, who had known only Breton society, should in
so short a time have made herself familiar with the manners, airs, and language
of the Court, and have become one of the best guides to good deportment.
Throughout their entire marriage, she was a strong support to her husband,
who made no mistakes when he heeded her advice, and went astray only when
he ignored her.

No one was better at entertaining. She vastly enjoyed it, was most enterpris-
ing, and very lavish both in- and out-of-doors; but she gave no parties without
good reason, and those she gave were quiet and modest, never unbecoming to
her age, rank, and status. As a relation she was ever willing to assist; as a friend,
most staunch, most obliging, the best and truest in every possible way. She was
delightfully at ease in her country home; but was a menace at meals because she
so prolonged them, for she understood good food, and although she scarcely
pecked herself, would encourage her guests to stuff themselves to bursting point.
She was occasionally extremely funny, but never at all vulgar, and always she was
gay, although there were times when she allowed it to be seen that she possessed
a temper. Her piety and virtue increased with her wealth. What she gave in
pensions; what impoverished girls she settled in matrimony; what nuns she made
(but only when she was sure of their vocation); how many others she rescued;
how many she put in the way of earning a living, cannot be counted. Her charity
deserves a single example. One Sunday, as she was leaving the parish church
of Versailles with Mme de Saint-Simon, she lagged behind a little. My wife,
who was in a hurry because she was dining at Meudon with Mme la Duchesse
de Bourgogne, made her come on, asking with some surprise the name of the
little guttersnipe to whom she had been speaking. 'Isn't she pretty?' said Mme de
Pontchartrain, 'I was so struck by her that I asked who the parents were. The child's
dying of hunger, aged fourteen or fifteen. With that lovely face she would soon
learn the trade; poverty will drive people to anything. I gave her a little talking-
to, and she is coming to see me tomorrow morning. I shall send her at once into
some safe place where they will teach her to earn an honest living.'

She did the like day after day, all unknown, for she told no one about her charities except Mme de Saint-Simon, whom she regarded as her *alter ego*. But in addition to such chance encounters, she maintained an entire community for poor girls, at Versailles, and brought them up to be pious and industrious, and fed and found them in everything as well as providing for them after they had grown up. She and the Chancellor built and endowed a hospital at Pontchartrain, where the spiritual and bodily needs of the sick were abundantly supplied, and where they themselves went often to care for the poor. It cost them more than two hundred thousand livres a year. Of all the good that they did, nothing was visible except that hospital, and the community at Versailles, which could not be hidden, although only the outside walls were known. All the rest remained a profound secret.

She gave her orders every morning, and attended to her domestic affairs. After that the subject was never mentioned, and yet everything in her house ran on oiled wheels. What betrayed her was the year 1709. The scarcity and high prices then caused a kind of famine in France. She doubled the amount she customarily gave in alms, because the country people were dying of hunger, she set up ovens and soup-kitchens at Pontchartrain, where her servants gave loaves of bread to all comers, and roasted meat to most of them as well, from sun-up to sunset. No one was sent away without enough to feed two or three people for several days, and with soup for one day. The crowd sometimes numbered more than three thousand persons, but they were so well marshalled that no one was pushed or suffered to miss his turn, and everything was ordered so quietly that no one would have guessed that more than fifty were present. The greater the crowd the better Mme de Pontchartrain was pleased; and she continued in that way for six or seven months. The Chancellor was delighted to share in these good works, and allowed her complete freedom. Their union, their affection, their respect were mutual and very great. Only on rare occasions were they separated by distance; and they shared a bedroom. They shared the same friends, the same relations, the same society. In everything they were united. Such was the Chancellor's wife, whom God tried more and more with long and painful illnesses, ending with dropsy of the lungs, which she bore with a patience and courage that were an example to the Court and Society. For several months before she died, she lived secluded in the midst of Versailles, seeing only her immediate family, Mme de Saint-Simon, and the good women who nursed her night and day. There she died on Thursday, 12 April, mourned by the entire Court, who all loved and esteemed her, and by the poor, who wept for her as though their hearts would break. The Chancellor retired to his small apartment at the Oratory in order to hide his sorrow. Mme de Saint-Simon and I were most deeply afflicted; we never had a kinder friend. Of her entire family, not excluding her servants, the only one who took her death calmly was her son.

Peace with the Emperor and the Empire was declared, a *Te Deum* was sung, and there were fireworks in the evening. The King, happening to be at Marly, where the *Te Deum* could not be sung at mass, went to hear it at five o'clock in the evening, at the parish church. The Duc de Tresmes[1] gave a great supper at the Hôtel de Ville, and another, at midnight at his own house, for a vast number of ladies, foreigners, and courtiers.

That particular Marly was once again very tragic. It will be best to start from the beginning; for it was on that excursion also that the Marquis de Brancas arrived, and Cardinal del Giudice saw the King, with many other events that I have already described.

A few days earlier, Mme de Saint-Simon had felt unwell and returned from Versailles to our house in Paris. She fell sick there with measles. Towards the end of her illness, the King went to Marly. A few days later, Mme de Lauzun[2] and I each received a note from Blouin, to inform us that the King was giving us lodgings at Marly; that measles was not like smallpox, and that we had his permission to appear on the following day. That kind of permission was an order, and such an order was a favour and distinction that made other people jealous. As soon as Mme de Saint-Simon was able to travel, she went to Mme de Lauzun's at Passy for a change of air, intending to return to Versailles on the same day as the King; for the Marly was announced as of long duration. Mme la Duchesse de Berry, who was with child, felt indisposed and was very glad to remain behind at Versailles, as she often did during the Marlys; and although the King did not care for such separations, he was somewhat relieved, for she had no such talent as Madame la Dauphine had possessed, for amusing him and Mme de Maintenon.

On Monday, 30 April, the King took physic, and worked after dinner with Pontchartrain. At about six o'clock, he visited M. le Duc de Berry, who had been feverish throughout the night. He had said nothing about it when he rose, and had attended the King's physicking, with the idea of stag-hunting later; but when he left the King at nine o'clock, a severe attack of the shivers sent him back. A high fever developed. He was bled, with the King standing by his bedside. They found his blood in a very bad state. The doctors told the King at his *coucher* that the nature of the illness was such as to make them hope it was a poison.[3] He had vomited very much, and the vomit was black. Fagon said confidently that it was blood; the other doctors blamed some chocolate which he had taken on the Sunday. From that time onwards, I knew what to believe. Boulduc, the

---

[1] The Duc de Tresmes was governor of Paris and therefore gave the official banquets on public occasions.
[2] The Duchesse de Lauzun, Geneviève Marie de Lorges, Mme de Saint-Simon's sister and greatest friend. She was aged thirty-four in 1714. Saint-Simon and his wife were aged thirty-nine and thirty-six, respectively.
[3] Because poisons were what the doctors knew most about.

King's apothecary, who was deeply attached to Mme de Saint-Simon and me, and whom I have more than once mentioned, whispered to me that he would not recover, and that, with little alteration, it was the same as with Monsieur and Madame la Dauphine. He confirmed that opinion on the following day, and did not change it, neither during the course of the short illness, nor later. On the third day, he said that none of the doctors attending the prince had any doubts about it and that they had said so to Boulduc himself. The doctors concerned were quite certain, and spoke to him fairly frankly.

On Tuesday, 1 May, after a miserable night, he was bled from the foot at seven in the morning. He was twice given an emetic with copious effect, and then some manna;[1] but there were two more attacks. The King went to him after mass; held the finance council; did not go shooting, as had been his intention, and walked instead in his gardens. The doctors, against their usual custom, had offered him no hope. It was a dreadful night. On Wednesday, 2 May, the King again went after his mass to M. le Duc de Berry, who had once more been bled from the foot. The King held the council of State, as usual, dined with Mme de Maintenon, and afterwards reviewed his bodyguard. Mme la Duchesse de Berry had sent her equerry Coëtanfao earlier in the day to beg the King to allow Chirac, M. le Duc d'Orléans's celebrated physician, to see M. le Duc de Berry. The King refused, on the grounds that since all the doctors agreed, a different opinion could only embarrass them. During the afternoon, Mmes de Pompadour and de La Vieuville[2] came to beg the King's leave for Mme la Duchesse de Berry to appear, explaining many times how anxious she felt, and that if necessary she would come on foot.[3] But had she truly so desired, she might have travelled in her coach, and asked the King's leave before stepping out of it. The truth is that she had no more desire to see M. le Duc de Berry than he to see her, for he had never so much as uttered her name, nor even referred to her indirectly. The King reasoned with those ladies, but when they insisted, he said that he would not absolutely shut the door in her face, but that in her condition she would be most unwise to travel. He then desired Madame and M. le Duc d'Orléans[4] to go to Versailles and dissuade her. On his return from the review, he again called on M. le Duc de Berry. He had been bled once more, this time from the arm. There had been great vomitings all through the day, with much blood, and in order to stop them he had been given as much as three doses of Rabel water.[5] Owing to the vomitings, they had delayed in giving him

---

[1] Manna, in this case, meant the sugary juices of certain trees, such as the larch; it was used as a purge.
[2] Mmes de Pompadour and de La Vieuville: the children's governess, and the Duchesse de Berry's woman-of-the-bedchamber.
[3] Because she was pregnant and the jolting of the coach would have been bad for her.
[4] Madame her grandmother, and the Duc d'Orléans her father.
[5] Rabel water: a mixture of sulphuric acid and alcohol, prescribed for fevers.

the Sacraments. Père de La Rue had been with him continuously since the Tuesday morning, and had found him wonderfully patient and resigned.

On Thursday the 3rd, after a still worse night, the doctors declared that he had, beyond any doubt, ruptured a vein in his stomach. On the previous evening there had been a rumour that this was the result of a strain he had suffered out hunting, on the Thursday before. They said that the Elector of Bavaria had joined the hunt; that in trying to check his horse M. le Duc de Berry had caused it to stumble so badly that his body was thrown against the pommel, and that every day since then he had spat blood. The vomitings ceased at nine that morning; but he was no better. The King was to have gone stag-hunting, but he cancelled the hunt. At six o'clock in the evening, M. le Duc de Berry was suffocating and could not stay in bed. At eight, he felt better and said to Madame that he hoped not to die; but soon afterwards the fever increased so greatly that Père de La Rue told him it was time to think only of God and receive the viaticum. The wretched prince seemed himself to desire it. Shortly after ten that same evening, the King went to the chapel, where the consecrated host had been kept ready since the first day of the illness. M. le Duc de Berry received it with deep reverence and piety. The King was with him nearly an hour, and then returned to his own room to sup alone. He did not see the princesses after his meal, but went straight to bed. M. le Duc d'Orléans went to Versailles at two o'clock in the morning, in case Mme la Duchesse de Berry should still wish to go to Marly. Just before he died, M. le Duc de Berry informed Père de La Rue, at least so that Father said, of the mishap with the stumbling horse; but from what was afterwards reported, his mind was already confused.[1] When speech failed, he took the crucifix from Père de La Rue's hand, kissed it, and laid it on his heart. He expired on Friday, 4 May, at four o'clock in the morning, in his twenty-eighth year, having been born at Versailles on the last day of August 1686.

M. le Duc de Berry was of average height for a man, somewhat large everywhere, with pale golden hair and a fresh-complexioned, rather handsome face that proclaimed an excellent constitution. He was made for Society and pleasures, all of which he enjoyed. The best and gentlest of men, he was also the kindest and most approachable, without pride or vanity, but not without dignity or a sense of rank. His mental powers were only mediocre; he was lacking in imagination and had few ideas; but he possessed excellent common sense and a sense of justice, and was capable of listening and understanding, and of choosing the right course amid many that were speciously attractive. He liked truth, justice, and fair play. Anything contrary to religion pained him excessively, although he was not remarkable for piety. He had a will of his own and resented any form

---

[1] Saint-Simon still seems convinced that they were all poisoned. But he was certainly wrong.

of constraint. This had given those about him cause to fear that he had not the docility required of a third Son of France, for as a boy he could never understand why any difference should be made between himself and his eldest brother, which was why their youthful quarrels had caused alarm.

He was the best-looking and most affable of the three brothers, and consequently the best liked, most petted, and most subjected to the attacks[1] of Society. Since he was frank, gay, and independent by nature, his boyish retorts to Madame and M. de La Rochefoucauld were repeated everywhere, for they assaulted him all day long. He made fun of his tutors and masters, and often of his punishments. He was taught no more than how to read and write, and learned nothing after being released from the need to study. His education was so oppressive that it dulled his faculties, broke his spirit, and made him so excessively timid that he was left unfit for most things, even for the ordinary duties of his rank. He never knew what to say to people outside his usual acquaintance, and dared not answer them or say a civil word, for fear of making a blunder. In the end, he convinced himself that he was no more than a fool and good for nothing. You will recall his misadventure at the Parlement. Mme de Saint-Simon, whom he entirely trusted, was quite unable to reassure him; indeed, his great lack of confidence did him untold harm. He cast all the blame on his education, and retained very little love for those who had been in charge of it.

Mme la Duchesse de Bourgogne had been devoted to him, and was as eager to give him little pleasures as if he had been her own brother. In return he had loved her truly, and had lived on terms of friendship and affection with the prince her husband, showing sincere and most marked respect for them both. Their deaths had afflicted him deeply, especially that of Mgr le Duc de Bourgogne, who was then the Dauphin, and his grief was very real, for no man was ever less able to dissemble. As for the King, he hardly dared to approach him; indeed, his fear was so extreme that King Louis had only to look gravely at him, or to speak of other matters than cards or hunting, and he would become giddy and confused. You may well imagine that such fear could not exist alongside strong affection.

In his marriage with Mme la Duchesse de Berry, he had begun in the way of most young bridegrooms, by falling passionately in love with his wife, and this, combined with his kind and easy-going temper, had had the effect of spoiling her completely. It was not long before she made him aware of that; but his passion was too strong for him. He found that she was haughty, vain, ill-tempered, and incapable of returning his love. She despised him, and allowed him to see it, for she was by far the more intelligent, but utterly faithless, and quite devoid of compassion. She was even proud of the last two qualities, and of making sport

---

[1] *Attaquer*: people battered him with questions in the hope of making him talk.

of religion, and jeering at M. le Duc de Berry because he was a believer. That he did find insufferable, and her attempt to spoil his relations with Mgr and Mme la Duchesse de Bourgogne finally provoked him beyond endurance. Her amorous adventures were sudden, swift, and immoderate; he could not ignore them. Her daily private sessions with M. le Duc d'Orléans, which relapsed into dullness, to say the least, as soon as her husband entered, made him boil with rage. There were violent and appalling scenes,[1] the last of which took place at Rambouillet after an unlucky encounter, and earned for Mme la Duchesse de Berry a kick on her backside and a threat to imprison her in a convent for the remainder of her life. That had occurred just before he had fallen ill, and he had already begun to dodge around the King, twisting his hat like a little child, trying to make up his mind to tell all and beg to be rescued from her. Let us not go into details. Such scenes are sordid and unhappy. Let one example suffice. She resolved at all costs to allow herself to be abducted by La Haye, her chamberlain. The maddest and most passionate letters were intercepted; but with such a scheme, when the King, her father and the prince her husband were all living, it was not hard to guess which of them had planned it and was clamouring for action. Thus, when M. le Duc de Berry died, she felt less distress at her reduction in rank than joy at her deliverance. She was pregnant, hoping for a son, and reckoned on having complete freedom now that the cause of so many tedious scoldings from the King and Mme de Maintenon had finally departed. She supposed that they would no longer take the same interest in her conduct.

The obsequies of M. le Duc de Berry were rather casually conducted. It was lamentable that, at the Tuileries, where the bishops seized possession both of armchairs and hassocks, Dreux did not see fit to intervene. This was the first example of that particular form of encroachment. The princes of the blood, the ambassadors and the dukes went in robes to sprinkle holy water, and the magistrature also. All were received and escorted to the door by the principal officials, acting as officers of the household. The Comte de Charolais and the Duc de Fronsac[2] took the heart to Val-de-Grâce, on Thursday, 10 May. M. le Duc d'Orléans should have accompanied the body to Saint-Denis; but he asked the King to relieve him of that task, and Monsieur le Duc was sent in his place, with the Duc de La Trémoïlle. That was on Wednesday, 16 May. The decencies were observed in Mme la Duchesse de Berry's apartment; Mme de Saint-Simon saw to that. The rooms were kept completely dark, with every window shuttered. At least, that was so in her bedroom; in the other rooms only the curtains were

---

[1] The Duchesse de Berry is believed to have been going mad. She had lost both her babies.
[2] The Comte de Charolais was Charles de Bourbon-Condé (1700-1760), son of Monsieur le Duc and Madame la Duchesse. The Duc de Fronsac et Richelieu became Duc de Richelieu at his father's death in 1715.

drawn close. This was done as a precaution, so that no one should see her in bed; but when the King first visited her, they allowed in sufficient light, for a moment only, as he entered, in order that he might get his bearings. No one else was so favoured, and thus the most absurd situations occurred, causing unseemly laughter that was hard to suppress. Those living in the room had become used to the darkness; but those who entered from daylight saw nothing, staggered, and had to be assisted. Père Trévou, and Père Tellier after him, paid their respects to a wall, and others bowed low over the foot of her bed; it gradually became a household joke. The ladies and the domestic staff were truly affected, but comic incidents do occur to surprise laughter out of people who are then ashamed. This artificial night was kept up for the shortest period that decency would allow.

The King resumed his customary life at Marly immediately after his grandson's death; but the concerts in Mme de Maintenon's room did not begin again until soon after his return to Versailles. He invited Cardinal del Giudice into his study one morning, much to that prelate's astonishment. But King Louis believed that the cardinal was charged with some affair which he wished kept secret from the ministers, and thus he saw him alone. It then appeared that del Giudice had nothing new to impart, and the emptiness of his whole mission became obvious.

The dowager Maréchale d'Estrées died in Paris. She never missed an excursion to Marly; but during that visit she was allotted a brand-new lodging, and it killed her.[1] She fell mortally ill there; had herself transported back to Paris, and died very soon afterwards. She was the daughter of a rich banker named Morin, who was invariably known as Morin the Jew.[2] She was a big and rather stout woman, good-looking notwithstanding a slight squint, with a proud, audacious countenance, resolute and full of character; indeed, you cannot imagine any woman having more, or knowing so much, or being more excellent company. She was brusque, but with politeness, understanding very well to whom she owed respect, and from whom she might demand it. Her entire life had been spent at the Court, among the best people in the highest Society, playing for high stakes with firmness and good judgment. People feared her, yet her company was much sought after. They said that she was spiteful; but if so, it was only through speaking her mind freely and frankly on every subject, often with much wit, and always with spirit and force, and by not having the temperament to suffer fools gladly. She could be dangerous at such times, when she let fly with an economy of words, speaking to people's faces such cruel home-truths that they felt like sinking

[1] Mme de Maintenon said that she died of quinsy, that is to say, of tonsillitis. She was Marie Marguerite Morin, who married Jean, Comte d'Estrées, Maréchal de France, in 1658. She was seventy-five when she died in 1714.

[2] Jacques Morin, nicknamed the Jew. First usurer, then tax-farmer, who bought a place as one of the King's secretaries, so as to be ennobled, and another post as major-domo in ordinary to the King.

through the floor; but truly, she did not enjoy quarrelling or scandal for its own sake; she simply wished to make herself redoubtable and a person to be reckoned with, and in that she succeeded, living the while very happily with her own family. She was avaricious to excess, as she was the first to admit and to laugh at herself. But she loved a bargain, possessed a good knowledge of objects and their prices, had excellent taste, and refused herself nothing. When the mood seized her to give a dinner, everything was exquisitely provided, the food was of the choicest, the setting magnificent. She was a good friend and a wise counsellor, both loyal and secret; and even those who were not her friends ran no risk by speaking in her presence. Her daughter Mlle de Tourbes[1] was an equally strong personality, but more arrogant and sharper. She slipped and fell at Marly, one day, in the middle of the drawing-room when she was covered with jewellery, dancing at a ball, before the King. Her mother, who was sitting among the older ladies in the second row, scrambled over the row in front, and rushed to her daughter, not asking whether she was hurt, although she still lay on the floor, but intent on gathering up the jewels. Everyone laughed heartily, and she joined with them. She left her more than eight hundred thousand livres, almost as much to her son the Maréchal d'Estrées,[2] and, to her other son, the Abbé d'Estrées, six hundred thousand livres, not counting an incredible amount of furniture, jewels, porcelain, silver plate, and precious stones. She was seventy-seven or -eight years of age, had the health and spirits of a woman of forty, and, without that new lodging, might have lived much longer. Although she cared for very few, she was regretted; but, with all her brilliance, she could never have endured life away from the Court and high Society.

The loss of Dunkirk, where the English had insisted on demolishing the port and the fortifications, produced the idea of making a canal to Mardyck, so as gradually to create an additional port there. Le Blanc, who was intendant of that province, put the proposal to Le Peletier,[3] who had the charge of fortifications and engineering works. It was much relished, and the works were begun with great enthusiasm. The English have always been disgusted by our behaviour; but the answer is that we have done nothing contrary to the peace terms, and the work, although sometimes interrupted by their threats and complaints, has proceeded satisfactorily, and continues to grow.

My sister-in-law, the Duchesse de Lorges, Chamillart's third daughter, died in Paris, giving birth to a second son, on the last day of May, on the feast of Corpus

---

[1] Mlle de Tourbes was Elisabeth Rosalie d'Estrées (1673-1750).

[2] He was Victor Marie, Comte, later Duc et Maréchal de Cœuvres, and later still d'Estrées (1660-1737).

[3] Louis Claude Le Blanc (1669-1728), the Intendant of Dunkirk, was minister for war from 1719 to 1723. Michel Le Peletier de Souzy (1640-1725) was controller-general of finances and director-general of fortifications from 1691 to 1715, and was later a member of the regency and finance councils during the minority of Louis XV.

Christi, in her twenty-ninth year. She was a great big girl, very well built, with a
pleasant face, a certain radiance, and a nature so open, true, and resilient that it
made her enchanting.[1] She was the best company imaginable, mad for all diversions, and especially for playing high. She showed no vestige of nonsensical vanity
or glorying in being the daughter of a minister, but she brimmed over with every
other kind of pride. From her girlhood onwards, she had been spoilt by a Court
eager to take advantage of her father's favour, and by a mother quite incapable
of giving her any sort of an education. She had never conceived it possible for
France or the King to exist without her father. She recognized no obligations, not
even to propriety. Her father's ruin taught her nothing, nor did it at all lessen her
passion for gambling and pleasure. This she frankly admitted in the most innocent way imaginable, adding that it was beyond her powers to mend. No one was
ever more untidy, more bedraggled than she, with her head-dress crooked, her
gown dropping down at one side, and all the rest of her dress completely awry;
yet she had a grace that redeemed all. Her health she ignored, and as for money,
she seemed to imagine that she would always have land to sell. She had a delicate
constitution, and a weak chest of which the doctors had warned her; she knew
it herself, but was utterly incapable of self-restraint. Thus she persisted with her
card-playing, her gadding about, and her late nights until the very end of her
pregnancy, staying up until the dawn, and returning each day lying outstretched
across the seat of her coach. When people asked what possible pleasure she could
derive in her condition, she replied in a voice almost inaudible from weakness
that indeed, she had vastly enjoyed herself. Thus she burned herself out before
her time. I was devoted to her, but used always to tell her that I would not for
anything have been her husband. She was a most gentle soul and, for those who
bore no responsibility for her, infinitely agreeable. Her father and mother were
deeply grieved.

Chalais arrived in Paris, sent from Spain by the Princesse des Ursins, with
letters for Cardinal del Giudice. The King had severed the link with her sovereignty, and the peace was at long last concluded with Spain, without mention of
it. The many delays had all been connected with that one subject. During the
interval, the King had been to Marly on 29 May, and had given a lodging there
to Cardinal del Giudice.

I was, as usual, of the party, although Mme de Saint-Simon had remained
at Versailles with Mme la Duchesse de Berry. The King had as yet heard nothing from the King of Spain regarding his intention of remarrying; still less that
the lady under consideration was a Princess of Parma. That piece of news had,

[1] Saint-Simon loved her and used to call her 'my big sweetheart (*ma grande biche*)'.

however, reached him from another source.[1] This last affair, coupled with Mme des Ursins' claim to royal rank, and her whole conduct towards the King of Spain since the death of the queen, had set the seal on King Louis's resolve to destroy her. It then happened that he, who was normally so completely master of himself and his words, gave utterance to a certain remark, with a smile so enigmatical, so altogether startling, that Torcy, to whom it was addressed, could make nothing of it. So astounded was he that he told his friend Castries, who confided in his close friend Mme la Duchesse d'Orléans, who repeated all to M. le Duc d'Orléans and myself. We racked our brains uselessly to discover a meaning; but such a cryptic utterance concerning one who had been in the King's and Mme de Maintenon's highest favour seemed ominous to me. I was confirmed in that view by all that had passed regarding her sovereignty; but I was miles from foreseeing the thunderbolt about to descend on her. It is not yet time to speak of that.

The marriage with Parma was already firmly settled; and still the King had received no news of it from Spain. There was, however, every reason to think that Chalais had come only for that purpose, and that his dispatches for Cardinal del Giudice were also concerned with it. Those emissaries may perhaps have felt too much embarrassed to make their reports to the King. I know no more as to that. Perhaps their entire mission related to the refusal of sovereignty, and the orders bidding the plenipotentiaries sign without further ado. Be that as it may, Chalais delivered his dispatches personally to Cardinal del Giudice, at Marly, and returned to Paris without seeing the King or anyone else. That was on Saturday, 2 June. On the following day, Sunday the 3rd, the King, having ascertained that the King of Spain's couriers were gone to Utrecht, summoned Berwick to his study, and ordered him to be ready to leave for the siege of Barcelona, with sixty-eight French battalions who received their marching orders at the same time, four lieutenant-generals, and four French brigadier-generals, in addition to those already in Spain.

On Saturday, 16 June, Mme la Duchesse de Berry injured herself giving birth to a daughter who lived only twelve hours. The King was at Rambouillet, and from there appointed Mme de Saint-Simon as the duchess to accompany the little body to Saint-Denis, and the heart to Val-de-Grâce, on the return journey. Two hours later, he announced that my wife had been the first duchess to come to his mind as being at Versailles. Had he recollected that she was also the lady-in-waiting, he would have nominated someone else; but the order was already dispatched and she was obliged to undertake that duty. The Bishop of Séez, first almoner to the late M. le Duc de Berry, went with her on the back seat, on the right-hand side; Mmes de Pompadour and de Vaudreuil, as governess and under-governess of the Berry children, sat in front; the

[1] The King had already heard the news from Brancas.

curé of Versailles sat by one door, and the little body was placed by the other. There was an escort of guards, pages, and the carriages of members of their household. She was away for fourteen or fifteen hours.

Princess Sophia of the Palatinate,[1] widow of the Elector of Hanover and mother of the first Hanoverian King of England,[2] died at the age of eighty-four. She was the daughter of a sister of King Charles I of England (the one whose head they struck off), and of the Elector Palatine who so much vexed that monarch by aspiring to be King of Bohemia. It was through her that the right to the English throne passed to the House of Hanover, notwithstanding that there were many closer heirs, apart from the Stuarts; all of these were, however, Catholics; she was the nearest Protestant. She was a princess of very great merit, and had brought up Madame, her brother's child, who had remained devotedly attached to her ever since, and twice a week wrote her letters that were often twenty or twenty-five pages long. It was she to whom Madame had written those terrible letters at the time of Monsieur's death, which the King had intercepted, and which very nearly destroyed her, as I have already mentioned.[3] Thus Madame's grief at the death of her aunt the Electress was very real indeed.

On Tuesday, 19 June, the King returned to Marly, and thence went to Versailles to visit Mme la Duchesse de Berry; but he did not stop the night. I went as usual to Marly, but I mention the fact only because the excursion was so full of interest. Cardinal del Giudice was also of the party. Chalais returned there on the morning of 27 June, and was summoned with Torcy to the King's study. Chalais's task was not easy, for he came to inform King Louis of the King of Spain's second marriage, as an event arranged and settled—which was the first mention King Louis had received of it from Spain. As soon as his audience was over, Chalais took his leave and returned immediately to Spain; Mme des Ursins, who must have felt anxious regarding her bold enterprise, wished to learn from someone she could trust how the news had been received. A few moments later, Cardinal del Giudice was admitted to the study on the same business, although we none of us knew this until much later. The King appeared to accept this unseemly alliance and the mystery surrounding it with the utmost calm, as though he thought it the most ordinary event imaginable. He could not have prevented it, and now he was sure of his revenge on the woman who had devised it and had brought it in such a manner to finality.

At this time the Chancellor took an action for which there was then no precedent, and which came as an unexpectedly terrible, indeed one might almost say a mortal, blow. He had planned all his life to place an interval between life and

---

[1] Sophia, Electress of Hanover (1630-1714). She was described by La Fontaine as '*La mère des amours et la mère des Graces*'.
[2] George Louis (1660-1727), Elector of Hanover. He became George I of England, August 1714, on the death of Queen Anne.
[3] See Vol. I, p. 161.

death; he had very often told me so. His wife on several occasions had dissuaded him from retiring even before he became Chancellor; had restrained him many times since then, and on her deathbed had extracted a promise that he would reflect well for at least six weeks, before finally deciding to retire. Yet from the first moments after her death, when he went to seek refuge in his little lodging at the seminary of the Oratory fathers, he was determined to carry out his plan, and began secretly to make his arrangements. He could not completely hide his intentions from his family. La Vrillière took fright and confided in me, and together we consulted the master of the horse;[1] they then both entreated me to speak to the Chancellor, reminding him of the great disadvantages of retirement to himself, and to his hated son, whom he would leave without protection. Say what I might, however, I spoke in vain. He served for the promised time, and then told the King, who was mightily astonished, for he did not believe that a Chancellor could resign, and truly there was no precedent. Although Mme de Maintenon's hatred of him had even increased since the death of Mme de Pontchartrain, whom she had liked; and although the King's opinion of him had been altered by her loathing and by a strong suspicion that the Chancellor inclined to Jansenism, long habit and memories of old friendship prevailed when the time came to face absolute separation. King Louis did all that was possible to persuade him to change his mind, adding tokens of affection calculated to show his high esteem. Pontchartrain still remained firm. The King then asked him to postpone his decision for two weeks. When that time had elapsed, at the end of June, the Chancellor renewed his request and at last, with enormous difficulty, won the freedom he so much desired, and of which he was to make a most courageous and saintly use.

The rumour of what was about to happen broke only four or five days before the event, even then uncertain. On Sunday, 1 July, the Chancellor was with the King alone for a long time after the other ministers had left the council, and it was then that, despite the King's final efforts, he gained permission to depart. Neither when he entered, nor when he left the study, nor at any time during the council, at least so said the other ministers, could anything be discerned from the Chancellor's manner or expression; and thus the greater part of the Court was still in uncertainty. Next day, after the King had returned from mass, the Chancellor was seen to arrive in his chair at the door into the little drawing-room between the King's apartments and those of Mme de Maintenon. Since there was no council at that time, people flocked into the great drawing-room. He was then observed, as he entered the King's room, to be carrying the case with the seals, and no one any longer doubted his retirement. Everyone began to praise him, and there was

---

[1] *Le Premier Ecuyer:* sometimes called *Monsieur le Premier,* Jean Louis, Marquis de Beringhem (1651-1723). His sons succeeded him as master of the horse, in 1723 and 1724 respectively, in the reign of Louis XV.

widespread dismay. He had already told all to me, and thus it was with a heavy heart that I watched him enter and depart; he, on the other hand, looked well content. The King had overwhelmed him with tokens of affection, esteem and regret, and all unasked had given him a pension of thirty-six thousand livres, and the right to keep his rank and privileges as Chancellor. Towards the end of his audience he had asked the King to protect his two secretaries who were, in very truth, most worthy men, and immediately the King had granted each of them a pension of two thousand livres.

The news had spread while he was still with the King, and thus, when he came to leave, all the gentlemen at Marly formed a crowd around him. He left as he had come, behaving in no way differently from usual, bowing to right and left, but speaking to no one, and no one speaking to him. He found his chair where he had left it; returned to his pavilion, and immediately stepped into his coach and went to Paris. He remained at his house[1] for nearly a month, in the first few days a victim to every caller, and then more and more in seclusion. The house which Charmel's death had left vacant, and which was being made ready for his residence, was not yet in order; but as soon as it was fit to live in, he went there.

Very soon after he had gone, the King, who had been given plenty of time to choose a replacement, sent for Voysin, gave him the seals, and proclaimed him the new Chancellor. Everyone expected that he would resign his post as secretary for war, since there was no precedent for a Chancellor's holding two offices. But this one had a large enough appetite and greedily swallowed them both.

I must now describe two persons of minor interest, Maisons,[2] président-à-mortier, and his wife, the elder sister of the Maréchale de Villars. Maisons's grandfather,[3] also a président-à-mortier, was a surintendant des finances into the bargain, and built for himself the magnificent Château de Maisons. He had been a friend of my father's, who to oblige him let him purchase for next to nothing the captaincy of Saint-Germain-en-Laye,[4] because his new house was in that district and the centre of that hunt. It was that same Maisons who said loudly when he was dismissed from the finances, 'They are making a very big mistake; I had made my pile, and was just about to make theirs'. His friendship with my father endured throughout their lives. His son, the father of the one we are about to discuss, and likewise a président-à-mortier, was the magistrate who so iniquitously presided in our suit against M. de Luxembourg;[5] and his conduct then left me with no desire to continue the acquaintance. Nor did I at all wish to know his son,

[1] In the Rue Neuve-des-Petits-Champs.

[2] Claude de Longueil, Marquis de Maisons (1668-1715). His wife was Marie Charlotte Roque de Varengeville. She was his second wife, and died, aged forty-five, in 1727.

[3] Maison's grandfather, René de Longueil, Marquis de Maisons, had died in 1677.

[4] The Captain of Saint-Germain-en-Laye was master of the royal hunts, a post which Saint-Simon's father had held under Louis XIII.

[5] The Maréchal de Luxembourg's claim to ducal precedence. See Vol. I, p. 42 et seq.

for I had never so much as heard mention of him until the beginning of that year 1714. This preamble was necessary for the understanding of what follows.

Maisons was a big man with an imposing presence, but only a very superficial knowledge of his profession. He was immensely wealthy and very ready with his tongue, with a high-bred air, not at all foppish, without the complacency of most lawyers, and quite devoid of the président-à-mortier's usual impertinence. No doubt M. de Mesmes's example had taught him to shun the buffoonery in which that magistrate was pleased to indulge. Far from aping the airs of the great nobles and the best Society, he was content to spend his leisure with well-bred company from Paris and the Court, whom he and his wife attracted to their house by their polished, unassuming manners, never neglecting the courtesy due to each individual, showing respect to some, marked attention to others, all with an easy, friendly bearing that, far from displeasing their guests, gave the hosts a reputation for putting people at their ease.

His wife, although she possessed little or no radiance, knew the art of gracious and lavish entertaining, and had the good sense to be ruled by him. She did not affect the lofty airs of the wives of other présidents-à-mortier and magistrates; was only a touch more stylish than himself, and behaved with the same carefully graded politeness. She was tall, and had she been less stout, might have been called a fine figure of a woman, of the Roman matron type. To many people her beauty was infinitely preferable to that of her sister,[1] with whom she had the good judgment to live at peace, without showing jealousy for her high rank, or vying with her in appearance. Maisons himself was notably respectful towards the Maréchal de Villars, and yet on friendly terms with him. He soon realized that the Parlement was the foundation on which he had to build; that his social standing would depend on his reputation in that place, and that the company with whom he mixed would oblige him only so long as magistrate's rank lent him importance. He was therefore wise in making that his chief concern, welcoming other magistrates to his house, cultivating those who were highly esteemed in the courts, persuading them that he felt honoured by their company. He attended regularly at the Palais de Justice, and made himself popular with the more lowly placed, such as the rising advocates, attorneys, and clerks, by graciousness, and affability blended with praise, that made him generally beloved. By such conduct his reputation in the Parlement was undisputed, and universally acknowledged at the Court and in Society, which had made Président de Mesmes more than a little jealous when he discovered that Maisons was capable of leading the Parlement wherever he desired.

---

[1] Mme de Maisons's sister, the Maréchale et Duchesse de Villars, who died in 1763, aged eighty-eight.

The fact that his house was near Marly gave him plenty of opportunities to entertain distinguished members of the Court. It became the fashion to visit him, and for a long time he had the pleasure of seeing the courtiers walking on his terraces. At first he seldom went to Versailles, then gradually increased his visits to once a week; after which, because so many eminent courtiers dined with him during the long Marlys, the King took to asking him about his house almost every time he saw him; yet even that did not make him swollen-headed. Indeed, he behaved so well that Monsieur le Duc and M. le Prince de Conti took notice of him, with the result that he regarded their deaths as almost a personal loss. Then, someone, I know not who, introduced him to M. de Beauvilliers, and they did business together, although when, and about what, I never discovered. He later became acquainted with M. le Duc d'Orléans, who imagined that he had found a treasure.

At that point Maisons set his cap at me, whom I think he feared, on account of my opinion of his father. He had an only son of about the age of my children,[1] and for a long time made overtures to them and saw them often. That, however, had brought him no closer to me, and in the end he persuaded M. le Duc d'Orléans to speak to me; which was when I first learned of their attachment, and of Maisons's desiring my friendship, on the grounds of his esteem, admiration, and the mutual acquaintance of our fathers—all of which the prince rehearsed to me. I remained unmoved; sent my compliments; regretted that I went so little to Paris, and supposed myself well rid of him. A few days later, however, M. de Beauvilliers, much to my surprise, for I did not know they were acquainted, also tried to tell me that friendship with Maisons might advantage me in many ways, and when I was frigid, used all his authority, saying that he begged me to comply; that he desired it, and that I appeared to have no real reason for objecting. I plainly saw that Maisons, having failed with M. le Duc d'Orléans, felt sure that I should not resist M. de Beauvilliers. None the less, I waited until the prince returned to the attack, for I would not have had him think that I would do for M. de Beauvilliers what I had refused to do for him.

M. le Duc d'Orléans then begged me to spend one night in Paris; where, on my arrival, I found a note from Maisons asking me to meet him that same night, at eleven o'clock, very secretly, in the plain[2] behind the Invalides. I therefore took with me an old coachman of my mother's and one of her footmen, so as to put my people off the scent. There was a little moonlight. Maisons, with a small escort, was waiting for me. He stepped into my coach. I have never understood his desire for secrecy, for all that he did was to make advances to me, pay

---

[1] Saint-Simon's two sons were aged sixteen and fifteen respectively in 1714; his daughter was eighteen.
[2] It was indeed a plain, in those days covered with gardens and market-gardens, and was called La Plaine de Grenelle.

me compliments, protest his esteem, remind me of our fathers' long acquaintance, all, in fact, that becomes a man of substance when he wishes to form an attachment. He also praised M. le Duc d'Orléans and M. de Beauvilliers, and remarked generally on the situation at the Court. In short, he said nothing of any consequence. I replied to his spate of words with all the graciousness I could muster, and then expected something more to justify the peculiar time and place; but to my amazement nothing more was forthcoming. He simply said that our first meeting was best kept secret, but that he saw no reason why he should not now call on me occasionally at Versailles, and then gradually lessen the intervals between calls—once people had grown used to seeing him at my lodging. He requested me, however, not to visit him in Paris, saying that there was always too great a company at his house. We separated in a flow of compliments, and the very next time that he visited Versailles, he called on me in the morning. It was not long before he came every Sunday. Slowly our talks became more serious. I still remained on my guard; but I tried him on various topics and found him very ready to speak frankly.

We were on those terms when I returned to Marly late in the morning of Sunday, 29 July. I found one of Maisons's footmen waiting for me with a note entreating me to leave all and go that instant to his house in Paris. He would be alone, he said, and I should then realize the extreme urgency and importance of the matter. The footman had been waiting some considerable time, and my servants were looking for me everywhere. Mme de Saint-Simon was at Versailles with Mme la Duchesse de Berry, and I was bidden to dine with M. and Mme de Lauzun. To have absented myself would have aroused M. de Lauzun's malice and curiosity; thus I dared not fail them, but ordered my coach, and left as soon as the meal was over. No one saw me depart. I went at once to my house in Paris, and thence to Maisons. You may picture my intense curiosity.

Maisons I found closeted with the Duc de Noailles. I saw before me two utterly distraught individuals who, after a short preamble, told me in trembling voices that the King had declared his two male bastards and their male progeny to be for ever, in all respects, princes of the blood and capable of the succession. At this news, to me entirely unexpected, for no rumours had emerged, my arms fell to my sides. I bowed my head, and so remained in deep silence, buried in my thoughts. Cries and groans aroused me. The two men had risen, and were stamping around the room, banging with their fists on the furniture, shouting with rage, making the whole house re-echo with the din they were creating. I must confess that so much fury and noise appeared highly suspect to me, coming, as it did, from two gentlemen, one of whom was normally grave and moderate, and who was, after all, unaffected by this announcement; and the other, generally so calm, subtle, and composed. I failed to understand why this violent rage should have succeeded their dejection, and I could not help suspecting that it was all done for the purpose of exciting me. If that had been their intention, they were disappointed, for I remained seated, and coldly desired to know with whom they were so much vexed. My coolness served only to increase their fury. Never in all my life have I seen such an astounding scene. I asked if they were mad, and whether it would not be better to cease from storming and consider what, if anything, might be done.

They shrieked out that there was nothing to be done; that the matter was not only settled, but proclaimed and sent to the Parlement for registration; that it was outrageous; that M. le Duc d'Orléans, being as he was with the King, would not dare to protest; that the princes trembled like the children they were, that the Parlement was reduced to subjection and abject silence. And thereupon they began to shout and rave once more, and even louder, sparing neither their words, persons, nor even the furniture. I too was extremely angry; but the fearful racket they were creating made me want to laugh, and helped me to remain calm. I agreed that there seemed to be no remedy, at present, but said that on the whole I preferred the bastards to be full princes of the blood, rather than at the half-way stage at which they had been of late. Indeed, that was how I felt when I came to my senses and the noise had somewhat abated. We then began to converse. They informed me that the premier président had gone early to Marly with the Chancellor; that they had seen the King in his study after his *lever*, and had immediately after returned to Paris, with the proclamation signed and sealed. Yet Maisons must have known something rather earlier, for the footman whom he sent to me at Marly had left Paris before those gentlemen returned. At that point, seeing that the discussion would lead nowhere, I took my leave, and drove quickly back to Marly so that my absence would not be noticed.

It was almost the hour of the King's supper. I went straight to the drawing-room, where the atmosphere was very lugubrious. People stood gazing at one another, not daring to speak or, at the most, making furtive signs, or breathing some remark into a passing ear. I watched the King as he sat down to table; he appeared haughtier than usual, and stared hard at those to his right and left. It was barely an hour since the news had broken; people were still petrified, everyone very much on his guard. But when there is no remedy one must submit, and this came the more easily since there was no urgency about the matter. At the time when the bastards were promoted to an intermediate rank they got no compliments from me, nor the smallest semblance of any such. I had now to make a decision.

After the King was seated, and he had gazed fixedly at me as he passed, I went to call on M. du Maine, notwithstanding that the hour was somewhat irregular.

Both doors[1] were opened to receive me. I found him surprised, but pleased by my visit for, despite his limp, he seemed to tread on air, as he came forward to welcome me. I stated that the present was an occasion when I might sincerely offer him my congratulations; we dukes had no claims on princes of the blood. We claimed nothing but our rights, namely that no new rank should be interposed between the princes and ourselves. He was now one of them; we therefore had no objections to make; only to rejoice that we need no longer suffer that intermediate rank which, I had to confess, I found intolerable. M. du Maine's gratification was supreme. I shall not repeat all that he said and did with infinite politeness, and that deceptively humble air which often accompanies the first moment of triumph.

On the following day I offered my congratulations also to M. le Comte de Toulouse and to Mme la Duchesse d'Orléans—a hundred times more pro-bastard, more enraptured than her brothers, whom she saw already wearing the crown. Madame la Duchesse, on the other hand, was very much the princess of the blood, behaving quite unlike her sister, looking very grave, and opening her door to no one. M. le Duc d'Orléans was vexed after his fashion, but did not find it hard to dissemble. The dukes and foreign princes were outraged but dumb. At the Court, there was far more grumbling than might have been expected. In Paris and the provinces, and in private houses, the people's anger knew no bounds. Mme de Maintenon, triumphant at her great achievement, basked in the adoration of her cronies. But although she and M. du Maine feared none of the legitimate princes, they were none the less anxious and watched the King closely, priming him with lying reports of general rejoicing. Mme du Maine, at Sceaux, delighted in the universal dismay; gave twice the usual number of parties, took at their face value the driest and most formal compliments, and ignored those who would not consent to worship at her shrine. The deified bastards appeared for only a few moments at Marly, M. du Maine finding it prudent to assume a modest and diffident air. He was wise. As for M. le Comte de Toulouse, he had benefited by this most abominable deed without having done anything to further it. It had been all his brother's doing, aided by his most devoted and powerful protectress, and by her cunning (which was then perceived for the first time), in arranging for Voysin to keep his post of Secretary of State after he had been promoted to Chancellor. Had he been only Chancellor, he would have had no reason to approach the King, no work to do with him, no excuse for seeing him whenever he so desired.

Let us pause here to reflect, for the steps which the King took to establish the unrestricted grandeur of his bastards belongs to his testament, for which it is not yet time. Although he was, in fact, composing it at this very moment, the terms were made known only at the opening of his will and its codicil, fifteen days after

[1] For dukes and above, both sides of the double doors were flung wide open.

his death, as you will discover in due course. No one, until then, had had a notion that he was engaged in drafting his testament.

When you consider the vast array of persons working to bring the fruits of double adultery from their profound nonentity to the throne itself, you will be less stunned by the poets' imagination that sets the hands of giants piling mountain upon mountain to scale the heavenly heights. Moreover, the fate of Enceladus and Briareus[1] will appear the only just punishment for such ambitions.

That kings should become the absolute lords of giving, raising, lowering, or transposing ranks, and prostituting the highest honours, just as lately they have assumed the right to encroach upon the wealth of all their subjects, and violate at will their liberties with one stroke of their pens (or, more often, the pens of their ministers and favourites), is a misfortune to which those subjects' abuse of free-dom[2] opened the way that continued unobstructed to the bitter end of the reign of Louis XIV. Thus the very words law, right, privilege became crimes. Such a total reversal engenders universal slavery. Such rulers, after long experience of boundless and unopposed authority, hearing only the worship that drowns the bitter groans of every order in their oppressed kingdoms, become habituated to all that total power may offer them.[3]

Such princes, beginning and growing old in the possession of excessive power, forget that their crowns are in trust, and not their absolute property. They may not dispose of them elsewhere, for they received them by right of succession from their ancestors, and by entail, not by free bequest. They may not tamper with that entail, because until it ends with the extinction of the legitimate line, neither they nor any other may dispose of the succession, which never falls vacant while a rightful heir lives. After their deaths, the right returns to the nation from which they first received it, as did all the other heirs-male of their line.

You will find it easier to imagine the effects of such encroachments (plain as they are to every eye), than to credit the publication of this edict—the first of its kind in all the centuries that the monarchy has existed in three estates[4]—or realise that it was possible to carry the abuse so far. You must, however, carefully recall all the minor infringements from which came the total destruction of all rights, laws, oaths, and promises, causing havoc to the estates, ranks, and condition of every subject of the realm.

---

[1] Briareus, son of heaven and earth, had fifty heads and a hundred arms. Poseidon hurled him into the sea and Zeus chained him up under Mt. Etna to punish him for rebelling against the gods. Encelades was another of the giants who attacked Olympus. Athene buried him also under Etna.

[2] Saint-Simon is referring to the revolt of the nobles during the minority of Louis XIV.

[3] Saint-Simon's violent invective has some justification. What he so hated was not Louis XIV, but the absolute rule that had reduced the nobility to dumb obedience, depriving them of their right to be the King's counsellors and support him in his rule. His hatred of Mme de Maintenon thus becomes more understandable, but she probably does not bear as much responsibility as he supposes for the elevation of the bastards.

[4] The three estates: the Church, the nobility and the third, comprising all who were commoners.

What must you now think of that avowed Creole, kept relict of the legless poet,[1] and of him, the first fruit of double adultery to be made the equal of other men, who together so gulled a great king, and would not be satisfied with all their wealth and honours, and a grandeur, so outrageous that it was an open attack on public decency, morals, and religion, if not yet a direct assault upon the throne itself? Is it so rash to assume that this monstrous edict, giving the bastards the throne after the last true prince of the blood, and endowing them with the name and title, and all else enjoyed by those princes now and in the future, was the final step towards bringing them to the Crown itself, before all others save only a Dauphin and his posterity? Surely a greater distance was travelled in lifting those shady offspring from nonentity to rank, and from rank to the degree of grandeur in which we now see them; surely there is a greater gap between nothingness and their present state than from their present state to the throne. The whole picture is, in truth, one of violence, injustice, and a continual abuse of power; but once made princes of the blood, there remained only one step for them to climb, and it were easier for one prince of the blood to take precedence over another in order to gain the succession than to fabricate such princes with ink and wax, and make them royal without a murmur of dissent.

The Court, Paris, and Society in general were rudely shocked by the abominable toadying of the Maréchal d'Huxelles, who went to thank the King formally, as for a personal favour, for what he had done for the bastards. He canvassed for guests to a great dinner which he proposed giving for them on one of the days when they made their formal applications to the Parlement. He dared not invite dukes or other distinguished persons and thus finally settled for receiving only congratulations. He was burning to enter the council; he was consumed with desire to become a duke; his toadying brought him neither the one nor the other. But what did give me cause to reflect was that on one of those same two days the Duc du Maine and the Comte de Toulouse dined privately with Maisons. I cannot conceive how any man of intelligence could have hoped to keep it secret. Yet he did so hope; and therefore invited no other guests. He seemed much embarrassed when I tackled him on the subject. I pretended not to notice, and took in good part his excuse that they were so hard pressed for time, after making their applications, that they could only snatch a bite, not dine, before returning to Marly. Such behaviour on his part seemed to me ill-suited to those rages of which I had been a witness a few days earlier; and surely those gentry, at the summit of their favour and glory, would not have been reduced to seeking high and low

---

[1] Not strictly accurate: Mme de Maintenon was born in the gaol at Niort, where her father was a political prisoner. He emigrated to Martinique when she was four, and died there six years later. His family then returned to France. The poet, Paul Scarron, whom she married, was not legless *(cul de jatte)* but twisted and crippled with rheumatism.

for a snack—especially since they both had houses in Paris. Maisons would never have been granted that favour and privilege had he not solicited it. That is what I said to M. le Duc d'Orléans, with whom Maisons had been letting fly against the bastards. Indeed, I have always believed that Maisons had staged that scene at his house, in order that I might retail it to M. le Duc d'Orléans.

The two brothers, accompanied only by their personal suites, called without previous warning on all the peers and on all the magistrates of the great chamber. When every voice had been silenced, and even sighs were smothered, you may well believe that it would have been considered a crime to refuse to receive them, even on the plea of most grave and evident illness. Thursday, 2 August, was the great day appointed for the ratification of their new rank as princes of the blood. Monsieur le Duc and M. le Prince de Conti, and twenty or so of the peers, that is to say all who were able to attend, were present. I saw with my own eyes the tremor that went through the chamber when the two bastards appeared, and how it changed to a subdued murmur as they slowly crossed the floor. Hypocrisy was writ plain on the face and bearing of M. du Maine, and shamefaced modesty all over the person of the Comte de Toulouse. The elder brother, stooping over his cane[1] with most notable self-abasement, paused to bow and scrape at every step, bending low in all directions. He bowed more and more often; he stayed bent double in moments of deep respect; I really thought, when he came to my corner, that he would prostrate himself. His countenance was disciplined to gravity and sweetness, seeming to convey *non sum dignus* from the very bottom of his heart; but his eyes, dancing with joy, gave the lie to that, as he darted furtive glances all about him. On reaching his seat, he bowed again and again before sitting down, remaining most admirably grave throughout the whole session and when he departed. The princes of the blood he treated less well in the matter of bows and scrapes—they were too young for him to mind them. The Comte de Toulouse, stiff and formal as usual, kept his eyes lowered, his bows in moderation. His whole person bore witness to the fact that he was led, and also to his embarrassment. He remained motionless and silent, gazing into space, withdrawn, unlike M. du Maine, who was plainly labouring to contain all the feelings that none the less escaped him. He had leisure to savour the grim silence, broken occasionally by a dull murmur with difficulty stifled, and the glances that showed the full horror of what everyone, save for the premier président, was feeling.

M. de Mesmes gave a great dinner for those new admissions to the succession, at which the Maréchal d'Huxelles surpassed himself. There were present numerous of those gentry's servants, some magistrates on the look-out for jobs,

[1] The Duc du Maine was lame with a club-foot.

d'Antin, no other duke, no persons otherwise of distinction, one or two présidents-à-mortier. Maisons attended with the rest; he had kept throughout the session a grave and attentive countenance, vastly stiff and formal. The two bastards returned that same evening to Marly.

Despite the King's displeasure with Mme la Duchesse de Berry, and his animosity against her and M. le Duc d'Orléans—an estrangement which Mme de Maintenon encouraged with skill and care—his actions on behalf of the bastards persuaded him to remove some of her bitterness by a kindness from which he expected results. M. and Mme la Duchesse de Berry had contracted since their marriage more than five hundred thousand livres of debts; they had commissioned a great quantity of extremely beautiful furniture, and had bought a great deal of jewellery, although they already possessed much. Mme la Duchesse de Berry had been insatiable. The King paid four hundred thousand livres for her and, because there were no children, gave her all the furniture and all the jewels, even those which M. le Duc de Berry had owned before his marriage, and those which had been Monseigneur's property.

It became the fashion in Paris to drive out at midnight on the Cours la Reine, by the light of torches, and with an orchestra and dancing on the circus in the centre. For a long time all Parisian Society joined in the parade, and although there were several scandals, people still continued to go. There were almost as many carriages as in midsummer. That craze ran its course and ended only when the nights became altogether too cold to be endurable.

The perilous state of Queen Anne's health sent the Duke of Marlborough back to England, where fortune smiled on him once more.[1] On 1 August, Queen Anne died, at the age of fifty-three, a widow and childless, after a twelve-year reign, the end of which was marred by faction and sorrow. It was generally believed that she had wished to arrange matters so that her brother might succeed her;[2] and that she had persistently worked to that end, which was the real reason for the revolutionary change in the policy of the English government at the fall of Godolphin and Marlborough, and also for the peace. The King lost a true friend in her; she had ardently desired him to accept the Order of the Garter, following the precedent of his father before him, and of the other Kings of France. King Louis would gladly have received it from her, but he could not bring himself to hurt the rightful King of England, or the queen his mother, at Saint-Germain, by any other sign of recognizing Queen Anne. He had good cause to regret her death. Court mourning lasted for six weeks, during which time he wore violet. The Elector of Hanover was at once proclaimed king, in London, and soon after

[1] Since Marlborough's dismissal and the fall of the Whig government in 1712, he had been living in exile.
[2] Queen Anne's half-brother, was the Old Pretender.

there was a change of government; thus those to whom we owed the peace were abandoned to hatred and questionings.

We now come to the King's will and testament, which was later to appear amid the most remarkable precautions, devised not so much to keep the contents secret as to ensure the inviolable safety of the document itself.[1] The King was rapidly ageing; not that there was any marked change in his daily life, but those nearest him were beginning to fear that he had not long to live. This is not the place to enlarge on a constitution that, until then, had been so uniformly robust; let it suffice to say that there were ominous signs. He, who for so many years had been master of his fate, had latterly met with humiliating defeats; but more dreadful to him had been his family tragedies. All his children had died before him, leaving him a prey to dreadful suspicions,[2] so that at every moment he feared to meet their fate; yet instead of having comfort in the circle of friends who were with him continually, he found there only fresh cause for anxiety.

Maréchal his chief surgeon was the only one who strove to allay his fears. Mme de Maintenon, M. du Maine, Fagon, Blouin, and the confidential servants, all of whom were creatures of the bastard and his former governess, sought only to increase them, and, to say truth, they did not find it difficult. Everyone, indeed, suspected poison, no one could seriously have imagined otherwise; and Maréchal himself was convinced of it, although he said differently because he wished to save the King useless torment. M. du Maine, however, had too many personal interests at stake not to wish to increase his alarm, and Mme de Maintenon (pursuing her hate, and anxious to serve the one she loved) allowed the horrible suspicion to fall on the one remaining prince old enough to oppose her. Indeed, they had already determined to ruin M. le Duc d'Orléans, and now constantly encouraged the King in his sinister thoughts. You may well imagine his state of mind, seeing, as he did, the supposed perpetrator of these awful crimes at his table and at certain hours in his study.

Together with that of his children he had suffered by similar means the loss of an incomparable princess[3] who had been the life and light of his court, his joy, his darling, his great resource in his hours of leisure. Never in all his life had he felt perfectly at ease with anyone but her, and I have already described to what lengths he would go with her. Nothing filled that terrible void, and his grief was all the greater because he found no other diversion. In that unhappy state he took

---

[1] All that is known of the original document, which has since disappeared, is that it was a deed drawn up on four sheets of ordinary paper, folded, the last page being blank; that it was encased in a fifth unfolded sheet of the same paper, and was sealed seven times with the King's private seal. On it, written by the King's hand, were the words *Ceci est notre testament,* signed Louis, beneath. (From the Archives Nationales).

[2] Saint-Simon here refers again to the quite unfounded rumours of poison.

[3] The Duchesse de Bourgogne.

such comfort as came to hand, turning more and more to Mme de Maintenon and M. du Maine. In their seemingly unending devotion and the fact that they were constantly with him he found some reassurance; they had long since persuaded him that M. du Maine, although sufficiently intelligent to be consulted over the smaller details of State affairs (and small details were the King's particular weakness), was without aims or ambitions, and wholly incapable of harbouring any such. King Louis pictured him as being entirely engrossed with family concerns, and interested in glory only so far as it reflected that of the monarch whom he loved simply, honestly, transparently, and above all else. He imagined him, after a day spent dutifully in striving to please the King, and devoting long hours to prayer and meditation, going off to hunt alone, or exercising his charm and wit in the bosom of his family, often quite ignorant of what happened at the Court.

To think thus pleased King Louis greatly, and helped him to feel at ease with M. du Maine, who was, in any event, his favourite and constantly by his side amusing him with jests and anecdotes. To speak truly, I have never known a more accomplished talker than M. du Maine. He could be most charming, and so friendly that one was almost tempted to confide in him. Yet, at the same time, he was sly and malicious, and would mock most cruelly at absurdities. His words were carefully weighed to suit all occasions and the King's moods, which he understood to perfection.

He and Mme de Maintenon having become thus firmly established in the King's heart and trust, it only remained for them to make good use of a precious moment which they thought could not long endure. If the Crown itself was not their immediate aim, which is hard not to credit when one considers that abominable edict, they were, at least, determined to hold on to what they had gained, to make the future secure, and force the Regent to reckon with them when the time should come. Fortune seemed to smile on their wicked plans. They had prepared the way by most atrocious slanders, artfully sustained, designed to blacken the character of the one prince who possessed an indisputable right to the regency. With immense skill and cunning they had convinced the mean and foolish, and put doubts into the minds of others, thus rendering M. le Duc d'Orléans highly suspect in Paris and the provinces, and especially so at the Court, where no one either dared or cared to be seen with him. How could this friendless prince defend himself in the deplorable situation to which he was reduced? How disprove a negative accusation, particularly of that personal nature? How clear himself in the eyes of a king thus bedevilled? M. du Maine could scarcely have held better cards. He and Mme de Maintenon saw this so clearly that they resolved immediately to harvest all that they desired both for the present and the future.

For them it had become no longer a matter of dignities, high office, governorships, and reversions—still less one of rank and honours. They were aiming at something far greater now, namely to be what no man can achieve, to take to themselves what no subject, although crowned, can ever assume—the Divine Right.[1] They wished to defraud the princes of the blood of the sublime birthright that distinguished them from all other men, to introduce a tyrannical and wicked precedent, to destroy a holy and most ancient law, making a mockery of kingship, and trampling upon the State. Worst of all, for that dreadful deed they used a man who had not the power to change nature nor make what is not become what is, a man who, as head of an unique line, should have been doubly anxious to preserve its sanctity, since he was King solely by right of inheritance. They caused the King of a most loyal and faithful nation to disavow and cast aside its sacred laws in order to make possible the crowning of the fruit of double adultery. Louis XIV was the first King of France to raise from nothingness what all other nations, including barbarians, have from the beginning of time kept hidden. The plot was cunning enough; but it would certainly have failed, for even had it been mooted it would have gone down in a general conflagration that would have lost them all they had gained.

Be that as it may, their only concern at that time was to make the King sign a will drawn up at their dictation, by means of which they might be sure of the permanence of their new status, and gain wider powers in the future. Not that M. du Maine had any illusions as to the general fate of such documents; but the present situation was exceptional, since he had managed to persuade the King and the bulk of the nation of the criminality of M. le Duc d'Orléans. All that remained for him now was to gather the fruit. He had only to persuade the King, for conscience's sake, for the safety of his one remaining heir, and for the security of his kingdom, to reduce as far as possible the authority of a prince who had become suspect, by dividing the regency and making M. du Maine the keeper and absolute master of that precious infant the future King.

One other difficulty remained, how to ensure the safety of the aforementioned testament once the King had signed it; for it must be kept inviolate, and hedged about with precautions well calculated to increase the respect with which it would be received. Moreover some means must be devised of making its administration a matter for the Parlement, and of finding some way to overcome the King's aversion to that authority.[2] To those who knew him well, his obstinate clinging to principles, his refusal to break habits, his extreme sensitiveness regarding his absolute power, might have made the task appear impossible. But Providence decreed

[1] William of Orange would not touch for scrofula because he was elected, not king by divine right. Queen Anne consented to touch only after long self-questioning regarding the Old Pretender, and after convincing herself, temporarily at least, of the 'warming-pan plot'—If James Francis Edward had been a strange baby smuggled in merely to provide a male heir, Queen Anne would unquestionably have succeeded by divine right.
[2] Louis XIV wrote: 'An obligation that places the sovereign in the position of having to accept the law from his people is the worst calamity that can befall a man of our rank. It is perverting the natural order of things to give the decision to subjects and demand deference from the sovereign.'

otherwise. To punish himself, perhaps, for the public scandal of the double adultery, the King, fully recognizing the wickedness of his act and the shame of it, was yet impelled to perform it, bit by bit, against his will, until at last, groaning in bitterness of soul and despairing at his own weakness, he crowned his sin with this most dreadful apotheosis.

We have already seen from the King's unguarded words when he informed M. du Maine of all that he had done to include him in the succession, and from his tone and manner of speaking, how unwillingly that first disgraceful concession had been wrung from him. You shall now hear how that monarch, usually so much his own master, betrayed his feelings no less clearly in the matter of his testament. A few days before the news broke, when the King was still full of that monstrous thing, he was in his study with the two bastards, d'O, and d'Antin, and some of the personal valets. He turned to M. du Maine and, with a sour, disgruntled air, said sternly, 'You would have it so; but remember, however high I may raise you in my lifetime, when I am dead you are nothing. It will be for you to make good use of what I have done—if you can.' All present trembled at this thunderclap, so sudden, so totally unexpected, so foreign to the King's nature and habits. It clearly revealed the ultimate ambitions of M. du Maine, and the violence he did to the King in his weakness, for King Louis plainly reproached himself for his softness and the bastard for his pride and ambition.

Then it was that the curtain began to rise before all that inner circle who, until then, had been so baffled and troubled by the changes that were taking place. M. de Maine's dismay at this outburst, for which he had been quite unprepared, was so intense that the spectators held their breath and gazed fixedly at the floor. There followed a long silence that lasted an appreciable time. It was broken only when the King moved into his dressing-room and everyone could breathe again. King Louis's heart was very heavy because of what they had made him do;[1] but that was only the beginning. He had delivered himself of one monstrosity but, like a woman who gives birth to twins, there still remained another to come; he felt all the anguish of the second without any relief after the first.

The Court at that time was at Versailles. On Sunday, 26 August, Mesmes the premier président and Daguesseau the procureur général entered the study after the King's *lever*; they had already seen the Chancellor, and had agreed on the means to safeguard the precious testament. You may be sure that as soon as M. du Maine had secured his document he had discussed it thoroughly with his tool,

[1] Louis XIV's testament established a council of Regency expressly in order to reduce the Regent's powers. When he became Regent, the Duc d'Orléans would be chairman of that council, but its decisions would be made by majority vote, and the little king would be in the charge of the Duc du Maine and the Comte de Toulouse. The Regent's hands were thus tied. It was a complete contradiction of the King's absolutist principles.

the premier président. When they were alone, the King pulled open a drawer and took from it a large packet sealed with seven seals—I do not know whether M. du Maine, when he had it so sanctified, was thinking of that mysterious Book of the Seven Seals which is mentioned in the Apocrypha. However that may be, the King handed them the package, saying, 'Messieurs, this is my will; no one but myself knows its contents; to your care I consign it for safe keeping by the Parlement, to whom I can show no higher proof of my trust and esteem. The fate of the wills of earlier kings and of my royal father makes me well aware what may become of it. But they would have it. They pestered me. They gave me no peace, no matter what I said to them. Now at least I have earned my rest. Here it is! Take it now! Come what may, I shall have peace of mind and hear no more of it.' Then, turning on his heel with a curt nod, he went into another room, leaving them almost petrified with fright. They gazed at one another, deeply alarmed by what they had heard and by the King's look and expression, and as soon as they had come to their senses they left and returned to Paris. It was not known until after dinner that the King had made a will and had given it into their keeping. As the news spread, the entire Court was filled with dismay; but the toadies, who were at heart as deeply shocked as the rest, surpassed themselves in praise and eulogies.

On the following day, 27 May, the Queen of England, came from Chaillot, where she spent most of her time, to visit Mme de Maintenon. The King went in to see her, but no sooner did he clap eyes on her than he burst out with, 'Madame, I have made a will; they badgered me until it was done,' then, turning to Mme de Maintenon, 'I have bought my rest now. I realize the futility of it all; we may do as we wish while we live; afterwards we have less power than ordinary folk. You have only to think what happened to my royal father's will—and that immediately after he died.[1] I knew all this; but they would have it; they gave me no peace. Well! Madame, I have done it now; perhaps it may have some influence. At least they will stop tormenting me.'

Words so expressive of the King's outraged feelings, and of the long and bitter struggle before he yielded from misery and exhaustion—words so plain and so momentous—require proof of authenticity. Here it is! What the King said to the premier président and the procureur général, I learned from the former, who could never forget it. It is true, for I must be quite accurate, that he told me a long time afterwards; but he then repeated the King's speech to me, word for word, as I have written it here. During the interval, I had not been on good terms

---

[1] Regarding the King's doubts about his will, Madame wrote in 1716, 'The late King never believed that his will would have any effect. He said to a number of people, "They have forced me to make a will and do various other things; I have done them to get some rest; but I know that they will not be lasting." '

with him; but after his daughter's marriage to the Duc de Lorges[1] he made great efforts to be reconciled. Indeed, we patched up our quarrel so well that he kept me informed of everything, and his sister Mme de Fontenilles[2] became one of our closest friends.

What the King said to the Queen of England was much more direct and emphatic, partly because he was more intimate with her, partly because Mme de Maintenon was present, and he intended her to feel his reproaches. I heard of it two days later from M. de Lauzun, to whom the queen repeated it all in her first astonishment; and she did not need pressing, so full was she of the King's terrifying remarks, which she recounted to M. de Lauzun, word by word, just as he reported it to me, and as I have written it here. Further proof was in the unusually disagreeable expression on the King's face, his curt and haughty tone, which was so unlike him, his angry answers to every question, Mme de Maintenon's acute embarrassment, and the low spirits of the Duc du Maine, whose ill-humour lasted more than a week, and was only gradually dissipated. It became very plain that they were having to endure recriminations; but they had what they wanted, and might think themselves lucky to have only passing tantrums to bear. They well knew that by patience and courtesy, and by being more than ordinarily attentive, they would soon make the King glad he had surrendered, and could enjoy the repose he had purchased so dearly.

As soon as the premier président and the procureur général reached Paris, they sent for workmen and took them to the tower behind the robing-room of the great chamber, and the premier président's office. There they made them hollow out a large hole in the wall which is very thick at that point, and there they placed the testament. The opening was closed, first with an iron door, then with a grille, and was then walled up. The iron door and the grille were each given three locks, arranged in such a way that the three keys each opened only two of the locks. The premier président and the procureur général kept two of the keys, and the third was given to the chief clerk. The Parlement happened to be in session, and thus the premier président was able to give them a most gratifying account of the King's respect and esteem, and of his confidence that his will would be safe in their keeping, and its provisions put into effect when the time came.

I have already said that consternation reigned when the existence of the will became known. It was M. du Maine's misfortune that he always obtained his desires amid public execration; this occurred also in the affair of the King's will. When he realized the general sentiments he became frantic.

---

[1] The Duc de Lorges's second marriage took place on 14 December, 1720. The bride was Marie Antoinette de Mesmes (1696-1767).
[2] The Marquise de Fontenilles: Louise Marie Thérèse de Mesmes (1668-1755); she married François de La Roche, Marquis de Fontenilles, in 1693.

Mme de Maintenon was furious, and both redoubled their efforts to prevent any
whispers from reaching the King. They set themselves more than ever to keep him
happy and amused, and saw to it that he heard nothing but praise, rejoicings, and
general congratulations for his great, wise, generous, and beneficent gesture, which
was, so they said, needed to maintain the peace, and to extend the glory of his reign
beyond the span of his life. The public dismay was only natural in the circumstances,
but M. du Maine had not expected it, and he was deeply pained. He had persuaded
himself that the abominable suspicions he had cast on M. le Duc d'Orléans had
cleared his own path; and, indeed, he had partly succeeded, but not to the extent he
supposed. His own wishes and his spies had greatly magnified his achievement; thus
when, instead of applause, he received the opposite, he was vastly discomfited.

People saw very clearly that the will was aimed against M. le Duc d'Orléans, for
had there been no desire to obstruct him, there was no need for a will, and matters
might have been left to take the normal course. The doubts and suspicions, so carefully maintained, were not diminished; but whatever people may have believed,
however much they disapproved, no one was so blind as not to realize that M. le
Duc d'Orléans must be regent because of his incontestable birth-right. No will could
destroy that, unless some newer power, equal to his own, were to be established. But
that would be to create two parties within the State, which the rival leaders would
support by every possible means. Every man would then be forced to choose his side,
and in such a choice lie a thousand dangers and no good hope. Such considerations,
more or less understood by people according to their lights, lay at the root of the
murmurs and whispered arguments. Fear kept them muffled, but they were audible
none the less, and as time went on they increased.

What reason demanded, what most men of rank desired, what even those
commonplace minds that form public opinion dumbly conceived, was that the King
during his lifetime should establish the government that he wished to continue after
him, bring into his councils those whom he intended to leave in power, and give
them at once their offices and functions. He, meanwhile, ruling with the same absolute authority, would train the future regent and those who were appointed to serve
under him in a new administration. Thus might the King become executor of his
own testament, and his death bring no sudden change, but all proceed smoothly, in
the way that he had ordered and desired.

As for M. le Duc d'Orléans, he was stunned by the blow. He could feel how
closely it touched him, but saw no remedy while the King still lived. A deep, respectful silence seemed to him the only possible course, for any other would have led
to the redoubling of precautions. There I shall leave the affair for the present; it
is not yet time to discuss the prince's plans and intentions. The King avoided all
speech with him on such matters; except for one bald statement after the event.

M. du Maine the same. M. le Duc d'Orléans replied with a simple 'yes' to both, like a well-trained courtier who never argues. He refrained even from discussion with his wife. I was the only one to whom he dared speak openly. With all the rest he took pains to appear as usual, and avoided looking displeased or opening his mind to prying tongues. His utter isolation at the Court and in Society saved him from hearing comments, for no one would mention the subject to him; even Maisons failed him.

For some time past, the King must have been considering how best, after his death, to provide for the Dauphin's education. It was only natural, thinking as he had been led to think of M. le Duc d'Orléans, that he should have been unwilling to leave the charge to him. Mme de Maintenon and M. du Maine may well have used that very argument to open their campaign, and thence all the rest had followed. Be that as it may, when, shortly after M. le Duc de Berry's death, I went to Vaucresson where M. de Beauvilliers was lying indisposed, he asked to speak with me alone. Thereupon, without further preamble, he said that he wished to ask me a question, but only on condition that I answered him truly and precisely, without either fear or favour. I asked whether his kindness and trust for so many years, and the frankness with which I habitually addressed him did not guarantee a straight answer. He replied with all his usual affection, adding that if I would give my promise I should soon see that he had a special reason. I then gave my word, much surprised by his insistence, and even more curious to know his reasons.

He proceeded to tell me that the King believed he would not live to see the Dauphin pass into the care of men, and thus felt it his duty to provide in advance for his upbringing. He wished M. de Beauvilliers to take sole charge of him and his education, acting in every way as he had done for the prince's royal father and uncles. M. de Beauvilliers had excused himself on the plea of age and infirmity, which seemed to offer him no chance of completing such a task. King Louis had none the less insisted, and had finally consented to his doing only so much as he felt able and willing to undertake. At this point, looking me straight in the face, M. de Beauvilliers thus addressed me: 'You are duke and peer and senior to me in rank; would you consider it an indignity to be made joint-governor with myself, to do what I cannot manage, in a word, to share equally in my work, and yet, although the senior in rank, not be the first? That is what I want you to answer truly. Do not be afraid to hurt me.' I answered that I should speak the absolute truth; I fully understood that such a post would mean acting as assistant governor; that for no other man would I consent, but that for him, whom I had always looked on as a father, I agreed with all my heart. He embraced me, saying that I had greatly relieved him, with many other touching expressions of his love and gratitude. He then asked me to be very secret, and continued in a way which I understood to mean that when the details were arranged the King would speedily make an announcement.

This was the last mark of esteem and affection which M. de Beauvilliers was able to give me; it was also the last of so many which he had received from the King, despite the persistent dislike of Mme de Maintenon. His failing health did not allow him time to see the decision take effect. He had always been delicate; a life divided between the practice of his religion, his official functions, of which he never missed one unless two overlapped, and his affairs, left him little time for recreation within the narrow compass of his immediate relations, and the still smaller circle of his friends. Thus his health could never improve. The loss of his children had left him deeply afflicted; you know what courage and remarkable piety he and Mme de Beauvilliers showed in that fatal hour;[1] but neither of them ever recovered. The Dauphin's death affected him as much in another way, as he more than once told me. All his affection had been turned on that prince, whose nature, talents, industry, and plans he had so greatly admired, and whose complete confidence in him he had found deeply touching. Convinced though he was of the Dauphin's saintliness and present happiness, his death had so overwhelmed him that ever since he had languished—wretched, bitter, inconsolable; and the death of the Duc de Chevreuse, his bosom friend, the one who had shared and often influenced his most secret thoughts, dealt him the final blow. He lay for nearly two months ill at Vaucresson and there died the death of the just, on Friday, 31 August, in the early evening, retaining all his faculties unimpaired until the end. He was nearly sixty-six years of age, about three years younger than the Duc de Chevreuse, having been born on 24 October, 1648, of extremely ancient lineage,[2] with many very noble alliances, especially in the more remote past.

Mme de Beauvilliers, who had been so tenderly and piously joined in union with him throughout their married lives, remained inconsolable, but bore her grief like a Christian and a woman of strong character. He wished to be buried in the Benedictine convent where seven of his daughters[3] had asked to be professed, and where his eldest daughter was the perpetual prioress, the others all having refused to accept abbeys. Mme de Beauvilliers went there also, and by an act of devotion too dreadful to contemplate was present at his interment. It was a place at which she liked to make retreats, going there each year for a long period, and often more than once, living among her daughters and other close relatives in bitter sorrow and with severe penances, although she allowed nothing of that to appear during the community's times of recreation. To continue to live in Paris at their vast mansion,[4] far from those nuns, was a sacrifice which she made for the sake of Mme de Chevreuse, for, having no children in the world and

[1] See Vol I, p. 280.
[2] The Duc de Beauvilliers's family claimed descent from Louis le Débonnaire (778-840), son of Charlemagne and Hildegarde, King of France and Emperor of the West.
[3] The Beauvilliers had nine daughters. The first died at the age of two, in 1674, the fifth became the Duchesse de Mortemart, and the remaining seven were nuns at Montargis.
[4] The Hôtel de Beauvilliers.

no social duties, she did not feel it incumbent on her to live like other widows. Her retirement was complete, no dinners, nor even the most innocent diversions; everything tending that way was banished from her life, and all connection with Society severed. She saw only close relatives and a very few friends who had also been the friends of M. de Beauvilliers, with whom she had shared everything. Her days were spent in prayer, either at her home or in church; but sometimes she visited her sisters, or Mme de Saint-Simon, after we came to live in Paris. She went nowhere else, or almost nowhere. For a great part of each summer she went to her estates in order to busy herself with good works, and there she was, if possible, more alone even than in Paris. She lived nigh on another twenty years in this most solitary and penitential vacuum and died in 1733, aged seventy-five, infinitely rich in alms-giving and in good deeds of every kind.

I confess that I find it hard to tear myself from persons who were, and always will remain, dear to me; but it is time to return to my situation at the Court, so different now from what it once had been. The deaths of the Dauphin and the Dauphine and the dispersal of their ladies, Chamillart's disgrace, the Chancellor's retirement, the deaths of the Maréchal de Boufflers, the Duc de Chevreuse and, lastly, of the Duc de Beauvilliers, had left a blank which nothing could fill. I had been the intimate friend of all these ministers and great nobles, just as I had been friends with many well-informed ladies of the highest standing, who in one way or another had since disappeared. Those friendships, and especially my attachment to the Dauphin at the end of his life, a relationship that became known despite the most careful precautions, had turned all eyes upon me. Envy far exceeded any future prospects I might have enjoyed. I was considered so ripe for the council that my enemies took fright, and Blouin, M. du Maine's tool, hinted as much to the King, which in itself was enough to obstruct me. Among those surrounding the King, I had now only Maréchal, who more than once broke a lance in my defence when I was attacked in the royal presence. Among the ministers I had no one, for Desmaretz avoided me without cause, and, as soon as I perceived this, I avoided him. I have already mentioned that I had no acquaintance with Torcy, and with Pontchartrain I still remained on bad terms. Voysin, the Chancellor and secretary of State, I barely knew and, in any case, he was the tool of Mme de Maintenon and M. du Maine. Thus the successors of my great friends were either opposed or, at the very least, indifferent to me. In short, I had no one to support me, for Charost, despite his post,[1] was nothing, and Noailles, endeavouring to keep up appearances and gnawed by the cancer of concealed disgrace, was

---

[1] The Duc de Charost was captain of the King's bodyguard.

in greater need of me than I of him. The ministers and the King's family circle were against me, and at the Court many daggers were pointed at me, either from fear or jealousy, or from the thought of a not too distant future when M. le Duc d'Orléans would be regent.

He and I were lifelong friends, and people now were aware that his separation from Mme d'Argenton, his reconciliation with Mme la Duchesse d'Orléans, their present harmony, and the marriage of Mme la Duchesse de Berry had been my work. His manifest disgrace with the King, the dangers of the Spanish affair, the repeated cries of poison, the general avoidance of him still continued. Warnings and dark threats reached my ears, but did not affect me, and I remained the only courtier to be seen with him in the gardens at Marly, publicly, under the King's very eye. My conduct gave the direct lie to the loathsome slanders by which M. du Maine, in partnership with Mme de Maintenon, had so greatly profited. I still retained my reputation for truth, honour, and integrity, which no quarrels over rank had ever impugned. Mme de Saint-Simon's reputation was of the highest in every possible way. Everyone had some conception of the enormous loss we had suffered by the deaths of the Dauphin and the Dauphine, both then and for the future. They knew also how much we had loved them. I was never noted for restraint; and it was thus plain to all that, had I suspected M. le Duc d'Orléans in the slightest degree, I should have broken with him absolutely, without a care for the future. So much, indeed, was generally recognized; moreover, I saw him too often and too intimately not to have had some knowledge of his crime, no matter how hard he might have tried to conceal it. That was one cause of my disregarding the warnings that reached me from every quarter urging me to change. My steadfast attitude towards him had brought upon me the anger of Mme de Maintenon and M. du Maine who, in addition to all else, wished to deprive him of the only friend who still sought his company and whom he might consult.

Although the King's health was beginning to fail, there was no immediate cause for alarm, and I envisaged a long and lonely passage between all these rocks and shoals. But God would not let me be discouraged. I resolved to be very prudent, but to continue as before, to seek no one's friendship and, above all, to let my conduct towards M. le Duc d'Orléans be as before, both in public and private, and to give no one the pleasure of watching me weaken or attempt to trim. This short explanation was needed to understand what follows, although it is not yet time to describe what passed between Mme la Duchesse d'Orléans and myself. In the meanwhile, let us return to world affairs, which I have too long neglected.

You will recall that it was on Sunday, 26 August, that the King gave his testament into the keeping of the premier président and the procureur général, and that it was registered and locked away on Tuesday, the 28th. On the following night the King slept at Petit-Bourg, and reached Fontainebleau on Thursday, 30 August. It was on Friday, the 31st, that the Duc de Beauvilliers died at Vaucresson.

In Spain there had been great displeasure at the continued absence of the grand inquisitor, who was also a counsellor of State. Mme des Ursins was enchanted by Cardinal del Giudice's non-appearance, since it was for that very purpose that she had dispatched him to France with most unseemly haste; but her other purpose, the King of Spain's second marriage, had not yet been achieved. She therefore conspired to make King Philip still more vexed with the cardinal; but delayed his recall until his mission had been accomplished, as it was when he at last gave King Louis official notice of the approaching marriage, on the morning of the day when that monarch left Versailles to sleep at Petit-Bourg. The cardinal had been invited to the next Marly, and had been allotted a fine, large bedroom; but Mme des Ursins, having been informed of the exact date of the announcement, so arranged matters that he received his recall immediately afterwards. Giudice was astounded. He went to Fontainebleau on Monday, 3 September; had a long audience of the King in his study; took leave of him, and returned at once to Paris, where he told everyone of his grief at parting, and hinted something of his fears. He did not hesitate to say that he felt he was quitting a terrestrial paradise, and returning to a country where he would find only troubles and no one on whom he could rely. He added that he would gladly resign all his offices if King Philip would make him his ambassador to France, and thus make it possible for him to live there permanently.

Two days later King Louis sent him a diamond worth ten thousand écus, and he forthwith set out for Spain, travelling by post-chaise with his nephew. When he reached Bayonne, however, he found an order forbidding him to enter Spain, and commanding him to wait in that city until further notice. There we will leave him, for he remained a very long time without a summons, and he had the extra humiliation of being forbidden to meet the new Queen of Spain as she passed through the town. We shall learn in due course what became of him.

I do not know what the Princesse des Ursins had discovered of the character of the Princess of Parma; but she became so apprehensive of the latter's arrogant and high-handed ways that she repented of ever having made the match, and did her best to undo it. With that intention she created all manner of obstacles, and sent a courier to Cardinal Acquaviva, the Spanish chargé d'affaires in Rome, giving him instructions to delay his departure for Parma. He was under orders from King Philip to go there bearing the proposal of marriage, and to witness the proxy-wedding. Mme des Ursins, however, had changed her mind too late, for Acquaviva had started by the time her courier arrived, and was already approaching Parma, which would have made his sudden return extremely difficult to explain. He was received with all honour and much ceremony, and made the proposal; but the actual wedding he was able to postpone, although this caused a great scandal. In the meantime Parma was finding the expense hard to bear; but the marriage at last took place, on 16 September, and was performed by Cardinal Gozzadini, the legate appointed by the Pope for that especial function, and to convey his congratulations to the new Queen of Spain. She left immediately afterwards with the intention of embarking at Genoa and going by sea to Alicante, accompanied by the Marquesa de los Balbases and the Princesse of Piombino, a brilliant woman and a close friend of the Princesse des Ursins.

The new envoy from Parma had an audience of King Louis on 11 October, at Fontainebleau, to report, if somewhat belatedly, the celebration of the marriage. The queen had a dowry of a hundred thousand pistoles, and three thousand livres in jewellery and precious stones. The King sent the Duc de Saint-Aignan to convey his compliments, and also a present. This consisted of his portrait set with four diamonds and certain other jewels. It reflected King Louis's displeasure at the marriage, for its entire value did not amount to more than a hundred thousand francs.

The King had been in a remarkably bad temper during the journey to Fontainebleau, becoming angry over trifles (which was unlike him), dismissing his coachman and flying out at the master of the horse, of whom he was fond; at least so said Mme de Saint-Simon, who travelled in the same coach as the King and the princesses. He had plainly not yet recovered from the 'torments' to which M. du Maine had subjected him, and of which he had complained to the Queen of England. He had found his apartments at Fontainebleau completely altered; I do not know whether they were any more comfortable; but they were certainly not more beautiful. The Elector of Bavaria arrived a few days later, and set up residence at d'Antin's house, with card-tables and the highest stakes imaginable, beginning soon after dawn. He was for ever gambling at Madame la Duchesse's house, and she sometimes went to him. She frequently took him in her gondola on the canal, when the King, followed by the entire Court, went out driving. The Elector joined in all the hunts, and saw the King then, but very rarely entered the study. Mme de Maintenon made every effort to keep the King amused with dinners, concerts, and games within their private circle. She had a gallery constructed in the play-room opposite the theatre, and went there from her apartments. The King, who for many years past had ceased to go to the theatre, sometimes watched an act or two, with certain ladies chosen from among those at dinner. I noticed Mme d'Espinay on one occasion. He saw whole plays by Molière in Mme de Maintenon's room, acted by professional actors, with music in the intervals.

The Comte de Luc's son arrived on the morning of Wednesday, 12 September, bearing the news that the peace-treaty between the Emperor and the

King had been signed at Baden. Prior[1] came also, on behalf of the new King of England,[2] to acquaint the King at a private audience of his accession to that throne, of his imminent departure from Hanover to London, and of his wish to maintain peace and good neighbourliness. King George made his entry into London with great pomp and ceremony on 1 October. He dismissed the Duke of Ormonde, Lord Bolingbroke and several other noblemen from their posts, changed Queen Anne's government for the opposition, and restored Marlborough to all his offices and commands, thus giving power to the Whigs at the Tories' expense. This boded no good for France.

The King returned from Fontainebleau on Wednesday, 23 October. He slept at Petit-Bourg, and on the following day arrived at Versailles. Mme de Saint-Simon, who was in his coach, said that he was in no better mood than on the previous journey, and that from seeing him on those two occasions, she thought that his health had deteriorated. That was his last visit to Fontainebleau.

He was harassed also by the affair of the constitution,[3] for Père Tellier had laid the whole burden of it on his conscience and authority. There had been much negotiation with Cardinal de Noailles. Cardinal d'Estrées, who by order of the King had been forced to intervene, had soon after retired in disgust at the knavery of Père Tellier and Bissy, concerning whom he was most outspoken. Cardinal de Polignac then intruded himself. The result was the same; he displeased the King, and quarrelled so violently with Cardinal de Rohan that he refused to compliment him on his brother's becoming a duke and peer. All who were learned and honest in the episcopate followed Cardinal de Noailles. The famous universities, the religious orders, the chapters, the curés of Paris and a vast number in the provinces, the parlements, and those scholarly laymen who were not slaves of the Jesuits were all on his side; even at the Court only one voice was faintly heard. Among those who accepted the constitution, there was not even a glimmer of unanimity; everyone explained it differently; there was utter chaos, a very tower of Babel. It became more than ever plain that without menaces, promises, rewards, and the severest punishments, the constitution would be universally refused, and that for those who accepted it the problem was to find some pretext for receiving the words and rejecting the sense. The Pope, becoming more and more vexed at not finding the blind obedience promised him by Père Tellier (without which he would never have embarked on the detestable affair), issued a brief expressing his anger against those who opposed him. Faced with all these troubles,

---

[1] Matthew Prior (1664-1721), the poet and diplomat. He already knew Louis XIV because he had brought to France the articles of the Peace of Ryswick in 1697. He entered Parliament in 1701, joined the Tories, and became Queen Anne's ambassador to Paris in 1712. In 1715, he was impeached, and imprisoned until 1717.

[2] George I.

[3] The affair of the Bull *Unigenitus*.

King Louis was finally persuaded to entreat the Pope either to provide some explanation of his bull, or alternatively to allow a national council to be held in France; but as you may well imagine, that council, when held, was merely the tool of Rome.

During the afternoon of 28 November, I spent an hour with M. le Duc d'Orléans, who appeared in his usual robust health. Mme la Duchesse d'Orléans had remained at Versailles[1] suffering from a slight fever. I then joined the King in his gardens. After a time the cold drove me indoors, and I went to warm myself in the little drawing-room between the King's room and that of Mme de Maintenon, until he should come back to change his coat before going to her room. I had been there nigh on a quarter of an hour, quite alone, when I heard cries of, 'M. Fagon! M. Maréchal!' and the names of other doctors, who might be thought to be in the King's study, awaiting his return. Almost at once the shouts grew louder, and blue footmen[2] came running through the drawing-room. I inquired what was amiss. They said that M. le Duc d'Orléans had been taken very ill. I at once rushed to his side. I found him with his buttons all undone, his cravat missing, being dragged, rather than supported, by two of his servants, up and down the length of his room before the open windows. His face was redder than usual but in no way contorted; his eyes were fixed and staring; his speech easy and unaffected. He at once told me that he had had a sudden fit of giddiness, but thought that it was of no consequence. Soon afterwards Fagon appeared, followed by Maréchal and some others. They let him walk a little while longer, then gave him some essences and recommended him to go to bed, but on no account to sleep. They also wished to bleed him; but he would have none of that, and they left him alone for the time being. I remained with him. He told me that not knowing the cause of his sickness, and seeing that his head was clear and that he felt no constriction anywhere, he had thought it wiser to let them feel and sound him, but to wait for any after effects before being bled, because with certain poisons blood-letting is fatal.[3]

When the King returned, he sent Maréchal to inquire, with a message to say that, since Fagon reported that there was no danger, he would not visit him because the stairs were tiring. I stayed with him, almost always alone, until past midnight. There were very few callers, and for the most part they came in groups, doing no more than enter and leave. Mme la Duchesse de Berry and Madame had both been to Versailles to see Mme la Duchesse d'Orléans, to whom I sent two notes during the course of the evening. The bleeding was done later on. Maréchal called four or five times before the

---

[1] The King and the Court were at Marly.

[2] The footmen in blue liveries who waited on the Court and carried the fleet of chairs put at the service of the courtiers in the gardens of Versailles and Marly.

[3] Fear of poisoning was in the air. On the other hand, some people were beginning to think that bleeding might in itself be dangerous, as was only too probable because of dirty knives especially when, as in measles, the blood was already infected.

King's *coucher*. He told me two days later that on each occasion the King had asked to know who was with M. le Duc d'Orléans, and that each time he had mentioned me. On the last occasion the King, who until then had made no comment, remarked, 'M. de Saint-Simon is a good friend of my nephew; I wish he had no other, for he is an honest man and always gives him good advice. I am never anxious on that account. I only wish he did not follow the advice of others.' I felt greatly relieved at this information, although I must confess, without vanity, that I did not fear my reputation with the King—nor with anyone else for that matter. None the less, M. le Duc d'Orléans had been so cruelly abused in the intimate circle around the King; and I had received such a hailstorm of threats and warnings concerning him, that I had every reason for thinking that the King disliked our friendship. Life became very much easier when I knew the facts to be otherwise.

The King's remark led me to wonder whence he had gleaned such a flattering impression of me, despite those who had tried to persuade him to the contrary. It was more than plain that I had neither Mme de Maintenon nor M. du Maine to thank, nor any of the ministers. It might have been Maréchal (but he would have told me), or possibly the Duc de Beauvilliers. What seemed more likely was that I had never been suspected of having had any part in the more serious crimes for which M. le Duc d'Orléans was blamed; not even the smallest rumour had come from that hostile and envious cabal, whom I had done nothing to appease. Moreover, I had dissociated myself entirely, and at all times, not only from his mistresses, debauches, and private suppers, but also from his boon companions in Paris. The most likely explanation was that the King had learned at last that it was I who had parted him from Mme d'Argenton, reconciled him with his wife, and helped them to remain united by giving them a common friend. Perhaps Mme la Duchesse d'Orléans, herself, may have said something to the King, for she greatly approved of my being her husband's constant companion. If that were so, she never gave me the smallest hint to that effect.

Maréchal also said that he had taken the opportunity, when the courtiers who possessed that entrée had left the King after his *petit coucher*, to mention M. le Duc d'Orléans again, in the hope that the King would speak of him, for he had been singularly unforthcoming during the earlier reports. He set to praising his ability, enumerating the sciences and arts in which he was skilled, and ended by saying jokingly that, had M. le Duc d'Orléans been obliged to earn his living, he might have made a handsome fortune in five or six different ways. The King let him speak; then, after smiling at Maréchal's last remark, he grew more serious, turned to face him, and said, 'You know my nephew. He is just as you say; but he likes to flaunt his vices.' When Maréchal repeated those words to me I was quite overcome by the King's brilliance, for it was M. le Duc d'Orléans to the life; but I confess that I should never have imagined the King capable of understanding this.

M. le Duc d'Orléans recovered so quickly that he was able to attend the King's *lever* on the following morning, and immediately afterwards went to Versailles, where he remained. There being only two or three days left of that Marly, he took one or two gentle remedies,[1] and did not go there again.

Sceaux had become the scene of the ever wilder follies of the Duchesse du Maine, to the shame, embarrassment, and ruin of her husband, who was obliged to pay for her monstrous extravagance. Her house was a perpetual source of amusement for Parisian Society and the courtiers, who went there in vast numbers, and much despised her. She spent entire nights with lotteries, gambling, feasts, and fireworks; and every day there were entertainments of various kinds. She played *Athalie* several times a week in a company of professional actors and actresses. She revelled in her new grandeur; she multiplied her follies on that account, and the Duc du Maine, who lived in terror lest the slightest opposition should drive her frantic, was constrained, albeit with a very bad grace, to do the honours for her, when that did not too much interfere with his assiduous watch over the King's leisure.

Great though his joy undoubtedly was, and unbelievable the height to which he had climbed, M. du Maine's mind was far from easy. Like tyrants who illegally seize the sovereign power, and for ever after live in dread of their fellow-countrymen, he felt that the sword of Damocles hung over him. He, who so often made a jest of grave matters, admitted freely to his friends that he felt like a flea between a thumb and fingernail (the princes of the blood and the peers), and that sooner or later they would unite to crush him. Such reflections prevented him from enjoying all the glory that his schemes had brought him. He dreaded the time when the princes of the blood would be old enough to comprehend the monstrous wrong he had done to that royal blood which made them unlike other men. He feared lest, even in his presence, the Parlement should be unable to conceal its abhorrence at the violation of most sacred laws. Not even the doglike devotion of the premier président had power to reassure him, for de Mesmes was too much despised for his ignorance, and too notorious for his loose-living and immorality, to have much influence over his colleagues. He feared even the dukes, so abject does tyranny and injustice make a man. All these terrors led him to devise a plot to sow discord among his enemies, in order that they might forget him in quarrelling with one another, or, at least, lose the desire to unite against him, an eventuality which he most of all dreaded. So that you may know how he achieved that purpose, I must

[1] In such cases remedies nearly always signified purges.

first explain certain matters concerning the peers and the Parlement. Although I shall be very brief, necessity forbids my being as brief as I could wish.[1]

First let me explain the rank of a peer of France,[2] for it is not what it was in former days; also the functions of the Paris Parlement, and of the other parlements throughout the kingdom. An acquaintance with these matters is essential for what follows.

We know as a certain fact that the early successors of Pharamond[3] were less like kings than captains who led their warlike followers to break their boundaries and increase their lands by force of arms and conquest. Clovis[4] was perhaps our first king, in the true sense of that word, for he gave some kind of stability to the new State, reigned with a certain majesty and, after embracing Christianity, created order and discipline among his subjects, and encouraged trade with neighbouring kingdoms. His rule was wholly military, but never despotic. The principal chieftains who had helped him to form his kingdom were summoned to his councils for war and peacemaking, to make and enforce the laws, and decide every other thing that concerned internal and external affairs. As their conquests spread, these Franks gave the name of France to defeated Gaul, and received from their king large tracts of conquered territory, in proportion to their services and importance. Such estates took the place of pay for assistance rendered. At first they were held for life; only later did they become family possessions. As time went on, those with the greatest estates gave away portions to Franks of lower degree, under the same terms as they had received their own lands from the king—that is to say, under an oath of fealty, which bound them to maintain troops at their own expense and to lead them in the wars under the king's command. The earliest of these great nobles were thus feudal lords, having vassals holding feoffs from them, with similar obligations to their lords of loyalty and military service as those which their lords owed to the king. That is how the nobility came into existence. They were not sufficiently numerous to cultivate their land unaided, and accordingly they gave portions of it to certain serfs under their jurisdiction—not as rewards for military service, but in exchange for rent and other dues, out of which have arisen the various manorial rights. Some serfs thus became landowners, while others remained landless, and these two groups combined to form the common people, since called the third estate, which, even today, is divided into townsfolk and peasants.

---

[1] Saint-Simon apologizes on the score of length, as well he may, since his 'brief account' covers nearly a hundred pages in the *Pléiade* edition. This editor therefore does not apologize for very drastic cutting; this is one of Macaulay's 'very dry deserts', but to Saint-Simon himself the affair was of the very first importance.

[2] There were three kinds of dukedom: (1) dukedoms with a peerage, (2) dukedoms verified by the Parlement, (3) so-called brevet-dukedoms, not registered by the Parlement by the date of their creation, not hereditary but for life only, and not privileged to receive all ducal honours.

[3] Pharamond, a legendary Frankish king of the fifth century.

[4] Clovis (*c.* 466-511), king of the Franks.

The Church also received land through the bounty of the kings and nobles. Bishops and abbots became nobles by owning vast stretches of land; and they also bestowed estates in feoff, which became the rich benefices of today, and carried then similar obligations of loyalty and military service. On account of their temporal power, such bishops were regarded as being on a par with other feudal lords, until the lay nobles in their innocence gave the prelates pride of place, as a religious principle, and because they also possessed ecclesiastical rank. It was thus that the early nobility who, alone at first, had power under the king, allowed a second power to come into existence; which was how the remaining land-owning and landless serfs came to be known as the third estate.

The government, a purely military one, was administered by an army council called the *Champs de Mars*. Each year in March or, latterly, in May, the king summoned an assembly and named the place and date. Every bishop and great noble attended with his vassals and their troops. Two courts were then set up in the open air, one for the prelates and the other for the nobles, while round them, in the open field, stood the crowd of men-at-arms—in other words the troops commanded by subsidiary vassals. The king sat on a raised throne to hear the answers to his proposals, and when all were agreed, he proclaimed the military or civil decisions that had been taken. Thereupon the great crowd of warriors burst into a shout of '*Vivat!*' This crowd discussed nothing, nor were their opinions asked; their lords represented them, and their only function was to applaud the decisions which the king proclaimed. There is very much that requires amplifying in this brief account; but an account (very brief of necessity) is what was needed here, not an exact history.

The title 'peer of France' was not used until a later date; but those early feudal lords, great vassals of the crown, were none the less peers in all but name, for they fulfilled the same function, and had the right to sit beside the throne from the very beginning. The word 'peer' comes from the legal right of every man to be judged by his peers, that is to say his equals. Thus the owner of each great feoff had his peers, and the title came to be held by the most important of those powerful vassals who held land from the king, sat with him in judgment, and assisted him in governing the kingdom.[1] Moreover, the king himself bore subsidiary titles on a par with theirs; he was, for instance, Duc de France and Comte de Paris.

As time went on, quarrels over inheritance, debts, the division of spoils, terms of service, and crimes, vastly increased, as did the ordinary business of governing the kingdom. Thus the grand assembly came to be held more often, and since the

---

[1] The oath taken by a duke and peer at his reception by the Parlement was 'to serve well and faithfully, to assist and counsel the King in his most high and mighty affairs, and, holding sessions at the Court, to do justice to poor and rich alike, guarding the laws, keeping secret the deliberations of the council, and in all things to conduct himself as befits a virtuous, wise, and merciful peer of France'.

problems were no longer purely military, the crowd of warriors ceased to attend. Later, the king, the peers with some of their vassals, and certain of the bishops, whom the king specially appointed, formed other courts, and the *Champs de Mars* was no longer held. In the reign of Saint Louis,[1] the king appointed jurists to explain the law and assist the peers by giving them the benefit of their professional knowledge.

These jurists were commoners, men versed in the arts of the law. They sat on the steps of the high seats on which the peers had their places, so as to be near them for consultation, if required. But such consultation was a purely voluntary matter, and the peers were by no means obliged to follow their advice. Jurists had no say in lawsuits; their only function was to enlighten the peers on points of law, if consulted, after which the peers voted according to their own lights. Hence the legal title of counsellor; the jurists attended to give counsel to the peers. Judges they were never called, for judging was not their business.

Little by little, the peers who were usually occupied in the wars, or in other great affairs, ceased to attend every trial. The lesser lords, summoned a few at a time, began also to send excuses. The king likewise was often absent. Thus, because lawsuits continued to increase, the king granted permission for the jurists to speak and vote in unimportant cases, and the jurists, having gained that privilege, managed to keep it, even when peers were present. No one at that time, or until much later, ever conceived that those same lawyers had either received or requested permission to speak and vote in important trials, or in cases affecting the good of the State. Apart from the fact that there was no precedent for any such thing, you have only to consider the difference in their status and that of the peers and the lesser lords of that time. Moreover, you shall see in due course that the peers of today are exactly similar to their forebears, in rank, quality, and functions. Let us now, however, pursue the jurists.

At a later period, the ever increasing number of lawsuits required the courts to be held more often, and the king accordingly named certain festivals on which they might assemble in one or other of his palaces. These courts came to be called parlements, because men parleyed there together. The peers attended when they so pleased; they were the judges and did not receive summonses. Lesser lords and jurists were appointed by the king, but they all attended by royal summons, and none sat during two successive assemblies. So things continued until the time of Charles VI.[2] During that disastrous reign, the rival factions of Bourgogne and

---

[1] Louis IX (1214-1270), King of France from 1226. He directed the sixth crusade, 1249, built the Sainte-Chapelle, authorized the Sorbonne, embarked on a new crusade against Tunis, and died of the plague while besieging that city. He was canonized in 1297, an event which confirmed later French Kings in the agreeable belief that they were of semi-divine birth.

[2] Charles VI (1368-1422), Le Bien-Aimé or, to the English, the Foolish. In his reign the French lost the Battle of Agincourt (1415), and most of his kingdom went to the English. He died insane.

Orléans packed the parlements for their personal advantage when the king was unfit to make nominations. In the resulting chaos, it was thought best to make life appointments to the courts, instead of issuing summonses for one session only. That was the beginning of offices and office-holders. The parlements tended to occupy ever greater periods of time; the peers were forced to choose between the claims of sword and pen, and the lesser lords, with no time to spare on account of the wars, ceased altogether to attend, with very few exceptions; their families, all now extinct, were the highest-ranking members of the Parlement of Paris. This account is, of necessity, more like a précis than a history, but the historical truth has none the less been rigidly preserved.

Such then were the first jurists, and that was how the parlements first came into being. Their power has since steadily increased, owing to wars that made possible the sale and re-sale of offices, and multiplied *ad infinitum* the number of the courts and their officers. It is thus that the jurists, from being mere prompters, consulted at will, allowed only to whisper into the ear of a peer in judgment, have gradually become equal judges with the peers. This they made plain first by placing a partition between their backs and the peers' feet, and then by quietly raising the step of the peers' bench, on which was their proper place, until they had made of it a bench for their own use. That is the origin of the high and low benches in the great chamber in Paris, and in all other great chambers of the provincial parlements.

Thus the jurists became, first assistant-judges, then judges in their own right, and finally judges by inheritance. Defeats in war and a pressing need for money led the kings to make profit from their appointments by selling them, and later by creating offices that were both saleable and hereditary. By that time the magistrates had assumed the title of président, and had swelled in numbers until they had formed the great host that swarms over Paris today, and proliferates in the provinces under various other titles, attaching to the upper and lower courts of justice.

When the Paris Parlement went into permanent session and increased its jurist-membership, a staff of magistrates was formed to function throughout the year, and that staff also became permanent, as did the staffs of jurists in the provincial parlements. In time, the magistrates came to be accepted as the absolute rulers of the courts of justice, above all the lords except the peers, and sitting on the highest seats. Later, the premier président continued to act as such, even when peers were present, then did so as a right, just as the jurists, from having been mere consultants, developed into magistrates. Thenceforward, on the pretext that justice was done in the King's name, those who filled the office of magistrate began to call themselves his representatives. Other presidents did likewise, especially those known as présidents-à-mortier from the shape of their bonnets, which have grown so large that they can no longer be worn on the head.[1] These claims also have been allowed, and thus every magistrate-president, so-called, stands superior even to the Dauphin, or to the Regent, if there be one, yielding place to no one except the Chancellor of France.

[*For a further twenty pages Saint-Simon continues the history of the parlements and recites the encroachments of the jurists, from the reign of Louis XI onwards. He then lists and comments on every premier président after 1664. Lamoignon, of whom he elsewhere says 'corruption in that office dates from him and has continued ever since'; Novion, his successor, 'dismissed for jobbery in that noble office, in 1689, and for wrongful arrests by changing the name on the warrants which he signed.' Finally the atrocious Harlay, whom we already know. (See Vol. I, index, Harlay, Achille III.)*]

This preamble has been entirely necessary, partly to give dates, partly to show the kind of presidents with whom the peers had had to deal. For, indeed, it would be hard to find three men who, one after another, on any tribunal, were more abundantly corrupt than Novion, Harlay, and de Mesmes, with widely varying kinds of corruptness, although no one could say which of them was the worst. Each, however, was corrupt through and through, each differently, and each had precisely those talents and qualities that in combination made their knavery most highly dangerous.

Novion was not long in office before he began to take liberties that at first passed unnoticed, then became habitual, and at last developed into most disgraceful encroachments. Since the peers did not at once perceive what was happening, and complained only much later, I cannot mark the date of each seemingly trivial move; but such small liberties were followed by a far graver infringement, introduced as it were by chance, or through absence of mind. When lawsuits take place, the premier président rises to take the vote, turning first to one side, then to the other. He removes his bonnet, and stays uncovered from the moment of rising until he resumes his seat; he then pronounces judgment covered. At closed sittings, for example, when new peers are received, the premier président takes the vote of the entire chamber with his bonnet on his head and without rising. When he comes to the peers, on the other hand, he uncovers, and calls on the senior peer by name to be the first to vote. Princes of the blood then vote without being named, and so do the presidents. The premier président finally covers and pronounces judgment.

Novion began by pretending carelessly to drop his bonnet on the table when he called the counsellors by name, and thus avoided having to remove it when he called on the senior peer to speak. Later, he carried this play of forgetfulness still further, by remaining covered for several peers, and suddenly removing his bonnet for the remainder, as though he had only that instant remembered the

---

[1] The evolution of the *mortier:* it started as a soft velvet cap or bonnet; it was then heightened and stiffened; it finally took the shape of a funnel, and became so impractical that it was impossible to wear it, and it was carried.

observance. For a long time the peers were so guileless that they perceived no harm, and, indeed, the reception of a new peer was a rare event. Novion's behaviour was noticed, but everything was forgotten until the next occasion, which evoked the same astonishment, but still no complaint was made. None the less, the peers should have taken warning. The final insult occurred when the Comte-Evêque de Châlons, long since known as Cardinal de Noailles, Archbishop of Paris, was received into the Parlement, in 1681. It was at his reception that Novion threw off his mask by remaining covered for all the peers, and uncovering only for the princes of the blood. The Duc d'Uzès had thereupon completely lost his temper, and cramming his hat on his head had voted covered, with a look of inexpressible fury. The dukes exploded in complaint to the King, but King Louis liked to reduce and lower the ducal authority by every means in his power,[1] and such quarrels did not displease him. He preferred not to intervene, but rather to let them continue, hoping that the rift might become permanent, leaving both sides the more dependent on himself. He merely said that, since the Duc d'Uzès had taken justice upon himself, there was no occasion to do more. None the less, the dukes might easily have cornered the King by pressing him for a ruling; for he could not possibly have supported behaviour so novel, unseemly, and aggressive. I might have been astounded at the dukes' returning to the Parlement and consenting to vote uncovered while the premier président still continued to wear his bonnet, had I not, with my own eyes, seen sufficient to make me ready to believe anything concerning the dukes' conduct towards the Parlement. Let me say only that this affair of the bonnet is still a matter for dispute, and that M. du Maine's black treachery renders this digression wholly necessary.

For very many years past, those gentry of the Parlement had been in tranquil enjoyment of their encroachments on the rights of the dukes and peers, whose weakness and inertia had kept them equally serene, despite the many warnings they had received. When I had congratulated M. du Maine on his new rank, he had mentioned the affair of the bonnet among his other protestations of goodwill towards the dukes in general and myself in particular. At the time, I thought this merely the exuberance of a man who, having succeeded beyond measure, wished to soften anger and restore peace. I therefore touched only lightly on the matter, drowning some vague acknowledgment in a flood of compliments. On reflection, I conclude that already at that time he had concocted the foul plot which I shall now reveal, and was simply testing my reactions. You must also bear in mind

[1] Louis XIV could never forgive or forget the part which the old nobility had played in the revolt, 1648-1653, when he was ten to fifteen years old. In 1649, King Charles I of England, his uncle by marriage, had been beheaded by the Parliamentarians, and the boy Louis must have suffered an appalling shock. No wonder his distrust persisted.

the character of Premier Président de Mesmes, and the fact that his complete surrender to M. du Maine had gained for him an office far beyond his reach unaided. Lastly, I must warn you that the affair of the bonnet, which began in the November of this year (1714), did not end until March of the following year. Since it is of a nature to interrupt the flow of the narrative, I have placed it last in this year, and shall not begin the new year until the account is finished.[1]

One morning when the King, according to his usual custom, was giving his orders for the day, M. du Maine approached d'Antin, and without further preamble mentioned the gross impropriety of the affair of the bonnet. He repeated the same two days later to the Duc d'Aumont and the Duc d'Harcourt, offering them his support with many compliments, and doing all in his power to arouse their interest. Both replied with cold reluctance, for neither wished to take active steps in the matter until the time was ripe. They marvelled at his offer, but allowed the subject to drop. That, however, did not deter M. du Maine. Some days later he took d'Antin and M. de Noailles on one side, saying that he failed to understand their present indifference to an affair that more than once had rightly aroused their wrath; that he, himself, was continually shocked by the abominable discourtesy, but that he had not said anything because an exception had been made for him. Now that he had risen to higher rank, he found the novel practice quite intolerable. He was, he said, the friend of many dukes and the servant of them all. He honoured them for their rank, desired their good-will, and hoped to win it by serving them in this affair that touched their honour. He added, as proof of sincerity, that he had sounded the King, who seemed favourably disposed, and was ready to vouch for the premier président, and for the Parlement as well, under his influence. He then invited the two dukes to discuss the whole matter and to let him know how he could best oblige them.

M. du Maine was too urgent, too persistent to be ignored, and thus the Duc d'Harcourt, although so weak that he could hardly walk, went that very day to ask some of the most senior dukes to call on him shortly before noon. De La Rochefoucauld, de Villeroy, de Noailles, d'Aumont, Charost, and I[2] visited him all together. Harcourt explained the matter to us in detail, and the need to give M. du Maine some answer. We conferred. None of us swallowed the bait except Noailles and d'Aumont, and even they were not entirely convinced. We all knew how false he was, and how little he was disposed to love us at that moment. We all

---

[1] The affair of the bonnet, which now appears so trivial, was to the dukes a most deliberate insult. Lifting the bonnet was an ordinary courtesy offered even to the lowest members of the Parlement. Had the president decided never to lift it at all, that might have been accepted, but to lift it for some and not for dukes was too rude to be borne. *Opiner du bonnet* (voting by bonnet) signified that, when a person was individually addressed, he raised his bonnet in approval, or remained covered in dissent.

[2] Saint-Simon's peerage dated from 1635. At the beginning of 1715 he was eleventh duke and peer in order of seniority, not counting the seven ecclesiastical peers who ranked above him.

suspected that his first desire was to embroil us with the Parlement, and thus prevent our uniting against him after the death of the King, and that his second was to reduce us still further by a defeat. We could see no other reason for his sudden offer, nor for the urgency with which he had pressed it on us.

We had no difficulty in agreeing so far. What line to take with him was another matter altogether. Two chasms opened before us. The dangers of the future were plain enough; but almost equally plain was the danger of refusing, for he would then see that we had read his mind, or else were so bent on his destruction that we would take no help from him. Whatever we did would be fraught with every kind of danger and difficulty, because of his and Mme de Maintenon's influence with the King. We argued at length, and at last concluded that it would be an infinitely greater risk to give him cause to represent us as his enemies. Thus the second alternative became a question of necessity, not of choice, and we sent our acceptance on the following morning. M. du Maine appeared enchanted, eager to act on our behalf, full of delicate compliments, lavish with promises, urging d'Antin to speak at once to the King, saying that he, himself, would immediately go to the premier président.

That jurist, according to M. du Maine's report, responded warmly, and was certainly all sweet reason when visited by d'Aumont and d'Antin. Nor was there any difficulty in tackling the King, for he, himself, spoke first, telling d'Antin that M. du Maine had mentioned the bonnet; that provided all was settled harmoniously, he would be glad to have the scandal ended, adding that he considered it wholly unwarrantable (his very word), and would be pleased to serve the dukes in such an undertaking. The stumbling-block was the word harmoniously, and from that moment I despaired. M. d'Harcourt also feared that impediment; I was therefore not alone. D'Antin did not know what to think. There was nothing to be done, however, for we had already embarked. All that remained for us was to steer our course with the utmost care. M. du Maine, acting as helmsman, then asked us to compose a short memorandum to offer the King as a basis on which to form his judgment. I saw the trap, and so did d'Harcourt, but there appeared no way of escape, and d'Antin was given the task of preparing the document, which he accordingly did, in temperate and well-chosen words. He showed it to M. du Maine, who approved, and then read it aloud to the King, who thought it good and requiring no alteration. It was next sent to the premier président, with a note asking him to correct it, if he so desired, and to return it to us for presentation to the King.

Two days later, the paper was returned to d'Antin without comment; he gave it to the King, saying that, since it had not been altered, the premier président was presumably content with it. The King agreed, or pretended to agree, praised the memorandum and our action for the second time, and promised to give it with a recommendation to the premier président. You shall soon see the reason for de Mesmes's conduct.

In the meantime, I had undertaken to speak to M. le Duc d'Orléans, and the Dukes of La Rochefoucauld and Villeroy went to Madame la Duchesse. None of us met with the least hindrance. We obtained their absolute consent regarding the matter of the bonnet, and they both said that they had thought the affair an unwarrantable discourtesy. They both kept faith with us absolutely and entirely.

The memorandum had been sent to the premier président from Marly; and it was at Marly that we returned it to the King, to be handed over, as I have already described. There was an interval before M. de Mesmes's next appearance, and when he did arrive d'Antin was in bed with a bad cold. De Mesmes went straight to M. du Maine's lodging, remained there a long time, and afterwards visited d'Antin, where he found MM. de La Rochefoucauld, de Noailles, and d'Aumont. He was quite different from what he had been in his own house, for he now frowned and seemed ill at ease, saying only that he had thought it better to speak to no one before receiving the King's orders. He did, however, let slip the remark that the bonnet was an ancient privilege which the Parlement might find it hard to relinquish, letting them perceive that he was in great haste to go to the King, and leaving them much perturbed by his sudden and unexpected recoil.

I lay in wait for him in the salon, talking to M. le Duc d'Orléans, who immediately went up to him, saying that he understood the matter in question, and not only did not object to our claim, but thinking it very just and reasonable, would support us in every possible way. The premier président deflected him with generalizations on the antiquity of the bonnet and its significance, adding that he was about to go to the King and take his orders. He then at once entered the study; remained only a short time, and emerged flushed and excited, to find the Dukes of Villeroy, Noailles, Aumont, Charost, and Harcourt, waiting in a body to intercept him. He curtly informed them that the King had given him a memorandum, with permission to consult the Parlement, graciously assuring him at the same time that he had no wish to influence their findings. Passing thence to the so-called antiquity of the bonnet, he grew heated and abruptly quitted them, leaving them in a state of even greater bewilderment. He then took his leave of M. du Maine, entered his coach, and returned to Paris.

Next morning the King informed d'Antin, through Bontemps, that he had given the memorandum to the premier président who, so the King said, had made no objection, and had even admitted that there might be some grounds for complaint. The soft answer in the King's study was so much at variance with de Mesmes's demeanour both before and after that some of us concluded he was anxious to oblige, but at the same time wished to preserve his dignity, and to show his colleagues that he cared for their supposed interests—for in many ways they were ill-pleased with him. To me the risks appeared as great as ever; what is more, I distrusted the entire affair of the memorandum—demanded for no specific reason, and returned without comment, spoken or written. I could not persuade myself to believe what my eyes did not see, and M. d'Harcourt entirely agreed with me.

Until then the secret had been so closely guarded that it seemed hard to credit that many people had known, for the past six weeks, what was in the air; but four days later, the silence was broken by loud complaints from the Paris magistrates. The premier président had called a meeting at his house, attended by the présidents-à-mortier, and various other lay and clerical counsellors. They had pretended to find in the opening words of the memorandum a wicked regression to the troubles of the King's minority, had appeared scandalized, and had found nothing to reassure them in the premier président's address. He, indeed, had been the first to cry the alarm, arousing their passions, and striving with might and main to spread trouble throughout the Parlement. D'Antin then wrote a very mildly worded letter, which he first showed to several of the dukes, reminding the premier président of his having been sent the memorandum for correction and comment, and of how he had returned it without a word, That, said d'Antin, should give him no cause for complaint, for the dukes' conduct was not that of men wishing to give offence. He ended with a clear explanation of the passage in question, though truly it needed to be marvellously contorted to convey what was not intended. Nevertheless, the first stone had been cast.

At that precise moment, the premier président fell ill, or pretended to be so. He said he thought he had an abscess in the head, a malady that is invisible. He said that a holiday in the country was essential for recovery. He returned with the gout, and thus, for two entire months, the affair languished. On the same pretext he postponed his reply to the King; but used the interval to stir up indignation and to lay plans, or so, at least, we all suspected. Be that as it may, our suspicions brought him a visit from the Ducs de Noailles and d'Antin, who said on entering that they did not come on business, but simply to ask after his health. He, however, broached the subject himself, and after touching lightly on the memorandum (he could find no excuse for returning it without comment), he suddenly made them a proposition.

The premier président could be haughty or affable to suit his company; he now proceeded to explain most amiably that although he was the first president, he was not the only one, and had no authority over his colleagues, who viewed the affair very differently. He said that he had encountered loud and unanimous opposition; but knowing the dukes' desire to settle amicably the ancient quarrels, he felt sure that all would end happily if they, on their side, would yield in some small matters.

Such an offer from men who by force or cunning had gradually deprived the dukes of all their rights, evoked the answer that our claims were either right or wrong, that the matter concerned the abolition of a flagrant encroachment, and that we asked only for a return to the *status quo*.

Still vastly urbane, the premier président continued to harp on the need for a *quid pro quo*, if only, as he several times repeated, for the sake of peace. He then produced two suggestions: first, that it ill-befitted those who complained of new ways and encroachments to err in an exactly similar way, and was not the peers' novel habit of remaining seated, when the lower benches rose, an insult to the Parlement as a whole?; secondly, that the peers should submit to following the presidents when they entered or left the chamber. With those two points conceded, all the rest could be settled harmoniously. MM. de Noailles and d'Antin, had they only remembered it, possessed the perfect answer to the first demand. They might well have said that if the small door through which the jurists entered to terminate the session were left open, as in the past, there would be no need for any change. It was the closing of that door that had obliged the peers to remain seated. Until then, the upper and lower benches had risen together; the senior peers, followed by the others, had processed along their bench towards the little door, whilst the magistrates at the same time made their way to the opening between the desks of the expositor and the clerk. They forgot, however, and thus had no answer ready; but, in any case, they had not gone to argue, and the president's only desire was to make difficulties, although, in view of all that had passed, the peers had no call to expect that from him. The tale which they brought back aroused serious doubts as to M. de Mesmes's intentions; as for his honesty, no one for years past had credited him with any, if, indeed, anyone had ever done so.

The Marly excursion was nearing its end. The premier président was visible in Paris, but showed no sign of returning. M. du Maine thought it strange, but offered excuses, and continued to vouch for him. We, however, wished to know more, and d'Antin invited him to dinner, ostensibly to run his cultured eye over the fine house and decorations, but in reality to bring matters to a head. He also invited the Dukes of La Rochefoucauld, La Force, Guiche, Villeroy, Noailles, and Aumont. It was d'Aumont's year in waiting as first gentleman and, by a most unlucky accident, neither M. de Bouillon the chamberlain nor any other of the King's gentlemen was within reach. They were all sick or far away, and thus there was great matter for gossip at the Court. The King, who attached immense importance to outward forms, had never seen the functions of his high officers divided among so few, and no one could remember a time when he was reduced to substitutes. Yet, despite his care for ceremony, he absolutely insisted that MM. d'Aumont and de La Rochefoucauld should go to Paris for the dinner, saying that he would do very well with Souvré, the master of his wardrobe. I merely state the facts; I make no comment. These nobles, all of whom were known personally to the premier président, who prided himself on moving in high Society, arrived at d'Antin's house. They waited for a long time. At last, Maisons appeared bearing the premier président's excuses. He was, he said, somewhat indisposed (although that did not prevent his supping that same night with the Marquise de Créquy and Mme de Vassé). It was a bad beginning; but the affair was none the less discussed both before and after dinner, especially concerning the antiquity, or otherwise, of the bonnet, the gross impropriety, the tit-for-tat of following the presidents. Maisons, for all his brilliance, was more than once reduced to embarrassed silence. Yet he would not budge, and the party broke up without any advance having been made. One thing that the evening did achieve was to force him to show his true colours. Of late he had seen little of M. du Maine, for after courting him assiduously for many long years he did not relish seeing de Mesmes made premier président and Voysin Chancellor, both of whom were young and healthy, while he was left rotting on the long bench.[1] After that dinner-party he suddenly began to haunt Sceaux, where M. du Maine went every other day, and Mme du Maine resided permanently. He took to visiting them several times a week, was often found closeted with Mme du Maine, and at Versailles enjoyed long private conversations with her husband in his study. From that time onwards all resentment vanished, and he no longer pretended to be otherwise than against the dukes, though his words were smooth enough.

Two days later the Duc d'Aumont invited me to meet him next morning in the King's bedroom. I already suspected what I could scarcely bring myself to believe, but I did not like to refuse him. In the event, I was put to no trouble, for as I was about to go to him, he entered my apartment. He straightway began to enumerate the difficulties; attacked the premier président as a liar and a cheat, ready to go to any length in order to keep his bonnet safe, mentioned the King's strong dislike of giving judgment, and ended by averring that, since nothing could be worse than outright failure, we had best consent to follow the presidents. I listened attentively and in silence. I then said that such conduct would be a fine reward for discourtesy and for the closing of the small door through which the peers had been wont to leave; that consenting to follow would be the final blow and reduce us to the level of mere counsellors. It would mean raising jurists of the third estate above great nobles who, sitting covered on the high benches, had seen them pleading capless, on their bended knees, from the lower bench, which had once been the step on which we had set our feet.

The Duc d'Aumont persisted in trying to convince me that we had nothing to fear, since the princes of the blood sat between us and the presidents, and in urging

[1] The bench of the présidents-à-mortier.

me to gain M. le Duc d'Orléans's consent on their behalf. I coldly replied that I should make a bad advocate in that cause, seeing that the prince and I had laughed at the idea of agreeing to something so belittling to their rank, so plainly injurious to that of the peers. At last, wearied by his nagging, I said that at the very most I would consent to discuss the situation regarding the princes of the blood, but only on condition that a large number of dukes attended for an open debate, and that a vote was taken. If the majority wished the princes to follow after the presidents, I would see M. le Duc d'Orléans, not to persuade him, but merely to express their wishes. For the sake of peace, or from other motives, M. d'Aumont made do with that offer; but before leaving me he asked for another interview next morning, to discuss our second thoughts, if any. That conversation was shorter, and left our minds totally unchanged.

Meanwhile the dukes had grown tired of M. de Mesmes's tardiness. He could not blame his colleagues, for many meetings had been held at his house; as for his health, he sat in the great chamber each morning, and every afternoon was abroad in the streets of Paris. It showed scant respect for the King to make him wait so long for an answer on a matter which he had recommended to the Parlement, and at last d'Antin spoke out. The King then sent for de Mesmes, who had no choice but to obey, and, reminding him that he considered the dukes' claims to be reasonable, said that he should be glad of an immediate decision in their favour, although he did not wish to issue an order. The premier président excused himself as best he might and left the study scarlet in the face. We were still at Marly. He had entered the study, calm and serene, giving gracious bows to all, including such dukes as were lying in wait for him. When he emerged, he seemed a different man. Greatly to the surprise of the dukes who encountered him, he addressed them angrily, asking whether they wished to destroy their case, grumbling at the unnecessary haste, mentioning his state of health, even going so far as to accuse d'Antin of having primed the King. He then left in high dudgeon.

In the interval, Maisons had decided to work upon me. You will recall how he had striven to make my acquaintance, and how carefully he had cultivated it. He now ignored all the ill-feeling, or worse, that the affair of the bonnet might have aroused, and set himself to persuade me to change my mind and bring my influence to bear on the rest. I thus had to endure from him frequent and lengthy visitations, with much speechifying, during which, despite my impatience, I could not but marvel at the resourcefulness and versatility with which, by twists and turns, he pursued his aims. That persecution continued until the explosion of the bombshell, already being prepared against us.

Black treachery is never trouble-free, even when devised with the utmost skill and backed by most powerful interests. I omit many details because they throw no new light on M. du Maine,[1] who hatched the plot and directed its operation. Respect for the memory of that great King, whose subject I was, forbids me to believe that he acted in concert with his cherished bastard. Be that as it may, M. du Maine, wishing to lure the dukes into a permanent quarrel with the Parlement, had not found it over-hard to persuade King Louis to oppose them in the affair of the bonnet when it suited the interests of the bastards, and then to encourage them when their interests coincided with those of the princes of the blood, and they needed to be appeased. Once sure of the premier président, M. du Maine risked nothing by appealing to the King, whose extreme dislike of pronouncing judgment he well knew. That was why he represented the affair as having been agreed in principle, but prudently arranged for the King to state that he did not wish to order compliance. M. du Maine thus ensured that, no matter what happened, King Louis need decide nothing, and that the dukes would be trapped. He acted with the utmost secrecy, and in such a way that no one could force his hand. None the less, the affair was bound to end in an explosion, and that caused him great anxiety. He would vastly have preferred not to appear; but the premier président refused to budge unaided, which was why the matter had been so long drawn out.

M. de Mesmes fully realized his own danger, but was under considerable pressure from M. du Maine's persuasive tongue and Mme du Maine's hasty temper. He saw also that apart from the advantages to himself and his colleagues from an exchange of the bonnet against precedence over the dukes, such a bargain would preserve him from future trouble and leave M. du Maine trapped; for the bastards would gain nothing, whereas even a temporary truce between the dukes and the Parlement might suffice to endanger all that he had recently acquired in the way of rank and power—the very situation which he most wished to avoid. In that dilemma M. du Maine did not hesitate. He knew that any sign of fearing a reconciliation would be construed as weakness, and he therefore did nothing, being confident that the dukes were not such coarse feeders. He was right. The premier président, on his side, continued to hedge, hoping that d'Aumont and Maisons would between them persuade the dukes to reconsider; after which he might excuse himself to M. du Maine, by saying that he had been outvoted by the other presidents. That was the reason for his long delay in answering the King.

When at last he was summoned, he informed the King that the dukes had been meeting, ostensibly to discuss the affair of the bonnet, but actually to plan for an event which those on whom the King had showered his favours must regard with horror. Sworn enemies of the bastards, they were, he said, plotting to despoil

---

[1] In defence of Saint-Simon's hatred of the Duc du Maine, this is what the Marquis de Lassay had to say of him. After noting that his mind was more crooked and defective even than his body, he continues, 'He is weaker than anyone could well imagine, averse from Society, timid, superstitious, made only to be ruled.'

them after His Majesty's death, in order to make themselves masters of the State. Worse still, confident that the tragedies which had destroyed so many of the royal line would continue and would wipe out those who still remained, they planned thereafter to make the crown elective, as in Sweden or Poland, and to choose one of themselves to wear it. Such were the suggestions which the premier président advanced, to the accompaniment of horrified reflections on the abomination of them. The King himself was duly scandalized. He repeated everything to d'Antin, expressing his distress and alarm, but as one not wholly convinced, and requiring an explanation. D'Antin then spoke so bluntly of lies and fabrications that the King was first ashamed, and then angered by the insolence of such absurd and awful accusations. He immediately desired d'Antin to inform the dukes, so that they might know the kind of men with whom they had to deal. D'Antin thereupon seized the occasion to contrast the dukes with the men of the Parlement as regarded loyalty, obedience, and devotion to the King's service. Had not the artful Duc du Maine already obtained the King's promise not to give an order, the whole affair of the bonnet might have been settled there and then. Enough of that! The plain, unvarnished truth is more telling than any comment. Suffice it to say that the instrument matched the user of it, who was not too nice to employ it for most loathsome purposes, as when, with a front of brass, he promised everything to the King himself, as well as to the dukes, who perceived no evil and made no demands.

D'Antin spent the rest of that day in warning the dukes, with the King's approval. You may picture their feelings. Less than forty-eight hours later, they resolved to sever all communications with the premier président, and to make their families do likewise, treating him thenceforward as a public enemy, a treacherous and flagrant liar—which was not saying too much. M. de Mesmes, himself, was astonished to find such unanimity; even M. d'Aumont dared not visit him, with the result that he, who had so prided himself on being of the Court and of High Society, found himself suddenly shunned by both. No one greeted him; short of personal insult, which would have been improper to a professional man who wore no sword, there was no rudeness that he did not daily have to endure. At last, seeing that his wretched state showed no sign of betterment, he complained to the King when on one occasion the Duc de Tresmes left him kicking his heels in the ante-room, long after everyone else had been admitted to the *lever*. He succeeded in having the Duc de Tresmes told that he should not use his official post for private vengeance; but the King spoke without anger, remained deaf to all de Mesmes's other complaints, and flatly refused to grant him an interview.

M. du Maine was enchanted at having brought the dukes and the premier président to open warfare, but he was no less troubled regarding the outcome. The slander on the dukes had not produced the desired effect, and much to his chagrin, he could now neither hide behind the premier président, nor risk a quarrel with him. In the end, he decided to seem eager to go to all lengths in support of the dukes; and to rescue M. de Mesmes later, if that should still be possible. He began by assuring the dukes of his disappointment, his continued good wishes, his hopes not yet dead, sliding in a word here and there in aid of his ally. He was heard in silence, with an occasional stiff bow that gave him much food for thought. He then tackled the two dukes to whom he had at first spoken, suggesting that one of us should visit Sceaux for a discussion with Mme du Maine, who might be able to suggest some new expedient. What follows is the final proof of his power over the King, and of his fear of losing all.

The dukes at first refused, but after repeated assaults they again yielded, although they suspected his motives; but not one duke would volunteer. At that point d'Aumont, ceasing to pretend that he was not a tool, ventured to propose himself. We looked at one another; but he had not yet sufficiently incriminated himself to warrant our insulting him. Thus we were to accept him; but since we by no means trusted him we insisted on his being accompanied. The difficulty was to find someone else who would go. The mission itself was distasteful enough; partnership with M. d'Aumont made it positively repellent. In the end, however, M. de La Force offered and was joyfully received. He was highly intelligent, privy to the entire affair, careful of our rights, and incapable of weakness. Moreover, he was d'Aumont's senior and would take the lead. Amid so much that had gone amiss, the Duc de La Force's willingness to serve was wholly to the good.

They went on the appointed day, Mme la Duchesse du Maine received them with every courtesy, and almost immediately led them to her private room. There after some preliminary compliments she bluntly informed them that M. du Maine, having led them to resist, would do everything possible to bring them success; but they, on the other hand, must promise him some token of their gratitude. The dukes expressed complete astonishment at this novel proposal, which may not have appeared quite so new to d'Aumont, although at first he spoke up loyally.

Mme du Maine tried coaxing and flattery, saying that it would as much benefit the dukes to agree, as it would strengthen M. du Maine to gain their support. He had long been aware of their dislike of his advancement; he wished only to have their friendship, and to make sure that their success would form the basis of a strong attachment (what a word!). The dukes expressed good feeling in a flow of compliments; but she declared that that was not enough. They then stated that they could say no more, since there had been no definite proposal.

After a long pause Mme du Maine continued that since her husband had been admitted to the succession he had no further ambitions. He was aware, none the less, that the provisions of the King's will might not so much be revoked, for that could never be (which she did not believe); but might give cause for grumbling (what a word!), discontent, and the resentment of the young princes, with whom the peers might be tempted to unite. M. du Maine's only wish was to avoid trouble and enjoy the King's bounty in peace and comfort. It was now for the dukes to decide if they could strike a bargain that would cost them nothing, namely, give him a written promise to defend the King's last wishes for his natural children and their heirs.

M. de La Force had soon seen where the conversation was leading. He asked her to reflect that no subject, without treacherous intentions, could assume the right to fulfil the King's wishes while he was still living and reigning, especially not those of King Louis who so jealously guarded his supreme authority. At that point, Mme du Maine interrupted him excitedly, saying that she had expected some such excuse, but could give them positive assurance that the King not only would not be vexed by such a promise in writing, but would be grateful for it, and that M. du Maine would vouch for the truth of her assertion. The Duc d'Aumont swiftly took advantage of the Duc de La Force's stupefaction to say, 'Monsieur, we need not be afraid, since Madame vows that there will be no anger, and M. du Maine will vouch for the King. Moreover, we owe it to him to give him the promise he desires.' M. de La Force, restraining himself with difficulty, replied smiling, 'But, Monsieur, who will guarantee that what the King approves today he will not condemn tomorrow? Even M. du Maine cannot be so sure of the King's authority if he needs the dukes to buttress him.' He then turned to Mme du Maine. 'Madame,' said he, 'this matter is altogether too dangerous; none of us would dare to touch it.'

Mme du Maine seethed with rage, as her expression betrayed, but she managed to control herself, relying upon her wits and her rank to overthrow M. de La Force who, now that d'Aumont had deserted him, remained her only adversary. D'Aumont had several times tried to intervene, but on each occasion M. de La Force had frustrated him by continuing to speak, and laying a hand on his arm. At last Mme du Maine's fury overcame her. She burst out that it was quite apparent that neither the dukes before her, nor any of their fellows would ever regain their rights; that it was folly to fear the King when she had given her word; that they evidently considered only their own interests; that both she and the Duc du Maine could protect themselves, and, lastly, that she wished to tell them once and for all that having been made capable of the succession they would sooner set the kingdom on fire from end to end, than have it snatched away from them. That was the end. She rose suddenly, and they parted with many insincere compliments from the one side, and expressions of respect just as false from the other. M. de La Force kept close all the while to M. d'Aumont, so as to prevent his following her, or speaking to her in private. They then returned to make their report, What I have said above is taken word for word from M. de La Force's account, given to us in the presence of the Duc d'Aumont, who had nothing to add or subtract, nor anything to change in any way whatsoever.

What was her true purpose? Was it a trap? Did they hope that the dukes, in their eagerness to succeed in the affair of the bonnet, would be so foolish as to sign a pact certain to ruin them in the eyes of the King, the princes, the Parlement, and the kingdom as a whole? Did M. du Maine, in his alarm for the future, snatch at this chance of obtaining a written guarantee? Did he really mean to win the bonnet for us, and leave the premier président in trouble? Who could plumb the depths of his black heart, when he thus made use of his wife because he, himself, was too closely implicated in the premier président's execrable conduct? God has judged them both; it is not for me to speak ill of them.

However that may be, the plot was foiled thanks to the staunchness of the Duc de La Force, who stood firm when his comrade abandoned him, and coolly extricated himself without yielding an inch. M. du Maine had not forgotten his original intention of quietly deserting the dukes at the critical moment, in order to rescue M. de Mesmes. He began to fear, however, that the King might fore-stall him by impulsively ruling in our favour, and he now produced an entirely new conspiracy in which Madame la Princesse[1] played the chief part. At the beginning of the affair he had openly boasted to us that she was a fool and a puppet who dared not oppose the King, and was sure to remain inactive if her son-in-law gave her the slightest hint. So he had informed us, not once but many times, in order to show how little notice need be taken of her. But time pressed, and since no one else presented himself, he made use of her. Thus, for the only time in her life, Madame la Princesse became a woman of affairs with a master-ful nature, ready to do battle with the King in defence of her family. She said to King Louis that Monsieur le Prince had considered the bonnet a most precious token of the princes' more elevated rank, as compared with that of the dukes, and she respected his memory too much not to plead most earnestly against any change. Whereupon the King told d'Antin that much though the whim of Madame la Princesse had grieved him, he had not the heart to overrule her, and therefore hoped to hear no more about it. D'Antin perceived that the scene was pre-arranged, but he none the less spoke out. It was soon made plain, however, that the King was in conspiracy with M. du Maine to extricate himself on that plea, and that nothing would shake him.

---

[1] Madame la Princesse, widow of Monsieur le Prince de Condé, was the Duc du Maine's mother-in-law, the mother of the Monsieur le Duc who died in 1710, and grandmother of young Monsieur le Duc, the Comte de Charolais, and the Comte de Clermont, all three of whom were princes of the blood, and thus involved in the bonnet affair. She herself was a Palatine princess, and a first cousin of Madame. Her husband, Monsieur le Prince, had been a bully, and had broken her spirit.

I had been involved in the affair since that first conference of the dukes in the Maréchal d'Harcourt's lodgings, when we discussed whether or not to take action. Moreover, although I had done my best to avoid him, M. du Maine had several times cornered me before the premier président's outburst. I do not pretend that I was not outraged at our having been made use of to further M. du Maine's ambitions, and as the target of the premier président's malice. It was on a Saturday evening, at Versailles, that d'Antin had given us the King's final answer. I had had the entire night for reflexion, yet I could not persuade myself to let M. du Maine enjoy in peace the entire success of his snakiness. That word is not, I think, too strong. To me, personally, as well as to the dukes in a body, he had vouched for Madame la Princesse, the princes, the premier président, and the Parlement. He had protested his loyalty and good intentions; he had, in the early days, even gone so far as to beg me to obtain M. le Duc d'Orléans's co-operation. No thought of danger could deter me now from telling him my mind. I wished for no man's support; to leave him ignorant of my sentiments towards him was more than I could bear.

My lodging was in the new wing, on the same level as the tribune of the chapel. His was on the floor below, close by the main entrance. On the following day, Sunday, I had him watched when he emerged after mass. He never missed on saints' days and Sundays, but his hypocritical piety deceived no one. He usually attended Compline and prayers, always went to hear the sermon, when there was one, and was present at Salut[1] every Thursday evening. As soon as I heard that he was back, I went downstairs, and found him alone in his study. He suspected nothing, and greeted me in the most civil and obliging manner. I did not utter until I was seated in one armchair, and he in another.[2] Then, very gravely, I told him what I knew. M. du Maine blamed Madame la Princesse, roundly abused her, defended his own conduct, expressed great regret. I interrupted him, with the bare mention of the premier président's name, most solemnly pronounced. M. du Maine tried to excuse him, adding very promptly that we must not despair nor think the matter closed, for he would continue to support us and never rest until we had succeeded. I heard him unmoved. Then I related to him the whole truth of M. de Mesmes's slander, the King's repetition of it to d'Antin, and his warning to the dukes. Thereafter, I spoke my mind freely of de Mesmes, not in anger, but showing my real contempt for him, and my disgust at his villainy. Not that I was telling M. du Maine anything he did not already know; but I wished him to understand that I knew all. I then looked him straight between the eyes. 'Sir!' said I, 'You are the man who lured us into this affair against our inclinations, who

---

[1] Evening prayers to salute the Host.
[2] Did Saint-Simon almost hope that the Duc du Maine would be so uppity as to try to offer him a chair without arms?

vouched for the King, the premier président, and the Parlement, who first assured us that Madame la Princesse would be neutral, and then incited her to intervene. You, Sir, have made us dupes of the Parlement and a subject for ridicule!' M. du Maine, usually so ruddy, became as pale as death. He stammered out excuses, protested his regard for the dukes in general and myself in particular. I let him have his say without for an instant lowering my gaze. Then, riveting my eyes on his face, I interrupted, saying with proud haughtiness, but still calm and unruffled, 'Sir, you may have all the power, we and the entire kingdom are left in no doubt as to that. Enjoy it while you may; but' (here I raised my head and voice, piercing him to the very soul) 'a time may come when you will have cause to regret your misuse of that power; for you have duped and callously betrayed the greatest nobles in the land, and they will not forget it.'

I quickly rose and turned to go, allowing him no time to think of a reply. He was most completely taken by surprise, and perhaps ashamed, for he followed me, still murmuring excuses and compliments. I did not turn until I reached the door. There, however, I stopped, and turning furiously in his direction, I exclaimed, 'Sir! to escort me to your door, after what has passed, is adding ridicule to insult!' After which I crossed his threshold without a backward glance, and went my way.

After dinner, that same day, I described my visit, moment by moment, to the other dukes. I cannot say how many of them would have wished to imitate me, but all appeared well satisfied. No one more so than I. I never learned the effect on M. du Maine, of what must have been, for him, a new experience. I never discovered and little cared whether or not he told the King, or confided in Mme de Maintenon. If the King ever knew he made no sign, nor did Mme de Maintenon show any difference. Mme de Saint-Simon and I watched them both; but we learned nothing. Not one of M. du Maine's household, nor any of the people at Sceaux mentioned the scene. As you may well imagine we ceased to be on calling-terms. On the rare occasions when we met, he would stop to make me a particularly low and stately bow; for his club-foot obliged him to come to a halt for a formal salute. I invariably returned a half-bow, still continuing to walk, and we lived thus until after the King's death.

Enough of this monstrous intrigue that dragged on until the end of March 1715. Its extreme importance has obliged me to pursue it without interruption. Let us now return to the narrative, and retrace our steps to New Year's Day, 1715.

CHAPTER VI

1715

Death of the Comte de Grignan - Death of Fénelon, Archbishop of Cambrai - Fleury's plot to be made tutor of Louis XV - Fall of the Princesse des Ursins - Voysin drives in State to the Parlement - A highly dubious ambassador from Persia - The Princesse des Ursins in Paris - Lord Stair the English Ambassador - Mme de Coëtanfao leaves me her all - Sickness of Mme la Duchesse d'Orléans - Death of Nesmond, Bishop of Bayeux - Death of Cardinal Sala - The Princesse des Ursins takes her leave - M. le Duc d'Orléans and the Abbé, later Cardinal, Dubois - Character of M. le Duc d'Orléans, of Mme la Duchesse d'Orléans, of Mme la Duchesse de Berry, and of Madame - My own prospects - I firmly refuse the finances - Consultation on the proclamation and form of M. le Duc d'Orléans's Regency - The Duc de Noailles turns against me - His black ingratitude - The last days of the King - Unhappiness of M. le Duc d'Orléans - Death of the King

THE YEAR began with the Queen of Spain thanking the King for the presents he had sent her by Saint-Aignan. The Marquis de Chamilly died in Paris, on 7 January, after a long illness, at the age of seventy-nine. He was tall and stout, remarkably well formed, highly distinguished for his valour in several battles, and famous in particular for his defence of Grave.[1] He was most notably a man of honour, wealthy, and lived everywhere as a gentleman should, but his dullness was a continual surprise and often embarrassed his wife, who was very much the reverse. In his youth he had served in Portugal, and it was to him that the famous *Lettres Portugaises*[2] were addressed by a nun who fell madly in love with him. He died childless. His family, by name Bouton, had provided several chamberlains for the later Dukes of Burgundy, from which province they had sprung. The only vacancy created by his death was the governorship of Strasbourg, which the King gave to the Maréchal d'Huxelles. It was a handsome addition to his other

---

[1] A hero himself, Noël Bouton, Marquis de Chamilly had a great understanding of the fears of others. A young man was reported to him for cowardice by some brother officers. Chamilly refused to believe them despite all the evidence. He said that such things were impossible in his regiment. The young man retrieved his character with glory next day.

[2] See *Letters from a Portuguese Nun*, 1666, translated by Lucy Norton, with a foreword by Raymond Mortimer, Hamish Hamilton 1956. These letters created a tremendous stir in France; they were so passionate, so touching. Mme de Sévigné said of a friend's love-letter: 'Wonderful! a positive *Portugaise.*' All the smart literary people in France copied the style and discussed whether or not the letters were fakes.

governorship of Alsace: in spite of which, he never once visited it. The truth is that although Strasbourg was worth thirty thousand livres to him, he was obliged to pay out twelve thousand in salaries for the government of Brisach.

The Comte de Grignan,[1] a lieutenant-general and commandant of Provence and a Knight of the Order, the son-in-law of Mme de Sévigné who often spoke of him in her letters, died at the age of eighty three in a hostelry on the road from Lambesc to Marseilles. He was a big man, extremely well formed, ugly, highly conscious of his rank, a very good fellow, vastly polite, exceedingly dignified, most particularly obliging, and universally loved and esteemed throughout Provence, where he ruined himself by subsisting without other support. Two daughters survived him: Mme de Vibraye (his daughter by the Duchesse de Montausier's sister), whom his third wife, Mme de Grignan Sévigné,[2] forced into a most unsuitable marriage, and continually quarrelled with; and Mme de Simiane, his third wife's own daughter, whom she doted upon with the same passion that her mother had expended upon her. The marriage with Simiane was a love-match. He saw little service, and became M. le Duc d'Orléans's first gentleman—a secondary post when he first took it; but events brought him the lieutenant-generalcy of Provence, which was still vacant at the King's death.

At the beginning of that same month of January, Fénelon,[3] now Councillor of State, lieutenant-general, Governor of Le Quesnoy, and Knight of the Order, called on me at my lodging in Versailles, as we were finishing dinner. In great distress, he informed me that he had just learned, by courier, of the mortal illness of his great-uncle the Archbishop of Cambrai,[4] and begged me to entreat M. le Duc d'Orléans to send Chirac his doctor immediately, asking me furthermore to lend him my post-chaise. I left the table, ordered the chaise, and went at once to M. le Duc d'Orléans, who gave orders for Chirac to leave forthwith, and to stay at Cambrai as long as his presence was required. Scarcely an hour had elapsed between Fénelon's appearance at my lodging and the departure of Chirac. At Cambrai, he found the Archbishop past hope, and in no condition to be given remedies. He none the less remained with him for twenty-four hours, at the end of which time Fénelon expired. It was thus I, whose presence near M. le Duc d'Orléans he had so much dreaded for the future, who could render him that final service. This prelate was so well known and is so famous that it would be useless to add much more to what I have already said

[1] François Adhémar de Monteil.
[2] Françoise Marguerite de Sévigné (1646-1705).
[3] Gabriel Jacques de Fénelon, Marquis de Salignac (1688-1745).
[4] François de Salignac de La Mothe-Fénelon (1651-1715). He had been Archbishop of Cambrai since 1695. See Vol. I, p. 72 and index.

in other parts of these Memoirs. Yet I must linger for a little while.[1]

You already know his ancient lineage, and his excellently noble family, distinguished, as they were, by embassies, various kinds of official employment, a collar of the Order under Henri III, and very great alliances; of his poverty and obscure beginnings; how he made tentative approaches to the Jansenists, the Jesuits, the Oratory Fathers, and the seminary of Saint-Sulpice, to which in the end, and without much enthusiasm, he attached himself. You know how that connection gained him the acquaintance of the Dukes of Chevreuse and Beauvilliers, how he rose swiftly in their esteem, how it brought him the post of tutor to the Children of France, how he succeeded in that office, and the origins and calamitous progress of his views and fortunes. You will remember his writings and the replies of his opponents; the tricks that he used, which failed to save him; the disgrace of his supporters, his friends, his patrons; how nearly he brought about the ruin of the Dukes of Chevreuse and Beauvilliers, and the incomparably fine action of Noailles, Archbishop of Paris, later Cardinal. The twists and turns of that affair, which he finally submitted to the judgment of Rome, where the King appealed against him, caused him to be condemned by canon law, a judgment that was accepted by all the ecclesiastical courts in the provinces owing obedience to the King. The promptness, the entirety, the publicity of his submission, and his admirable conduct before his own provincial assembly, did him much honour. He had, indeed, the happiness of retaining wholly and for ever the love and esteem of Mgr le Duc de Bourgogne, the Dukes of Chevreuse and Beauvilliers, and of all his old friends, despite the harshness and depth of his disgrace, the active persecution of Mme de Maintenon, the precipice on which he stood in relation to the King, and his seventeen years' exile from the Court. His friends were all equally vigilant, making his interests their first object, equally subject to his spiritual direction, equally keen to seize every possibility of restoring him to favour, showing the King their deep respect, yet never hiding their sentiments, especially not the Dukes of Chevreuse and Beauvilliers, and their entire families, and Mgr le Duc de Bourgogne also.

Fénelon was a tall, lean man, well built, with a large nose, eyes that danced and sparkled like a torrent, and a countenance that, once seen, could never be forgotten. It displayed all his qualities, and their contrasts never clashed. It combined gravity with humour, seriousness with gaiety; it expressed in full measure the scholar, the prelate and the great noble. The chief impression made by his

---

[1] Fénelon fascinated Saint-Simon although they never met. There are several sketch-portraits of him in the memoirs; this is the finished article.

face, as by his whole person, was of discretion, humour, radiance, grace, decency, and above all nobility. It required an effort to avert one's gaze. All his portraits are eloquent likenesses; but none catch the delicate harmony so striking in the original, nor the true refinement of all the qualities displayed. His manners were in keeping with the rest—a graciousness that put others at their ease, a poise which frequenting the best people and the highest Society alone can bring, and which was quite unconsciously apparent in all his conversation. In addition he possessed unstudied eloquence, natural, gentle, polished. He was charmingly courteous, but dignified and with discrimination. His elocution, clear and precise, was most agreeable; he gave the impression of being anxious to make himself understood in difficult and tortuous matters; indeed, he was one who never tried to appear cleverer than the person with whom he spoke, who could bring himself down to anyone's level without condescension, who seemed delighted to put people at ease; so much so, in very truth, that one could neither bring oneself easily to leave him, nor oppose him, nor cease to come again and again into his presence.

That most rare of qualities he possessed in the highest degree. It kept his friends wholly devoted to him throughout his entire life, despite his disgrace. It was that which, after they had been dispersed, made them meet together to speak of him, lament for him, and cling to him ever more closely, like the Jews to Jerusalem, longing for his return, always in hope; just as that unhappy race still waits and yearns for the coming of their Messiah. It was, moreover, by prophetic power that he had gained authority over his followers, and had grown accustomed to ruling them in a manner which, for all its gentleness, brooked no opposition. Thus, had he returned to the Court and become a member of the Council, which was always his chief ambition, he would not long have tolerated his colleagues, and, once established and beyond the need for protection, it would have been highly dangerous not merely to oppose him, but to be anything other than his admiring and subservient ally.

Exiled to his diocese, he combined the busy, pious life of a diocesan bishop with the style and magnificence of one who renounces nothing, and who respects himself, others, and the world at large. No man had ever such a passionate desire to please, and to please servants as well as their masters; no man ever carried it further, with more persistent, continuous, and widespread application; no man was ever so completely successful. Cambrai is a much frequented town, full of travellers; nothing could have equalled the discriminating courtesy, the charm with which he received them all. In the first years of his disgrace he was avoided; he made advances to none; gradually, his delightful manners attracted a certain number. Emboldened by this little crowd, many of those whom fear had kept away, but who wished to sow their seed against better days, were glad to find excuses for visiting Cambrai. For one reason or another, everyone hastened thither. When Mgr le Duc de Bourgogne began to appear there, Fénelon's court increased in size, and when his pupil was the Dauphin became of real importance. The numbers of persons whom he had welcomed, the great number who had lodged with him on their journeys to and from the war, the care which he had taken of the sick and wounded who were brought to the town, won him the love of the troops. He visited the hospitals constantly, and the most junior of the officers; was attentive to the needs of the higher ranks, and received very many to stay at his palace, sometimes for several months on end until they were perfectly recovered. He showed the vigilance of a good shepherd for the welfare of their souls, with a knowledge of the world that drew them to him, and persuaded many to seek him out on their own account. He never refused the least of those who applied to him, but ministered to them as though they were his only care. He was just as active in relieving their physical sufferings; soups, food and wine, bodily comforts, even remedies, were issued in vast quantities from his palace; and in all that abundance, immense care was taken to see that everything was of the best. He attended with the doctors at the most vital consultations; how could he be other than worshipped by the soldiers, or his name other than famous even at the Court?

He gave alms and made pastoral visits several times a year, and these regular visitations taught him to know all the various groups in his diocese. The wisdom and gentleness of his rule, his sermons in the town and in villages, his approach-ability, his sweetness with children, his politeness to all, the grace which enhanced his every word and action, made him adored by his people and his priests, whose father and brother he declared himself to be; and he treated them all as such, winning their hearts completely. With so much skill and ardour in the art of pleas-ing, there was nothing mean or common, affected or out of place, but always perfect decorum. At his palace, he was of easy access, swift and impartial in action. One spirit, his own, governed all those who worked under him in his diocese; there were never any scandals nor any violence; everything about him and in his see was done with the greatest propriety. His mornings were spent working on diocesan affairs; but since he had firm principles and a quick brain, was always in residence, and never let a day pass without settling the business on hand, the morning's work was neither long nor arduous. He then received call-ers, went to say mass in his private chapel, except on days when he officiated, or had some particular reason for saying it elsewhere. On his return, he dined in company, eating little himself and not much that was solid, but staying long at table for the sake of others, and delighting them by the pleasantness, variety, and charm of his conversation, that never descended to anything unworthy of a great prelate and a great noble. After leaving the table he stayed only a little while with his guests; they were used to living with him without constraint, and he had none with them. He then went to his study and worked for several hours, prolonging that time if the weather was bad or if he had no engagements abroad. After that he paid his visits and went out on foot into the town. He loved walking and gladly extended the time so spent. If there were no visitors, or no person of distinction, he would take with him some vicar-general, and other ecclesiastics, and converse with them on matters concerning religion, scholarship, or his diocese. He spent the evenings with those who were lodging with him, supping with the high-ranking officers when they journeyed to or from the army, with a table no less well furnished than for his dinner. He, himself, ate even less at supper time, and always retired to bed before midnight. Although his table was sumptuously and delicately supplied with everything, in the style of a great noble, there was nothing unbecoming to the episcopate, or to the most rigid rules of the Church; all was redolent of digni-fied luxury and sweet liberty. He himself was a living example, but one to which no other could attain. He appeared everywhere as a true pastor, a great noble, the author of *Télémaque*.[1] Never did he say a word regarding the Court or State affairs, never anything that could be used against him. Despite the grand scale on which he lived, his domestic affairs were kept in perfect order, and his diocese under firm control; but without meanness or pedantry, and without questioning persons of any sort or condition on matters of doctrine.

The Jansenists in his diocese of Cambrai—and there were many—lived in uninterrupted peace. They remained silent, and so did their Archbishop. It might have been better had he been equally blind to those beyond its boundaries; but he held too closely to the Jesuits, and expected too much advantage from them, not to satisfy their wishes when his peace was not disturbed. He was likewise too much attached to his Little Flock[2] not to send them from time to time the nourishment for which they craved, in the form of books that were eagerly passed from hand to hand and praised resoundingly.

His theories were strongly refuted by the Jansenists, and indeed silence on matters of doctrine would best have suited the author of a work so absolutely condemned as had been the *Maximes des Saints;* but his ambitions were far from dead. The blows he suffered from the Jansenists were seen as fresh proofs of merit by his friends, and by the Jesuits as new reasons for endeavouring by every means to procure him rank and high office in Church and State. As the storms receded and the Dauphin's reign approached, his impatience must have been hard to restrain. Bossuet, Bishop of Meaux, was dead; so also was Godet, Bishop of Chartres; the bull had removed Cardinal de Noailles; Père Tellier, the King's

---

[1] *Les Aventures de Télémaque:* the novel which Fénelon wrote in 1699, for the education of the Duc de Bourgogne.
[2] For Fénelon's 'Little Flock', see Vol. I, p. 74. They were the devout group at the Court, headed by the Duchesse de Béthune (1650-1716), the Chevreuses and the Beauvilliers, and, at the beginning, Mme de Maintenon.

confessor, was all powerful and wholly on his side, as were the cream of the Jesuit administration. As for the Society as a whole, it had professed attachment to him since the deaths of Père Bourdaloue,[1] Père Gaillard, and other prominent clerics who had opposed him unchecked by their superiors, who feared to arouse the wrath of the King and Mme de Maintenon against them all. But such times were past, and all that formidable concourse was united in his support. Even the King had latterly praised him, albeit unwillingly, on two or three occasions, for his action in opening his storehouses to the army in times of scarcity.

You may well imagine that that service was not allowed to lie hidden; indeed it was that which emboldened his friends to speak his name to the King. The Duc de Chevreuse at last dared to visit him, and to receive him at Chaulnes and, as you may guess, he made very certain that the King would not take this amiss. Thus Fénelon, enjoying the highest and most agreeable expectations, allowed them to germinate unaided; but they never reached maturity. The Dauphin's sudden death prostrated him; that of the Duc de Chevreuse, soon afterwards, re-opened the wound, the death of the Duc de Beauvilliers crushed him utterly. Beauvilliers and he had been one in heart and soul, and although they never saw one another after his disgrace, Fénelon had directed, from Cambrai, the smallest details of the duke's life. After the Dauphin's death, despite his deep affliction, Fénelon still clung to the wreckage of his hopes. His ambition survived; he clutched at every straw.

His intellect had always appealed to M. le Duc d'Orléans; M. de Chevreuse had continually encouraged their mutual regard, and I also did my part, out of love for the Duc de Beauvilliers, who could persuade me to anything. You already know what those noblemen had required of me on his behalf; how I had so well succeeded that the highest offices were reserved for him, and how I had been able to give them that assurance. For religious reasons they were deeply concerned for his reinstatement, and were sure that nothing would better advantage the Church and the State than to place the tiller of government in his hands. It was written, however, that he should have no more than hope. As I have already said, he harboured suspicions concerning me; the Dukes of Chevreuse and Beauvilliers had told me as much. Perhaps their deaths increased his doubts, for he may have believed that without their guidance I should think differently of him, with whom I had had no acquaintance, having been too young before his exile, and with no opportunity to know him since. Be that as it may, his frail constitution could not support so many trials and tribulations, and the death of the Duc de Beauvilliers proved to be the final blow. For a little while his courage kept him afloat; but his

---

[1] For Père Bourdaloue and his hellfire sermons, see Vol. I, p. 57.

strength was exhausted. As with Tantalus,[1] the water had receded too often when he had tried to quench his agonizing thirst. He made a tour of pastoral visits, during which his coach overturned at a dangerous spot; no one was injured, but he comprehended the peril, and his feeble health was shattered by the accident. He returned shaken to Cambrai; he developed a fever, and for these mishaps coming so swiftly one after another there was no remedy, although his head remained clear and sound. He died at Cambrai, on 7 January of that year, filled with regrets, and on the threshold of his heart's desire. He knew of the King's declining health; he knew all that he might expect after his death. He was already consulted and courted, for the rising sun was slowly becoming visible. How much he must have longed for life! How bitter must death have been, when on every side his prospects appeared so brilliant! Yet he showed nothing. Whether for the sake of his reputation, which had ever been his first care; whether his lofty spirit had learned at last to despise what it could not achieve; whether he felt disgust for a world that had so often cheated him; whether the religion which he had for so long practised revived under such sad and weighty thoughts—he appeared unaware of all that he was quitting, and wholly centred upon what was to come. He manifested a tranquillity of soul, a peace which nothing could disturb, that embraced penitence, detachment, a sole concern for the things of the spirit and the care of his diocese, displaying, in very truth, a faith that triumphed over humility and fear. In that frame of mind, he wrote a letter to the King[2] on the spiritual state of his diocese, saying nothing of himself, evincing only sentiments of a most touching nature, well becoming the death-bed of a great prelate. His death in his sixty-fifth year, fortified by the rites of Holy Church, and surrounded by his household and clergy, might well have served to edify those who survived him, and to bring hope to those who had received the call.

Consternation reigned throughout the entire Low Countries, where he had won the love of all, even including the enemy armies, who took as much, or perhaps even more care, than our own soldiers to protect his property. Their generals and the court at Brussels gloried in giving him every token of esteem; indeed the mourning was sincere and universal, among Protestants and Catholics alike. His friends, especially the Little Flock, were stricken. All in all, he had nobility of soul and was a great man. Humanity blushed for him on account of Mme Guyon, for whom he retained, or pretended to retain, a life-time's admiration; yet his morals were never suspected. He died a martyr to her theories, from which he could never be dissociated. Despite the notorious failure of all her prophecies,

---

[1] Tantalus, a son of Zeus: he offered the flesh of his son Pelops in a pie to the gods, in order to prove the divinity of himself and his son. For that crime he was cast hungry and thirsty into Tartarus with water all about him and rich fruits over his head. Whenever he tried to drink the waters sank, and when he reached to pick the fruit the branches flew up out of his grasp.

[2] The letter was dated 6 January, on the eve of his death.

she remained the centre of everything for the Little Flock, and the oracle through whom Fénelon lived and guided them. If I have spread myself too much over this personage, his great talents, his life and its contrasts, the figure and the scandal that he made in Society have induced, nay impelled me to write this much in memory of the Duc de Beauvilliers, whose friend and beloved master he was. I hope to have shown that it was not extraordinary for the duke to have fallen so completely beneath his spell; for in his innocence he had seen only the most sublime piety, and never so much as suspected the over-riding ambition.[1] Everything in Monsieur de Cambrai's domestic affairs was so perfectly ordered that when he died he owed not a sou and possessed nothing.

Another prelate, happier in worldly life, yet careful of no one's happiness except his own, now laid the first foundation of a reign that astonished Europe, and at the same time proved the greatest disaster France has suffered. I refer to the all too famous Fleury, who, more than two years ago,[2] was called to answer to God for his long life and all-powerful, most pernicious governance, of which it is not yet time to speak. You already know his obscure origins, his progress by more than shady intrigues, how late, and with how much difficulty he contrived to become Bishop of Fréjus, and of the King's prophecy concerning him to Cardinal de Noailles, who at last persuaded him to grant Fleury that see.[3] For a long time he had languished far from the Court and High Society, not daring to show his face at Versailles, except on rare occasions. He had, however, spent his life in courting the Maréchal de Villeroy, and through him Mme de Maintenon, by whose agency he finally secured the Abbey of Tournus, which brought him nearer to the centre.

Fleury, who never made learning, morals, and religion the first objects of his career, had carefully avoided questions of doctrine. Being little esteemed by the Jesuits (who knew him too well to trust him), and with many attachments in High Society, he had not restrained himself in blaming the inquisition and cruel treatment of the Jansenists, and had always left his diocese in peace. The notion of becoming preceptor to the little Dauphin made him change his conduct. He decided to play for safety and to arm himself against all criticism in this dangerous matter. He therefore spent the last six months of his episcopate in studying doctrine, examining books and confessors, tormenting the nuns of the few convents within his diocese, and composing a farewell address to his

[1] Mme de Maintenon's rather surly comment in a letter of 10 January: 'I was sorry to hear of M. de Cambrai's death. I lost a friend because of Quietism; but they say that he would have done well on the Council, if one cared to look so far ahead.' She was speaking of the Regency.

[2] Saint-Simon must have added this when he was revising the memoirs, for André Hercule de Fleury, made Bishop of Fréjus in 1698, tutor to Louis XV in 1715, and Cardinal and Minister of State in 1726, did not die until 1743.

[3] The King thought Fleury dissipated, did not approve of his conduct, or of the company he kept, and said that too many people were trying to advance him. When, in 1698, Cardinal de Noailles at last induced him to make Fleury Bishop of Fréjus, the King said: 'I consent, to stop you from pestering me; but I do so with the greatest reluctance. Remember my words; you will live to regret this.'

diocesans, the tenor of which was not much appreciated. Since his chief desire
was to create a stir, he made more noise than trouble; but the sound of it penetrated far into the Low Countries, to the retreat of the famous Père Quesnel who,
having finished his seventh report (published only in 1716) on the constitution[1],
was now compiling a preface. Quesnel was already displeased with Fleury for
taking upon himself the unaccustomed rôle of an inquisitor, and when he received
a copy of the address, he could not resist the opportunity of chastening him with
ridicule. He accordingly quoted it in his preface, and, with the most bitter and
contemptuous irony, completely demolished it. *Inde irae!*[2] Fleury, for all his smiling
pretence of humility, was the vainest and most unforgiving man I ever encountered. He never forgave Père Quesnel for that injury, which was the sole cause
of the unparalleled fury that during the remainder of his life continually vented
itself in acts of extraordinary cruelty and oppression towards the Jansenists and
anti-constitutionalists, and which led him to take devilish measures to perpetuate
those acts after his death, to the great detriment of Church and State.

You already know that the Princesse des Ursins had at last ruined herself with
the King and Mme de Maintenon. The King could forgive her neither for her
temerity in demanding royal rank, nor for the way in which she had continued
to work secretly to prevent King Philip from signing the peace. He was at first
mortally afraid lest King Philip should marry her, and then feared her absolute
dominion over him during his solitary confinement at the Medina-Celi palace.
Lastly, the Parma marriage and the manner of its negotiation had cut him to
the quick; the choice of such a bride would in no circumstances have pleased
him, and the machinations used to bring it about had been the last straw. As for
Mme de Maintenon, she had assisted Mme des Ursins' incredible rise for the sole
purpose of governing Spain through her agency, more directly than she could ever
have achieved through the ministers. The princess's assumption of independence
after the death of the queen, and her impudent abuse of the King of Spain's
confidence, had compelled Mme de Maintenon to consider her own position.
Indeed, she was more distressed even than King Louis by the thought of her
becoming Queen of Spain, especially remembering that she herself had twice
missed being proclaimed Queen of France, despite a firm promise to that effect.
Royal rank for the princess would have left her far behind; it had aroused her
permanent enmity, and the Parma marriage, negotiated without her knowledge
or the King's, left her hopeless of ever again using the Princesse des Ursins as a
tool. Those were the reasons that made both the King and Mme de Maintenon

---

[1] The constitution was the name used in France for the Bull *Unigenitus*. Père Quesnel was the Oratorian father who, since
1694, had been supporting the Jansenists against the Catholic authorities.
[2] Hence these rages!

determined to ruin her,[1] but in a manner so secret, both before and after, that I never met anyone who knew whom they had employed, or what means they selected for their purpose. It is only honest to confess ignorance, and forbid imagination to invent a fiction. The facts must be recorded exactly as they are, with the addition of my own opinion, for what that may be worth.[2]

The Queen of Spain continued her progress towards Madrid with a great train of coaches and guards, and the special escort of the King of Spain's bodyguard, which had been sent to meet her at the frontier. Alberoni had been with her since she left Parma, and the Duc de Saint-Aignan had joined her when she passed through France. Mme des Ursins had assumed the post of duenna, which she had held during the reign of the late queen, and had made all the other appointments in her new household, cramming it full of men and women who were dependent on herself. In the meanwhile she took good care not to let the king far out of her sight; and accordingly followed him when he went to Guadalajara, a little town owned by the Duke of Infantado who had constructed a family tomb there at the Franciscan monastery, far smaller than the royal tombs in the Escorial, but designed on the same pattern, and scarcely less rich in beauty and art. I shall have occasion to speak of it later. Guadalajara is on the way from Madrid to Burgos, and consequently on the road to France, and is only slightly farther from Madrid than Fontainebleau is from Paris. The palace owned by the Dukes of Infantado is vast, beautiful, luxuriously appointed, and occasionally lived in. It was the place chosen for the King of Spain to meet his queen, and the wedding was to be celebrated in the chapel, although, as you already know, he had been married at Parma by proxy. The two journeys were so well timed that the king reached Guadalajara just two days in advance of the queen.

He made that short excursion surrounded by courtiers specially appointed by the Princesse des Ursins, so that others should be prevented from approaching him. She followed in her coach, arriving at the same moment; and immediately afterwards, the king was closeted alone with her, seeing no other person until his *coucher.* Bad roads and wintry weather had delayed matters, and Christmas was approaching. It was already 22 December when the king arrived at Guadalajara, and on the following day, the 23rd, Mme des Ursins set out with a very small suite to drive a further seven miles to the little village of Jadraqué,[3] where the queen was due to sleep. Mme des Ursins greatly looked forward to receiving abundant thanks for the incredible honour for which she had been responsible; to spending the evening alone with the queen, and to accompanying her in her

---

[1] Mme des Ursins had probably done quite enough harm in Spain to warrant her exile, without the need for any intervention from Louis XIV or Mme de Maintenon.

[2] Saint-Simon seems none the less to have added a good deal of local colour.

[3] Jadraqué or Quadraqué, in New Castile, is on the road from Madrid to Saragossa.

coach, on the following day, to Guadalajara. At Jadraqué, she found the royal party already established. She alighted at the lodging prepared for her opposite to, and quite near, that of the queen. She had travelled decked out with jewels, and in full court-attire, and thus had no more to do than to tidy herself before being presented to the new queen. The coldness and formality of her reception greatly surprised her; she thought at first that it was due to shyness, and did her best to melt that icy front. The company meanwhile respectfully withdrew, so as to leave them alone.

Then conversation began. The queen brought it to an abrupt conclusion with a stream of rebukes, taxing her with want of respect for appearing before her attired as she was, and accusing her of bad manners.[1] Mme des Ursins, who knew that her dress was proper in the circumstances, and believed that her respectful bearing and conciliatory speeches had warranted no such attacks, made as though to retire; but the queen immediately fell to reviling her, screaming, calling for assistance, summoning the guard, and rudely ordering her to leave her presence. When Mme des Ursins tried to defend herself, the queen became still more abusive and furious, bidding them put the mad woman out of her lodging, and forcing them to eject her bodily. An instant later, she had sent for Amezaga, the lieutenant commanding her escort, and for the equerry in charge of her coaches. The former she directed to place Mme des Ursins under arrest and to stay beside her until he had seen her put into a coach, guarded by two trustworthy officers and fifteen soldiers. The equerry she sent to fetch a coach and six, with two or three grooms, ordering him to set her upon the road to Burgos and Bayonne without delay for any reason whatsoever. When Amezaga endeavoured to explain that only the King of Spain possessed so much power, she proudly asked him whether he had not received the king's order to obey her implicitly and without protest. In point of fact he had indeed received such an order, but thought that no one else knew of it.

The Princesse des Ursins was accordingly arrested, and placed in a coach with one of her maids; she was allowed no time to change her dress or her hair style, or to make any provision against the cold. Without money or other necessities for herself or her maid; without food for the journey, or a change of linen; without even the requisites for undressing or spending the night, she was simply put aboard the nearest coach, with the two officers of the guard who happened to be at hand. She was in full court dress, with all her jewels, just as she had come from the queen's presence. During the very short interval allowed her, she

---

[1] Was the Queen perhaps still in her travelling dress? Should Mme des Ursins have been waiting to receive her on her arrival?

managed to send the queen a message; but that lady, falling into an even worse passion because her orders had not yet been obeyed, merely ordered them to remove the princess at once. It was close on seven in the evening, only two days before Christmas; the ground was covered with snow and ice, and the cold was bitter, intense, and piercing, as it always is during the Spanish winter. As soon as the queen learned that Mme des Ursins was gone from Jadraqué, she dispatched a letter to the King of Spain by an officer of the guard. The night was so black that nothing could be seen, save in the light reflected by the snow.

It is no easy task to describe the plight of Mme des Ursins in that coach. Her first overpowering sensation was one of shock, fury, and despair. There followed deep and melancholy reflections on an action so brutal, so shameful, so wholly without cause or excuse. This led to conjectures as to the extent of the queen's authority, and the impression that she would make at Guadalajara; then to hopes of the King of Spain's anger and surprise, to thoughts of his affection and dependence on herself, and of the efforts of that group of loyal servants with whom she had surrounded him, and who, from motives of self-interest, would be eager to rescue her.[1] She spent thus the whole of that long winter's night, totally without protection against the terrible cold, in which the coachman lost the use of a hand from frost-bite. As the morning wore on, the need to feed the horses compelled them to halt; but at Spanish inns nothing is provided for human beings. They merely direct you where to buy necessities. The meat is usually sold on the hoof; most of the wine is coarse, dull, and cloudy, the bread like putty, the water undrinkable. As for beds, none exist, except for muleteers. In short, travellers must take with them everything needed on a journey; and neither Mme des Ursins nor those accompanying her had brought provisions of any kind. Eggs, where they were to be found, were their sole support throughout that long journey, and these had to be plain boiled, fresh or otherwise.

Until they stopped to feed the horses deep silence had reigned unbroken. It was now time for speech. During the long hours of darkness, the Princesse des Ursins had had leisure to consider her plans and to compose her countenance. She spoke of her intense astonishment, and described the little that had passed between the queen and herself at their interview. The two officers who, like all Spaniards, were accustomed to hold her in even greater awe and respect than the king, said what they might from the abyss of stupefaction in which they were still sunk. It was soon time to harness the horses and depart. By then Mme des Ursins had begun to feel that the aid which she expected from King Philip was

[1] She was thinking of her nephews Chalais and Lanti, the Prince de Robecq and the Marquis de Crèvecœur, whom she had made the king's constant companions

very long in appearing. But there was no rest for her, no food, no possibility even of loosening her clothing until they reached Saint-Jean-de-Luz.[1] The farther they travelled, the longer she remained without news and the more desperate became her situation. You may imagine the fury which possessed that ambitious woman; so long accustomed to queening it in public, and so ignominiously overthrown by the very hand which she had chosen to support and guarantee her continuing grandeur. The queen had not answered her last two letters,[2] and that pointed omission must have seemed ominous to her; but who could ever have foreseen treatment so brutal, so totally inhuman?

Her nephews Lanti and Chalais, who received permission to join her,[3] destroyed her last hopes. She remained none the less steadfast. No tears or complaints, not the smallest sign of weakness escaped her, not one murmur, even against the piercing cold, the lack of bare necessities, or the extreme fatigues of the journey. The two officers, keeping a close eye on her, were overcome with admiration. At last, on 14 January, they reached Saint-Jean-de-Luz, and the end of her physical sufferings. She found a bed, borrowed the wherewithal to undress, etc., and rested. There also she recovered her liberty.[4] The officers, the soldiers, and the coach returned to Spain, while she remained with her nephews and her maid. She now had leisure to consider the kind of reception she might expect at Versailles; for despite that wild notion of claiming royal rank, which she had carried to such inordinate lengths, and her temerity in arranging a marriage for the King of Spain without King Louis's consent, she still believed that there would be room for her at that other Court where she had once held sway. It was therefore from Saint-Jean-de-Luz that she dispatched her first courier with letters to the King, Mme de Maintenon, and some of her friends, giving a brief account of the thunderbolt that had struck her, and asking leave to report the facts personally, and at greater length. She then settled down to await the courier's return, at this her first resting-place in freedom, and a very agreeable spot in any situation. Yet no sooner had this courier gone than she sent Lanti after him with other letters, less hastily composed, and containing further instructions. He saw the King for a few brief seconds in his study, at Versailles. Lanti afterwards reported that when the first courier had gone she sent another bearing her compliments to the Queen-dowager of Spain who was nearby at Bayonne, but that he was refused admittance. What cruel mortification attends the fall from a throne! Let us now return to Guadalajara.

[1] Beyond the Spanish frontier; in the present *département* of the Basses-Pyrénées.
[2] Others say that she had received a very amiable letter from the queen, dated 20 December, only three days before her disgrace.
[3] They did their utmost to persuade King Philip to treat her leniently, and had some success.
[4] If Saint-Simon is accurate, and he heard the story from Mme des Ursins herself, she was on the road in her tight stays and miserably stiff, low-necked court dress for just over three weeks, without sleeping in a bed, or undressing. She was seventy-three years old.

The officer bearing the letter dispatched by the queen to King Philip as soon as Mme des Ursins had left arrived as that monarch was about to retire. He appeared moved, wrote a short reply; but sent no orders. The officer at once returned. What was remarkable was that the secret was so well kept that nothing was divulged until the following day. You may picture the feelings of the entire court, and the various activities of those who were at Guadalajara. Yet no one dared speak to the king, although there was intense curiosity regarding his reply to the queen. As the morning wore on and nothing further transpired, the conviction grew that Mme des Ursins was finished—in Spain at any rate. It was then that Chalais and Lanti dared to ask the king's permission to join her in exile. He not only granted this, but sent her a decent, civil letter, expressing his distress at what had occurred, but saying that he felt unable to use his authority to countermand the queen's orders; adding that he would continue her pensions and see that they were paid regularly. He kept his word, and for the remainder of her life she received them punctually.

The queen arrived at Guadalajara at the time appointed, in the afternoon of Christmas Eve, and behaved as though nothing had happened. The king, appearing equally unconcerned, met her on the steps, gave her his hand, and led her at once to the chapel, where their marriage was celebrated for the second time; because in Spain it is customary to be married after dinner. He then led her to his bedroom, where they immediately went to bed (although it was not six o'clock), and they did not rise until midnight, in time for mass. What passed between them on the subject of Mme des Ursins was never revealed; and no explanation was ever forthcoming. On the morrow, which was Christmas Day, the king announced that there would be no changes in the queen's household, as appointed by Mme des Ursins; and thus confidence was to some extent restored. Next day, the king and queen, alone in their coach and followed by the entire court, took the road for Madrid, where there was as little mention of the Princesse des Ursins as if the King of Spain had never known her. Louis XIV, his grand-father, appeared in no way surprised when he received the news by a courier, dispatched from Jadraqué by the Duc de Saint-Aignan. The French Court, on the other hand, was both shocked and alarmed, having been accustomed to seeing the princess so triumphant.

Let us now piece together certain clues to the understanding of the mystery. First, King Louis's ominous remark to Torcy, which the Duchesse d'Orléans repeated to us, and which I guessed had boded no good to Mme des Ursins; secondly that quarrel over nothing—a quarrel that blew up in the first moments of a private conversation and was immediately pressed to the last extreme. Is it to be imagined that a Princess of Parma, brought up in an attic by a tyrannical mother,[1]

---

[1] Saint-Simon says elsewhere that she was so dull, and had so lacked support, that her life until then had been very hard.

would have dared to act in such a way towards one who was the intimate friend of King Philip, and was the real ruler of Spain, and to do so only six leagues distant from that monarch, whom she had never encountered? The explanation of that mystery may doubtless be found in the King of Spain's strange command to Amezaga to obey the queen implicitly, without protest or hesitation, a command of which nothing was known until the queen ordered the arrest of Mme des Ursins and sent her packing. Thirdly, consider the perfect calm with which both kings received the news, and King Philip's total unconcern as to the fate of the woman who had seemed so dear to him on the previous evening, and who was journeying, stripped of every comfort, by night and day, over icy, snow-covered roads. You will recall an earlier occasion[1] when King Louis desired to effect the dismissal of Mme des Ursins for having opened a letter from the French ambassador, and appending a note written in her own hand. They did not dare, at that time, to act in the King of Spain's presence. King Louis had urgently recommended him to visit the Portuguese frontier, and had waited until he was safely there before signing the order bidding her retire to Italy. These two incidents are very similar.

Let me add something which I was later told by the Maréchal de Brancas,[2] who had learned it long after the final disgrace of the Princesse des Ursins, from Alberoni, at that time a mere nobody,[3] attached to the queen's retinue on her journey from Parma to Madrid. Alberoni said that one evening, when he was alone with the queen, he had found her extremely agitated, pacing the room, and from time to time muttering inaudible, disjointed remarks. Then becoming angry, she had let slip the name of the Princesse des Ursins, followed by the words, 'I'll dismiss her first of all!' Alberoni had exclaimed in horror, wishing to warn the queen of the danger, folly, and complete hopelessness of any such enterprise; for indeed he was truly alarmed. 'Silence!' the queen had answered. 'Say nothing of all this, and do not speak of it to me. I know very well what I am about.' All this may throw light on a catastrophe that was equally astounding in itself and in the manner of its execution. It also shows King Louis to have been the prime mover, with the King of Spain the consenting party, aiding and abetting King Louis by that strange command to Amezaga, and with the queen charged by both of them to take action in whatever way she pleased. What later followed confirmed me in my opinion.

The fall of the Princesse des Ursins brought many changes in Spain. Countess Altamira[4] was appointed duenna in her place. She was one of the greatest ladies in Spain, hereditary Duchess of Cordoba in her own right. Her husband, who had been dead for some years, had held the highest offices of State, and was

[1] In 1704. See Vol. I, p. 336.
[2] Louis, Marquis de Brancas (1672-1750), made a Marshal of France in 1741.
[3] At that time Alberoni was the Duke of Parma's ambassador to the King of Spain.
[4] Angèle Folch of Aragon, daughter of the Duke of Segovia.

also ambassador to Rome. I shall have occasion to speak of her again, as well as of her children and their various marriages. Cellamare, Cardinal del Giudice's nephew, was promoted to be her master of the horse, and the cardinal himself hastened his return to Madrid and the king's favour. Orry received orders to leave Spain without bidding the king farewell, and did so amid public execration. Pompadour, who was made ambassador only to please Mme des Ursins, received thanks for his services, and the Duc de Saint-Aignan was appointed in his place, just as he was thinking of returning to France after escorting the Queen of Spain to Madrid. That lady made every endeavour to please the king her husband, and succeeded beyond all expectation. She felt very strongly for Italians, and advanced them whenever possible, regardless of their merit, which made the Spaniards and Flemings inordinately jealous. This slight sketch must serve for the present.

While the Princesse des Ursins slowly made her way to Paris, Voysin, glutted with the best that fortune can bestow—Chancellor and keeper of the seals, minister and secretary of State for war, with greater influence than ever Louvois possessed, the confidential adviser of Mme de Maintenon and M. du Maine, executor of the King's testament, and of all else which the ancient whore and the bastard wished to extort, minister in sole charge of the question of the constitution, implicitly trusted by the leaders of that redoubtable intrigue and with a heart as black and corrupted as theirs—basked in the King's favour and the enjoyment of boundless power. Wishing to savour his present glory, he decided to drive in state to the Parlement, in the rôle of Chancellor of France—to that same Parlement where his paternal grandfather had been for many years clerk of the criminal court, and without rising higher had thought himself wonderfully successful. Chancellor Pontchartrain and other chancellors before him had refused to set foot there; few or none had ever gone there without need; none, like Voysin, had ever gone purely out of vanity. He drove with an escort of more than a hundred officers, and accompanied by his full complement of counsellors of State and présidents-à-mortier. There was no pomp omitted on his drive, his reception, or his departure. His speech revealed better luck than brains. Neither the princes nor the peers attended; they do not displace themselves for officials.

In the meantime a Persian ambassador had arrived at Charenton, with all expenses paid from the moment when he disembarked. The King made a great occasion of his coming and Pontchartrain paid court to him assiduously. Pontchartrain was, in fact, suspected of having invented this ambassador, for there seemed to be nothing genuine about him, and his behaviour was as disgraceful as his wretched suite and miserable presents. Moreover he produced neither credentials nor instructions from the King of Persia or his ministers. He seems to have been no more than some kind of provincial intendant, entrusted by the governor of his province with business to transact in France. Pontchartrain blew him up to ambassadorial status but, in the event, only the King was deceived.

He entered Paris in state, riding between the Maréchal de Matignon and the Baron de Breteuil, head of protocol; but his manners were so bad, and he made so much difficulty over precedence, that they left him outside the Hôtel des Ambassadeurs, instead of escorting him to his door, as is the usual custom. They then returned straight to Versailles and complained to the King, who approved their conduct and said he thought the ambassador exceedingly ill-bred.

It so happened that the King's interpreter of oriental languages had recently died, and thus they were forced to send for a priest, living near Amboise, who had spent many years in Persia.[1] He did his work well, and was very poorly paid, for I came to be acquainted with this man and conversed with him. He was very gentlemanly and sensible, and was well versed in the manners and customs, as well as familiar with the government and language of the Persians. He said that from all he saw of the so-called ambassador, he felt sure that his mission was bogus, and the man himself merely a merchant in a small way of business, who felt greatly discomfited at having to sustain a rôle for which he was in no way fitted. None the less, they continued to speak of him to the King as though he were genuine, and thus, almost alone of the Court, the King believed in him, and was highly flattered that the Persians should have sent him an ambassador without an invitation. He often mentioned it with satisfaction, and he desired the entire Court to be very splendidly attired on the day of his audience, which was fixed for Tuesday, 19 February. He set the example himself, and the courtiers were most extravagant in copying him.

The long gallery and the state apartments were most beautifully decorated, and a magnificent throne was placed at the end of the gallery, with tiers of benches set at different levels along both sides. The rows nearest the throne were reserved for the ladies of the Court; the rest were for gentlemen and spectators;[2] but no one was admitted except in full court dress. The King lent M. le Duc du Maine a set of diamond and pearl buttons for the occasion, and one of coloured stones to M. le Comte de Toulouse. M. le Duc d'Orléans wore a blue velvet coat, embroidered in a mosaic pattern, overlaid with pearls and diamonds, which was a veritable triumph of richness and good taste. The courtyards, roofs, and approaches swarmed with onlookers, which vastly delighted the King as he looked from the windows. He greatly enjoyed waiting for the ambassador's arrival, which took place at eleven o'clock, in one of the royal coaches, escorted by the Maréchal de

[1] This priest was the Abbé Gauderau, Curé of Notre-Dame-en-Grève. He was rewarded with a permanent appointment as interpreter to the head of protocol.

[2] On public occasions everyone had the freedom of Versailles. The men had only to wear full court dress with a sword and to give their names to the official at the head of the stairs.

Matignon and the Baron de Breteuil. They stopped in the avenue to mount their horses, rode into the great courtyard preceded by the ambassador's suite, and up to the door of the apartment of the colonel of the guard, as is the custom. The suite appeared in every way poverty-stricken, and the supposed ambassador highly embarrassed and very ill-clad. The presents were beneath contempt.

At that point, the King, accompanied by those who filled his study, entered the gallery, and showed himself to the ladies on the tiers of benches, those nearest the throne having been reserved for the princesses of the blood. He wore a coat of black and gold cloth, with the Order outside, and so did those few knights who usually wore it under their coats. His coat was trimmed with the finest diamonds of the crown jewels, to the tune of more than twelve and a half million livres. He bent under the weight of them, looking worn-out, thin, and vastly ill-favoured as he seated himself on the throne, with the princes of the blood and the bastards standing uncovered on either side. A low step and an empty space had been left behind the throne for Madame, Mme la Duchesse de Berry, and their chief ladies-in-waiting, who were all in the first year of mourning. They were incognito, and few noticed them, but they were able to see and hear everything. It had been arranged for them to enter and leave by the late queen's apartments, which had been closed since Mme la Dauphine's death. The Duchesse de Ventadour stood by the King's right hand, holding the leading strings of the little king to be,[1] while on the second tier of benches were the Elector of Bavaria with the ladies of his retinue, the Comte de Lusace, Prince Elector of Saxony,[2] and the Princesse de Conti (Monsieur le Prince's daughter).[3] Coypel[4] the painter, and Boze, secretary of the Académie des Inscriptions, were placed below the throne to paint and describe the scene. Pontchartrain had forgotten nothing likely to flatter the King, or persuade him that this embassy was a revival of his glorious past. In short, he shamefully deceived him in order to give him pleasure, for by that time no one else was gulled.

The envoy mounted the grand staircase of the ambassadors, crossed the state apartments, and entered the long gallery by the salon opposite to the throne. He appeared completely bewildered by the magnificence, and more than once lost his temper with the interpreter, which showed that he knew some French. After the audience, he was entertained to dinner by the household, as is the custom; and then saw the future king in the apartments of the late queen, which were also most richly adorned. Thereafter he visited Pontchartrain and Torcy,

---

[1] There is a famous picture of the royal family, by Largilliére, in the Wallace Collection, London, with the Duchess holding the little prince's leading strings.

[2] Frederick Augustus, Electoral-prince of Saxony (1696-1763). He became Augustus III, King of Poland, in 1733.

[3] There were two Princesses de Conti: the dowager, Marie Anne de Bourbon, the illegitimate daughter of Louis XIV by Mme de La Vallière and the widow of Louis Armand Prince de Conti (d. 1685), and this one, Marie Thérèse de Bourbon, Monsieur le Prince's daughter, widow of François Louis, Prince de Conti, who died in 1709.

[4] Antoine Coypel, court-painter to Louis XIV (1661-1722).

stepped into his coach and returned to Paris. The gifts were as disgraceful to the King of Persia as they were to King Louis, consisting in all of four hundred very poor pearls, two hundred most commonplace turquoises, and two gold boxes of mumis—a precious balm that issues from one rock enclosed within another, and that congeals after a certain time. The King ordered nothing to be moved in the gallery and the state apartments, for he intended to hold a final audience at the same place and with the same ceremonies as at the bogus ambassador's reception. He ordered Torcy, Pontchartrain, and Desmaretz to attend together to the arrangements, which caused Pontchartrain a good deal of chagrin.

At long last the Princesse des Ursins arrived in Paris, and went immediately to lodge with her brother the Duc de Noirmoutiers,[1] who rented a little house, the property of the Dominicans, next to mine, in the Rue Saint-Dominique. How different must her journey have seemed to her, compared with that other journey through France, when she appeared to be mistress of the court![2] Few visited her regularly, except old friends and members of her late circle; but others called out of curiosity, and thus in the first days after her return there was something of a crowd in her salon; this was followed by a falling off, and, as soon as the outcome of her visit to Versailles became known, she was deserted. M. le Duc d'Orléans, now newly reconciled with the King of Spain,[3] felt strongly that his true interests, and perhaps a faint desire for revenge, required him to prove that the Spanish affair that had brought him so near the scaffold was the vindictive action of Mme des Ursins. Mme de Maintenon, with M. du Maine and their powerful allies at Meudon, had grossly exaggerated the rumours, but Mme des Ursins alone had been their inspiration. Times had changed, however; Monseigneur was dead; his cabal dispersed, and Mme de Maintenon no longer protected her. M. le Duc d'Orléans thus felt free to settle with his old enemy, and he saw no reason to be merciful. He was urged on by Mme la Duchesse d'Orléans, and even more powerfully by Madame, who persuaded him to ask the King to ban her from all those places, including Versailles, where she might be likely to encounter Mme la Duchesse de Berry, Madame, or the Orléans themselves. Those ladies, meanwhile, issued strict instructions to their households not to visit her, and required the same of their intimate friends. Such prohibitions provoked a great scandal, demonstrating, as they did, Mme de Maintenon's enmity and the King's indifference. They were also highly embarrassing for the Princesse des Ursins herself.

---

[1] Antoine François de La Trïmoille, Duc de Noirmoutiers (1652-1733). A charming character, he was made blind by smallpox, when he was only nineteen, and felt so desperate that he did not go out for the next twenty years. His friend, the Comte de Fiesque, came to live with him and refused to leave him. Eventually the count persuaded him to receive visitors. Twenty years of being read to had so cultivated his mind that he was discovered to be delightful company and his drawing-room was always crowded.

[2] Her journey back to Spain in triumph, in 1705. See Vol. I, p. 277.

[3] Philip V's quarrel with the Duc d'Orléans was made up only in 1715.

I could not blame M. le Duc d'Orléans for wishing to lay those false accusations squarely at her door, at the precise moment of his reconciliation with King Philip. None the less, I felt bound to say that, having always been a great friend of hers (apart from her behaviour to himself, and without comparing the personal devotion which I felt for him, and my affection for her), I could not forget her past kindnesses, especially not during that last triumphant visit, which I have described.[1] It would thus be hard for me, I protested, not to see her at all. We therefore reached a compromise. M. and Mme la Duchesse d'Orléans gave me leave to visit her twice, once immediately, and again just before her departure; but they made me promise not to go a third time, and Mme de Saint-Simon not ever, on account of Mme la Duchesse de Berry. That last veto we accepted with great reluctance; but there was nothing to be done. Resolved, therefore, to make the best use of such opportunities as I had been given, I informed Mme des Ursins of the obstructions, saying that since I particularly wished to find her alone in the very short time allowed, I would let pass the first few days and her visit to the Court, and only then would ask her to give me audience. She welcomed my letter, for, having known these many years of my friendship with M. le Duc d'Orléans, she was not surprised at the obstacles, but on the contrary thought me clever to have achieved so much. I waited on her, at two o'clock in the afternoon, just two days after her return from Versailles. She immediately closed her doors to every other visitor, and we were closeted together until after ten o'clock. You may imagine how much ground was covered during that long séance. I found her as always, just as affectionate and frank with me as of old, exceedingly discreet regarding M. le Duc d'Orléans and his family, and most outspoken about everything else.

She described her catastrophe without blaming either the King or the King of Spain, for whom she had nothing but praise; but she let fly on the subject of the queen, foretelling everything which we have since seen come about. She concealed neither her astonishment nor her ill-treatment, especially not those acts of deliberate cruelty in the manner of her departure, journey, lack of all creature comforts, and all the rest which she had been made to suffer. She spoke also very frankly of her visit to Versailles and of her disagreeable situation in Paris, of the King of Spain and his late queen, and of various other persons who, in her time, had been prominent in the government. Lastly she spoke of her hope of honourable retirement, although she had not yet decided on any particular place. This eight-hour conversation with one who had so much of interest to impart seemed like eight minutes to me. Supper, although postponed, forced us to separate, with many sincere and reciprocal protestations of friendship and

[1] See Vol. I, pp. 275f.

affection, and regrets that she and Mme de Saint-Simon were forbidden to meet. She promised to inform me well before her departure, so that another interview might be arranged.

Her visit to Versailles had been excessively disagreeable. She had gone there on the morning of Wednesday, 27 March; had dined with the Duchesse du Lude, who lodged there still; had remained with her until nigh on half an hour before the time when the King usually visited Mme de Maintenon, and had waited alone with that lady for his arrival. She stayed scarcely longer than that closeted with them both,[1] and then retired to the house of Mme Adam, in the town, who was the wife of a chief clerk in the foreign service, and who gave her supper and a bed. She had very few callers. Next day, she dined with the Duchesse de Ventadour, and afterwards returned to Paris. She was soon afterwards granted permission to exchange the King's pension for an increase in her annuity from the Hôtel de Ville, from which she was then receiving forty thousand livres. That exchange meant not only doubling the sum involved, but far greater security, for she firmly believed that she would lose her pension as soon as M. le Duc d'Orléans took charge. At first she thought of retiring to Holland; but the States General would have her neither at Amsterdam nor at The Hague, where she had counted on living. She then considered Utrecht; but soon grew bored with that idea, and turned her hopes to Italy. She did not return to the Court except to take her leave. It was M. du Maine, in gratitude for the honours which she had procured for M. de Vendôme in Spain, who gained her that pecuniary favour from the King.

Lord Stair[2] had been living in France for some considerable time. He had come with letters patent as the ambassador of the King of England; but it was a long time before he was able to assume that rôle. He was a tall, well-built Scotsman, a Knight of the Thistle. He went about with his nose in the air, appearing supremely insolent, making disparaging remarks about the fortifications of Mardyck, the demolitions at Dunkirk,[3] trade, etc., and stirring up all kinds of quarrels and arguments, until people began to believe that his mission was less concerned with keeping the peace and promoting his country's affairs, than with provoking another breach between England and France.

He tried Torcy's patience so high that the minister refused to have further dealings with him; and he used so little moderation in speaking to the King at his frequently requested audiences, and appeared so haughty and arrogant that

---

[1] According to Dangeau's journal: 'After dinner, the King heard the sermon, and then gave audience to the Princesse des Ursins, in his study. The audience lasted two hours.... Mme des Ursins went thence to Mme de Maintenon, where she stayed until the King appeared. She had arrived early in the morning, and had dined with the Duchesse du Lude.'

[2] John Dalrymple, 2nd Earl of Stair (1673-1747). He distinguished himself at Oudenarde and Malplaquet. As George I's ambassador in Paris, he undermined the plans of the Pretender and Alberoni. After his retirement he took to farming and made a special study of turnips.

[3] By the Treaty of Utrecht the French were bound to demolish the fortifications at Mardyck and Dunkirk, but had been understandably slow in the process.

King Louis at last refused to see him. Stair made every effort to mingle in the best Society; but his impudent speeches during the public outings and spectacles, and even at his house, where he tried to attract company by offering high living, soon made people weary of him. I shall have further occasion to mention this personage, who knew so well how to bully and bluster, whilst inwardly he was quaking, and with good reason. He was a man of parts and of many adventures; had served as a regimental officer during Marlborough's campaigns, and had retained an amazing hatred of France. He spoke on every subject without the slightest care or restraint.

The King left Versailles to hunt the stag in the forest of Marly, with horses provided for the Comte de Lusace (the Electoral Prince of Saxony), his governor, and the Princes of Anhalt and Darmstadt. Next day, in the gallery, he invited the Comte de Lusace to join him out hawking. While he was at Marly, the King one day went out into his gardens before mass, amusing himself by watching an eclipse of the sun, at nine o'clock in the morning. The ladies had assembled there much earlier. The famous astronomer Cassini[1] came from the Observatory with dark spectacles to enable him to see it more clearly. This occurred on Friday, 3 May. On the following day, the 'year's end' service for M. le Duc de Berry was held at Saint-Denis. M. le Duc d'Orléans attended with some of the princes of the blood. It was on the very next day that the King desired Mme la Duchesse de Berry to go out of deep mourning, although the correct period had another six weeks to run, and himself led her into the salon, and set her down to card-playing. I have mentioned several times already the King's great aversion to mourning, and the small account he took of it, even where his close family was concerned.

Mme la Duchesse de Berry had shown a desire to have ladies of her own since the death of Madame la Dauphine, and for some time past the King had allowed Mme de Saint-Simon to engage Mme de Coëtanfao to attend her, when neither she nor Mme de La Vieuville happened to be available. Mme la Duchesse de Berry now received permission to have four ladies of her own; but they were not to rank as palace-ladies. One whom she nominated was Mme de Coëtanfao, and the King agreed to her. The others were the Duchesse de Brancas, of whom I have already spoken,[2] Mme de Clermont, whose husband had been captain of M. le Duc de Berry's guard, and Mme de Pons, whose husband had been keeper of his wardrobe. These ladies were appointed to accompany Mme la Duchesse de Berry, and to go by twos to Marly, with salaries of four thousand livres. The Duchesse de Brancas was never on duty, and went away to Provence, never to return, and Mme de Coëtanfao died shortly after her appointment.

[1] Jacques Cassini (1677-1756), son of the founder of the Paris Observatoire.
[2] See Vol. I., p. 72.

Mme de Coëtanfao's demise involved me in a wholly unexpected lawsuit. She was of small account, her father having been a counsellor of the Parlement, and she died leaving no children or other close heirs. Her second husband was an old and a very dear friend of mine, for whom I had found a place as groom-in-waiting in Mme la Duchesse de Berry's household, and during the last three campaigns he had given me a box to keep safe for him, which was to be returned to his widow in the event of his death. When she fell ill, she sent to Marly, where I then was, and begged me to go at once to her in Paris. I immediately went. There she quickly handed me the said box, without comment or explanation, either as to its contents or as to what she wished me to do with it; and she contrived to do this behind a screen, for she was not yet bedridden, and was mortally afraid lest her mother enter and find her in the act. I took the box to my house and returned to Marly. A week later she was dead. It then became necessary for me to declare the box, and I accordingly sent it to the civil authorities to be opened. Inside was her will, leaving everything that she possessed to me, to the tune of more than five hundred thousand francs. I did not need anyone to tell me the nature of that princely gift but at once informed Coëtanfao and his brother, the Bishop of Avranches,[1] and with all speed made arrangements to collect my inheritance and immediately hand it over to them.[2] Her heirs and her mother prepared to dispute the will, and I to defend my legacy.

It appeared to me that I must have a pretty strong case, since no one had mentioned a legacy to me, still less told me what to do with it—that I could swear before the Parlement. Most unfortunately, a new judgment had very recently been delivered, aimed directly and with malice at such deeds of trust. In that case, Mme d'Isenghien Rhodes, who died childless, had bequeathed all her wealth to the Abbé de Thou, a man of high integrity, and her very good friend, as well as being a friend of M. d'Isenghien her husband. The abbé had not heard of his bequest until after the will was ready, still less had he received any hint of an underlying purpose. He had thus been in my own situation, and felt equally free to swear to that effect before the Parlement. That body, however, suddenly introduced a completely novel restriction. He was required to swear not only to having had no previous knowledge of the bequest, or of its being in the nature of a trust; but he was asked to take a second oath promising to use the money exclusively for his personal benefit, failing which the will would be declared invalid. I have no idea what may have been the Abbé de Thou's original intention; but

---

[1] Roland François de Kerhoent, Bishop of Avranches.

[2] According to the laws of the Paris Parlement, a husband could not inherit from his wife (whose only wealth was presumably the dowry given by her family), if her mother or any brother survived her. It was a fairly new law, and some of the provincial parlements had not yet brought their regulations into line with Paris, as will be seen. The sum in question was very great, and Mme de Coëtanfao's implicit faith in Saint-Simon is touching, for she obviously trusted him to be clever as well as honest.

confronted with the alternative of keeping his legacy or nullifying the will, he went through the hoop, took the oath, and received payment on that understanding.

In my own case, when my sole concern was to pass the legacy on to M. de Coëtanfao (since I realized that it was left to me for that purpose only), I was loath to risk having a similar oath required of me. I therefore arranged to have the case heard by the Rouen Parlement, both on account of the disputants' connections in Paris,[1] and because in Rouen, where I myself had friends, they might not yet have heard of that supplementary oath. Thus on the pretext of wishing to settle the affair as soon as possible, the preliminary hearing took place at Rouen. My opponents attended, and pleaded that I was defending my legacy merely for appearances' sake; that I was not interested in the result as far as it concerned myself, and that my absence from the proceedings was proof enough of my lack of interest. Coëtanfao and the Bishop of Avranches kept me informed of what took place, and of when that stage was reached. Two days later, despite all that was then occupying my mind, I went to Rouen; visited all the judges and all my friends; did everything possible to ensure success, and remained for a week or ten days, in order to show my deep concern at the outcome, and my determination to win. That journey of mine put a different complexion on the affair. The mother and the heirs immediately took fright and offered to settle out of court. I refused; but at once informed Coëtanfao and his brother that, since not a halfpenny would enter my pocket, the question of whether or not to settle made no difference to me. It was for them, I added, to decide what best suited their interests, and to instruct me accordingly. At that point, my opponents made a better offer, and finally proposed surrendering the larger half to me. Coëtanfao then resolved to accept, preferring that to the anxieties and delays of litigation and pettifoggery. I accordingly signed the required papers, and a moment later did everything that was needed to place the money straight into his hands, without its ever having entered mine. He received immediately the full amount of his share.

Four or five months later, Coëtanfao and his brother had a fine set of heavy silver plate made and engraved with my coat of arms, and did it all so quietly that I knew nothing of it until two days after it was delivered at my house by porters, who departed forthwith without saying what the various packages contained, or whence they came. Mlle d'Avaise, a young woman of good family, and much virtue, who had served Mme la Duchesse d'Orléans with some distinction, and whom I had placed as head waiting-woman with Mme la Duchesse de Berry, ultimately discovered the name of the senders and told us who they were. In all,

---

[1] Because Mme de Coëtanfao's heirs had many relations in the Paris Parlement.

it amounted to more than twenty thousand écus' worth of silver.[1] We then challenged Coëtanfao, who at first denied all knowledge, and then confessed under our pressure; but although Mme de Saint-Simon and I did our best to persuade him, nothing would induce him to take it back. We had been using only china, since the time when everyone sent their silver to the mint.[2] Thus the affair of my unexpected legacy ended with great advantage to everybody concerned.

I afterwards discovered that the box which Coëtanfao had put into my care during the last three campaigns had all the time contained Mme de Coëtanfao's will. He had money of his own; but this increase was most acceptable, for he lived like a gentleman both in the army and elsewhere. He was a lieutenant-general, equally distinguished for bravery in action and for devotion to the service. In the *Maison du Roi*,[3] where he was senior subaltern of the light horse, he was very popular and most highly esteemed. I prevailed on M. le Duc d'Orléans to promise, in my presence, that he would make him a knight of the Order at the next promotion; but the prince had given so many such promises that in the event he preferred to fail everyone rather than satisfy a few, since he could not appoint more than the hundred allowed by statute.

The King left for Marly on Wednesday, 12 June: it was his last visit. The Queen of England left by litter, on the following day, to take the waters at Plombières, and, more especially, to see the king her son. Chamlay,[4] who attended every Marly, had a fit of apoplexy and immediately departed to Bourbon. His lodging was given to the Marquis d'Effiat.[5] The King's health visibly declined, and M. du Maine, who had long since taken possession of the Marquis d'Effiat (which M. le Duc d'Orléans would not admit, nor trust him any the less), needed to have him on the spot. If, as appeared highly possible, the King should die during the long Marly excursion, M. du Maine would wish to know what measures the Regent intended taking, so as to persuade him into making mistakes. Effiat was an utter rogue, all the more dangerous because he had good sense and intelligence. He was also most monstrously grasping, cunning, and debauched, yet with sufficient restraint to keep his health unimpaired. He was a keen huntsman, and until latterly had been wont to spend whole days on his estates with M. le Duc d'Orléans's hounds. It was well known that he had poisoned Monsieur's first wife Henrietta of England, with a concoction sent from Rome by his lifelong friend the Chevalier de Lorraine. I never spoke to the man, at Marly; I was well aware

---

[1] One *écu* equalled three francs, very approximately ten shillings.
[2] After the terrible winter of 1709, Saint-Simon had very unwillingly contributed his second-best set of silver plate; but what had happened to the other? See Vol. I, p, 441.
[3] The famous household troops.
[4] Jules Louis Bolé, Marquis de Chamlay (1650-1719), who had 'expert knowledge of Flanders down to the smallest brooks and hamlets'. See Vol. I, p, 400.
[5] Antoine Coiffier-Ruzé, Marquis d'Effiat. He was the Duc d'Orléans's master of the horse, and master of hounds. He was also a friend of the Lorraines, which was enough to make him hated by Saint-Simon.

that he was plotting with M. du Maine, and with Mme de Maintenon too; I disliked everything about him.

As soon as he arrived at Marly, which was some four days after the King, Mme la Duchesse d'Orléans started complaining bitterly to me of the great disorder and maladministration of M. le Duc d'Orléans's affairs, praising to the skies the merits of the Marquis d'Effiat, his attachment to her husband, the distress which he felt at seeing his fortune go to wrack and ruin, and the ease with which he could set matters right, had he only the authority. She said that she had already spoken to him, and that although he would never ask for such authority, he was prepared to accept it in the way of friendship. She added, praising us both, that she would dearly love to see me acquainted with him, and ended by desiring me to tackle M. le Duc d'Orléans on the subject of his finances, stressing the bad impression that such chaos gave of a prince soon to be Regent. I was then to propose that the Marquis d'Effiat should be given sole charge of his affairs. Such suggestions I found wholly displeasing, for not only did I avoid new acquaintanceship, but I well knew that Mme la Duchesse d'Orléans was far less to be trusted as a wife than as a sister. I therefore replied that all my life I had taken care not to embroil myself with M. le Duc d'Orléans's private affairs or with the Palais Royal, and that I was now too old to change. My firmness had no effect. She pressed me; she teased me; finally she compelled me to promise to choose a time when I was alone with them both, in order to warn him of the dangers of such confusion in his finances, and afterwards to make the proposal she desired. She vowed that Effiat would support me; that M. le Duc d'Orléans would never rebuff him to his face, and that the marquis would then agree to take charge of the situation and rectify it.

I did not see the Marquis d'Effiat until two days later, when I joined him in conversation with M. le Duc d'Orléans; needless to say that in no other circumstances should I have made a third with them. For a while we spoke on general matters. I then made my observations and followed them with my proposal. They heard me without interrupting; but after I had finished speaking M. le Duc d'Orléans remarked that he could not imagine whence I had gained the idea that there was any confusion capable of destroying his public reputation. His affairs, he said, were in admirable order. I replied that I had better information, from those whose interests coincided with his own. At which point I turned to the Marquis d'Effiat, who hitherto had preserved total silence, and requested the prince to ask his opinion, since he probably knew even more than I. Whereupon d'Effiat calmly stated that he had not inquired closely into matters which did not concern him, but could affirm quite positively that M. le Duc d'Orléans's fortunes were in excellent order and well administered, and he proceeded for some considerable time to enlarge and improve on the prince's reply. They then, with obvious enjoyment, passed the ball from one to the other, whilst I sat furious and amazed. At last I managed to extricate myself by saying that I was glad to hear my informant was so wide of the mark. The conversation gradually reverted to general topics, which gave me sufficient excuse to raise the siege.

I went straight to Mme la Duchesse d'Orléans, exclaiming as I entered that I trusted she would never mention the Marquis d'Effiat's name to me again, and described what had happened. She seemed surprised, but not at all displeased. His value to her more closely concerned her heart than her husband's interests.[1] None the less I benefited to the extent that she never again spoke of him, and I found little difficulty thereafter in avoiding him in M. le Duc d'Orléans's apartments, or in keeping my distance in the salon, for he took equal care to avoid me. In public places he was noticeably polite, and appeared quite unmoved by the coldness of my response. It is not yet time to speak of the domestic life of M. and Mme la Duchesse d'Orléans, nor of the few persons who still sought his society.

Those same enemies who had endeavoured by intrigue and secret agents to convince King Louis, Paris, and foreign countries that M. le Duc d'Orléans was to blame for all the royal tragedies, did not fail to make capital from a most strange and continued sickness which his wife contracted and the doctors professed not to understand. Yet there was nothing very mysterious about it, and I, who am no doctor, had warned her that it would happen. All the Princesses[2] had their fads, from which nothing could dissuade them. This one, not content with her magnificent apartments at Versailles replete as they were with every imaginable luxury, took it into her head to create a minute boudoir from an unsavoury closet, which one entered through the wall beside her bed. It had served her as a privy, and its only light came from a high window giving on to the gallery. She built a hearth there, and added as much ornamentation as the space would allow. The room was so small that it held no more than five persons, and so many only because of a deep recess, contrived by digging and excavating into the thickness of the wall opposite to the fireplace. It had to be plastered over to hide the gaps and roughnesses, for wooden panelling would have shrunk in that situation. She hung tapestries over the still wet plaster, and at once began to spend most of her day there. I had warned her that nothing was more dangerous than to live with wet plaster. I had quoted several examples, even mentioning the death of the vastly stout, vastly healthy Maréchale d'Estrées, which was caused solely by her having been given a newly constructed room at Marly. Nothing deterred her, however,

---

[1] Saint-Simon means that she cared more for the Duc du Maine and what would happen to him in the Regency.
[2] 'The Princesses' was the collective term for the King's three illegitimate daughters, the Dowager Princesse de Conti, Madame la Duchesse, and the Duchesse d'Orléans.

and she was punished for it—pains all over, pulse erratic, sometimes strong, sometimes weak, a constant thirst, and no appetite whatsoever. It was not so much an illness as an intolerable feeling of lassitude. After a time she grew tired of doctors and remedies,[1] emancipated herself from both, and recovered without assistance, to the profound regret, or so I should imagine, of those who were preparing to lay that monstrous accusation also to the account of M. le Duc d'Orléans, despite his many weighty reasons for wishing to keep her alive.

Although it is not yet time to describe the King's decline, his health was swiftly and visibly deteriorating, and his appetite, hitherto so exceedingly large and constant, was much diminished. The courtiers watched him intently, although nothing in his life was changed, or in the daily routine, which, although it varied in detail, was in essence always the same. In foreign countries there was fully as much interest, and scarcely less information. In London, wagers were laid that he would not live beyond 1 September; which was to say not more than three months; but despite the King's anxiety to hear all, you may be sure that no one rushed to impart that piece of news. He was in the habit of having the Dutch gazettes read to him, generally by Torcy, after the council of State. One day, when Torcy had begun to read without previously skimming the article, he suddenly came upon the London wagers. He stopped, hesitated, and skipped the paragraph. The King, seeing plainly that something was amiss, demanded to know what was wrong, what he had omitted, and why. Torcy, blushing to the whites of his eyes, passed it off as best he might, saying that it was nothing but impudence, and not worth repeating. The King insisted; Torcy likewise, but he became ever more entangled. At last, unable to resist further, he read the entire passage. The King tried to appear unmoved; but he was so deeply shaken that he could not help mentioning the wagers when he sat down to his dinner, looking round the assembled company, but not naming the gazette.

This occurred at Marly, where I often paid my court at the beginning of *petit couvert*,[2] and thus I happened to be present. The King looked at me with the rest; but as though he expected me, in particular, to reply. None the less, I was very careful to keep my mouth shut and my eyes lowered. Cheverny,[3] who in most respects was exceedingly tactful, did not behave so prudently. He embarked on a long, superfluous rigmarole concerning similar rumours that had spread from Vienna to Copenhagen at the time when he was ambassador there, seventeen or eighteen years earlier. The King let him have his say, but did not listen. He was

---

[1] Remedies almost certainly meant purges.

[2] When the King's meal was laid for him alone, at a small table.

[3] The Comte de Cheverny (1654-1722), Saint-Simon's friend, with whom he had stayed at Cheverny, in 1708. He had been the French ambassador to Denmark from 1685 to 1693. See Vol. I, p. 369.

obviously deeply distressed, but was unwilling to let that appear. It was noticeable that he did his best to eat and to simulate an appetite; but morsels of food swelled in his mouth.[1] After this, the courtiers watched him still more closely, especially those whose situations gave them most cause for alarm. Rumour had it that one of Lord Stair's aides-de-camp, lately returned to England, had been responsible for the wagers because of the way in which he had described the King's condition. When Stair was told of this he appeared much vexed, declaring that the man was a scoundrel, whom he had already dismissed.

Sainte-Maure,[2] the late M. le Duc de Berry's first equerry, ventured, on coming out of mourning, to ask the King's permission to continue using that prince's liveries and the royal arms on his coaches, for his life, and at his own expense. He needed the arms in order to enjoy the honours of the Louvre;[3] the liveries he wished to wear out, for they were made to last a lifetime, and he would otherwise have been obliged to buy new coats. It appeared that Hautefort, first equerry to the late Queen and paternal uncle of all the present Hauteforts, had received a similar concession, and on that precedent, the King granted Sainte-Maure's request.

The Comte de Lusace, then Electoral-prince of Saxony, and today Elector and King of Poland, in succession to his father, took leave of the King in his study, at Marly. King Louis was exceedingly polite to him, and to the Palatine of Livonia[4] also, who had controlled the Electoral-prince's journey and behaviour, and had himself gained a reputation for good manners, both in France and in other countries. The King sent the Comte de Lusace a diamond-hilted sword worth forty thousand écus, and to the Palatine of Livonia his portrait set in very fine diamonds, with a similar present, although less costly, for the Count's governor, Baron Hagen. The Count had expressed a strong wish to see Saint-Cyr, but for one reason or another the visit had been postponed. Mme de Maintenon had made an appointment with him for 2 June. She had waited for him there, and had intended, after showing him the school, to have a performance of *Esther*[5] given by the young ladies; but the Count developed a fever, and sent his excuses. The visit eventually took place on Tuesday, 11 June, by which time he had recovered. He returned to Saxony a few days later. He conducted himself with extreme discretion and courtesy, even with dignity, and was often to be seen in high Society.

---

[1] Because he had difficulty in swallowing, the pieces of food seemed bigger.
[2] Comte Honoré de Sainte-Maure (1653-1731). Later became first equerry to Louis XV.
[3] The right to park coaches and hunting carriages in the courtyard of the Louvre.
[4] Livonia: a region of Northern Europe, on the Baltic. Once a Russian province, it covered South Estonia and North Latvia.
[5] Racine's play was written in 1689 especially for the schoolgirls of Saint-Cyr. Sainte-Beuve said that it was an outpouring of purest poetry, the most exquisite lament of the tender heart of Racine. It is said that, after *Phèdre*, Racine had such qualms over what was called the wicked incestuousness of that play, that he ceased to write, and sank into a period of brooding piety, from which Mme de Maintenon rescued him by commissioning *Esther*.

Nesmond, Bishop of Bayeux[1] died about this time, at the age of eighty-six. He was doyen of the French episcopy, and one of those true saints who, all unwillingly, inspire veneration, yet at the same time quite innocently provide a constant source of merriment. It was told of him that he said mass every morning, but never knew what he was saying during the remainder of the day. His complete innocence, combined with very limited intelligence, caused him to let fall obscenities at every turn, and to remain totally unaware of them. It made his company an embarrassment to the ladies; so much so, indeed, that his niece, Mme Présidente Lamoignon, sent her daughter from the room whenever he called. For similar reasons he was a danger in regard to the coming reign, for he spoke far too freely; when tackled, he merely said that such matters were of public interest and no news to anyone. On the other hand, if he felt he had hurt someone's feelings, he never hesitated to go and ask their forgiveness.

He admonished one of his priests for attending a wedding. The priest defended himself by the example of Our Lord at the marriage of Cana. 'Come, come! Monsieur le Curé,' said Nesmond, 'that was not one of the best things He did.' What blasphemy, had it come from the mouth of any other! But the good bishop sincerely believed that his retort had been proper, and entirely edifying. It is also worth mentioning that, coming from him, it was received in the way he had intended. He was a good shepherd, always in residence, always busy with the cure of souls in his diocese, visiting the sick, until the very end of his life fulfilling all his functions with understanding and the good sense which God had in other ways denied him. He was wealthy by inheritance and by his rich benefice, and had been clever enough to double his fortune without falling foul of anyone. He lived in a gentlemanly way, not luxuriously, but quietly and frugally, as befits a prelate. By the end of each year he had saved nothing; all was gone in good works, or to the poor. So long as King James remained in France, he gave him each year ten thousand écus; which no one knew of until after his death. Nor did anyone know of many other large charitable gifts which had enabled the impoverished noblemen[2] in his diocese to marry and subsist.

His clergy did their best to keep him on a tight rein to prevent his giving alms out of his pocket; but he was always eluding them and making surreptitious contributions whenever he could manage it. On one occasion, when he was about to go to Paris, someone asked him as a favour to allow one of his attendant clergy to take charge of a hundred gold louis, which he owed to a friend in Paris. The

---

[1] François de Nesmond (1629-1715), He had been Bishop of Bayeux for fifty-four years.
[2] H. Carré in *La Noblesse de France et l'Opinion Publique au XVIII me siècle*, Paris, 1920, says that examples of needy gentlefolk reduced to extreme poverty might be multiplied indefinitely. It was usually accepted that most of the nobles were in that category.

worthy bishop offered to take the money himself, and would not rest until it had been given him. On the road, he gave alms to every beggar and hospital, and to all the poor convents in every place through which he passed. His people could not imagine how he had the means for such munificence; but by the time they reached Paris he was down to his last pistole. Next morning, he told the priest in charge of his finances to take a hundred louis to a certain person, and that was how they discovered whence those great sums had originated.

The King, who knew his goodness, treated him kindly, even with respect, during the short periods when he came to the Court, and the bishop himself was as much at ease with the King as though he saw him every day. He was, indeed, the best and the mildest of men; something of a scold at times, but as far removed as he could possibly be from any abuse of the law or of his power. There was never a breath of scandal in his diocese; he departed from it in perfect peace, and with his affairs in excellent order. His death caused dismay among the poor, and bitter grief throughout his see. He could, none the less, be an ugly customer in delivering rebukes; but only to those whom he could reach in no other way. The following anecdote, among many, may serve to show the zeal that drove him on. He was once involved in an important lawsuit that necessitated his appearing before the Rouen parlement. One of the senior présidents-à-mortier, a man of such vast influence and ability that he could sway the great chamber and his fellow magistrates, openly kept and lived with a married woman, having ill-treated his wife to such an extent that she had been forced to enter a convent. The good bishop paid a formal call on this président, who was one of the judges, in order to state his case. The porter maintained that he was not at home. The bishop insisted. The porter confirmed the fact that he was out, but asked if the bishop would care to wait with Madame, who was receiving in the salon, until his return. 'Madame!' exclaimed the bishop. 'How truly glad I am. When did she return to M. le Président?' 'But, my Lord,' said the porter, 'this is not Madame his wife; it is Madame....' 'Fie! for shame!' cried the bishop in great anger. 'Indeed I shall not enter! She is a vile creature; do you hear me? a vile creature, and I refuse to see her. Be sure to repeat that from me to M. le Président. Say that I think it disgraceful for a judge to ill-use his wife, good, virtuous woman that she is, and to create a scandal by living openly with this bitch, and at his age, too. Fie! Fie! I find it most shocking—be sure that you repeat my words—and then say that I shall not return.' Such was the Bishop of Bayeux's peculiar manner of calling to solicit votes. The strange thing was that he won his suit, and that the président served him marvellously well. Yet even that did not appease him. This tale set all Rouen laughing, and even spread to Paris. I have known so few bishops like him that I could not resist telling the whole story.

Cardinal Sala, a prelate of a very different order, died a few days later, as he was on his way to Rome to receive the hat. He was a Catalan of the very dregs who, discovering brains and ambition in himself, had taken Benedictine orders in his native province, in the hope of pulling himself out of the gutter and making his fortune. It so happened that when the Archduke[1] came to Barcelona, his equerries mistook Sala's father for the coachman. The son managed to turn that mistake to excellent account by using it to become acquainted both with Archduke himself, and with his ministers. He was indeed of great use to them, for his mind being wholly intent on sedition and intrigue, he stirred up every monastery in the town and province, appearing everywhere in the rôle of leader, organizer, and arch-rebel. His successes were such that the Archduke found it necessary to train him for something higher, which was what brought him the bishopric of Gerona, and later promotion to the see of Barcelona itself. In that sphere, he so much distinguished himself that he received the Archduke's nomination to the cardinalate. When the allies' victories eventually compelled the Pope to recognize the Archduke as King of Spain, that pontiff thought himself obliged also to accept Sala, despite his repugnance for prelates of that type. Sala was thus obeying the summons to Rome, when death took him only a short distance from that city.

The Sacred College immediately and more suitably replaced that worthy cardinal with a prelate of less lowly birth, but fully as violent and ambitious, and equally careless of the means by which he attained the cardinalate, that pinnacle of a churchman's aspirations. Bissy had long been working in that direction; his actual methods may not have been so blatantly odious as Sala's—he did not have the same opportunities; but in other ways there was little to choose between them, as you will have observed from various items throughout these memoirs, and from the prophecy of his father concerning him, which showed perfect knowledge of his character.[2] I am speaking, of course, of Bissy, Bishop of Meaux and Abbot of Saint-Germain-des-Prés, who, by the King's influence and the self-interested manœuvres of the Jesuits (who had bought him body and soul), obtained the consent of the various sovereigns to having his promotion advanced by nearly four years.

You will recollect that there was a fashion for driving by night beside the river, and for holding concerts and supper-parties there on occasion. This foolish craze had continued to flourish; but despite the fact that most of the coaches were illuminated with torches, indelicate lapses, or even worse, caused a ban to be placed on nocturnal driving, and it was forbidden altogether at the beginning of this July.

[1] Charles Francis Joseph, Archduke of Austria (1685-1740), recognized as King of Spain by the Allies in 1703, became Holy Roman Emperor as Charles VI in 1711.
[2] In 1701, Bissy's father Jacques, Marquis de Bissy, had told some friends who praised his son: 'You do not know him! See that mild little priest. He is so eaten up with ambition that he is quite capable of setting Church and State alight if that would serve his interests.'

The Spanish ambassador, the Prince of Cellamare,[1] arrived in Paris at this time. He came to Marly four days later, in time for the King's *lever*, and was immediately granted an audience in the study. He went thence to M. le Duc d'Orléans, bearing a vastly civil letter from the King of Spain, in answer to one sent by the prince, and returned soon after to attend the King. He had been promised the first vacant lodging at Marly, for in France as in Spain ambassadors, as members of the royal household, have the right to join every excursion. Mme de Saint-Simon, who felt in need of the waters at Forges,[2] asked for leave of absence.

Our lodging was on the lower floor of the first pavilion, on the chapel side. On the day when she was going to Paris, we were surprised, as we were sitting down to table, by the arrival of Blouin, accompanied by some of the porters from the furniture store. He said that he came from the King to request me to give up my ground floor rooms to the Prince of Cellamare, and to move to another lodging, opposite the chapel, on an upper floor. He did not say how it had fallen vacant; but assured me that the King wished me well-lodged, and vowed that I should find the new rooms very comfortable. He added that the King hoped I would move and settle in immediately, and attached so much importance to speed that he was sending porters to help my servants with the furniture. We ate our dinner; Mme de Saint-Simon departed, and I forthwith moved house. My servants reported that a very large number of porters had arrived; that Blouin himself had returned to superintend, and that all was accomplished in a moment. I failed to understand the reason for so much haste; but when bedtime came I learned all.

My people told me that I had been transferred to the lodging of Courtenvaux who, by virtue of being captain of the Hundred Swiss, had permanent quarters near the Guards in the ante-chamber, the *garde-robe*, and the chapel, and that at ten o'clock a post-chaise had drawn up at my door. It contained Courtenvaux himself, much disturbed to see lights in the windows and demanding to know what was going on. His footman, dashing upstairs with his boots on, was still more astonished to find my servants in residence, and quickly returned to tell his master. Courtenvaux at once sent him back to say that it was his lodging and that he needed it to sleep in. My people informed him of the reason for my removal; that they could not turn me out, and that his master had best find Blouin to discover what new arrangements had been made for him. Courtenvaux, indeed, had no other alternative. What he learned from Blouin on the King's behalf was that he had been absent without leave for nearly three weeks; that this had occurred on other excursions; that the King was tired of his neglecting his duties, and had disposed elsewhere of his lodging so as to prevent his return. The King

---

[1] Antoine Joseph del Giudice, Prince of Cellamare (1657-1733). He was Cardinal del Giudice's nephew.
[2] Forges-les-Eaux, a spa in Normandy.

had said that this should be a lesson to teach him better behaviour, by giving him the disgrace of exclusion from Marly for the rest of that visit. Petty malice of that kind will never help the Crown to liberate humanity!

Père Tellier, having failed with his national Church council, by means of which he and Bissy had undertaken to gain acceptance for the constitution, viewed with despair the possibility that the King might die before their aim was achieved. He therefore made one last effort and, in order to clinch matters, advised the King to summon the premier président and his deputies to Marly. Daguesseau,[1] the procureur général, was the one most against the bull. Mesmes, the premier président, vacillated between the Court and his colleagues. Fleury,[2] the premier avocat général, used all his unequalled wit and cunning to play for time and avoid a conflict. Chauvelin,[3] another avocat général, brilliant, learned, percipient, knew no god nor law other than those which served his interests. He was sold to the Jesuits, and to anyone capable of promoting or assisting him. Tellier, having made sure of him, had placed him in the King's confidence to such an extent that for the past year he had been summoned for secret conferences, and frequently given entry through the back offices. Blancmesnil,[4] Lamoignon's son, a general dogsbody[5] and, like the rest of his family, a slave of the Jesuits, was born only to bow and scrape. It was generally expected that these Jesuits would reach a sudden decision after some sharp words by the King, uttered for the sole purpose of intimidating them. Daguesseau's wife[6] exhorted her husband to stand all the firmer if his colleagues proved weak, and when he left for Marly, she kissed him and solemnly charged him to forget that he had a wife and family, to hold his wealth and office as nothing, and his conscience and honour as above price. Her brave words had their effect. He bore the first onslaught almost alone; but continued to speak out with so much respect, albeit with learning and authority, that the others felt too much ashamed to desert him; even although the King was so furious that Daguesseau was within an ace of dismissal. Fleury was his strongest supporter; but he, too, was consumed with fright lest he lose his office.

Such violent measures, sure to arouse antagonism, were not, however, what Père Tellier required. He was not insensible to the delights of vengeance, but would not be distracted from his main purpose. Using all his influence to

---

[1] Henri François Daguesseau (1668-1751), later Chancellor of France.

[2] Guillaume François Joly de Fleury (1675-1756). Not to be confused with Cardinal de Fleury. He was the deputy director of prosecutions in the court of appeal.

[3] Louis IV Chauvelin (1683-1715).

[4] Guillaume de Lamoignon de Blancmesnil (1685-1772). He was avocat général, but became Chancellor of France in 1750. Saint-Simon's objection to him may have come from a loathing for the whole family who had assumed the particule to which, springing as they did from the gutter, they had no vestige of a right.

[5] *Valet-a-tout-faire*, a contemptuous term for a handyman. 'Dogsbody' suggested itself as a Saint-Simonian equivalent. It was naval slang for a pease-pudding boiled in a cloth, also for a lower officer, a drudge. Saint-Simon's nurse came from a seafaring family.

[6] Anne Françoise le Fèvre d'Ormesson (1678-1724).

overcome the King's almost insuperable reluctance, and even his failing health, he prevailed upon that monarch to announce his intention to visit Paris and hold there a *Lit de Justice*, after which they would see whether the King's authority sufficed to have the constitution enregistered, as it stood. The Parlement received the appropriate instructions, and a general panic ensued; but not so great a one as to decide the issue in advance. It was at the Court that the alarm was greatest   it became the sole subject of conversation.

M. le Duc d'Orléans, who was well aware of my views on the constitution and had often given me his own opinion, asked me how I should act on the appointed day. My answer was that my duty and my peer's oath both required me to assist the King in high and weighty questions concerning the State; that they had succeeded in turning a piece of sharp practice into such a question; that the King would summon me among other peers to the *Lit de Justice*, and that I should perforce obey him. Nevertheless, before starting out, I should take care to see that no one would find anything among my papers, except such as I desired them to find, and that I had ready money and my post-chaise packed and prepared. That done, I should go to the *Lit de Justice* with conscience, justice, and truth to support me, and, making very sure not to seem to vote with my bonnet, should protest with all my strength against the constitution, its enregistration, and its acceptance. Having done so, even although I might act with the greatest moderation, showing all proper respect for the King's authority, I was morally certain I should not be allowed to return home after the session, and should think myself lucky if I was sent only into exile and not to the Bastille. At this short answer, M. le Duc d'Orléans, who knew me too well to doubt my courage, gazed hard at me and then embraced me, saying that he was glad to find me of that mind, for he himself was resolved to do likewise. There was, however, a certain difference, for he would speak in full view of the King, who would hear every word he said, glare at him from top to toe, and be so shaken by passion that the consequences were unpredictable. We discussed the affair again and again, endeavouring to give ourselves courage, and so we continued until the King had returned from Marly, and the day arrived for him to attend the Parlement. At that point, however, his health would not permit him to undertake the journey. Thus the *Lit de Justice* came to nothing, and so did the enregistration on which he had set his heart. I should not have spent so long over an event that never happened, did I not think it both interesting and important to depict M. le Duc d'Orléans as he then showed himself to me, so that you may compare his later behaviour in the same matter, when it was in all respects the same, only further developed, more understandable and, if possible, still more odious.

At this time, in England, the persecution of the leading Tories was at its height, especially those who had been ministers of the late Queen Anne and all those who had helped in negotiating the peace. The new court had been clamouring in particular for the head of the Earl of Oxford,[1] lately Chancellor of the Exchequer, but he had defended himself so bravely at the bar of the House of Lords that against all expectations he had been acquitted. The Duke of Ormonde was also in the greatest danger, and surrounded in his house at Richmond, near London, but he somehow managed to escape and appeared in Paris at about this time.

The state of the King's health, with his strength visibly declining, gave Mme des Ursins some cause for alarm, lest she suddenly find herself in the power of M. le Duc d'Orléans. She therefore determined to put herself quickly beyond his reach, even though she had not yet decided where to settle, and she begged the King's permission to bid him farewell at Marly. She came from Paris on Tuesday, 6 August, at a time to coincide with the King's leaving his table; was at once summoned to the study, and was with him a good half-hour, after which she went straight to Mme de Maintenon, remained closeted with her for an hour, and thereafter proceeded immediately to her carriage for the return journey to Paris. I did not know of her coming until some time after her arrival, and I was therefore in doubt how best to see her. As luck would have it, it occurred to me to go to her coach and question her servants, and, by another stroke of luck, she appeared in a sedan-chair as I was speaking to them. She seemed glad to see me, and made me sit beside her in the coach, where we remained talking very freely for just under the hour.

She made no attempt to hide her fears from me; spoke of the coldness shown her by the King and Mme de Maintenon, despite all their civility, of how deserted she had felt at the Court, and even in Paris, of her uncertainty regarding her choice of a place of residence. All this she discussed in great detail, yet without complaint, regrets, or tears, showing moderation always, as though, rising above all her troubles, she were speaking of some third person. She touched very lightly upon Spain, describing the influence, nay the growing ascendancy, of the queen over the king; making me understand that it was bound to happen; mentioning the queen in passing, and expressing with modesty her gratitude for the King of Spain's generosity. Fear of being seen by passers-by made her bring our conversation to a close. She was extremely affectionate, said how sorry she was at having to end our talk, promised to warn me before her departure and to devote another day to me, sent many messages to Mme de Saint-Simon, and appeared to

---

[1] Robert Harley, 1st Earl of Oxford (1661-1724), a Tory and Marlborough's enemy. He had been dismissed from office in 1714 and, in 1715, was sent to the Tower on suspicion of conspiring with the French.

appreciate my friendly gesture in seeking her out despite my promise to M. le Duc d'Orléans. When she was gone, I went at once to that prince, and told him what I had done, saying that it was in no way a visit, but only a chance meeting; that I could not have resisted seeing her, but without prejudice to the farewell visit, for which I had his leave. M. and Mme la Duchesse d'Orléans were not in the slightest degree ruffled, for their victory had been complete. The Princesse des Ursins was about to leave France for ever, and without hope of ever returning to Spain.

Until then, she had diverted herself with her few remaining friends and acquaintances, and some of M. de Noirmoutiers's circle. She had spent her time quietly putting her affairs in order and transferring her belongings from Spain. The fear of finding herself in the hands of a prince whom she had most cruelly wronged made her hasten her plans; and panic had gripped her when she observed the prodigious change in the King's appearance since her first audience on her return from Spain. She felt convinced that the end was near, and thenceforward made every effort to be well informed regarding a health which, so she thought, alone ensured her safety in France. Still more alarmed by later reports, she decided to wait no longer and, on 14 August, left in a violent hurry, accompanied as far as Essonnes[1] by her two nephews. There was no time to think of warning me, and thus our conversation in her coach, at Marly,[2] was the last I ever saw of her; for she did not draw breath until she reached Lyons. She had long ago abandoned the idea of living in Holland—the States General would not receive her, and she was disgusted by the absence of rank, the lack of distinction in a republican society which, in her eyes, quite destroyed the pleasures of its freedoms. On the other hand, she could not bring herself to return to Rome, the scene of past triumphs, for fear of appearing an outcast begging for asylum. Moreover, she dreaded a hostile reception, for she did not forget the closed residence of the nuncio at Madrid,[3] and the quarrels between the two courts.[4] She had lost many of her old friends and acquaintances; much had changed during her fifteen years' absence, and she foresaw the embarrassment of meeting the ministers of the Emperor, and of the two crowns, and their partisans. The court of Turin was unworthy of her; the King of Sicily had not always approved her conduct, and in both countries she was all too well known. In Venice, she would have nothing to occupy her. In this agitated state of mind, she received greatly exaggerated reports of the King's being *in extremis,* and left Lyons on the instant, lest his death should find her still in France. With no fixed destination in

---

[1] Essonnes, now linked with Corbeil to form Corbeil-Essonnes in the District of Paris; it was a posting-stage on the main road to Fontainebleau and the South.

[2] A week earlier, on 6 August.

[3] In 1709, the Emperor had persuaded the Pope to recognize the Archduke Charles as King of Spain; and, in consequence, Philip V broke with Rome and refused to receive the nuncio, at Madrid.

[4] The Pope, on his side, was not anxious to receive her for fear of annoying Philip V.

mind, she made for Chambéry in Savoy as the nearest place of safety, and arrived there breathless.

That was her first abode; and there she allowed herself leisure to decide where next to go, and where to find a home. After weighing every possibility, she fixed on Genoa, because she liked its freedom, the society of its numerous rich and noble families, its pleasant situation and climate, and the fact of its being a kind of halfway-house between Madrid, Paris, and Rome, where she still had correspondents, whom she avidly plied for news. The relinquishment of so much real power, and of so many equally important plans, had not succeeded in destroying her hopes—still less her ambitions. Having settled on Genoa she made her way thither and was warmly welcomed. She thought at last to have found a settled home, and did, in fact, remain there several years; after which boredom set in, and perhaps annoyance that she was not of more consequence. Life was nothing to her without intrigue, and what was there to aspire to, at Genoa, for a woman past her prime? She once again turned her thoughts to Rome; took soundings at the Vatican; became reconciled, although with difficulty, with her brother, Cardinal de La Trémoïlle; revived old friendships when that could decently be managed; feeling her way delicately, in order to discover what sort of treatment she might expect from those who were attached to France or Spain.

She eventually left Genoa and returned to her old home. It was not long before she had attached herself to the English court, and in next to no time she was ruling it entirely, and quite openly.[1] What a sorry descent! But it none the less gave her the sensation of being at a court, with a ferment of petty intrigues to divert her who could not dispense with them. Thus her life drew to its close, in magnificent health both bodily and mentally, and most prodigious opulence, which did not come amiss in that lamentable circle. For the rest, she was not much regarded at Rome. She was thought to be of little consequence, shunned by all who inclined to Spain, rarely visited by the French, but in no way harassed by the Regent, well fortified with money from both countries, wholly engrossed with Society and with what she was and once had been, never stooping to flatter, always well bred and courageous. The death of Cardinal de La Trémoïlle, in January 1720, left her life emptier, although there had been little affection between them. She survived him by three years, retaining her health and energy, with her faculties unimpaired until the day of her death, and was carried off, after a remarkably short illness, on 5 December, 1722.

She had the joy of seeing Mme de Maintenon forgotten and discredited at Saint-Cyr, the pleasure of outliving her, and the rapture of watching her two

---

[1] The English court at Rome was the court of the Old Pretender, whom Louis XIV had been forced to banish from France by the terms of the Treaty of Utrecht.

great enemies, the Cardinals del Giudice and Alberoni, appear at Rome one after the other, in disgrace as deep as hers had been, and one of them fallen from a equally great height. She was able to rejoice at the complete neglect, not to say contempt, with which they were treated. Her own death, which only a few years earlier would have rocked Europe, raised not the smallest ripple. The little English court mourned her, as did certain of her old friends, myself included—a fact which I did not attempt to conceal, although I had not written to her, on account of M. le Duc d'Orléans. The rest of the world appeared not to notice that she was gone. Nevertheless, during the whole course of her long life, she figured so nobly and so publicly (although in many different ways), had such radiance, courage, industry, and rare attainments, ruled so absolutely and openly in Spain, and possessed a character of such extraordinary interest, that her biography deserves to be written, and would find a place among the most fascinating episodes in the history of her times.

The reign of Louis XIV has now been brought nearly to its close; nothing more remains to tell, save the events of the final month. These, however, were of such importance that they need to be recorded with the utmost precision and clarity, and in their right order, for they are linked very closely with all that followed after the King's death. Yet it is no less necessary to describe the plans, thoughts, and diffi-culties of that prince who, despite all the endeavours of Mme de Maintenon and the Duc du Maine, would inevitably rule the State during the minority of the future King. Now therefore is the time to explain many of these things, after which I shall return to the final month of the King's life, and to what followed thereafter.

Before venturing upon that thorny path, however, I shall try, if I can, to describe the character of the leading figure, his private and official troubles, and all that concerned him personally. I say, 'if I can', because never in all my life have I met a man so conspicuously and perfectly inconsistent as M. le Duc d'Orléans. You will soon see that although I had known him intimately for many years, during which he never tried to deceive me—although latterly I had been the only man to visit him, and positively the only person to whom he could speak freely, and he did so speak, openly, trustfully, and, indeed, of necessity—yet I still did not know him; nor did he fully understand himself.

M. le Duc d'Orléans was of medium height, at most, stout without being obese, with a bearing that was easy and extremely noble, a large pleasant counte-nance, a high colour, black hair, and a wig to match.[1] He was always an abominable dancer, and had little success at the academy;[2] but he possessed so much natural

---

[1] Madame described him as follows: 'When my son was only about fourteen or fifteen he was not ill-looking; but the suns of Spain and Italy so bronzed his skin that his complexion turned dark red. He is not tall, but in no way fat. His bad eyesight causes him to squint a little sometimes, and he carries himself badly. I love him with all my heart; but I can understand that women are not attracted to him, for he is not gallant and possesses no tact.'

[2] The academy for the education of young nobles, which the Duc d'Orléans attended.

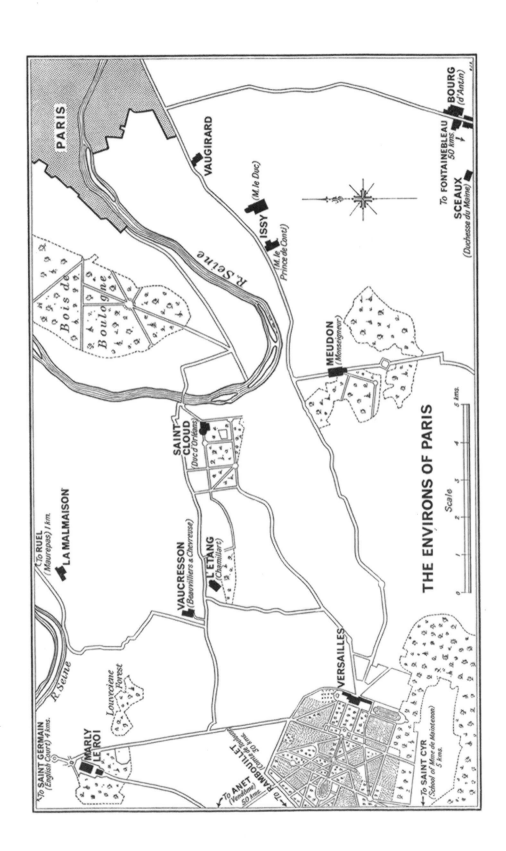

PARIS

VAUGIRARD

ISSY (M. le Duc)

(M. le Prince de Conti)

R. Seine

Bois de Boulogne

BOURG (d'Antin)

To FONTAINEBLEAU
50 kms.

SCEAUX
(Duchesse du Maine)

MEUDON
(Monseigneur)

SAINT-
CLOUD
(Duc d'Orléans)

L'ETANG
(Chamillart)

VAUCRESSON
(Beauvilliers & Chevreuse)

LA MALMAISON

To RUEL
(Maurepas) 1 km.

Louveciene
Forest

R. Seine

To SAINT GERMAIN
(English Court) 4 kms.

MARLY
LE ROI

To ANET
(Vendôme) 50 kms.

RAMBOUILLET
(Comte de Toulouse)
50 kms.

VERSAILLES

To SAINT CYR
(School of Mme de Maintenon)
5 kms.

THE ENVIRONS OF PARIS

Scale

0   1   2   3   4   5 kms.

charm of manner that it enhanced his every action, even the most commonplace.
When not crossed he could be gentle, cordial, frank, easy of access; he had a
most agreeable voice, and an original turn of phrase. He conversed lucidly and
fluently on any subject, never feeling for his words, and often remarkably interesting. What is more, he could be just as sensible and as eloquent on the abstract
sciences, State affairs, finance, the law, military matters, and the doings of the
Court, as in polite conversation, or in the discussion of engineering or the arts.
He had read the histories and memoirs of great men, and put them to excellent
use. He was familiar with the lives of the leading personalities in other periods,
and with the intrigues in ancient courts as well as in those of his own day. To
hear him talk, you would have thought him vastly learned. Not so, indeed, for
he was a skimmer; but his memory was so uniformly good that he forgot nothing, not even names and dates, which he quoted accurately. His grasp was so
complete that in glancing through a book he took in as much as though he had
read it carefully, and he excelled at impromptu speeches, being very quick with his
sallies and in repartee. I never flattered him, for which he reproached me, as did
others, but I used often to praise him for a quality which few possess, and which
he had abundantly, namely great intelligence supported by excellent good sense.
Had he followed his instincts in every matter he would not have made mistakes.
He sometimes took such praise as though it were meant as a reproach, and there
he was not always wrong; but it was none the less true. Despite all these gifts, he
never put on airs or paraded superior knowledge, but spoke to each man as to
an equal, and often surprised scholars by his brilliance. In Society he was neither
pompous nor overbearing, but retained a just sense of his rank and position, so
that no one forgot himself in his presence; yet everyone was at ease, because he
brought himself to their level.

With the princes of the blood he was especially careful to preserve his dignity.
No one was more respectful in speech and manner, no one more noble in his
attitude towards the King and the Sons of France; for he had inherited Monsieur's[1]
inordinate pride in his royal ancestry. Although not prone to say ill-natured or
spiteful things, he was a dangerous critic of other men's courage. He never boasted
of his own and, indeed, was unusually modest and silent regarding events in
which he had distinguished himself. He gave others their due; but found it hard
not to round upon those whom he described as 'not pulling their weight',[2] and
made his scorn and dislike very evident.

Another of his weaknesses was to imagine that he greatly resembled Henri
IV, and to imitate him in his conduct and sayings. He even managed to convince

---

[1] Monsieur was Philippe I, Duc d'Orléans, father of this Duc d'Orléans, and the only brother of Louis XIV.
[2] 'Franc du collier': used of carthorses willingly throwing their weight into the collar to pull a load uphill.

himself that he looked like that monarch in face and figure, and no flattery pleased him more than a remark to that effect. This, however, I would not stoop to, for I knew only too well that he tried also to copy that great monarch's vices, and that he admired them equally with his virtues. As a matter of fact, he did somewhat resemble Henri IV, in being by nature good, kind, and compassionate. He was accused of most brutal crimes, yet I never met a man more violently opposed to murder, or even to causing pain. You might say that he carried kindness and even tolerance too far, for I maintain that he made a vice of the sublime virtue of forgiving one's enemies, and that such indiscriminate generosity verged on blindness to crime, and caused him much trouble and annoyance in later years, as will be seen in due course.

I remember, for example, that at Marly, about a year before the King's death, I went upstairs soon after dinner to pay a call on Mme la Duchesse d'Orléans, and found her in bed, suffering from a migraine. M. le Duc d'Orléans was alone with her, sitting in an armchair by her bedside. No sooner was I also seated, than Mme la Duchesse d'Orléans began to speak of Cardinal de Rohan's part in the plot against the duke, and of his supporting Mme de Maintenon and M. du Maine in their efforts to give credence to the abominable accusations so prevalent at that time. I exclaimed all the more indignantly because M. le Duc d'Orléans had for some unknown reason favoured the cardinal and his brother and had thought of them as friends. 'What do you think of M. le Duc d'Orléans now?' she added. 'He knows that all this is true, and yet he persists in treating them in the same friendly way.' I looked at the prince lolling back in his chair and saying nothing beyond a word or two in confirmation; then I said, 'Truly, Monsieur, I believe that no one has been so meek since Louis le Débonnaire.' At those words he leapt to his feet, blushing scarlet to the whites of his eyes, and, spluttering with rage, began to accuse me of envy and malice, whilst the duchess laughed at him and egged me on. 'That is right, Monsieur,' said I, 'scold your friends and spoil your enemies. I am glad to see you so angry; it shows that I have put my finger on an abscess; when I press, the patient yells. I wish I might squeeze all the poison out of your system; you would then be a better man, and far more respected.' He continued growling a little longer and then subsided. That was one of the only two occasions when he was really vexed with me. The other I shall now recount.

It happened two or three years after the King's death, when I was chatting one day in a corner of the long gallery at the Tuileries, waiting for the Conseil de la Régence to begin, whilst M. le Duc d'Orléans talked to someone in a window recess at the other end of the room. I then heard my name being called, and learned that he wished to speak to me, as often happened before those meetings. I accordingly went to him, to find him looking grave, thoughtful, and annoyed, which much surprised me. 'Monsieur!' said he abruptly, 'I have much to reproach you with; I thought you were my friend!' 'Reproach me, Sir?' I exclaimed, still more astonished, 'Pray what have I done?' 'What you have done,' he retorted, 'is something which you cannot deny; writing verses, Sirrah! Verses against me!' 'Verses?' I exclaimed in bewilderment, 'Who on earth has reported such nonsense? You have known me forty years, and are well aware that I cannot string two lines together, let alone write a verse.' 'Disgraceful lies,' said he, 'you cannot possibly deny writing these,' and bursting into laughter, he there and then began to sing a street ditty with the refrain, 'Our good Regent is meek and mild; La la, he's mild as milk!' 'Bless my soul!' I cried, 'so you remember that incident. Well, now that you have had your revenge, try to make good use of it.' And I, too, began to laugh. He was still laughing when he sat down at the council table. I do not hesitate to record this absurd encounter, because it so well portrays him.

He truly loved freedom, and for others as much as for himself. He one day praised the English to me because they had no system of sending people into exile and no *lettres de cachet*,[1] and because their king can forbid no one anything except the entrée to his own palace, and can keep no one in prison without trial. He then recounted that King Charles II had many minor mistresses beside the Duchess of Portsmouth, and that the Grand Prieur [2] (in those days young and charming) sought refuge in England after being banished for some foolish prank, and was given a warm welcome by the English king. He showed his gratitude by seducing one of these lesser mistresses; but King Charles was so devoted to her that he cried for mercy, offered bribes, and finally promised so to mend matters that his rival might return to France. The Grand Prieur refused to deliver up the lady. Charles forbad him his palace; but he cared nothing for that and took his conquest to the play every night, sitting opposite to the king's box. At last King Charles, unable to get rid of him, so pestered King Louis for his recall that he was summoned to France. The Grand Prieur none the less remained, pretending that he was comfortable in England, openly enjoying his love affair. In the end King Charles was reduced to telling our King, in confidence, of the situation in which the Grand Prieur had placed him, which brought so peremptory a summons that M. de Vendôme returned forthwith. M. le Duc d'Orléans appeared to admire him for his conduct, and I am not at all sure that he would not have liked to be in his shoes. I said that for my part I was astounded that the great-grandson of a King of France should have lent himself to such an insolent manœuvre, and that

---

[1] Orders signed by the King and a secretary of State, by means of which a person could be imprisoned and kept indefinitely, without a trial, and on no specific charge.
[2] Philippe de Vendôme and his brother were the grandsons of a bastard-son of Henri IV; thus, though connected with the royal family, they had no right to the succession.

speaking as a subject who, like the Grand Prieur, had no claim to the throne,[1] I thought that he had behaved scandalously and richly deserved punishment. M. le Duc d'Orléans, however, would not have it so, and continued to tell the story with enormous gusto.

He had no real desire to reign or rule, and although he had acted very foolishly in Spain,[2] it was solely because others put the idea into his head. In very truth, he had never seriously considered governing this country until forced to choose between exercising his birthright or being dishonoured, and as for reigning, I can honestly say that he had no ambitions that way. Had the need arisen, it would have troubled and embarrassed him. What did he desire? you may ask. To command armies while the war lasted, and for the remainder of the time to find diversions without putting any restraint upon himself or on others.

Soldiering was what he most enjoyed. He was by nature calm and courageous, able to foresee difficulties and to apply suitable remedies. He had great aptitude for campaigning, for making plans and carrying them out, for mustering his resources, taking full advantage of them, and making prompt use of good opportunities when they came his way. It is not too much to say that he was a most able commander, engineer, and commissary-general. He knew the effective strength of the troops under his command, the names and capabilities of his officers, and the particular merits of the various regiments. The troops adored him; he kept them under strict discipline, and inspired them to achieve almost impossible tasks, even when they lacked everything. Both his military and his administrative plans were remarkably wise and practical; it was really amazing to see how well he grasped the details of several courses of action, never confusing the issue, but weighing the relative advantages and drawbacks, and explaining them most lucidly to others. In short, he had good and varied capabilities and knowledge; but he never paraded them, for truly he had no very great opinion of his own qualities.

What a man he was! So superior in every way, so well-informed! So capable of bringing happiness to France when he came to power! Moreover, he had one other excellent qualification for governing; he was more than thirty-six years old when the two Dauphins died, and nearly thirty-eight at the death of the Duc de Berry. During all that time he had lived like a private individual, an ordinary subject, with no prospect of ever taking the helm. Like other courtiers he was buffeted by every storm and tempest, and had learned to know all the leading personalities, and many others also. Thus he had the advantage of having led a private life, and had gained a knowledge of the world which he would not otherwise have acquired.

---

[1] Because he was descended from a bastard.
[2] In 1708 the Duc d'Orléans was accused of trying to dethrone Philip V, in order to succeed him.

All that was the good side, and very good it was, and no doubt very precious. Unfortunately he had another side, which must also be described, at the risk of repeating some things that have already been said.

This prince, so well endowed by nature to do honour to a good education, was not fortunate in his masters. His first tutor, Saint-Laurent,[1] was of no account and even in Monsieur's household had held no higher post than that of assistant to the head of protocol. He was none the less the man best fitted in all Europe to educate a king. He, however, died before his pupil was out of the schoolroom, and by the worst mischance died so suddenly that there was no time to consider the underling left in charge, or the probability of his inheriting the post. You have already encountered the Abbé Dubois, who began life as valet to Saint-Laurent's friend the Curé of Saint-Eustache. That cleric, finding him intelligent, set him to study, with the result that the valet became marvellously well versed in literature, and even in history. His master was pleased with his progress, but being unable to advance him, offered him to Saint-Laurent, in the hope that he might do better for him. Saint-Laurent accepted Dubois, and made increasing use of him in writing out lessons for M. de Chartres.[2] Then, wishing to advance him still higher, he made him wear clerical bands[3] to raise his status, and quietly inserted him into the prince's schoolroom, to help in preparing the lessons, writing compositions, generally assisting, and looking up words in the dictionary. In those early days, I saw him often when I went to play with M. de Chartres. As time went on and Saint-Laurent's health declined, Dubois took over much of the teaching, and did it very well, yet succeeded in making it palatable to the young prince. He managed at the same time to insinuate himself into the affections and confidence of a boy who knew no one else, and took most abominable advantage of that affection to promote his own interests and keep his bread well buttered. Dubois soon realized that the post of tutor would not always advantage him, especially not when he saw that his labours in extracting M. de Chartres's unwilling consent to marriage did not bring the expected rewards; and when he disgraced himself with the King by asking for, and obtaining, a secret audience, to demand a nomination to the cardinalate, as the price of his efforts. He then discovered that he was entirely dependent on M. de Chartres's favour, and turned his whole mind to ruling him. He has since become so great a personage that you will need to know him. We shall return to him anon.

Monsieur, who was inordinately proud of his rank, was made still more so by his governor's having been created a duke and peer while still in his

[1] Nicolas Parisot de Saint-Laurent, who died in 1687.

[2] The Duc de Chartres was the courtesy title borne by Philippe II, Duc d'Orléans, before he succeeded his father. His marriage to Mlle de Blois, an illegitimate daughter of the King by Mme de Montespan, took place in 1692. See Vol. I, pp. 12 et seq.

[3] *Le petit collet*: a clerical collar worn by priests in orders or by those studying for the priesthood.

service,[1] and he accordingly resolved that his son also should have noblemen to educate him. Volunteers were not easy to find; but some were not unwilling, and nothing else concerning them at all signified to Monsieur. The first to accept was M. de Navailles.[2] He was a brevet-duke[3] and a Marshal of France, virtuous, respectable, in every way worthy, but scarcely the man to train a prince. He seldom appeared, and died in February 1684, aged sixty-five. He was succeeded by the Maréchal d'Estrades, who might have suited very well, had he not been so extremely old. He died, aged seventy-nine, in February 1686. M. de La Vieuville, a brevet-duke, then took the post, but died in 1689, a month after being made a Knight of the Order. He was wholly unfit to be a governor; but all the same his death was a loss to Monsieur, since no other nobleman was willing to replace him. Saint-Laurent, however, had his entire confidence and all the real authority; the other posts were merely honorary.

The last of M. de Chartres's governors was the Marquis d'Arcy,[4] who had served with distinction in various embassies, and also in the army. He was a man of quality, very conscious of that fact, and a Knight of the Order since 1688. You already know how he conducted himself with M. le Duc de Chartres, especially in battle. His death, at Maubeuge, in June 1694, was the greatest possible misfortune for his pupil, over whom he possessed full control, and, even better, whose full confidence he enjoyed. His manners and character had charmed the young prince and inspired him with a respect which, in such circumstances, often includes obedience. After the death of this wise guide, whom he never ceased to regret, as he continually made plain to members of his family, M. de Chartres fell completely under Dubois's influence, and that of the young rakes who paid their court to him.

The domestic scandals in Monsieur's court, and in what those thoughtless greenhorns took to be high Society, soon obliterated all the good which Saint-Laurent and the Marquis d'Arcy had achieved. M. de Chartres allowed himself to be led into debauchery and the worst of bad company because even the best of that low kind avoided him for fear of the King's anger. Forced into a marriage whose unworthiness he realized too late, he listened to the blandishments of certain nobodies, who wished to keep him in Paris. There he sowed his wild oats, feeling perfectly justified in so doing, in view of Monsieur's indignation at being unable to obtain for him the governorship or military command[5] which he had for so long been promised. He thereafter set no limits to his wild speeches or his debauchery, acting partly from self-indulgence, partly from boredom at

---

[1] He was the Maréchal du Plessis-Praslin.
[2] Philippe de Montault, Comte de Navailles (1619-1684).
[3] A dukedom à brevet was a personal, not a hereditary honour; it did not carry a peerage.
[4] See Vol. I, p. 28.
[5] See Vol. I, p. 155.

the Court (his relations with his wife being as they were), partly from jealousy at seeing M. le Duc and M. le Prince de Conti surrounded by all the most brilliant young men; but chiefly with the suicidal notion of freeing himself from the King by giving him offence, and thus revenging himself for his want of employment. He lived among actresses and suchlike, in most unseemly obscurity, and appeared at the Court as seldom as possible. Sad to relate, Monsieur, who bore the King a similar grudge, and Madame, who never forgave the King or her daughter-in-law for her son's misalliance, did not try to restrain him. Madame, although she strongly disapproved of his way of life, scarcely mentioned it to him, for she secretly delighted in his wife's unhappiness, and in the King's distress on her account.

Monsieur's sudden and untimely death ended that situation. You already know what occurred then; how the new M. le Duc d'Orléans lived for a time quietly enough; was assiduous at the Court, and on better terms with his wife; although they still felt for one another a secret aversion that lessened only when I had mended matters by parting him from Mme d'Argenton. Love and idleness made him cling to this mistress, who kept him away from the Court. In her company, he found others equally determined to keep him to themselves, and the leader of them all was the Abbé Dubois. This must suffice to show by what sorry methods his noble nature was warped. Let us now see the effects of this long, pernicious process, which you will comprehend only by a knowledge of that man who was entirely responsible.

The Abbé Dubois was a little lean man, slight, blond-wigged, weasel-faced, furtive, keen, the very spit of what illiterate Frenchmen term a blood-sucker[1]— but, indeed, there is no better word. All the vices fought for mastery in him, each continually striving and clamouring to be uppermost. Avarice, debauchery, ambition were his gods; treachery, flattery, subservience, his expedients. In perfect godlessness he was at peace, and in the confirmed opinion that honour and credit were mere shadows, to be donned for show, having no substance in anyone. Hence his principle that all means were good. He excelled in base intrigues; he lived by them, he could not do without them, always working with some aim in view, to which all his actions tended, and with a persistence that yielded only to success or the certainty of failure; unless by tunnelling in subterranean darkness he could find fresh hope by opening still another sap. He thus spent his entire life in underground workings. Barefaced lies became his second nature, though he preserved an honest, sincere, often a deprecatory air.[2] He could have been a ready and an eloquent speaker, had not the desire to probe into the minds of others, and the fear of conceding more than he wished, given him an affected stammer,

---

[1] '*Un sacre*', a hawk or bird of prey; used in slang to describe a voracious thief.
[2] Madame called him 'a treacherous cur', a man debauched, 'without loyalty or decency', 'the most thoroughgoing swindler and hypocrite in all Paris', 'without his equal in knavery'.

which became intolerable when he intruded himself into matters of importance, and often rendered him unintelligible. Without his evasions, and the hypocrisy that was discernible despite all his endeavours, his conversation might have been agreeable. He had some wit, a certain acquaintance with literature and history, much worldly wisdom, and a great desire to please and flatter; but all was marred by an odour of falsity which oozed from him and mingled with his jollity to make one turn against him.

Withal he was spiteful, both by nature and intentionally, treacherous and thankless, expert in concocting villainous plots, shameless when caught red-handed, avaricious in all things, demanding every reward. Only later, when he felt safe enough to cast away restraint, did it appear how self-seeking, how thoroughly dissolute, irresponsible, and commonplace he was, always prejudiced, blasphemous and wrong-headed. For truly he scarcely deigned to disguise the contempt he felt for his master and the State; for all men without exception, and for State affairs, sacrificing them gladly to serve his personal ambition, importance, and influence, his fears, or his revenge. Such was the mentor to whom Monsieur confided the education of his only son.[1]

So capable a master lost no time in dominating a pupil who was still very green, and in whom Saint-Laurent's excellent principles had had no time to take root, despite the affection and esteem which he all his life conserved for that good man. Here, I must sadly confess, for truth is everything, that M. le Duc d'Orléans was born with readiness to comply that continually marred his talents and was of the utmost service to his tutor. Dubois, whose rash request for a cardinalate had lost him all hope of the King's favour, now turned his entire mind to making his young master like unto himself. He so far favoured him in his lack of morals as to encourage him to live dissolutely, teaching him that such was the way to shine in the world, and that a show of contempt for duty and decorum was more likely to succeed with the King than steadier conduct. He flattered him so grossly regarding his intellectual powers that he persuaded him of his being too clever to be duped by religion which, so he averred, was a mere political contrivance, used in every age to frighten ordinary mortals, and to keep the rabble in subjection. He instilled into him his own favourite maxim that integrity in men and virtue in women are chimeras, wholly without substance save, perhaps, in a few simpletons who allow themselves to be laden with such burdens, even as they support religion, and are consequently perpetual underlings—and in a very few others who, despite their intelligence and capabilities, let themselves be bound by an outmoded education. Such was the doctrine of that unworthy prelate, by which the young

---

[1] They say that in the little room which Saint-Simon used as his privy, he had a portrait of Cardinal Dubois, framed and glazed, hanging opposite his chaise-percée.

prince received licence for treachery, lies, tricks, scepticism, infidelity of all kinds; in short for all crimes and knavery, provided that these could pass as being clever, able, in the grand manner, showing independence and strength of intellect, provided also that they could be concealed from the doubts and prejudices of ordinary folk.

Unhappily, M. le Duc d'Orléans's whole nature and circumstances inclined him to swallow this accursed poison. He was very young, full of health, vigour, the joys of freedom from the schoolroom, and the embarrassments of his marriage and his timidity. The ensuing boredom, a love-affair of the kind that so often proves fatal in early youth, blind admiration for people of fashion and the desire to emulate and surpass them, the allurements of passion, the young men whose pride and tool he had become, some of whom had persuaded him to live like them and with them, all served to accustom him to loose-living, and, worse still, to the scandal which it created, until the time came when he could no longer exist without it, and found relaxation only in the midst of noise, confusion, and excess.

That is what led him to commit such terrible, such shocking improprieties and, as though wishing to exceed the worst rakes, to mingle blasphemies with his ordinary conversation, and to engage deliberately in scandalous debauches on saints' days. Thus during the Regency, even, he several times indulged in amorous escapades by choice on Good Friday, and on other holy days too. The more persistently experienced, the more steeped in sin a man's reputation made him appear, the more M. le Duc d'Orléans respected him; I myself can bear witness to his blind admiration—his reverence almost—for the Grand Prieur, merely because he had not been to bed sober for the past forty years, and publicly and continuously kept mistresses, never ceasing to utter impious, nay, blasphemous remarks. It is scarcely to be wondered at that, having such principles, and acting in accordance with them, he was openly unfaithful, even boasting of it, and priding himself on being the most sophisticated, the cleverest of deceivers. He and Mme la Duchesse de Berry would sometimes argue to prove which of them took the palm in that line, and this kind of discussion would take place while she dressed, in the presence of Mme de Saint-Simon and those who entered before the general public, with M. le Duc de Berry, who was extremely proper, listening in horror and disgust, and Mme de Saint-Simon quite unable to quell them by turning their tone to jesting, or by indicating the door to show their lack of discretion. M. le Duc d'Orléans was incredibly indiscreet about himself in all that concerned his daily life. He was not unjustly given the name for being unable to keep a secret. The fact is that, having grown up amid all the malicious tittle-tattle of the Palais Royal and Monsieur's court, he had developed the odious habit of setting people at each other's throats, so as to have nothing to fear from their attachments, and to learn by allowing them to speak against one another. That was one of his chief occupations, all the time that he was at the head of the State. He profited by it at first; but it was soon discovered, and he then became unpopular, and suffered in many ways. Not being wicked in himself (indeed, far the reverse), he never overstepped that state of debauchery and impiety into which Dubois first initiated him, and which long practice, combined with the streams of confidences which he received regarding everyone (for, in very truth, none was sacred) confirmed in him. Yet he went no further in vice than his tutor had taught him.

More frequent attendance at the Court after Monsieur's death brought boredom, and led to those experiments in science which I mentioned earlier,[1] and which were so spitefully used against him. It is hard to conceive how utterly incapable he was of attracting a circle, how totally unfitted to hold court, even before the devilish plots of Mme de Maintenon and the Duc du Maine succeeded in isolating him completely. High society harassed and wearied him, despite his air of cheerful detachment;[2] yet in his private rooms, and later, when everyone shunned him and he was left alone, he found himself without resources, notwithstanding the many talents that should have provided him with endless entertainment. He was born bored, and by that time had become so accustomed to seek for outside amusements that he could not bear the thought of creating his own, and became incapable of making the attempt. He could not live away from the hurly-burly of administration, for instance in supplying the needs of armies at war, or from the excitement of amorous adventures. Once the bustle had ceased, he began to flag, and found it hard to pass the time. When his passion for chemistry was exhausted, or had been destroyed by the unkind things that were said of him, he turned to art. He painted during the greater part of every afternoon at Versailles, or at Marly, knew a great deal about pictures, loved them, and made for himself a collection as good as the King's own. Later he amused himself by making compositions of stones and seals, which he smoked,[3] thus often driving me from the room; and also compounds of strong perfumes: but in that I discouraged him, for the King detested such odours, and he nearly always smelled strongly of them. Never was there a man born with so many gifts, such facility and eagerness to use them, never one whose private life was so idle, so much given up to dullness and boredom.

Madame summed him up as pithily as did the King in his remark to Maréchal, which I related earlier. She, who loved fairy-tales, used to say that all the fairies

---

[1] See Vol. I, pp. 460, 462.

[2] Madame wrote: 'I wish my son took more pleasure in the company of men of quality, and less with actors, painters, and doctors. When he is with them he can converse; but when people visit him, he hangs his head, bites his nails, refuses to speak, and they go away much vexed.'

[3] *Les Aberrations* or *Les Bizarreries du 18me Siècle*:—a hobby of that time (like *petit-point* in England before the Second World War) was to detect a face, a flower, an animal in the graining of a piece of marble or onyx, improve the resemblance with a needle and paint, and fix the result with the smoke from burning charcoal.

were invited to his christening, and that each one gave him a different talent, until
he possessed them all. Alas! one ancient dame had lived so long in retirement that
she was forgotten. She arrived late, bent over her crutch and in a perfect fury;
but, when she heard what had happened, she grew angrier still, and nullified
all the gifts by decreeing that though possessing every talent, he should be
incapable of using any of them. Indeed! indeed! I must confess that that portrait
is a speaking likeness.

One of M. le Duc d'Orléans's chief misfortunes was to have so little perseverance that he scarcely understood the meaning of that word. Another weakness,
as I have already said, was a kind of toughness that rendered him insensitive to
the most mortal and dangerous slanders; thus since the origins and principle of
hatred and love, gratitude and vengeance are the same, and he lacked the instinct
to distinguish between them, the consequences were serious. He was by nature
excessively shy; he knew it, and was so much ashamed that he pretended to the
contrary, by boasting of his firmness. The truth, however, was that, as everyone
realized when he came into power, nothing could be extracted from him—neither
favours nor justice—without importuning him or playing on his fears. He would
try to escape with promises, with which he was most liberal; but only the strongest
could force him to keep his given word. At last, he broke so many pledges that his
word ceased to have any meaning, for he many times promised to several people
what he could grant only to one. Many were discontented and he ceased to be
respected. In the end, no one believed him, even when he spoke in good faith,
and his glibness in speech greatly discredited him. Finally, the low and knavish
company which he kept, and from among whom he chose those boon companions, whom, he openly referred to as his 'roués',[1] drove better men from his side,
and did him infinite harm, even after he came into power.

His readiness to suspect everyone was particularly displeasing, especially after
he became head of the State, and his monstrous way of including in his suspicions even those of his acquaintance who were not confirmed in debauchery.
That fault, which led him to make serious errors, sprang partly from diffidence,
which made him fear his proven enemies so much that he treated them with
more respect than he did his friends; and partly from his inclination to imagine
a likeness between himself and Henri IV (and not even with the better side of
that monarch), and thus to believe that integrity had no reality, and that everyone therefore was suspect. None the less, he was very certain of my sincerity, for
he often reproached me with it, as a fault caused by my education that, so he
thought, had made me narrow-minded. He believed the same of Mme de Saint-
Simon, for he was persuaded of her virtue. I had, moreover, given him too many

---

[1] He meant that they were scoundrels who deserved to be broken on the wheel (roué).

proofs of my attachment, especially in times of danger, for him to doubt me; yet this was precisely what he did in the second or third year of his Regency—and I shall relate the story because it is one of the most telling features of this portrait.

It was autumn, and M. le Duc d'Orléans had prorogued the councils for a fortnight. I had decided to spend that time at La Ferté; had been closeted with him for the past hour; had taken my leave, and had returned to my house, shutting my door in order to rest. Before an hour had passed they came to tell me that Biron[1] was at the door and refusing to go away, saying that M. le Duc d'Orléans had ordered him to give me a personal message. I must add, at this juncture, that my two sons[2] commanded cavalry regiments and, like all the other colonels, were with their troops. I bade Biron enter, with considerable surprise, seeing that I had only just quitted M. le Duc d'Orléans; and I asked him to tell me quickly what had occurred. Biron, looking highly embarrassed, asked me where the Marquis de Ruffec was at that moment. Still more astonished I asked why. Biron, growing scarlet in the face, said that M. le Duc d'Orléans was worried and wished to know my son's whereabouts. I said that he was at Besançon with his regiment, lodging with M. de Levis, the general commanding in Franche-Comté. 'I know that,' said Biron, 'but have you not had letters from him?' 'Why?' said I. 'Well, if you insist,' replied Biron, 'M. le Duc d'Orléans wishes to see his hand-writing.' He then explained that shortly after I left him, M. le Duc d'Orléans had gone to Mme la Duchesse d'Orléans's little garden, at Montmartre,[3] with his usual crowd of *roués* and w....,[4] that a courier had arrived with letters, and that he had talked with the man alone for some minutes. He had then called for Biron and, showing him a letter from the Marquis de Ruffec to his mother, dated from Madrid, had ordered him to find me at once. I was seized by a mixture of anger and pity, which I made no effort to disguise from Biron. As a matter of fact I had no letters from my son, because I always burned them immediately, along with other papers of no further importance. I charged Biron to convey at least some of my feelings to M. le Duc d'Orléans; to tell him that I had not the slightest acquaintance with anyone in Spain, nor at the place where my son was stationed, and to suggest his sending a courier forthwith to Besançon, so as to set his mind at rest. Biron shrugged his shoulders, saying that it was all very well; but if I did happen to have such a letter, he begged me to send it at once, whereupon he would have it given to them at table, even although their suppers were strictly private. I did not wish to make a scene at the Palais Royal, and I therefore let Biron return

[1] Charles Armand de Gontaut, Duc de Biron (1663-1756). Maréchal de France, 1734.

[2] Jacques Louis de Rouvroy, Vidame de Chartres, Marquis 1722, later Duc de Ruffec (1698-1746), who married the Princesse de Bournonville in 1727 and had one daughter. Also Armand Jean de Rouvroy, Marquis, later Duc de Ruffec (1699-1754), who died childless.

[3] The Duchesse d'Orléans's little garden was probably in the grounds of the abbey.

[4] In the manuscript, only the initial of the word appears.

with my message. Luckily, Mme de Saint-Simon, appearing soon after, had kept the Marquis de Ruffec's latest letter, and we sent it at once to Biron. They took it to him at supper, as had been promised, and M. le Duc d'Orléans fell upon it immediately. What amazed me was that he did not already know my son's writing. He not only examined the writing but, since he found the letter amusing, read it aloud to the assembled company. It became a topic of conversation, and from that moment the prince ceased to suspect him.

When I returned from La Ferté, M. le Duc d'Orléans came to me very penitent, and what I said to him made him still more so. Other letters then began to arrive from this bogus Marquis de Ruffec. Long afterwards he was arrested at Bayonne while dining with d'Adoncourt,[1] in command there, who suddenly became suspicious of him when he saw him eating olives with a fork. At the gaol he confessed, and his papers disclosed the exploits of a young adventurer who, in order to be received and obtain credit, had assumed the name of the Marquis de Ruffec. He put it about that he had quarrelled with me and written for pardon to Mme de Saint-Simon, begging her to pay his debts—all this in order that his letters might be seen and confirm his belonging to our family. He was indeed believed to be my son, and thus gained many benefits. He was a tall, well-built, young fellow, clever, attractive, and sufficiently impudent, the son of one of Madame's ushers. He thus had some acquaintance with the Court, and when he took it into his head to pose as my son, he made a study of our family, so as to say the right things, and not be caught out. He was gaoled for a time. Before this he had journeyed under other names but thought that being of the same age as my son, the title of Marquis de Ruffec might bring better results.

M. le Duc d'Orléans's lively mind, coupled with his wrong-headed notions of firmness and courage, had early made him determined to call up the devil and to speak with him. He did everything, even down to reading the most wanton and maniacal books, in order to convince himself of there being no God; and he believed in the devil to the point of wishing to see and argue with him. Such a contradiction seems impossible to believe; yet many people are so persuaded. He worked with all manner of obscure persons. They spent entire nights in the quarries of Vanves and Vaugirard[2] attempting to summon up the fiend. M. le Duc d'Orléans admitted that he had never had any success, and at last given up that particular folly. It was at first only to please Mme d'Argenton that he took to gazing into glasses of water to see the present and the future, but after he had seen some marvels which he described to me,[3] and he was no liar, his interest

---

[1] Dominique Stuart d'Adoncourt. He had been a major-general of the Spanish army in 1703 and, in 1710, was a major-general of the army in Roussillon, in the south of France.

[2] The stone quarries of Vanves and Vaugirard, over which those two villages were built, to the south-west of Paris. They are now in the XV *arrondissement*.

[3] See *Saint-Simon at Versailles*, pp. 118-120.

was kindled. Deception and lying, although very close, are not the same, and he never lied, unless pressed regarding a promise or a love-affair, when he did so unwillingly, to get himself out of a scrape.

Although we often spoke of religion—for, so long as I entertained any hope of reclaiming him, I took immense pains to discuss it with him, but from different angles so as not to fatigue him—I never discovered what convictions he held, if any. At last I decided that he had formed none, and was still uncertain. Like his debauched companions, he longed to persuade himself that God did not exist; but he was far too intelligent to be an atheist, which is a rarer type of madness than most people imagine. That glimmer of enlightenment worried him; he did his best to extinguish it, but never entirely succeeded. It would have comforted him to believe that he had no soul but, despite all his efforts, he could not quite convince himself of that; the idea of a living God and an immortal soul greatly disturbed him, yet he could not blind himself to the fact that both do exist. I could only discover what he was not, for I never found in him any positive feelings. Yet I did know his extreme discomfort regarding that vast mystery, and I believe that had he undergone some dangerous illness and been given time, he would have needed no urging to put himself into the hands of those same priests and friars whom he made such a parade of despising and ridiculing. His besetting sin was to pride himself on irreligion, and to try to out-mock the most brazen scoffers.

I remember one Christmas Eve, at Versailles, when he accompanied the King to matins and the three midnight masses,[1] and astonished the Court by appearing to be absorbed in a book that looked like a prayer-book. Mme la Duchesse d'Orléans's head tiring-woman,[2] who loved them both and, like all old retainers, was very free in her speech, was so much overcome that she congratulated him in public, before his wife and a very large company. M. le Duc d'Orléans let her run on for a while, and then said, 'You are a great ninny, Mme Imbert. If you must know what I was reading, it was Rabelais. I brought it with me for fear of being bored.' You may imagine the effect of that reply. It was true, but done out of pure bravado, for beyond all question of subjects and places the music in the chapel was far better even than at the opera, or for that matter anywhere else in Europe. Moreover, as matins, lauds and the three Christmas Eve masses lasted a very long time, the music had been even better than usual. In any event, nothing could have been more exquisite than the decorations in the chapel, and the way in which it was illuminated. Every corner was filled; even the bays between the tribunes were crowded with the ladies of the Court, not in full court dress, but none the less glamorous for that. The scene was therefore as beautiful as possible

[1] Matins is usually said after midnight; but on Christmas Eve it comes before the midnight mass.
[2] She was Henriette Prieur, the wife of Pierre Imbert, who was apothecary to the Orléans family.

and the music was transporting. M. le Duc d'Orléans was fond of music. He composed a little himself, and had even written a short opera for which La Fare supplied the words;[1] and it was performed before the King. Listening to the music in the chapel would have been quite enough to occupy his mind delightfully. His Rabelais was not necessary; but he had to make a show of being a mocker and free-thinker.

Mme la Duchesse d'Orléans was of quite a different type. She was tall and in every way stately, with an admirable complexion, bosom and arms, fine eyes, a mouth that was not ill-formed, and good, if rather long teeth. Her full, pendulous cheeks a little spoiled her beauty; but her most unbecoming feature was the arch of her eyebrows, for there her skin looked red, as if it were peeling, and the hairs were scanty. On the other hand, she had good eye-lashes and her hair grew prettily. Although not lame nor in any way deformed, one side of her was bigger than the other, which made her walk like a crab,[2] and that physical defect matched another that was a greater handicap in Society, and troubled even herself, as I shall now recount.

She possessed as much intelligence as M. le Duc d'Orléans, or even more, for she had a greater sense of continuity. Words came easily to her, with a gift for choosing the apt and unexpected remark that was always a delightful surprise. What is more, she used that enchanting turn of phrase that belonged only to Mme de Montespan and her sisters, or to those brought up in that family. Mme la Duchesse d'Orléans could say whatsoever she pleased with emphasis, tact, and charm. She could speak without uttering a word, and make her meaning plain to the precise degree that she chose. But her voice was so thick and hesitant, so difficult to unaccustomed ears, that this disability, although she did not regard it as such, took much of the charm from her conversation.

Reserve, propriety, good manners were born in her. She was the very essence of pride and nicety. You will scarcely believe me when I tell you, what is no more than the precise truth, that from the bottom of her heart she believed that she conferred a great honour on M. le Duc d'Orléans by marrying him, and sometimes dropped an almost imperceptible hint to that effect. She was too sensible not to see that such an attitude would be thought intolerable, but too proud to discard it altogether. She was relentless, even with her brothers, in sustaining the rank into which she had married, and even upon her *chaise-percée* remembered that she was a Daughter of France. M. le Duc d'Orléans would often laugh about it, and when they were alone called her Mme Lucifer, which she averred she did not mind. She was, moreover, very much alive to the benefits and favours that, after Monsieur's death, accrued to M. le Duc d'Orléans because of his marriage.

---

[1] He wrote several operettas, including *Penthée* and *Daphnis et Chloé*.
[2] It is possible that she had a curvature of the spine.

Her annoyance at his behaviour towards herself, although he was most punc-
tilious in company, came not so much from jealousy as from resentment that he
would not treat her as a goddess. On the other hand, she made no advances to
him, and did nothing to win his affection, nor did she ever refrain from doing
what she knew he disliked. She was never kind to him, never took those small
liberties that women who live happily with their husbands delight in. She received
such demonstrations of regard as came from him with coldness, and a kind of
patronizing superiority. That was one of the main reasons for their estrangement,
and even after their reconciliation politics counted more with her than all the
endeavours of M. le Duc d'Orléans.

As for her court, which was how one was required to speak of her household
and the company who frequented her, she preferred to be worshipped rather than
paid court to. Indeed, I think I may truthfully state that, in all her life, she found
only the Duchesse de Villeroy and myself who were not ready to toady to her, but
always did and said as we thought right. Yet at the same time, she was painfully
timid. The King had only to look at her with a little severity, and she was immediately discomfited. It is possible that Mme de Maintenon produced the same effect
on her, for she trembled at both, and even in public, in the most ordinary conversations, would mumble her answers and appear terrified. I say answers advisedly,
because it would have required more courage than she possessed to have spoken
first, especially to the King.

Her life, for the most part, was monstrously dull to one who enjoyed such
robust health—solitude and reading in the morning, dinner alone, needlework for
the remainder of the day, and company between five and six in the evening; but
even then she had no freedom or amusement, because she never learned to put
people at their ease. She thus had no friendly intercourse, save for infrequent visits
of courtesy from Mme la Duchesse du Maine. You already know how badly she
agreed with her sisters;[1] which is to say not at all. When I first knew her, her favourite
was her little brother, as she liked to call the Comte de Toulouse. He visited her
every day in company, and saw her fairly often alone in her boudoir. M. du Maine
very rarely saw her in those early days, and scarcely ever in company. They came
together after the marriage of M. le Duc de Berry, and after that prince's death he
was attentive to her, but only so as to use her influence over M. le Duc d'Orléans,
in which he was marvellously successful. As for me, I hardly ever visited her at her
receiving time; but nearly always tête-à-tête, with M. le Duc d'Orléans sometimes
making a third. Very occasionally, more especially before the King's death, M. le
Comte de Toulouse would join us, but never M. du Maine. Neither of them set
foot in M. le Duc d'Orléans's apartments, except on formal occasions. Neither

[1] At the time of M. le Duc de Berry's marriage.

of them liked him. The Duc du Maine had very little inclination to like anyone, except from motives of self-interest. He later adopted all Mme de Maintenon's likes and dislikes; and you will recollect how he endeavoured to steal away M. le Duc d'Orléans's birthright and seize the sovereign power for himself.[1] The Comte de Toulouse, who was something of a cold fish, led a life of a different kind. He strongly disapproved of M. le Duc d'Orléans's habits, sympathized with his sister's distresses, and held aloof from him because of the King's anger. In all the events that followed, I never found him otherwise than truthful, honourable and prudent, doing his duty by M. le Duc d'Orléans, but never becoming either friendly or affectionate.

When M. le Duc d'Orléans was abandoned by the Court and completely isolated, his wife was too proud and too lazy to make advances to anyone. She seemed perfectly content to wait for Society to pay homage to her without the least encouragement. Thus their lives became tedious, ignominious, unbefitting their rank, altogether despicable. That was one of the first obstacles to be overcome. Both were aware of that, and to do her justice, once her mind was made up, Mme la Duchesse d'Orléans set about the task with much more courage and perseverance than her husband. I expressly say courage, because her pride suffered many hurts during her long struggle to extricate herself from their unhappy situation. At first, the ladies she invited to dinner were fertile in inventing excuses. They feared to be seen in company with M. le Duc d'Orléans, and the cleverest waited for one of his excursions to Paris before they consented to dine with his wife. They then considered themselves absolved for several months to come. What they most feared was the King's displeasure, which meant that of Mme de Maintenon and, for those most in the know, the enmity of the Duc du Maine. For a long time it was considered fashionable to refuse at first, and later to be persuaded into going, pleading that continual invitations made it impossible always to escape. The men were a harder problem than the women, because on account of her rank as a Daughter of France she could invite only noblemen.

Once Mme la Duchesse d'Orléans was thoroughly convinced of the need to break down the most unseemly barrier that, on account of her husband, separated her from Society, she did not flinch. Realizing that people would not come to her unless they accepted him also, she assumed, in so far as she was able, an affable and gracious manner, so as to melt the ice, and make her apartments and table attractive. Such endeavours were odious to her and very hard, but by persistence she finally triumphed. People gradually grew bolder, following the example of the more courageous, and little by little the numbers of her guests increased, after the manner of a snowball.

---

[1] This refers to the circumstances of the King's testament.

The food and wine which she offered them were exquisite, and after a time the constraint was less obvious, although respect for rank and the proprieties was still very strictly observed. M. le Duc d'Orléans kept a guard upon his lips, and began to converse on general topics, such as the nation's affairs, in a way that embarrassed no one, not even himself. Card-parties were often arranged when the meal was over, and thus the company remained until the time came for the King's drawing-room. Soon, one began to hear people praising her dinner-parties, and expressing astonishment that they had ever been shunned. The fact that the King and Mme de Maintenon appeared unmoved seemed reassuring, and many felt ashamed of having feared their displeasure. None the less, frequenters of the King's circle did not soften towards M. le Duc d'Orléans himself. At her dinners, one dined in the apartment of the King's illegitimate daughter: her husband merely happened to be included among her guests. In the King's drawing-room, where most of the gentlemen in attendance had not been present at the dinners, he was still deserted; and even some of those who had just left his table avoided him absolutely. That state of affairs did not change until the King's last illness.

Boredom drove him often to Paris for wild supper-parties and debauches. We tried to divert him with other parties, given by Mme la Duchesse d'Orléans at Saint-Cloud, or Étoile, the most charming little house imaginable, which the King had given her in the park at Versailles, and which she had decorated to perfection, for she had excellent good taste. She loved entertaining, her guests all liked her, and at table she was a different person, easy-going, radiant, charming. M. le Duc d'Orléans wanted nothing but noise, and as he was always completely unrestrained at such parties, it was extremely hard to find suitable company, since both their ears and eyes were prone to be embarrassed by his loud pronounce-ments and by seeing him drunk from the very start of the meal, amongst people whose only thought was to entertain him and enjoy themselves decently, and who none of them would have been in the least degree tipsy on such an occasion. During that period, which lasted until the King's death, people's politeness to him and their embarrassment were equally evident, as I shall attempt to describe, after explaining, for your better knowledge, the family situation with Mme la Duchesse de Berry and Madame.

You will already have acquired some notion of the character of Mme la Duchesse de Berry; but you shall soon see her cutting so eccentric a figure, both on her own account and because of her relations with her father (then Regent), that I make no apology for repeating myself. She was tall, handsome, well-built,[1] yet somewhat graceless, and with a look in her eye that made one fear for her

[1] Madame, her grandmother, said that she was stout, thickset, disagreeable. She must have looked very different before her marriage, when she was grossly fat. She was almost certainly mad, and the loss of her babies may well have made her worse.

understanding. Like her parents, she had the gift of words, and could use them freely to convey what she wished with clarity, precision, and in language that came always as a surprise. Although nervous in certain trivial matters, she was terrifyingly bold in others, wildly proud, vulgar beyond the bounds of decency. One may almost say that, avarice excepted, she was the very image of all the vices, and the more dangerous because she had no equal for cunning and wit. I am not accustomed to exaggerate the portraits which I give for the sake of your enlightenment; and you will have noticed how restrained I always am when ladies are in question, and on all love-passages that are not essential to the understanding of more important affairs. I shall restrain myself here also, so far as maybe, for my own self-respect, not to mention my respect for the sex and rank of the object here referred to. The very considerable part I played in the marriage of Mme la Duchesse de Berry, and the post which Mme de Saint-Simon was so unwillingly forced to occupy, and continued to hold until the princess's death, would in themselves be quite enough to keep me silent, did silence not cast a shadow obscuring the truth about the history of that time. It is therefore only for the sake of truth that I swallow my pride, and at the same time truly confess that had I discerned or suspected one fraction of the entirety that was disclosed regarding that princess after her marriage, she should never have become the Duchesse de Berry.

You must recollect the supper-party at Saint-Cloud immediately after the wedding, and my delicate but none the less clear intimations of what had happened during the following Marly; her furious attack on the usher who inadvertently opened both doors to admit her mother; her despair at the death of Monseigneur and the cause; the wild and most alarming admissions which she made to Mme de Saint-Simon; her hatred of Mgr le Duc de Bourgogne and, more especially, of his wife, and her conduct towards them, notwithstanding that she owed everything to their kindness; her endeavours to make her unwilling husband quarrel with them; the reasons for the angry scolding (not by any means the last) which she received from the King and Mme de Maintenon, the advice which the persecution of Mme la Duchesse d'Orléans, and the most undeserved public outcry, caused me to give M. le Duc d'Orléans regarding his daughter; finally, my brief description of her behaviour towards M. le Duc de Berry, and his feeling for her at the time of his death.

She did everything in her power to turn that prince from religion, although he was a true believer and exceedingly straitlaced, persecuting him for keeping the fasts (which he hated but none the less strictly adhered to), teasing and mocking him until sometimes, for love of her, he broke them, and then covering him with ridicule. His sense of justice suffered equally from her furious outbursts and her unfair treatment of members of his household—in matters concerning her own, he never dared to interfere. Often she tried his patience beyond endurance, and more than once they were on the verge of an appalling scandal. When she ate a meal in public, and such occasions were frequent, she scarcely ever failed to drink herself into unconsciousness, rendering in all directions the wine she had swallowed; but if that were all, it was considered nothing. Neither M. le Duc de Berry's presence, nor that of her mother and father, nor of ladies with whom she was barely acquainted, at all deterred her. She even thought ill of M. le Duc de Berry for not doing likewise. Fear of the King kept her a little more restrained with her lady mother; but her manners were, if possible, worse on that account, so bad, indeed, that none of the three dared to cross her, far less offer the least criticism. If on very rare occasions, for some pressing reason, one of them felt compelled to speak the result was an explosion, after which both father and husband would come to offer submission and beg her pardon, for which they had to pay dearly.

Love-passages, usually difficult for one in her position, were not confined to one object, and were conducted with scant discretion. Latterly, however, she had settled upon La Haye,[1] who had risen from being one of the King's pages to the rank of personal equerry to M. le Duc de Berry. He was a tall, gaunt, dull sort of fellow, both stupid and conceited, but a good horseman, whom she had allowed to amass a considerable fortune (for one of his kind) in her husband's service. Their fond glances in the Marly drawing-room were apparent to all, but no one's presence deterred them. Finally (since this portrays her to the life), she resolved to have him abduct her from Versailles, with the King and her husband both very much alive, and to escape with him to the Low Countries. La Haye almost expired with terror on learning this plan, and she with rage when he expostulated. He was the victim of terrible scenes, when she attacked him with every insult her mind could devise, and her torrents of tears allowed her to utter. He suffered many such assaults of tenderness and fury mixed. At last, his fear of what she might do next and his dread of being taken for her accomplice obliged him to be prudent and to reveal the whole story. His secret was faithfully guarded, and the necessary measures taken; but La Haye dared not completely vanish, partly for appearances' sake, but chiefly on account of M. le Duc de Berry who, although not as mad as his wife, could be excessively passionate on occasions. Mme la Duchesse de Berry did, in the end, recover her senses sufficiently to realize that La Haye would not be wooed, and she ceased her pursuit of him. But her love for him persisted until the death of M. le Duc de Berry, and for some time after. Such was she who was the confidante of M. le Duc d'Orléans and the object of his adoration. He knew every detail of all that history, and had been in a state of

---

[1] Louis Berault de La Haye (1677-1754). Saint-Simon says elsewhere that he was 'as thin as a lath, with a cadaverous face that was far from handsome'. In October 1710, he was gratuitously appointed chamberlain to the Duc de Berry; but in the following December, M. de Berry gave him sixty thousand francs, with which to buy the post of master of his hounds.

absolute panic, not for fear of an abduction, but on account of the violent scenes and outbursts when she let herself go beyond control. Yet, both before and after these events, he made her the repository of all his secrets so long as she lived; and she gave him many another occasion for alarm, as you shall see in due course.

Her conduct, after reprimands and threats had proved useless, succeeded at last in turning the King and Mme de Maintenon against her. King Louis gave an appearance of icy formality in his relations with her; both he and Mme de Maintenon completely ignored her. He put up with her from necessity; she altogether ceased to see her, and Mme la Duchesse de Berry dreaded them both like the plague. When with them, she remained silent and shy in the extreme, and was only slightly less so with the King in public. All their complaints fell plumb on to the head of M. le Duc d'Orléans who, so they reckoned, had deceived them when he gave them his daughter, knowing her for what she was. They moreover despised and hated him for his weakness in adoring her, and for the spoiling affection that did nothing to change her.

Madame, on the other hand, was a princess of the old stamp, who attached importance to honour, virtue, rank, nobility, and was inexorable in the matter of propriety. She was not without understanding and what she saw, she saw very clearly indeed. A loyal and faithful friend, she was true and honest, easily shocked and prejudiced, and once lost very hard to recapture. In speech she was vulgar, and dangerously prone to rant; very German in her ways, frank, ignoring all contrivance and niceties both for herself and others. She was also sober, unsociable, and full of likes and dislikes.[1] She liked dogs and horses, doted on hunting and the play, was never seen out of court dress, unless she wore a man's wig and a riding habit, and for more than sixty years, well or ill, which last she seldom was, had never been known to wear informal attire. She passionately loved the prince her son, and, strangely enough, her native country and the relations whom she never saw. You will recall how at the time of Monsieur's death she spent her whole life in writing to them, and how close it brought her to ruin. In later days, she became reconciled, not to the birth of the princess her daughter-in-law, but to her nature, and was very kind to her before the rupture with Mme d'Argenton. She respected, pitied, in time came almost to love her, and deeply disapproved of the life which M. le Duc d'Orléans had been lead-ing. The conduct of Mme la Duchesse de Berry she considered outrageous, and on occasions let fly with extreme bitterness when speaking of her to Mme de Saint-Simon, whom she had liked and esteemed from the first moment of her appearance at the Court. She thus had little sympathy for the princess, and felt real hatred for M. du Maine and the aggrandisement of the bastards. It much

---

[1] Saint-Simon would naturally have tended to approve of Madame, with her plain-speaking and love of the proprieties.

displeased her that the prince her son should be less violently opposed to them.[1]

Notwithstanding such excellent qualities she had her faults, among which was a pettiness touching the respect that was owed to her; wherein she was ever on the look-out for a slight. I remember one winter during the Regency, when she had established herself in her little apartment at the Palais Royal, which she seldom visited, for she hated Paris and lived always at Saint-Cloud, that M. le Duc d'Orléans asked me to do him a particular favour, namely to call on her. It appeared that she said she never saw me and that I despised her. You may imagine how I answered for you may well believe that there was no foundation for that last accusation; indeed, contempt was something which no one could feel for Madame. As for my not calling on her, that was partly true. I paid my respects to her at Versailles on formal occasions; but at other times, when there was no real need to visit her, I had quite other occupations to fill my leisure hours. After that incident, however, when she was in Paris I attended at her *toilette* every fortnight or so, and she always gave me a very warm welcome.

M. le Duc d'Orléans was the best of fathers, the best of sons, and, after his rupture with Mme d'Argenton, the best of husbands. He dearly loved Madame, his mother, paid her constant attentions, and very frequently visited her. He also feared her; but having no real appreciation of her quality he told her little, and only half trusted her. Although secrets were safe in her keeping, nothing but dire necessity ever prompted him to tell her his; he kept her informed in family matters, such as the marriages of his children; but when he came to power said as little as possible regarding public affairs. Thus she had little influence on his private or his public life, and rarely asked questions, although he never refused her a favour. All of this makes it unnecessary for me to mention those few who had power to sway her. Suffice it to add that she was one with the King and Mme la Duchesse d'Orléans in their horror of the conduct of Mme la Duchesse de Berry, with whom she sometimes had terrible scenes; that the King trusted her implicitly, and for a time put Mme la Duchesse de Berry in her charge; but she soon tired of that odious responsibility, and gave it up as King Louis himself had done; for she regarded with similar disfavour the relationship of M. le Duc d'Orléans with his daughter, which made it impossible to influence her behaviour.

Before continuing to speak of events in the outside world, I must mention my own situation. I had long been meditating on the future, for I realized that I needed to reflect very seriously on a period that would be equally important and critical for me. The more I considered what I should do, the more I grieved for the loss of that prince who was born to deliver France and all Europe. Alas that we had proved unworthy of enjoying so much happiness. In him we had been

[1] Neither could Saint-Simon ever forgive the Duc d'Orléans for carrying the virtue of forgiving his enemies to the point where it was almost a vice.

shown the picture of good and prudent government; but we had also learned that God would neither lift his hand nor allow our country to prosper and be happy, until we deserved a King after His own image. The prince who would inherit the regency was far from being that; but, in any event, a regent, no matter how perfect, can never be the equal of a king. That I realized to the full, and I found it very hard not to despair.

I had now to deal with a prince of remarkable intelligence and good education, who had all the advantages of having lived his own life far from the throne or expectations of a regency. He was very conscious of his great faults, some of which had been brought home to him, causing him bitter unhappiness. None the less his idleness, weakness of character, and his liking for bad company, made it hard, if not impossible to change, or even to improve him. We had often discussed the defects in the government of France, and the consequent disasters. Every event, even minor ones at the Court, gave us food for conversation. He and I were of the same mind as to causes and effects. Thus we had only to apply our ideas fairly and consistently in order to rid the administration of its failings and arrange for a new system, in so far as a regent's power would permit, with the further aim of confirming the young King in good and rational principles, so that he continue in them when he came of age. That was my sole object, and my mind had been wholly set on instilling into M. le Duc d'Orléans all that he was capable of assimilating. As King Louis's age increased and his strength diminished, I began to enter into more detail; and this is what I must now explain....

[*At this point, Saint-Simon devotes more than twenty pages to describing all over again the decline in the power of the nobility during the past five reigns, and his belief that the French disasters were attributable to the fact of the hereditary peers having been deprived of their share in the government. He realized that, after so long a lapse, the peers might at first be incapable of legislating. His plan was therefore to substitute for Louis XIV's professional administrators a number of Councils, whose members would be drawn mainly from the nobility. On these Councils the peers would serve their apprenticeship, and, after a suitable interval, replace the gens-de-robe in all the high offices of State, except those whose functions were purely juridical. Saint-Simon states that his plan was wholly approved by the saintly Duc de Bourgogne, and that M. le Duc d'Orléans showed much interest in it; 'for many and many a time we had argued and discussed it between us.' He then goes on to suggest names for the heads of the various Councils, and to comment on them in great detail. The Memoirs continue:*—]

The names were soon agreed upon, but before making the decisions final M. le Duc d'Orléans turned to me and said, 'And you? You have mentioned all these people but never spoken of yourself. What place do you want?' I replied that it was not for me to appoint myself, still less to pick and choose. He must say whether he thought me capable and wished to give me employment, and then indicate where he wished me to serve. We were in his room, at Marly. Never shall I forget that moment. After a few interchanges of what might have been termed compliments between men of equal rank, he proposed to make me president of the finance Council; in other words, to control the finances, with the aid of the Maréchal de Villeroy or some other such imbecile. He added that he believed the post would best suit both himself and me.[1] I thanked him for the honour and for his confidence in my ability; but I refused with all due respect—president of the finance Council having been the office for which I had previously designated the Duc de Noailles. M. le Duc d'Orléans appeared amazed and did his utmost to persuade me to reconsider. I said, however, that I had no aptitude for the finances; that their administration had become a science, with a technical language that quite escaped me; that I knew nothing of commerce, currencies, exchanges, or circulation, beyond their bare names; that I was ignorant even of the primary rules of arithmetic, and for that very reason had never managed my own fortune or my household expenses. How much less fit was I to control the finances of an entire kingdom, especially in their present state of embarrassment.[2] M. le Duc d'Orléans reminded me of the advice and assistance which I might expect to receive from other members of the Council, and from experts outside. He said everything best calculated to flatter and encourage me, stressing particularly my integrity and altruism—qualities vital in those who have the care of public funds. To this I replied that whether I personally robbed the finances or allowed them to be robbed by others, the result would be the same; that although I could swear to my own honesty, I must also confess that I had not the experience necessary to detect the most glaring frauds, let alone the petty pilfering that so often occurs. After an hour of argument, he was left at first angry with me, then determined to make me reconsider, and forming plans for a further discussion next day.

My mind had long been made up. I had not spent so much time since the demise of our noble Dauphin, and so much more since M. le Duc de Berry's death, in arranging the various Councils and all the posts in a future government, without considering where I myself might most usefully serve. The finance

[1] The Duc d'Orléans was probably thinking of the documents which Saint-Simon had prepared on the tax-system for the Duc de Bourgogne and the Duc de Beauvilliers, his strong views on Vauban and his idea of a single tax. Certainly the control of finances was the most important department in the government, because it included agriculture, commerce, industry, and communications, as well as the financial administration of the entire country. It is noteworthy that the Duc d'Orléans believed his friend to be so capable.

[2] Saint-Simon dreaded taking responsibility. He saw himself as an adviser to the throne. When he was later appointed to the Council of Regency, which was at first thought to be the most important of all, he showed himself to be passionate about details, but very unsure of himself when decisions had to be made. As he himself says he had no aptitude for administration; but, as Winston Churchill said, diarists seldom make statesmen. Saint-Simon, the greatest memoirist in history, proved a complete failure when the time came for him to act.

Council had suggested itself amongst others, for I shall not be so vulgar as to
pretend that I did not expect M. le Duc d'Orléans to offer me some place in the
government, and thus I had not thought him tyrannical for trying to over-rule
me. The finances indeed repelled me for the reasons which I gave to M. le Duc
d'Orléans, but there were other objections less concerned with the actual work.
What frightened me was the unavoidable injustice. I could not bring myself to
become the hammer of the peasants and the people, to listen to the miseries of
the impoverished, and the false, but often plausible complaints of rascals, trick-
sters, and profiteers. What, however, had finally decided me against them was
the appalling situation to which wars and other monstrous expenses had reduced
our nation. I could see only two alternatives; to pay the huge debt by raising
taxation to the highest possible limit, thereby oppressing the entire population,
or to declare national bankruptcy, thereby relieving the future King of all debts,
including those of his predecessor, but also most unjustly ruining a vast number
of families, either directly or indirectly. My horror of both these evil courses
prevented my sponsoring either. As for the middle way, the cataloguing of the
various debts, so as to ensure the payment of genuine claims and the cancellation
of fraudulent ones, this would mean the examination of witnesses and evidence,
and the scope of such an inquiry appeared to me to resemble a fathomless sea,
in which my soundings would find no bottom. In any event, what opportunities
would it not give for deception and knavery! Dare I admit to a still more personal
reason for refusing? Had I found myself in charge of the finances, I should have
discovered in myself a strong bias in favour of total bankruptcy, and that was a
responsibility which I was unwilling to bear in the eyes of God and man.

Of the two fearful injustices, bankruptcy appeared to me to be the less cruel,
since at the cost of ruining certain creditors, most of whom had lent voluntarily
in the hope of gain, and many of whom had already profited, the general public
might be saved and the King also. It would mean an immediate and large reduction in taxation that would be a blessing to those townsmen and countryfolk, who
form beyond comparison the great majority of the nation, and are the very life's
blood of France. All these reasons, which I might have stated openly, had a strong
influence on me; but there was still another which I scarcely dare to mention,
even here, in these memoirs.

In the prevailing circumstances there is no possibility of curbing the expenses
of the government. However much the discovery of treasure in America may have
increased the stocks of gold and silver in Europe as more and more is transported
from overseas, it offers no comparison with the colossal increase in the revenues
of our recent kings, nor were theirs one half so great as those which Louis XIV
received. Yet, despite this almost incredible expansion, I was constantly reminded

of our deplorable situation at the close of a long, rich, and glorious reign—a reign laid most manifestly bare by the need for Torcy's journey to The Hague and the events that followed, and again afterwards, at Gertruydemberg, when by the sudden intervention of Heaven, France was saved only because of domestic quarrels in England. All this may be found among my documents, together with the original dispatches and the explanations which Torcy himself gave me.

The inevitable conclusion is that no amount of wealth can compensate for inefficiency in government, and that the well-being of a nation depends entirely on the wisdom of its administrators, as also does its prosperity and happiness, its lasting fame, and its influence over other peoples. It was Louvois, in his eagerness to rule single-handed and destroy Colbert, who first inspired the King with the desire for conquests. He raised vast armies; he invaded the Low Countries as far as Amsterdam, and by so doing frightened Europe into forming the League against France. Hence the wars that have continued since then almost without interruption. Hence the impoverishment of a State (albeit very great and most abundantly furnished) through having stood so long alone against the whole of Europe. Hence the desperate situation in which the King found himself at last, when he could neither wage war, nor obtain peace, except on the most humiliating terms. How much larger were the sums spent on the vast buildings of his reign, those useless fortresses and pleasure houses:[1] what immense amounts wasted in mere frivolity! All these various spendings brought us back to the same point of financial crisis, which was not hard once that point had been reached. Thus not only are our kings with their mistresses, favourites, and expensive tastes responsible for such calamities, but their ministers also, as it was with Louvois, at the beginning. Everyone will agree, I feel sure, that nothing more urgently required remedying; nor that the safeguard had long ago been discarded.

What then might still be done to secure our kings and our kingdom from experiencing another similar catastrophe? The incomparable Dauphin saw clearly what to do and had determined to act; but for such action a king not a regent is required; a man, moreover, still mightier than a king—a sovereign capable of ruling himself, who by divine guidance is greater even than his throne. But who could hope for such a monarch, having seen the very pattern, God-given, snatched from us on the eve of his accession? Thus it was that after deep reflection I had convinced myself that the best service a man could render to the State (for which Kings are made, and not the State for Kings, as the Dauphin fully realized and publicly acknowledged) was to save it from the abyss that had opened beneath the feet of King Louis. The only means of doing this was to preserve the sovereign from the ambitions of a second Louvois, and at the same time from his own selfish

[1] Yet, after three centuries, Versailles remains one of the world's finest monuments.

desires and indulgences; to protect him also from becoming drunk with his own power and splendour, through weakness of will and lack of intellect which, in its fullest capacity, is not always given to crowned heads.

On the following day, M. le Duc d'Orléans thus found me just as unwilling to accept the finances. There were the same blandishments, the same pleading, the same arguments from him; from me, the same answers and the same firm refusal. His anger then changed to such marked displeasure that I took to seeing him less often, and for shorter periods, which he appeared not to notice, for we conversed only on general matters of no particular interest; in other words, on the weather and the crops. This bout of sulking, icy on his side, obstinately calm on mine, endured for more than three weeks. He was the first to tire of it. In the middle of a vastly dull discussion, during which I had thought him more frigid than ever, he suddenly exclaimed: 'Oh! well; so it's settled. I suppose you are still determined to refuse the finances?' I lowered my eyes respectfully, murmuring that I thought it no longer a matter for debate. He could not suppress a little more grumbling; but not angrily, nor condemning me. He then began to pace up and down the room, silent, head bent, as was his way when embarrassed, and abruptly turning to face me, cried, 'But whom then shall we appoint?' I left him in doubt for a while, and then said that there was someone close at hand far more suitable than myself and, in my opinion, unlikely to refuse. He thought hard, but could by no means guess, and I finally named the Duc de Noailles.

Thereupon he flew into a rage, declaring that this would simply mean filling the pockets of the Maréchale de Noailles, the Duchesse de Gramont[1] (who openly boasted that she lived by speculating), and all the rest of that greedy and prolific family. I allowed him to run on for a time, and then remarked that the Duc de Noailles had amply sufficient intelligence, and so much already in the way of wealth, land, offices, governorships, and alliances, that he would be relatively safe from temptation. If His Royal Highness thought a nobleman desirable, none better could be found. As for his relations, his children were too young to count, and his wife, notwithstanding her aunt,[2] who had been the first to snub her, was regarded as a nonentity by his entire family. As for the Maréchale de Noailles and the Duchesse de Gramont, there was no reason to suppose that either of them influenced him in the slightest. There was always some objection to be found in a candidate; but this seemed insufficient to bar M. de Noailles who, being what he was, would desire only to make a reputation, without regard for his family, on whom he had hitherto lavished remarkably little affection. All these arguments for and against were rehearsed many times in subsequent conversations; but at

---

[1] The Maréchale de Noailles and the Duchesse de Guiche, later de Gramont, were the mother and the sister of the Duc de Noailles.

[2] His wife Françoise Charlotte, Demoiselle d'Aubigné, was Mme de Maintenon's niece and had been brought up by her. See Vol. I, p. 95.

last M. le Duc d'Orléans made up his mind to offer him the presidency of the finance Council. I honestly believed that he would do well in that office, and I was glad also to be able to assist Cardinal de Noailles by promoting his nephew, who was eminently capable of becoming of great importance and establishing a reputation.

When all had been settled between us, M. le Duc d'Orléans turned to me saying, 'And yourself? Tell me your whole mind; just what do you wish to be?', and he pressed me so hard for an answer, that I finally declared myself in the spirit of what I have explained above. I then said that if he cared to place me on the Council for the interior, which would replace the Conseil des Dépêches, I felt that I might be of more service there than elsewhere. 'President, then,' said he swiftly. 'No, not president,' I answered, 'just an ordinary member.' We continued to argue that matter for some considerable time, until I had explained that the duties of a president, and the task of reporting to the Council of Regency filled me with alarm and, what is more, that there would be nothing left for Harcourt were I to take that office. 'A mere membership of the Council for the interior is absurd for you; indeed, quite out of the question,' said M. le Duc d'Orléans. 'If you absolutely refuse to be president, there is only one place left for you, and that will greatly please me. You shall sit on the supreme Council, the Council of Regency.' I did accept that, and I thanked him. From that moment onwards the matter was settled, and he at the same time decided to make Harcourt president of the Council for the interior. There was no question of a supreme president being placed over him, because the business of that Council did not require one. Only in the marine and finance Councils were there to be assistant-presidents, so as to offset the dangerously great power of a single president and, in the finance Council, to compensate for the stupidity of the Maréchal de Villeroy.

Having thus settled the matter of the Councils, their presidents and assistant-presidents, I suggested to M. le Duc d'Orléans that he might profitably use the remainder of King Louis's reign in considering his nominees for membership of the councils. I urged him to select the smallest possible number to do the work of each Council, and to add others later from a list known only to himself, when deaths rendered replacements necessary. Thus, when the King died there would be no more to do than announce the names. At that moment, I said, he would be so inundated by orders, ceremonies, disputes, claims, rulings, decisions, and hosts of petitioners, that he would have time for nothing, scarcely even for thought. If his nominations were not already written down and placed under lock and key, he would have no leisure to ponder them, but would appoint regardless of merit, experience, or even his own best interests, running a grave risk later of having cause to repent, if nothing worse.

This is what I constantly urged on him during the rest of the King's reign. This is what he continually promised me to do, sometimes assuring me that he had already begun; this is what, from sheer idleness, he never did do. I did not ask him the names, for fear of losing his confidence; I simply laid down the broad outlines, and established the presidents and assistant-presidents, as being the most important. He had already consulted me as to the forms of the future govern-ment, and had encouraged me to make suggestions. I then prudently waited until he pressed me to say more, which, as you shall see, he did. All of this took place long before there was any question of the King's testament.[1]

Soon afterwards he discussed with me the Council of Regency, for which the nominations were proving exceedingly hard. In order to clear the field and limit the scope of our choice, we first reviewed the members of the existing Council of State. Of all the ministers, I proposed retaining only the Maréchal de Villeroy, not because I liked the man, or in any way respected him, but in consideration of his rank, offices, and family connections. The Chancellor[2] himself was in every way worthless, a commonplace, self-seeking official, without a friend (save for those who desired favours or places), hated at the Court, and loathed in the army, because of his arrogant heartlessness. He had gained his reputation solely by toadying to Mme de Maintenon and the Duc du Maine, by serving Cardinal de Bissy, Rome, and the red-hot constitutionalists, and by acting in opposition to M. le Duc d'Orléans. I therefore proposed that his office of Secretary of State should be abolished, and that he be retired to some such town as Moulins or Bourges. The seals might then be transferred to Daguesseau,[3] a magistrate of the old school, universally liked and respected, one who served honour, justice, and the true religion, with an untarnished reputation, and vast skill and experience in his profession. M. le Duc d'Orléans fully agreed that he could not do better than rid himself of an enemy, whose dismissal would please everyone with the exception of the Duc du Maine, and at the same time benefit himself by an appointment sure to win general approval.

Torcy was another minister whom I wished to have dismissed. He was the Maréchal de Villeroy's closest friend, not attached to the Duc du Maine or to Mme de Maintenon, but possessing friends who opposed M. le Duc d'Orléans, which had made me think that he also was against him. I had not forgotten his words to the King regarding the renunciations, which I recounted earlier. He was a man with whom I had had no dealings, nor the slightest personal acquaintance;

[1] See p. 352. The situation was completely changed when, by the King's will, the two bastards were appointed to assist the Duc d'Orléans on the Council of Regency, possibly because he was suspected of plotting to secure the throne for himself and his immediate family.

[2] Voysin had become Chancellor of France in 1714.

[3] Henri Daguesseau (1636-1716), a member of the finance Council at the beginning of the Regency. Saint-Simon forgot; it was not he, but his son Henri François Daguesseau, who succeeded Voysin as Chancellor in 1717.

but the Dukes of Chevreuse and Beauvilliers had always disliked him, believing him to be a Jansenist. Thus all that I really knew of him was that he had once tried to ruin me, and that his manners were stiff and formal, which I mistook for pride, but which was, in fact, shyness and reserve. I therefore desired to exclude him also by abolishing the office of Secretary of State, and I many times attacked him when speaking to M. le Duc d'Orléans, with much inward displeasure because I made slow progress. There, I must admit, is clear proof of the fact that ignorance and impulsiveness make blind guides. It is not yet time to tell how glad I became of my failure to remove Torcy.

As for Desmaretz; I had long vowed to destroy him, and for some considerable time had been working to that end. It was repayment for his ingratitude, and for the gross discourtesy which I mentioned earlier. His retention was incompatible with the kind of finance Council for which I had planned, and which had already been accepted. It was, moreover, a public benefaction to rid Society of a man so ill-tempered and possessing so avaricious a wife. In procuring his removal I was entirely successful, for M. le Duc d'Orléans did not even question it.

From all that you have learned of Pontchartrain, you will not find it hard to guess that I had long since been endeavouring with all my might to ruin him. His conduct and character gave me ample excuse to wreak vengeance on a most hateful and despicable man who, throughout the whole of France, and in every other country with which he had had official dealings, was regarded as such. You know how and for what reasons he had deliberately weakened the navy;[1] you have yet to learn how he plundered it. He was far too base not to have won the favour of Mme de Maintenon, M. du Maine, and the World of Fashion by siding against M. le Duc d'Orléans. To destroy him was therefore an act of public justice, and a vastly agreeable one into the bargain. He was quite friendless, possessing not one redeeming feature to set off so many that were repulsive. His destruction was long since arranged, and I secretly gloated at having had my part in it.

Another matter on which I had for a considerable time been meditating was the summoning of the States General.[2] I carefully weighed the pros and cons of so vital a decision, ransacking my memory for the other occasions on which meetings had been called, and the losses and benefits resulting from them. At last I had become convinced that one should be summoned, as I thought of the changes that had occurred. There were no longer parties in the State, for that of the Duc du Maine had dwindled to an odious cabal, supported only by the vulgar, the

[1] See Vol. I, p. 261. Saint-Simon thought that Pontchartrain deliberately kept the fleet ill-supplied in order to prevent the Comte de Toulouse from winning victories.

[2] The national assembly consisting of representatives of the three estates (the Church, the nobility, and the third, which comprised all who were neither prelates nor nobles). They met, in assembly; and then separately drew up their lists of grievances (their *cahiers*) in full assembly. The last meeting of the States General had been in 1614.

seekers after present favour, the cunning intriguers. Its mean and cowardly leader, and the insensate ravings of a wife whose sole respectable quality was her birth,[1] inspired fear only through ignorance, its usual prompter. The ancient factions of Orléans and Bourgogne no longer existed. No member of the House of Lorraine possessed the talents, force of character, reputation, or, indeed, the power to stir up memories of the *Ligue*. No Huguenots remained; no outstanding personality in any walk of life. Such had been the result of long rule by low-born professionals, clever enough to govern in their own interests by pandering to the foibles of the King, and deliberately crushing and preventing other men from developing their capabilities, by obliterating all competition, all talents, all the rewards of education, and carefully removing any man from office who displayed the faintest trace of application and decent feeling. This was the sad situation that continually obstructed M. le Duc d'Orléans and myself, as we sought to find persons suitable to sit on the Council of Regency; but it was also a defence against the dangers inherent in an assembly of the States General. That is why, after long and frequent deliberations, I finally decided to speak to M. le Duc d'Orléans.

I began by imploring him not to take fright until he had heard my arguments; then, after giving him the above explanation, I proceeded to catalogue the advantages. I emphasized that the only possible danger was to those who administered the affairs of State, and possibly to those who had appointed them; that His Royal Highness ran no kind of risk, since he was well known to have had no share in the government. That alone should persuade him that he might safely order the Secretaries of State, immediately after the King's death, to prepare to summon the States General, and to issue that summons at the earliest possible moment. Frenchmen, so fickle, so eager for change, so crushed by increasing taxation, would be overjoyed at the return of a privilege withheld for more than a century, and react with love and gratitude towards the prince whose first deed on gaining power had been to grant them this boon. What a beginning to his Regency!

Apart from the very real benefits which M. le Duc d'Orléans would clearly derive from the summoning of the States General, I believed that there might be little harm in attempting another advantage, perhaps not impossible to win during the first transports of delight. Although the nation had been reduced to a state near to serfdom, there still remained certain matters on which the mind of the public was clear, although fear prevented any discussion. One such was the legitimization of the bastards, their grandeur, above all their regality. Everyone, even at the Court, was secretly horrified by their very existence, their ennoblement, their admission to the succession. This last was generally recognized as being

[1] The Duchesse du Maine was a granddaughter of the Grand Condé.

a reversal of the laws of God and man, a sign of bondage, an attack on God himself, a most present danger to the State and all its subjects. Such, at that time, were the inmost feelings of all the princes of the blood and all the great nobles, even including those who owed most to the King's favour and that of Mme de Maintenon, and who seemed most closely attached to the Duc du Maine. All kinds and conditions of men were incensed by such unseemly aggrandizement, and the very rabble showed its anger when the bastards appeared in public. Thus I was fully persuaded that their case might be presented as highly dangerous and of immense urgency.

It appeared to me that we had all the ingredients for rousing the States General to action without M. le Duc d'Orléans even having to make a sign. We had the means to work upon the members sorrowfully, gently, plaintively, first gaining their interest, then stiffening their courage by demonstrating the danger to justice, religion, and their country; finally convincing them that honour required them to immortalize their assembly and themselves also by becoming liberators of all that men held most dear and most sacred.

Thoughts without deeds are reverie, to write of them in such detail mere romancing. I realized this even before I began, but I thought I owed it to myself to show the need, justice, and importance of such an enterprise, and to prove that I was not hatching hare-brained schemes. Daydream is not the word for a plan to restore good and prudent government, reinstate the oppressed nobility, return peace to the Church, and, without in any way diminishing the King's authority, bring relief from the intolerable burden of taxation that had led Louis XIV to the brink of total disaster. If these plans came to nothing, it was because we had a Regent without enough ruthlessness and determination to carry them out when the time was ripe. During the course of that same year and the year that followed, many similar projects came to nothing. Should I regret ever having conceived or proposed them? I do not believe that success is the only criterion of the worth of such designs; still less is it valid when all depends on one who is not willing to study them, much less to act upon them. What follows will show the prince's disinclination to move.

After a long and frequent discussion of these matters, M. le Duc d'Orléans and I proceeded to the manner of his taking up his Regency, on which I had much reflected. I reminded him of the Parlement's jealousy of the peers, and their usurpation of our privileges without a just cause. After producing incontrovertible proofs to that effect, I proposed that immediately after the King's death he should summon the peers and officers of the Crown to meet in the King's apartments, with Monsieur le Duc (the only prince of the blood who was of age), the Duc du

Maine, and the Comte de Toulouse. There in session, seated and covered, with the three Secretaries of State standing behind the table at the farther end of the room,[1] he should speak in praise of the late King, and of the pressing need to form a new administration with himself, as Regent, at the head. Then, looking at them all firmly and with confidence, he should invite them to attend him that same afternoon (or next morning should the King die in the evening) at the Parlement, it being all important to prevent the Duc du Maine from spending the night in plotting, or the premier président from delivering a harangue.

Immediately after his arrival, he should address the members, stating that respect for their assembly had prompted him to come in person to condole with them on the loss which France had suffered, and to proclaim the Regency that had fallen to him by right of birth, assuring them that he intended to seek their counsel in times of need. He should then add that in order to prove his sincerity he would acquaint them with the plans made by M. le Duc de Bourgogne, of which he thoroughly approved, and which had been discovered in that prince's desk after his death. Then he should at once announce the setting up of the various Councils, mentioning no names, and so end the session. As the Regency was already in existence, there would be no occasion for the officers of the Crown to reply, or for the Parlement to give its views. If M. du Maine made any sign, M. le Duc d'Orléans should interrupt, saying that there was no cause to question a procedure that had been adopted in every Regency except the last two, when the circumstances were abnormal. Then, without waiting for a reply, he should dismiss the assembly.

I dealt finally with two matters in a way that should have brought much comfort to the Duc du Maine, considering the general opinion of the bastards at that time, and thus of the validity of any provisions made for them by the late King. I was inclined to think that, in any matter not directly concerned with the State or its government, M. le Duc d'Orléans would be in honour bound to carry out the King's wishes—not by law, but gladly, as a token of respect to the dead monarch, and to avoid any imputation of acting spitefully. For similar reasons, I felt that Mme de Maintenon and her school at Saint-Cyr should receive the full benefit of any bequest, and that if none had been made, she should be permitted to retire to wherever she pleased and no pecuniary favour refused her. There was nothing more to fear from that eighty-year-old witch; her mighty and malevolent wand was broken, and she had reverted to being once again old widow Scarron. I believed also, however, that after granting her personal liberty and sufficient funds, all rank and honours should most firmly be refused her. She deserved far worse from M. le Duc d'Orléans.

---

[1] The King sat in council at the head of a long table, with the princes and other members in order of rank along the sides. Ministers spoke facing him at the farther end. Members of royal councils had perroquets, special folding camp-stools with arms, of which they were very proud. The perroquets went with them everywhere, so that they need never be reduced to the indignity of sitting on a stool without arms.

Another matter to which I drew the prince's attention was that, although we had very freely criticized the King's administration, we had been in one mind regarding his two greatest assets, which his successor should by every means be encouraged to emulate, and which I passionately desired M. le Duc d'Orléans, modelling himself on the King, to strive to adopt also. These priceless adjuncts to royalty were the King's unshakeable dignity, and the perfect regularity of his public life. The first had ensured that, at whatever hour he was seen, he presented an appearance of majesty inspiring awe in his beholders; the other that one had only to know the date and the time to know also what the King was doing, excepting during his leisure hours when he hunted or was merely out of doors. You will scarcely believe the benefit which this regularity conferred on his service, on the magnificence of his Court, the convenience of his courtiers, and on those who desired speech with him but had little to say,[1] on the harmony of his private life, and the smooth-running of the business of the State. What is more, the fact that his permanent residence was far from Paris entailed a stricter ordering of his daily work, and provided a meeting place for everyone, so that it was possible to approach more ministers and their offices in a single day than could be done in a fortnight at Paris, where the distances between offices and private houses were often very great.

For quite other reasons I feared the establishment of the Court nearer to Paris. I knew M. le Duc d'Orléans's nature, his readiness to be waylaid by and to hear people who, by their rank and lives, were far removed from the Court, and who could not have approached him at Versailles; who were ignorant of State affairs, low-born, self-confident, but very sure of their capacity to govern. I equally dreaded another group, quite as vulgar and no less avaricious—his intimates in pleasure and exotic studies, and all the more dangerous because they were well acquainted with him. Such men would try to keep him continually amused, making him waste his time, diverting him with malicious jests, whose effects might well prove fatal to State and Regent alike. No less dangerous were his debauches, mistresses, and frequent attendance at the opera, which was on the same floor as his apartments, with a thousand improper amusements of a similar kind, such as his dissolute supper-parties, and the nocturnal adventures that were the climax of them all.

After mentioning all these at some considerable length, I said to M. le Duc d'Orléans that, as he well knew, it was a long time since I had discussed his way of life, being quite aware that it would have no effect. Now I felt I must speak, imploring him to reflect seriously how he himself would view a Regent who, at over forty,

---

[1] Anyone with sufficient courage might approach Louis XIV and whisper a request into his wig on his swift passage from his study to the chapel and back, or as he was walking in his gardens. He invariably answered, 'We shall see', and remarkably enough he nearly always did see and returned an answer.

led the life of an eighteen-year-old musketeer, with the kind of companions whom no man of rank would condescend to know. What result would his conduct have on his influence at home, his credit abroad, his reputation with the young King when he grew old enough to see and understand! Most damaging of all, I continued, would be to proclaim his godlessness, or anything approaching atheism; for it would make enemies of all religious bodies and at the same time antagonize every decent person who cared for morality, sobriety, and religion. He would then find turning against himself that licentious maxim which he was so fond of quoting—namely that religion is a bogy which clever men have invented in order to govern, and which is therefore necessary for Kings and republics. If for that reason only, he might think it in his best interests to respect the Church and not bring it into disrepute. I dwelt long on this important subject, adding that he need not be a hypocrite, only avoid plain speaking, observe the conventions (which was not hard if one confined oneself to appearances), refuse to countenance improper jests or remarks, and generally live like an honest gentleman who respects his country's faith and conceals the fact that he, personally, sets no store by it.

I represented also how dangerous, in his position, it would be to keep a mistress, and I besought him, if he could not do without one, at least to change continually, so as to avoid the love that comes from habit. If he did find himself in that sorry pass, let him conduct himself with the caution of prelates, who safeguard their reputations by secrecy in their debauchery. I said that with so many new and interesting occupations he should not, unless his mind were entirely corrupted, find it hard to practise restraint; that in his urgent need to be liked, respected, and obeyed, he would find a system of greater use than he supposed. A regular routine to bring order into his affairs would prevent things from going awry, and himself from regretting the pleasures of debauchery. He should be particularly careful in granting audiences, especially to women, who were apt to beg one on the slightest pretext, and then use the time for conversing over trifles, with often some hidden purpose which the prince might fail to perceive, for they would boast of the length and, if possible, the frequency of such interviews. He would do well to make them await his pleasure in the ante-rooms of Madame's or Mme la Duchesse d'Orléans's apartment, at his usual visiting hour, and listen standing, following the King's excellent practice of seldom saying more than 'We shall see', and then very civilly cutting them short. He would do well to make it a rule that, after entering his mother's or his wife's drawing-room, no lady might draw him aside to talk on her affairs. By showing the first offenders to the door with icy courtesy, he would prevent others from copying their example.

I was, however, most careful to say nothing of Mme la Duchesse de Berry.

The incident at Fontainebleau had taught me prudence. None the less, my silence on a matter which it would have been so natural to mention must, in itself, have said volumes. Although what follows will show that all my time and efforts were wasted, truth demands that I should tell everything and keep nothing back.

The further the King's health deteriorated (although his daily routine remained unchanged), the more people's thoughts turned to their own futures. Yet such was the awe in which King Louis, though visibly decaying, was held, that M. le Duc d'Orléans still remained completely isolated in the drawing-rooms of Marly. I did observe, however, that people began to seek my own society, both ordinary folk and men of high standing, as well as those schemers who, when they think it profitable, shamelessly chase after persons whom they do not know. I had often mocked such bursts of friendship for office or self-esteem; I could not help laughing at this sudden enthusiasm for a man who as yet possessed nothing but hope, and I made a joke of it to M. le Duc d'Orléans, so that he, too, might be on his guard.

The Duc de Noailles who had hitherto sought him out rather after the manner of Nicodemus,[1] now began to visit him more often, trying without success to learn something of what lay ahead. He repeatedly complained of the awkwardness of knowing nothing for certain of the posts which I had said I hoped to obtain for him and his uncle; but I kept him in suspense, merely saying that my suggestions had been well received and that I knew no more. Sometimes he begged me to inquire; sometimes, vowing that he knew I knew, he besought me to be frank with him. I saw that he passionately desired a post with the finances; but even after he had made his will, the King did not seem close enough to death to warrant my discussing the future with anyone. I therefore said no more to the Duc de Noailles at that time, nor did I mention him again to M. le Duc d'Orléans.

Mme la Duchesse d'Orléans was no less eager to have the veil removed from the future. She foresaw the danger of M. du Maine's position, for she had to admit that he deserved little good of her husband. But apart from that (to her) paramount concern, she was also interested in M. le Duc d'Orléans and his plans. Her talk, when we were alone together, turned for the most part on the bastards' right to the succession, and she put me on the rack. She knew very well that M. le Duc d'Orléans trusted me implicitly, and that with me alone he would freely consult and discuss his ideas. Experience had taught her that he was ill-equipped for making such plans or for putting them into action, and that when a difficulty presented itself he was all too ready to rely on my ideas and suggestions. His approaching vast responsibilities made it impossible for her not to believe that we had discussed them, and experience had also shown her that although M. le Duc

[1] John iii, 1-2.

d'Orléans might well have no ideas at all, the same was unlikely to be true of me.

Her curiosity was therefore extreme, her questions inexhaustible. She used clever shifts to take me by surprise, for example asking my opinion of some person, with apparent lack of interest, trying to pump me with all the power that cunning, rank, argument, condescension, or friendship could bring to bear, and all in the most artful, reasonable, and persuasive way imaginable. I thus continually had to trim, being doubly careful neither to let anything be known or even suspected of secrets which were not mine to tell, nor to forget that she was the sister of the Duc du Maine, for whose benefit she would gladly have sacrificed husband, children, and herself as well. The best I could do was to make long speeches in an effort to gain time, stressing the difficulties, the complications, not to say the dangers of preparing any plans during the King's lifetime, and the futility of them should he have made provisions in his will, for no one would be so foolish as to go against his wishes. Yet despite my flow of words, Mme la Duchesse d'Orléans remained unsatisfied. She had too often heard my liberal views and seen me kick against the pricks to put any faith in my answers, and I immediately felt her disbelief.

Although I tried by all means to avoid the snares of every imaginable kind which she set to trap me, the deceit involved was so prodigiously painful that I went in constant dread lest my face or voice betray me. Impossible to describe the agony in the heart of one who was by nature frank, truthful and honest, who, amid all the hazards of the most dangerous Court on earth, had never brought himself to dissemble, and had often paid dearly for it, as these memoirs have shown. What torture, I repeat, must such a man suffer, faced with the alternative, either of ruining the State, which I hoped to save and renew; betraying M. le Duc d'Orléans, whose secrets I alone knew, and destroying myself with him; or else of using my whole strength and cunning to deceive a princess with whom I had lived for years in an atmosphere of mutual trust and friendship, but who now battered me daily with questions, whilst I continually parried and eluded her. I often left her presence and went straight to that of M. le Duc d'Orléans, weeping tears of rage and despair, which he made worse by laughing at me. I would then turn furiously upon him, speaking my thoughts with something more than freedom; and so we continued until the death of the King.

During the second half of that Marly, the King appeared to be sinking so rapidly that I felt the time had come to relieve the Duc de Noailles's anxiety and thus be able to discuss with him the finances. When I asked M. le Duc d'Orléans, he agreed with me, giving me leave to reveal the duke's future appointment, and that of his uncle also;[1] and he confirmed the news on the next occasion when M. de Noailles visited him. That nobleman could scarcely contain his delight;

---

[1] Cardinal de Noailles was to be at the head of Church affairs, and dispenser of benefices.

expressions of emotion were his first reaction, vanity his second. His speech was full of the benefits to Cardinal de Noailles, and he also admitted that the finances were vastly to his liking because, so he said, he had always been interested in them and had studied them under Desmaretz; he therefore flattered himself that he would prove as good as any other candidate. He then showered on me promises of eternal friendship, his entire confidence, his desire to work with me in every way and, above all, his undying gratitude for all my efforts on his behalf.

Once the door lay open on the future, we consulted him on the other nominations for presidents and assistant-presidents of the Councils. He mentioned d'Antin (who, since his dukedom, had been courting me assiduously), expressing surprise and gratification that his name was not included. We discussed him frankly, he not denying d'Antin's faults, and I speaking well of him where I might truthfully do so. We both agreed, however, that the names selected for the heads of the Councils were preferable, and that the Council for the interior was the only one suitable for him as a member, or as its head, if that post should fall vacant. He thoroughly approved of the dismissal of the Secretaries of State and the disgrace of the Chancellor, and we argued amicably about his successor. He was in favour of the procureur général, whereas I thought that the seals would be safer in his father's hands.[1] There were many other subjects on which he spoke his mind, and I listened gladly, for there were some others on which I preferred to keep him in ignorance, and was therefore very willing to let him delude himself. As he became increasingly free with me regarding the future, he gave vent to such violent utterances concerning the bastards that I shall not repeat them; and going on from one thing to another, he proposed as a prudent and most necessary measure that Paris be immediately fortified. 'Fortify Paris!' I cried, 'and where shall we find the necessary materials, the millions of francs, the years needed for such a work? And if it could be done merely by waving a wand, what garrison would man it? Where should we find ammunition and food for the troops and inhabitants? What about the artillery? Finally, what advantage would accrue, when the whole scheme was so demonstrably impracticable?' He continued to offer feeble arguments for the next few days, and I let him ramble on, having no fear of that folly becoming a reality.

Observing that he made no progress, he proposed another scheme, namely to move the law courts, the law schools, and all the public business transacted therein, bodily to Versailles. I stared at him in utter blank amazement, asking when, and how, and at what cost he proposed to house all these establishments at Versailles, which had no river or other drinking water, whose foundations were only sand and mud, where nature had provided not so much as a pond for horses,

---

[1] This refers to Henri François Daguesseau and his father.

and where nothing grew for miles around. What possible advantage would come from a removal, even supposing it could be done, that brought only confusion and discomfort to the Court, and left Paris a vacuum, with plaintiffs, magistrates, officers of the law, and universities, all alike ruined? Where, in short, would be the benefit, for nothing of the smallest use would be achieved? He replied that the object was to decrease the size of Paris, the nourishment of which had laid bare the surrounding country, and secondly to separate the law courts from the vast numbers of the citizens, because in the past their union had sometimes proved dangerous. Gradually, however, he came to admit the disadvantages of Versailles, loudly exclaiming against the huge establishment which the King had formed there, praising Saint-Germain, on the other hand, and going on to propose, as the simplest thing imaginable, that Versailles should be entirely dismantled and everything transferred thence to Saint-Germain which, he averred, could be made the healthiest and most enviable resort in all Europe.

Words failed me at this third *postulatum*. 'He's raving mad!' I thought. 'What have I done? What will become of our finances?' Whilst I thus murmured through my closed lips he continued to hold forth, delighting at the prospect of the marvels to be wrought at Saint-Germain with the spoils from Versailles. Aware, at last, of my silence, he begged me to say something. 'Sir,' said I, 'when the fairies lend you their magic wands I shall be of your mind. Nothing, indeed, could be better, for I never have understood how that cesspool Versailles came to be chosen in the first place, still less preferred to Saint-Germain. But to bring about such a change we should need the help of fairies. Until you can enlist their aid, it is no use even to discuss it.' He began to laugh, and confessed that the whole thing was impossible. Of his three proposals the last was the least alarming; but I trembled none the less.

Some time before this conversation took place he had made yet another suggestion, which I had equally firmly rejected, but he continued to press it none the less. The objections I raised he was quite unable to counter, but still he persisted. Events will soon reveal his reasons for promoting that ridiculous plan; and in due course you shall know all.

Towards the end of that Marly, I discovered that M. le Duc d'Orléans had consulted M. de Noailles regarding the States General. He explained that the matter was too closely bound up with the finances to conceal it from that nobleman, once he had been told his destiny. The latter described their discussion with some signs of embarrassment, and I soon after became aware that M. le Duc d'Orléans no longer favoured the idea. I then found that he had yielded altogether in the matter of the Parlement. I knew him too well to hope to move him on both counts, and the States General appeared to me of such vast importance that

I unhesitatingly sacrificed the Parlement. I hoped to please him by sparing him one argument, and at the same time to save all my ammunition for the States General, which was what I continued to strive for, without making much progress until the eve of the King's death, when M. le Duc d'Orléans told me flatly that it was no longer in question. From that moment I despaired. I perceived the selfishness of the Duc de Noailles, who stood to lose some control of the finances by a meeting of that assembly; and I guessed that he had pointed out to the Regent that his authority also might be weakened. I could not pretend that it would be otherwise, nor that I thought such an event undesirable. Experience has since demonstrated that I was not wrong. With the failure of my plan to summon the States General went also my proposal for national bankruptcy; it would have removed too many opportunities for fishing in troubled waters. Liquidations and the continuance of taxes and covenants opened wide the door for bestowing fortunes, favours, and the opposite, to which M. le Duc d'Orléans, and especially the Duc de Noailles, would hold the key. It is not yet the moment to describe my sorrowful reflections on this bad beginning, nor the events that confirmed them.

On Friday, 9 August, Père Tellier instructed the King at some length on the enregistration of the constitution,[1] entire, as it was written; and the King gave audience to the premier président and the procureur général, who had been sent for on the previous day. He went stag-hunting after dinner in his new calash, driving himself as usual, for the last time in his life, and returned exhausted. That same evening there was a full orchestra in Mme de Maintenon's room. On the Saturday, he walked before dinner in his gardens, at Marly, and about six o'clock returned to Versailles for the last time in his life, never again to contemplate that monstrous work of his creation.[2] In the evening he worked with the Chancellor in Mme de Maintenon's room. Everyone thought him looking gravely ill. On Sunday, 11 August, he held the council of State, and in the afternoon he drove to Trianon. He never again went out.

On the following day he took physic as was customary, and followed his usual routine for such days. It was reported that he complained of sciatica in his leg and thigh. He had never before suffered from sciatica, nor from rheumatism; he had never even had a cold, and for a long time past had had no attacks of gout. That evening they had the small orchestra at Mme de Maintenon's; and that was the last time he walked.

---

[1] The Bull *Unigenitus*. Saint-Simon, himself, has been called a bigot, or alternatively one to whom religion meant little. He was certainly deeply religious, and made retreats each year to La Trappe. He was not narrow-minded, but wished to see a free Church of France established; he suspected the Vatican of wishing to interfere and dominate, and hated the Inquisition as 'abominable in the sight of God and execrable in that of men'.

[2] Saint-Simon strongly disapproved of Marly. It cost 'several thousand million at a time when France could least afford it', and was 'a haunt of snakes and vermin, typical of the King's bad taste.' Boislisle, on the other hand, says: 'From all that we know of Marly, its decorations and its wonderful gardens, it must have been a model of good taste and true magnificence. Its disappearance is an irreparable loss.'

On Tuesday, 13 August, he made one last effort, on returning from mass in his chair, to give the final audience, standing without support, to that dubious ambassador from Persia. His weakness did not allow him to repeat the magnificence of the first audience, and he had to be content to receive him in the throne room, where nothing was out of the ordinary. This was the last public engagement which the King fulfilled, one in which Pontchartrain played vilely upon his vanity in order to press his court. Indeed, he was shameless enough to conclude the farce with the signing of a treaty, whose effects amply demonstrated the fraudulence of the whole affair. The audience was long and tiring, but after it was over, the King did not rest although he must have longed to do so. He held the finance Council, dined in private, and was carried to Mme de Maintenon's room for a concert by the smaller orchestra. As he left the study, he stopped to allow the Duchesse de La Rochefoucauld to present her daughter-in-law the Duchesse de La Rocheguyon, the last lady ever to be presented to him. She took her *tabouret* that night at the King's supper, the last time that he ever ate in public. Afterwards he worked alone with the Chancellor, and on the following day he sent gifts, including some jewellery, to that bogus ambassador who, two days later, was escorted to the house of a merchant at Chaillot and shortly afterwards left for Havre-de-Grace, where he embarked. It was on this same day that the Princesse des Ursins, fearing for the King's health, had left Paris by diligence for Lyons. The next day was Wednesday.

The King's health had been failing for more than a year. The personal valets were the first to notice it, and observed every symptom without daring to speak. Then the bastards, especially M. du Maine, also perceived it, and with the assistance of Mme de Maintenon acted with all dispatch.[1] Fagon, now weak in body and mind, was the only one of all that great household who noticed nothing. Maréchal the chief surgeon spoke to him several times, but was harshly rebuffed. At last, out of duty and devotion to the King, Maréchal was driven to go to Mme de Maintenon to warn her how completely Fagon was mistaken. He assured her that the King, whose pulse he took often, had for a long time been suffering from a slow internal fever, that his constitution being so robust there would be no danger, given proper care and remedies, but that if the fever went unchecked it might soon prove fatal. Mme de Maintenon lost her temper, and what his loyalty induced him to tell her only served to make her angrier still. She said that only Fagon's personal enemies believed such tales about the King's health, and that the chief physician's skill, wisdom and experience could not be deceived. Maréchal told me indignantly that he felt there was nothing more that he could do. From that moment he began to mourn the death of his master. Fagon had indeed once

---

[1] Saint-Simon means that they scurried to get his will signed and sealed.

been the first physician in all Europe; but for a long time past his health had prevented him from continuing to broaden his experience, and his unlimited authority and favour with the King had spoilt him. He would brook neither argument nor discussion, continued to treat the King's health as in earlier days and, by his stubbornness, killed him.

Because he had once been afflicted with long attacks of gout, Fagon had taken to swaddling him, as it were, every night, in a great heap of feather pillows, with the result that he had to be changed and rubbed down each morning before the great chamberlain and the first gentleman of the bedchamber were allowed to enter. For years past he had been drinking, instead of the best Champagne wine which until then he had used exclusively, nothing but watered-down Burgundy, so old that it had lost its potency. He sometimes said laughingly that foreigners often felt swindled when they asked to taste his wine. Never at any time did he drink his wine without water, and he had never been accustomed to drink sweet wines, or even tea, coffee, or chocolate. When he rose, instead of a little bread with wine and water, he had, for a long time past, been having two cups of sage and veronica. Between his meals, and always at his bedtime, he drank more than a pint-sized glass of water flavoured with orange-flowers, and these drinks were always iced. Even on the days when he was purged he took this drink, and always at every meal; and he never ate anything between meals, except for a few cinnamon lozenges, which he put in his pocket at dessert, together with a great many dry biscuits for the bitches in his dog-room.

During the last years he became increasingly constipated, and Fagon used to make him begin his meals with iced fruit, such as mulberries, melons, and figs, often half-rotten with over-ripeness, and he ate still more for dessert, with an astonishing number of sweetmeats. All the year round, he consumed an immense amount of salad at his supper. His soups (of which he drank several different kinds, both morning and evening, taking a full cup of each regardless of what came after) were strong meat-juices, exceedingly rich, and all that was served to him was very highly spiced, at least as much as is normal, and very hot. Fagon did not approve of the spices and sweetmeats, and often made a face when he saw the King eating them, but he dared not say anything, except once in a way to Livry and Benoist,[1] who replied that their business was to make the King eat, not to purge him. He never touched venison or water-fowl, but with those exceptions he would eat everything, on feasts and fast-days alike, apart from Lent, which he had observed for the past twenty years, but only for a few days. In that last summer he had greatly increased his consumption of fruit and liquids.

In the end, the fruit taken after soup flooded his stomach and took away his

[1] Louis Sanguin, Marquis de Livry, and Georges Benoist, respectively the King's steward and his taster.

appetite, which never before had failed in the whole course of his life, although he never felt hungry, even when his meals were unavoidably delayed. With the first spoonful of soup his appetite came, as I have many times heard him say, and he ate prodigiously of solid meals each morning and evening, and so steadily that one never grew accustomed to watching him.[1] So much water, so much fruit, unrelieved by any alcohol, turned his blood gangrenous by lowering his vital spirits, and weakened his digestion by nightly sweatings. This diet finally caused his death, as was proved when they opened his body, for all the vitals were found to be perfectly healthy, and so strong that he might well have lived for more than a century. His stomach and bowels were particularly noteworthy, because their size and capacity were double that of any normal man, which explains why he was so huge and regular an eater.

They turned to remedies when it was too late, because Fagon would not admit that the King was ill, nor would Mme de Maintenon, although she took good care to safeguard her own future at Saint-Cyr, and M. du Maine's future as well. The King himself was one of the first to recognize his condition, and he sometimes spoke of it to his personal valets; but Fagon always reassured him and would do nothing. The King listened to him but remained unconvinced. Nevertheless, his old friendship for Fagon and, more especially, Mme de Maintenon's influence prevented him from taking action.

On Wednesday, 14 August he was carried to mass for the last time, and afterwards held a council of State. He ate meat, although it was a fast-day, and went to the concert in Mme de Maintenon's room. He supped alone in his room and was seen by the Court at his dinner-hour. He stayed only a short time among his family, in the study, and retired to bed soon after ten o'clock.

On Thursday, the Feast of the Assumption, he heard mass in bed. He had been restless and thirsty during the night. He dined in his bed before the entire Court, rose at five o'clock, and had himself carried to Mme de Maintenon's, where there was the small orchestra. Between mass and dinner he had spoken separately with the Chancellor, Desmaretz, and Pontchartrain. He supped and retired to bed as on the previous day. There was the same routine every day afterwards, as long as he was able to leave his bed.

On Friday, 16 August his night was no better; he suffered much from thirst and drank a great deal. He did not hear mass until ten o'clock, dined in bed, as he continued to do every day afterwards, gave audience to an envoy from Wolfenbuttel,[2] had himself carried to Mme de Maintenon; played cards there with the usual ladies, and afterwards listened to the full orchestra.

[1] Madame wrote: 'I have often seen the King consume four full plates of different kinds of soup, a whole pheasant, a partridge, a large dish of salad, two great slices of ham, mutton served with gravy and garlic, a plate of sweet cakes, and, on top of that, fruit and hard-boiled eggs.'
[2] A German town in the Duchy of Brunswick.

On Saturday, 17 August, the night was as before. He remained in bed during the finance Council, saw the Court at dinner, rose immediately after, and went to Mme de Maintenon's room, where he worked with the Chancellor. That was the first night on which Fagon slept in his room.

Sunday, 18 August was like the other days. Fagon still denied that he had a fever. The King held a Council of State, worked as usual with Le Peletier[1] on the defences, and went to Mme de Maintenon for the concert. On that same day, the Portuguese ambassador extraordinary, the Count of Ribeyra,[2] whose mother, then dead, had been a sister of the Prince and the Cardinal de Rohan, made his entry into Paris in the grand manner, throwing a great number of silver medals and a few gold ones into the crowd. The King's condition showed very plainly that he could not last more than a few days; for I had, through Maréchal, a truer account than that with which Fagon strove to deceive himself and others. This made me remember Chamillart who, since his retirement, had been receiving a pension of sixty thousand livres from the King. I asked M. le Duc d'Orléans for his promise to continue it, to which he at once consented, and gave me leave to write to Chamillart, in Paris, to that effect. Chamillart was greatly distressed by the King's illness and affected by little else; but my letter came to him as an agreeable surprise, and he was obliged to me for my pains; he had had no thought for himself. He enclosed a letter of thanks. I never did anything that gave me more pleasure. It was kept secret until the King's death; but I lost no time in announcing it after the Regency was proclaimed.

That same day, I went to visit the Duc de Noailles at about eight in the evening, on the floor below my lodging. He was in his study, and came out to greet me in his bedroom. After some preliminaries regarding the state of the King's health and the future, he began a long discourse on the Jesuits, at the end of which he proposed driving them all out of France, returning to their original owners the benefices which they had seized for their monasteries, and giving all their wealth to the universities near where they were situated. Although the Duc de Noailles's wild projects should have taught me that he might propose others even wilder, I must confess that this one took me as much by surprise as though it had been the first of its kind. He perceived my horrified expression and began to argue and, at the same moment, the door of his study opened and I saw the procureur général[3] emerge and approach us. Several members of the Parlement had come during the morning to inquire for the King, as they frequently did on Sundays; but I believed the Duc de Noailles to be alone in his study, and the procureur général to have left very early for Paris, as those magistrates always did.

[1] Le Peletier de Souzy, director-general of fortifications.
[2] Louis de Camara who died, aged thirty-eight, in 1723. His mother was Constance Emilie de Rohan-Soubise, née de Frontenac.
[3] Henri François Daguesseau.

He had scarcely drawn up a chair before the Duc de Noailles acquainted him with what we had been saying—I myself had not yet uttered a word—but my surprised gesture forced him to defend himself. He repeated what little had been said, and the procureur soon interrupted him to gaze coldly at me, remarking that it was the best plan imaginable, and quite the most useful with which to begin the Regency. I cannot express my feelings at such a speech from the procureur général. That such utter folly should bamboozle a sensible man, whose office must have taught him something of administrative action and its effect, made me fear for my own reason. My astonishment made me think that I had not understood, I made them repeat, and remained completely stupefied. They soon saw from my countenance that I was engulfed in my own thoughts; and they begged me to give my opinion.

I told them plainly that I thought their project so dreadful that I could scarcely credit what I heard. They then attacked me together, the one furiously, the other gravely and seriously, telling me that everyone knew the Jesuits, how they dominated everything, how dangerous they were to Church, State, and individuals also. At last, overcome by impatience, I interrupted them; and it appeared to me that they were not ill-pleased, so eager were they to hear what I had to say. I said that I agreed with all their complaints against the Jesuits and concerning the benefit to France if they could be removed—I might say much more on that subject; but that now I wished to speak only of how and what next. As to how, we were no island, like Sicily, with a barren interior, a few Jesuit houses in the two principal cities, such as Palermo and Messina, and a few others in smaller towns along the coast. It had been easy for the viceroy, Count Maffei,[1] to arrest and embark them at one blow, and immediately dispose of their lands and monasteries as the King of Sicily commanded.[2] But as for doing the like in France, my mind boggled at the thought of dealing with the vast quantity of Jesuit houses throughout the provinces, and the infinite numbers of Jesuits filling them.

What an uproar there would be! What troubles! What resistance to the very first move against them! Think of the enormous regiments of Jesuits, their families, pupils, and penitents, the families of these pupils and penitents, the masses of people at their retreats and in their congregations, the lovers of their sermons, their friends, and the followers of their doctrine! What a turmoil would be aroused even before the first province was cleared of them; and even supposing that that were done successfully, where to banish them? Beyond the nearest frontier, you may reply, but who would prevent their return? We have no sea surrounding us as in Sicily, no great wall like China, our country is open on

---

[1] Annibal, Count Maffei, Viceroy of Sicily, 1714. He had visited London as envoy extraordinary of Victor Amadeus II, Duke of Savoy, in 1706 and 1709.

[2] In fact the expulsion had not occurred until 1714.

every side. The whole idea is thus plainly impossible. But even suppose it were managed, what would Rome say? The French Jesuits are her best agents, and uphold her claims with devotion. What about the King of Spain, so religious, so openly attached to the Jesuits, whose feelings regarding M. le Duc d'Orléans need not be described? What about the Catholic peoples of Europe, amongst whom the Jesuits have so many powerful friends and partisans, not to mention our own regular orders, among whom only the Benedictines and Dominicans might perhaps be called their enemies?

I ended by saying that such a project, however well-organized, would be the ruin of M. le Duc d'Orléans, and produce such confusion that I saw no way of restoring order. My speech was longer than I have recounted; but they did not interrupt me. When I had finished, I saw two surprised and angry faces, quite unable to argue against my objections, yet both declaring that they were by no means convinced. Then again, cutting in on each other, they reverted to the Jesuits being a danger to the State and the Church, and to individuals also, whilst I continued to repeat that the question was not so much that, but the cause, the means, and the effects—three things which they must demonstrate to be both possible and guaranteed. It was of no use; they persisted in—shall I call it?— baying the moon. Their want of success with me, and the unsuitably late hour for a magistrate to return to Paris caused us to separate without the smallest progress having been made on either side. I left at the same time as the procureur général, and returned to my lodging, still overcome with astonishment that a sensible, intelligent man like Daguesseau could seriously have been debating such an issue (as I am sure he was) with the Duc de Noailles before my arrival; that the duke should so suddenly have broached it to me, and then have thrown the ball to Daguesseau when he came to join us.

On the night of Monday, 19 August the King was just as restless; but Fagon still refused to admit that he had a fever. He expressed a desire to have water brought from Bourbon. The King worked with Pontchartrain, heard the small orchestra in Mme de Maintenon's room, announced that he would not go to Fontainebleau, but that on the following Wednesday he would watch the review of the household troops from his balcony. He had summoned them, from their headquarters, to be reviewed; but it was only on that day that he realized the impossibility, and announced that he would watch them from a window overlooking the great courtyard of Versailles.

On Tuesday, 20 August, the night was like the previous ones. In the morning he worked with the Chancellor, but saw only a few of the foreign noblemen and ministers, who had, and still have, Tuesday as the day appointed for their going to Versailles. He held the finance Council and afterwards worked alone with

Desmaretz. He could not go to Mme de Maintenon, but sent for her to come to him. Mmes de Dangeau and de Caylus were admitted later to help in the conversation. He supped in his armchair, wearing his dressing-gown. He never again left his apartments or put on his clothes. The evening was as short as the preceding ones. Fagon at last suggested a consultation with the ablest doctors of Paris and the Court.

On that same day, Mme de Saint-Simon, whom I had been urging to return, arrived back from Forges, where she had been drinking the waters. The King noticed her as he entered his study after supper. He stopped his chair, and said many civil things to her of her journey and the return, before making Blouin wheel him into the other study. She was the last court-lady to whom he spoke, for I do not count Mmes de Levis, Dangeau, Caylus, and d'O, who always came to him for cards and music at Mme de Maintenon's. Mme de Saint-Simon told me later that she would not have recognized him had she met him elsewhere. It was only on 6 July that she had gone to Forges.

On Wednesday, 21 August, four doctors saw the King; but all they did was to praise Fagon, who prescribed senna. The King put off until Friday the review of the *gendarmerie*, held the State Council after dinner, and then worked with the Chancellor. Mme de Maintenon visited him later, followed by the usual ladies and the full orchestra. He supped in his armchair, in his dressing-gown. For some days past they had noticed a difficulty when he swallowed meat, or even bread, of which he ate sparingly throughout his life, and for a long time past nothing but the crumb, because he had no teeth. He took rather more soup than usual, and some very light mince, with eggs to supplement it; but he ate extremely little.

By Thursday, 22 August, the King's health had deteriorated. He saw four other doctors, but like the four who had preceded them, they only applauded the admirable learning and treatments of Fagon, who prescribed quinine and water for that evening, and asses' milk for the night. Since he no longer saw any likelihood of being able to watch the troops from the balcony, the King, even in his extremity, thought of the Duc du Maine's advantage. He commissioned him to review the flower of his army in his stead, with all a sovereign's majesty; thereby offering a foretaste by accustoming them, in his lifetime, to regard his bastard as on a level with himself, and allowing him to do them the favour of a flattering report. That, at least, was what this rotten image of the Guises and Cromwell wished to extract for himself; but having none of their courage, panic gripped him lest M. le Duc d'Orléans should know his own strength and decide to use it. He therefore looked about for a protector, whom Mme de Maintenon provided without the least difficulty; for Mme de Ventadour, urged thereto by her close friend and one-time lover, the Maréchal de Villeroy (who very well knew what he did), gave Monseigneur le Dauphin a fancy to attend the review. He had begun to ride a little pony, and he went to ask for the King's permission. The cat was out of the bag with a vengeance when a uniform of a captain of the *gendarmerie* was found to fit Monseigneur le Dauphin to perfection, though he had only very recently been breeched. The King was delighted by his childish eagerness, and very willingly gave him leave to go.

Now that no one any longer doubted the King's condition, M. le Duc d'Orléans's once deserted apartments became crowded with callers. I suggested to him that he should attend the review, on the pretext of honouring the King, impersonated, for that occasion, by M. du Maine. I instructed him to follow the latter like a courtier, as though he were the King himself; to ride fifty paces forward when they approached his companies, in order to salute him at their head; then to rejoin his suite, and follow him bare-headed along the line, glancing repeatedly at the suite and then at the soldiers, letting no one miss the sarcasm in his insultingly respectful bearing, so as to show them that pasteboard monarch in the last stages of fright and embarrassment.

Greater even than the delight of shaming M. du Maine at the height of his triumph would have been the advantage of proving him a coward, and thus showing the troops and the crowd, and thereafter the Court and Paris, the terror that rightful authority inspires in usurpers. I confess that I would have given much to have been in M. le Duc d'Orléans's shoes for those twenty-four hours. M. du Maine being what he was, I swear that he would have died of fright; but alas the prince's soft nature prevented his acting out the pleasant comedy. He attended the review, inspected his companies, saluted Monseigneur le Dauphin at their head, and scarcely noticed M. du Maine, who paled at the sight of him, appearing vastly upset and embarrassed, especially when his retinue left him to follow M. le Duc d'Orléans. Everyone unanimously expressed their indignation at his having taken the salute in M. le Duc d'Orléans's presence. How much more telling it would have been had he found the resolution to act as I suggested. Indeed, he came to be of the same opinion later, and was ashamed of himself, a feeling which I encouraged in an effort to make him bolder.

That same evening, at his *coucher*, the King ordered the Duc de La Rochefoucauld to show him some coats on the following morning. He wished to choose one against the time when he ceased to be in mourning for Mme la Duchesse de Lorraine's son[1]—barely twenty-six, yet already endowed with the Abbeys of Stavelot and Malmédy. You will remember that the King had not walked for some time past, nor worn clothes, not even when they carried him to Mme de Maintenon's room; that he never now left his bed, except to sup in a

---

[1] Prince Francis (1689-1715), the fifth son of Charles V and Maria Eleonora of Austria. Saint-Simon was mistaken. He was the brother-in-law of the Duchesse de Lorraine, not her son.

dressing-gown, and that he could no longer eat solid food. Yet, as you will observe, he still expected to recover. What is more, he still continued his daily round of Councils, work, and leisure. So true it is that men are determined not to die, and disguise the facts from themselves as long and as much as they can.

It was desirable to continue with the King's illness to the very gates of death despite all that had been happening elsewhere, for fear of losing the narrative by overlong digressions. On the other hand, what took place at his actual death should not be interrupted, and I shall therefore include here certain matters that have been left on one side for the sake of clarity. Let us now retrace our steps, and afterwards continue this day-to-day account, which I shall not again interrupt until the King's death.

I mentioned earlier that the Duc de Noailles made me yet another proposition which I flatly rejected. Now is the time to describe it. He proposed that, immediately after the King's death, all the dukes should go in a body to salute the successor, in the train of M. le Duc d'Orléans and the princes of the blood. He pressed the matter again and again without moving me in the slightest; and then urged the other dukes to work on me, taking advantage of the many small gatherings in our various homes, as the King's life drew to its close. Several of these meetings took place at my house, which, more often than not, was full of my close friends, eager to hear the latest news at this critical and heart-rending time. I soon learned, what is more, that the footmen and valets of every kind of person attached to the Court sat all day outside my door, taking note of the comings and goings, so as to discover what was happening, in so far as their situations allowed.

One evening, I went downstairs earlier than usual, to call on the Duc de Noailles. He was alone, and almost at once entered into a conflict with me in an attempt to dissuade me from the idea of summoning the States General. Interlarding his objections with many congratulations on my extraordinarily brilliant plan (which he well knew was designed to hinder him from using the finances for his own benefit), he produced every possible obstacle. So he rambled on for some time, saying nothing of any particular note, and then, suddenly, as if on an impulse, although, in fact, every word and glance was nicely calculated, he abruptly exclaimed, 'You refused the finances [M. le Duc d'Orléans must have told him that]; you preferred to have no direct responsibility? You were right. You mean to have a finger in every pie, and to stick to M. le Duc d'Orléans. In your solitary position, you could scarcely do better. But if we worked together, you and I could do with him what we chose. But the finances are not enough, we should need other departments as well; we cannot do with opposition.'

I heard this highly confidential revelation in utter amazement, and was sharpening my ears and brain to discover where it led, when he put me out of suspense. 'As for the States General,' he continued, 'you would never be quit of them. I myself enjoy such work—I freely admit it—and thus I have had an idea, and an excellent one, or so I believe. Let us first come to a clear understanding; then make me prime minister, and we will rule the country together.' 'Prime minister!' I exclaimed, with all the anger at my command, which I had been repressing with great difficulty. 'Prime minister, Sirrah! I would have you know that if a prime minister were needed, and if I desired that office, it would be given to me, for I do not suppose you could hope to be above me. Let me inform you, however, that so long as M. le Duc d'Orléans honours me by consulting me, neither I, nor you, nor any other man shall ever be prime minister, an office which I regard as a scourge and poison to any State, and a disgraceful curb on the authority of any king or regent, for, despite all appearances, such an office-holder would be his master.'[1] Whilst I added other facts to that simple, unvarnished truth, my eyes remained fixed upon my victim, over whose entire face there spread the blush of shame, a sign of total discomfiture. He none the less retained enough self-control to appear outwardly unruffled, even to the point of replying that he would not insist, but that it had seemed to him a good idea. Thereafter the conversation languished, and lapsed altogether as soon as we could with decency separate. Thus ended an interview that had become painful to us both. I leave you to imagine my thoughts; yet even I was far from realizing the whole truth, as you shall learn in due course. Meanwhile M. de Noailles called on me next morning, and behaved as though there had never been any mention of a prime minister. Three days then elapsed, which will bring us to the King's last moments; for he lived another three days after what I must now recount.

I have already said that when the King's condition was declared hopeless, the dukes had taken to meeting quietly in small groups, at each other's houses, in order to discuss their future actions in the affair of the bonnet, which would become of first importance when they assembled at the Parlement for the announcement of the Regency. At about six or seven o'clock, on the fourth evening, the Duc de Noailles entered my room, where there were already Mailly, Archbishop of Rheims, the Dukes of Sully, La Force, Charentais, with others whom I forget, and also the Duc d'Humières who, although not a peer, had for some time past been

---

[1] In Saint-Simon's plan, which, to his huge satisfaction, the Duc d'Orléans had accepted, there were six councils of ten members each, and each with a duke and peer as president. Saint-Simon, having nominated the Duc de Noailles for the key post, President of the Finance Council, as being incomparably the best and ablest of the peers, it is no wonder that he despaired. The experiment did not long endure; the aristocratic oligarchy of his dreams was not possible, for the nobles, so long confined in their gilded cage, at Versailles, had neither the experience nor the capabilities needed. He himself later realized that the Councils did nothing but quarrel and cause delay. His system was discarded and replaced by a plan on the lines of the old one under Louis XIV, with individual ministers responsible to the King for the departments of finance, foreign affairs, war, and commerce. There was never a prime minister; the government acted under the direct supervision of the Regent, and of Louis XV, when he came of age.

interested in the affair. The discussion continued in M. de Noailles's presence. He said little at first; then suddenly broke in with the proposal that we all go in a body to salute the new King—the very same project which he had suggested to me. I was the more astonished because, after teasing me unmercifully, he had not referred to it for the past fortnight, and I had thought him convinced by my objections. You must bear in mind that news of our meetings had leaked out some days earlier, and that they had become the topic of the day, everywhere.

M. de Noailles persisted in holding forth, interrupting me in loud, authoritative tones, stating that he had the support of the dukes who met at the Duc d'Harcourt's, and by sheer lung-power (far exceeding my own)[1] shouting me down to monopolize the discussion. I was so bursting with fury and indignation that I climbed on to the step of the window recess and sat down on the cupboard,[2] saying that I wished to hear him better, and then to speak when he had finished. I was so excited that the others tried to silence Noailles, who continued despite them, interrupting me again several times as I began. But at last I gained the upper hand by declaring that I must insist on being heard, and that we would not be treated like schoolboys. The other dukes wished to hear me, and thus he was forced to let me speak. I said that the Duc de Noailles's proposal was an unprecedented novelty, without a parallel in past history, even at the coronation of Louis XIV; that the first salutation was never made in a body, but individually, as each duke appeared, early or late, and that it thus differed from the homage, which was paid by all the nobles together, usually at the first *Lit de Justice*. Such an innovation, I continued, would be of no benefit to the dukes, for the lower nobility, egged on by the Duc and Duchesse du Maine, might easily take offence, averring that we wished to be a class apart. Indeed, I added, as they knew very well, such ambitions had already been imputed to us, with all the cunning and malice imaginable, and the best way to substantiate the rumour was to act as M. de Noailles proposed.

I spoke with more violence and at far greater length than space allows me to report here. Noailles shouted and blustered, swearing that all he had said was perfectly reasonable, and all my arguments futile. It was a stream of words that came from him, bellowed at the top of his voice, containing not a single argument, good or bad, intended to terrify the others into consenting, rather than convince them. I interrupted him, from time to time, but observing that the dispute was becoming personal, and that the rest were too much bewildered to utter a word, I merely restated my objections and my firm refusal to give my consent. When I had finished I was completely breathless. You will see in due

[1] Saint-Simon's voice was regrettably squeaky.

[2] In the great houses of those days, a low cupboard or chest was often placed on the step below the windows.

course that M. de Noailles never seriously contemplated acting on his proposal; that he had mentioned it to none of the other dukes, and that the entire scene was directed against me, and for a particular purpose. After he had gone, I once more explained my views to those who remained. They could not deny the truth of them; but for the sake of peace, and because they were exhausted by that long and stormy session, they also departed. I then found Mme de Saint-Simon and told her all.

The dukes who had been with me had no time to warn the other peers of what had happened, for by then the crazy notion of our all saluting the new King together was being spoken of as our serious intention. Coëtquen, Noailles's brother-in-law, and on excellent terms with him, although far otherwise with his sister,[1] rushed through the Château alerting the various lords, who behaved exactly as I had predicted, with the result that by the evening a vile and slanderous rumour was afloat which, spreading throughout the night to new arrivals and departures, had reached Paris by morning. The vast crowds, flocking to Versailles on account of the King's extremity, were much swollen by this rumour. The nobodies who came from curiosity, self-interest, or from fear for the future, made a point of aligning themselves with the men of quality (who perforce endured them), thus increasing the general excitement until a great outcry arose against dukes. Those noblemen, apart from the few who had been present in my room, had heard nothing of any salute to the new King. It was only by slow degrees and with considerable difficulty that they discovered what was amiss; and then, some from timidity, some from annoyance at not having been consulted, they all joined in the clamour against their fellow peers. Until that moment no names had been mentioned, but anger was rising, and anonymity was not long preserved.

First Saint-Hérem,[2] and after him several others, called to warn Mme de Saint-Simon that all the blame was being laid on me, as the prime mover and originator of the idea, and as having used my growing influence to persuade certain dukes against their better judgment to stand out against the rest. They said that feelings were running so high that I might be in personal danger, and strongly advised her to take precautions. All of this surprised Mme de Saint-Simon prodigiously because she knew what had happened with M. de Noailles; but what left her dumbfounded was to hear that Noailles himself was saying I had made the proposal, and that he had opposed it. This news Mme de Saint-Simon heard on the evening of the third day before the King's death; and she made them repeat again and again that they had it from the lips of the Duc de

---

[1] The Marquis de Coëtquen (1678-1727), had married Marie Charlotte de Noailles in 1696, and disliked her extremely. She died, aged sixty-two, in 1723.

[2] Louis Charles de Montmorin, Marquis de Saint-Hérem (1675-1722). He was the son of the lady who boiled her own leg while bathing in the Seine. See Vol. I, p. 163.

Noailles himself, and that he was spreading the lie everywhere through Coëtquen and other of his spies.

It so happened that on the following morning she encountered the Duc de Noailles in the great gallery, which at that time was always full of courtiers. She drew him apart into a window-recess, and asked him the reason for the scandal. He endeavoured to put her off, saying that it was nothing and would soon blow over; but she pressed him, letting him see that she already knew much, and finally declared her surprise at my being held responsible. This made Noailles look thoroughly uncomfortable. He said that was the first he had heard of it, to which Mme de Saint-Simon retorted that seeing what had taken place in my room, he should know better than anyone who had proposed and who opposed the project. That remark appeared to floor him, for he stammered out a kind of apology, but my wife obliged him to stay and hear some short, sharp observations on his ingratitude to me, and the filthy slander with which he had rewarded me. What effect, however, has a reprimand, no matter how severe, on a thorough-going villain when he is profiting from some well-laid plot? Although he promised Mme de Saint-Simon to tell everyone that I had opposed his scheme, he had no such intention, and he continued to spread the libel; the only difference being that he took care thenceforward to select his company, and whenever possible avoided us in the public rooms. It was not until that moment that the scales fell from my eyes. I recalled our conversation regarding the office of prime minister, and his delight at having the finances; I remembered how firmly he had opposed the summoning of the States General, and how, two days before that final outburst, I had failed to obtain the consent of M. le Duc d'Orléans who, until then, had talked of little else. I perceived, in short, that such an intrigue, so well contrived, so wholly false, so quickly set in motion at the crucial time, must be the work of his diabolical ambitions, bitter jealousy, and black ingratitude. Noailles had suddenly realized that he would have to consider me; but he wanted no opposition, for he was determined to govern alone, in other words to be the prime minister. Hence his mad proposal; he was digging a pit hoping that I should fall into it, and when I did not fall, he unhesitatingly pushed me in.

You may imagine my feelings; but the storm had come upon me so fiercely and suddenly that it was hard to retaliate, especially since he took good care to avoid me, and thought it unsafe to appear at the Château de Versailles. My best defence was the testimony of those dukes who had been present, and that of my friends among the lesser nobility, who repeated their assurances everywhere. I myself spoke with considerable violence, sparing neither facts nor words relative to the Duc de Noailles. I spoke also to M. le Duc d'Orléans, but he was so burdened with affairs of State that he could pay little attention to private business. Even there

M. de Noailles avoided me, for fear lest I insult him in the prince's presence, for he was learning from all sides of the intolerable things that I said of him. He armed himself with silence and a face of brass, and continued to press his attack among the dukes, who despite all the evidence to the contrary were still not convinced of my innocence. He had seen to it that their views and emotions coincided with his interests.

He and M. du Maine so worked on people's credulity that I had no chance of persuading them to listen to reason; but in the end Providence cheated them of their highest hopes. I came and went about my business as usual; no one said anything to make me angry, nor anything unfriendly, for that matter. The worst disposed bowed formally as they passed, and thus I was not obliged to retreat, defend myself, or challenge them. I still fail to comprehend how this came about, with such vast numbers of furious and excitable people, and all the supporters of the Duc de Noailles, who must often have heard me speak of him in the most slanderous and intemperate manner. I shall continue with this narrative until the affair is concluded, so as to be done with it once and for all. It will serve also to shed light on many things that occurred during the Regency and after.

Noailles suffered the torments of the damned, but despite the insults which I forced him to endure he was not deterred. He never failed to greet me with a very low bow, when we met at the Regent's apartment, or on entering and leaving the Regency Council; whereas I invariably walked straight on, never bowing to him, and sometimes insulting him by turning my face in the opposite direction. What is more, I let fly at him on every possible occasion, in such a tone, and with such words that the bystanders were positively alarmed. He, however, never replied, merely turned pale, or else blushed, not daring, or so it appeared, to risk a renewed attack. None the less, I did not allow State business to suffer in any way; on that I was firmness itself. I supported him when I thought his advice good; but other than that, my behaviour to him was arrogant and insulting. He sometimes quitted the Palais Royal or the Tuileries in such a state of indignation that he was obliged to return home and fling himself on his bed, exclaiming that he could not stand such treatment. One day, at the Council, I forced him to quash a measure which I knew he greatly favoured, and left him flayed after a merciless attack. I followed this up by dictating the repeal, and reading it aloud to the entire assembly; thus plainly showing my contempt and suspicion of him. That was too much. He rose and hurled his *tabouret* ten paces from him—he who at the table had dared say nothing except regarding the measure itself, and only with the deepest respect. Then, exclaiming, 'S'death! This is beyond endurance,' as he turned to go, he went home (whence his lamentations were reported to me) and contracted a fever.

Not long after, he made several vain attempts to pacify me, having lost hope of securing the desired result. He next tried praise; but there rarely passed a week in which he did not suffer from me some public insult, such haughtiness as I passed that everyone stared at him, or some caustic personal remark. He then took to saying that he could not imagine what had vexed me; that there must be a misunderstanding; that he would do everything to win back my regard. They assailed me by every possible channel, both direct and indirect. His mother,[1] whom I had good cause to like, was sent to intercede for him. Mme de Saint-Simon was appealed to on religious grounds, my dearest friends were implored to intervene. I invariably replied that one might be duped once, but not twice by the same individual. The facts were clear; there was no denying the black treachery, thought out with malice, and carefully planned. Why should people imagine that its victim was a fool and without sensibility, or believe that he might be persuaded to forget such perfidy—a slander of such magnitude? The criminal responsible would continue for ever to be the object of my public and implacable hate—let him be sure of that.

I behaved towards him precisely on that basis, and he to me with the utmost servility. What most vexed him, amid all his later prosperity, was that although he remained unreconciled to me, my friendship with his uncle did not suffer in the slightest and was generally known. Indeed, I became more than ever active on behalf of Cardinal de Noailles, who was constantly at my house, and I at his, on terms of mutual confidence, and I openly served his interests to the best of my abilities. That contrast spoke ill for the Duc de Noailles, and at last he was driven to beg my pardon in the proper terms, through the intermediary of M. le Duc d'Orléans, whom I answered in a way that made him careful not to involve himself again. M. de Noailles was prostrated by my rejection. He let me hear such things of him as I scarcely dare to repeat; for, although true, they are almost unbelievable. It was said, for example, that could I but see the state to which I had reduced him, I should be obliged to pity him, and many other such despicable statements. Cardinal de Noailles often tried to change me, and spoke to me twice, saying that the quarrel was making him very miserable. On both occasions I gave him the same answer, namely that if he so desired, I would give him an exact account of the cause, that he should be prepared for terrible revelations, but that thereafter I should desire no other judge. That silenced him, and he never mentioned the subject again. I am sure that he already knew enough not to wish to hear more, and that he ceased on that account; but our quarrel did truly grieve him, for he was fond of his graceless nephew, who was ungrateful to him also, as will in due course appear. For twelve years we continued in that way without the least sign of softening on my part, and without my relations with the rest of his family

---

[1] The Duc de Noailles's mother was the Maréchale-Duchesse de Noailles (1654-1748). See Vol. I, pp. 207, 227, 359.

in any way suffering. The private prosecution of a crime is indeed a dreadful thing, and this has been a very long digression, but you must hear the end.

This occurred long after I had resigned from the Regency Council. My influence had ceased after the death of M. le Duc d'Orléans; I no longer held any offices, and was living in almost complete retirement. M. de Noailles, by contrast, with his governorships, and his post of senior captain of the King's bodyguard, was head of the most powerful family in France, most of whose members held offices of one kind or another. Yet despite the vast difference in our worldly situations, neither he nor his relations could bear that we should be on such bad terms. The reconciliation came about in this fashion. The Duc de Guiche, who was made a Maréchal de France in 1724, and thereafter called the Maréchal de Gramont, had living two daughters. The elder was married to Biron's eldest son, and the younger[1] to the Prince de Bournonville, son of a first cousin of the Maréchale de Noailles and of a sister of the Duc de Chevreuse, both now deceased. The Bournonville marriage had taken place towards the end of March 1719, notwithstanding that the bridegroom's nerves were already so sadly afflicted that he could hardly stand. He very shortly afterwards became impotent, then completely crippled. He had for a long time past been expected to die young. The mother of the bride was the eldest of the Duc de Noailles's sisters, all of whom regarded her with respect. They all took a fancy to gain my elder son for her daughter the moment she was free, in order to effect a reconciliation. The girl was a beauty, well-made,[2] had never come out from under her mother's wing, and, regarding wealth, was the greatest heiress in France at that time, among the nobility. They dared not make any move in my direction; but they thought that Mme de Saint-Simon might prove more approachable. They were not mistaken. She dropped me a few vague hints from time to time with little success, but did not lose hope. At last she came out into the open with the worldly temptations of riches and a great alliance, and pious arguments about an honourable way of ending the continuing scandal of a public quarrel. None the less, a year passed before I could overcome my disgust at the thought of a reconciliation. But, to be brief, when I eventually did give my consent, all was most swiftly accomplished.

Chauvelin, a président-à-mortier and later keeper of the seals, who had been courting me for some time past, acted as the Maréchale de Gramont's ambassador. As soon as he learned of my surrender, for until then he had not dared to speak, he declared that although the Maréchale could do nothing while her

---

[1] Catherine Charlotte Thérèse de Gramont (1707-1755) married Philippe Alexandre, Prince de Bournonville in 1719. He died, aged twenty-eight, on 5 January, 1727, and two months later she married Saint-Simon's son, Jacques Louis, Duc de Ruffec.

[2] The poor Saint-Simons naturally set great store by the shapeliness of their daughter-in-law elect. With their two sons, the 'basset-hounds', and their poor sickly daughter Charlotte, 'twisted like a vine', they must have felt most anxious about grandchildren.

son-in-law still lived, he himself would make all the arrangements; and, indeed, he and Mme de Saint-Simon had already done all, in the conviction that there would soon be no obstacle. During the short interval that ensued, Cardinal de Noailles never ceased to talk of the match, and the Maréchale and her daughters did everything to make themselves agreeable to our friends and relatives. Their prime object was a reconciliation between the Duc de Noailles and myself. I laid it down firmly that there was to be no more discussion, and that at no time should more be asked of me than ordinary politeness. No one disputed with me over that.

It so happened that one afternoon, when I was calling at the Hôtel de Lauzun, I found Mme de Bournonville there, playing ombre, chaperoned by Mme de Beaumanoir,[1] who lived with the Maréchale de Gramont, her sister. Soon afterwards, Mme de Beaumanoir was asked for; she left the room and immediately returned, whispering something to Mme de Lauzun, and looking at me meanwhile with a very broad smile. She told her niece to ask permission to leave the game, adding in a low voice that she must go at once to her husband, who lived with his sister Mme de Duras, for he had been taken very ill. This kind of thing used often to happen, and with illnesses of that sort one expects a false alarm, for they seem never-ending.

That same evening I chanced to go to the archbishop's palace, and met both the Maréchale de Gramont and Mme de Beaumanoir, who had taken and desposited her niece, but was speaking of M. de Bournonville as though she expected him to live a long time yet. Cardinal de Noailles and she, after expressing certain Christian sentiments, allowed their impatience to be seen, and gave me a knowing look. The Maréchale looked at me also, smiled, as they did, simpered a little, and then rising, laughed out loud. Addressing herself to me, she announced that they had best be taking their leave. The good cardinal was later overcome by emotion. That night, Chauvelin sent to say that the illness was growing worse, and next morning, when I was at home with company, they called me out with a message to say that M. de Bournonville was dead. I sent at once for Mme de Saint-Simon, who was at mass nearby with the Dominicans.[2] She instantly returned, found me still with my guests, and I told her before them all what had taken place.

We had already agreed that when the event occurred we would go immediately and make the offer to the cardinal, who would then take charge of all the rest. Mme de Saint-Simon accordingly started at once. She found him having his supper, before taking Vespers, at Notre Dame. He left the table and came to meet her with arms outspread and a beaming smile; then, before all his people, giving her no time to speak, he cried, 'Quick, harness my horses!' Turning again to her,

---

[1] Marie Françoise de Noailles, widowed in 1703, had married the Marquis de Beaumanoir.
[2] The Dominican monastery was at that time in the Rue Saint-Dominique.

he said, 'I can see what brings you. God's will be done! We are free. I shall go at once to the Maréchale de Gramont, and you shall hear from me very soon.' He led her for a moment into his private room; but as he was accompanying her to the door, his people reminded him of Vespers. 'Hurry, fetch my coach!' he said once more, 'Vespers must wait tonight, hurry! hurry!' Mme de Saint-Simon came home and we sat down to supper. Just as we were finishing, we heard a coach in the courtyard; it was the cardinal. I went down to greet him, and he embraced me repeatedly, exclaiming before all our servants. 'Where is my nephew? I must see my new nephew, send for him at once!' Much astonished, I explained that he was at Marly. 'Well, send for him then! I long to embrace him; he must go straight to see the Maréchale de Gramont and his intended.' I could not get over my surprise at his frankness, or his allowing the servants, both his and ours who had flocked to greet him, thus to know everything.

By that time we were beginning to go upstairs, but Mme de Saint-Simon, on her way down, made me turn again and take the cardinal into my study, so as to spare him the climb.[1] Never have I seen a man more delighted. He told us that the Maréchale and her daughter were in raptures; that all was in train, and that he had wished to have the pleasure of telling us himself, and of calling the news out loud, as he had just done. In view of the number of eligible bachelors, all eagerly waiting for that moment to come in order to propose, he had considered it wiser to speak out, so as to stop their mouths, and squash any idea that it would be possible to break the engagement in favour of someone else. He added that he had rather be thought senile than let that happen. Then, with many tokens of affection, he went off to Vespers.

We had already made arrangements for Mme de Saint-Simon to go to the Bon-Pasteur[2] on that day, and to meet the Maréchale de Gramont there, in her tribune. My son returned later in the evening. Next day, we were dining at home with guests, when the entire Gramont family and many of the Noailles called on us, but without the young lady, her mother, or her grandmother. They could not have made themselves more conspicuous, and the Maréchale herself visited us that same evening. My son called on them, in return, and I afterwards took him to the cardinal. He then returned to Marly, in order to obtain the King's consent,[3] and to give the news to such of our kindred and friends as happened to be there, in advance of the public announcement. Meeting the Duc de Chaulnes in one of the smaller drawing-rooms, just after he arrived, he whispered the event into his ear. 'Impossible!' said Chaulnes, refusing to believe it, despite my son's telling him that he had seen Cardinal de Noailles, the Maréchale de Gramont, etc. This was

---

[1] Saint-Simon's study was behind the room on the ground floor of his apartment.
[2] A house for fallen women in the Rue du Cherche-midi.
[3] All this took place on 6 January, 1727; the King referred to was Louis XV.

because he had been certain of the match for his own son, through the agency of Mme de Mortemart, the Maréchale's old and dear friend. She had, however, been given hope, but no definite promise, on the pretext that nothing could be done while M. de Bournonville lived. Chauvelin had every document ready to be signed and witnessed in the space of three or four days. The Duchesse de Duras strongly approved of our not waiting, and wished to have the marriage celebrated at once; but all whom we consulted strongly advised three or four months' delay, for fear of a pregnancy,[1] even though M. de Bournonville had been always quite incapable of lying with his wife, and for the past two or three years had not even lived with her.

Until then everything had gone well. Never was there so much rejoicing and eagerness, a particular mark of which had been the visit already mentioned; for it is usually the bridegroom's family who pay the first call. After that, however, the hour came for the reconciliation. Président Chauvelin, on behalf of the Duc de Noailles, paid me the most handsome compliments imaginable, and begged me, for the sake of Cardinal and the Maréchale de Noailles, to allow M. de Noailles to visit me. I feared that any such encounter would be too long for my taste, and I therefore refused; and I insisted so strongly on his meeting me at the archbishop's house, that they dared not gainsay me. I remained silent after that, not mentioning whether I wished anyone or no one to be present, and again they did not say a word. On the day appointed, the Duc de Noailles came to Paris. Mme de Saint-Simon and I were dining with Asfeld (later a Maréchal de France), our next-door neighbour, in company with the Maréchal and Mme de Berwick, and some of our intimate friends. I was in a monstrously bad temper; I kept them at table as long as I could, and when we finally rose, they had to make several attempts before they could drive me out. They well knew that the interview would be no lovers' meeting, but they exhorted me to do the thing well, and with a good grace. I then went home, to draw breath and start afresh, as they say, while Mme de Saint-Simon went on before me, and they harnessed my horses. At length I, too, set out, and arrived at the archbishop's palace like a man on the way to the scaffold.

The Maréchale de Gramont, Mme de Beaumanoir, Mme de Saint-Simon, and Mme de Lauzun were in the drawing-room. Cardinal de Noailles, as soon as he perceived me, advanced towards me holding the Duc de Noailles by the hand. 'Sir!' said he. 'Allow me to present my nephew; I pray you, be so good as to embrace him.' I stood stiff and cold, eyeing the Duc de Noailles for a moment, and then said dryly, 'Sir! At the cardinal's request', and I moved forward one pace. Thereupon the Duc de Noailles flung himself upon me, encircling me with both

---

[1] They did not wait so long, however, for the marriage took place only two months after M. de Bournonville's death. The families may have been less heartless than it appears, since marriages were not made for love, nor was love expected to come from them.

arms far below the level of my chest, and in that position kissed me warmly on both cheeks.[1] Once that was accomplished I greeted the cardinal, who embraced me also, as did his two nieces,[2] and I sat down beside them, close to Mme de Saint-Simon. I was by that time trembling from head to foot, and the little that I added to the disjointed conversation was quite incoherent. The talk was confined to the wedding, the delight of the family, and other trifling matters. The Duc de Noailles appeared excessively embarrassed. He more than once addressed me with a respectful, somewhat sheepish air, and I answered him shortly, but civilly enough. After a quarter of an hour I rose, saying that we must not waste the time of M. le Cardinal. The Duc de Noailles wished to accompany me but the ladies said that he must not pester or try to persuade me; and thus I escaped. I returned home, my brain reeling, my head as thick as a drunkard's, and, indeed, very shortly afterwards I was actually sick. Such was the agitation wrought by the violence done to my feelings that I was within an ace of having myself bled. The truth is that I had been under a very great strain; but I thought myself well rid of him for some time to come.

Not at all! He called on me the very next morning and found me at home. We were alone; it was towards the end of the morning. The talk was still only of the wedding and of some trifling matters. He held the floor unchallenged for as long as he desired, and seemed less constrained, more his old self. As for me, I was very much the reverse, finding it extremely hard to endure a conversation that lasted half an hour and appeared to me unending. Our deportment was the same as it had been at the cardinal's. Next day I called on the Maréchale de Noailles, who seemed enchanted; and I inquired for her son, but fortunately he was not at home. Ever since then he has made constant efforts to come to terms with me, and I have striven to avoid him. We have seen each other on formal occasions at his house, rarely elsewhere—which means to say scarcely ever. To my house he came whenever he could, or, not to mince words, as often as he dared. He attended the wedding. It was the last ceremony at which Cardinal de Noailles officiated. The couple were married in his great chapel, and he provided a most sumptuous and delicious banquet. I gave one on the following day, to which the Duc de Noailles was invited and came.

Many years later when we were living at La Ferté, my daughter-in-law informed me that M. de Noailles pined to visit us, and after some beating about the bush said that he was preparing to start out. I was extremely cold to her, and answered almost nothing. When she left me, however, I called to my son, who had heard the beginning of the conversation, and bade him tell his wife that for

---

[1] Saint-Simon was minute, despite the highest red heels at the Court. Noailles was a reasonable height. It must have looked extraordinary, as though he were picking up a furious child.

[2] Mmes de Gramont and de Beaumanoir, Noailles's sisters.

her sake I had not expressed my true feelings; but that although she might treat her uncle as she pleased, I would never receive him at La Ferté, even if she had to tell him so herself. I was determined not to let him make the journey a pretext for renewing our friendship, still less expose myself to tête-à-tête conversations with him on morning walks; for he would certainly spread reports of discussions that had never taken place, if that should suit his interests. That was why, whenever he did find me at my house, I took good care as soon as he was announced to beg the company to stay until after his departure. At last he tired of repeated failures. My firm adherence to bare politeness had delivered me, and obliged him to accept my terms. God bids us forgive, but not surrender our self-respect, or humble ourselves after such bitter experiences. The world has since recognized him for what he is; for it has observed his conduct at the Court, in council, and at the head of armies.

Let us now return to the point at which we digressed, that is to say Thursday, 22 August, 1715, a date made memorable by the review of the *gendarmerie* by the Duc du Maine, representing the King, and with all the authority of the sovereign who, meanwhile, was choosing a new coat, against the time when he would again be able to wear clothes.

The night of Friday, 23 August, was much as usual, and the morning also. The King worked with Père Tellier, who made vain efforts to obtain nominations for the many rich benefices lying vacant. In other words, he wished to dispose of them himself, and not leave their distribution to M. le Duc d'Orléans. Let me say here and now that the worse the King grew, the more insistent Père Tellier became, for he loathed losing such spoils, and the opportunity to gain loyal supporters who, having no money to offer him, would assist him in intrigues. He did not succeed, however. The King stated firmly that he had already enough to account for to God without adding those nominations, and he refused to hear more of them. He dined standing in his dressing-gown and saw the courtiers; he did the same for supper, and went afterwards to his bedroom with the two bastards, Mme de Maintenon, and the ladies of their circle. The evening was the same as usual. It was on that same day that he heard the news of the death of Maisons, to whose son, at the Duc du Maine's request, he gave his father's offices.

Before proceeding further, I had best explain the arrangements in the King's apartments, now that he no longer went out. The entire Court spent all day in the *Galerie des Glaces*. No one waited in the ante-chamber[1] nearest his bedroom, except his personal valets, and the dispensers who heated there whatever was needed. The rest passed quickly through, from one door to another. Those with the entrée went to the studies by the mirror-door leading into the gallery, which was always shut unless someone scratched on it, when it was opened and closed again immediately.

[1] The *Salon de l'Œil de Bœuf.*

Ministers and Secretaries of State entered also by that door, and stood grouped in the room[1] adjoining the gallery. No one, not even the princes of the blood or the Princesses, was allowed farther unless the King especially asked for them, which he never did. The Maréchal de Villeroy, the Chancellor, the two bastards, M. le Duc d'Orléans, Père Tellier, the Curé of Versailles,[2] Maréchal, Fagon, and the head-valets (when not required in the bedroom) waited in the Council-chamber between the King's bedroom and the other room, where the princes and princesses of the blood, the entrées, and the ministers were all assembled.

The Duc de Tresmes, on duty as first gentleman, stood at the open door between these two rooms, and entered the King's bedroom only when it was absolutely necessary for his service. During the day, no one entered the King's room, except by the Council-chamber, save only the personal valets and the dispensers (who waited in the first ante-room), Mme de Maintenon and the intimate ladies, and, during his dinner and supper, such of the household officers and courtiers as he permitted. M. le Duc d'Orléans carefully restricted his entrances to one or, at the most, two a day, going in for a moment only with the Duc de Tresmes, and at other times showing himself at the door leading into the Council-chamber, so that the King might see him from his bed. The King sometimes asked for the Chancellor, the Maréchal de Villeroy, or Père Tellier, rarely for any of the ministers, often for M. du Maine, seldom for the Comte de Toulouse; but for no one else at all, not even for Cardinal de Rohan or Cardinal de Bissy, who were often waiting in the same room as the other entrées. Occasionally, when he was alone with Mme de Maintenon, he asked for the Maréchal de Villeroy or the Chancellor or both, and very often for the Duc du Maine. Neither Madame nor Mme la Duchesse de Berry ever waited in the studies; they had scarcely seen the King in his last illness, but when they did so, they came and left at once by the antechambers.

The night of Saturday the 24th was only a little worse than usual, for all had been bad; but his leg was considerably worse, and gave him more pain. Mass was as usual; dinner in his bed, where the chief courtiers without the entrée were able to see him; the finance Council followed; he then worked with the Chancellor alone, and Mme de Maintenon and the ladies of his circle joined him afterwards. He supped standing in his dressing-gown in the presence of the courtiers, for the last time. I noticed that he swallowed only liquids, and that it distressed him to be looked at. He could not finish, and asked the courtiers to move along, that is to say, to leave him. He made them put him back into bed, and they examined his leg, on which black spots had begun to appear. He sent for Père Tellier, and confessed. Panic set in among the doctors. They had been trying milk, and quinine with

[1] The *Cabinet des Termes*.
[2] The Curé of Versailles was Claude Huchon.

water; now both were cancelled and no one knew what to try next. They admitted that they had thought him suffering from a slow fever since Pentecost, and excused themselves for doing nothing about it on the pretext that he had refused remedies, and that they themselves had not believed him to be very ill. You will know what I think, from my description of all that had happened between Mme de Maintenon and Maréchal even befoie that time.

Sunday, 25 August, was the feast of Saint Louis; the night was far worse. They made no mystery now of the danger, and suddenly it was seen to be serious and imminent. None the less, he expressly ordered that nothing should be changed in the ordinary routine for that day; that is to say, the drum and fife band stationed beneath his windows struck up as usual as soon as he woke, and the four-and-twenty fiddlers played as usual in the ante-room during his dinner.[1] He was then left alone with Mme de Maintenon, the Chancellor, and, for a short while, the Duc du Maine. He had sent for pens and ink on the previous evening when he was working with the Chancellor; he had them brought again that day when Mme de Maintenon was with him; and it was on one of those two days that he dictated to the Chancellor a codicil to his will. Mme de Maintenon and M. du Maine, who constantly thought of their own advantage, decided that the King had not done enough for him in the will. They desired to remedy matters by a codicil that plainly evidenced both their shameful abuse of the King's extremity and the lengths to which ambition can lead a man. By this codicil, the King handed over to the Duc du Maine his entire household, both civil and military, immediately and without reserve, with the Maréchal de Villeroy to act as his deputy, thereby making them sole governors of the person and residence of the King; of Paris, on account of the guards regiments and the two companies of musketeers stationed there; of all the guards both indoor and outdoor, and of the whole household staff, bedchamber, wardrobe, chapels, kitchen, and stables. Thus the Regent was left without authority—not so much as the faintest shadow of power, and entirely at their mercy, in continual danger of arrest, or worse, at any time that the Duc du Maine so pleased.[2]

Soon after the Chancellor quitted the King, Mme de Maintenon, who had remained, sent for the ladies of his circle, and the orchestra arrived at seven in the evening. Yet the King fell asleep while the ladies conversed. He woke up in confusion, which caused them some alarm, and made them send for the doctors. They found his pulse so weak that they did not hesitate to recommend the King, whose senses had returned, to delay no longer in receiving the Sacraments. They

---

[1] Louis XIV is supposed to have said, 'I have lived among the people of my Court; I should like to die with them. They have been with me all my life; it is only right that they should witness my end.'

[2] In actual fact, the Duc du Maine's powers were set out in the will, not in the codicil. At that anxious and critical time, the King may have been influenced by suspicions of the Duc d'Orléans, and suddenly not dared to leave him with all the power.

then sent for Père Tellier, and informed Cardinal de Rohan, who was at his home with company, his thoughts quite otherwise employed, and in the meanwhile they sent away the musicians, who had set out their books and instruments; the ladies also left. It so happened that I was at that precise moment walking through the gallery and the ante-rooms, on the way from my apartment in the new wing to Mme la Duchesse d'Orléans's rooms on the other side, and then on to see M. le Duc d'Orléans. I even observed some of the orchestra, and thought that the rest had entered. Just as I passed the entrance of the guard-room, Pernoist, the usher in the ante-chamber, came up to me and asked if I knew what had occurred, and told me all. I found Mme la Duchesse d'Orléans in bed with the remnants of a migraine, surrounded by ladies who were conversing and who knew nothing. I went up to the bed and told Mme la Duchesse d'Orléans what had happened; but she refused to believe me, saying that the concert was in progress and the King no worse; then, as I had been whispering, she asked the ladies out loud if they had heard anything. Not one of them knew anything, and Mme la Duchesse d'Orléans was reassured. I repeated that I was quite certain, and that I thought it might be advisable to send to inquire, and in the meantime for her to dress. She believed me then, and I went to M. le Duc d'Orléans and warned him also; but he rightly thought it best to remain in his own room for the time being, since he had not been summoned.

In the quarter of an hour that had elapsed since the dismissal of the musicians and the ladies, everything had been accomplished. Père Tellier had confessed the King, whilst Cardinal de Rohan went to fetch the viaticum, and sent for the curé and the Holy Oils. Two of the King's almoners, summoned by the cardinal, had come in haste, together with seven or eight blue footmen, carrying torches, two of Fagon's lackeys, and a servant of Mme de Maintenon. This very small escort went up to the King's bedroom by the narrow staircase in his studies, and the cardinal also passed them, on his way to the King. Père Tellier, Mme de Maintenon, and a dozen of the entrées, masters and valets, preceded or followed the Holy Sacraments. The Cardinal spoke briefly of this great, final act, during which the King appeared perfectly collected, but deeply moved. When he had received Our Lord and the Holy Oils, all those who were in his room left, either preceding or behind the Host. Only Mme de Maintenon and the Chancellor remained. Then immediately, and that word immediately appears rather dreadful in the circumstances, they placed on his bed a kind of book or small table. The Chancellor presented the codicil, at the end of which the King wrote four or five lines in his own hand, afterwards returning it to the Chancellor. The King asked to drink; then called for the Maréchal de Villeroy who, with a very few of the notables, was at the door opening into the Council-chamber, and talked with him alone for nigh on a quarter of an hour. He sent also for M. le Duc d'Orléans, with whom he talked alone for a somewhat longer period. He expressed his esteem, affection, and confidence; but, and this was terrible with Jesus Christ upon his lips, assured him that nothing in his will was calculated to displease him; and recommended to his care the State, and the person of the future King. Not half an hour had passed since he had received Extreme Unction. He cannot already have forgotten those vile provisions, extracted from him with so much suffering; and, what is more, during that short interval he had added words to a new codicil that held a knife to M. le Duc d'Orléans's throat, and presented the handle to the Duc du Maine. The strange thing is that the rumour after that interview, the first that the King had given to M. le Duc d'Orléans, was to the effect that he had just been appointed Regent.

As soon as he was gone, the Duc du Maine, who had been waiting in the study, was sent for. The King spoke with him for longer than a quarter of an hour, and then asked for the Comte de Toulouse, who spent a further quarter of an hour alone with the King and M. du Maine. Only very few of the most necessary valets remained in the bedroom with Mme de Maintenon. She had not approached while the King was speaking to M. le Duc d'Orléans. All this time, the King's three bastard daughters, two of Mme la Duchesse's sons,[1] and the Prince de Conti had been arriving in the study. When the King was finished with the Duc du Maine and the Comte de Toulouse, he called for the princes of the blood, whom he had noticed standing in the study-doorway, and spoke a few words to them altogether, but nothing private nor in a whisper. The doctors came to dress his leg; the princes withdrew; only those persons who were absolutely essential remained, and Mme de Maintenon. While all this was happening, the Chancellor took M. le Duc d'Orléans aside in the Council-chamber, and showed him the codicil. After the dressing, the King was told that the Princesses were in the Council-chamber; he called for them, said a couple of words to them out loud, and made their tears an excuse to beg them to leave him, as he wished to rest. They left with those few who had entered; the bed-curtains were drawn, and Mme de Maintenon went into the outer studies.

The day and the night of Monday, 26 August, were no better. His leg was dressed, and he heard mass. Only those who were indispensable remained in his room, and they left after mass. The King made Cardinals de Rohan and Bissy stay with him. Mme de Maintenon remained, as she invariably did, and with her were the Maréchal de Villeroy, Père Tellier, and the Chancellor. The King addressed the two cardinals, protesting that he died in the Faith and submissive to the Church. Then, looking them in the eyes, he said that it grieved him to leave

[1] The Duc de Bourbon and the Comte de Charolais.

the Church's affairs in such a sorry state;[1] that he was perfectly ignorant in such matters; that they well knew, and he called them to witness, that he had done nothing except what they had advised, and that therefore it was they, not he, who would have to account to God for all that had been done, whether too much or too little. He once more protested that he held them responsible before God, and that his own conscience was clear; for, being so ignorant, he had trusted them entirely throughout the whole course of the affair. What a thunderbolt! But the two cardinals were not of the kind to be appalled; their hides were too thick for that. They only soothed and praised, while the King continued to repeat that, being so ignorant, he believed that he could do no better than trust them implicitly to act for the best, and that having done so, he had, in God's eyes, laid all the burden upon them. He added that, regarding Cardinal de Noailles, as God was his witness, he had never hated him, and had always been deeply distressed at having, so he thought, been obliged to act against him.

At the last words, Blouin, Fagon (servile courtier though he was) and Maréchal, who was in full view and rather close to the King, gazed at one another, inquiring in low tones whether the King could be allowed to die without seeing his archbishop, in token of reconciliation and forgiveness, for not to do so would inevitably provoke a scandal. The King, overhearing, answered at once that not only did he feel no aversion to seeing him, but positively wished to do so. Those words disconcerted the two cardinals far more than the charge which the King had laid on them before God. Mme de Maintenon was alarmed; Père Tellier trembled. A revival of the King's former trust, a generous and sincere impulse on the part of the archbishop—the very thought terrified them. They dreaded those moments when awe and respect are forgotten in the face of graver issues. Silence fell on them in that awful predicament. It was broken when the King ordered the Chancellor to send immediately for Cardinal de Noailles, provided that those gentlemen (looking at Cardinals de Rohan and Bissy) saw no objection. They looked at one another, and then went over to the window, with Père Tellier, the Chancellor, and Mme de Maintenon following them. Tellier expostulated in an undertone, and de Bissy supported him; Mme de Maintenon thought the whole thing most dangerous; Rohan, gentler and more far-sighted, said nothing, and neither did the Chancellor say a word. They finally decided to end their audience as they had begun and conducted it until that moment, by deceiving the King and mocking him. They once more approached him, and made him understand, with fulsome flattery, that he should not allow his enemies to triumph over righteousness, for they would certainly take advantage of a gesture that sprang from

[1] The bitter quarrel over the constitution, which Cardinal de Noailles, Archbishop of Paris, had at last accepted subject to many subtle changes and reservations. His obstinate refusal to accept it as it stood had led Louis XIV to forbid him to appear at the Court.

the King's kind nature, and excessively tender conscience. They said that they certainly approved of Cardinal de Noailles's having the honour of seeing him, but only on condition of his accepting the constitution, and giving a promise to that effect. The King obeyed them in this also, and the Chancellor at once wrote to Cardinal de Noailles on those lines.[1]

As soon as the King had signified his agreement, the cardinals fell to praising him for the great work he would accomplish by winning Cardinal de Noailles back to the fold, or making him proclaim, by a refusal, his stubborn determination to trouble the Church, and his black ingratitude to a King to whom he owed all, and who held out to him his dying arms. Cardinal de Noailles preferred the second alternative; but he was grief-stricken by this crowning act of duplicity. He might have been right or wrong in the affair of the constitution; but the King's immi-nent death had no bearing on the truth of it, or otherwise, and, consequently, he could not change his views. The circumstances were deeply afflicting, but the alternative was horrible, and so, too, was the trap which had been laid, taking advantage of the King's extremity, to muzzle or slander Cardinal de Noailles. This terrible deed turned public opinion against them, all the more violently because the King's condition freed men from the fear which for so long had kept them dumb. Indeed, when all the circumstances became known, everyone was indignant, but no one blamed the cardinal, whose brief reply to the Chancellor had been a model of piety, sorrow, and wisdom.

That same Monday after the two cardinals had left, the King dined in his bed in the presence of those who had the entrée. He made them gather round him when the meal was being removed, and uttered these words, which were recorded at that very time. 'Gentlemen, I ask your pardon for having set you a bad example. I have much to thank you for in the manner in which you have served me, and for your constant devotion and faithfulness. It saddens me to think that I have not done for you all that I could have wished. The bad times were the cause. I pray you, show my great-grandson the same devotion and fidelity that you have shown to me. He is a child who may have many troubles to bear. Set an example for all my other subjects. Obey the orders which my nephew will give you; he will rule the kingdom; I hope he will rule well. I hope also that you will all remain united, and that if one should stray, the rest will help to bring him back. I feel moved to tears, and I think that I am moving you, too. I beg your pardon. Gentlemen, farewell; I trust that you will sometimes think of me.'

[1] Mlle d'Aumale, Mme de Maintenon's secretary, gives a somewhat different account: 'As I had been present almost the entire time, in the King's room with Mme de Maintenon, the Maréchal de Noailles [father of the Duc de Noailles] asked me to say something to the King of his brother the Cardinal, and try to persuade him to see him. I did so speak, asking him if he had anything against M. le Cardinal de Noailles. "No," he replied, "I have nothing against him personally, and if he comes now, I will gladly embrace him provided he submits to the Pope; for I wish to die as I have lived, catholic, apostolic, and roman." I carried that message to M. le Cardinal, who said, "In that case, I am sorry that you spoke to him." There was no more said about it, and the King never saw him.'

Soon after the rest had gone, the King asked for the Maréchal de Villeroy, and said these same words, which he noted well, and has since recorded: 'M. le Maréchal, in dying, I offer you one further proof of my affection and confidence. I appoint you Governor of the Dauphin, the most important office that I have to give. In due course, you will learn from my will how you must act regarding M. du Maine. I do not doubt that after my death you will serve me as faithfully as in my lifetime. I hope that my nephew will treat you with the respect and confidence due to one whom I have always loved. Farewell, Monsieur le Maréchal; I hope you will remember me.'

After an interval had elapsed, the King called for Monsieur le Duc and M. le Prince de Conti, who were in the study, and not letting them come too close, he reminded them of the unity desirable among the princes, urging them not to follow the tradition of trouble and strife in their families.[1] That was all he said. Then, hearing the voices of women in the studies, he recognized them and bade them enter. They were Mme la Duchesse de Berry, Madame, Mme la Duchesse d'Orléans, and the princesses of the blood, all sobbing, and he told them that they must not weep like that. He spoke to them briefly, but affectionately, paid particular respect to Madame, and concluded by exhorting Mme la Duchesse d'Orléans and Madame la Duchesse to make up their quarrel. It was all quickly over, and he dismissed them. They withdrew through the studies, weeping and sobbing so loud that people heard them from outside the open windows and spread the news to Paris and far beyond, that the King was already dead.

Later on, he sent orders to the Duchesse de Ventadour, telling her to bring the Dauphin. He called the child to him, and said these words, in the presence of Mme de Maintenon and a few of the more intimate of his friends and valets, who wrote them down: 'My child, you will soon be a great king. Do not imitate me in my love of building, or my liking for war; try to live at peace with your neighbours. Render to God that which you owe Him; remember your duty to Him; see that your subjects fear Him. Always follow good counsel; try to lighten your people's burdens, as I, alas! could never do. Never forget your debt of gratitude to Mme de Ventadour.'[2] 'Madame,' said he, turning to her, 'let me embrace him', and, so doing, he added, 'Dear child, I bless you right gladly.' As they lifted the little prince off the bed, the King asked for him again, and again embraced him, raising his eyes and hands to heaven. It was indeed a touching sight. Mme de Ventadour then swiftly removed the Dauphin, and took him back to his apartments.

After a short interval, the King sent for the Duc du Maine and the Comte de Toulouse, dismissing those few who still remained in his room, and ordering the doors to be shut. This private interview lasted rather a long while. When every-

[1] He was remembering the *Fronde*.
[2] Louis XV never did forget that Mme de Ventadour had saved his life.

thing was restored to order, he sent for M. le Duc d'Orléans, who had remained in his own apartments. He talked to him for a very short time, but called him back as he was leaving, to add a brief word.[1] It was then also that he ordered him to have the future King taken, immediately after his death, to Vincennes,[2] where the air is good, and to keep him there until all the ceremonies were done with at Versailles, and the château had been properly cleansed. Then only was he to be brought back, for the King expected him to make Versailles his residence. It seems that he had already discussed this matter with the Duc du Maine and the Maréchal de Villeroy, because after M. le Duc d'Orléans had left, he gave orders for furnishing Vincennes, and making it ready to receive his successor immediately. Mme du Maine, who until then had not taken the trouble to remove herself from Sceaux, her visitors and pastimes, had meanwhile arrived at Versailles, and had sent asking the King's permission to see him for a moment, when his orders were given. She was already in the ante-chamber; she entered, and a moment afterwards left.

On Tuesday, 27 August, no one entered the King's room, save for Père Tellier, Mme de Maintenon, and, for his mass only, Cardinal de Rohan, and the two almoners on duty. At two o'clock, exactly, he sent for the Chancellor and, alone with him and Mme de Maintenon, made him open two boxes full of papers, making him burn many of them, and giving him orders for the disposal of the rest. At six o'clock in the evening, he asked again for the Chancellor. Mme de Maintenon did not leave his room the whole of that day, and no one else entered it except the valets and, from time to time, those who were essential for his service. During the evening, he sent for Père Tellier and, almost immediately after, for Pontchartrain, commanding him to have his heart taken to the professed house of the Jesuits in Paris, as soon as he was dead, and to have it placed opposite to the heart of the King his father, and after the same manner. Shortly after that, he recollected that Cavoye, the grand-marshal of his household, had never yet had occasion to arrange for the Court to be in residence at Vincennes, for it was fifty years since they had last been there. He directed them to a box that contained a plan of that château, and commanded them to take it to Cavoye. Later on, when he had given these orders, he said to Mme de Maintenon that he had heard tell of the difficulty of resigning oneself to death; but that as he approached the awful moment, he did not find it too hard to submit. She replied that it must be very painful if one were attached to people, or hated them in one's heart, or had restitutions to make. 'Oh!' said the King, 'as for restitutions I owe nothing to any

---

[1] The King was recommending Mme de Maintenon to the prince's care.
[2] Vincennes was a strong fortress. Enemies of the Duc d'Orléans might have drawn the implication that Louis XIV thought the future King in danger of assassination.

individual; and for what I owe to the kingdom, I trust in the mercy of God.' The following night was terribly agitated. He could be seen continually pressing his hands together, and they heard him reciting the prayers which he had been wont to say when well, and beating his breast at the *Confiteor.*

On the morning of 28 August, he gave a word of comfort to Mme de Maintenon, which she so little relished that she did not answer. He said that the thought which consoled him in parting from her was the hope that, considering her age, they would soon be reunited.[1] At seven that morning he had sent for Père Tellier and, as they spoke of God, he had seen reflected in the mirror above the chimney-piece two of his pages in tears, sitting at the foot of his bed. He said to them, 'Why are you crying? Did you think I was immortal? I, myself, have never thought so, and considering my age, you should have been prepared to lose me.'

A countryman, a sort of squire from Provence, a monstrous rough fellow, who had learned of the King's condition on the road from Marseilles to Paris, now arrived at Versailles with a remedy which, so he said, was a certain cure for gangrene. By that time, the King was so bad, and the doctors so desperate, that they gave it him without hesitation, in the presence of Mme de Maintenon and the Duc du Maine. Fagon did try to object, but the countryman, whose name was Le Brun, turned on him so fiercely that Fagon, who usually bullied others into fits of terror, was completely silenced. They gave the King ten drops of that elixir in a glass of Alicante wine, at eleven in the morning. For a short time he felt stronger; but when, his pulse being weak and almost failing, they offered him a second dose at four o'clock, saying that it would revive him, he answered as he took the glass, 'Life or death, as God pleases.' Mme de Maintenon had just left the room with her hood drawn down; the Maréchal de Villeroy led her past the door of her apartments, which she did not enter, and down the grand staircase, where she stopped and raised her hood. Then, completely dry-eyed, she embraced the Maréchal, saying, 'Adieu, M. le Maréchal,' and stepping into the King's coach that was always at her disposal and in which Mme de Caylus was waiting, she drove away to Saint-Cyr, followed by a second coach containing her women. That evening the Duc du Maine made an excellent story of Fagon's encounter with Le Brun. I shall return later to his conduct, and that of Mme de Maintenon and Père Tellier during the last days of the King's

---

[1] Mme de Maintenon's account of the King's three farewells is as follows: 'On the first occasion he assured me that his only regret was in leaving me. "But," he continued with a sigh, "we shall meet again soon." I begged him to think only of God. The next time, he asked my forgiveness for not having considered me enough, and for not making me happy; but he vowed that he had always loved and esteemed me. Then feeling moved to tears, he bade me be sure that no one was listening, adding, "But no one will ever be surprised at my being moved by you." On the third occasion, he said, "What will become of you? You have nothing." Again, I begged him to think only of God; but after reflecting that I did not know how the prince would treat me, I asked him to recommend me to M. le Duc d'Orléans.'

life.[1] Le Bran's remedy continued to be given as he advised, and he was always present when the King took it. When they wished the King to drink some soup, he said that they should not speak to him as to other men; that what he needed was not soup but his confessor, and he had him recalled. One day when he came to his senses after a period of unconsciousness, he asked Père Tellier for general absolution from his sins, and Père Tellier inquired whether he suffered very much. 'No, alas!' replied the King, 'that is what distresses me; I should prefer to suffer more for the expiation of my sins.'

On Thursday, 29 August, the previous day and night having been so very bad, the absence of the dispensers, who had done all that they could, left more room in the King's bedchamber for the high officials who until then had been excluded. There had been no mass the day before,[2] and there seemed no prospect of one in the future. The Duc de Charost, captain of the guard, who had stolen in with the others, rightly thought this very bad, and asked the King through one of the personal valets whether he did not desire to hear one. The King replied that he did so wish. The necessary clergy and materials were at once sent for, and mass was said every day afterwards. On the Thursday morning he seemed somewhat stronger, and even a shade better, although this was so greatly exaggerated that the news spread in all directions. The King was even able to eat two biscuits in a little Alicante wine, and appeared to enjoy them. I went on that day to call on M. le Duc d'Orléans, at about two in the afternoon. His apartments had been swarming with visitors at all hours of the day for the past week; truly, you could not have dropped a pin between them so that it reached the ground. No one was there. As soon as he saw me he burst out laughing, saying that I was the first person he had seen all day, and he remained completely deserted until the evening.[3] But that is the way of the world.

It was then I realized that he had changed his mind regarding the summoning of the States General, and that except for what we had decided about the Councils, he had not given such matters another thought—nor many other matters either, and I took the liberty of speaking to him very plainly. He was still minded to dismiss Desmaretz and Pontchartrain, but had weakened over the Chancellor, which made me press for an explanation. He confessed, at last, somewhat out of countenance, that Mme la Duchesse d'Orléans (whom the Maréchal de Villeroy had visited so secretly that even he had not known of it) had begged him to see Villeroy to reach agreement over some extremely important matters in

---

[1] Lest Mme de Maintenon be thought as heartless as Saint-Simon makes her out, it should be remembered that she was eighty, and had been for many days in the fetid air of the King's room, and under the terrible strain of his long-drawn-out dying. She must have been exhausted by the stench of gangrene and his suffering. She may also have been terrified lest the Duc d'Orléans arrest her at Versailles, and have felt it safer to be at Saint-Cyr when the King died.

[2] Because the King could not have heard it.

[3] The Duc d'Orléans is supposed to have said, 'If the King eats any more, no one at all will visit me.'

absolute secrecy, warning him that if he refused he would find himself in serious difficulties, and excusing herself from saying more, on the pretext of a promise to the Maréchal. M. le Duc d'Orléans had delayed for a time; but had finally consented to see him.

The Maréchal came, and for four or five days everything was shrouded in mystery, after which, as the price of the information to follow, he had asked M. le Duc d'Orléans for his promise to keep the Chancellor in office and in charge of the seals, against the Chancellor's word (of which the Maréchal would stand guarantor) to hand in his resignation as Secretary of State, as soon as His Highness had reimbursed him in full. After a violent dispute, and the promise given, the Maréchal had informed him that M. du Maine was made superintendent of the future King's education, and he his governor, with absolute authority.[1] The Chancellor had afterwards told him of the codicil, and its effects, but the Maréchal said he did not wish to take advantage of that. This had brought on a lively dispute between them, resulting in no stipulations of any kind from the Maréchal, but from the Chancellor a request for the above promise concerning his dismissal; in return for which he had thanked M. de Villeroy, in the King's study, and had even shown him the codicil.

I must confess to having been angered by his weak, deceitful opening, and I did not hide my feelings from M. le Duc d'Orléans, who appeared exceedingly embarrassed. I asked him what had happened to his perceptions, he, who had never seen any difference between M. du Maine and Mme la Duchesse d'Orléans, who so often had warned me to beware of her and tell her nothing, and who repeatedly averred that she was as impenetrable as a forest. Did he not perceive that M. du Maine and Mme la Duchesse d'Orléans were using the Maréchal de Villeroy to scare him, so as to discover how he would take the news, the secret of what was nothing less than his own murder? They stood to lose nothing by trying to keep their tool in office at so cheap a price,[2] for having been their pernicious servant in all their actions against M. le Duc d'Orléans, he would thus continue to hold a key post in his Regency, which they fully intended to reduce to a mere shadow. We argued this for a considerable time; but his word had been given. He had not had strength enough to resist them, and although so brilliant, had been duped into believing that he made a good bargain by dismissal with repayment; although the Chancellor himself made a far better one by ensuring full reimbursement[3] for an office which he could never have held, and when the slightest word would have sufficed to make him return the seals and even go into exile, had that seemed desirable.

[1] In other words the secret of the King's will was out, which had been known only to Mme de Maintenon, the Duc du Maine, the Maréchal de Villeroy and the Chancellor. It was a betrayal of the King's trust.

[2] Their 'tool' was of course Chancellor Voysin.

[3] The King, had he lived, would have repaid him only in part for the return of his office.

The thing was done, and there was no help for it; but I exhorted M. le Duc d'Orléans to learn by this wretched lesson, and to be on his guard thenceforward against enemies of all kinds, against deceit, good-nature, and weakness, and especially to realize the affront and the danger to him of the codicil, if he allowed it in any way to become law. He never told me what agreement, if any, he had made with the Maréchal de Villeroy; only that there had been no question of any understanding with the Duc du Maine, who thus reckoned on remaining the absolute and independent controller of the King's household, both civil and military, and governor of the palaces, with M. le Duc d'Orléans no more than an absurd puppet in his Regency, living in perpetual fear of the governor's axe. M. le Duc d'Orléans, with all his intelligence, had discerned nothing of all this. I left him both thoughtful and repentant. He spoke again to Mme la Duchesse d'Orléans, and this time with so much firmness that they began to fear he would hold to nothing because of having promised too much. The Maréchal was accordingly instructed to proceed slowly, and limited his efforts to consolidating his gains, assuring the prince meanwhile that he would give no offence. But the King's life was moving so rapidly to its close that he easily avoided further enlightenment, and because of what had taken place in the King's study, with the Chancellor, and with M. le Duc d'Orléans, their fish remained hooked—if I may be permitted so vulgar a phrase.[1]

The late evening did not fulfil the much vaunted promise of that morning, at which time the Curé of Versailles had taken advantage of the emptier room to tell the King that the people were praying for his life. The King had replied that it was not now a question of that, but of his salvation, for which prayers were badly needed. When he had given his orders that morning, he had let slip the words, 'the young King', when speaking of the Dauphin. He observed the sudden movement among the onlookers and said, 'Well, what of it? That does not trouble me at all.' At eight o'clock he took some more of the elixir of that man from Provence. His head appeared to be confused, and he said himself that he felt very bad. At eleven, they examined his leg. Gangrene had spread all over his foot and knee, and his thigh was much swollen. He fainted during the examination. He was distressed to notice the absence of Mme de Maintenon, who had not intended to return. He asked for her several times during the day;

---

[1] Mlle d'Aumale gives the following account: 'The King's approaching death put the whole Court into a great state of agitation. The contents of his will, which he had entrusted to the Parlement, had become known, and had reached the ears of the Duc d'Orléans, who felt that the King's dispositions did not treat him according to his desires or deserts. He had already taken certain measures to secure what he believed to be his rightful place in the government. As soon as the King's illness was pronounced fatal, he began to work more seriously in order to complete his plans. He had, moreover, secretly consulted with several nobles who were attached to him. His schemes were not at first noticed, but during the last days of the King's life, it became perfectly clear that the duke's only concern was for his own interests, and everyone was talking about it in whispers.'

and they were unable to conceal from him that she had gone. He sent to fetch her from Saint-Cyr; she returned in the evening.

Friday, 30 August was as distressing as the night before had been; a deep coma set in, and in the intervals his mind wandered. From time to time he swallowed a little jelly in plain water, for he could no longer take wine. Only the valets essential for his service remained in the room with the doctors and Mme de Maintenon; Père Tellier appeared on rare occasions when Blouin or Maréchal summoned him. Few remained even in the studies; M. du Maine not amongst them. The King quickly responded to words of piety, when Mme de Maintenon or Père Tellier found the moments when his head was less confused; but such moments were rare and of short duration. At five that evening, Mme de Maintenon went to her apartments, distributed such furniture as belonged to her among the members of her staff, and departed to Saint-Cyr, never to return.

The day and the night of Saturday, 31 August, were horrible indeed. There were only brief and rare moments of consciousness. The gangrene had reached his knee and spread over his entire thigh. They gave him the late Abbé Aignan's[1] remedy, which the Duchesse du Maine suggested as being an excellent thing against smallpox. By this time, the doctors were agreeing to anything because they had lost all hope. Towards eleven in the evening, they thought him so ill that the prayers for the dying were said over him. The bustle brought him to his senses. He recited the prayers in a voice so strong that it could be heard above those of the many priests, and above those of all the people who had entered with them. When the prayers ended he recognized Cardinal de Rohan and said to him: 'Those are the last blessings of the Church.' That was the last person to whom he spoke. He several times repeated, *'Nunc et in hora mortis'*, then said, 'O God help me! Haste thou to succour me.' Those were his last words. He lay unconscious throughout the night. His long agony ended at a quarter past eight, on the morning of Sunday, 1 September, 1715, three days before his seventy-seventh birthday, in the seventy-second year of his reign.

He had married at the age of twenty-two, after signing the famous Peace of the Pyrenees, in 1660. He was twenty-three when death delivered France of Cardinal Mazarin; twenty-seven, when he lost the Queen his mother, in 1666. He became a widower at forty-four, in 1683; lost Monsieur his brother when he was sixty-three, in 1701, and survived all his sons, grandsons and great-grandsons, excepting only his successor, the King of Spain, and the sons of that monarch. Europe had never known so long a reign, nor France so old a king.

---

[1] The Abbé François Aignan, a mendicant friar known as '*le Père Tranquille*'. He concocted a number of different remedies from therapeutic recipes which he brought back after a journey to the Far East, chief of them being his 'Tranquil Balm' (*le baume tranquille*), a narcotic ointment, perhaps the first record of a tranquillizer.

When his body was opened by Maréchal his chief surgeon, with all the attendant ceremonies, they found every organ intact, and so healthy, so perfectly formed, that it made them believe that he might have lived beyond a century, had it not been for those weaknesses of which I have spoken, which introduced the gangrene into his body.[1] They found that the capacity of his stomach and entrails was at least double that of the average man of the same height, which was truly extraordinary, and the reason for his appetite having been so huge and so regular.

[1] Saint-Simon is referring to his theory that over-indulgence in soup and fruit had caused the King to die prematurely.

INDEX

NOTE: As in Volume I, it has been found necessary, for reasons of space, to omit names occurring only once and of no particular interest in the context: apologies to readers for any resulting inconvenience. 'f' after a number indicates that the name occurs on two, 'ff' on three, 'fff' on four consecutive pages; mentions on more than four consecutive pages are indicated, e.g., 36-45 passim. Subjects discussed over not more than three consecutive pages are indicated by consecutive numbers; if discussed over a longer series of pages, by the first page number followed by 'et seqq'.

Historical Books from

A Year with a Whaler by Walter Noble Burns
Able-bodied seamen, great mammals, and the ever-changing sea are the central figures in this narrative of a carefree boy shipping out and a wise man returning.

The Private Life of Marie Antoinette by Madame Campan
An intimate account of the intrigue and drama at the royal court, from the queen's Lady-in-Waiting.

A New Voyage Round the World by William Dampier
Explorer, naturalist and pirate William Dampier provides one of the earliest and most eloquent accounts of discovery and piracy on the high seas.

To Cuba and Back by Richard Henry Dana
With keen observations and a riveting narrative, the author of the seafaring classic Two Years Before the Mast tells of his journey to this lush and beautiful island.

Foreign Devil by Richard Hughes
Inspiration for Ian Fleming and John LeCarré, the memoirs of a Far East reporter during the tumultuous 1940s and '50s.

A Minstrel in France by Harry Lauder
A world famous performer's life is forever changed by the loss of his beloved son in World War I. With a piano lashed to his jeep, Lauder tours the battlefront paying tribute to the troops.

Thirty Years a Detective by Allan Pinkerton
From the founder of the Pinkerton agency, an insider's look at criminals, their mindsets, and their most famous schemes.

The Dukays by Lajos Zilahy
Hungary's foremost novelist tells the story of the momentous changes in Europe after WWI through the eyes of an aging aristocrat and his children.

For excerpts to these and other books, please visit 1500Books.com.

The Legendary Memoirs of Duc de Saint-Simon

Memoirs of Duc de Saint-Simon 1691-1709:
Presented to the King

With a passionate eye for detail, brilliant character sketches and devastating wit, Saint-Simon, a duke and a peer during the reign of the Sun King Louis XIV, paints a dramatic portrait of his early years at the French court. Known for its treacherous conspiracies, pompous rituals and ribald debauchery, it remains one of the most famous royal courts in history. In Saint-Simon's first-hand account we meet the legendary Sun King, his powerful mistresses and bastards, his decadent nephew---and Saint-Simon's confidant---Duc d'Orléans, and a broad cast of characters worthy of the most imaginative novels.

Memoirs of Duc de Saint-Simon 1710-1715:
The Bastards Triumphant

The Sun King, Louis XIV is dying, and the French court is erupting in a frenzy of twisted alliances and dark schemes in the struggle for power. As if we are eavesdropping in the chambers and hallways of Versailles, eyewitness Saint-Simon details the plots and counter plots, his own involvement, and his close relationships with some of most fascinating and vividly sketched characters in history.

Memoirs of Duc de Saint-Simon 1715-1723:
Fatal Weakness

Now that the King is dead, intrigue and espionage run rampant at a royal court where indulgence and excess are the norm. Saint-Simon now has close ties to the most powerful man in France, the Regent Duc d'Orléans, but he also has enemies stronger than ever before. Both high drama and frivolous escapades reach new heights as he takes us breathlessly into his final days at the French court, and the conclusion of the Memoirs.

1500Books.com.